YOU ARE YOUR FIRST NAME

YOU ARE YOUR FIRST NAME

Ellin Dodge

A FIRESIDE BOOK
PUBLISHED BY SIMON & SCHUSTER, INC.
NEW YORK

*To Sadie Rothner Leibowitz
with love*

Acknowledgments

Special thanks to a rare woman, Joanne Marritt Benjamin. Hugs to Robert Strom, Sandra Karlik, and the A.C.I. team for generosity, hospitality, and encouragement.

For helping me to watch my p's and q's, thanks to Babs, Norman, and Jane Klein.

To Lucille Lowy Solomon, catalyst and friend; Alexandria Hatcher, agent and booster; and gutsy Long Shadow publisher Martin Asher—thank you. You have dared to recognize nonconformity and helped to make my visualization a reality.

To Wingate Holmes Paine, my dear inspiration, thank you for "tilling the soul."

To Adrianne Grayson Batlin, for over twenty-five years of adventurous, culturally expanding (if often hilarious), character-challenging, and heartfelt memories . . . through the clarity of numerology, our friendship has groped, scoped, and coped.

To Martin Schneider, Joan-Jennifer Bassey-Bassie, Philip Cusack, Lorrie B. Turner, Barbara Hinton, Drs. Evelyn and Paul Moschetta, Eileen and Robert X. Young, Patricia and Charles Treves, Lona Holland Buyuksoy, Adelle Sardi, Carla and Harvey Saunders, Evelyn Bender of New York, Arthur Gross of Connecticut, Lottie Schlamm of Florida, Joan Leonard of Wisconsin, and Bernice Fischer and Lou Miller of Nevada—bless you all for enriching my destiny.

To my dividends, Ivy and Jeff Dodge; my ever-supportive father, Bill; and surprising Jack—hooray, we did it!

CONTENTS

YOU ARE
YOUR FIRST
NAME

Introduction

Wouldn't it be great to meet someone on a first-name basis and know if you should put out your hand with a crush of sincerity, touch fingers lightly, or wait until a hand is offered? "Hi, this is Herbert" at the beginning of a blind-date phone call gives Mary enough information to reply yes or no without hesitation. His first name tells her he's not a glib talker, though she knows that most Herberts are stubbornly headed for affluence and power. And Herbert's sure that Mary will be a down-to-earth, practical, structured kindred spirit who'll say yes to a fashionable evening. Numerology's first-name descriptions turn prospects into promises. On a job interview, at a cocktail party, or for naming a baby, it's comforting to open a new door with the up-front knowledge that everyone with the same first name shares specific character traits. Just as the sun sign of astrology keys into personalities, numerology's first-name description has your number too.

With the first letter of the first name as it appears on the birth certificate, numerology tells you what to expect at an introduction. You can anticipate whether to be the first to extend your hand in greeting or whether your two hands will meet in midair. The last letter clues you in to what triggers an overreaction in someone, and the total of the numerical values assigned to the letters in the first name identifies the ingredients of the major career talent. Simple? It sure is—and faster, more direct, and more on target than popular newspaper astrology.

Without having to ask for a birthdate, which might not go over too well when you meet your future mother-in-law, you can get the identical information from a first name. Numerology's nine character traits are indicated by the numerical values allocated to the letters of the alphabet. Each letter has its own personality, but their general characteristics and experiences can be inferred as follows: $A, J, S = 1$; $B, K, T = 2$; $C, L, U = 3$; $D, M, V = 4$; E, N, W = 5; $F, O, X = 6$; $G, P, Y = 7$; H, Q, Z = 8; and I, R = 9. Each of these letter values represents the interpretation of the vibration of sound established by the Greek mathematician Pythagoras (remember him from ninth-grade geometry?) and may be equated with the effects that astrology's planetary movements have upon people and their lives.

Numbers are the scorekeepers of the material world, and they graphically suggest their spiritual meanings. Look at the shapes of the numbers; then apply a bit of imagination when you read their meanings. The number 1 *(A, J, S)* represents the creative, changeably progressive loner who is motivated by the ego. The number 2 *(B, K, T)* cooperatively follows or supports leadership, is receptive, and collects people and things that develop ambitions. The number 3 *(C, L, U)* communicates, loves a party, and adds spice to a variety of imaginative interests. The number 4 *(D, M, V)*—visualize the four-sided square—is a systematic, disciplined worker, while the number 5 *(E, N, W)* enthusiastically focuses upon sensuality, experimentation, and the unconventional and is an entrepreneur and a catalyst for change in the conservative. The number 6 *(F, O, X)* is responsible, instructional, and comfort-loving and is motivated to serve the community and give sympathy, parental guidance, and love. The number 7 *(G, P, Y)* is analytic and aristocratic and strives for spiritual, scientific, or technical perfection in order to provide authoritative theories. The efficient, executive, and strongly disciplined number 8 *(H, Q, Z)* seeks material power. Brotherly love motivates the number 9 *(I, R)*, and it is up to its nines in all personality ingredients. Number 9 would philosophically give the shirt off its back or work without pay, and it is dedicated to perfecting a skill or performance in order to serve humanity.

The high-strung, visionary, sensitive letters *K* (the 11th letter of the alphabet) and *V* (the 22nd letter of the alphabet) are spiritually special. They sense the future with emotional intensity, hyperactivity, and an elitist desire to uplift mass tastes and expectations creatively or materially.

"What's in a name?" Just about everything. *You Are Your First Name* touches only the tip of the iceberg. The vowels, the consonants, all the letters in the entire name round out the personality picture in numerology. The missing letter/number values reveal unfamiliar areas of experience and point out things that must be experienced to be learned. An overabundance of one or more letter/number values indicates a deep, innate knowledge of that area. There is a positive and a negative side to each number/letter; therefore we can be wonderful or terrible, depending on the side we use, but the trait remains the same. For example, a number 4 name could be very disciplined or very disorganized.

You are your first name as it appears on your birth certificate. Nicknames or name changes are influential, but the name as it is spelled on the birth certificate is the first record of the new soul on earth and evokes the self-chosen character of the infant. Even if the first record is Baby, Infant, Boy, Girl, an initial, or a misspelled name, or is changed later, we still learn about that person from the first recorded letters. To do a total numerology chart to compare a personality to the path its life will take, a numerologist needs only a name and a birthdate. Each letter of the name tells the story of the deepest self. The month, date, and year of birth predict the opportunities that the name will have in life. Don't make it complicated; that's all there is to it. Don't fear its simplicity or negate its integrity just because you can work with it immediately.

From the birthdate, numerology opens the door to the future. Add all the digits in multiple-digit numbers together to reduce them to a single number, and you will have the exact definition. (Example: $12 = 1 + 2 = 3$. We would read 12 as the number 3.) For the birthdate October 8, 1983, we add 1 (the 10th month, $1 + 0 = 1$) for October, 8 for the day, and 3 for the year ($1 + 9 + 8 + 3 = 21, 2 + 1 = 3$). The equation for the date is $1 + 8 + 3 = 12, 1 + 2 = 3$. Thus, we would predict that a person born on October 8, 1983, will be offered a life of meeting people and will have experiences that are socially oriented, good outlets for creative expression, and filled with a variety of up-to-date activities. This is the path where friends bring in business as well as social activity.

When you name a baby or contemplate a name change, think before you print a name on a birth-certificate form. Check out a nickname, a stage name, or a spelling change to see what you're getting and what you're giving up. A Stanley Otis Berns will never be able to put his initials on anything. Hesitate before you tag a child Cornubia, especially if your sense of humor runs rampant and your last name is Bliss. Ming Toy Shapiro, Ima Hogg, Hannibal O'Brien, and Pandora Box didn't develop a sense of humor until they matured. That's just common sense. But if you want to introduce "my son, the doctor," be sure to select a number 9 name with the appropriate humanitarian vibes. If you want him to be the toast of Broadway, the reincarnation of Mike Todd, or FDR reborn, then choose a number 3, 5, 6, or 9 for a self-expressive, entrepreneurial, people-oriented name. If domesticity is important, a person with a number 2 or 6 name will be responsible, companionable, loving, and dedicated to service. If you use your nickname for business, be sure that the career numbers or dictionary definition is similar to that of your real name; personality conflicts may occur when opposing traits clash. Marilyn Monroe's first birth name was Norma. The first letter *N* (5) indicates a point of view that is curious, nonconformist, and experimental. The point of view of the name Marilyn is exemplified by the down-to-earth, practical, and conservative letter *M* (4). The letter values are dissimilar, as are the last letters. Emotional balance is difficult to maintain when aggressive odd numbers are put into conflict with receptive even numbers.

You are only the tool for naming a child. That's a tough one to accept, isn't it? You have to have faith in the things that are beyond your perception, and you have to accept the fact that these age-old parasciences are more than coincidence. You have to be ready to take all the help you can get. Now let's try again. The incoming soul selects its name and the date it will arrive. Premature and late babies simply can't make up their minds about getting into this world. However, most of us are preprogrammed, ready, and need the vibes of our names to fulfill our purpose. True, some people do not like their names. That's part of their personalities. They may change them, but that's all in keeping with their character. The child will use its parents, sisters and brothers, or rich Aunt Honoria's name selection, but it's really all in the spiritual cards that the child selects the name.

No two people are exactly alike. Children with the same name as one of their parents will have the same personality ingredients, but the month, day, and year of birth are different. The people, environments, and educational opportunities that they are offered will influence their personality's *modus operandi*. Generally, fathers and sons with the same name are either like fire and water or like peas in a pod. If they clash, it's because each sees in the other a mirror image of the character traits that he does not like in himself, or because they embody the negative and positive sides of the same trait. When sharing the same name, father and son may react with inappropriate hostility or they may be inseparable comrades.

Some names are popular for particular generations, some names seem to have a special quality, and there are names that have "good" or "bad" connotations throughout the ages. When I was a child, there were always a few Joans, Michaels, and Alans in my class. When my children came along, more than one annoyed voice would answer when I called my son Jeffrey to come in to dinner. Today's homes are filled with Justins, Carolines, and Jennifers. Some names call to mind specific personality traits—like David, the constructive, strong, determined builder; Ivan, the "terrible"; and Percy, who is supposed to be a milquetoast. Some of these preconceptions are numerologically accurate, as you will see when you look them up, and others just ain't so. Some names have power. Their bearers are able to attract followers to their personal ideals, and they may bring about changes through their ability to capture the imagination or uplift man's expectations. Adolph (Hitler) and Jesus (of Nazareth) have the same numerical value (11) in numerology. Adolph captured man's imagination and brought destruction to the world. Jesus evangelized, just as Adolph did, but he brought a loving message to mankind. It's interesting, too, that Zoroaster, the Persian prophet, and Siddhartha (Buddha's real name) both total 11.

Numerology elongates the vision of the nearsighted, blasts through tunnel vision, and just plain sheds light when we want clarity. Numbers are not just cumulative values to be totaled by a calculator or applied to odds at a crap table. This is the eighties, the age of numbers, and the duality of their importance is even more in focus. We are drawn to people, places, and things that vibe with us, and most of us find one or two numbers that feel lucky or seem to turn up in addresses or phone numbers no matter how often we change them. When you understand the gist of the number meanings, you will be able to understand the types of people and experiences that your changing home, phone, and auto repeatedly attract.

Clients have sent their astonished therapists to me, and I have been told that numerology identified problems that took years for analysis to pinpoint. Numerology cannot change behavior, but it can reinforce the inner awareness that we have of mistakes that we made repeatedly and help us to want to work to change behavior patterns that have reappeared and brought about disappointments. If you make a muck of things in one area of your personality, that's the negative. Remember, you have two sides to a trait. You can turn the coin to its positive side with self-awareness and self-discipline, and numerology can help by telling you what you already know about yourself. It's true that when children are told something by a stranger, they do it willingly, but when a parent wants something, it's a big deal. When a total stranger or a parascientist reinforces thoughts that you have been unsure about but have dwelled upon as a project to improve upon, you listen. There are facets of numerology that still astound me, and I hope that you will take the time to dig more deeply into a total charting of your full name and birthdate. Numerology's first name definition sets the stage for the unfolding drama of life.

Remember that you have choice and you may use your traits for positive or negative results. The sound of your name sparks feelings in you and the listener. Some will be attracted to you and some will reject you because of it. Your first name has vibes. Learn to love them, understand them, and use your birth name's positive traits without looking in other people's windows. *You are your first name,* and you are marvelous!

How to Use This Book

This is a dictionary. Look up names alphabetically. Origins are listed in parentheses. Female (F.) and male (M.) names are mixed; unisex names are identified as F. & M.

Birth certificate names show the bearer's true nature. Nicknames, diminutives, and variants tend to mix into the character and are therefore noted in the origins.

Interpretation may be positive or negative. If you are not comfortable with the interpretation, look to the opposite meaning of the words. All numerology descriptions have a positive and a negative aspect to the character trait. A person will have the trait but will also have a choice as to which way it will be used. For example, if the description says you are practical and you know you are not practical, then you embody the opposite side of the trait—impracticality. Simply by knowing that an aspect of your character exists, you can use it for positive or negative results, and you may find yourself vacillating between one extreme and the other. Another example: If the words say that you are responsible, but you just left your wife and twelve children destitute, then you are the opposing meaning of the word: irresponsible.

People are complex. We may be practical one day and foolish the next, or impractical in youth and extremely sensible in middle age. The trait will always show up in one extreme or the other. If we are not compulsively responsible then the burdens of caring for others do not feel heavy and we need no escape from them. The "irresponsible" husband cited as an example is really a person who does not take responsibilities lightly, is intensely dedicated, and burns out when overloaded. He runs away from responsibility to recharge his ego. The talents and personality ingredients (character traits) will show themselves during the lifetime.

Read a name description over again. You Are Your First Name encourages positive focus, but clear–cut negatives are explained too. As you read a name description, remember that you have control of your character ingredients and may turn negatives to positives, or find the greys in a black and white description of a trait. Read name interpretations more than one time and additional insights will come to light.

Read letter descriptions and number descriptions to learn more.

If a name is not in the dictionary or you wish to commit the numerology system to memory, see the following chapter for simple directions, interpretations of the letters and their number correspondents.

If Your Name Is Not in the Dictionary . . . Do It Yourself!

Some of you will not be able to find your name or its exact spelling in this dictionary. This section is for you. It is also for those of you who wish to commit the numerology system to memory.

Anyone can become an instant personality analyst by memorizing the nine generalized number meanings. The fine points of each letter are explained on the following pages, but general insight comes from thoughtful consideration of the positive and negative aspects of the number value. If you are a whiz at arithmetic or just interested enough to concentrate upon simple addition, all the information a name offers can be yours a few seconds after being introduced to a prospective employer, a new friend, or a blind date.

1. The number value of the first letter of the first name reveals the *strong point* or *point of view* of the personality.
2. Add up the total number value of the first name for identification of the name's *major talent*.
3. A quick look at each letter in the first name pinpoints the basic *personality ingredients*.
4. The last letter of the first name reveals the *personality extreme,* or area of conflict.

The number meanings apply to two or three letters, and each meaning has possible variations. If number 1 (the letters *A, J,* and *S*) signifies independence, creative action, and progress through change, then the variations of that definition would be in the areas of leadership, ambition, and originality. Let your common sense and natural intuition add aggressive, not passive, tendencies. A word like *action* hardly implies receptivity or someone who wants to take a backseat. Think about the negatives that these qualities may indicate. The opposites of leadership would be imitation, passivity and fear of creating change. Ambition could negate itself and become stagnation. All number meanings have positive and negative effects that depend upon the focus of the bearer. Ill health, mental depression, or even stress may cause a person to activate the negative meaning of a number value. It could affect some or all of the letters in the name or only the one that is having its button pushed at the moment. As you get more comfortable with interpretation, it becomes habit, and you will be able to add more analysis.

Nothing is simple. People surely are complex and often confuse us and themselves by demonstrating the opposing forces in their nature. The letter/number interpretations reveal these conflicts in the personality.

If you have the desire, this is an exact science that is easy to master. When you use it to your own benefit, "I've got your number!" will become your motto.

Components by Number

Number 1—Letters *A, J, S*
Independent ego; creative action; progress through change; *ambition.*
Number 2—Letters *B, K, T*
Cooperation; diplomacy; receptivity; personal sensitivity; *support-iveness.*
Number 3—Letters *C, L, U*
Communication; imagination; sociability; optimism; creation and appreciation of beauty; *self-expression.*
Number 4—Letters *D, M, V*
Practicality; organization; conservatism; trustworthiness; problem-solving ability; *self-discipline.*
Number 5—Letters *E, N,W*
Physical freedom; mental versatility; adventurousness; cleverness; sensuality; *speculativeness.*
Number 6—Letters *F, O, X*
Social responsibility; adjustment to others; protectiveness; domesticity; comfort-consciousness; *showmanship.*
Number 7—Letters *G, P, Y*
Introspection; perfectionism; scientific/logical/technical/spiritual/investigative ability; *aristocratic nature.*
Number 8—Letters *H, Q, Z*
Material power and organization; management; practicality; ambition; problem-solving ability; *efficiency.*
Number 9—Letters *I, R*
Selfless service; compassion; artistic ability; broadness of scope; romanticism; brotherly love; *polish and skill of performance.*

The First Letter of Your First Name Reveals Your Strong Point or Point of View

Letters *A, J, S* = Number 1
Independent leadership, creative mental energy, and ambition strongly influence the personality. There is a natural inclination to make pioneering changes, which may restrict or vitalize lifetime activity.
Letters *B, K, T* = Number 2
Receptivity, cooperation, and adaptability strongly influence the personality. There is a natural inclination to be emotionally supportive, which may restrict or vitalize lifetime activity.
Letters *C, L, U* = Number 3
Creative self-expression, imagination, and versatility in communica-

tions strongly influence the personality. There is a natural inclination to be optimistic, which may restrict or vitalize lifetime activity.

Letters *D, M, V* = Number 4

Self-discipline, organization, and practical application to work strongly influence the personality. There is a natural inclination to be dutiful and conservative, which may restrict or vitalize lifetime activity.

Letters *E, N, W* = Number 5

Mental curiosity, nonconformity, and unexpected changes strongly influence the personality. There is a natural inclination to experimentation and learning through experience, which may restrict or vitalize lifetime activity.

Letters *F, O, X* = Number 6

Assumption of responsibility, adjustments for others, and maintenance of family/community harmony strongly influence the personality. There is a natural inclination to protect and be protected, which may restrict or vitalize lifetime activity.

Letters *G, P, Y* = Number 7

Introspective analysis, aristocratic tastes, and technical, scientific, or spiritual curiosity strongly influence the personality. There is a natural inclination to specialize, seek perfection, and become an authority, which may restrict or vitalize lifetime activity.

Letters *H, Q, Z* = Number 8

Influence over others, material accumulation, and disciplined, practical, problem–solving judgment strongly influence the personality. There is a natural inclination to seek affluence and power, which may restrict or vitalize lifetime activity.

Letters *I, R* = Number 9

Compassion, empathetic philosophical judgment, and a need to creatively communicate and serve humanity strongly influence the personality. There is a natural inclination to polish skills or performance, expand culturally, and to impractically romanticize, which may restrict or vitalize lifetime activity.

The Last Letter of Your First Name Reveals Your Personality Extremes and Overreactive Tendencies

Letters *A, J, S* = Number 1

Indecision and emotional judgments weaken the personality. If the first and last letters of the first name have the same number value, there will be too much independence or a lack of self-assertion, resulting in conflict within the personality.

Letters *B, K, T* = Number 2

Personalized sensitivity and preoccupation with petty problems weaken the personality. If the first and last letters of the first name have the same number value, there will be too much concern about peaceful surroundings or constant nitpicking at others, resulting in conflict within the personality.

Letters C, L, U = Number 3
Scattering interests and concentrating upon surface values weaken the personality. If the first and last letters of the first name have the same number value, there will be too many superficial social concerns or reclusiveness, resulting in conflict within the personality.

Letters D, M, V = Number 4
Dislike for down-to-earth work and commonsense discipline weaken the personality. If the first and last letters of the first name have the same number value, there will be too much caution or a lack of self-protective practicality, resulting in conflict within the personality.

Letters E, N, W = Number 5
Inability to learn without experiencing everything and a subconscious desire to be free of responsibility weaken the personality. If the first and last letters of the first name have the same number value, there will be too much curiosity about physical sensations and life or a fear of sensuality and trying new experiences, resulting in conflict within the personality.

Letters F, O, X = Number 6
Stubborn sense of responsibility and jealous misgivings weaken the personality. If the first and last letters of the first name have the same number value, there will be too strong a desire to adjust to others' needs or to impose personal standards on others, resulting in conflict within the personality.

Letters G, P, Y = Number 7
Aloofness and a faultfinding lack of faith weaken the personality. If the first and last letters of the first name have the same number value, there will be too strong a need to question everything or gullibility in relationships, resulting in conflict within the personality.

Letters H, Q, Z = Number 8
A need for material recognition and an intolerance for less efficient people weaken the personality. If the first and last letters of the first name have the same number value, there will be a drive for influence and affluence or a lack of ambition or respect for established material values, resulting in conflict within the personality.

Letters I, R = Number 9
Misplaced sympathy and impracticality weaken the personality. If the first and last letters of the first name have the same number value, there will be too strong an emphasis upon serving the needs of others or egocentricity, resulting in conflict within the personality.

The Total Value of the Letters in Your First Name Reveals Your Major Talent

LETTER VALUES

1	2	3	4	5	6	7	8	9
A	B	C	D	E	F	G	H	I
J	K	L	M	N	O	P	Q	R
S	T	U	V	W	X	Y	Z	

To find the Major Talent number, refer to the letter values listed in the Letter Values chart above.

Step 1. Print your first name._____

Step 2. Write the number of each letter value above each letter. Let's use the name JUSTIN for an example.

EXAMPLE: 1 3 1 2 9 5
                JUSTIN

Step 3. Add the numbers. You will probably end up with a double number.

EXAMPLE: $1 + 3 + 1 + 2 + 9 + 5 = 21$
                J U S T I N

Step 4. Reduce the double number to a single number by adding from left to right. Example: $12 = 1 + 2 = 3$, $28 = 2 + 8 = 10$, (reduce again to end up with a single number), $1 + 0 = 1$. The basic rule in numerology is to reduce all multiple numbers to a single number for direct interpretation.

EXAMPLE: Justin
                $1 + 3 + 1 + 2 + 9 + 5 = 21$
                J + U + S + T + I + N
                $2 + 1 = 3$

The Major Talent number for the name Justin is 3.

Note: If your name adds up to 11 or 22, you have two number interpretations to read. Read the definitions of 11 or 22, then read their reduced values, 2 or 4, ($11 = 1 + 1 = 2$, $22 = 2 + 2 = 4$) to find the practical/ mundane meanings of spiritually–special numbers 11 and 22. They have the creative vision to leave a lasting mark on humanity, and their reduced numbers explain their day to day aspects.

EXAMPLE: **David**
                $41494 = 4 + 1 + 4 + 9 + 4 = 22$
                David = D + A + V + I + D
                $2 + 2 = 4$

Read the 22 and the 4 interpretations for the name David. Here's another example: Jennifer

                $1 + 5 + 5 + 5 + 9 + 6 + 5 + 9 = 45$
                J + E + N + N + I + F + E + R
                $4 + 5 = 9$

The Major Talent single reduced number for the name Jennifer is 9.

You've done it. Now look at the following pages to find your own Major Talent number interpretation.

Number 1

Incorporate initiative, independence, and originality into your career. Expect to succeed through aggressive leadership, self-reliance, and individualistic methods. Develop courage, patience, and a pioneering spirit.

Number 2

Incorporate tact and diplomacy into a cooperative group effort. Your career deals with partnerships and boosting the original ideas of innovative leaders. Detail–consciousness, patient collecting, and the ability to bring harmony to opposing forces are a few of your strong talents. Develop an interest in the arts, share experiences, and try a nonaggressive approach.

Number 3

Incorporate self-expression through writing, speaking, or entertaining into your career. The ability to use your imagination and your gift for optimism bring you to people and attract people to you. Develop your interest in fashion, beautification, theater, opera, literature, writing, acting, or speaking to enhance your ability to attract money and friends.

Number 4

Incorporate honesty, conscientiousness, and commonsense managerial ability into your career. Use self-discipline and assume responsibility. Practical problem solving is your greatest strength. Build through systems, efficiency, and attention to economy, detail, and routine. Develop your determination, sincerity, and ability to structure to protect others.

Number 5

Incorporate unconventional ideas, experimentation with a confident approach, and enthusiasm for changing established impressions and procedures into your career. You can be quick and clever and have unusual versatility. Avoid planning tight schedules, seize spontaneous opportunities, and expect to be able to do more than one thing at a time. Develop contacts with nonroutine people and consistently update daily and long-term goals. Contact with the public and promotion of new concepts should be cultivated.

Number 6

Incorporate home or community service, a sense of showmanship, and responsibility into your career. Creating beauty and music and maintaining group harmony are important, as is a secure, comfortable, opulent life style. Your work will be negatively affected if there is discord at home or in the office. Cultivate your voice (singing or speaking), express your knowledge to uplift others, and recognize your need to give and receive protection.

Number 7

Incorporate a spiritual, technical, or scientific speciality into your career. You have the ability to attract money by questioning, investigating, and broadening your expertise. Take private time to study, analyze, and receive inspiration from within yourself. Avoid partnerships and expect to be discriminating when you decide to share your information. Cultivate educational opportunities, independent thought, aristocratic instincts, and your talents for seeking depth and perfection in your interests.

Number 8

Incorporate finance, executive leadership, and organizational structure into your career. Keep tuned to civic and governmental affairs and focus upon influential, talented, or prominent persons who cross your busy path. Depend upon your work effort, discipline, and judgment, not luck, for success. Aim high, be just, and cultivate patience with less efficient associates who will detail, administer, and boost your ambitions. Develop a businesslike attitude.

Number 9

Incorporate concern for artistic quality, skill of performance, and the welfare of others into your career. Try to keep your emotions out of business as you employ compassion, understanding for the human condition, and generosity to solve material problems. Your talents for communication and artistic expression should be recognized and broadened; cultural growth, not material or practical accumulation, brings fulfillment. The rewards of this talent are harvested through humanitarian, empathetic and selfless service.

Number 11

Add the ability to juggle decisions, inspire future generations, and change the ideals of man to the interpretation of the 2. The number 11 brings a duality to the number 2 if it is derived by the $11 = 1 + 1 = 2$ reduction. The desire to be elite and uplift the expectations of humanity, either artistically or spiritually, is incorporated into the other talents of the 2. These talents attract followers and heighten nervous tension; emotional calm must be cultivated.

Number 22

Add the ability to change the future by creative improvement, to bring that change to form, and to solve far-reaching problems to the interpretation of the 4. The number 22 brings a duality to the number 4 if it is derived by the $22 = 2 + 2 = 4$ reduction. It has a spiritual quality that forecasts high-powered practical work which produces tangible results that last after the name bearer has passed on. The number 22 forecasts the master architect, problem solver and builder.

Each Letter of Your First Name Reveals Ingredients of Your Personality

The letter meanings and interpretations are listed below. They are consolidated because this is basically a dictionary for easy reference. If your name is not in this dictionary, the letter interpretations that follow will give you character insights.

A adds impulsiveness, active energy, the desire for sudden change, and intellectual planning. It is inspired by self-reliance and constant ideas for progress.

B adds caution, nervous energy, and the desire for domestic love, emotional serenity, and cooperation. It is inwardly focused and avoids self-assertion, personal ambition, or changing attitudes.

C adds vocal expression, concern for beauty, and social consciousness. It brings optimism, imagination, and intuition with it, but needs the attention of the opposite sex, a variety of interests, and concentration on priorities.

D adds emotional discipline, earthy honesty, and a realistic attitude. Its practical work efforts must produce tangible results, even at the expense of personal freedom. *D* builds for the future.

E adds emotional impulsiveness, changeableness, versatility, and varied financial experiences. It brings creative ideas, enthusiasm for unconventional opportunities, and material awareness.

F adds strong family ties, compassionate helpfulness, and the ability to assume responsibility or duties willingly. It causes vacillation in decisions where personal ambitions are concerned. A youthful need for maturity, physical comforts, and social involvement govern priorities and ambitions.

G adds unique mental qualities, the courage to be innovative, the willingness to take credit for innovation, and a talent for balanced analysis. It dislikes taking advice, brings extreme need for methodical perfection, and attracts intensified, unconventional love interests.

H adds the strong desire for financial freedom, leadership, influence, and impatience with petty distractions. It brings the courage to work, discipline, and the willingness to apply stamina to accumulate tangible assets. Physical fitness is important to mental well-being.

I adds an intense emotional desire to serve humanitarian needs, fulfill commitments, and grow culturally. It brings charm, artistry, and an erratic but powerful, empathetic, and practically organized need to relieve the suffering of others.

J adds the ability to see all sides of a picture to its need to be a creative leader. It signals a clever innovator who reflects upon past experiences and has self-promotional ambitions.

K adds the ability to get recognition for elitist ideas and contagious enthusiasm. It brings dedicated idealism, personalized sensitivity, nervous energy, need for sexual activity, and strong intuition. *K* needs associates to implement its unique concepts. Personality balance is difficult where creative ideas and material accumulation conflict.

L adds gifts of communication, with writing as a forte. Emotional detachment and a balanced personality help it to accumulate material for expressive activities. Often takes on more than it can handle and attracts surprises.

M adds dedication to established procedures, binding self-control, and emotional detachment. It makes one a practical taskmaster who has the determination to finish what it starts or is started by others. Wants to do the right thing.

N adds intellectual restlessness, an inability to learn from past experiences, and a love for physical pleasure and long-shot opportunities. It adds a tendency to bypass established successful procedures.

O adds a strong emotional sense of responsibility, a touch of paranoia where loved ones are concerned, and the inability to burden others with its personal problems. It brings concern about material ambitions, family/community involvement, and concentration on teaching or learning.

P adds a strong desire for intellectual and spiritual perfection. It senses that it is a loner and often will not be pushed into an established mold. Its heightened sense of pride and introverted tendencies cause difficulties in partnerships.

Q combines good luck with the need for power and material accumulation. It is impatient with little steps up the ladder and often pursues ambitions off the beaten track. *Q* is outwardly secure, inwardly questioning.

R adds active energy to serve mass needs through established procedures. It brings involvements that detract from personal commitments. It cannot expect to get back all that it gives.

S adds personality fluctuations that affect creative energy. Emotional reactions inspire progressive changes. Nerves often affect physical stamina. It strives to be honest, practical, and aggressive, which is difficult with the impractical intuitional and emotional reactions that it has.

T adds the emotional strain and sensitivity of a martyr. It takes on family burdens and is very affectionate and cooperative. *T* needs spiritual peace but has a strong awareness of the attitudes of others and may get involved in petty problems, self-pity, and depression.

U adds sociability, emotional involvement in all areas of experience, and a tendency toward extreme behavior. Its physical appetites, aesthetic idealism, and inability to concentrate on one material ambition often bring confusion.

V adds the ability to get things done in a big way. It demands results from associates, although it is often hyperactive, unpredictable, and extreme in its efforts to work with others. It brings material achievement, attention to long-term goals, and determination to maintain a practical routine.

W adds an impulsive, often unrealistic, need for change and variety. It can bring self-destruction if forced to conform to rigid co-workers' respect for established procedure. It can benefit from its diagnostic abilities, human understanding, and cleverness. It must learn to change and when to do it. It must have freedom but cannot abuse it.

X adds concern for family and community and it adjusts to their needs through self-sacrifice. Its artistic, high-strung, possessive qualities bring on emotional highs and lows. It strives for beautiful, comfortable, harmonious surroundings and aims to teach or raise standards.

Y adds strong intuition, intellect, and exactitude to its confusing personality trait of preaching one thing and doing another. It needs to be recognized for its inner wisdom in order to avoid vacillation, escapist antics, or introversion due to lack of self-respect.

Z adds artistic gifts to its powerful need for influence over others, for affluence, and for the power that these bring. It projects strength and stamina and an intelligence that touches on slyness. It is governed by executive intuition.

The Numerology Name Dictionary

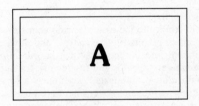

All names that begin with the letter *A* have the *Strong Point* of independent leadership—creative energy—ambition—mental attitude.

AARON (Egyptian/English)—M.

MAJOR TALENT: Ability to incorporate practical vision, philanthropic purpose, and organizational structure into career. Builds through common sense to identify essentials, produce tangible returns, and provide long-lasting benefits. Industry, politics, or the professions are possible career opportunities.

PERSONALITY INGREDIENTS: Employs intuition, courage, and strong opinions in policy making. Often impatient, stubborn, and idealistic. Feels that family/community are roots and digs them in securely. Socially adept, musical, and culturally appreciative. Appears to be adventurous, sexy, and fashionable, but down deep is all business.

PERSONALITY EXTREME: Too curious, or afraid to gamble.

ABEL (Hebrew/English)—M.

MAJOR TALENT: Ability to incorporate sensitive support, diplomacy, and evangelistic ideals into career. A dual personality: the power behind the throne or the zealous moralizer. Naive in commercial manipulations, but attracts practical partners. Enlightened teacher, writer, or preacher with appreciation for the fine points of an effort. Art, theater, and sales management are possible career opportunities.

PERSONALITY INGREDIENTS: Attracts accidents/surprises. Family oriented, protective, and affectionate. Appears to be physically attractive, energetic, and enthusiastic. Wants love.

PERSONALITY EXTREME: Too inventive, or lacking imagination.

ABIGAIL (Hebrew/English)—F.

MAJOR TALENT: Ability to incorporate predictive, progressive, and promotional concepts into career. Pursues a variety of artistic, political, or unconventional interests. Clever, dexterous, and curious. Provides enthusiasm for alternatives. Learns by experimentation. Advertising, travel agencies, and government policy making are possible career opportunities.

PERSONALITY INGREDIENTS: Impatient, adaptable, romantic, generous, empathetic . . . and very human. Occasionally petty or depressed, but generally self-confident. Cosmopolitan encounters provide educational refinements. Desires loving partner, but may attract flirtations.

PERSONALITY EXTREME: Too concerned about appearances, or indifferent/sloppy or inconsistent.

ABNER (Hebrew/English)—M.

MAJOR TALENT: Ability to incorporate wide-scoped administrative resources, broad-termed reconstructive energy, and powerful potential for humanitarian wisdom into career. Practical coordination, system, and down-to-earth judgments provide the framework for subjective and objective goals. With ethical emphasis, may amass a fortune. Careers in earth products, contracting, and government are possible opportunities.

PERSONALITY INGREDIENTS: Workaholic energy must not be wasted on exploiting others. Too many petty acquisitions may bring about emotional stress. Most progressive in groups. Desires to have a peaceful homelife and to appear cultured. Difficult outer personality: naive, questioning, moody.

PERSONALITY EXTREME: Too sentimental, or too unemotional.

ABRAHAM (Hebrew/English)—M.

MAJOR TALENT: Ability to incorporate efficiency, executive organization, and confident expectation into career. Detailed work and problem solving analysis, not lucky gambles, offer positions of trust and valuable service. Relates to everyone, but must not become annoyed with less mentally energetic types. Finance, industry, and government are possible career opportunities.

PERSONALITY INGREDIENTS: Strives to be unconventional, enthusiastic, broad-minded. Inwardly craves charming, attractive people and environment to lift spirits. Empathetic, humanitarian instincts and generosity turn to petty criticisms or snide personalizations when disappointed. High physical energy must be displaced constructively or it internalizes to self-destructive actions.

PERSONALITY EXTREME: Too honest, or a conniver.

ADA (Hebrew/Egyptian/Greek/English)—F.

MAJOR TALENT: Ability to incorporate personal warmth, artistic expression, and responsible opinions into career. Brings imagination to life-support services. Sympathetic listener, gracious hostess, protective volunteer who should always express the Golden Rule. Home products, educational systems, and medical facilities offer possible career opportunities.

PERSONALITY INGREDIENTS: Desires beautiful surroundings, opulent home, and works to maintain conventions and material security. Appears to be conservative, practical, and sturdy. May assume responsibilities early in life. Must avoid jealousy or whining discontent. Has expressive hands.

PERSONALITY EXTREME: Too bossy, or too subordinate.

ADAM (Hebrew/English)—M.

MAJOR TALENT: Ability to incorporate original ideas, ways, and means into career. Succeeds when left to own devices. Develops willpower, quick mind, and courage for material rewards. Commercial sales, engineering, and aviation are possible career opportunities.

PERSONALITY INGREDIENTS: Strains against the system. Impatient with less efficient personalities. May exaggerate prospects or problems. Experiences major changes every five years and must plan long-term regenerative goals to maintain financial security. Desires autonomous executive power, but appears to be an accommodator.

PERSONALITY EXTREME: Too nonconformist, or swims with the stream.

ADDISON (English)—F. & M.

MAJOR TALENT: Ability to incorporate imagination in large-scale projects into artistic, judicial, or scientific career. Very versatile; skillful communicator. Voice or appearance usually attracts attention. Writing, designing, and the professions are possible career opportunities.

PERSONALITY INGREDIENTS: Desires perfection and strives for security. Appears energetic, sexy, and adventurous, but prefers quiet gentility. Must seek a specialty to bolster confidence. Usually inwardly disappointed in accomplishments until area of authority is established.

PERSONALITY EXTREME: Too impulsive, or too unchanging.

ADELA (German/English)—F.

MAJOR TALENT: Ability to incorporate speculative writing, fiery ideas, and nonconformity into career. Versatility, cleverness, and invigorating approach attract all types of friends. Can be all things to all people and benefits from all interaction. Copywriting, politics, and theatrical production are possible career opportunities.

PERSONALITY INGREDIENTS: Transparent outer personality obscures analytic/intellectual/secretive inner voice. High physical energy supports focus upon sex, sports, and sensationalism. Scatters interests; should be cautious and less impulsive. Gives refined impression and desires to have the best of everything.

PERSONALITY EXTREME: Too self-promoting, or self-deprecating.

ADELAIDE (English/German/French)—F.

MAJOR TALENT: Ability to incorporate promotional concepts into career. Talent for communication is coupled with enthusiasm that entrains the listener. A catalyst for progressive change in others' lives.

Theater/art production, politics, and advertising are possible career opportunities.

PERSONALITY INGREDIENTS: Able to structure chaos. Practical, romantic, and empathetic, with a voracious appetite for people-contact and living. Often repressed by responsibilities and pride. Desires center stage, but appears to be a modest, supportive partner.

PERSONALITY EXTREME: Too conservative, or a nonconformist.

ADELE (German/French)—F.

MAJOR TALENT: Ability to incorporate humanitarian and artistic expressions into a communications career. Shows empathy for others. Seeks a far-reaching marketplace. Elevated concepts overrule commercial rewards. Universities, charitable agencies, and government offer possible career opportunities.

PERSONALITY INGREDIENTS: Enjoys travel, progressive ideas, and intellectual/spiritual enlightenment. Appears and would prefer to be a supportive, modest listener. Has vivid imagination and memorable dreams. Should organize time to include undisturbed, restful sleep and vacations to relieve nervous habits.

PERSONALITY EXTREME: Too intense sexually, or out of touch with physical senses.

ADOLPH (German/English)—M.

MAJOR TALENT: Ability to incorporate personal ideals, evangelistic magnetism, and practical alliances into career. Creative vision is coupled with detail consciousness and emotional sensitivity for noncommercial goals. Material security is an offshoot of gifts of persuasion. Private secretary, diplomat, and statistical professions are pragmatic career opportunities. Other career possibilities require personal commitment to a cause and offer possibility of fame connected with changing the attitudes of man.

PERSONALITY INGREDIENTS: Desires spiritual/intellectual nonconformity, privacy, meditation, secrecy. Appears to be a dynamic go-getter who identifies with conventional society. Strong need for family pride.

PERSONALITY EXTREME: Too intent upon rulership, or a mundane lackey.

ADRIAN (Latin/English)—M.

MAJOR TALENT: Ability to incorporate stimulation and inspiration for social betterment into career. Diplomatic approach, tempered with patience, and tenacity bring rewards. Analyzes detailed information with ease. Attracts financial guidance and profitable partnerships. Any positions of power behind the throne in the arts, government, or the professions are possible career opportunities.

PERSONALITY INGREDIENTS: Appears worldly, but needs to mature to give impersonal love. Impresses others with idealism, emotional sensitivity, and benefits gained through elevated experiences. Autocratic attitude is an asset when tempered with cooperation, resourcefulness, and reliable judgment. Lacks sophistication in financial dealings, singularity of purpose, and emotional control.

PERSONALITY EXTREME: Too finely tuned sexually, or inhibited and sophomoric.

ADRIANNE (Latin/English)—F.

MAJOR TALENT: Ability to incorporate idealistic and creative expression into career. Innovative crusader, with compulsion to complete commitments. Attracts the limelight personally and brings efforts to a broad marketplace. Mixes business and friendships successfully. Communication media, fashion design, and publishing are possible career opportunities.

PERSONALITY INGREDIENTS: Sensual indulgences lead to nonproductive and insensitive existence. Strengths lie in imagination and intellect, not in physical senses. Needs area of research/interest to provide authority status, which will strengthen the ego and ease feelings of separatism/loneliness. When positive, a "regular gal"; but when moody, haughty/questioning.

PERSONALITY EXTREME: Too experimental, or too fearful.

ADRIENNE (Latin/French)—F.

MAJOR TALENT: Ability to incorporate intellectual curiosity into career. Speaks with authority and knows when to be silent. Fascinated by perfection and power, and geared to constructive planning. Attracts awards and bonuses. Technical, scientific, and spiritual organizations offer possible career opportunities.

PERSONALITY INGREDIENTS: Wants closeness, tenderness, and sentimentality, but prefers to conceal personal thoughts and private life. First impression is exciting, clever, and seductive. Has a well of energy for emergencies, but is most comfortable in a sedate, refined, polished atmosphere.

PERSONALITY EXTREME: Too poised and cautious, or revealing and erratic.

AGATHA (Greek/English)—F.

MAJOR TALENT: Ability to incorporate discerning sensitivity into career. Binding, bolstering, detail-oriented asset to groups and organizations. Gets recognition through diplomatic leadership. The arts, government, and data processing are possible career opportunities.

PERSONALITY INGREDIENTS: Must learn not to judge a book by its cover, to be decisive, and to adapt to change. Wants to appear authoritative, affluent, and energetic. Inwardly desires a life of cheer, imaginative interests, and generous philosophy. Needs emotional control.

PERSONALITY EXTREME: Too efficient, or too slow.

AGNES (Greek/Latin/English/Italian/French)—F.

MAJOR TALENT: Ability to incorporate originality, foresight, and management into career. When educated to a specialty, excels in public service. Self-taught do well in large organizations. High vitality fosters regeneration when chips are down. Attracts love, material contentment, and esteem. Lecturing/speaking, agriculture, and military service are possible career opportunities.

PERSONALITY INGREDIENTS: Should cultivate patience and personal sensitivity. Desires beauty, peace, and pride in family. First impression is conservative, organized, and dependable. Enjoys life's simple pleasures.

PERSONALITY EXTREME: Too compliant, or too assertive.

AILEEN (Greek: Helen/Irish)—F.

MAJOR TALENT: Ability to incorporate competitive energy, executive responsibility, and originality into career. Always ready for a challenge. Enjoys using scientific procedures. Prefers material rewards, but will forgo them to maintain relationships. Artistic production, commercial production, and transportation sales are possible career opportunities.

PERSONALITY INGREDIENTS: Full of contradictions: petty and generous. Appears to be efficient, affluent leader, but desires to be supportive partner in peaceful, harmonious life-style. Should avoid rash judgments and learn to profit from past experiences.

PERSONALITY EXTREME: Too preoccupied with sex, or indifferent to sexual explorations.

AIMEE (Latin/French)—F.

MAJOR TALENT: Ability to incorporate responsibility into a career geared to improving home/family/community conditions. Employs music, beautification, and verbal expression. Protects and serves influential people for generous compensation. Creates abundant life-style, nurtures relationships, and can be social and financial success. Practical nursing, hotel/restaurant management, and teaching are possible career opportunities.

PERSONALITY INGREDIENTS: Emotionally impulsive but financially practical companion. Personal standards are high; expects that everyone will be truthful, just, and dependable. Strong parental nature. Must avoid jealousy.

PERSONALITY EXTREME: Too seductive, or too coltish.

ALAN (Celtic/English/Scottish/Irish)—M.

MAJOR TALENT: Ability to incorporate innovative ideas to improve, advance, and challenge generations to come into career. Assumes leadership to link, influence, and revitalize groups of people. Needs no directions or urging when goals are set. Theatrical production, international politics, and inventing are possible career opportunities.

PERSONALITY INGREDIENTS: Faith, optimism, and courage to take first step top a tender, gentle, modest psyche. First impression is efficient, trustworthy, and powerful. An "old soul" that understands the depth and complexity of human emotions and life experience. Lucky when tuned to intuition, patience, and the human angle.

PERSONALITY EXTREME: Too melodramatic and changeable, or opinionated and stubborn.

ALANA (Irish/English)—F.

MAJOR TALENT: Ability to incorporate personal perceptions, detailed analysis, and sound partnership into career. Diplomatic, supportive, inspirational administrator. Benefits from charitable work, visionary salesmanship, and a noncommercial attitude. Magnetic speaker when expounding ideals. The arts, religion, and government are possible career opportunities.

PERSONALITY INGREDIENTS: Versitile, sensual, dramatic, and progressive; should be more practical. Needs attractive surroundings, friends, and avenues for self-expression. First impression is executive, but must learn to be decisive. Scatters nervous energy.

PERSONALITY EXTREME: Too willful, or too docile.

ALANNA (Irish/English)—F.
MAJOR TALENT: Ability to incorporate authority, faith, and nonmanual
skills into career. Should strive for specialized education or technical
expertise to find happiness. Writing, analysis, and counseling are possible career opportunities.
PERSONALITY INGREDIENTS: Prefers a world where nobody burps. Uncomfortable with earthy realities. Disappointed in speculation and partnerships. Succeeds materially and is happy when goals are intellectually
or spiritually oriented. First impression is down to earth, but desires
lighter pleasures.
PERSONALITY EXTREME: Too modifiable, or too resolved.

ALASTAIR (Greek/English)—M.
MAJOR TALENT: Ability to incorporate public attraction, service, and
elevated artistic expression into career. Noble instincts, compassionate
nature, and empathetic insights round out a broad philosophy. Develops
unique character through inspirational life experiences and sets standards for others. Theater, government, and any service profession are
possible career opportunities.
PERSONALITY INGREDIENTS: First impression is responsible, concerned, parental. Inwardly expansive, dramatic, and happy-go-lucky. If
decisive and nonjudgmental, may experience universal stature.
PERSONALITY EXTREME: Too philosophical, or too narrow.

ALBERT (German/English/French/Danish)—M.
MAJOR TALENT: Ability to incorporate imagination and practical results into career. Ideas are timely, constructive, and futuristic. Gener-
ates organization, practical system, and economy. Production for
industry/arts/government, technical design, and real estate are possible
career opportunities.
PERSONALITY INGREDIENTS: First impression is quiet, moody, and
aristocratic. Inwardly desires affection, family harmony, and cheerful
life-style. Needs privacy to think and develop a specialized interest.
PERSONALITY EXTREME: Too easily hurt, or too cool; self-protective.

ALBERTA (German/English)—F.
MAJOR TALENT: Ability to incorporate a mosaic of interests and contagious enthusiasm into career. Offbeat people, nonroutine schedule, and a
clever mind advance goals. Youthful zest for experimentation is an asset.
Politics, advertising and the travel industry are possible career opportunities.
PERSONALITY INGREDIENTS: First impression is inconsistent. Often
puzzling to associates. When at ease, gracious, generous, tactful, warm,
and sensitive. Inwardly requires solitude, without loneliness, and cultural stimulation. Gains self-approval through spiritual or professional
expertise. Sensual, but has difficulty identifying physical feelings.
PERSONALITY EXTREME: Too impatient, or too considerate.

ALBIN (Latin/Celtic/English)—M.
MAJOR TALENT: Ability to incorporate group cooperation, statistical
detail, and emotional sensitivity into career. Services a mass need and is
a devoted booster. Collects information, people, and things. Psychology,
accounting, and government are possible career opportunities.

PERSONALITY INGREDIENTS: A self-starter with pioneering ideas, but thrives with a secure partnership. First impression is individualistic, and inwardly really is a distinct identity. Should investigate to enlarge perspective and welcome a change of goals in midlife. Makes contribution to society after forty.

PERSONALITY EXTREME: Too speculative, or too conservative.

ALEC (Greek/English)—M.

MAJOR TALENT: Ability to incorporate a diplomatic attentiveness to the interactions of diverse personalities into career. Aesthetic, imaginative, and gifted with uncommon poise. Has choice of communication abilities: drama, painting, decorating; unusual voice attracts attention. Has star quality, dramatic imagination, and responsible follow-through. Writing, beauty products and sales, and decorating are possible career opportunities.

PERSONALITY INGREDIENTS: First impression is paternally protective, emotionally expressive, and genuinely concerned. Inwardly has unique philosophy/ideals that spark negative reactions in others. When contrary, suffers through these beliefs in strong emotional drain. Gains by remembering to live and let live.

PERSONALITY EXTREME: Too superficial and modish, or brooding and unfashionable.

ALEX (Greek/English)—F. & M.

MAJOR TALENT: Ability to incorporate imagination, emotional response and useful service into career. Attracts gifts and favors. Perseveres for both material and idealistic motives. Music, art forms, and instructive communications may blend or switch in importance throughout maturity. Civic improvement, theatrical agency, and home products/services are possible career opportunities.

PERSONALITY INGREDIENTS: Should be more discerning. Must not judge by appearances or expect everyone to abide by personal standards. Enjoys an appreciative audience and strong family pride.

PERSONALITY EXTREME: Too custodial, or avoids obligations.

ALEXANDER (Greek/German/Danish/English)—M.

MAJOR TALENT: Ability to incorporate social service, self-expression, and intense persistence into career. Optimism, enthusiasm, and inspirational/imaginative magnetism blend in a responsible nature to tackle large enterprises. Writing, entertaining, and health/beauty/fashion products are possible career opportunities.

PERSONALITY INGREDIENTS: First impression is trustworthy and broad-minded. Desires more fun and less depth to life . . . a lighthearted existence. The look of the thespian, the soul of the actor. Intense emotional outbursts and overly generous material display lose opportunities and destroy ground that has been gained. High capability when not too diversified to finish commitments.

PERSONALITY EXTREME: Too depersonalized, or too concerned.

ALEXANDRA (Greek/English)—F.

MAJOR TALENT: Ability to incorporate resourcefulness, determination, and dynamic energy into career. Understands what the public wants,

how to overcome obstacles, and how to produce tangible results. Attracts powerful associates, rewards, and recognition. Executive administration, entertainment/fashion industry, and sports are possible career
opportunities.

PERSONALITY INGREDIENTS: Needs establishment prestige. First impression is culturally developed. Usually benefits from legacy/gift of
status or money . . . or both. Travel, refinements, and social involvements check emotional insecurities. Should avoid mundane goals, unrea-
sonableness, and arrogant overconfidence.

PERSONALITY EXTREME: Too self-propelled, or stagnating.

ALEXANDRIA (Greek/Russian/English)—F.

MAJOR TALENT: Ability to incorporate diversified and far-reaching executive organizational skills into career. Realizes that steadily progressive goals, discipline, and common sense support success. Resourceful,
cautious, and efficient achiever. Attracts powerful associates. Military/
government, financial and psychiatry offer possible career opportunities.

PERSONALITY INGREDIENTS: First impression is philosophically expansive and cultured. Inwardly strives for material accumulation and
financial security. When engaged in social service, assuming responsibility and accepting burdens for the helpless, realizes healing potential,
emotional release, and extraordinary life perspective. Powerful name is
expected to serve humanity and has fortunate regenerative opportunities.

PERSONALITY EXTREME: Too willful, or too servile.

ALEXIS (Greek/French/English)—F. & M.

MAJOR TALENT: Ability to incorporate culture, refinement, and reflective wisdom into career. Questions, analyzes, and strains for perfection.
Speaks with authority, and usually is expert in a career choice. Unusual
childhood experiences encourage early maturity and self-confidence.
Education and life experience add polish. Any technical, scientific, or
spiritual interest is a possible career opportunity.

PERSONALITY INGREDIENTS: Understands quality. Inwardly desires
loving, beautiful, idyllic home/family. Enjoys responsibility and learning
from and teaching others. Absolutely a unique individual.

PERSONALITY EXTREME: Too indecisive, or too commanding.

ALFRED (Teutonic/English/German/Danish/French)—M.

MAJOR TALENT: Ability to incorporate responsible judgment, new
ideas, and boldness into career. A forerunner who takes direct action to
improve existing conditions. Inventive, courageous, competitive. Successful when motives are aboveboard. Not at best trusting to partners.
Sole proprietorship, home-product design and theatrical production are
possible career opportunities.

PERSONALITY INGREDIENTS: Takes pride in family/community. Wants
a gracious, beautiful, culturally–expansive home and life style. Appears
solid, conservative, and controlled.

PERSONALITY EXTREME: Too impractical, or too economical.

ALFREDA (Teutonic/English)—F.

MAJOR TALENT: Ability to incorporate detailed observations, methods, and analyses into career. Commercial success can be achieved with foresight, tactful interaction, and cooperative partnership. Data processing, inspirational writing/teaching/lecturing, and metaphysics are possible career opportunities.

PERSONALITY INGREDIENTS: First impression is sturdy, practical, and composed. Inwardly reflective, perfecting, and quality-conscious. Struggles with material aspects of personality. Often picks the wrong friends/business associates. Less pride and stubborn emotionalism will open doors to greater discernment and healthier decisions.

PERSONALITY EXTREME: Too strong, or too weak.

ALGERNON (Old French/English)—M.

MAJOR TALENT: Ability to incorporate a variety of enthusiasms, commitments, and methods into career. Inspires and promotes, and challenges outworn conditions. Unusually fertile; breeds ideas and children. Imports/exports, communications, and language teaching are possible career opportunities.

PERSONALITY INGREDIENTS: First impression is modest, but seems special. Inwardly desires beauty, love, and pleasure seeking. Strong protective and reflective needs. Dislikes vulgarity, ugliness, and impracticality. Usually a closet sensualist.

PERSONALITY EXTREME: Too conservative, or too unconventional.

ALI (English diminutive of names that begin with *Ali,* or foreign)—F. & M.

MAJOR TALENT: Ability to incorporate a sixth sense of life's true values into career. Intuition to see through people and experiences provides a special skill for transforming and rebuilding when others give up. Employs practical common sense and structure to ensure durability. Farming, efficiency engineering, and the communications trades are possible career opportunities.

PERSONALITY INGREDIENTS: Appears charming, stylish, and imaginative. Inwardly feels competitive, assertive, and individualistic. Less carelessness, impatience, and indiscretion will make changing direction easier. Wants to be unique.

PERSONALITY EXTREME: Too sympathetic, or unemotional.

ALICE (Greek/English)—F.

MAJOR TALENT: Ability to incorporate presence, good memory, and delicate artistic inspiration into career. Diversifies interests through travel. Applies charm, concentration, and positive thinking. Cosmetics, voice teaching, and writing are possible career opportunities.

PERSONALITY INGREDIENTS: Appears to be and feels protective, comfortable, and parental. Either very natty or a sloppy dresser. Likes an audience, and often talks too much. Must avoid living in the past to spark visionary gifts.

PERSONALITY EXTREME: Too experimental, or too conservative.

ALICIA (Greek/Italian/Spanish/English)—F.

MAJOR TALENT: Ability to incorporate positive action, executive self-

All names that begin with the letter *A* have the *Strong Point* of
independent leadership—creative energy—ambition—mental attitude.

27

control, and magnetic attraction into career. Benefits group ambitions,
financial institutions, and athletic organizations. Theater arts, health
products, and investigative services are possible career opportunities.

PERSONALITY INGREDIENTS: Attracts attention. Sensitive, artistic, caring, responsive, and very idealistic.

PERSONALITY EXTREME: Too self-concerned, or drained by emotional
relationships.

ALISA (Greek/Hebrew/English)—F.

MAJOR TALENT: Ability to incorporate artistic attraction, perseverance, and a strong will into career. Good student/imaginative teacher.
Plans carefully and is usually rewarded by favors, gifts, and/or money.
Decorative products, theater, and marriage/divorce industries are possible career opportunities.

PERSONALITY INGREDIENTS: Appears average, but feels special. Sensitivity and structured thinking may cause difficulties. Should develop a
lighter attitude to relieve self-induced pressures. Matures to realize
benefits from forgiveness. Always wants tangible evidence of accomplishments.

PERSONALITY EXTREME: Too easily discouraged, or too bent upon
change.

ALISON (Latin/English/Irish/Scottish/Spanish)—F. & M.

MAJOR TALENT: Ability to incorporate observation, detail awareness,
and intuition into career. Expresses novel ideas, has quality consciousness, and is accepted by everyone. Has the knack of making changes
based upon past experiences. Photography, medicine, and research are
possible career opportunities.

PERSONALITY INGREDIENTS: Appears to be socially adept, artistically
gifted, and broad-scoped. Inwardly requires privacy to reflect upon ways
to perfect growth. Strives for self-confidence through cultural polish and
a sense of authority. Dictates, but cannot take orders comfortably. Quick
temper when insecure intellectually.

PERSONALITY EXTREME: Too impulsive, or procrastinating.

ALISTAIR (English)—F. & M.

MAJOR TALENT: Ability to incorporate executive decisions, financial
judgment, and practical methods into career. Attracts powerful people,
growth opportunities, and strenuous activity. Very industrious, resourceful, and innovative. Business/political adviser, architecture, and
investigative professions are possible career opportunities.

PERSONALITY INGREDIENTS: Appears to be charming, expressive, and
genuinely concerned. Inwardly too personalized, often petty. Desires
loving mate; easy-going home life; and to collect people, facts, and
things. Improves material worth through dedication to convictions, unbiased relationships, and an innate comfort/empathy for breaking lan-
gauge barriers.

PERSONALITY EXTREME: Too emotional, or too detached.

ALLAN (Celtic: Alan/English)—M.

MAJOR TALENT: Ability to incorporate practical methods for rebuilding, transforming, and renewing tangibles into career. When others give

up a business, relationship or a humane cause, the mental agility to reevaluate emerges. Down-to-earth insights make it difficult to be fooled. Accountancy/law, construction trades, and efficiency engineering are possible career opportunities.

PERSONALITY INGREDIENTS: Appears to be and is unpretentious, supportive, and sensitive. Detail conscious. Strives to maintain partnerships. Unexpected upheavals and idealistic crusades slow long-term goals. Optimistic sense of humor, easy-going nature and receptivity to creative leadership softens rough spots.

PERSONALITY EXTREME: Too cautious, or too erratic.

ALLEN (Celtic: Alan/English)—M.

MAJOR TALENT: Ability to incorporate research, efficiency, and executive judgment into career. Innate intelligence, persuasive eloquence, and intuitive decisions inevitably will contribute to a rise in status. Should aim high. Government, brokerage, and criminal investigation are possible career opportunities.

PERSONALITY INGREDIENTS: Outwardly modest and full of idealistic persuasions. Inwardly responsible, "domesticated," and expressive. Strong personal standards tend to create demanding judgments. Responds to artistic touches, music, and stimulating companionship.

PERSONALITY EXTREME: Too curious, or too indifferent.

ALLISON (Teutonic/English)—M.

MAJOR TALENT: Ability to incorporate cautious judgments, direct actions, and pioneering ideas into career. Courage supports intuition. Receives tangible rewards for inspirational group work. Learns from past mistakes. Program planning, communications, and brokerage are possible career opportunities.

PERSONALITY INGREDIENTS: First impression is socially attractive, artistic, and expressive. Inwardly unable to accept ordinary people and circumstances. Expects perfection, polish, and quality. Feels need for authority.

PERSONALITY EXTREME: Too reckless, or too controlled.

ALLISTER (Greek/Gaelic/Scottish/English)—M.

MAJOR TALENT: Ability to incorporate enlightened teaching, beneficial reforms, and responsible service into career. Honesty, determination, and self-sacrifice attract supporters. If a heartfelt purpose can be identified, lasting improvements will result. If focus is personalized, domestic instincts take over. Decorative/theatrical/musical arts, home products, and credit unions offer possible career opportunities.

PERSONALITY INGREDIENTS: First impression is magnetic, enthusiastic, and empathetic. Inwardly feels protective and strives for family/community advantages. Happiest when in love and advising others.

PERSONALITY EXTREME: Too worldly, or too unsophisticated.

ALLYN (Celtic: Alan/English)—M.

MAJOR TALENT: Ability to incorporate invention and theorization into career. Accepts and overcomes challenges to reach broad opportunities. Attracts cooperation and is able to sell original concepts. Able to lead a double life and usually does. Production, promotion, and designing are possible career opportunities.

PERSONALITY INGREDIENTS: Appears low-key, but really is a high-powered producer. Desires the independence that money and power bring. Emotionally tender, sensitively attractive, and intellectually versatile.

PERSONALITY EXTREME: Too promiscuous, or too inhibited.

ALMA (Latin/Arabic/Celtic/Italian/English)—F.

MAJOR TALENT: Ability to incorporate inspirational guidance, humanitarian service, and emotional wisdom into career. Understands how people feel and why they do, or want, something that is unique to their personality. High standards, broad philosophy, and artistic discrimination attract noteworthy personalities. Medicine, music, and research are possible career opportunities.

PERSONALITY INGREDIENTS: Combines emotional sensitivity and cultural perfection. Desires comfort, serenity, and material security. Appears to be a loner.

PERSONALITY EXTREME: Too self-indulgent, or a martyr.

ALOYSIUS (Old German/Latin; English Lewis)—M.

MAJOR TALENT: Ability to incorporate practical judgments, tenacity, and a fighting spirit into career. Influences associates as a loyal, honest, and steadfast force. Diligent research and positive action will bring successful outcomes if confirmed by professional counsel. Mechanics, farming, and theatrical production are possible career opportunities.

PERSONALITY INGREDIENTS: Appears to be easygoing, attractive, and multifaceted. Inwardly wants to be boss. Offers intense courage, inspiration, and strength in times of trouble.

PERSONALITY EXTREME: Too disdainful, or too easily satisfied.

ALPHONSO (Teutonic/Old German/Latin/English)—M.

MAJOR TALENT: Ability to incorporate contagious inspirations, mature judgments, and controlled reactions into career. Aspires to prominence, and succeeds when home/family relationships are secure. Travel offers fortunate meetings. International banking, religious philosophies, and poker playing are possible career opportunities.

PERSONALITY INGREDIENTS: Takes pride in emotional control. Explodes when plans are jeopardized. Motivated to preserve, build, and accumulate. First impression is kindly, concerned, and responsible. Requires cooperation, individualism, and authority.

PERSONALITY EXTREME: Too conscientious, or too irresponsible.

ALTHEA (Greek/English)—F.

MAJOR TALENTS: Ability to incorporate detailed perceptions, adaptability, and diplomatic courtesy into career. Faces diverse factions and joins opposing forces. Grows through balancing sensitive relationships, and the inner strength that develops toughens thin emotional skin. Can be depended upon to keep a secret, boost initiative in others, and overcome obstacles. Arbitration agent, private secretary, and legislator are possible career opportunities.

PERSONALITY INGREDIENTS: Has a special sparkle. Appears to be conventional, practical, and organized, but inwardly strives for quality embellishments, cultural poise, and perfection in all things. Needs physical stimulation.

PERSONALITY EXTREME: Too indecisive, or too tenacious.

ALVA (Latin/Spanish/English)—F. & M.

MAJOR TALENT: Ability to incorporate inspirations and aspirations for benefiting others into career. Unbiased, concerned, and elevated to a broad philosophy due to empathetic attitudes. Understanding of universal standards attracts opportunities to meet the famous and become one of them. Exploring, science, and medicine are possible career opportunities.

PERSONALITY INGREDIENTS: Inwardly wants attention, is shy and keenly aware of details. First impression is reserved and quietly authoritative. Secretive nature creates tensions. Should avoid living in the past.

PERSONALITY EXTREME: Too ambivalent, or too sure.

ALVIN (Old German/English)—M.

MAJOR TALENT: Ability to incorporate constructive personal concepts, hard work, and ethical authority into a career that raises expectations for others. Solves problems, builds a better mousetrap, and implements improved conditions. Fluctuates between intuitive and workaholic drives. Puts strong opinions and wisdom to practical use. Government, any profession, and property development are possible career opportunities.

PERSONALITY INGREDIENTS: Appears to be empathetic, reasonable, and a communicator. Actually wants to be the boss. Has a sense of responsibility to mass needs, and aims for enduring results.

PERSONALITY EXTREME: Too improvisational, or too structured.

ALVINA (Old German/English)—F.

MAJOR TALENT: Ability to incorporate a clever, quick, articulate delivery of ideas into career. Passionately loyal, investigative, and enthusiastic; attracts supporters and rewards. Intuitive decisions and remedies work best. Reporting, body building, and any field that offers on-the-job training are possible career opportunities.

PERSONALITY INGREDIENTS: Inwardly high-strung and sensitive. First impression is affable, expressive, and multifaceted. Sometimes patronizing or argumentative. Makes a good marriage.

PERSONALITY EXTREME: Too hasty, or too rooted.

ALYCE (Greek/English)—F.

MAJOR TALENT: Ability to incorporate nontraditional ideas into a mass-service industry. Overcomes obstacles through perseverance. Effective speaker; scientifically or artistically oriented. Attracts love and money. Theatrical production, designing, and selling are possible career opportunities.

PERSONALITY INGREDIENTS: Appears to be a conservative, effective, practical person. Inwardly strives for recognition, family/community improvement, and a gracious life-style. Complex personality wants companionship and privacy.

PERSONALITY EXTREME: Too spontaneous, or overreacts when surprised.

ALYSON (Greek: Alyssa/English)—F.

MAJOR TALENT: Ability to incorporate physical attributes, cleverness, and enthusiasm into career. Benefits from knowledgeable business associates and friends and from flexible daily schedule. Open-minded: coordinates a variety of commitments. Communications, research, and politics are possible career opportunities.

PERSONALITY INGREDIENTS: Inwardly fears loneliness and poverty. Desires cultivated life-style. First impression is inconsistent. Often the authority; other times uncommunicative.

PERSONALITY EXTREME: Too cautious, or an opportunist.

ALYSSA (Greek/English)—F.

MAJOR TALENT: Ability to incorporate clever adaptations of personal experiences into career. Attracts education through unusual opportunities and people. Physical appetites are strong. Can exert self-control to balance business and homelife when overcommitted. Vivid imagination; should write for profit or pleasure. Cautious gambling, entertainment industries, and counseling are possible career opportunities.

PERSONALITY INGREDIENTS: First impression is personable, articulate, and onstage. Inwardly desires serenity and security. Empathetic psychologist. Has problems with narrow thinking and book learning.

PERSONALITY EXTREME: Too innovative, or too modified.

AMANDA (Latin/English)—F.

MAJOR TALENT: Ability to incorporate dignity, refinement, and expertise into career. Magnetic, decisive, but lacks faith in intellectual self. Focus on noncommercial work presents situations which build authority. Then others seek you out, and money comes through them to provide financial security. Deception, disappointment, and insecurity may come through greed. Photography, research, and healing are possible career opportunities.

PERSONALITY INGREDIENTS: Appears to be practical, but inwardly would spend last penny on a beautiful flower.

PERSONALITY EXTREME: Too dependent, or overly assertive.

AMBER (Arabic/English)—F.

MAJOR TALENT: Ability to incorporate beauty, optimism, and sensitivity into career. Exhibits imagination and administrative ability, and often sets inspirational examples laced with humor or ESP. Art, sales, and medicine are possible career opportunities.

PERSONALITY INGREDIENTS: Desires love, roots, and harmony. Shares obligations and responsibilities. Very levelheaded when unemotional.

PERSONALITY EXTREME: Too romantic and compassionate, or indifferent and too personalized.

AMBROSE (Greek/English)—M.

MAJOR TALENT: Ability to incorporate organization, leadership, and detail into career. Enterprising, materialistic, and trustworthy. Rises above self-interest. Large service organizations, inventive products, and directorships offer possible career opportunities.

PERSONALITY INGREDIENTS: Understands practical economy and strategy, and respects established procedures. Tactful, sensitive, and

cooperative when prepared. Dislikes surprises. Generous to family and
universally understanding.

PERSONALITY EXTREME: Too persevering, or an adventurous butterfly.

AMELIA (Teutonic: Emily/English)—F.

MAJOR TALENT: Ability to incorporate versatility, promotional skills,
and the ability to learn by trial and error into career. Enthusiastic, open-
minded, and imaginative. Copyreading, interpreting, and advertising are
possible career opportunities.

PERSONALITY INGREDIENTS: Follows directions and works with a plan,
but needs exciting daily routine or subject matter. Benefits from physical
exercise.

PERSONALITY EXTREME: Too persistent, or constantly changing.

AMOS (Hebrew)—M.

MAJOR TALENT: Ability to incorporate social contacts and imagination
into a practical career. Assumes responsibility for group commitments.
Employs words, humor, and appearance for success. Nursing, the arts,
and vocational guidance are possible career opportunities.

PERSONALITY INGREDIENTS: Conservative attitude when family or
community is involved. Protective, structured, and very emotional. Unusual point of view; not one of the crowd.

PERSONALITY EXTREME: Too commanding, or too submissive.

AMY (Latin/English)—F.

MAJOR TALENT: Ability to incorporate inspiration, imagination, and
communication talents into career. Can be prolific writer. Enjoys a variety of interests. Health improvement, artistic crafts and supplies sales,
and spiritual advising are possible career opportunities.

PERSONALITY INGREDIENTS: Prefers to feel useful. May overtalk or
clam up. Rare combination of down-to-earth qualities and creative expression.

PERSONALITY EXTREME: Too insecure intellectually, or the authority
on everything.

ANABEL (English/Scottish)—F.

MAJOR TALENT: Ability to incorporate executive and administrative
skills, technical expertise, and mental endurance into career. Works
either alone or with others to produce tangible results. Benefits through
travel. Business law, criminal investigation, and banking are possible
career opportunities.

PERSONALITY INGREDIENTS: Needs quality cultural opportunities, personal privacy, and time to develop depth of character. Appears energetic
and individualistic. Must curb impulsiveness and stubborn streak.

PERSONALITY EXTREME: Too serious, or too flighty.

ANASTASIA (Greek/English/Irish/Russian)—F.

MAJOR TALENT: Ability to incorporate problem-solving activities and
practical solutions into career. An ethical, constructive, wise, visionary
powerhouse. Strong opinions attract policy-making positions. Industry,
politics, and any of the professions are possible career opportunities.

PERSONALITY INGREDIENTS: High-strung energy and impatience may

cause reversals. Intuitively builds toward financial security. Should rise
above mundane experience, aim for universal service and avoid overindulgence, gambles, and physical limitations.

PERSONALITY EXTREME: Too headstrong, or lacking self-determina-
tion.

ANATOL (Greek/English/French)—M.

MAJOR TALENT: Ability to incorporate artistic, governmental, or
humanitarian service into career. Intuitive organizer with leadership
drive. Employs vivid imagination. Superb counselor. Any creative or
performing art, crime investigation, and medicine are possible career
opportunities.

PERSONALITY INGREDIENTS: Intensely emotional reactions often cause
repeated nightmares. Health depends upon positive life-style. Prefers a
gentle approach, though unaccountably irritable when daydreaming.

PERSONALITY EXTREME: Too communicative, or taciturn.

ANDRE (Greek: Andrew/French/Portuguese)—M.

MAJOR TALENT: Ability to incorporate comforting service, communication and a strong sense of responsibility into career. Attracts the support of powerful people. Sincere, just, and practical. Teaching, the
decorative arts, and the theater are possible career opportunities.

PERSONALITY INGREDIENTS: Attracts family life-style and community
participation. When negative, jealous, stubborn, and a vengeance
seeker. Generally, provides and receives material comforts.

PERSONALITY EXTREME: Too sensual, or disconnected from physical
impressions.

ANDREA (Greek/Scottish/English)—F. (Italian)—M.

MAJOR TALENT: Ability to incorporate cultural refinements, intellectual questioning, and specialization into career. Combines intuition, detail analysis, and cultural awareness. Thrives on a changing schedule.
Can rise above mundane life-style. Photography, parasciences, and land-
scaping are possible career opportunities.

PERSONALITY INGREDIENTS: Would prefer a life where nobody
burped. Earthy encounters rattle the senses. Keeps a youthful vigor,
employs conventions of society, and benefits from quiet time near the
water.

PERSONALITY EXTREME: Too bossy, or lacking autonomy.

ANDREW (Greek/Scottish/English)—M.

MAJOR TALENT: Ability to incorporate partnership into career. Attracts peer relationships and assistance in visionary commercial ventures. Eloquent speaker when selling personal ideals. Vital, generous,
enthusiastic supporter. Public affairs, space-age electronics, and education offer possible career opportunities.

PERSONALITY INGREDIENTS: Must overcome anxiety and harness nervous energy. Has to have the last word. Has difficulty understanding the
business world initially, but learns to cooperate and finds success. Very
individualistic.

PERSONALITY EXTREME: Too unconventional, or Hoyle-bound.

ANDRIA (Latin)—F.

MAJOR TALENT: Ability to incorporate authority through tact, diplomacy, and boosting into career. Absorbs details. Sensitive to family/group thinking and emotions. Commercial success comes through associates. Dance, government, and inspirational forms of communication are possible career opportunities.

PERSONALITY INGREDIENTS: Feels special. Expects recognition. Empathetic nature affects emotions and health. Impractical; too compassionate and generous. Enjoys travel, unique people, and futuristic artistic expression.

PERSONALITY EXTREME: Too controlled by others, or unrestrained.

ANGELA (Greek/Latin/Old French/English)—F.

MAJOR TALENT: Ability to incorporate constructive planning, industrious habits, and wide-scoped tangible results into career. Practical, honest, ethical organizer. Attracts attention through voicing strong opinions. Mediation, school administration, and cataloguing are possible career opportunities.

PERSONALITY INGREDIENTS: The original Ms. Fullcharge. Works hard at everything. Suffers through overestimating energy. Employs practical wisdom to build strong personal relationships.

PERSONALITY EXTREME: Too precautionary, or bold and impatient.

ANGELICA (Greek: Angela/Latin/English)—F.

MAJOR TALENT: Ability to incorporate orderly system, levelheaded practical analysis, and formal conventions into career. Deals in facts, and employs gifted intuition. Strong sense of right and wrong. Legal profession, archaeology, and dentistry are possible career opportunities.

PERSONALITY INGREDIENTS: Extreme desire for perfection in self and others. Enjoys cultural associations, travel, and philosophical personalities. Overcomes self-doubt if considered an expert. Needs privacy. Attracts admiring friends.

PERSONALITY EXTREME: Too inoffensive, or self-important.

ANGELINA (Greek: Angela/English)—F.

MAJOR TALENT: Ability to incorporate a nonprovincial approach and empathy for all into career. Gives more than is received. Imaginative communicator, with a need to help and protect. Any field that requires emotional response, healing inspiration, and realistic judgment is a possible career opportunity.

PERSONALITY INGREDIENTS: Lacks faith in intellectual self. Needs academic education or a field of expertise. Appears to be modest, passive, and supportive.

PERSONALITY EXTREME: Too thoughtless, or overly considerate.

ANGUS (Celtic/English)—M.

MAJOR TALENT: Ability to incorporate executive organizational skills, commercial awareness, and investigative curiosity into career. Benefits through solitude to research ideas and concentrate upon plans. Always produces tangibles. Aviation, exploring, and science are possible career opportunities.

PERSONALITY INGREDIENTS: Suffers through stubbornness, pessi-

mism, and lack of true understanding of spiritual values. Wants and
appears to be practical, economical, and self-disciplined.

PERSONALITY EXTREME: Too personalized, or lacking sensitivity.

ANITA (Hebrew: Hannah-Ann/Spanish)—F.

MAJOR TALENT: Ability to incorporate a broad philosophy into artistic/
spiritual/practical service career. Combines organizational instincts with
innate magnetism. Should allow for human frailty. Any art form, horticulture, and medicine are possible career opportunities.

PERSONALITY INGREDIENTS: Enjoys physical pleasures, variety, and a
sense of humor. Sensitive emotionally; a martyr when depressed.

PERSONALITY EXTREME: Too aggressive, or overly congenial.

ANN (Hebrew: Hannah/English)—M. & F.

MAJOR TALENT: Ability to incorporate idealistic leadership, inspirational artistry, and devotion to a goal into career. Draws upon sensitivity
to detail, communication gifts, and desire to open doors to information
that may benefit others. Possibility of fame through charitable works.
Public affairs, writing, and metaphysical instruction are possible career
opportunities.

PERSONALITY INGREDIENTS: Desires to be an individualist and appears
to be one. Must develop patience and emotional detachment, and learn
to examine the fine print before making commitments.

PERSONALITY EXTREME: Too impulsive, or too deliberate.

ANNA (Hebrew: Hannah-Ann/English/Italian/Dutch/Danish)—F.

MAJOR TALENT: Ability to incorporate social relationships, imagination, and uncommon poise into career. Employs tolerance, unique
understanding of humanity's realities, and personal sacrifice to benefit
others. Happiest when nonmaterialistic. Natural go-between. Art, fashion, or cosmetics sales, philosophy, and service professions are possible
career opportunities.

PERSONALITY INGREDIENTS: Appears independent; desires to be supportive.

PERSONALITY EXTREME: Too mental, or too emotional.

ANNABELLE (English, combining Hebrew: Hannah + Latin:
Belle)—F.

MAJOR TALENT: Ability to incorporate extraordinary goals, system,
and a practical application of sex appeal into career. Attracts attention; is
versatile, clever, idealistic. Lucky in love and material rewards.
Medicine, the judicial system, and all artistic media are possible career
opportunities.

PERSONALITY INGREDIENTS: Desires security and a happy home, and
to be the center of attention. Appears magnetic, empathetic, and
humanitarian.

PERSONALITY EXTREME: Too filled with enthusiasms, or discontented
through boredom.

ANNE (Hebrew: Hannah-Ann/English/French/German)—F.

MAJOR TALENT: Ability to incorporate splendid logic, excellent taste,
and a drive for perfection into career. Knows how to read between the

lines. Most competent in position of authority. Advances through research and specialization. Library work, photography, and playwriting are possible career opportunities.

PERSONALITY INGREDIENTS: Appears capable, self-assertive, and singular, but lacks intellectual self-esteem. Desires love, family harmony, and affection, but may lose warmth by expecting too much of loved ones. Generally chooses service career and suffers disappointments through legal or family misunderstandings.

PERSONALITY EXTREME: Too apprehensive, or foolishly fearless.

ANNEMARIE (English/French, combining Anne + Marie)—F.

MAJOR TALENT: Ability to incorporate a proclivity for executive organization, constructive application, and regard for profit into career. Fortunate when dealing with finance, but must master an appreciation for nonmaterial values. Disciplined, resourceful, and steadfast. Has opportunity to bring lasting benefits to others. Construction industry, medicine, and government are possible career opportunities.

PERSONALITY INGREDIENTS: Desires beauty and attracts excitement.

PERSONALITY EXTREME: Too centered on youth, or too old-fashioned.

ANNETTE (Hebrew: Hannah-Ann/French)—F.

MAJOR TALENT: Ability to incorporate a perfectionist attitude toward details and gifted intuitive abilities into career. Thrives when mobile in a specialized field. Photography, research, and spiritual work are possible career opportunities.

PERSONALITY INGREDIENTS: Appears devil-may-care, but wants a sensitive one-to-one partner. Suffers through emotional reactions and nervous energy.

PERSONALITY EXTREME: Too impulsive, or too cautious.

ANTHONY (Latin/English)—M.

MAJOR TALENT: Ability to incorporate practical organizational skills, communication devices, and down-to-earth analysis into career. Employs determined approach, lateral vision, and trustworthy instincts. Enlarges expertise through air travel, formal procedures, and patient study. Attracts success. Lecturing, writing, and scientific/technical processes offer possible career opportunities.

PERSONALITY INGREDIENTS: Needs physical pleasures, progressive opportunities, and freedom of expression. Prefers to seem modest/indulgent/conservative, but surprises intimates with offbeat enthusiasms.

PERSONALITY EXTREME: Too blunt, or too cunning.

ANTOINE (Latin: Anthony/French)—M.

MAJOR TALENT: Ability to incorporate imaginative artistry into a service career. Discriminating reformer when a worthy mission is offered. Protective family/community adviser. Offers self-sacrifice, martyrdom, or a passion for uplifting humanity when pursuing ideals. Alleviates problems for others. Public service, interpretation of religion, and family counseling are possible career opportunities.

PERSONALITY INGREDIENTS: Born communicator. Needs variety, beauty, and a sense of humor.

PERSONALITY EXTREME: Too innovative, or invariable.

ANTOINETTE (Latin: Antonia/French)—F.

MAJOR TALENT: Ability to incorporate personal charm, social responsibility, and artistic discrimination into career. Knows how to make people comfortable, entertained, and loved. Family/community services, interior decoration, and theater work are possible career opportunities.

PERSONALITY INGREDIENTS: Needs warm personal relationships, but must learn to balance imagination and emotions. Serves as a harmonizer, desires material accumulation, and gives cultured/refined/intellectual impression.

PERSONALITY EXTREME: Too adventurous, or too timid.

ANTON (Latin: Anthony/German/Slovak)—M.

MAJOR TALENT: Ability to incorporate managerial and regenerative attitudes into career. High energy, courage, and quick thinking turn problems into projects that bring benefits to others. Distributes reasonable and enduring guidance through pioneering concepts. Learns quickly from mistakes. Creative work, the military, and theatrical production are possible career opportunities.

PERSONALITY INGREDIENTS: Prefers intellectual and cultured people and surroundings. Appears light and extroverted. A fooler—really a thoughtful perfectionist.

PERSONALITY EXTREME: Too experimental, or too theoretical.

ANTONY (Latin: Anthony/English)—M.

MAJOR TALENT: Ability to incorporate enthusiasm, speaking abilities, and courage into a materialistic career. Develops self-confidence, wisdom, and endurance through trial and error. High-powered executive. Strong sense of physical balance. Sports, finance, and communications are possible career opportunities.

PERSONALITY INGREDIENTS: Desires adventure. Needs freedom, but must control impulsiveness. Physically attractive, colorful, and sensual. Love relationships are problematic.

PERSONALITY EXTREME: Too melancholy and withdrawn, or displaying haughty authority.

APRIL (Latin/English)—F.

MAJOR TALENT: Ability to incorporate successful partnerships, artistic/uplifting vision, and contagious eagerness into career. Succeeds after learning to understand commercial/business world. Multifaceted abilities, almost regal bearing, and virtuous ideals attract a unique social circle. Inspirational writing, public welfare promotion, and electronic sciences are possible career opportunities.

PERSONALITY INGREDIENTS: Must avoid pride, arrogance, and stubbornness. Nervous energy causes uncertainty and anxiety.

PERSONALITY EXTREME: Too animated and optimistic, or dull and uninspired.

ARCHER (English/German diminutive of Archibald)—M.

MAJOR TALENT: Ability to incorporate individualistic, forceful decision making, exceptional vitality, and mass-market service needs into career. Charming, dedicated, and usually inherits money, power, or position. Confident executive, responsible, and able to maintain success. Business and the teaching and legal professions offer possible career opportunities.

PERSONALITY INGREDIENTS: Expects that everyone will live up to personal standards. May be unreasonable or unbending where family/community responsibilities are concerned.

PERSONALITY EXTREME: Too compassionate or uninterested.

ARCHIBALD (Teutonic/German/Latin/English)—M.

MAJOR TALENT: Ability to incorporate mathematics, material planning, and well-rounded analysis into career. Honorable, confident, wise individual. Investment counseling, real estate, and accounting are possible career opportunities.

PERSONALITY INGREDIENTS: Dislikes arguments, confusion, and rudeness. Will subordinate self to keep the peace. Must not be indecisive, petty, or overly sensitive. Enjoys nature, and attracts lasting benefits for self and others.

PERSONALITY EXTREME: Too methodized, or disorganized.

ARDIS (Latin: Ardelia/English)—F.

MAJOR TALENT: Ability to incorporate a magnetic personality combined with artistic and responsible service into career. Fortunate materially, socially, and in family growth. Convincing talker; rarely indifferent to others' needs. Home/community improvement, music, and practical nursing are possible career opportunities.

PERSONALITY INGREDIENTS: Needs autonomy and recognition. Self-importance may bring out a domineering/jealous/stubborn streak. Looks sexy, dashing, and enthusiastic. High physical energy should be disciplined.

PERSONALITY EXTREME: Too self-sacrificing, or too headstrong.

ARLENE (Celtic/Irish/English)—F.

MAJOR TALENT: Ability to incorporate unique personal characteristics, bold ideas, and the courage of strong convictions into career. Generous, emotional, daring goals will be achieved through patient determination. Attracts help from the opposite sex. Must learn from experience and partnerships. Management, retail ownership, and program planning are possible career opportunities.

PERSONALITY INGREDIENTS: Wants recognition, a loving partner, and serenity. Impresses others as establishment power type. Suffers if impatient, lazy, or inconstant.

PERSONALITY EXTREME: Too apprehensive, or in constant motion.

ARLINE (Celtic: Arlene/German)—F.

MAJOR TALENT: Ability to incorporate foreign-language aptitude, social confidence, and promotional communications into career. Attracts help from friends by exhibiting modest pose. Experiences prophetic dreams. Versatile opportunist, gambler, counselor. Teaching, import-export, and theatrical production are possible career opportunities.

PERSONALITY INGREDIENTS: Needs and creates homey atmosphere everywhere. Wants love, protection, and beauty. First impression is businesslike and successful.

PERSONALITY EXTREME: Too enthusiastic, or too blasé.

ARLO (Old English: Harlow)—M.

MAJOR TALENT: Ability to incorporate public-service organization, regenerative concepts, and expressive communicating into career. When emotions are mastered attracts money, a good homelife, and recognition. Overcomes a variety of obstacles through great endurance. Lecturing, agriculture, and theater arts are possible career opportunities.

PERSONALITY INGREDIENTS: When dependent or feeling self-pity, loss of courage causes escapist tactics. May lead a double life. Needs serene environment, but appears to want social variety. Talented introvert/extrovert.

PERSONALITY EXTREME: Too idealistic, or wishy-washy.

ARMAND (Old German: Herman/Latin/French)—M.

MAJOR TALENT: Ability to incorporate an attractive personality into a sympathetic, responsible, and trustworthy family/community service career. Attracts music, beauty, and influential friends. Business judgment, patience, and disciplined instruction come naturally. Family pride and abundant life-style are important. Marriage counseling, medicine, and artistic instruction are possible career opportunities.

PERSONALITY INGREDIENTS: Collects everything. Appears masterly, conservative, and durable, but needs gentle touch; a sensitive mate.

PERSONALITY EXTREME: Too practical, or too disorganized.

ARNOLD (Old German/Teutonic/Italian/English)—M.

MAJOR TALENT: Ability to incorporate trend-setting authority, accountability, and realistic foresight into career. Analytic, inspirational, and courageous. Expects financial remuneration. Learns to avoid fence sitting, tactlessness, and impatience from group participation. Scientific procedures, theatrical production, and any creative business are possible career opportunities.

PERSONALITY INGREDIENTS: Needs cultural stimulation. Prefers refined people and atmosphere. Attracts attention through appearance and personality.

PERSONALITY EXTREME: Too rigid, or a rule-bender.

ARTHUR (Welsh/French)—M.

MAJOR TALENT: Ability to incorporate versatility, promotion, and adventurous activity into career. Usually understands why people tick; intuitive diagnostician. A catalyst for personal change in others' lives. Should aim high, take mental responsibility, and persist despite the judgments of associates. The communications, investigation, and teaching fields offer possible career opportunities.

PERSONALITY INGREDIENTS: Haughtiness may be self-defeating. Progress may seem to come too easily; avoid guilt feelings that may explode on loved ones. Appears to be different, but comfortable when practical and organized in an Everyman life-style.

PERSONALITY EXTREME: Too generous and romantic, or unimaginative and self-oriented.

AXEL (Teutonic/English/Danish)—M.

MAJOR TALENT: Ability to incorporate determination, cleverness, and understanding for others' frustrations or weaknesses into career. A sense

of humor should be developed to lighten the restraints of the desire for
status and possessions. Very strong ambition is aided by focus upon
learning from others' mistakes. Fund raising, fashion, and acting are
possible career opportunities.

PERSONALITY INGREDIENTS: Must laugh in the face of adversity, and
learn to be discerning and to control emotional reactions. Appears to be
compassionate, worldly, and philosophical. Desires roots, beauty, and
gracious living.

PERSONALITY EXTREME: Too eloquent, or too silent.

ASA (Hebrew)—M.

MAJOR TALENT: Ability to incorporate writing, music, painting, and
the performing arts into career. Honest, imaginative, affable personality.
Lucky if not overindulgent. Any career that offers star status offers a
career opportunity. Counseling, social work, and the law utilize complexity of personality.

PERSONALITY INGREDIENTS: Impatient/sensitive dreamer; can make
dreams come true just by wishing. Uses words and unusual voice to
advantage. Does everything in a big way. In constant motion; scatters
interests, energy, and money. Should avoid gossip, superficiality, and
isolation. Must have people.

PERSONALITY EXTREME: Too self-centered, or too eager to please.

ASHER (Hebrew/Old English)—M.

MAJOR TALENT: Ability to incorporate strong sense of symmetry, justice, and responsibility into career. Succeeds in harmonious atmosphere
where trust, emotional response, and uplifting standards are shared.
Home products, music, teaching, and medical administration offer possible career opportunities.

PERSONALITY INGREDIENTS: Desires attractive home, beauty, and
abundant comforts. Provides protective, comforting shelter. Jealousy,
self-pity, and martyrdom drain productivity when environment is inharmonious. Appears to be more worldly than he is.

PERSONALITY EXTREME: Too filled with inspiration, or living in the
past.

ASHLEY (English)—M.

MAJOR TALENT: Ability to incorporate self-examination, testing experiences, and a gift for observation into career. Energetic mind seeks a
variety of enterprises. Impulsive gestures should be curbed by hard work
and perseverance to attain success. Photography, engineering, and research are possible career opportunities.

PERSONALITY INGREDIENTS: Youthful years may be unorthodox. Insecurity brings about a thirst for a cultural, refined maturity. Clever questioner progresses through travel, physical challenges, and beach/
waterside relaxation. Should seek legal counsel to avoid conflict. Appears to be comforting and empathetic, and gains self-assurance through
privacy and perfection.

PERSONALITY EXTREME: Too analytic, or too accepting.

AUBREY (Teutonic/English)—M.

MAJOR TALENT: Ability to incorporate social welfare, cultural aspirations, and clear-sighted problem-solving methods into career. Unusual

gifts of communication: the thespian in comparison to the actor. Combines business capability, enduring philosophy, and mass-market acceptance. Diplomacy, creative arts, and exploring are possible career opportunities.

PERSONALITY INGREDIENTS: Should develop tolerance for self/others and ability to make firm decisions. Appears empathetic, enduring, and impressive: a champion. Yearns to relax in a peaceful, gracious, model environment.

PERSONALITY EXTREME: Too aloof from practical realities, or authoritatively involved while lacking any real world experience.

AUDREY (Teutonic: Ethel/English)—F.

MAJOR TALENT: Ability to incorporate magnetic personality while pursuing an extraordinary idea into a commercial career. Gets help from sheltering/boosting authority figures. Should stick to one belief and welcome partnerships. Perseverance wins special recognition. A career in any innovative business or the arts or as a social secretary, is possible.

PERSONALITY INGREDIENTS: Regal bearing attracts attention. Always feels different. Must learn practical economy and to touch ground with Everyman. Expresses modesty and sensitivity, but is able to console humanity. Generous, empathetic nature.

PERSONALITY EXTREME: Too affected, or too simple.

AUGUST (Latin/German/English)—M.

MAJOR TALENT: Ability to incorporate judgment, authority, and methodization into career. Strives for perfection and specialization. Attracts quality in scientific, technical, or esoteric interests, and achieves tangible results. Has business sense. Pharmacy, brokerage, and investigative professions are possible career opportunities.

PERSONALITY INGREDIENTS: Expressive, imaginative, analytic, versatile, discerning introvert/extrovert. Avoids contact with mundane or earthy associations. Prefers lofty pursuits and cultured social interaction. May be haughty, but brilliant.

PERSONALITY EXTREME: Too concerned with details, or sweeping and insensitive.

AUGUSTA (Latin/English)—F.

MAJOR TALENT: Ability to incorporate an active imagination, empathetic nature, and physical consciousness into career. Benefits from dream interpretation. Succeeds when investigative and emotionally detached. Natural healer; gentle, compelling adviser. Medicine, the arts, and welfare work are possible career opportunities.

PERSONALITY INGREDIENTS: Mental or physical exhaustion and irritability or touchiness blind practical judgment. Should exercise and vacation often to eliminate nervous habits. Desires big results. Appears highstrung and energetic. Needs restful sleep and an organized mind.

PERSONALITY EXTREME: Too opinionated, or too permissive.

AURELIA (Latin/English/Italian/Spanish)—F.

MAJOR TALENT: Ability to incorporate emotional generosity, determination, and administrative techniques into career. Gets down to basics with positive approach. Skillful with words/voice. Succeeds when singularly motivated, cooperative with associates, and not impelled by a chip on the shoulder. Theater, research, and laboratory work are possible career opportunities.

PERSONALITY INGREDIENTS: Understands human nature to influence others. Appears to be an efficient powerhouse. Wants to rise above birth environment and usually does.

PERSONALITY EXTREME: Too actively competitive and slender, or frustrated and fighting fat.

AUSTIN (Latin: August/English)—M.

MAJOR TALENT: Ability to incorporate a good memory, inspirational personality, and detailed planning into a communications career. Talent, charm, and luck combine when changes/variety/intangibles are accepted as part of life. Succeeds through optimism, travel, and allowing transitional changes to be made. Administration, science, and the performing arts are possible career opportunities.

PERSONALITY INGREDIENTS: Attracts admirers through service and material attainment. Desires practical, organized, secure life-style. Appears efficient, affluent, and authoritative.

PERSONALITY EXTREME: Too glib and promotional, or mutely conservative.

AVA (Latin/English)—F.

MAJOR TALENT: Ability to incorporate artistic expression, strong judgment, and responsibility into career. Defends ideals, teaches, and enhances associates/family/community. Strong parental drive. Protective, generous, and tolerant. Generally communicates with hand gestures. Arts, fashion, and home decorating are possible career opportunities.

PERSONALITY INGREDIENTS: Attracts heavy responsibilities. Should avoid self-pity or martyrdom. Appears to be extremely capable, but desires to be a support for a loving partner.

PERSONALITY EXTREME: Too self-centered and demanding, or unsure of personal convictions.

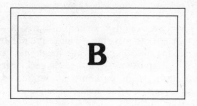

B

All names that begin with the letter *B* have the *Strong Point* of adaptability—receptivity—devotion—emotional sensitivity.

BABETTE (Greek: Barbara/English)—F.

MAJOR TALENT: Ability to incorporate an instinct for acquiring or compiling and endurance in overcoming obstacles into career. Attracts love, money, and emotional extravagance. Success comes when independence, courage, and compliance are learned, then applied to self-image. Cannot mix emotional judgments and business relationships. Designing, managing, and program planning are possible career opportunities.

PERSONALITY INGREDIENTS: First impression is efficient, controlled, and impressive. Inwardly inspired and inspirational; has nervous energy; needs an understanding, supportive mate. May waste exceptional imagination in self-pity.

PERSONALITY EXTREME: Too open-minded, or too intolerant.

BABY (often in place of first name on birth certificate)—F. & M.

MAJOR TALENT: Ability to incorporate a unique impression and presence of mind into career. Is better suited to nonmaterial goals and dealing with psychology, science, or the arts. Deals in the abstract, and should let money come through sharing a special wisdom. Art, the clergy, and Dr. Schweitzer–type callings are possible career opportunities.

PERSONALITY INGREDIENTS: First impression is ordinary, but different. Inwardly efficient, trustworthy, and organized to get things done. Needs reflective time, and must learn to recognize that tact, sympathy, and passivity attract people who solve practical problems.

PERSONALITY EXTREME: Too reclusive, or too authoritative.

BARBARA (Greek/German/English)—F.

MAJOR TALENT: Ability to incorporate a developed skill for observation and detail into career. Energetic mind seeks new experiences, ideas, and locations. Achieves through perseverance, hard work, and tackling problems head-on. Expands culturally in a serene environment. Research work, the law, and elite clienteles or emporiums are possible career opportunities.

PERSONALITY INGREDIENTS: First impression is contemporary, industrious, and judicious. Inwardly wants the spice of life. Emits beauty, imagination, and responsibility. Creates problems with impulsive remarks and reactions. Introvert/extrovert: wants both companionship and peace and quiet for inner analysis.

PERSONALITY EXTREME: Too uncompromising, or too accountable.

BARBRA (Greek/German/English: variant of Barbara)—F.

MAJOR TALENT: Ability to incorporate magnetic personality, powers of suggestion, and responsible material judgment into career. Ambitious temperament and high spirits are softened by generosity and sunny outlook. Inspires assistance from harmonious relationships. Creates a nurturing atmosphere; has a parental nature. Teaching, interior decorating, and any artistic/service profession are possible career opportunities.

PERSONALITY INGREDIENTS: First impression is custom-made, in command, and deliberate. Inwardly wants to love and be loved, to pamper and be pampered, never to be hurt or to hurt another. However, emotional sensitivity, a plus, becomes a minus when insecurities turn a pussycat into a cougar. Jealous, unfaithful, and domineering; revengeful when negative.

PERSONALITY EXTREME: Too emphatic, or too implied.

BARNABY (English diminutive of Aramaic/Greek Barnabas)—M.

MAJOR TALENT: Ability to incorporate a presence, profound intuition, and inventive ideas into career. Expresses beauty and artistry, and implements ideas commercially. Chivalrous benefactor surging to better the world. Decisive action, and allowing for human frailty in self and others, speed success. Doctor, musician, and lawyer are possible career opportunities.

PERSONALITY INGREDIENTS: Appears to be and really is very philosophical, empathetic, and universally integrated. Prefers to see the world as King Arthur's Round Table; romantic, broad-scoped and compassionate. Should avoid habit of rounding shoulders. Is usually virile and prematurely gray.

PERSONALITY EXTREME: Too introspective, or too bluntly authoritative.

BARNARD (German/French/English)—M.

MAJOR TALENT: Ability to incorporate an intense independent competitive drive into career. Organization is the key to directing energy efficiently and to identifying practical goals. Is positive, thorough, and strong-willed. Must harmonize with others for success. Real estate sales, accounting, and executive technician are possible career opportunities.

PERSONALITY INGREDIENTS: Appears energetic, interested, and inspirational. Inwardly sensitive, adaptable, and helpful. Wants serenity, but may be too personalized and pick at minutiae. Gets heart's desire when tactful, cooperative, and gently decisive. Good memory, gifted imagination, and dramatic flair should be used positively.

PERSONALITY EXTREME: Too economical, or too extravagant.

BARNEY (Irish diminutive of Barnaby, Bernard)—M.

MAJOR TALENT: Ability to incorporate the inclination to commercialize on unique skills and attract supportive partners into career. Extraordinary foresight/wisdom/individuality jell when goals are secured. May achieve lasting fame when stubborn pride is overturned and flexibility with associates is maintained. Sales, public affairs, and space-age electronics are possible career opportunities.

PERSONALITY INGREDIENTS: First impression is adventurous, but is really home/family/community oriented. Desires love, harmony, and traditional life-style abundance. Appears devil-may-care, but assumes responsibility and respectability. Musically expressive.

PERSONALITY EXTREME: Too analytic, or easily fooled.

BARRON (Old German/English)—M.

MAJOR TALENT: Ability to incorporate facility with language and speech into career. Is charming, dominating, and determined to enjoy life's pleasures. Has extreme self-confidence, which may rise to prideful haughtiness when success comes easily. Clever, sensitive, and imaginative skirmisher. Fights to influence the future with strong sense of duty and responsibility. Government investigating, advertising, and any communications profession are possible career opportunities.

PERSONALITY INGREDIENTS: Avoids manual labor, mundane attainments, and unpolished personal relationships. Can get along with anyone for commercial gain. Appears and wants culture, intellectual stimulation, and peaceful time to think. Carries an air of mystery.

PERSONALITY EXTREME: Too active, or too thoughtful.

BARRY (Celtic: Barrie/English)—M.

MAJOR TALENT: Ability to incorporate responsible leadership, a zesty approach, and open-mindedness into career. Efficient, innovative, and courageous. Produces tangibles from ideas. Works best with groups and following intuition. Business executive, military officer, and theatrical producer are possible career opportunities.

PERSONALITY INGREDIENTS: First impression is not dynamic, but inwardly is extremely organized and powerful. Likes easy-to-wear expensive clothes and wants material possessions. Should cultivate tolerance and patience, and avoid acting contradictory.

PERSONALITY EXTREME: Too brash, or too high-toned.

BARTHOLOMEW (Aramaic/Hebrew/English)—M.

MAJOR TALENT: Ability to incorporate the teachings of truth, justice, and mercy into career. Is intelligent, perceptive, and authoritative. Uses bravado as well as careful communication or appraisals to ensure steady progress. Should aspire to prominent positions. Judge, elected official, and the musical theater are possible career opportunities.

PERSONALITY INGREDIENTS: First impression is modest, humble, and charitable. Inwardly imaginative, compassionate/generous, and strongly intuitive. Understands the laws of give-and-take, but may be very firm and attract unbridled enemies. Should maintain vigilance and impartiality, and act as a force for balance.

PERSONALITY EXTREME: Too gutsy, or too fearful.

BASIL (Greek/English)—M.

MAJOR TALENT: Ability to incorporate a forceful, magnetic, and cleverly expressive personality into career. Intellect is unobstructed, and accurate assessments of people and circumstances attract supportive friends. Overconfidence brings on a tendency to gamble, and material loss accompanies this aspect. Emotional self-indulgence, impatience with regulations, and the illusion that money conquers everything lead to repeated disappointments. May focus on awakening the inner being for

success. Antiques, metaphysics, and investigative research are possible
career opportunities.

PERSONALITY INGREDIENTS: First impression is comforting, artistic,
and reliable. Inwardly highly individualistic, determined, and impatient.
Receives illuminating insights that bring tangible rewards, but nothing
will last if goals are based upon ownership and not the quality of the
effort.

PERSONALITY EXTREME: Too extroverted, or too veiled.

BAXTER (Teutonic/English)—M.

MAJOR TALENT: Ability to incorporate retrospective observations, prophetic imagery, and contemplation of details into career. Resourceful,
enterprising, and progressive instincts often are best suited to adventurous professions. Perseverance overcomes threats to success. Photography, archaeology, and farming are possible career opportunities.

PERSONALITY INGREDIENTS: First impression is parental, easy to
know, and trustworthy. Inwardly creative, energetic, and assertive. Appears to be pliable and sociable, but requires solitude and often becomes
a loner. Best suited to refined, cultured, individualistic life-style.

PERSONALITY EXTREME: Too romantic, or too disenchanted.

BAYARD (Old English)—M.

MAJOR TALENT: Ability to incorporate influential social relationships,
Svengali-type personality, and the knack for exemplary behavior into
career. Is trustworthy, stately, and kind. Exhibits parental tolerance for
business associates. Gets assistance from the opposite sex. Domestic
services, all theater work, and vocal coaching are possible career opportunities.

PERSONALITY INGREDIENTS: First impression is of being a bit above
the crowd in masterfully handling all situations; basic appearance is
Brooks Brothers custom-made. Inwardly desires peace, and aims for tact
when differences arise. Strongest asset is optimism. Stubborn judgments
cause serious problems. Happiness is deeply dependent on love.

PERSONALITY EXTREME: Too rigid, or too lazy.

BEATRICE (Latin/Italian/English)—F.

MAJOR TALENT: Ability to incorporate determination, common sense,
and inspirational resources into career. Is not afraid to assume responsibility, and directs large projects kindly, imaginatively, and justly. Should
attempt to raise living standards for others. Medicine, artistic professions, and horticulture are possible career opportunities.

PERSONALITY INGREDIENTS: Appears to be standoffish, but inwardly
desires to give and receive companionship, serenity, and emotional expression. Is often misunderstood at first blush, but is appreciated by
close associates and family. Should temper the great highs and lows that
arise when earthy strength is overburdened.

PERSONALITY EXTREME: Too sensual, or too repressed.

BECKY (English nickname of Rebecca)—F.

MAJOR TALENT: Ability to incorporate organization, management, and
vocal self-expression into career. Intellectual vitality finds positive directions where others are blind. Has faith to regenerate when growth is
stymied. Has difficulty balancing home and business if emotionally

All names that begin with the letter *B* have the *Strong Point* of adaptability—receptivity—devotion—emotional sensitivity.

47

motivated. Any creative work, business executive, and theater/industrial production are possible career opportunities.

PERSONALITY INGREDIENTS: First impression is private, detached, and well groomed. Inwardly sociable, optimistic, and imaginative. Needs glitter; wants culture. Definitely a polarity personality.

PERSONALITY EXTREME: Too aristocratic, or too unrefined.

BELINDA (Italian/Old Spanish)—F.

MAJOR TALENT: Ability to incorporate emotional sensitivity, intuitional pursuits, and commercial innovations into career. Is immensely talented, but must learn to balance business and artistry. A unique individualist who will succeed through perseverance in one area. Always recognized and offered assistance; may become famous. Communications idea person, film producer and political reformer are possible career opportunities.

PERSONALITY INGREDIENTS: Appears adventurous and attractive to the opposite sex. Inwardly responsible, family/community oriented, and artistically ambitious. Strong morals, ethics, and judgments are not obvious. Should aim to give love without smothering the recipients. Natural educator. Should not overdo generosity.

PERSONALITY EXTREME: Too submissive, or too independent.

BELLA (Italian/English)—F.

MAJOR TALENT: Ability to incorporate persuasive gifts, diplomatic action, and prospering through daily experiences into career. Rarely learns without testing, and often gets fingers into the fire. Material success comes slowly. Competitive situations must be handled patiently to become profitable. Teeming with vitality, imagination, and open-mindedness. Best to avoid petty mentalities and prepare to learn by trial and error. Sales, publishing, and psychology are possible career opportunities.

PERSONALITY INGREDIENTS: Appears organized, ethical, and materialistic. Inwardly needs love, generous homelife, and family attainment. Appreciates beauty, music, and position. Enjoys sensuality and attracts admirers. Must develop forethought before taking actions to avoid unwanted responsibilities.

PERSONALITY EXTREME: Too bossy, or too agreeable.

BELLE (English)—F.

MAJOR TALENT: Ability to incorporate innovative energy, natural advisory skills, and empathetic service into career. Is a force for relieving the emotional and physical suffering of others. Benefits from dream interpretation and organized personal health habits. Medicine, psychological testing, and public affairs are possible career opportunities.

PERSONALITY INGREDIENTS: First impression is substantial, influential, and as affluent as possible. Inwardly independent, capable, and ambitious. Understands executive leadership and applies efficient management to projects that entertain, elevate, or soothe people.

PERSONALITY EXTREME: Too emotionally impulsive, or too mental.

BEN (English diminutive of Benjamin)—M.

MAJOR TALENT: Ability to incorporate abstract thought, often anties-

tablishment actions, and enigmatic appearance into career. Is inwardly
strong and outwardly uncommonly poised. May be a peaceful haven for
the troubled. Not materialistic, but a survivor. The arts, medicine, and
philosophy are possible career opportunities.

PERSONALITY INGREDIENTS: First impression is a loner. May appear
poetic, mystical, or observing. Inwardly wants all the tastes, touches,
smells, feelings that life can offer . . . and freedom to pursue them. Very
sensual, curious, and experimental. Is an escapist.

PERSONALITY EXTREME: Too unconventional, or too proper.

BENEDICT (Latin/English)—M.

MAJOR TALENT: Ability to incorporate inherited money, power, or
position, tremendous vitality, and acceptance of trustworthy responsibility into career. Is expected to use mind and body to maintain status.
Overcomes obstacles easily when self-confident, reasonable, and open-
minded. Sports businesses, mortician, and any financial manipulation
profession are possible career opportunities.

PERSONALITY INGREDIENTS: Appears secretive, introspective, and
gloomy one time, but poised, self-assured, and aristocratic at other
times. Inwardly very independent, ambitious, and innovative. Needs to
feel authoritative; expertise in any area provides inner security to
brighten outer image. Extremely persuasive; natural fund raiser with an
innate understanding of public demand.

PERSONALITY EXTREME: Too emotionally tender, or too callous.

BENEDICTA (Latin/English)—F.

MAJOR TALENT: Ability to incorporate universal love, burden bearing,
and practical common sense into career. Is dependable, trustworthy, and
inspirationally directive. Offers artistry, spirituality, and earthy consciousness to tackle far-reaching humanitarian goals. Compassionate
undertakings for others will relieve the emotional extremes experienced
with this name. Any projects that need completion, physical/emotional/
spiritual healing, and horticulture are possible career opportunities.

PERSONALITY INGREDIENTS: Appears preoccupied, but if interested/
knowledgeable will attract attention. Inwardly is easily upset. Desires
peace and gentle partnerships, and to be a supportive asset to family/
community understanding and achievement. Too self-demanding, and
unrealistic in relationships. Expects a perfect world, and perseveres to
enrich and expand human concepts.

PERSONALITY EXTREME: Too self-sacrificing, or too aggressive.

BENJAMIN (Hebrew/English)—M.

MAJOR TALENT: Ability to incorporate a catalystic effect on others into
career. Is active, determined, and persistent, and aims high. A confident
leader; at home in any environment, with all people. Advertising, government, and educated gambling are possible career opportunities.

PERSONALITY INGREDIENTS: First impression is authoritative, successful, and impressive. Inwardly home/family/community conscious, socially attaining, and appreciative of beauty. Needs stabilized roots to
balance diversified interests. Juggles a multitude of interests skillfully.
Usually lucky and intuitive.

PERSONALITY EXTREME: Too enthusiastic, or too subdued.

All names that begin with the letter *B* have the *Strong Point* of adaptability—receptivity—devotion—emotional sensitivity.

49

BENNETT (English, from Latin Benedict)—M.

MAJOR TALENT: Ability to incorporate enthusiasm, courage, and a yen for power into career. Gifted with words slated for mass-communications market. Self-control is the key to enduring relationships. Cannot mix need for loving partner and commercial interests, or stressful situations result. Physical coordination/sports bring recognition. Physical education teaching, carpentry, and any financial organization are possible career opportunities.

PERSONALITY INGREDIENTS: First impression is cultured: quiet, aloof, and often mysterious. Inwardly ambitious, energetic, and innovative; very individualistic and directive. Not antisocial, but conversationally selective.

PERSONALITY EXTREME: Too emotional or too unexcitable.

BERENICE (Greek/French/English)—F.

MAJOR TALENT: Ability to incorporate true friendships, determination, and an insight for silence into career. Is clear-thinking, positive, and self-disciplining. Emits poise, sensitivity, and active energy. Generally does research and develops expertise to exhibit authority in hobbies or career. Teaching, writing, and game analysis/teaching are possible career opportunities.

PERSONALITY INGREDIENTS: First impression is individualistic, but wants secure/quiet/quality life-style, and takes responsibility for the attainments of the family. Deeply emotional, sentimental, and progressive, with great strength in an emergency or time of trials. Enjoys power, but must avoid overindulgence in the freedoms that money/position buy. Excesses lead to emotional instability and internal physical problems. Charitable focus secures well-being.

PERSONALITY EXTREME: Too fickle, or unchanging.

BERNADETTE (French/Old German)—F.

MAJOR TALENT: Ability to incorporate method, economy, and tangibles into career. Innate builder, with mathematical mind. Is a cautious planner. Successful in business. Best in peaceful, orderly, discriminating life-style. Statistical analysis, literature, and construction trades are possible career opportunities.

PERSONALITY INGREDIENTS: Inwardly wants to save the world and keep the peace. High intuitive ability provides futuristic vision. Appears modest, adaptable, and sensitive. Enjoys collecting, playing the piano, and sharing an honorable, emotionally balanced, considerate existence.

PERSONALITY EXTREME: Too illusionary, or too materialistic.

BERNARD (German/French)—M.

MAJOR TALENT: Ability to incorporate a knack for perceiving trends into career. People always want something new, and the bearer of this name identifies what it is and how to supply it. Usually wealth, power, or status is given at birth, and the insight, vitality, and individualism inherent in this name betters the birthright. Material judgment, charm, and consideration for others blend with foresight and fortunate opportunities. Must be disciplined, employ planning, and patiently expand for success. Executive in any business, professorship, and financial adviser are possible career opportunities.

PERSONALITY INGREDIENTS: First impression is modest, inspirational, and different. The impression hints of genius and/or eccentricity. Inwardly responsible, parental, and artistically appreciative. Wants peace, love, and family/community attainment. Generous, and a bit flaky at times.

PERSONALITY EXTREME: Too practical, or too undisciplined.

BERNICE (Greek: Berenice/English)—F.

MAJOR TALENT: Ability to incorporate poetic/imaginative ideas into a materially secure career. Is able to blend career and marriage successfully. Has unique dream energy that may be utilized for goal planning. Should engage in charitable work and be of service to others. Religious administrator/organizer, professional metaphysician, and communications teacher are possible career opportunities.

PERSONALITY INGREDIENTS: Appears to be and is a projects organizer who collects, synthesizes, and regenerates expressive changes. Can move mountains through faith, persuasive techniques, and creative insights. Usually lucky in love, family ties, and self-expression.

PERSONALITY EXTREME: Too extravagant, or too low-key.

BERT (Teutonic/English variant-nickname)—M.

MAJOR TALENT: Ability to incorporate emotional imagination, counseling, and health/hygiene into career. Physical stamina is governed by mental organization. Benefits from restful sleep and dream memories. Successful when careful of personal health balance and creatively or medically serving the needs of others. Any humanitarian profession, research, and the theater are possible career opportunities.

PERSONALITY INGREDIENTS: First impression is conservative, practical, and self-disciplined. Inwardly desires sensual pleasures, freedom of self-expression, and progressive opportunities. Can be a fooler. May display nervous habits and irritability when too intellectual and ignoring private time for contemplation.

PERSONALITY EXTREME: Too vinegary, or too saccharine.

BERTHA (Old German/Danish/English)—F.

MAJOR TALENT: Ability to incorporate problem-solving originality into career. Fertile business ideas impress supporters, who implement the perfection this name requires. Is very intuitive, intelligent, and constructive. May create a foundational fortune that benefits future generations. Engineering, dentistry, and any nonmanual labor are possible career opportunities.

PERSONALITY INGREDIENTS: First impression is sociable, expressive, and conversational. Inwardly tuned to home/family/community responsibilities, artistic beauty, and material attainment. Affectionate, loyal, sympathetic to loved ones. May be intolerant of self and others, which produces indecision/confusion to stymie expectations. Goes a long way from birthright during lifetime.

PERSONALITY EXTREME: Too independent, or too submissive.

BERTRAM (Old German/Old French/English)—M.

MAJOR TALENT: Ability to incorporate patient determination, enthusiastic promotion, and language skills into career. Is personable, and attracts leadership, supporters, and progressive actions. Legislator, foreign correspondent, and travel agent are possible career opportunities.

PERSONALITY INGREDIENTS: First impression is businesslike. Inwardly personally idealistic and desirous of beauty, and strives for family/community harmony and status. Must avoid impatience, impulsiveness, and being influenced by others. Usually self-confident, but will alienate potential and existing friends if haughty or humorless. Rewards may come easily, but any show of pride will detract from the pleasures and recognition that accompany success.

PERSONALITY EXTREME: Too economical, or too impractical.

BERYL (Sanskrit/Greek/English)—F. & M.

MAJOR TALENT: Ability to incorporate attention to detail, comforting service, and learning from experience into career. Is broad-scoped; has communications skills and an interest in sports. Usually benevolent, jovial, and influential. Machinery design, financial advising, and any executive administrative position are possible career opportunities.

PERSONALITY INGREDIENTS: First impression is socially attractive, expressive, and imaginative. Inwardly impulsive, curious, and sensual. Mail/telephone/conversational interactions are important throughout lifetime. Benefits from travel, speaking many languages, and being cautious in love relationships. Very enthusiastic, courageous, and ambitious.

PERSONALITY EXTREME: Too fashionable, or too inelegant.

BESS (English/Scottish diminutive of Elizabeth)—F.

MAJOR TALENT: Ability to incorporate humanitarian service, selflessness, and intense short-term aspirations into career. Is attractive to notable persons, sets high standards, and thrives when free to lighten others' burdens. Provides empathy, wisdom, and tolerance for all when using positive aspects of the name. Faith is the key to transcending mundane negative aspects. Welfare work, repertory theater, and charity patronage are possible career opportunities.

PERSONALITY INGREDIENTS: Appears to be practical, orderly, and dependable. Inwardly stimulating, adventurous, and progressive. Needs change, variety, and experimentation. Feels everything deeply and must avoid petty self-concerns. May be quick to anger; is a clever adversary. Prone to nervous tensions when too introspective.

PERSONALITY EXTREME: Too sarcastic, or too charming.

BETH (English diminutive of Elizabeth)—F.

MAJOR TALENT: Ability to incorporate investigative instincts into career. Is independent, logical, and determined. A leader for truth, with the gift of gab to promote social or business goals. Profits from joining intellect and pioneering spirit. Public affairs, legal research, and architecture are possible career opportunities.

PERSONALITY INGREDIENTS: Appears to have depth of character. Feels individualistic, enthusiastic, and free to express ideas and ideals. Detests intolerance, tunnel vision, and rigid structuring. Strives to appear attractive, cheerful, and multifaceted. Often hasty putting ideas into motion. Reflection brings long-lasting happiness.

PERSONALITY EXTREME: Too impatiently efficient, or too purposeless.

BETTE (English diminutive of Elizabeth/German)—F.

MAJOR TALENT: Ability to incorporate a magnetic manner, a dynamic
personality, and clever interpretation of ideas into career. Is a remark-
able, straight-thinking communicator. Is most fortunate when efforts are
directed to attaining perfection or expertise in an intuitional interest. If
accumulation of assets is not the only ambition, rewards are far-reaching
and long-lasting. Bearer of this name suffers losses in business, reputation, and romance if unrestrained, overconfident, and dependent upon
money or power for feelings of security. Psychologist, technical expert,
and university administrator are possible career opportunities.

PERSONALITY INGREDIENTS: First impression is of good taste. There is
a look of steadiness, reliability, and adult concern. Wants to be the boss
and takes the initiative. Superstition has it that the bearer of this name
will atone for a promiscuous past and must learn to separate false from
true values before she can maintain success.

PERSONALITY EXTREME: Too sensual, or too mental.

BETTINA (Italian/English diminutive of Elizabeth)—F.

MAJOR TALENT: Ability to incorporate detail work and service to
families, homes, and communities into career. Is ambitious and courageous, and has a natural gift for communications. Should focus upon use
of legs in physical fitness/sports/dance. Balance and coordination are
innate skills. Military, orchestra leading, and public service administration are possible career opportunities.

PERSONALITY INGREDIENTS: First impression is different; appears to
be in another world. Inwardly aims to keep harmony in family and community life. Wants the best for everyone and takes responsibility for
everyone/everything. Wants roots and attainment, and to beautify and
assist. Never showy or tasteless, but can be a bit exotic. Benefits from
broadening scope, developing artistic talents, and being cautious in love
commitments.

PERSONALITY EXTREME: Too strong, or too easily swayed.

BEULAH (Hebrew/English)—F.

MAJOR TALENT: Ability to incorporate practical capability and intuitional wisdom into career. Is hardworking and resourceful, and finds the
answers when everyone else has given up. Honest, ethical, and, when
balanced emotionally, able to benefit future generations and reshape
destinies. Any industry, public service, and architectural engineering are
possible career opportunities.

PERSONALITY INGREDIENTS: Emits a strong impression; appears to
draw attention in a dramatic, empathetic, charming way. Inwardly not
the romantic/impulsive/emotional person of the impression. Is organized, economical, and self-disciplined. Greatest cautions for bearers of
this name are overwork, obsession for power, and abusing gift of trust
that is given by others.

PERSONALITY EXTREME: Too conscientious, or too imprudent.

BEVERLY (Old English)—F. & M.

MAJOR TALENT: Ability to incorporate executive judgment, research,
and personal charm into career. Is always prepared—for travel, business, or a party. Has defensive abilities, vision, and inner strength to

juggle any inherited responsibilities or daily obligations. Requires stable
life-style to control dynamic energy and emotional highs and lows. Theater, politics, and financial professions are possible career opportunities.

PERSONALITY INGREDIENTS: First impression is magnetic, entertaining, and unforgettable. Inwardly efficient, ambitious, and authoritative.
Wants respect and the freedoms that money and power purchase. Has
nobility, charm, and a vivacity that is infectious. Must be patient with
less organized associates, and never doubt self-worth with unreasonable
demands or undisciplined self-indulgences. Should carefully seek the
middle path to find success.

PERSONALITY EXTREME: Too authoritative, or intellectually insecure.

BILL (English diminutive of William)—M.

MAJOR TALENT: Ability to incorporate independent investigation, research, and a quiet strength into career. Is on an intellectual/spiritual/
refined road and needs private thinking time to commercialize upon
ideas. Changes, travel, and strong/helpful friendships are rewarding.
Usually respected for wisdom; must be careful when advising others in
order to always be on top of any situation. Gifts of persuasion can be
used for power plays or humanitarian motives. Engineer, comptroller,
and tax consultant are possible career opportunities.

PERSONALITY INGREDIENTS: Rich or poor, looks efficient, authoritative, and prosperous. Inwardly emotional, romantic, and sympathetic.
Most at home with literate, dramatic, and broad-scoped environment.
Sound business concepts should be directed to a mass market. May
suffer through emotions or retreat into cool contemplation.

PERSONALITY EXTREME: Too introverted, or too conversational.

BILLIE (Old English diminutive of William or Wilhelmina)—F. & M.

MAJOR TALENT: Ability to incorporate independence, competitive
idealism, and stick-to-it-iveness into career. Is a communicator with a
fighting spirit. A survivor, with strong vitality, retentive memory, and
sincere, loyal, and honest ambitions. Succeeds through organization of
goals and a less dogmatic attitude with associates. Nursing, proofread-
ing, and building trades are possible career opportunities.

PERSONALITY INGREDIENTS: Appears efficient, ambitious, and authoritative. Desires freedom for self-expression. Repression of curiosity,
experimentation, and social conviviality bring out self-destructive energy. Best work is done in a changing environment offering spontaneous
activities. May dramatize too much, but is never dull.

PERSONALITY EXTREME: Too busy, or bored.

BILLY (English diminutive of William)—M.

MAJOR TALENT: Ability to incorporate attractiveness, ambition, and
group activity relationships into career. Is kind, generous, and patient;
presents an image. Should focus upon family/community promotion and
provide and receive an abundant life-style. Gains financially when practical and cautious. Home-care products, innkeeping, and any counseling
profession are possible career opportunities.

PERSONALITY INGREDIENTS: First impression is of great affluence;
seems strong, businesslike, and sociable. Inwardly feels like a loner and
is often difficult to understand. Unfulfilled without academic or technical
education. Desires cultural environment, but has strong self-doubt that

inspires disappointing experiences. May have irrational fears of loneliness and poverty.

PERSONALITY EXTREME: Too pensive, or too unreasoning.

BLAINE (Anglo-Saxon/Celtic/English)—M.

MAJOR TALENT: Ability to incorporate cool evaluations, technique, and an adventurous nature into career. Is intuitive, nature-loving, and extremely observant. Pays attention to the little things and always finds a way to overcome difficulties. Succeeds through diligent work. Journalistic photography, psychology, and insurance appraising are possible career opportunities.

PERSONALITY INGREDIENTS: Appears ready to take charge, but is not bossy; just enjoys giving advice. Prefers to have pleasant relationships and keeps harmony as long as personal standards are at the core. Desires to feel loved and needed; assumes responsibility, and is generous and attaining for loved ones.

PERSONALITY EXTREME: Too unconventional, or too structured.

BLAIR (Gaelic/Scottish/English)—M.

MAJOR TALENT: Ability to incorporate practical counseling, protective instincts, and artistic/musical creativity into career. Is family focused, assists others, and can be firm in personal idealism. Should attract friendships with magnetic personality. Influential associates promote ambitions. Animal welfare work, medical professions, and interior decorating are possible career opportunities.

PERSONALITY INGREDIENTS: First impression is friendly, unconventional, and exciting; a clever conversationalist who attracts sensual activity. Inwardly bossy, proud, and extremely innovative. Self-starter, courageous, and impatient for success. Vivid imagination may cause jealousy and stubborn petty vengeances. Negatives arise when too concerned with the welfare of loved ones or business associates. Should be careful to live and let live.

PERSONALITY EXTREME: Too unselfish, or too impersonal.

BLAISE (Teutonic: Blaze/French)—M.

MAJOR TALENT: Ability to incorporate patient administrative skills, imagination, and dependable memory into career. Is charming, inspirational, and lucky. Thrives on a variety of expressive interests, and benefits through the mails and telephone. Must be adaptable to change for major success. Fiction writer, entertainer, and lawyer are possible career opportunities.

PERSONALITY INGREDIENTS: Appears to be and inwardly desires to be the perfect host or manager. Assumes responsibility and feels genuine concern for everyone. Enjoys family attainments and a beautiful/abundant home, and has an open-door policy. Solves all problems at the kitchen table, surrounded by friends and family whenever possible. This name exemplifies the motto on the Statue of Liberty: "Give me your poor, your tired . . ."

PERSONALITY EXTREME: Too sexy, or too virginal.

BLAKE (Anglo-Saxon/English)—M.

MAJOR TALENT: Ability to incorporate keen social perception, com-

All names that begin with the letter *B* have the *Strong Point* of adaptability—receptivity—devotion—emotional sensitivity.

55

monsense systems, and a knack for salvaging people or projects into career. Is apt to carry the ball in order to alter relationships for the better. Has the skill to rebuild when others falter. Family stability, sensual self-discipline, and conventional reactions activate possibilities of lasting fame. Economist, printer, and landscaper are possible career opportunities.

PERSONALITY INGREDIENTS: First impression is cultured, sometimes cool, and analytic. Speaks with authority or not at all. Inwardly needs/ desires emotional tenderness, peaceful-artistic environment, and mature companionship. Prefers to guide rather than listen. The push-pull of needing warmth and remaining above emotional turmoil is difficult to handle or understand. Very mysterious type.

PERSONALITY EXTREME: Too changeable, or too self-limiting.

BLANCHE (Old German/English/French)—F.

MAJOR TALENT: Ability to incorporate personal presence, artistic/ creative skills, and executive organizational strength into career. Is a unique problem solver. Should follow intuitional insights for success. Positive approach inspires support from associates. Must not show intolerance or lack of purpose. Publishing, medical receptionist, and any artistic/humanitarian service are possible career opportunities.

PERSONALITY INGREDIENTS: First impression is sedate, retiring, and sensitively agreeable. Shows a love of music, fine art, and technical expertise. Would be happy in a world of cashmere sweaters, leather-bound books, and Louis XV furniture. Is happiest in quiet, introspective, classy surroundings. However, we live on a planet where most people burp . . . and life will never be as perfect as the bearer of this name would desire.

PERSONALITY EXTREME: Too human, or a prima donna.

BLAZE (Teutonic/English)—M.

MAJOR TALENT: Ability to incorporate management of innovative and ambitious undertakings into career. Is active in projects that require great endurance. Has possibilities of happiness, luck, and financial success when courageous, expressive, and overtly optimistic. Facade/image is a prime factor in quality of life. Must not put up a false front and avoid living the individualistic destiny required by this name. Communications pioneer, program planner, and theatrical producer are possible career opportunities.

PERSONALITY INGREDIENTS: Looks like a pillar of the community. Never flashy; neat, determined, and practical. Inwardly wants to give and receive love, artistic beauty, and family pride. Loyal friend, mentor, and guardian. Tenderhearted, but adheres to high personal standards . . . and expects everyone else to live up to them too. When pacifying society, leads a double life to avoid facing independent action.

PERSONALITY EXTREME: Too impulsive, or too staid.

BLOSSOM (Anglo-Saxon/Danish/German/Irish/English)—F.

MAJOR TALENT: Ability to incorporate cleverness, physical agility, and inventive ideas into career. Is helpful, aspiring, and passionately loyal. Fortunate in love, with children, and with inheritances. Thrives upon change and variety. Communications, research, and travel businesses are possible career opportunities.

PERSONALITY INGREDIENTS: First impression is not ordinary. Refined, aesthetic, and unique. Inwardly tries to laugh at problems, enjoy people, and flirt a bit. Dislikes sameness, complainers, and being alone. Imaginative, and sometimes naively childlike. Can be a modest listener or a super salesperson. Revitalizes from intellectual stimulation, and glows when really feeling needed. Tact, calm reactions, and carefully directed goals are the keys to success.

PERSONALITY EXTREME: Too rigid, or too easygoing.

BLYTHE (Anglo-Saxon/English)—F.

MAJOR TALENT: Ability to incorporate independent beliefs, determined leadership, and artistic/technical expertise into career. Is romantic, deep, and versatile. Impresses others, who help materialize creative concepts. Provides tangibles that improve existing conditions. Social worker, hair colorist, and publicist are possible career opportunities.

PERSONALITY INGREDIENTS: Appears trustworthy, generous, and interested; enjoys beauty, people, and humor. Inwardly responsible, optimistic, and imaginative. Enjoys being helpful and giving advice. Should be decisive and practice tolerance for all . . . including self.

PERSONALITY EXTREME: Too physical, or too mental.

BOB (English diminutive-nickname of Robert)—M.

MAJOR TALENT: Ability to incorporate a knack for forming alliances and influencing people into career. Is a productive leader, clear-thinking, understanding, and wise. Must learn to give new plans time to jell before changing course. Success comes easily when goals are products of intuitional feelings and each patient step is taken. Architect, credit adviser, and politician are possible career opportunities.

PERSONALITY INGREDIENTS: Appears average, practical, and neatly organized. Overall is conservative family/community builder, guardian, and economist. Needs beauty, love, and harmonious environments. Strives for attainment, but isn't showy about it. Parental/brotherly nature often leads to overburdening by others. Must avoid stubborn beliefs and opinions that stunt growth.

PERSONALITY EXTREME: Too petty, or too uncaring.

BOBBY (English diminutive of Robert or Roberta)—F. & M.

MAJOR TALENT: Ability to incorporate concern for others, communications, and unaffected values into career. Is individualistic, organized, and energetic. Succeeds when honestly courageous and has mastered emotional distractions. Usually attracts good marriage and material happiness. The bearer of this name will endure changes until true independence is learned. Musical professions, piloting, and any creative work are possible career opportunities.

PERSONALITY INGREDIENTS: First impression is concerned, parental, and conservatively tasteful; appears dependable and mature. Desires respectability, tradition, and practical achievements. Dislikes waste, insincerity, and inefficiency. Enjoys giving advice. May lead a double life.

PERSONALITY EXTREME: Too aloof, or too involved.

BONITA (Latin)—F.

MAJOR TALENT: Ability to incorporate definitive judgments, cautious observations, and enterprising ideas into career. Is geared to fact finding and natural environments, and has a thirst for knowledge. Childhood experiences provide foundation for meeting obstacles and overcoming them. Succeeds through tenacity. Technical/scientific professions, auditing, and editing are possible career opportunities.

PERSONALITY INGREDIENTS: Outwardly magnetic, sympathetic, and artistic. Finds intellectual stimulation, cultural environments, and a quality life-style desirable. Must develop expertise/authority in one area to experience contentment. May not understand inner drives until midlife. At best in the country or by the sea.

PERSONALITY EXTREME: Too self-important, or too demuring.

BONNY (English; variant Bonnie)—F.

MAJOR TALENT: Ability to incorporate observation, technical analysis, and cleverness into career. Is progressive, questioning, and persevering. Best suited to cultural atmospheres and nonmanual work. Cataloguer, photographer, and psychoanalyst are possible career opportunities.

PERSONALITY INGREDIENTS: Appears to be animated, imaginative, and optimistic. Inwardly practical, organized, and conservative. May seem flighty, but can be depended upon. Benefits from researching and detailing plans. Haste and impulsive actions cause conflicts.

PERSONALITY EXTREME: Too unrefined, or too elaborate.

BORIS (Russian)—M.

MAJOR TALENT: Ability to incorporate detailed analysis, wide-angle philosophy, and empathetic service to others into career. Is romantic, culturally progressive, and emotionally tuned. High ideals may create self-dissatisfaction. Success comes through clear understanding of goals, inventive mind, and a sense of justice. The arts, judicial reform, and teaching are possible career opportunities.

PERSONALITY INGREDIENTS: Inwardly family/community focused, idealistic, and artistic. Needs secure and harmonious relationships, but may find marriage difficult. Good conversationalist, imaginative, and noticeable. Prefers others to mind their own business and keeps an inner privacy that may reflect a moody or mysterious nature.

PERSONALITY EXTREME: Too creative, or too repressed.

BOY (often in place of first name on birth certificate)—M.

MAJOR TALENT: Ability to incorporate magnetic influence over others into career. Is materially oriented, strong-willed, and observant. Understands people and tries to provide for their needs. Takes things too seriously and finds contentment when a sense of humor is applied to own foibles. Medicine, counseling, and communications professions are possible career opportunities.

PERSONALITY INGREDIENTS: First impression is vigorous, romantic, and impressive. Provides human understanding, charm, and artistic embellishments. Impulsiveness, sensual obsessiveness, and selfish motives cause emotional ups and downs continually. Must strive for unselfishness as a life-style.

PERSONALITY EXTREME: Too trusting, or too cunning.

BOYD (Celtic/Scottish/English)—M.

MAJOR TALENT: Ability to incorporate high energy, initiative, and

creative ideas into career. Is instigative, impatient, and empathetic. Best
when left to own devices and providing an artistic or beneficial service.
May be melodramatic to make a point and influence others. Any communications profession, sales management, and psychiatry are possible
career opportunities.

PERSONALITY INGREDIENTS: First impression is sturdy, honest, and
determined. Needs to feel needed. Wants to prosper with family and
community welfare in mind. Enjoys counseling others, and is inclined to
be too helpful at times. Very tenderhearted, protective, and conscious of
beauty.

PERSONALITY EXTREME: Too conventional, or too undisciplined.

BRADFORD (Old English)—M.

MAJOR TALENT: Ability to incorporate independent leadership, practical planning, and offbeat ideas into career. Is versatile, enthusiastic, and
courageous. Attracts life's pleasures and material success. Succeeds easily when reflective and receptive to progressive concepts. Politics, entertaining, and detective work are possible career opportunities.

PERSONALITY INGREDIENTS: Strives for perfection in personal evaluations and relationships. Prefers to speak when sure of subject matter.
Needs intellectually stimulating people and environments, and also privacy in which to analyze, plan, and meditate. Originated the question,
"Why is the sky blue, Daddy?"

PERSONALITY EXTREME: Too routined, or too unscheduled.

BRADLEY (Old English)—M.

MAJOR TALENT: Ability to incorporate aggressive energy, determination, and dramatic concepts into career. Is generous, mentally restless,
and prone to extravagance in conversation and with money. Success
comes through organizing, working harmoniously with others, and establishing a clear direction. Dentistry, skilled manual labor, and the military
are possible career opportunities.

PERSONALITY INGREDIENTS: First impression is dignified, refined, and
unruffled. Inwardly tender, generous, and paternal. Wants artistic
beauty, family security, and serenity. Strongly idealistic, and expects the
best from everyone. Should learn to accept people for what they are and
avoid trying to change them.

PERSONALITY EXTREME: Too opinionated, or too vague.

BRENDA (Teutonic/Scottish/Irish)—F.

MAJOR TALENT: Ability to incorporate enthusiasm, spunk, and unsus-
picious nature into career. Is well coordinated, adds artistic touches, and
pays attention to the little securities that less sensitive people overlook.
May have impulsive loves that are stressful and curtail material achievements. Succeeds after learning to form enduring relationships. Has inner
strength. Any business, musical groups, and promotional professions are
possible career opportunities.

PERSONALITY INGREDIENTS: First impression is supportive, diplomatic, and soft. Inwardly wants attainment in home/family/community
affairs. Needs love, generous life-style, and praise. Enjoys power people
and status. Superb when self-confident; should take self-improvement
courses.

PERSONALITY EXTREME: Too independent, or too obliging.

All names that begin with the letter *B* have the *Strong Point* of
adaptability—receptivity—devotion—emotional sensitivity.

59

BRETT (Celtic/English)—M.

MAJOR TALENT: Ability to incorporate pattern planning and observation for details into career. Takes things at face value until preconceived notions are changed by unsettling events. Must develop broader and deeper perceptions of life and people to maintain success. Bookkeeper, fiction writer, and professional collector are possible career opportunities.

PERSONALITY INGREDIENTS: Desires adventure, freedom, and sensual pleasures. Speculates, and is not bound by conventional procedures or life-styles. May be a wise guy, but looks conservative, concerned, and trustworthy. Good politician, entertainer, or teacher. Will experience restlessness and indecisiveness. Must learn to be firm when planning long-term goals and to be flexible in getting to them.

PERSONALITY EXTREME: Too silent, or too quarrelsome.

BREWSTER (Teutonic/Old English)—M.

MAJOR TALENT: Ability to incorporate futuristic imagination, educational contributions, and responsibility to community into career. Is family oriented, proud, and inclined to do the right thing. Sets an example for others and provides perceptive counsel. Film/TV work, clergy, and public service projects are possible career opportunities.

PERSONALITY INGREDIENTS: First impression is ambitious, responsible, and independent. Wants to be the boss and influence others. High energy causes impatience, exaggerated reactions, and self-insistence. Fortunate in friendships, family, and material accumulation.

PERSONALITY EXTREME: Too worldly-wise, or too narrow-minded.

BRIAN (Irish/English)—M.

MAJOR TALENT: Ability to incorporate physical activity, expansive thinking, and courageous expectations into career. Is outwardly self-assured and concerned with justice, truth, and family/community attainment. Gifted communicator who finds success when business and love relationships are separated and carefully structured. Should aim high. Demolitions expert, law enforcement, and financial institutions are possible career opportunities.

PERSONALITY INGREDIENTS: Appears serious, analytic, and difficult to read. Inwardly individualistic, courageous, and creative. Takes the lead when sure of the facts. Admires intellect, culture, and quality. Strives for self-perfection and courts personal disappointments. Should have technical or academic expertise to experience contentment.

PERSONALITY EXTREME: Too impulsive, or too restrained.

BRICE (Anglo-Saxon/Celtic)—M.

MAJOR TALENT: Ability to incorporate social improvement, individualistic concepts, and mental resourcefulness into career. Is daring, impatient, and geared to produce tangible results. Attracts love relationships, intuitional guidance, and competitive experiences. Responsible, progressive, generous leader. Actor, psychiatrist, and business owner are possible career opportunities.

PERSONALITY INGREDIENTS: Appears to be and inwardly feels friendly, clever, and experimental. Enjoys travel, sexual pleasure, and youthful vigor. Must be free to explore the latest fads/fashions/

60

All names that begin with the letter *B* have the *Strong Point* of
adaptability—receptivity—devotion—emotional sensitivity.

philosophies. Born politician and promoter. Can sell anything with great
enthusiasm, and usually touches upon many careers.

PERSONALITY EXTREME: Too speculative, or too cautious.

BRIDGET (Sanskrit/Irish)—F.

MAJOR TALENT: Ability to incorporate visionary judgments into
career. Is dreamy, poetic, and imaginative. Parental, ambitious, and productive. Success comes with dedication to a better way of life for family/
community. Benefits materially from charitable efforts. Crusades for
ideals, and is a zealous evangelist. Welfare worker, biographer, and
reformer are possible career opportunities.

PERSONALITY INGREDIENTS: First impression is loving, peaceful, and
conservative. Inwardly fiery, progressive, and physically energetic. Desires fast-moving experiences and unconventional people. May enjoy
many deep love affairs until a kindred spirit comes along.

PERSONALITY EXTREME: Too excitable, or too withdrawn.

BRIGHAM (Old English)—M.

MAJOR TALENT: Ability to incorporate method, economy, and mathematical or statistical interests into career. Is dutiful, studious, and
meditative. Has emotional control and compassionate understanding for
others, and is a realist. Invests wisely for constructive growth. Building
trades, printing professions, and auto mechanic are possible career opportunities.

PERSONALITY INGREDIENTS: Appears to be an expressive, inventive,
spotlight-stealing communicator. Inwardly independent, pioneering, and
assertive. Capable leader, with strong sense of pride and honor. If negative, very pessimistic, disorganized, and prone to chasing rainbows. May
leave a lasting mark on humanity when building for the benefit of others.

PERSONALITY EXTREME: Too principled, or too aimless.

BROCK (Old English)—M.

MAJOR TALENT: Ability to incorporate original problem-solving techniques, broad planning, and an ethical nature into career. Has strong
opinions, practical attitudes, and mature wisdom. Magically gets others
to perform their best efforts, and works harder than any associate. Attracts good marriage and strong friendships. Any industry, government,
and all professions are possible career opportunities.

PERSONALITY INGREDIENTS: Appears to be a loner—mysterious, introspective, and refined. Often misunderstood socially. Desires beautiful,
generous, and attaining life-style. Responsible to family/community/
universal needs. Protective and parental to a point of self-sacrifice. Has
quality value system and enjoys cultural interests. Must be known to be
loved.

PERSONALITY EXTREME: Too personalized, or too detached.

BRODERICK (Old German/English)—M.

MAJOR TALENT: Ability to incorporate emotional control, strong sense
of justice, and attraction for the financially successful or well-known
personalities into career. Is patient, intuitionally tuned, and prone to
have a hearty appetite. Enjoys accumulating property and an abundant
life-style. Successful when conservative and routined physically and

All names that begin with the letter *B* have the *Strong Point* of
adaptability—receptivity—devotion—emotional sensitivity.

61

mentally. Must maintain a steady, persevering, honest course. Land
development, mechanical professions, and high-quality manufacturing
are possible career opportunities.

PERSONALITY INGREDIENTS: Very sensitive, peace-loving, and modest, but expects to do something or be someone special and has an
unusual first impression. May be high-strung and nervous. Knows how
to keep a secret and relishes close confidences. Hypersensitivity invites
petty jealousies, anxieties, and insecurities.

PERSONALITY EXTREME: Too naive, or too deceptive.

BROOKE (Old English)—F. & M.

MAJOR TALENT: Ability to incorporate quality consciousness, magnetism for the opposite sex, and wide-scoped goals into career. Is systematic, versatile, and imaginative. Should focus upon mind-stimulating
arts, technical sciences, and family ties. Lucky when practical, just and
conventional. Charming, agreeable, and clever personality attracts special attention. Entertainment industry, animal training, and writing are
possible career opportunities.

PERSONALITY INGREDIENTS: First impression is honest, sturdy, and
healthy. Inwardly efficient, organized, and courageous. Wants affluent
and powerful life-style. Has good financial judgment, and organizes to
live on a grand scale. Balances personality extremes by traveling and
investigating a variety of philosophies.

PERSONALITY EXTREME: Too sensual, or too virginal.

BROTHER (Nickname, or found in place of first name on
birth certificate)—M.

MAJOR TALENT: Ability to incorporate independent action, practical
economy, and curiosity into career. Is clever and learns from experience. Understands people and relates best in nonroutine situations. Very
intuitional/spiritual/conceptual. Has faith, enthusiasm, and courageous
love. Innovative ideas and commonsense values seek pragmatic outlets.
Most successful when able to curb pleasure seeking or sensual tendencies. Any sales position, navigation, and personnel director are possible
career opportunities.

PERSONALITY INGREDIENTS: First impression is freedom-loving,
clever, and understanding. Invites nonroutine experiences and is accident prone. Inwardly not materialistic. Wants serenity, partnerships, and
a gentle life. Feels a calling to improve the quality of life for others, but
cannot be cloistered.

PERSONALITY EXTREME: Too unselfish, or too stingy.

BRUCE (Old French/Scottish/English)—M.

MAJOR TALENT: Ability to incorporate strategic administration, a
statesmanlike approach, and visionary concepts into career. Is persevering and untiring, and senses what the public will understand or purchase.
Has strong opinions, and leads others into serving a common cause.
Succeeds through aiming high and avoiding the easy way to financial
power. Must work to prosper. Politics and any industry or profession are
possible career opportunities. The bearer of this name builds for generalized lasting results.

PERSONALITY INGREDIENTS: Strives for affluence, efficiency, and recognition. Appears attractive to the opposite sex, companionable, and unregimented. Has choice to be a great power for development or a destructive force. Unusual communications gifts should be recognized and encouraged.

PERSONALITY EXTREME: Too enthusiastic, or too embittered.

BRUNO (Teutonic/English; variant Bron)—M.

MAJOR TALENT: Ability to incorporate perception of details, progressive action, and intellectual analysis into career. Is impulsive, observant, and enterprising. Succeeds through difficulty and hurdles obstacles to achieve expertise in any field that doesn't include dirty work. Prefers refined, quiet, cultural working areas. Law, psychoanalysis, and technical professions offer career opportunities.

PERSONALITY INGREDIENTS: Difficult to read at first meeting; may appear aloof, mysterious, and introspective. Needs to show some authority to express self conversationally. Inwardly generous, empathetic, and a great lover . . . in spirit a humanitarian. Prefers the philosophical approach and sees more than surface values. Must balance search for perfection and everyday need for tangible necessities.

PERSONALITY EXTREME: Too jealous, or too trusting.

BRYAN (Irish/English variant of Brian)—M.

MAJOR TALENT: Ability to incorporate a trustworthy, sympathetic, inducingly magnetic nature into career. Is attaining for family; kind, generous, and patient. Practical attitude attracts social and business success. Builds influential relationships, and is boosted and assisted by females and authority figures. Therapist, doctor, and decorator are possible career opportunities.

PERSONALITY INGREDIENTS: Appears quiet, thoughtful, and mentally tuned; a keen judge of people with a natural love of imaginative wheeling and dealing. Takes charge efficiently, and drives for status in the community. But keeps a secret self that is only understood in a love relationship . . . if at all. Must avoid pessimism and moody facade. Luck is enhanced by optimistic outer personality.

PERSONALITY EXTREME: Too open-minded, or too stubborn.

BRYANT (Irish/English variant of Brian)—M.

MAJOR TALENT: Ability to incorporate a confident facade, physical coordination, and an engaging presence into career. Is ambitious. Combines eagerness, keen observation, and courage. Achieves major success when able to control headstrong love involvements. Born communicator, organizer, and leader. School administrator, insurance agent, and musician are possible career opportunities.

PERSONALITY INGREDIENTS: First impression is unruffled, poised and quietly authoritative. Respects cultured, knowledgeable, dignified associations. Inwardly efficient, exacting, and determined. Should maintain tactful attitude to promote large scale goals.

PERSONALITY EXTREME: Too uncompromising, or too adaptable.

BUD (Old English: Budd-Boda/nickname)—M.

MAJOR TALENT: Ability to incorporate humanitarian instincts, self-expression, and emotional nature into career. Is inspirational to others, tolerant, and intuitive. Has many friends and varied interests. Best suited to serving others and putting material values on the shelf. Welfare work, government, and artistic professions are possible career opportunities.

PERSONALITY INGREDIENTS: Appears to be responsible, trustworthy, and interested. Feels optimistic, and needs attractive surroundings and people. Imaginative, friendly to children/animals, and may enjoy flirtations. Likes to give advice, and is a parental guide. Must learn to be discriminating in emotional responses and not build personal ego upon the dependency of others.

PERSONALITY EXTREME: Too smug, or too insecure.

BUNNY (American variant of Bernice, Bonnie, etc.)—F. & M.

MAJOR TALENT: Ability to incorporate high practical energy, service to groups, and organizational control into career. Is able to comprehend, structure, and produce tangible results. Has firm opinions and an addiction to work. May leave a lasting result for the constructive use of future generations. Land investments, top-notch manufacture, and reconstruction challenges offer career opportunities.

PERSONALITY INGREDIENTS: Appears pleasant, friendly, and expressive. Inwardly very individualistic. Needs creative freedom, independence, and ambitious goals. Enjoys humor, beauty, and dramatic/theatrical experiences. Inspirational/powerful in difficult situations.

PERSONALITY EXTREME: Too sarcastic, or too aloof.

BURGESS (Teutonic/English)—M.

MAJOR TALENT: Ability to incorporate unbiased leadership, visionary creativity, and unclouded perception into career. Is startlingly direct, constructively progressive, and resourcefully bold. Although the bearer of this name requires independent leadership, he finds greater success working with colleagues. Theatrical director, business owner, and idea person are possible career opportunities.

PERSONALITY INGREDIENTS: Appears modest, self-possessed, and quietly supportive. Inwardly wants to mold an empire based upon justice, efficiency, and continued growth. A diplomatic powerhouse, but prefers gentle, discreet, amiable companionships.

PERSONALITY EXTREME: Too crisp, or too powdery.

BURKE (Teutonic/English)—M.

MAJOR TALENT: Ability to incorporate imaginative ideas, animated conversation, and shuffling interests into career. Is patiently guiding, pays attention to details, and always sees alternatives. Best when able to balance family responsibilities and business interests successfully. Literature, fashion photography, and sales are possible career opportunities.

PERSONALITY INGREDIENTS: Splendidly confusing but sensible daredevil. In mental perpetual motion, but appears conservative, dependable, and practical. Wants sensual pleasures, has unabashed curiosity, and relaxes in spontaneous situations. Remains youthful, and must learn to accept constant change to harvest dazzling potential.

PERSONALITY EXTREME: Too revolutionary, or too rooted.

BURL (Old English: Burleah-Byrle/Middle English: Burleigh)—M.

MAJOR TALENT: Ability to incorporate intellectual curiosity, prophetic vision, and outstanding leadership into career. Is thoughtful, efficient, and courageous. Integrates material results and meditative study to acquire an expertise/authority in a contemporary society. Best when expressing creativity after doing investigative research. Compiler, consultant, and public welfare official are possible career opportunities.

PERSONALITY INGREDIENTS: Needs people, attention, and optimism. Enjoys humor, beauty, and imaginative interests. Must feel free to experiment, travel, and use clever inner resources. Has a roving eye and stubborn or pessimistic lapses. Must concentrate on one thing to be self-confident.

PERSONALITY EXTREME: Too extravagant, or too fundamental.

BURNETT (English: Bron/Old French)—M.

MAJOR TALENT: Ability to incorporate a cooperative attitude and executive leadership into career. Is definite, capable, and ambitious. Develops own way of doing things, and is quick and inquiring. Best suited to positions where detailed analysis, group input, and tangible results are obvious. Most successful when receptive, not competitive, in communications with others. Illustrator, telephone operator, and psychiatrist are possible career opportunities.

PERSONALITY INGREDIENTS: Appears agreeable, studious, and helpful; may seem subdued. Inwardly businesslike, determined and a hard worker. Comfortable with affluent people and assuming an authoritative position. Experiences delays in material progress that introduce a much-needed awareness for patience. Self-pity causes rash behavior, which delays ambitions.

PERSONALITY EXTREME: Too soft, or too hard.

BURT (Teutonic/English variant of Bert or nickname for Burton)—M.

MAJOR TALENT: Ability to incorporate research, communications resources, and individualistic actions into career. Is at best when technically or academically expert. Should serve and assume responsibility, but is most content when nonmaterialistic. Needs spiritual or intellectual outlet for probing intellect. Newscaster, engineer, and appraiser are possible career opportunities.

PERSONALITY INGREDIENTS: Appears conservative, sturdy, and practical, but may scatter money or love and be a faddist. Inclined to see life as a game of chess, but sometimes forgets that chess is a quality game of intellect, practice, and nobility. Comfortable when surrounded by beautiful people, entertaining personalities, and a variety of interests.

PERSONALITY EXTREME: Too envious, or too self-satisfied.

BURTON (English variant of Old High German)—M.

MAJOR TALENT: Ability to incorporate impressive streams of creativity into career. Attracts a following, and supporters implement ideas for tangible rewards. Grows culturally, and learns tolerance and when to take decisive actions. Succeeds through diplomacy and technical/scientific analysis. Composer, doctor, and inventor are possible career opportunities.

PERSONALITY INGREDIENTS: Totally sympathetic, generous, and magnetic person. Empathetic, romantic, and noble. Dislikes petty details and people and mundane practicalities. Has great highs and lows. Expresses

self artistically with a charming and dramatic flair. Needs to help or raise
standards for humanitarian causes.

PERSONALITY EXTREME: Too sensual, or too high-minded.

BYRON (Greek/Old French/Middle English)—M.

MAJOR TALENT: Ability to incorporate idealistic, artistic, or humanitarian service into career. Is attentive to details and diplomatic, and
strives for a peaceful home and community. Will have commercial opportunities and should capitalize on them intuitively. Best as a middle-
man, administrative assistant, or instrumental salesman for a
commendable cause. Inspirational welfare worker, novelist, and character analyst are possible career opportunities.

PERSONALITY INGREDIENTS: First impression is refined, unfathom-
able, and aloof. Speaks when knowledgable, and prefers to give a
dignified impression. Inwardly a planner. Needs practicality, economy,
and constant relationships. Detests insincerity, pretension, and waste.
Nervous energy may produce physical or emotional instability. This
same energy may offer fame through extraordinary foresight. Must persevere and learn to admit mistakes.

PERSONALITY EXTREME: Too procrastinating, or too hurried.

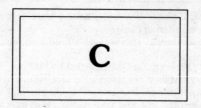

C

All names that begin with the letter *C* have the *Strong Point* of self-expression—words—imagination—inspiration—congeniality.

CAESAR (Latin/English)—M.

MAJOR TALENT: Ability to incorporate decisive actions geared to maintaining tactful, diplomatic, and unemotional reasoning into career. Must expect to adapt to changes and examine the depth of situations before drawing conclusions. May be a master tactician, craftsman, or visionary adviser. Music, civil service, and any detail-oriented profession are possible career opportunities.

PERSONALITY INGREDIENTS: Desires cultural advancement, but appears to be quietly conservative and of average tastes. Intellectually perceptive, questioning, and extremely intuitive inwardly. This name has far-reaching power when emotions are controlled and the compulsion to maintain a status quo is released.

PERSONALITY EXTREME: Too tempestuous, or too dispassionate.

CALEB (Hebrew/English)—M.

MAJOR TALENT: Ability to incorporate flow of unusual ideas and clever observations into career. Learns from exposures and experiences. Best when an opportunist. Is lucky, but must learn to be cautiously experimental and free of sexual obsessions. Should balance intellect and physical feelings to maintain financial stability. Law, the advertising professions, and psychology are possible career opportunities.

PERSONALITY INGREDIENTS: Appears organized, efficient, and powered for affluence. First impression: Let's get down to business. Needs roots, family attainments, and harmonious relationships. Has high ideals which tie into strong personal judgments that should not be imposed upon others. If too judgmental, beautiful protective feelings turn love relationships to jealous arguments. Impulsive angry words will cause problems until life experience provides opportunities for self-understanding.

PERSONALITY EXTREME: Too tender, or too tough.

CALVIN (Latin/English)—M.

MAJOR TALENT: Ability to incorporate a regard for meticulous attention to details and mentally tuned perceptions into career. Is meditative, intellectually alert, and often too impulsive. Success comes through hard work for recognition as an authority on a subject. Must hang in and conform to practical routines. Clergy, medicine, and any research-oriented business are possible career opportunities.

PERSONALITY INGREDIENTS: First impression is sensible, interested,

and responsible. Seems to be unselfish and loving. Inwardly individualistic, ambitious, and intent upon leadership. Finds contentment in meta-
physical/spiritual/academic pursuits.

PERSONALITY EXTREME: Too free-living, or too sober.

CAMERON (Celtic/Scottish)—M.

MAJOR TALENT: Ability to incorporate an exemplary image, concerned
guidance, and communication skills into career. Is protected financially
when helping others or performing artistically. Natural teacher. Gifted
with human wisdom; has ability to command respect although quiet and
thoughtful conversationally. Credit union reformer, politician, and conservationist are possible career opportunities.

PERSONALITY INGREDIENTS: Unusual as a youngster; eager to please,
fanciful, and unlike other children in depth of emotional generosity. Inwardly and outwardly needs beauty, variety, and patient understanding.
May have temper tantrums if misunderstood, but generally is cheerful,
optimistic, and gifted with a delightful personality. Unburdens the
young/needy/elderly, entertains, or provides service as a life-style. Must
avoid scattering energy and leaving things unfinished.

PERSONALITY EXTREME: Too irresponsible, or too protective.

CAMILLA (Etruscan/Italian/English)—F.

MAJOR TALENT: Ability to incorporate trustworthy image, practical
judgment, and focus upon responsible service into career. Is generous,
kind, and socially adept. Attracts help from financially influential or
authoritative people. Ambitious, but not just for money. Teaching, civil
service, and home-improvement products are possible career opportunities.

PERSONALITY INGREDIENTS: Feels special and is unusually inventive
and intuitive. Needs loving mate, peaceful environment, and to give and
receive emotional tenderness. Very sensitive, high-strung, and modest.
Appears to be respectable, sturdy, and dependable. Is often lost in own
world . . . daydreamy or crusading. Bows to conventions—usually.

PERSONALITY EXTREME: Too independent, or too obliging.

CAMILLE (French, from Camilla)—F. & M.

MAJOR TALENT: Ability to incorporate affinity for detail, independent
decisions, and mental organization into career. Is geared to influence
others. Attractive charmer; uses gentle/tactful/subtle approach to gain
power. Extremely resourceful individualist. Designing, theatrical production, and any creative work are possible career opportunities.

PERSONALITY INGREDIENTS: Wants beauty, balanced relationships,
and emotional expression. Deepens roots and seeks abundant life-style.
Appears honest, hardworking, and down-to-earth. Rarely gets anything
for nothing; must be practical, economical, and organized to maintain
stability. Has sex appeal and is full of interesting inconsistencies.

PERSONALITY EXTREME: Too unrestrained, or too conventional.

CAMPBELL (Old French/Scottish)—M.

MAJOR TALENT: Ability to incorporate innovative ideas and a self-
starter quality into career. Is determined and explorative, and has firm
personal opinions. Concerned with efficiency, organization, and material

results. Attracts cooperation from the opposite sex and in return is passionate, generous, and affectionate. Building contractor, credit worker, and inventor are possible career opportunities.

PERSONALITY INGREDIENTS: Needs comfortable, loving, respectable life-style. Takes pride in family and community image, and feels a sense of responsibility to nurture, teach, and counsel. Appears solid, conservative, and dependable. Has fondness for the earth and tries to retain real estate for future generations. Must learn patience and when to temper judgments.

PERSONALITY EXTREME: Too easygoing, or too regimented.

CANDACE (Greek/English)—F.

MAJOR TALENT: Ability to incorporate the gift of castle building into career. Is visionary, constructive, and able to turn ideas into tangibles. Needs to benefit others and has great love for humanity. Strong opinions are delivered with diplomatic flair. Inner faith brings out the master builder who leaves a mark on humanity. Writing, government, and structural analysis are possible career opportunities.

PERSONALITY INGREDIENTS: Combines refined/cultured intellect and parental, sociable, responsible facade. Needs time to think and opportunity to enjoy family/friends and be the just adviser to anyone in need of help. Displays classic but comfortable taste. Does not lose poise easily and juggles material and spiritual goals as a life-style.

PERSONALITY EXTREME: Too mental, or too physical.

CANDICE (Greek: Candace/English)—F.

MAJOR TALENT: Ability to incorporate practical personal philosophy, scientific or artistic versatility, and sex appeal into career. Is entertaining, agreeable, and humor-loving. Attracts pleasures, material security, and beautiful family relationships. Creates a special quality in life and can be the star. Theater, home decoration, and the legal professions are possible career opportunities.

PERSONALITY INGREDIENTS: The cosmic mother who adjusts all wrongs, assumes responsibility for harmonious family relationships, and wants to feel pride in home and community life. Is morally strong, ethical, and bound to have her personal standards upheld . . . sometimes to a fault. Maintains ideals from a conservative life-style, though the glitter may be offered.

PERSONALITY EXTREME: Too eccentric, or too conventional.

CARA (Latin/Irish)—F.

MAJOR TALENT: Ability to incorporate education through experience and experimentation into career. Is clever and liberal, and strikes while the iron is hot. Tests theories in practical ways and strives for progressive and cultural expansion. Thrives on change, physical sensations, and varied interests. Financial balance comes when impulsiveness is curbed. Advertising, politics, and investigative professions are possible career opportunities.

PERSONALITY INGREDIENTS: Wants the perfect mate, and gains through tact, diplomacy and attention to personal sensitivities. Is expressive, charming, gracious and attracts good-looking men with unusual philosophies. Is self-deluding and must learn patience. Makes many

changes throughout life and must sustain inner concentration to maintain
self-confidence.

PERSONALITY EXTREME: Too forceful, or too fearful.

CAREY (diminutive of Welsh Caradoc, M; or diminutive of
German/English/French Caroline, F.)—F. & M.

MAJOR TALENT: Ability to incorporate hypothetical questioning, resourceful ideas, and sensitivity to people into career. Is careful,
weatherwise, and probing. Best in cultural climate, freewheeling, and
alert to offbeat invitations. Faces and is able to overcome obstacles to
financial stability. Works best alone. Photography, editing, and any
scientific/technical career are possible opportunities.

PERSONALITY INGREDIENTS: Appears individualistic and creative. Desires love, beauty, music, and comfortable life-style. Tenderhearted,
protective, and emotionally generous. Devoted, broad-minded friend,
although personally high-minded and disciplined morally and ethically. A
perfectionist. Succeeds through perseverance.

PERSONALITY EXTREME: Too suspicious, or too gullible.

CARIN (Danish/Norwegian variant of Catherine or Karen)—F.

MAJOR TALENT: Ability to incorporate sensitivity to details, intellectual analysis, and humanitarian philosophy into career. Is compassionate, just, and wise. A font of ideas and techniques for creative problem
solving. Attracts helpful admirers. Commercial success may be slowed
by selfless/tolerant attitudes. Best when decisive and broadly philosophical. Medicine, publishing, and judicial reform are possible career opportunities.

PERSONALITY INGREDIENTS: Independent, businesslike, artistically
talented and appreciative. Wants creative avenues for material ambitions. Appears efficient, honest, and affluent. Has magnetism, and is
financially successful when courageous, daring, and true to intuition.

PERSONALITY EXTREME: Too venturesome, or too scared.

CARL (Old German/French/English variant of Charles)—M.

MAJOR TALENT: Ability to incorporate unmistakable authority, mental
analysis, and communication gifts into career. Is most productive when
unconcerned about money. Overcomes problems through specialization
of interests. Attracts good fortune when concentrated and unemotional,
nonmaterial and intellectual, questioning and not assuming. The bearer
of this name cannot release pressures if physically self-indulgent. Has
potential for fame, prosperity, and respect for unique intellect. Administrator, psychologist, and historian are possible career opportunities.

PERSONALITY INGREDIENTS: Needs individuality, innovative goals,
and a leadership position. Outwardly interested, conservative, and parental. Enjoys being needed and strives for home/family/community attainments. A true introvert/extrovert.

PERSONALITY EXTREME: Too talkative, or too quiet.

CARLA (German/English/French/Italian)—F.

MAJOR TALENT: Ability to incorporate investigative instincts, meditative solitude, and tangible results of mental concepts into career. Is gifted
with insight, determination, and compassion for others. Outstanding

70

All names that begin with the letter *C* have the *Strong Point* of
self-expression—words—imagination—inspiration—congeniality.

powers of persuasion attract affluent/respected associations. Advancements bring recognition, possibly public acclaim. This is a financially fortunate name when untouched by pessimism, bullying, and instability. Compiler, financial adviser, and communications executive are possible career opportunities.

PERSONALITY INGREDIENTS: Very sensitive, devoted, and soft. Instinctively tactful, thoughtful, and modest. Feels happiest in a relationship and takes the good with the bad. Enjoys collecting things and knows how to keep a secret. Strives for family safety/harmony, generous home, and respectability. Expects everyone to live up to personal standards and may sit in judgment upon others.

PERSONALITY EXTREME: Too individualistic, or too dependent.

CARLOS (Spanish/Portuguese, from Charles)—M.

MAJOR TALENT: Ability to incorporate fast thinking, passionate loyalties, and adventurous challenges into career. Is agile in mind and body. Often receives an inheritance, builds pleasurable family life, and receives fortunate counseling. Is a willing, friendly, straightforward person whose enthusiasms, courage, and inventive nature spark interest and further ambitions. Any sales professions, politics, and navigation/surveying are possible career opportunities.

PERSONALITY INGREDIENTS: Outer impression may be cloudy. Gets chummy when able to speak authoritatively or philosophically. Needs cultural, intellectual, and spiritual stimulation. Rarely understands self-worth. May be lacking the drive for education and/or the relaxation in social interaction that brings out the brilliance of this name. Must strive for specialization. The bearer of this name learns easily and will advance if he remains even-tempered, instinctively seizes opportunities, and does not patronize others.

PERSONALITY EXTREME: Too ambitious, or too uninspired.

CARLOTTA (Italian variant of Caroline)—F.

MAJOR TALENT: Ability to incorporate emotional responsiveness, love of nature, and artistic skills into career. Is attentive, sensitive, and romantic. Has grace, charm and nobility. Adds kindness, human understanding, and empathy to any interest. Writing, welfare work, and the entertainment professions are possible career opportunities.

PERSONALITY INGREDIENTS: Appears energetic, self-directed, and capable. May be impatient and too decisive. Should be a sharp dresser. Inwardly efficient, and prefers to manage large-scale projects. Feels determined, works hard, and is thorough. Analyzes for perfection and cultural depth. Is intellectually stimulating, and fine-tuned for noting the little things that indicate the traits of a great lover. May be secretive, indiscreet, and as confusingly generous and selfish as described.

PERSONALITY EXTREME: Too self-centered, or too obliging.

CARMEN (Italian/Spanish/English, from Hebrew Carmel)—F.

MAJOR TALENT: Ability to incorporate voluntary service, creative artistry, and philosophical attitude into career. Best efforts are conceptual and inventive, but not geared toward commercialization. They are not marketable items. Ambitions must be pushed out of the idea stage to reality. Observers see talents and are inclined to help. Matures to under-

stand that wishing will not make it so. Encouragement is the key to
commercialization. Any artistic, humanitarian, or nature-related business is a possible career opportunity.

PERSONALITY INGREDIENTS: Wants to be needed and to protect, teach,
and counsel. Has high standards and expects family/community/
employer to live up to personal principles. First impression is charming,
well groomed and sunny. Strives for optimism, variety, and ease of
living. Assumes unnecessary responsibilities. Often expects too much of
self, overreacts emotionally, and loses personal incentive.

PERSONALITY EXTREME: Too open-minded, or too proper.

CAROL (Old French/English diminutive of German/English/French
Caroline)—F.

MAJOR TALENT: Ability to incorporate practical, constructive, farsighted ideas and workaholic energy into career. Is bent upon producing
tangible results. May choose a humanitarian or large-scale business. Impressive, positive thinking, intuitional executive. Self-assured reformer
with possibility of contributing lasting accomplishments. Economist, job
counselor, and diplomat are possible career opportunities.

PERSONALITY INGREDIENTS: Appears soft, responsible, and concerned. Strives for beautiful, comfortable, rooted life-style. A good listener, teacher, and guide. Outer shell belies inner strength. Feels special.
Needs to be independent and self-assertive. Takes courageous lead and
may be supercharged, definite, and capable. A powerhouse for humanitarian service.

PERSONALITY EXTREME: Too worried, or too optimistic.

CAROLA (from Caroline)—F.

MAJOR TALENT: Ability to incorporate research, writing, and understanding of people into career. At best in a changing routine and when
assisting influential associates. Attracts money, happy marriage, and
progressive life-style. Inventive nature is supported by fine memory and
clever wit. Travel professions, sports, and science or mechanics are
possible career opportunities.

PERSONALITY INGREDIENTS: Wants accomplishments, status, and
affluence. Organizes efficiently for large undertakings and is a just
leader. Seems to be affectionate, responsible, loyal and family/
community oriented. Strives for gracious living and artistic expression.
Is a gifted communicator. Must avoid temperamental outbursts, impulsiveness, and self-important attitudes.

PERSONALITY EXTREME: Too energetic, or too lazy.

CAROLINA (English/Italian/Spanish/Portuguese)—F.

MAJOR TALENT: Ability to incorporate creative leadership, family/
business partnerships, and emotional control into career. Is kind, generous, and geared to protecting others' interests. May be cute or cunning to
achieve aspirations. Born with wisdom and maturity. Overseas agent,
inventor, and retailer are possible career opportunities.

PERSONALITY INGREDIENTS: Appears supportive, adaptable, and diplomatic. Wants affluence, efficient organization, and constructive
growth. Should choose mate carefully and form allied ambitions to maintain high-quality life-style. Social relationships advance ambitions.

PERSONALITY EXTREME: Too bossy, or too inoffensive.

CAROLINE (German/French/English)—F.

MAJOR TALENT: Ability to incorporate enthusiasm, versatility, and catalystic effect upon others into career. Is overflowing with love of life and people. Shows courage and faith, and recovers quickly when things go amiss. Gets ideas and produces material results. Receives help and protection from family and associations. Politics, journalism, and psychology are possible career opportunities.

PERSONALITY INGREDIENTS: Extremely diplomatic impression. Modest, supportive, and a calming presence. Wants fun, beauty, and varied interests. Enjoys the clever, progressive, theatrical types, and keeps in touch with fashions, fads, and imaginative trends. Unusually creative, sensitive, and perceptive. Attracts good fortune.

PERSONALITY EXTREME: Too pleasure-seeking, or too restrained.

CAROLYN (Variant of Caroline)—F.

MAJOR TALENT: Ability to incorporate cultured tastes, conventional philosophy, and sharp analysis into career. Is a wise and honest counselor. Works best privately, and should bring completed projects to others' attention. Has unruffled approach, but churns internally. Combines practicality, intellect, and charm. Speaks when sure. Florist, editor, and appraiser are possible career opportunities.

PERSONALITY INGREDIENTS: First impression is adaptable, modest, and soft. Inwardly needs change, adventure, and physical freedom. Feels curious, impulsive, and likes the newest fads. Retains youthful attitudes and progressive interests. Should learn not to judge others by appearances and to be diplomatic in relationships.

PERSONALITY EXTREME: Too changeable, or too resolute.

CARON (French variant of Catherine)—F.

MAJOR TALENT: Ability to incorporate responsible, practical, diplomatic attitudes into career. Is geared to communicating trustworthiness, companionability, and attainment. Good material judgments flourish when stubborn values are balanced by consideration of the feelings and emotions of associates/family members. Is respected for wisdom. Nursing, teaching, and the artistic/theatrical professions are possible career opportunities.

PERSONALITY INGREDIENTS: Impression is classy. Seems to be refined, introspective, and unruffled. Inwardly warm, generous, and concerned. Wants to help, and sometimes becomes Ms. Fullcharge. Strives for quality and needs roots to feel secure. Happy approach to people brings success.

PERSONALITY EXTREME: Too experimental, or too structured.

CARRIE (English variant of Carol or Caroline)—F.

MAJOR TALENT: Ability to incorporate self-expression, executive responsibility, and humanitarian uplift into career. Is able to bear burdens that flatten others. Has inventive nature that gears to serving broad-scoped, just, merciful causes. May act earthy or noble . . . whatever is needed to get the job done. A born welfare worker. Any philosophical, charitable, or artistically idealistic profession is a possible career opportunity.

PERSONALITY INGREDIENTS: Appears conversational, optimistic, and imaginative. Likes people and variety, and is inclined to impetuous emotional reactions. Inwardly protective, generous, and dedicated to family/community attainments. If freed of personal responsibility, should aim to implement prophetic ideas for the public good.

PERSONALITY EXTREME: Too human, or too sublime.

CARROLL (Old German/English)—M.

MAJOR TALENT: Ability to incorporate intellectual discrimination, structured planning, and communication gifts into career. Is a clear-thinking perfectionist. Focus is upon the facts. Benefits from air travel, outdoor exercise, and cultural interests. May use sense of humor to soften blunt speech habits. Psychologist, historical writer, and preacher are possible career opportunities.

PERSONALITY INGREDIENTS: First impression commands attention. Appears empathetic, charming, and neat. Emits a youthful, sometimes dramatic flair. Inwardly conservative, home oriented, and inclined to be protective. Gets emotionally involved and may personalize too much.

PERSONALITY EXTREME: Too superficial, or too serious.

CARTER (Old English)—M.

MAJOR TALENT: Ability to incorporate inspirational ideas and a calling to uplift others into career. Is intuitive, sensitive, and concerned with the fine points. An individualist with farsighted vision. May benefit mankind when diplomacy in the commercial world is understood and petty anxieties are squelched by decisive action. High ideals bring recognition. Politics, all service jobs, and any religious or humanistic interest are possible career opportunities.

PERSONALITY INGREDIENTS: Wants strong family and community responsibility, trust, and respect. Is generous, artistic, and protective. First impression is attractive to the opposite sex. Seems impulsive, friendly, and enthusiastic. Benefits from physical exercise. Retains youthful appearance.

PERSONALITY EXTREME: Too understanding, or too bitter.

CARY (Old Welsh/English variant of Charles or of Latin Caradoc, M.; variant of Caroline, F.)—F. & M.

MAJOR TALENT: Ability to incorporate fine-quality diplomacy, tactful, controlling personality, and advancement through adaptation into career. Is a creature of habit, judges by appearances, and becomes unhinged by sudden events until emotional personalizing ceases and turns to a gift for sensing the details and facing logical decisions. Is a fine artisan and should aim high. Can turn disasters to successes with detached practical planning. Age adds wisdom. Theatrical group work, statistical work, or any service technique is a possible career opportunity.

PERSONALITY INGREDIENTS: First impression is fun-loving, charming, and versatile. Inwardly organized, dignified, and businesslike. Feels special. Desires position, money, and power. Strives to be attractive, and surrounded by beauty. Likes pets, people, and flights of fancy. Is easily bored.

PERSONALITY EXTREME: Too secretive, or too informative.

CARYL (variant of Carol or Caroline)—F.

MAJOR TALENT: Ability to incorporate multiple interests, cleverness, and skillful understanding of public acceptance into career. Has a way with people. Is energetic in mind and body. Attracts material comforts, family pride, and help from admiring friends. Combines attractive presentations, adaptability, and mental curiosity. Designer, flight attendant, and advertising copywriter are possible career opportunities.

PERSONALITY INGREDIENTS: Inwardly materially ambitious, persevering, and efficient. Impatient with less organized/courageous/disciplined people. Strives for family/group harmony, abundant home, and respectability. Seems to be a concerned listener and a parental counselor, and has a comfortable appearance. The bearer of this name suffers through selfishness and eccentric emotional outbursts. When balanced, has all-around good fortune.

PERSONALITY EXTREME: Too theatrical, or too subdued.

CARYN (variant of Caroline, Catherine, or Karen)—F.

MAJOR TALENT: Ability to incorporate appreciation of details, intellectual analysis, and progressive ideas into career. Is intuitive, clever, and enterprising. Childhood experiences develop problem-solving qualities that include perseverance and practical judgments. Success comes with hard work and careful planning. Photography, antiques, and collecting data or objects are possible career opportunities.

PERSONALITY INGREDIENTS: Wants affluence, power, and respectability. Appears efficient, organized, and well-informed. Has executive personality and pride in family/community attainments. Should specialize and handle finances. May be secretive and overly concerned with money.

PERSONALITY EXTREME: Too spontaneous, or too contrived.

CASEY (Gaelic-Irish/English)—M.

MAJOR TALENT: Ability to incorporate scientific or technical skills, investigative analysis, and independent leadership into career. Is creative and spiritual, and gets things done. Enjoys travel, has mental vitality, and is extremely convincing. Any business/profession, school administration, and promotion are possible career opportunities.

PERSONALITY INGREDIENTS: Strives for illumination. Works for causes and appears different. Inwardly family/community rooted. Wants harmony, beauty, and abundant life-style. Assumes responsibility, is protective, and gives emotional and material assistance. Is musical, a good teacher, and a fine companion.

PERSONALITY EXTREME: Too introspective, or too authoritative.

CASPAR (Persian/English)—M.

MAJOR TALENT: Ability to incorporate practical improvements, definite planning, and emotional control into career. May be sensitive to details, but usually separates business and personal sensitivity. Has unlimited vision, determination, and strong opinions. Usually secure in marriage and friendships. Real estate, quality manufacturing, and government are possible career opportunities.

PERSONALITY INGREDIENTS: Inwardly peace-loving, gentle, and supportive. Seems modest, and must learn not to assume anything. Is care-

All names that begin with the letter *C* have the *Strong Point* of
self-expression—words—imagination—inspiration—congeniality.

75

ful about little details and must avoid being trapped in minutiae. Needs a
mate and appreciates emotional support.

PERSONALITY EXTREME: Too compassionate, or too unconcerned.

CASSANDRA (Greek/Italian/English)—F.

MAJOR TALENT: Ability to incorporate responsible business leadership
into career. Is a gifted speaker and athletically inclined; should learn to
adapt to partnerships. Maintains an air of self-confidence under pressure.
Is ambitious. Expects the best from self and others. Coach, military
officer, and insurance agent are possible career opportunities.

PERSONALITY INGREDIENTS: Desires beauty, variety, and life's pleasures. Is inclined to humor, socializing, and flirting. Enjoys children,
animals, and fantasy. First impression is attention-getting. Attracts
friends, adventure, and surprises. May be accident-prone, curious, and
impulsive. Has high energy and should develop powers of expression.
Needs self-control, patience, and endurance.

PERSONALITY EXTREME: Too aggressive, or too shielded.

CATHERINE (Greek/French/Scottish/Irish/English, with variants in all languages; may be spelled with a K)—F.

MAJOR TALENT: Ability to incorporate influence over others, confident
nature, and attraction for affection into career. Is torn between practical
and emotional desires. Adaptable, determined, and spiritual by nature.
Strong character knows how to be flexible, and handles money well. Can
make dreams come true if discriminating, patient, and realistic. Religious
authority, political campaigner, and character analyst are possible career
opportunities.

PERSONALITY INGREDIENTS: First impression is generous, broad-
scoped, and youthful. Attracts listeners. Inwardly sensitive, detail-
minded, and geared for partnership. May court disappointment by
romanticizing to create the perfect mate. Must be cautious when placing
affections. The bearer of this name may experience thunderous domestic
changes and has all the qualities necessary to weather any storm. However, with decisive planning, determination, and objective analysis of
goals, she may achieve perfect happiness and security.

PERSONALITY EXTREME: Too sensual, or too mental.

CATHLEEN (Irish, from Catherine)—F.

MAJOR TALENT: Ability to incorporate communications, cleverness,
and adaptability into career. Is active, confident, and persuasive. Attracts helpful friends and is sensitive to their needs. Has progressive
ideas, prophetic dreams, and conventional procedures for expansion.
Flight attendant, advertising executive, and government service are possible career opportunities.

PERSONALITY INGREDIENTS: Has futuristic thoughts and may be
crusading an ideal to the point of exhaustion trying to be constructive.
Inwardly spiritual, philosophical, and illuminating. A critic, friend, and
reformer of society. Wants partnership, peace, and respect. May be a
personality kid. Appears sunny, pleasure-seeking, and conversational.
Should avoid carelessness, supersensitivity, and impulsiveness. Should
master a foreign language, be determined, and aim high.

PERSONALITY EXTREME: Too superior, or too inferior.

76

All names that begin with the letter *C* have the *Strong Point* of
self-expression—words—imagination—inspiration—congeniality.

CATHY (variant in many languages of Catherine)—F.

MAJOR TALENT: Ability to incorporate patience, personality, and positive thinking into career. Is a good administrator, conversationalist, and adventurer. Gains through emotional control, retentive memory, and inspirational ideas. Theatrical production, writing, and fashion are possible career opportunities.

PERSONALITY INGREDIENTS: Appears homespun and honest. Clean-cut looks and approach impress others as conservative, sturdy, and average. Inwardly strives for top slot. Wants power, affluence, and position. Feels organized, efficient, and ready to work. Attracts a tailor-made lifestyle; adds expensive tastes and some spice.

PERSONALITY EXTREME: Too cool, or too opinionated.

CECIL (Latin/English)—M.

MAJOR TALENT: Ability to incorporate an agile mind and body into career. Is clever, versatile, and detailed. Attracts inheritances, interesting companionship, and nonroutine experiences. Best when free to invent, travel, and progress through changing goals. Collective research, science, and the arts are possible career opportunities.

PERSONALITY INGREDIENTS: Improves upon birth environment. Inwardly optimistic, versatile, and dramatic. Needs beauty, stimulating wit, and time to relax. Appears to relate to people and empathize with their problems. Is romantic and may be the great lover. Strives for nobility, life's pleasures, and unique experiences. Should have large circle of friends.

PERSONALITY EXTREME: Too superficial, or too blunt.

CECILE (French, from Cecilia)—F.

MAJOR TALENT: Ability to incorporate innovative ideas, executive leadership, and adaptability into career. Is ambitious, but knows when not to push. Attracts fortunate communications, good supportive associations, and grand-scale challenges. Has the courage, intuition, and artistic resources to master own fate. Free-lance illustrator, telephone operator, and manager are possible career opportunities.

PERSONALITY INGREDIENTS: Can choose to appear independent or philosophical. Always creates a positive image. Inwardly a welfare worker. Needs to give generous, broad-scoped service. Is romantic, inspirational, and compassionate. Has highly developed foresight and depth of wisdom. Very emotional, and may have quick temper. Can serve humanity through inventive impersonal guidelines, and must never become petty or small-minded.

PERSONALITY EXTREME: Too stagnant, or too restless.

CECILIA (Latin/French/Spanish/Italian/Danish/English)—F.

MAJOR TALENT: Ability to incorporate universal or domestic welfare into career. Has special resources to teach, uplift, and assure responsibility. Emotional stability governs choice. Aimless energy may turn to escapism. Attracted to teaching, artistic trends, and love of nature's peaceful climates. Is honest, discriminating, and resourceful. Should strive to inspire, whether as mother or martyr. Teacher, welfare pioneer, and diplomat are possible career opportunities.

PERSONALITY INGREDIENTS: Is charming, conversational, and witty. If lazy and inactive, may appear unconcerned or uncaring. Has clear perceptions on a grand scale, and can be a stabilizing as well as practically helpful influence upon situations and people. This name has great power. Its bearer needs a cause or may internalize nervous energy and become a doormat for others.

PERSONALITY EXTREME: Too brave, or too fearful.

CEDRIC (Anglo-Saxon/Celtic/English)—M.

MAJOR TALENT: Ability to incorporate artistic, charitable, or executive service into career. Is capable of great sacrifice, artistry, or humanitarian understanding. Cannot diversify interests; loses the opportunity for lasting fame when personal dedication is not exclusive. When special cause is not found, the bearer of this name becomes dedicated to a family/community. A loyal, trustworthy, concerned student and teacher. Should set an example for others to admire. Musician, chef, and medical supply salesperson are possible career opportunities.

PERSONALITY INGREDIENTS: Appears individualistic, assertive, and energetic. Desires freedom to experience all that life has to offer. Is curious, clever, and changeable. Feels sensual, impatient, and inclined to humor. Should put quick mind to a responsible job.

PERSONALITY EXTREME: Too comical, or too dry.

CELESTINE (Latin/French/English)—F. & M.

MAJOR TALENT: Ability to incorporate dreams of beauty, poetic vision, and constructive administration for tangible results into career. Is able to guide talents to financial success and receives assistance from admirers. Should not aim for affluence without finding means of helping less fortunate dreamers. Metaphysical professions, science, and the arts offer possible career opportunities.

PERSONALITY INGREDIENTS: Appears bright, enthusiastic, and youthful. Is attractive to the opposite sex, active, and curious. Can be articulate to promote any worthy cause. Looks sexy. Really is conservative. Inwardly responsible, protective, and comforting. Needs a home/family/roots. Strives for truth, justice, and improvements and attainments.

PERSONALITY EXTREME: Too adventurous, or too sedate.

CELIA (Latin/English/Italian/Irish)—F.

MAJOR TALENT: Ability to incorporate glib tongue, observation of details, and independent action into career. Is personally sensitive and ambitious, and needs a place for everything and everything in its place. Has good memory for business and bad memory for petty slights. Is expressive and tuned to fashion; must learn when to be tenacious and when to change for the sake of progress. Administrator, decorator, and dietitian are possible career opportunities.

PERSONALITY INGREDIENTS: Appears to be genteel. Strives for culture, quality, and intellectual progress. Inwardly needs activity, mental freedom and sunshine. Likes the opposite sex, and is fascinated by life, people, and excitement. Keeps secrets, and may not speak until sure of authority . . . but will not be inexpressive for long.

PERSONALITY EXTREME: Too imitative, or too innovative.

CHAD (Celtic/English)—M.

MAJOR TALENT: Ability to incorporate a forceful image, crystal intellect, and investigative action into career. Has unusual mental abilities, creative energy, and strong judgments. The bearer of this name succeeds when he is not too intense about establishment power or ownership and avoids superficial extravagances. Best suited to a special area of authority or technical expertise where there are no risks involved. Watchmaker, librarian, and judge are possible career opportunities.

PERSONALITY INGREDIENTS: First impression is concerned, responsible, and parental. Strives for family/community pride. Seems to be helpful and a fine, interested counselor. Inwardly individualistic, assertive, and courageous. Wants to lead the way through creative applications to work or play. Must not become overconfident, take chances, and fail to do the right thing.

PERSONALITY EXTREME: Too dignified, or too crude.

CHANDLER (Old French/English)—M.

MAJOR TALENT: Ability to incorporate versatility, businesslike attitudes, and prophetic ideas into career. Is geared for bringing together imagery and tangibles. Has happy disposition that attracts friends, sensitive love, and family attainments. Is a strong supporter, a trustworthy leader, and a visionary creator. Name has power for lasting uplift. Spiritual/philosophical writing, fashion design, and the theatrical professions are possible career opportunities.

PERSONALITY INGREDIENTS: Has a friendly, open-ended, enthusiastic way with people. Curious nature tries new foods, fads, and fashions. Inwardly needs a harmonious home and beautiful decorations, and wants to be a family/community counselor and protector. Assumes the parental role and expects loved ones/friends/business associates to maintain proper standards. Loves good food, down sofas, and candlelight dinners by the fire; could be a Casanova. Tender, generous, and helpful. Takes an excess of burdens for those in need.

PERSONALITY EXTREME: Too law-abiding, or too disreputable.

CHANNING (Latin/French/English)—M.

MAJOR TALENT: Ability to incorporate constructive planning, creative ideas, and a fine mind into career. Is logical, progressive, and deeply emotional. Somewhat secretive; separates home and business. Knows the value of silence, but speaks at the appropriate time. Takes things calmly until the need for action arises. Attracts the good life. Quality fashion designer, lawyer, and psychological researcher are possible career opportunities.

PERSONALITY INGREDIENTS: May have been a temper-tantrum child, but matures to give the impression of great depth, love, and wisdom. May not care about appearances, but that is ignored due to exemplary character. Inwardly individualistic, courageous, and ambitious. Wants to be the boss and create new vistas. Has extremely high standards for self and others.

PERSONALITY EXTREME: Too quality-conscious, or too uncultured.

CHARITY (Greek: Charis/English/American)—F.

MAJOR TALENT: Ability to incorporate humanitarian service, romantic ideas, and loving nature into career. Is fighter for personal ideals, friendships, and the welfare of everyone. Everyone loves a lover, and the bearer of this name attracts adoration. Arts/crafts work, animal training or care, and the communications professions are possible career opportunities.

PERSONALITY INGREDIENTS: Is either saint or sinner. If serving others' welfare impersonally, life is protected. If self-indulgent, sensual, or blind to the suffering of others, life will be filled with disappointments. Inwardly organized, determined, and a dependable worker for big results. Appears poised and tasteful, and radiates a healthy attitude. Can be a practical yet fanciful powerhouse.

PERSONALITY EXTREME: Too analytic, or too shallow.

CHARLENE (variant of Caroline)—F.

MAJOR TALENT: Ability to incorporate generous, idealistic, optimistic nature into career. A goodwill emissary looking for a cause. Is best suited to sharing, serving, and sympathizing. May not receive all that this name is willing to give to others, but may reap abundant life-style when unselfish, energetic, and sensitive to the suffering of others. Decorator, social director, and arts/crafts teacher are possible career opportunities.

PERSONALITY INGREDIENTS: First impression is individualistic, capable, and courageous. Inwardly wants to share harmonious life-style with a sensitive mate. Happy to adapt desires to have serenity. May personalize too much or be too understanding when love relationships are threatened. Appears aggressive but really is shy and receptive.

PERSONALITY EXTREME: Too sensual, or too demure.

CHARLES (Old German/French/English)—M.

MAJOR TALENT: Ability to incorporate a lasting impression on any area of the communication professions/industries into career. Has an attraction for people through the voice, face, or personality . . . or all three. Is structured and clever, and respects the order of things. Finds rewards in work, homelife, and maintenance of personal ideals. Any art form, legislative professions, and, foremost, writing are possible career opportunities.

PERSONALITY INGREDIENTS: Appears to be and is a concerned person. Assumes responsibility, gives generously of time and money to help others, and is a doting parent and lover. If lazy, scattered, or too extravagant, turns the other side of the coin to become jealous, selfish, and judgmental. It is rare that the bearer of this name does not bounce back if he slips into bad habits.

PERSONALITY EXTREME: Too impatient, or too controlled.

CHARLEY (nickname of Charles, M., or Charlotte, F.)—F. & M.

MAJOR TALENT: Ability to incorporate empathy for the public welfare, strong leadership, and attention-getting ideas into career. Is not afraid of grand-scale responsibility. Has hope, faith, and optimistic approach, which may be applied to business or philanthropic interests. Should be cautious and avoid rushes of emotion that skim the surface of a project. Supersalesperson who can be sold. Entertainer, publicist, and do-gooder are possible career opportunities.

PERSONALITY INGREDIENTS: Is charming, sunny, and conversant. Is interested in everything. Inwardly strives for family warmth, artistic surroundings, and a respected life-style. Seems fun-loving and mature. Should control exposing feelings at inopportune times. May be misunderstood.

PERSONALITY EXTREME: Too secretive, or too obvious.

CHARLIE (Nickname of Charles, M., or Charlotte, F.)—F. & M.

MAJOR TALENT: Ability to incorporate original, inventive, and creative ideas into career. Is compassionate and humanistic, and spreads the word. Has futuristic imagery and the organizational traits to produce results. High energy surges to quicken the pace and offers possibility of fame to the bearer of this name. Must be honest, inspirational, and prepared for intuitive decisions. Practical reform, law, and any communications business are possible career opportunities.

PERSONALITY INGREDIENTS: May appear to be in another world. Seems to be adventurous, sensual, and enthusiastic. Needs warmth, respect, and a dignified life-style. Is responsible, trustworthy, and protective. Craves beauty in everything and everyone. May be accident-prone.

PERSONALITY EXTREME: Too impulsive, or too cautious.

CHARLOTTE (German/French/English)—F.

MAJOR TALENT: Ability to incorporate impersonal love, magnetic attraction, and responsibility to crusade for humanitarian principles into career. Is gentle, philosophical, and sympathetic. Combines romantic ideas, intellectual contemplation, and strength of purpose. May serve others through charity, the arts, or government. Commentary writing, linguistics, and the fashion industry offer possible career opportunities.

PERSONALITY INGREDIENTS: Can stop traffic. Personality, style, and nobility of nature shine through. Youthful in spirit and body, and dramatic in reactions. Feels sunny, and wants to bring light to everyone. Must avoid scattering interests, laziness, and being unconcerned about money or old-age security.

PERSONALITY EXTREME: Too glib, or too thoughtful.

CHARLTON (Old French/German/English)—M.

MAJOR TALENT: Ability to incorporate creative leadership, perceptive insights, and nobility of purpose into career. Is reserved and expansive, and attracts supportive listeners. Invests time and money with equal care. Charming manner hides skillful intellect. Home-loving, but inspired to travel. Any creative art form, science, and positions of protective authority are possible career opportunities.

PERSONALITY INGREDIENTS: Introspective, culturally attaining, and emotionally controlled. Benefits from a marriage partnership, although marriage is not necessary to happiness. First impression is attractive, calm, and friendly. Enjoys logic puzzles and clever humor. May conjure up hypothetical problems and proceed to solve them, which creates real problems. Should curb overperfectionist nature.

PERSONALITY EXTREME: Too wise, or too foolish.

CHARMAINE (Latin/English)—F.

MAJOR TALENT: Ability to incorporate practical economy, structure,

and progressive ideas for service into career. Learns from experience,
then adapts the information to a commonsense procedure. Senses a
strength within. Is tireless, resilient, and idealistic. Develops ESP
through patient retrenching. Social work, metaphysical research, and
any artistic occupation are possible career opportunities.

PERSONALITY INGREDIENTS: Appears soft, dreamy, and easygoing.
When changing others' perceptions, the bearer of this name becomes a
supersalesperson. Inwardly refined, intuitive, and secretive. Needs privacy, country or seaside life-style, and sensual balance to avoid misplaced affections.

PERSONALITY EXTREME: Too changeable, or too procrastinating.

CHAUNCEY (Latin/Anglo-Saxon/English)—M.

MAJOR TALENT: Ability to incorporate businesslike attitude, variety of
interests, and skillful communicating into career. Is geared for power,
money, and inheritance. Attractive to men and women. Adds physical
vitality, charm, and consistent effort to all relationships. May make some
mistakes through overconfidence, but high energy and expansive desires
can be controlled. Can take heavy-pressure job when emotionally balanced. Stockbroker, sports team owner, and TV executive are possible
career opportunities.

PERSONALITY INGREDIENTS: Appears efficient, tailored, and self-
assured. Enjoys travel, philanthropic interests, and strenuous activity.
Plays and works hard. A clever problem solver who needs social interaction, challenges, and individualistic leadership role. Has tremendous insight into people, foresight, and longterm philosophy.

PERSONALITY EXTREME: Too perfecting, or too incautious.

CHERIE (French/English)—F.

MAJOR TALENT: Ability to incorporate sharing of thoughts, feelings,
and beliefs into career. Is a top-notch communicator, able to approach a
broad marketplace and satisfy mass tastes. Not to be rushed, but gets
something done for everyone. A dreamer with depth of intellect. Generous offerings of love come back tenfold. Artistic expression, nursing,
and kindergarten teaching are possible career opportunities.

PERSONALITY INGREDIENTS: Needs independence, and innovative interests; does not want to be told how to do things. Appears to walk on
water. Tries to please, is sensitive, and prefers peaceful relationships.
May be inspirational to others and attract recognition. Likes being different, but is always refined, considerate, and emotionally in gear.

PERSONALITY EXTREME: Too attention-getting, or too muzzled.

CHERRY (diminutive of Charity)—F.

MAJOR TALENT: Ability to incorporate inventive ideas, courageous
leadership, and commonsense procedures into career. Invites success
through sunny attitude, strong beliefs, and positive intentions. Sparks
activity with enthusiasm. Is protective, loving, and bounding with
creativity. Should avoid mere pleasure seeking or impulsive changes and
expect all of life's goodies. Theatrical director, salesperson, and travel
agent are possible career opportunities.

PERSONALITY INGREDIENTS: Needs variety, beauty, and friendships.
Desires to make everyone happy. Appears soft, sensitive, and spacy.

Strives for inspiration and revelation; wants to follow a select course of lasting benefit to others. Can be a crusader. May be high-strung and overly emotional. Should find a special goal and hang in.

PERSONALITY EXTREME: Too reflective, or too thoughtless.

CHERYL (variant of Caroline or Charlotte)—F.

MAJOR TALENT: Ability to incorporate communications expertise, progressive methods, and efficient leadership into career. Is businesslike and wants success. Gives courageous, dedicated, and disciplined service. Can make work seem like play, and has the vitality and stamina to keep on the go. Will have to handle money or power during lifetime, and has the resources to improve upon any demands of the responsibility. Sales executive, promoter, and manufacturer of fashion products are possible career opportunities.

PERSONALITY INGREDIENTS: First impression is striking, inviting, and colorful. Appears energetic, adventurous, and likable. Inwardly desires beautiful people, products, and environments. Enjoys a variety of social interests, and may want to play life as a game. High constructive energy must not be wasted on extravagances, escapism, or knuckle cracking. This name has power for making money and enjoying a progressive future.

PERSONALITY EXTREME: Too superficial, or too depressed.

CHESTER (Latin/English)—M.

MAJOR TALENT: Ability to incorporate unselfish service to family, community, or the world into career. Is artistic, expressive, and versatile. Has inspirational energy to teach, entertain, and strive for a mainspring cause. May sacrifice homelife, ambitions, or personal love to assume a greater responsibility. May be a pioneer, an inspiration to others, or a martyr. Circumstances will dictate whether the bearer of this name serves the family or humanity. Union founder, political reformer, and teacher/counselor are possible career opportunities.

PERSONALITY INGREDIENTS: Appears to understand and enjoy people. Is noticed for unique appeal. Inwardly needs to be the boss. Is best when left to do things alone and to learn through trial and error. Feels courageous, independent, and decisive. The bearer of this name has high energy and must avoid burning the candle at both ends, or emotions may overload.

PERSONALITY EXTREME: Too charitable, or too selfish.

CHLOE (Greek/English)—F.

MAJOR TALENT: Ability to incorporate intellectual perceptions, skill with details, and adventurous nature into career. Is strengthened by difficult experiences in early years. Becomes resourceful, self-assured, and able to think carefully before taking challenges. Benefits from professional counseling before signing documents. Diplomatic approach, hard work, and striving for an area of expertise brings success. Photographer, lawyer, and astronomer are possible career opportunities.

PERSONALITY INGREDIENTS: First impression is sexy, energetic, and friendly. Inwardly delicate, peace-loving, and receptive. Has strong ideals that, once torched, bring out the wiles of a fiery crusader. Should

develop alone, but may broaden horizons through partnership. May have
a childhood health problem that eases after maturity.

PERSONALITY EXTREME: Too experimental, or too incurious.

CHLORIS (Greek)—F.

MAJOR TALENT: Ability to incorporate exceptional communication
skills into career. Is magnetic to large audiences when serving a
humanitarian cause, writing, or enriching others through artistic applications. Loves the world, and it comes across. Seems unhurried and ready
to relax at the drop of a hat. Should travel, have a large social circle, and
put executive ability to serve worthy causes into life plan. Decorating,
fiction writing, and the musical theater offer possible career opportunities.

PERSONALITY INGREDIENTS: Is stimulated by beauty, family attainment, and being needed. May be torn between home and career. Should
watch diet and not become too involved in protecting others to keep trim
and attractive. Has strong opinions and keen sense of smell. Must avoid
becoming possessive.

PERSONALITY EXTREME: Too bossy, or too meek.

CHRISTIAN (Greek/German/Danish/English)—M.

MAJOR TALENT: Ability to incorporate the need for adaptability, discrimination, and emotional control into career. Is able to fall, then rise to
greater heights when practical and emotional natures balance. Good
money manager, creative, and tuned to the fine points of detail. Succeeds
in business, but may choose unwise romantic alliances. Happiness
comes with discarding superficial values. Any creative industry, the
ministry, and reform are possible career opportunities.

PERSONALITY INGREDIENTS: Extremely individualistic character.
Must manage, direct, and lead. Bossy as a child, and matures to have
definite ideas. Keeps things moving and leaves laggards behind. Impatient achiever; inventive, clever, and decisive.

PERSONALITY EXTREME: Too experimental, or too structured.

CHRISTINA (Greek/English)—F.

MAJOR TALENT: Ability to incorporate questioning mind, practical
work, and visionary artistic gifts into career. Is unusually adaptable,
clever, and direct. Must balance emotions and material aspects of
character. Nervous energy needs a specific goal to get full use of charm,
magnetism, and cleverness. Must learn the power of silence and to dis-
tinguish the real values from the transitory. Can have dreams come true
when using logic, not illusionary emotions. Character analysis, biog-
raphy, and any creative interest are possible career opportunities.

PERSONALITY INGREDIENTS: First impression is positive, independent,
and determined. Inwardly assertive, regenerative, and faithful. Usually
attracts love, money, and esteem. To maintain good fortune must have
courage and patience, and base judgments upon reason.

PERSONALITY EXTREME: Too sure, or too uncertain.

CHRISTINE (Greek/German/French/English)—F.

MAJOR TALENT: Ability to incorporate strong leadership, sense of responsibility, and adventurous nature into career. Is a fighter. Very active

mind, firm authoritative delivery, and keen perceptions should be balanced with a merciful feeling for others. Must be alert to envious reactions. When just and caring, all dreams are possible. Musical professions, teaching, and marriage counseling are possible career opportunities.

PERSONALITY INGREDIENTS: Takes an adult approach and is very individualistic. Has high energy and curiosity, and enjoys physical pleasures. Is sensual, impulsive, and freedom-loving. Retains youthful/progressive attitudes, and can be fearless. May be impatient, accident-prone, and too experimental.

PERSONALITY EXTREME: Too confident, or too overwhelmed.

CHRISTOPHER (Greek/English)—M.

MAJOR TALENT: Ability to incorporate persistence, hard work, and methodology into career. Is trustworthy, understands how to handle money, and is accountable for own actions. Protective, inventive, and resourceful. Maintains stability in businesses that perform a vital service. Must enjoy type of work, keep a steady pace, and feel a sense of responsibility to achieve the powerful potential of this name. Federal housing, laboratory work, and undertaking suggest opportunities.

PERSONALITY INGREDIENTS: Must never judge a book by its cover, control for personal gain, or use old habits for emotional crutches. The bearer of this name will have to be adaptable to growth changes and be prepared to make swift/logical/parental decisions. Sees the pros and cons of everything in detail. Is sensitive, but must not personalize realizations. Common sense is best tool.

PERSONALITY EXTREME: Too philosophical, or too narrow.

CICELY (English, from Cecilia)—F.

MAJOR TALENT: Ability to incorporate conventional desire for security, a search for perfection of beauty, and broad-scoped communication arts into career. Has versatility in any industry where charm, affability, and sex appeal are assets. Attracts star status. Reaps rewards through travel, quality of life-style, and strength of character. May scatter interests, but success cannot be lost entirely. Fashion coordinator, advertising art director, and interior decorator are possible career opportunities.

PERSONALITY INGREDIENTS: First impression is magnetic, generous, and sympathetic. Retains youthful attitudes and appearance. Inwardly optimistic and sunny; enjoys artistic expression. Attracts a happy marriage and material comforts, and strives for noble ideals.

PERSONALITY EXTREME: Too dignified, or too coltish.

CINDY (nickname of Lucinda, Cinderella, or Cynthia)—F.

MAJOR TALENT: Ability to incorporate individuality and businesslike procedures into career. Is sensitive, detail conscious, and ambitious. Has good judgment and assumes responsibility. Is inspirational, kind, and generous. Theater, internal medicine, and business ownership are possible career opportunities.

PERSONALITY INGREDIENTS: Appears sunny, social, and charming. Loves to laugh, but is stimulated by logic problems. Inwardly perfecting, refined, and not too sure of intellectual abilities. Has self-doubt and tries

All names that begin with the letter *C* have the *Strong Point* of
self-expression—words—imagination—inspiration—congeniality.

85

too hard. May miss opportunities of the moment by ignoring first thought. Very intuitive, and must realize own depth of perception to relax.

PERSONALITY EXTREME: Too aloof, or too chummy.

CLAIRE (English/French variant of Clara)—F.

MAJOR TALENT: Ability to incorporate writing, versatility, and attraction for people into career. Is a seeker of perfection, and may be too picky. Attracts the opposite sex, and can hold center stage. Should aim high and approach goals through conventional methods. Judge, lawyer, and philosopher are possible career opportunities.

PERSONALITY INGREDIENTS: Appears to be and is a born teacher. Wants home/family/community to have beauty, harmony, and attainments. Should serve the young/old/needy. Has strong ethics and morals and a towering instinct for responsibility. Expects much from self and others. Should learn to live and let live.

PERSONALITY EXTREME: Too sensual, or too mental.

CLARA (Latin/Italian/Portuguese/German/Danish/English)—F.

MAJOR TALENT: Ability to incorporate efficient mental organization, cultural awareness, and expensive tastes into career. Is ambitious, intelligent, and introspective. Strives for honest, dignified, carefully investigated relationships. Overcomes obstacles easily, and has great vitality of spirit. Has strong persuasive qualities and must never abuse the gift. Researcher, buyer, and financial adviser are possible career opportunities.

PERSONALITY INGREDIENTS: Inwardly sensitive, diplomatic, and loving. Wants partnership, peace, and comfort. Is a collector, and takes pleasure doing things for others. Appears sensible, conservative, and tasteful. Keeps harmony in all things. Attracts burdens from less fortunate folks, and is a sincere/wise/mature counselor.

PERSONALITY EXTREME: Too impatient, or too inactive.

CLARE (English/French variant of Clara)—F.

MAJOR TALENT: Ability to incorporate individualistic ambitions, good memory, and patience into career. Is charming, artistic, and sensitive to people, nature, and details. Changes bring a step up, and the bearer of this name should never stay in a rut. Succeeds when able to emotionally balance home and profession. Administration, communications, and nursing are possible career opportunities.

PERSONALITY INGREDIENTS: Emits an air of protectiveness. Appears responsible, generous, and comforting. Is willing to listen to anyone's troubles and give a helping hand. Needs respectability, family unity, and roots. Is able to find sunlight on a cloudy day. Should avoid becoming too comfortable and losing youthful vivacity.

PERSONALITY EXTREME: Too curious, or too satisfied.

CLARENCE (Latin/English)—M.

MAJOR TALENT: Ability to incorporate practicality, charm, and intellectual development into career. Is honest, logical, and straightforward. Articulate, an outdoorsman, and inclined to clever humor, the bearer of this name benefits from all forms of communication. Lawyer, architect, and college administrator are possible career opportunities.

PERSONALITY INGREDIENTS: Prone to following proper procedures, but looks venturesome. First impression is friendly attention-getting, and confident. Inwardly sensitive, gentle, and inclined to want to save the world. Feels idealistic. Needs an outlet for nervous energy and to focus upon thoughts of beauty, inventions, and a rainbow behind every cloud. Introspective qualities need serenity. Should learn to follow intuition.

PERSONALITY EXTREME: Too rebellious, or too accommodating.

CLARICE (French variant of Clara)—F.

MAJOR TALENT: Ability to incorporate concern for social welfare into career. Is articulate and quietly authoritative, and has humility that belies the stunning and profound wisdom within. Teaches and sets a courageous example. Best suited to quiet, artistic, and harmonious environments. Union leader, conservationist, and musician are possible career opportunities.

PERSONALITY INGREDIENTS: Appears magnetic, noble, and romantic. Looks graceful, dramatic, and understanding. Neat or sloppy, is always comfortable; there is a depth to the first impression. Inwardly wants loving family and beauty, and to give and have protection. Enjoys abundant, gracious life-style that warms all who touch upon it. May be obstinate, too helpful, or too imbedded in family life, but when serving a community need is dynamic.

PERSONALITY EXTREME: Too adventurous, or too cloistered.

CLARISSA (English/Italian/German variant of Clarissa)—F.

MAJOR TALENT: Ability to incorporate ideas, organizational capability, and perception of details into career. Is neat, individualistic, and companionable. Works alone and with others with an ambitious eye on the future. Attractive to the opposite sex, inspirational, and kind. When patient and decisive, achieves success. Taking or giving self-development courses, accountant/lawyer, and coin collector are possible career opportunities.

PERSONALITY INGREDIENTS: Feels different, and sees people and life through rose-colored glasses. Is a dreamer, and strives for efficient, organized, positioned life-style. Would like to save the world and become an influential/wealthy power while doing it. Very intuitive and creative, but appears businesslike. Can be nervous as a child and an adult.

PERSONALITY EXTREME: Too independent, or too submissive.

CLARK (Anglo-Saxon/English)—M.

MAJOR TALENT: Ability to incorporate creative leadership, businesslike assessments, and vivid imagination into career. Mental health is allied to physical well-being. Benefits from dream interpretation and maintaining an organized life-style. Is gentle, empathetic, and very receptive. Medicine, welfare work, and journalism are possible career opportunities.

PERSONALITY INGREDIENTS: Needs independent action, inventive challenges, and courage to individualize. Is inclined to self-impatience. Appears affluent, organized, and sociable. Likes praise and efficiency, and wants to feel trust in relationships. May be torn by faith in humanity and disbelief in its inconsistency of purpose.

PERSONALITY EXTREME: Too agreeable, or too personalized.

CLAUDE (Latin/French/English)—M.

MAJOR TALENT: Ability to incorporate techniques for grand-scale problem solving into career. Effective speaker, enduring, and attractive. Must rely on reason and avoid impulsive changes to achieve potential. With courage to be an individual, the bearer of this name can move mountains. Business owner, inventor, and politician are possible career opportunities.

PERSONALITY INGREDIENTS: Inwardly generous, philosophical, and artistic. Loves to love and be loved. May tend to give more than is received and doesn't care. Hides deep emotions. Appears capable, creative, and in motion. Strives to be clever, active, and decisive. Must not placate others. Needs to accept unique ambitions and walk alone if necessary.

PERSONALITY EXTREME: Too changeable, or too relaxed.

CLAUDETTE (Latin/French)—F.

MAJOR TALENT: Ability to incorporate individualistic ideas, self-reliance, and responsibility into career. Is inspirational, kind, and generous. Has attraction for the opposite sex, courage, and ambition. Patience, adaptability to surprising events, and supportive peer partnerships bring success. Stockbrokerage, legal investigation, and promotion/sales/production in any creative work are possible career opportunities.

PERSONALITY INGREDIENTS: Appears to be and feels open to progressive activities. Wants adventure, sensuality, and emancipation. Loves excitement, travel, and anything that is new/unusual/physical. High energy needs direction. Tries everything and stays too long, or only sees the tip of the iceberg. May wrap most people around little finger with clever wit, friendly manner, and intoxicating intellectual curiosity. Must learn caution.

PERSONALITY EXTREME: Too tied down, or too free.

CLAUDIA (Latin/Italian/German/Spanish/English)—F.

MAJOR TALENT: Ability to incorporate attention to practical details, generous service, and artistic gifts into career. Is responsible, protective, and instructive. Knows how to harmonize groups and make people comfortable. Hotel manager, songwriter, and marital counselor are possible career opportunities.

PERSONALITY INGREDIENTS: First impression is independent. Appears capable, energetic, and inventive. Inwardly feels bored if not on the go. Wants excitement, physical pleasures, and nonrestriction. Can spark any group with unconventional ideas. Gains respect for wisdom, but may lose through temperamental jealousy, stubborn ideals, or tendency to be too helpful.

PERSONALITY EXTREME: Too changeable, or too unimaginative.

CLAY (Anglo-Saxon diminutive of Clayton or Clayborne)—M.

MAJOR TALENT: Ability to incorporate authority, commonsense reactions, and a special skill for handling people into career. Is able to juggle many responsibilities, seize opportunities spontaneously, and absorb knowledge through trial-and-error experimentation. Has vivid imagination and love of adventure, and dislikes day-to-day routine. Very open-minded to progressive ideas. Theater, politics, and private investigation are possible career opportunities.

PERSONALITY INGREDIENTS: Appears systematic, neat, and sturdy. May seem dull, but is very creative, independent, and ambitious. Wants to be boss, and has courage, insight, and foresight. Thrives upon travel, and gains through gift for communication. Will be required to make many decisions. Has fine intellect and intuition to cope with active life-style.

PERSONALITY EXTREME: Too perceptive, or too thoughtless.

CLEM (diminutive of Clement or Clementine)—F. & M.

MAJOR TALENT: Ability to incorporate artistic or home/community-uplifting service into career. Is personable, money-wise, and strong-willed. Understands what people want, and may be calculating. Physically adventurous, individualistic, and a good student, the bearer of this name must learn to laugh under pressure to maintain success. Clam-digging, creative retail sales, and teaching opportunities.

PERSONALITY INGREDIENTS: Wants freedom to experiment/travel/progress, and appears capable, sensual, and impulsive. Strives to be own boss and pioneer new concepts. Needs to be adaptable to change, erase fears experienced in the past, and be discerning in material judgments. When able to live and let live, may be an example for others to follow and raise living standards.

PERSONALITY EXTREME: Too hardworking, or too unstructured.

CLEMENT (Latin/French/English)—M.

MAJOR TALENT: Ability to incorporate implementation of broad-scoped inventive ideas into career. Has a fertile mind, and attracts cooperation and support for tangible production of ideas. Has positive approach that is contagious. May apply gifts to art, beauty, government, or business, and may inspire a dynasty. Adviser, lecturer, and any communications profession are possible career opportunities.

PERSONALITY INGREDIENTS: First impression is efficient, authoritative, and prosperous. Appears sociable, diplomatic, and businesslike. Desires to independently control situations. May be introverted, but may also be outgoing. Dislikes people who personalize everything. Can easily be embarrassed and is therefore fair, honest, and loyal. Must stick to beliefs and act upon intellectual reasoning to use the positive power of this name. Can be self-destructive if too intolerant of self; noble and humanitarian ideals require time to implement. Patient understanding of self and others offers the bearer of this name a promise of fame.

PERSONALITY EXTREME: Too sensitive, or too inconsiderate.

CLEMENTINE (Latin/English/French/German)—F.

MAJOR TALENT: Ability to incorporate impressive individualism, personal popularity, and purist principles into career. Is intensely idealistic, expectant, and dramatically enthusiastic. Has a unique, methodical, and dutiful manner. Music, science, and philosophy are possible career opportunities.

PERSONALITY INGREDIENTS: Inwardly attaining, nurturing, and striving for harmony, justice, and material stability. Appears to be constructive, opinionated, and unforgettably wise. Clean-cut appearance, vivacious delivery, and magnetic charm create an outstanding personality. May be childish, superficial, or tuned to the past when attracting the negative aspect of this name.

PERSONALITY EXTREME: Too energetic, or too easygoing.

CLEO (Greek)—F.

MAJOR TALENT: Ability to incorporate individualism, questioning intellect, and businesslike attitude into career. Is intuitive and creative, and takes time for mental analysis. Has gifts of persuasion, outstanding leadership and determination. Succeeds through faith and adaptability. Purchasing agent, financial adviser, and tax consultant are possible career opportunities.

PERSONALITY INGREDIENTS: First impression is dependable, comfortable, and understanding. Is a concerned listener, and should command respect. Inwardly is not as practical or accepting as indicated by appearance. Wants to put inventive visionary ideas to use, and may see everyday needs as unimportant. Prefers to relax with idealistic peers and dream of redesigning the wheel.

PERSONALITY EXTREME: Too self-insistent, or too helpful.

CLIFFORD (Old English)—M.

MAJOR TALENT: Ability to incorporate creative philosophy, passionate concerns, and individualistic leadership into career. Usually takes center stage, and can be charming, witty, and understanding. Works and plays with determination, practical organization, and responsible attitude. Finds opportunities everywhere, and bounces back if too idealistic for tangible results and economic stability. Works well with others and provides an enthusiasm that maintains youthful zest of interest in any effort. Original promotions, designing, and theater arts are possible career opportunities.

PERSONALITY INGREDIENTS: Wants family to have same or better quality of life than own stable childhood. Has good memories and strives for loving, protected, respected life-style. Seems to be determined, direct, and of average appearance. Fights for ambitions, and may be uncooperative when competitive nature is aroused. Understands the innate rules of survival and goes on automatic when threatened.

PERSONALITY EXTREME: Too patterned, or unmoldable.

CLIFTON (Old English)—M.

MAJOR TALENT: Ability to incorporate discriminating intellect, practical judgment, and gift for communication gifts into career. Is perceptive and culturally aware; works with structured planning. Usually articulate, and may have unique wit, voice, and delivery. Maintains success when unselfish, patient, and honorable. Writer, psychologist, and any technical or scientific profession are possible career opportunities.

PERSONALITY INGREDIENTS: Needs family pride, roots, and tasteful environments. Feels protective, idealistic, and responsible. May expect much of others, and court disappointment that shows itself in biting/aloof/icy tones of voice. First impression is individualistic. Appears to be courageous, capable, and creative. May be a loner.

PERSONALITY EXTREME: Too unconventional, or too conditioned.

CLINTON (Danish/Swedish/English)—M.

MAJOR TALENT: Ability to incorporate wise counsel, gentle authority, and concern for the betterment of others into career. Is unlikely to care about passing fads or shallow quests. Has gifts for communication, community uplift, and nonmaterialistic needs. Finds all personal necessities

90

All names that begin with the letter *C* have the *Strong Point* of
self-expression—words—imagination—inspiration—congeniality.

are provided when instructing, servicing, and setting an example for
human understanding. Artist, welfare worker, and instructor suggest opportunities.

PERSONALITY INGREDIENTS: First impression is noble, magnetic, and
empathetic. Appears to understand, and want to help. Inwardly is parental, protective, and trustworthy. Desires progressive attainments for
family/community, and wants to right all wrongs. May seem too bossy,
anxious, and overly inclined to artistic interests or physical comforts if
personalized. The bearer of this name has possibilities of lasting fame
when decisive, emotionally balanced, and impersonally compassionate.

PERSONALITY EXTREME: Too enthusiastic, or too worn out.

CLIVE (Old English; variant Cliff)—M.

MAJOR TALENT: Ability to incorporate observation of details, organized routine, and useful counsel into career. Is exacting, conscientious,
and punctual. Has strong powers of suggestion and family pride; strives
for social truths. Gets help from women, handles finances practically,
and attracts supporters. Communications, family service organizations,
and instructional professions are possible career opportunities.

PERSONALITY INGREDIENTS: Needs change, progressive interests, and
freedom to experience physical pleasures. Appears to be individualistic,
creative, and authoritative. Strives for independent thinking and may
have to walk alone when self-asserting. Should be a sensitive voice for
social betterment.

PERSONALITY EXTREME: Too sensual, or too intellectual.

CLOVIS (Teutonic/English)—M.

MAJOR TALENT: Ability to incorporate tactful interaction, instructive
counseling, and businesslike organization into career. Is enthusiastic,
courageous, and physically balanced. May combine love of outdoor activity and communication skills with an air of confidence even under
stress. Benefits from self-help courses, and is a student by nature. Needs
life experience to maintain success. Collector, accountant, and military
professions are possible career opportunities.

PERSONALITY INGREDIENTS: Appears special or different. May seem
lost in thoughts, dramatic, and filled with refined nervous energy. Inwardly responsible, protective, and dependable. Needs harmonious life-
style filled with family attainments. Has firm beliefs and is a willing
counselor.

PERSONALITY EXTREME: Too courageous, or too weak.

CLYDE (Greek: Glydias, M., and Glydia, F./Welsh/Scottish/English)—
F. & M.

MAJOR TALENT: Ability to incorporate precision, practicality, and constructive precepts into career. Has potential for wealth, stature, and
humanitarian service. Is able to find original solutions to broad-scoped
problems previously considered unsolvable. May be an overworked
genius or a ruthless achiever. The bearer of this name has power and
chooses whether to use it for betterment or downfall of others. Real
estate, government, and any profession are possible career opportunities.

PERSONALITY INGREDIENTS: Notices every little thing and is personally sensitive. Wants loving partner, serene life-style, and respectability.

All names that begin with the letter *C* have the *Strong Point* of
self-expression—words—imagination—inspiration—congeniality.

91

Appears modest, confident, and adaptable to helping others. May be a
fool or a hero.

PERSONALITY EXTREME: Too clever, or too inept.

COLBY (Old English)—M.

MAJOR TALENT: Ability to incorporate artistic expression into career.
Is sociable, conversational, and innovative. Adds patience, sensitivity,
and administrative qualities to inventive aspirations. Has bounce, and
recovers from mistakes quickly. Cosmetician, juvenile story writer, and
all areas of communication are possible career opportunities.

PERSONALITY INGREDIENTS: Needs conservative, practical, organized
life-style. Feels drawn to system and order. Appears very affluent.
Strives for efficient organization, management positions, and community
respect. May be extravagant, scattered, and fanciful. Prefers to seek
perfection, and often forgets ugliness. Must not hide from past experience, or life's lessons will not be learned.

PERSONALITY EXTREME: Too outspoken, or too introspective.

COLE (Latin/English)—M.

MAJOR TALENT: Ability to incorporate executive judgment, candor,
and logic into career. Is questioning, courageous, and persuasive. Attracts attention for individualism and creative leadership. Investigator,
quality furniture manufacturer, and financial adviser are possible career
opportunities.

PERSONALITY INGREDIENTS: Feels family oriented; strives for truth
and justice, and to provide responsible counsel. Has vision that inspires
supporters. Is strong-willed and idealistic, and may be saint or sinner.
Appears different, innovative, and distinguishable in a crowd. May be
eccentric.

PERSONALITY EXTREME: Too impulsive, or too strategic.

COLETTE (French/English)—F.

MAJOR TALENT: Ability to incorporate power, responsible judgment,
and diplomatic manner into career. Is geared for material success. Has
inner strength, confidence, and energetic nature. Generous, expansive,
and always striving for self-control. Patience, persistence, and emotional
control bring success. Orchestra/dance group leader, public official, and
bank loan officer are possible career opportunities.

PERSONALITY INGREDIENTS: Wants cultural refinements and to live in
a perfect society. Lacks faith in intuition, which is exceptional. Must
strive for expertise or authority in a particular interest to relax and feel
personally positive. Outwardly is individualistic. May appear dramatic,
inventive, and assertive. Thinks twice before sharing feelings, and keeps
a secret self. Can be dynamic when balanced intellectually and emotionally.

PERSONALITY EXTREME: Too eccentric, or too formal.

COLIN (Celtic diminutive of Nicholas)—M.

MAJOR TALENT: Ability to incorporate eagerness, strength of character, and expansive communication gifts into career. Is a student and
teacher, and perceives ambitions with sensitivity and attention to detail.
Enjoys sports, music, and spontaneous love relationships. Succeeds
through doing patient work and controlling temperament. Military in-

structor, purchasing agent, and union comptroller are possible career opportunities.

PERSONALITY INGREDIENTS: Has bravado, and may appear confident in times of stress. Needs group/family companionship and harmony. Enjoys beauty, praise, and emotional involvement. Inwardly needs to feel needed. First impression is quiet, refined, and offbeat. Has enthusiasm for idealistic causes that light a divine fire when expressed. May move others to follow beliefs, and has the gift of evangelistic impression. May have radical views that are intended to improve material attainments for others.

PERSONALITY EXTREME: Too explosive, or too calm.

COLLEEN (Irish)—F.

MAJOR TALENT: Ability to incorporate charm, wit, and optimism into career. Is bubbling with personality, conversation, and organization to secure a prosperous life-style. Has unique sex appeal and attracts material comforts, respectable home, and a variety of interesting associations. Provides entertainment, and requires quality. Advertising copywriter, welfare worker, and any communications profession with non-structured routine are possible career opportunities.

PERSONALITY INGREDIENTS: Has difficulty understanding true value. Needs education, cultural interests, and one area of specialization to gain self-confidence and be able to let go of materialistic attitudes. First impression is enthusiastic, adventurous, and friendly. Very quick on the trigger with words/wit/opinions. May be spoiled as a child due to exceptionally attractive qualities but rarely learns to use fine mind, and may be frustrated intellectually after maturity.

PERSONALITY EXTREME: Too excitable, or too subdued.

COLLIER (Old English)—M.

MAJOR TALENT: Ability to incorporate personal ideals, creativity, and futuristic vision into career. Is meticulous, discerning, and sharp. Attracts material advantages and is influential in others' lives. Provides new avenues and has bold poetic license. Film/TV production, religious reform, and electronic engineering are possible career opportunities.

PERSONALITY INGREDIENTS: Feels sensitive, and needs diplomatic relationships. Is a supportive partner and is usually a power behind the throne. Doesn't need recognition, but is magnetic, noble, and broad-scoped. Generally appears individualistic, philosophical, and empathetic. Relieves nervous energy by helping others and living up to high personal standards. Must avoid unethical or immoral actions.

PERSONALITY EXTREME: Too liberal, or too narrow.

CONRAD (Old German/English)—M.

MAJOR TALENT: Ability to incorporate diplomatic interactions, businesslike approach, and independent creative energy into career. Is very responsible and ambitious, and strives to better conditions. Adds a positive attitude and bold ideas; takes authoritative position. May depend upon female relationships too much. Needs to be firm, but not domineering. Lawyer, editor, and any position of sole ownership are possible career opportunities.

PERSONALITY INGREDIENTS: First impression is charming, attractive, and sunny. Inwardly is an introvert. Needs privacy, cultural interests, and a specialized field of authority to maintain confident air. Is a perfecting intellectual with social graces, wit, and conversational ease. May be full of contradictions due to emotional overreactions. Is often too personalized.

PERSONALITY EXTREME: Too regulated, or too unstructured.

CONSTANCE (Latin/French/English)—F.

MAJOR TALENT: Ability to incorporate practical judgment, competitive spirit, and an adaptability to foreign languages into career. Is articulate and individualistic, and relates to people. May be too aggressive or challenging to others to maintain consistently diplomatic relationships. Benefits from finding a clear direction, patiently building resources, and being generous in relationships. Is a survivor, but should avoid fighting every block to ambitions as if its outcome were a life-or-death matter. Resolute attitude overcomes obstacles. Full-charge bookkeeper, military officer, and piano tuner or teacher are possible career opportunities.

PERSONALITY INGREDIENTS: First impression is energetic, individualistic, and capable. Thrives on beauty, variety, and an optimistic tone to life-style. Wants people, crowds, and extravagances. Feels emotional highs and lows. Has strong communication with children and animals. If thoughtless/rash/self-centered, may incur legal problems.

PERSONALITY EXTREME: Too honest, or too promotional.

CONSTANTINE (Latin/English)—M.

MAJOR TALENT: Ability to incorporate high-powered physical stamina, common sense, and emotional insight into career. Can aim for the sky when tuned to intuition . . . a thought that may not be based upon logic pops into the mind. Is disciplined. Perseveres to useful goals. Is resourceful, sensible, and cautious. Vast material challenges are offered to the bearer of this name, and balance is demanded for the possibility of fame, fortune, and humanitarian benefit. Physical therapist, architectural engineer, and government adviser are possible career opportunities.

PERSONALITY INGREDIENTS: Feels expansive and optimistic; perceives a beautiful world. May seem childlike in positive expectations of others, but attracts what is expected. First impression is adventurous, physically striking, and tuned to people. May be a catalyst for change in other people's lives. Must expect the unexpected, adapt new concepts, and produce tangible results. When attainments are counted, that is the time to guard against being self-satisfied.

PERSONALITY EXTREMES: Too clever, or too dull.

CORA (Greek/English)—F.

MAJOR TALENT: Ability to incorporate independent and creative leadership into career. Is conversationally attractive, and reaches a broad marketplace. Wants to be at the top, and will fight city hall, if necessary, to live up to personal directives. Cannot lose courage and put one face to the world and lead a double life. The bearer of this name is lucky when truly independent. Fashion consultant, theatrical producer, and all artistic/scientific/humanitarian service organizations are possible career opportunities.

PERSONALITY INGREDIENTS: Gives love and service, and strives for the best of everything. Needs roots, and assumes responsibility to home, family, and community. Thrives upon beauty, abundant life-style, and sharing wisdom to ease the concerns of others. Appears to be a worker. Is dependable, understated, and practical. Has material aspirations and needs ambitious goals.

PERSONALITY EXTREME: Too impatient, or too easygoing.

CORETTA (combination of Cora + Etta)—F.

MAJOR TALENT: Ability to incorporate tact, efficiency, and individualism into career. Is sensitive, ambitious, and courageous. Gets things done, assumes responsibility, and is resourceful. Profits from independent past experiences, and learns to achieve goals through working with partners or groups. All art/music forms, managing, and promoting are possible career opportunities.

PERSONALITY INGREDIENTS: First impression belies friendly nature. Appears aloof and introspective, and may seem conceited. Inwardly wants beauty, happiness, and a variety of imaginative interests. Is creatively expressive, and has extravagant tastes and feelings. Should investigate before placing trust in others and control impatience, pride, and contradictory actions.

PERSONALITY EXTREME: Too dominant, or too submissive.

COREY (Anglo-Saxon/Irish/Scottish)—M.

MAJOR TALENT: Ability to incorporate versatility, attractiveness, and communication skills into career. Can tackle big jobs easily and reach the top. Has sex appeal, is charming, and is able to organize/systematize for practical results. Seeks to provide and receive quality. Able to maintain success when tuned to a conservative life-style. Improvisational writing-speaking-acting, fashion criticism, and law are possible career opportunities.

PERSONALITY INGREDIENTS: First impression is energetic, direct, and individualistic. Has style, flair, and a firm approach. Inwardly sensitive, high-strung, and idealistic. Prefers to relax with peers, but has a world of friends. Is romantic, extravagant, and lucky.

PERSONALITY EXTREME: Too regal, or too earthy.

CORINNE (French, from Cora)—F.

MAJOR TALENT: Ability to incorporate realistic appraisals, gentle sensitivity, and desire to bring pleasure or service to others into career. Is concerned, cooperative, and charming. Attracts companionship, is hospitable, and abides by commitments. Thrives upon beauty. Music, hotel administration, and home improvement are possible career opportunities.

PERSONALITY INGREDIENTS: Leaves a lasting impression. Is able to entertain, counsel, or relieve suffering for large groups. Must be totally aboveboard to maintain stability; cannot gamble, ignore established structure, or be dishonest. Should use innate gifts of tact, diplomacy, and adaptability for easing others' burdens. Is very lucky when discerning and willing to face the necessity for economy, patient planning, and down-to-earth goals.

PERSONALITY EXTREME: Too sensual, or too mental.

CORLISS (Latin/English)—F.

MAJOR TALENT: Ability to incorporate gift of gab, tact, and inspiration into career. Is active, progressive, and confident. Gets involved in speculative ideas and ventures successfully. Travel, cleverness with people, and expertise in foreign language are offered to the bearer of this name. Advertising, politics, and journalism are possible career opportunities.

PERSONALITY INGREDIENTS: First impression is businesslike, self-assured, and status-conscious. Strives for efficiency, authority, and possessions. Wants home/family/community attainments, comfort, and harmony. Needs artistic and attractive people and environments. Is helpful, parental, and trustworthy. Should learn how to be patient and persistent to reach top priorities.

PERSONALITY EXTREME: Too courageous, or too afraid.

CORNEL (Old French/English variant of Cornelius)—M.

MAJOR TALENT: Ability to incorporate independent creative leadership, practical productivity, and communication skills into career. Is determined. Combines organizational planning, optimism, strong competitive spirit, and depth of pride. Must not scatter interests or become too stubborn. Patience, adjustment to situations/people, and a little humility bring tangible results. Mnemonics instructor, architect, and landscaper are possible career opportunities.

PERSONALITY INGREDIENTS: Inwardly filled with idealistic zeal and nervous energy. Needs peace, sensitive partner/mate, and tolerance of less visionary and inventive talents. Needs to relate to everyone and find relaxation with peers. First impression is mild-mannered, pleasant, and easygoing. Should be an avid reader, supportive friend, and tenderly emotional lover.

PERSONALITY EXTREME: Too superficial, or too blunt.

CORNELIA (Latin/Italian/German/English)—F.

MAJOR TALENT: Ability to incorporate practical planning, creative ideas, and adventurous nature into career. Is enthusiastic, curious, and impulsive. Indulges self and brings excitement to others. Attracts family love, material gain, and recognition. Theater, investigative professions, and psychology are possible career opportunities.

PERSONALITY INGREDIENTS: First impression is subdued, refined, and diplomatic. Strives for sensitive partnerships, and enjoys collecting everything. Inwardly needs beauty, humor, and lightness. Has charm, flirts, and is optimistic. May appear unassuming, but desires the limelight.

PERSONALITY EXTREME: Too impatient, or too lazy.

CORNELIUS (Greek/Latin/German/French/English)—M.

MAJOR TALENT: Ability to incorporate all ingredients for financial success into career. Has mental, physical, and emotional balance. Is a disciplined, resourceful, strategic, and dedicated worker. Serves humanity practically when intuition is recognized as an equal to other abilities. This power may be used to help unfortunates, may be invested commercially, or may be applied to government/military affairs. Loses physical vigor when self-serving, money-hungry, or unconventional. Any profession that requires common sense, kindness, logic, and perseverance is a possible career opportunity.

PERSONALITY INGREDIENTS: Charm, friendliness, and well-tailored attire strike the first impression. Strives for gentle dignity, military bearing, and a generous/interested/charitable appearance. May seem modest, but feels adventurous, curious, and energetic. Happiest when in constructive motion and experiencing the five senses.

PERSONALITY EXTREME: Too individualistic, or too indistinguishable.

COURTNEY (Old French/Old English/English)—M.

MAJOR TALENT: Ability to incorporate economy, statistical skills, and realistic perspective into career. Is orderly, confident, and receptive. Knows the power of research, study, and integrity. Very constructive. Skilled craftsman, accountant, and piano player are possible career opportunities.

PERSONALITY INGREDIENTS: Wants freedom, experimentation, and physical pleasures. Feels curious and open-minded, and is clever. Appears businesslike, tailored, and very affluent. Strives for executive position and status. Impulsiveness causes material instability. Needs to maintain conservative judgments.

PERSONALITY EXTREME: Too analytic, or too misguided.

CRAIG (Scottish)—F. & M.

MAJOR TALENT: Ability to incorporate high-powered energy, empathetic service, and sensitivity to details into career. Is inspired, but not really best in the bustling business world. Has intuitional perceptions that adapt to quick decisions when a clear career purpose is determined. Creates and loves beauty, especially the delicate, refined, hazy imagery of a gossamer picture. Seems to be in another world when at creative best. Poet, teacher, and welfare reformer are possible career opportunities.

PERSONALITY INGREDIENTS: Wants to be and appears to be independent, assertive, and active. May be self-centered, thoughtless, and bossy as a child. With proper guidance, the bearer of this name can be directed to reach great heights. Must govern impatient nature.

PERSONALITY EXTREME: Too smart, or too unschooled.

CRYSTAL (Greek/English)—F.

MAJOR TALENT: Ability to incorporate physical coordination, perception of details, and innate air of confidence into career. Sparks and supports others, and may put too much stock in group accomplishment. Concrete plans must be developed independently and courageously to support enthusiasms. Has communication counseling, and diplomatic skills. Ambitions are satisfied after life experience teaches adaptability, self-control, and patience not to feel jealousy or envy. Financial adviser, manufacturer, and orchestra leader are possible career opportunities.

PERSONALITY INGREDIENTS: First impression is magnetic, youthful, and graceful. Leaves a lasting impression. Inwardly wants to manage, direct, and achieve financial success. Is dependable, determined, and trustworthy. Strives for mass-market exposure and the power that comes with it.

PERSONALITY EXTREME: Too superficial, or too honest.

CULLEN (Latin/Irish-Gaelic/English)—M.

MAJOR TALENT: Ability to incorporate practical, creative, and wide-angle executive/administrative skills into career. Is a constructive force. High nervous energy may be used for mundane or philanthropic goals . . . or both. Sensitive to people, and provides for their needs while gaining cooperation, respect, and control. Analyzes, organizes, and leads groups for realistic benefits. Needs to be kept busy to avoid destructive activity. Economics, appraising, and all building trades are possible career opportunities.

PERSONALITY INGREDIENTS: Attracts people. Inwardly businesslike, honest, and efficient. Keen judge of character. Appears to be very compatible, clever, and changeable. Seems broad-minded, sexy, and promotional. Can become infatuated/fascinated quickly, and must avoid scattering interests and energy.

PERSONALITY EXTREME: Too glib, or too serious.

CURT (diminutive of Old French Curtise/Latin/English)—M.

MAJOR TALENT: Ability to incorporate innovative ideas, logical analysis, and financial wheeling and dealing into career. Is honest, cultural, and trustworthy. Skilled researcher by nature due to fine powers of concentration. Attracts recognition. Engineer, statistician, and purchasing agent are possible career opportunities.

PERSONALITY INGREDIENTS: First impression is open, energetic, and zesty. Has a gift of relating to all people. Emits an air of masculinity. Inwardly wants beauty, gracious living, and sunny skies. Has charm, is articulate, and may be a good promoter. Clever and quick in times of trouble. Persuasive, perceptive, and unflappable conversationalist.

PERSONALITY EXTREME: Too tender, or too hard.

CURTIS (Old French: Curtise/English)—M.

MAJOR TALENT: Ability to incorporate sensitivity to details, refined judgment, and wide-angle vision into career. Is charitable and empathetic, and provides an original approach. Should attract supporters for artistic/skilled ideas and aim to reach a useful marketplace. Publisher, chemist, and lawyer are possible career opportunities.

PERSONALITY INGREDIENTS: Appears persevering, generous, and helpful. Listens to others' problems, tries to offer mature counsel, and is willing to assume responsibility. May take things too seriously and be too honest. Desires attractive environments, variety, and artistic stimulation. Is drawn to beauty. Feels an uncommon poise, and applies personal nonmaterialistic idealism that increases probability of personal sacrifice during lifetime. Requires quiet meditation to maintain equilibrium.

PERSONALITY EXTREME: Too accommodating, or too self-insistent.

CYNTHIA (Greek/English)—F.

MAJOR TALENT: Ability to incorporate efficiency, cleverness, and personal charm into career. Is friendly and tuned to understand what people want, and has inner strength. May be impulsive or pushy and seek unrealistic goals. Succeeds when emotionally disciplined and reasonably ambitious. Administration, public service, and educational research are possible career opportunities.

PERSONALITY INGREDIENTS: Needs quality, refinement, and serenity in surroundings. Lacks faith in self. Needs concentration for education or to develop an expertise. Appears both individualistic and empathetic, and attracts broad-scoped individuals. Makes people feel important. Imagines perfection in others, and the eventual disappointment breeds physical and emotional problems. Must use logic and maintain structured, economical, and practical life-style.

PERSONALITY EXTREME: Too submissive, or too independent.

CYRIL (Greek/English)—M.

MAJOR TALENT: Ability to incorporate artistic interests, independent leadership, and sensible administration into career. Is organized, routined, and competitive. Drives hard for achievements. Benefits from cooperative attitude, facing realities, and focusing in one direction. Has dramatic nature, and may intensify experiences. Theater, piano instruction, and nursing are possible career opportunities.

PERSONALITY INGREDIENTS: Seems generous, concerned, and instructive. Enjoys family/community relationships, assumes responsibility, and has strong personal judgments. Desires cultural, refined, quality environments and associations. Has untapped intellectual potential and superior memory. Needs to get in touch with emotional values and cease to remain aloof from the imperfections of people, life experience, and standardized ideals. Keeps a secret self until able to understand the real values in life.

PERSONALITY EXTREME: Too pretentious, or too plain.

CYRUS (Persian/English)—M.

MAJOR TALENT: Ability to incorporate mental and physical agility, communication skills, and practical ideas into career. Attracts and wants adventure, progressive experiences, and tangible support from affluent or powerful associates. Succeeds through maintaining friendly relationships. Booking agent, inventor, and promoter are possible career opportunities.

PERSONALITY INGREDIENTS: First impression is conservative, dependable, and trustworthy . . . basic Brooks Brothers brown. Inwardly is individualistic, ambitious, and aggressive. Feels courageous and innovative, and strives to pioneer new concepts. Takes a leadership role, and may surprise others who have accepted the first impression. Must avoid hasty actions, decisions, and self-importance. Selfish temper tantrums cause material losses.

PERSONALITY EXTREME: Too emotional, or too mental.

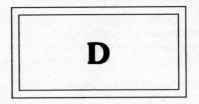

D

All names that begin with the letter *D* have the *Strong Point* of constructive effort—system—conscientiousness—structure—material judgment.

DAGMAR (Danish)—F.

MAJOR TALENT: Ability to incorporate gentleness, parental concern, and far-reaching communication skills into career. Is ambitious, physically tuned, and able to grow through self-improvement techniques. Has strong opinions and loving nature. Must take challenges to prove mettle. Buyer, lawyer, and critic are possible career opportunities.

PERSONALITY INGREDIENTS: First impression is concerned, generous, and comforting. Seems articulate and enjoys moderating. Inwardly feels sensitive, shy, and reserved. Desires partnership, musical pleasures, and collecting things. Wants to show and receive love, emits warmth, and strives for respectability.

PERSONALITY EXTREME: Too understanding, or too intolerant.

DAISY (Anglo-Saxon/English, from Candace or Margaret)—F.

MAJOR TALENT: Ability to incorporate careful, practical, and determined attitudes into career. Is not afraid to rise above average material goals or to work/rework to improve upon scheduled progress. Opinionated, visionary, and geared to be part of the policy-making decisions. The bearer of this name has to claim broad responsibilities, take a viable role in policy making, and avoid extravagant gestures to leave a mark for the future. Stage manager, diplomat, and C.P.A. are possible career opportunities.

PERSONALITY INGREDIENTS: Is a power pack of nervous, creative, determined energy. Wants affluence, potent authority, and an efficient, organized, and exemplary life-style. First impression is sexy, curious, and devil-may-care. Appears friendly, exciting, and liberal. Has infectious enthusiasm that sells high-heeled shoes to the Jolly Green Giant. Adheres to basic conservative code, but attracts offbeat interests.

PERSONALITY EXTREME: Too questioning, or too accepting.

DALE (Anglo-Saxon)—F. & M.

MAJOR TALENT: Ability to incorporate neatness, planning, and practical organization into career. Is geared to build and rebuild through honest, patient, and dedicated work. Brings the ideas of others to form and transforms lost causes. Has common sense. Real estate, office management, and accounting are possible career opportunities.

PERSONALITY INGREDIENTS: Needs home/family/community attainments. Feels protective, sympathetic, and burden-bearing. Gives wise counsel and has high standards. First impression is cool, refined, and

calm. Strives for quality and perfection. May be deeply spiritual and
experience intuitional triumphs. When unable to face earthy reality, can
be self-destructive, unconventional, and tempestuous.

PERSONALITY EXTREME: Too virginal, or too sensual.

DAMIAN (German variant of Damon)—M.

MAJOR TALENT: Ability to incorporate magnetic and influential attraction into career. Is encouraged financially and artistically due to generous, patient, and wise nature. Has sound judgment, but may be
domineering. Succeeds when helpful, unselfish, and companionable.
Teacher, performer, and marriage counselor are possible career opportunities.

PERSONALITY INGREDIENTS: First impression is conservative, dependable, and sturdy. Appears trustworthy and down-to-earth. Inwardly feels
idealistic, creative, and visionary. May be clairvoyant. Is courageous,
talented, and inventive. Needs to maintain faith, trust, and tolerance.

PERSONALITY EXTREME: Too different, or too ordinary.

DAMON (Greek/English)—M.

MAJOR TALENT: Ability to incorporate tact, patience, and keen perception of details into career. Is peace-loving, and attracts partnerships with
innovative types. Uses diplomatic authority, but must be adaptable to
new people and experiences to find alternatives when occasions demand
change. At best when balancing pros and cons. Should not judge by
appearances. Group musician/dancer, secretary, and columnist are possible career opportunities.

PERSONALITY INGREDIENTS: Inwardly very analytic. Needs thinking
time, refinement, and cultural stimulation. Secretly fears loneliness and
poverty. Collects tangibles to appease insecurities. Appears conservative, hardworking, and dependable. Strives to be inoffensive, financially
stable, and law-abiding. Occasionally surprises intimates with idealistic
daydreams.

PERSONALITY EXTREME: Too changeable, or too consistent.

DAN (diminutive of Daniel)—M.

MAJOR TALENT: Ability to incorporate inventive leadership into
career. Is an arbitrator, able to join forces to bring about constructive
change. Sees things clearly and inspires confidence. Makes ideas take
shape, and should progress through faith, optimism, and patient handling
of details. Must keep mentally active. Sales promoter, contractor, and
idea person are possible career opportunities.

PERSONALITY INGREDIENTS: Wants to be free to control, direct, and
originate. Has courage and pride in accomplishments. Appears understanding, articulate, and broad-scoped. Is fortunate when speaking to
groups, and attracts supporters. Strives for expansion, and responds to
major humanitarian causes. Seems ageless, and often gives more than is
returned. Emits sympathy, charm, and a special flair.

PERSONALITY EXTREME: Too enthusiastic, or too disinterested.

DANA (Anglo-Saxon/English, M.; Irish/Scandinavian, F.)—F. & M.

MAJOR TALENT: Ability to incorporate creative vision, fact finding, and
futuristic planning into career. Is not at best when materialistic. Has
inspirational gifts, foresight, and acute perceptions. Most successful

when selling own concepts or cooperating in a compassionate cause. Attracts unusual people and recognition. Creative writing, teaching, and all communications professions are possible career opportunities.

PERSONALITY INGREDIENTS: First impression is empathetic, philosophical, and attractive. Strives to appear noble, graceful, and impressive. Inwardly very sensitive. Craves peace, love, and softness. Uncomfortable with crude or gregarious types. Prefers not to be alone, and gives tenderness to loved ones. Keeps confidences, and wants to be helpful. When emotionally upset, may be strong-willed and unjust.

PERSONALITY EXTREME: Too impatient, or too easygoing.

DANIEL (Hebrew/English)—M.

MAJOR TALENT: Ability to incorporate cultured intellect, perception of details, and original ideas for humanitarian service into career. Attracts expansive projects, followers, and respect for honest judgments. Inspires peace, artistry, and faith. Must follow intuition to maintain success. Government service, medicine/law/teaching/any profession, and all forms of communication are possible career opportunities.

PERSONALITY INGREDIENTS: Feels strong family ties, and is protective, responsible, and uplifting. Wants to give wise counsel, and expects others to live up to high standards maintained personally. May not realize tendency to be bossy. Outwardly friendly, cheerful, and charming. Enjoys fashion, variety, and beauty. Likes to be noticed, and may use humor as a tool to popularity. Wants to see life as a sunny day, and is able to focus upon the rainbow if clouds appear.

PERSONALITY EXTREME: Too flashy, or too dignified.

DANIELA (Hebrew/English)—F.

MAJOR TALENT: Ability to incorporate sensitiveness, confident facade, and self-starter character into career. Is perceptive, organizational, and diplomatic. Must balance impatience and do research before taking action. Has attraction for material affairs, and should aim high. Real estate, design, and any administrative position are possible career opportunities.

PERSONALITY INGREDIENTS: Outwardly questioning, but too easily intimidated by authoritative people. Intuitively knows when something isn't right, and may not pay attention to feelings of apprehension. Needs to probe to avoid losing self-confidence through making naive judgments. Should concentrate upon gaining cultural advantages to improve self-esteem. First impression is self-assured, individualistic, and attaining. Is assertive, but requires meditative time to squelch impulsive moves. Needs outward display of affection, status, and quality until unrealistic fears of loneliness and poverty are eliminated.

PERSONALITY EXTREME: Too rash, or too conservative.

DAPHNE (Greek/English)—F.

MAJOR TALENT: Ability to incorporate versatility, sex appeal, and established procedures into career. Senses perfection and develops skills in an orderly, responsible, and philosophical way. Thrives upon beauty, art, and getting attention. Science, writing, and all communications professions are possible opportunities.

PERSONALITY INGREDIENTS: First impression attracts desires. Wants family/community harmony, respect, and abundance. Gives wise counsel, but may be too helpful. Magnetic to men, and must maintain conventional life-style to achieve celebrity potential.

PERSONALITY EXTREME: Too eccentric, or too bland.

DARCY (Old French/Irish/English)—M.

MAJOR TALENT: Ability to incorporate persuasive and companionable character into career. Is nurturing, generous, and patient. Attracts respect and material comforts, and applies practical organization. Hotel/hospital administrator, personnel director, and any musical/artistic professions are possible career opportunities.

PERSONALITY INGREDIENTS: First impression may be inscrutable. Seems refined, introspective, and either authoritatively concerned or aloof. May seem snobbish. Inwardly is businesslike. Needs affluent lifestyle. Has strong beliefs, and may be stubborn, jealous, or domineering.

PERSONALITY EXTREME: Too questioning, or too gullible.

DARLENE (Anglo-Saxon/English)—F.

MAJOR TALENT: Ability to incorporate mixing up business and pleasure into career. Has a charming, confident, and just manner. Is persuasive, futuristic, and speculative. Promoter, fashion consultant, and any policy-making position are possible career opportunities.

PERSONALITY INGREDIENTS: First impression is attention-getting, sunny, and friendly. Thrives upon beauty, humor, and experiencing extravagant emotions. Inwardly is loving, sensitive, and idealistic. Needs close relationships and creative opportunities; feels responsibility to help others. Gets things easily when relaxed, and should not feel guilty about being an opportunist. The bearer of this name must never be reclusive.

PERSONALITY EXTREME: Too confident, or too unsure.

DARRELL (Anglo-Saxon/Old French/English)—M.

MAJOR TALENT: Ability to incorporate systematic and logical approach into career. Is articulate, practical, and introspective. Best when unrestricted. Is discreet and optimistic, and respects conventional behavior. Psychologist, editor, and technical expert are possible career opportunities.

PERSONALITY INGREDIENTS: First impression is individualistic. Seems persuasive, independent, and creative. Inwardly parental, mature, and family conscious. Enjoys guiding, protecting, and expressing in artistic forms. Should be less blunt and curb selfishness.

PERSONALITY EXTREME: Too optimistic, or too melancholy.

DARREN (Irish/Gaelic)—M.

MAJOR TALENT: Ability to incorporate community consciousness, communication skills, and responsible character into career. Is capable of self-sacrifice for uplifting causes. Is inspirational, honest, and discriminating. Gifted teacher and concerned parent. Has great courage and assumes burdens for others. Can be a world beater through desires for social reform. Consumer sales, conservationism, and any profession that helps people are possible career opportunities.

PERSONALITY INGREDIENTS: Desires loving homelife. Wants to protect, provide, and feel pride in relationships. First impression is empathetic, attractive, and youthful. May act dramatic, charming, and philosophical. Is romantic, and appreciates all artistic expression. Must avoid overloading, or will be prone to emotional problems. Should learn to identify just causes and not martyr with false bravado.

PERSONALITY EXTREME: Too self-indulgent, or too repressed.

DAVID (Hebrew/Welsh/English)—M.

MAJOR TALENT: Ability to incorporate broad-scoped constructive planning into career. Is a worker. Strives to build a better mousetrap, sell it at a fair price, and eliminate the problem for humanity. Is a resourceful, practical, ethical, and wise problem solver. Attracts secure marriage, respect from community, and financial growth. Military/diplomatic/business professions, psychiatry and transportation are possible career opportunities.

PERSONALITY INGREDIENTS: First impression is articulate, attractive, and sparked with humor. Strives for variety and beauty, and to be a trend-setter. Inwardly needs creative freedom and independence—in short, to be boss. Avoids details, but wants exemplary home, family, and community reputation. Usually mental, and may be introvert or extrovert by choice.

PERSONALITY EXTREME: Too law-abiding, or too unconventional.

DAWN (Scandinavian)—F.

MAJOR TALENT: Ability to incorporate perseverance, clever planning, and attraction for people into career. Makes off-the-cuff judgments. Should be discerning and understanding, and learn to see the humor in life. Instructing, counseling, and public service are possible career opportunities.

PERSONALITY INGREDIENTS: Judges by appearances. Is too changeable, and must understand that it's always darkest before the dawn. Appears adventurous, physically attractive, and energetic. Wants individualism. Is ambitious, creative, and aggressive. Courts emotional and workaholic problems. Must cultivate patience.

PERSONALITY EXTREME: Too regimented, or too spontaneous.

DEAN (Late Latin/Anglo-Saxon/English)—M.

MAJOR TALENT: Ability to incorporate instigation, progressive action, and responsibility into career. Is a born counselor. Has clever ideas, individuality, and a strong will. May be too impulsive. Teaching, home services, and songwriting are possible career opportunities.

PERSONALITY INGREDIENTS: Desires harmony, artistic expression, and a comfortable life-style. Is companionable, and needs loving family to feel rooted. First impression is interested, interesting, and youthfully attractive. Seems empathetic, understanding, and a bit romantic. Has self-imposed disciplines that frustrate natural curiosity. Must relax codes to chuckle at people's foibles and life's inconsistencies. May be dogmatic and self-deluding, and misunderstand associates.

PERSONALITY EXTREME: Too lackluster, or too flashy.

DEANNA (Latin/English)—F.

MAJOR TALENT: Ability to incorporate gentle diplomacy, independent action, and communication skills into career. Has memorable voice or

delivery, or charming manner of speaking. Is patient and orderly, and
has a good memory. Needs to balance home and business responsibilities
to maintain emotional control. All artistic/musical professions, chemistry, and veterinary medicine are possible career opportunities.

PERSONALITY INGREDIENTS: Desires refinement, cultural stimulation,
and quality people and products. Needs thinking time and companionship. Dreads poverty and loneliness. Hides true feelings. Appears attractive to men, friendly, and free-spirited. Uncomfortable doing manual
labor or facing practical realities. Strives for perfection, and may be an
escapist.

PERSONALITY EXTREME: Too independent, or too accommodating.

DEBBIE (nickname for Deborah)—F.

MAJOR TALENT: Ability to incorporate analytic mind, adaptable nature, and appealing presence into career. Is diplomatic, artistic, and
original. Impressive positive attitude, fertile intellect, and attention to
details of wide-scoped projects attract supporters and financial assistance. Charitable organizations, communications professions, and research into religion are possible career opportunities.

PERSONALITY INGREDIENTS: First impression is clean-cut, conventional, and neat. Strives for practicality, security, and constructive life-
style. Desires change, physical activity, and unconventional experiences. Wants to travel and experience the unknown, and is either the
vestal virgin or intensely sexual. This nickname softens the businesslike
nature of the name Deborah.

PERSONALITY EXTREME: Too enthusiastic, or too undemonstrative.

DEBORAH (Hebrew/English)—F.

MAJOR TALENT: Ability to incorporate charm, dynamic energy, and
executive/administrative skills into career. Is efficient, honest, and trustworthy. Aims to get things done. Has inherited strength, money, or
position. Mainstay is ability to organize others. Banking, manufacturing,
and theatrical production are possible career opportunities.

PERSONALITY INGREDIENTS: Inwardly generous, but reserved. Feels
optimistic and resilient; enjoys practical artistic expression. First impression attracts men and women. Has youthful, friendly, and understanding
appearance. Is inspirational, progressive, and multifaceted. Must be
confident, reasonable, and flexible to overcome obstacles.

PERSONALITY EXTREME: Too materialistic, or too sanctimonious.

DEBRA (English, from Deborah)—F.

MAJOR TALENT: Ability to incorporate detailed, progressive, and instigative imagination into career. Is a loner one minute and a show
stealer the next. Vital, charming, youthful, and tactfully cautious nature
invites envious criticism. At best when flexible and progressive. All expressive art forms, performing, and teaching are possible career opportunities.

PERSONALITY INGREDIENTS: Inwardly loves home, and is able to
create a comfortable, companionable, and beautiful atmosphere anywhere. Is generous, helpful, and wise. Perceptive counselor with exemplary personal standards. May be stubborn, unprogressive, and selfish
when overextended emotionally.

PERSONALITY EXTREME: Too ambitious, or too unproductive.

DELANO (Old French/English)—M.

MAJOR TALENT: Ability to incorporate magnetic charm, persuasive communication skills, and parental nature into career. Is diplomatic, reserved, and practical. Assumes responsibility and makes personal adjustments for family, group, or community harmony and progress. Has mature judgment. Teacher, civil servant, and guidance counselor are possible career opportunities.

PERSONALITY INGREDIENTS: Needs people, artistic expression, and positive thinking. Appears to be and is extravagant, unpredictable, and entertaining. Strives for recognition, approval, and the humorous approach. May scatter energies.

PERSONALITY EXTREME: Too trusting, or too suspicious.

DELIA (English diminutive of Greek Cordelia)—F.

MAJOR TALENT: Ability to incorporate practicality, tact, and patient methodology for creating better products, services, or diplomatic relations into career. Must avoid inferiority complex and know no limitation. Uses common sense, strong opinions, and wide-angle viewpoint to re-shape existing conditions. Government, industry, and any profession are possible career opportunities.

PERSONALITY INGREDIENTS: Feels responsible and honorable, and assumes a parental attitude. Enjoys artistic stimulation, family attainments, and high standards. Appears refined, unruffled, and dignified. Strives for cultural improvement, serenity, and intellectual, or academic growth. Wants comfort, quality, and quantity; can have it all.

PERSONALITY EXTREME: Too impatient, or too placid.

DELLA (variant of Delia)—F.

MAJOR TALENT: Ability to incorporate sense of perfection, duty, and independence into career. Looks for the why of everything. Has quality taste, creative ideas, and artistic interests. Best when not motivated for material power. Needs to specialize research and achieve specific expertise to maintain emotional and material security. Designer, librarian, and technical/scientific/precision-oriented professions are possible career opportunities.

PERSONALITY INGREDIENTS: Feels the harmony of people, music, and experiences. Needs companionship, responsibility, and roots. First impression is individualistic. Strives for activity, innovation, and quick decisions. Must concentrate, mull things over, and avoid naive mistakes. Meditation, behavior-change training, or hatha yoga may unlock doors to superior intuition.

PERSONALITY EXTREME: Too bold, or too fearful.

DELPHINE (Greek/French)—F.

MAJOR TALENT: Ability to incorporate subtle strong will, showmanship, and creative leadership into career. Has a passionate nature, and is intense at work or play. Expects the best of everything; is generous, imaginative, and responsible. Must avoid living in the past. Has youthful vulnerability, dramatic/musical flair, and optimistic determination. Performing arts, science, and family or home improvement industries are possible career opportunities.

PERSONALITY INGREDIENTS: Inwardly flowing with fresh ideas. May reveal concepts and lose rewards. Must act independently to provide service, progress, and understanding. First impression is magnetic, empathetic, and graceful. Restores health to others, but experiences dramatic personal highs and lows.

PERSONALITY EXTREME: Too carefree, or too precautionary.

DEMETRIUS (Greek/French/German/English)—M.

MAJOR TALENT: Ability to incorporate practical work, tactful interactions, and service to family/home/community into career. Employs generous, artistic, cooperative nature to support sensitive imagination. Keeps commitments, is honest, and gives and needs love. House painter, writer of children's books, and welfare counselor are possible career opportunities.

PERSONALITY INGREDIENTS: First impression is modest, quiet, and reserved. Inwardly has broad vision for construction or improvement. Plans unemotionally, but is personally sensitive. Has limitless determination, courage, and humanitarian instincts.

PERSONALITY EXTREME: Too self-important, or too inferior.

DENISE (Latin/French/English)—F.

MAJOR TALENT: Ability to incorporate magnetic, supportive, and inventive ideas into career. Is farsighted, philosophical, and understanding. Attracts attention with joyous, noble, uncommonly wise attitude. Must face practical realities while maintaining personal ideals in order to attain commercial success. Filmed communications, social services, and inspirational writing are possible career opportunities.

PERSONALITY INGREDIENTS: Must have independent action, leadership, and changing goals. Is ambitious, courageous, and aggressive. Has own way of doing things and cannot be a follower. May tend to be self-important and ruthless.

PERSONALITY EXTREME: Too sensual, or too mental.

DENNIS (Greek: Dionysos/Latin/French/English)—M.

MAJOR TALENT: Ability to incorporate appreciation for small things, humanitarian instincts, and a desire to expound personal beliefs into career. Attracts respect, partnerships, and recognition. Is romantic, compassionate, and intuitive. Has an eager and enthusiastic quality that brightens but may seem to be a bit out of this world. Social reformer, musician, and preacher are possible career opportunities.

PERSONALITY INGREDIENTS: Has nervous energy, a clever mind, and unconventional desires. First impression is responsible, helpful, and conservative. Feels curious, impulsive, and sensual. Strives for family/community respect, attainments, and harmony. An individualist. Must maintain high ideals.

PERSONALITY EXTREME: Too uncertain, or too zealous.

DEREK (Gothic: Theodoric/English)—M.

MAJOR TALENT: Ability to incorporate perception of fine points, nonroutine experiences, and logical thinking into career. Is clever, progressive, and tuned to the physical senses. Awakens interest, perseveres, and succeeds through hard work. Childhood experiences teach lifelong lessons. Photographer, psychoanalyst and appraiser are possible career opportunities.

PERSONALITY INGREDIENTS: May appear stuck-up. Lacks congeniality at first meeting. Opens up to show generous, helpful, parental nature. Is reliable, trustworthy, and idealistic. Likes to guide, teach, and counsel. May be too judgmental. Should live and let live.

PERSONALITY EXTREME: Too attention-getting, or too modest.

DERMOT (Celtic/English)—M.

MAJOR TALENT: Ability to incorporate imagination, gift of gab, and practical/versatile nature into career. Attracts attention from the ladies and influential people. Creates, purchases, and collects fine/quality things. At best in conventional life-style and when visualizing a broad marketplace. Designer, promoter/salesman, and lecturer are possible career opportunities.

PERSONALITY INGREDIENTS: Full of ideas, evangelisms, and high ideals. Has nervous energy that needs an organized partner/mate to stay earthbound. First impression is individualistic, determined, and capable. Strives for independence, originality, and fast results. Must avoid extravagant gestures, scattering energy, and out-of-bounds flirtations.

PERSONALITY EXTREME: Too hot-tempered, or too unemotional.

DESMOND (Celtic)—M.

MAJOR TALENT: Ability to incorporate sensitivity to details, intuitional decisions, and universal empathy into career. Is high-strung, inventive, and attractive to groups. Gifted arbitrator. Defensively arrogant when misguided by taking face values. Firmness, commonsense practicality, and tact help to promote idealistic leanings. Welfare worker, inspirational leader, and political campaigner are possible career opportunities.

PERSONALITY INGREDIENTS: Is petty/generous, supportive/critical, revolutionary/peaceful . . . inconsistent. Appears graceful, tweedy, and romantic. Inwardly feels special. Sees things imaginatively, and wants respectable, gentle, quiet homelife. Can be saint or sinner.

PERSONALITY EXTREME: Too conforming, or too unconventional.

DEXTER (Latin)—M.

MAJOR TALENT: Ability to incorporate individualism, versatility, and determination into career. Is restless, energetic, and competitive. Has good memory, generous nature, and dramatic reactions. Must organize practical goals and maintain cooperative attitude for success. Military officer, architect/builder/real estate salesman, and mechanic are possible career opportunities.

PERSONALITY INGREDIENTS: Inwardly innovative, strong-willed, and independent. Is ambitious. First impression is attractive, pleasant, and optimistic. May scatter interests. Benefits from down-to-earth approach.

PERSONALITY EXTREME: Too expansive, or too narrow.

DIANA (Latin/Greek/Italian/German/English)—F.

MAJOR TALENT: Ability to incorporate feelings, fancies, and futuristic thinking into career. Is a working partner: cooperative, gentle, and peaceful. Grows through change and learning to look inside issues before making them personal crusades. Is magnetic and sheds light to uplift humanitarian causes. Musician, psychologist, and teacher are possible career opportunities.

PERSONALITY INGREDIENTS: Inwardly a dreamer and not always practical. Sensitive, emotional, and friendly. First impression is romantic, harmonious, and dramatic. Has nervous-energy drains that produce personal highs and lows, but appears understanding, sympathetic, and charming. Rarely shows signs of aging.

PERSONALITY EXTREME: Too innovative, or too old-world.

DIANE (Latin/French)—F.

MAJOR TALENT: Ability to incorporate persuasive, companionable, and socially adept characteristics into career. Is a responsible, attaining helpmate/lover/parent. Very sincere, hardworking, and a protective and willing counselor. Seeks status and comforts, and attracts help from influential people. Nursing, home/family products sales and service, and theater/art forms are possible career opportunities.

PERSONALITY INGREDIENTS: Inwardly a determined planner. Is prone to take things literally. Should be discerning and not make vice or virtue judgments. First impression is empathetic, compassionate, and cosmopolitan. Appears to have nobility of purpose, but happiness depends on love.

PERSONALITY EXTREME: Too maidenly, or too sensuous.

DICK (English nickname of Richard)—M.

MAJOR TALENT: Ability to incorporate independence, practical judgment, and compassionate nature into career. Has physical, mental and humanitarian focus. Is very active, has extraordinary dreams, and must pay attention to bodily needs. Tunes body to mental health. Medicine, aviation, and all art/communications professions are possible career opportunities.

PERSONALITY INGREDIENTS: From childhood throughout life is sympathetic and loving, and wants to please. Sports, entertaining, philosophical probing and daydreaming meld in this emotional, romantic, empathetic, and broad-scoped personality. Identifies with Casanova, Barrymore, and Gandhi . . . also sees the humor in self-image.

PERSONALITY EXTREME: Too idealistic, or too petty.

DIERDRE (Old Irish)—F.

MAJOR TALENT: Ability to incorporate humanitarian instincts, practical organizational skills, and desire for reform into career. Has fortitude. Sets example and teaches from experience. Gives more than is received. Missionary, publisher, and lawyer are possible career opportunities.

PERSONALITY INGREDIENTS: Inwardly courageous, closemouthed, and determined. Must learn to let go of outgrown habits and people. First impression is managerial, confident, and persuasive. Must give love, understanding, and tolerance without sacrificing material or emotional stability.

PERSONALITY EXTREME: Too sensual, or too temperate.

DINAH (Hebrew/English)—F.

MAJOR TALENT: Ability to incorporate desire for perfection, attention to details, and magnetic attraction for mass-market approval into career. Is loyal, philanthropic, and empathetic. Vivaciously mixes mental, emotional, and spiritual aspects to charm supporters. All communications professions, welfare services, and legislative work are possible career opportunities.

PERSONALITY INGREDIENTS: Desires independence and innovation, and switches from introvert to extrovert at will. Has extraordinary intuition. First impression is capable, businesslike, and very affluent. Strives for control and impeccable reputation; isn't easy on self or others. Self-made, expects to succeed, and reaches cultural heights.

PERSONALITY EXTREME: Too power-hungry, or too antiestablishment.

DIONE (French)—M.

MAJOR TALENT: Ability to incorporate universal service, perception of details, and creative energy into career. Has wisdom and futuristic concepts; is an individualist. Attracts beneficial commercial partnerships. Unique personality influences others. TV/film industries, religious reform, and any service business are possible career opportunities.

PERSONALITY INGREDIENTS: Enjoys giving advice, family/community attainments, and conventional standards. First impression is striking. Appears progressive, clever, and sensual. Is friendly, curious, and changeable. Must avoid pomposity, indecision, and gullibility.

PERSONALITY EXTREME: Too reflective, or too adventurous.

DIRK (Gothic: Derek/nickname)—M.

MAJOR TALENT: Ability to incorporate consideration of details, practicality, and artistic or social service into career. Is sensitive, instructive, and administrative. Has strong will and judgment, and parental nature. Counseling, theater arts, and economics are possible career opportunities.

PERSONALITY INGREDIENTS: Inwardly compassionate, romantic, and broad-minded. Has a way with words and people. Appears interested, comfortable, and durable. May be too serious.

PERSONALITY EXTREME: Too critical, or too adaptable.

DIXIE (English, from French and Latin)—F. & M.

MAJOR TALENT: Ability to incorporate attractive personality, communications skills, and social service into career. Is the cosmic parent. Has generosity, charity, and wisdom for family/community/humanity. Assumes responsibility for others' welfare. Teacher, union organizer, and personnel director are possible career opportunities.

PERSONALITY INGREDIENTS: Desires sensual pleasure, adventure, and unconventional experiences. Is impulsive, curious, and clever. First impression is individualistic. Seems energetic, capable, and firm. Can overdo burden bearing and become a doormat. Must be discerning to avoid self-destruction.

PERSONALITY EXTREME: Too relaxed, or too deliberate.

DOLLY (diminutive of Dolores)—F.

MAJOR TALENT: Ability to incorporate attention to details, optimistic personality, and material ideas into career. Is energetic, quick, and clever. Changeable, adventurous, enthusiastic nature has unique appeal and attracts supporters. Has catalystic effect upon the lives of others. Politician, promoter, and investigator are possible career opportunities.

PERSONALITY INGREDIENTS: Inwardly practical, economical, and conventional. Is organized, structured, and materially attaining. First impression is assertive, independent, and original. Strives to be unique.

PERSONALITY EXTREME: Too refined, or too earthy.

DOLORES (Latin/Spanish/English)—F.

MAJOR TALENT: Ability to incorporate self-expression, cultural stimulation, and commonsense judgments into career. Is organized and logical, and applies conventional methods to spiritual/intellectual interests. Is discreet but straightforward. Psychologist, antique dealer, and high-level administrator are possible career opportunities.

PERSONALITY INGREDIENTS: Desires affluence, power, and status. First impression is custom-made. Appears businesslike, sociable, and determined. Articulate, patiently understanding, keen judge of character.

PERSONALITY EXTREME: Too independent, or too submissive.

DOMINIC (Latin/English)—M.

MAJOR TALENT: Ability to incorporate method, economy, and orderliness into career. Is factual and honorable; expects to give and get consideration. Wants peace, constructive activity, and to make and abide by the rules. Building trades, literature, and investment counseling are possible career opportunities.

PERSONALITY INGREDIENTS: Has mathematical-statistical/black-white administrative judgment. Comfortable when responsible for control. Needs roots, respectability, and abundant life-style. First impression is quiet, introspective, and often mysterious or aloof. Lacks social self-esteem, and appears to be an observer. Strives for refinement, culture, and dignity. Academic, scientific or technical expertise turns the bearer of this name into an authoritative conversationalist.

PERSONALITY EXTREME: Too fanciful, or too unimaginative.

DONALD (Gaelic/Celtic/English)—M.

MAJOR TALENT: Ability to incorporate progressive, detailed, unconventional thinking into career. Is curious, articulate, and clever. Has an appealing approach, wants leadership, and attracts the unusual. Research, science, and communications are possible career opportunities.

PERSONALITY INGREDIENTS: Seeks prefection. Feels introspective, is culturally attaining, and uses logic. Desires serenity, privacy, and quiet for best efforts. Seems to be a loner, but dreads loneliness. May have security and fear poverty. First impression is deceptive. Hides a secret self. Must feel loved to give love.

PERSONALITY EXTREME: Too obedient, or too unconventional.

DONNA (Latin: Domina/Italian/English)—F.

MAJOR TALENT: Ability to incorporate individuality, good memory, and communication skills into career. Is artistically expressive, orderly, and admired by others. Enjoys variety, freedom, and cheerfulness. Must balance home responsibilities and career. Writing, animal training, and lecturing are possible career opportunities.

PERSONALITY INGREDIENTS: Inwardly desires perfection, quality life-style, and cultural attainments. Needs privacy for meditation, inspiration, emotional control. First impression is enthusiastic, friendly, and attractive. Strives for spiritual and material balance.

PERSONALITY EXTREME: Too impatient, or too tenacious.

DORA (Greek/English/diminutive and independent)—F.

MAJOR TALENT: Ability to incorporate alternative judgments into career. Is reconstructive, sensitive, and best suited to partnerships. Relates to the fine points, and is governed by emotional reactions. Has difficulty breaking habits, and grows through decisive changes and not taking things at face value. Managing, collecting and minute detail work are possible career opportunities.

PERSONALITY INGREDIENTS: First impression is different. Appears idealistic, cooperative, and refined. Inwardly thinks, plans, and aspires to quality life-style. Keeps secrets. Fears loneliness and poverty. Needs shows of affection, but may pout them away.

PERSONALITY EXTREME: Too innovative, or too commonplace.

DOREEN (French/Celtic/Gaelic/English)—F.

MAJOR TALENT: Ability to incorporate articulate/attractive personality, practical/economical organization, and a perfectionist/analytic mind into career. Is honest, logical, and discriminating. Enjoys the outdoors, a good joke, and spiritual/intellectual stimulation. Editor, appraiser/buyer, and researcher are possible career opportunities.

PERSONALITY INGREDIENTS: Highly intuitive, but ignores first thought and overthinks. Doubts fine taste, judgment, and logic. Needs education or concentrated study to provide proof of undeniable authority. Attracts friends; is generous and an empathetic humanitarian. Needs quiet, solitude, and cultural refinements. Happiest near water or in the country.

PERSONALITY EXTREME: Too busy, or too bored.

DORIAN (Greek/English)—F. & M.

MAJOR TALENT: Ability to incorporate dignity, authority, and conventional administration into career. Is attractive, articulate, and practical. Has analytic approach, powers of persuasion, and wisdom. Lawyer, technical writer, and accountant are possible career opportunities.

PERSONALITY INGREDIENTS: First impression is noble, sympathetic, and attractive. Strives for perfection and may feel dissatisfied. Needs cultural stimulation, quality products, and polished people. Tries to escape from mundane realities. Strives for universal recognition. May be cunning, too outspoken, or impulsive when in unconventional life-style.

PERSONALITY EXTREME: Too fast-moving, or too expectant.

DORIS (Greek/English)—F.

MAJOR TALENT: Ability to incorporate personal ideals, humanitarian service, and supportive instincts into career. Is high-strung, individualistic, and highly intuitive. Has inspirational effect on others, refinement, and a trusting nature. Beauty specialist, teacher, and artist are possible career opportunities.

PERSONALITY INGREDIENTS: Inwardly home/family rooted. Wants comfort, conventional attainments, and to be needed. Appears energetic, unusual, and clever. Has a way with people. May be impractical in business. Needs down-to-earth partnership.

PERSONALITY EXTREME: Too sure, or too compromising.

DOROTHEA (Greek/German/English)—F.

MAJOR TALENT: Ability to incorporate pioneering ideas, unconventional routine, and organizational practicality into career. Is creative, faithful, and courageous. Thinks before taking action. Can tackle anything. Theatrical production, travel agency and any selling job are possible career opportunities.

PERSONALITY INGREDIENTS: Relates to everybody and gives compassionate understanding. Feels deeply emotional, philosophical, and appreciates beauty, culture, and universal problems. Dislikes looking like everyone else, sameness, and not having money. May be an escapist.

PERSONALITY EXTREME: Too changeable, or too unaggressive.

DOROTHY (English, from Dorothea)—F.

MAJOR TALENT: Ability to incorporate helpful service, cooperative nature, and friendliness into career. Is peace-loving and understanding; creates an abundant homelife. Sees good, beauty, and hospitality as musts. Attracts friends, family focus, and love. Home decorator, caterer, and social secretary are possible career opportunities.

PERSONALITY INGREDIENTS: Needs independence, creative outlets, and innovations. Is courageous, ambitious, and imaginative. Appears adventurous, enthusiastic, and unusual. Has charm and gracious manner, and attracts male admiration. Thrives on respectability, pleasure, and harmonious relationships.

PERSONALITY EXTREME: Too aloof, or too down-to-earth.

DOTTIE (diminutive of Dorothy)—F.

MAJOR TALENT: Ability to incorporate adaptability, executive judgment, and inventive ideas into career. Is ambitious, responsible, and resourceful. Attracts money, men, and action. Best when intuitive. Internist, inspector, and owner of any business are possible career opportunities.

PERSONALITY INGREDIENTS: First impression is very affluent. Appears capable, self-possessed, and persuasive. Inwardly is soft, sensitive, and emotionally governed. Wants loving mate, respectability, and relaxed life-style.

PERSONALITY EXTREME: Too impulsive, or too incurious.

DOUGLAS (Celtic/Scottish/English)—M.

MAJOR TALENT: Ability to incorporate intellect, diplomacy, and promotional ideas into career. Is sensitive, physical, and culturally attaining. Has humor, compatibility, and keen perception of details. Thrives on new concepts and adventure; wins through hard work. High-level administrator, psychoanalyst, and architect are possible career opportunities.

PERSONALITY INGREDIENTS: First impression is tasteful, comfortable, and mature. Is concerned, articulate, and managerial. Inwardly wants to be boss. Feels creative, capable, and ambitious. Original methods are best suited to working alone. Impulsiveness causes problems.

PERSONALITY EXTREME: Too self-centered, or too dependent.

DOYLE (Celtic/English)—M.

MAJOR TALENT: Ability to incorporate adaptability, cleverness, and mental concentration into career. Is detail conscious, enterprising, and willing. Has unusual childhood experiences that develop wisdom. Must persevere, concentrate, and work patiently to overcome obstacles. Watchmaker, foreman, and accountant are possible career opportunities.

PERSONALITY INGREDIENTS: Inwardly compassionate, generous, and charitable. Feels romantic, brotherly, and noble. First impression is unruffled, quiet, and reserved. Does not show depth of feelings, and may confuse friends. Needs social confidence. May lack academic credits, but has exceptional intellect.

PERSONALITY EXTREME: Too unconventional, or too practical.

DRAKE (Old German/English)—M.

MAJOR TALENT: Ability to incorporate leadership, adaptability, and imagination into career. Is friendly, talented, and charming. Has optimistic attitude, loves beauty, and needs concentration. All theater arts, medicine/law, and cartooning are possible career opportunities.

PERSONALITY INGREDIENTS: Dislikes confrontations/arguments and attempts to take mature approach to everything. Feels responsible, understanding, and materially attaining. Needs family harmony for happiness.

PERSONALITY EXTREME: Too adventurous, or too cautious.

DREW (Teutonic/English)—M.

MAJOR TALENT: Ability to incorporate learning by experience into career. Is clever, passionate, and changeable. Has physical agility, retentive memory, and exceptional understanding of people. Fortunate with inheritances, marriage, and creature comforts. Advertising, politics, and investigative research are possible career opportunities.

PERSONALITY INGREDIENTS: Feels curious, progressive, and sexy. Needs freedom to explore new concepts. Is loyal, bold, and unpredictable. Appears capable, independent, and empathetic. Strives for broad-scoped markets, humanitarian service, and romantic life-style.

PERSONALITY EXTREME: Too physical, or too emotional.

DUANE (Celtic: Doane/English)—M.

MAJOR TALENT: Ability to incorporate empathy, friendliness, and voluntary service into career. Is dramatic and individualistic, and a great lover. Has active mind that governs health. Should focus on practical life-style. Charity administrator, publisher, and humorist are possible career opportunities.

PERSONALITY INGREDIENTS: Gives more than is received. Feels like and is a born welfare worker. Thrives on healing, helping, and handling everything and everyone. Has prophetic dreams, artistic interests, and magnetic personality. Needs physical-fitness program.

PERSONALITY EXTREME: Too eccentric, or too ordinary.

DUDLEY (Anglo-Saxon/English)—M.

MAJOR TALENT: Ability to incorporate tact, communication skills, and physical balance into career. Is instructive, helpful, and sensitive. Has artistic/expressive gifts, impulsive loves, and a self-development approach. Success breeds self-confidence. Arbitrator, druggist, and comptroller are possible career opportunities.

PERSONALITY INGREDIENTS: Wants affluence, influence, and power. Desires executive leadership, honest relationships, and organized life-style. Is ambitious, determined, and physical. First impression attracts attention. Appears charming, understanding, and dramatic.

PERSONALITY EXTREME: Too secretive, or too indiscreet.

DUKE (Anglo-Saxon)—M.

MAJOR TALENT: Ability to incorporate independence, conservative nature, and adventurous spirit into career. Is courageous, practical, and loyal. Has problem-solving ability, learns by experience, and considers all possibilities. Sexually attractive and active. Theatrical manager, electrical engineer, and politician are possible career opportunities.

PERSONALITY INGREDIENTS: Desires executive leadership, trustworthy associations, and influential position. Appears magnetic, parental, and instructive. Strives for respectability, useful service, and knowledge. Gains through tactful, diplomatic, and persuasive approach.

PERSONALITY EXTREME: Too curious, or too conventional.

DUNCAN (Gaelic/English)—M.

MAJOR TALENT: Ability to incorporate charm, cooperative nature, and creative ideas into career. Is versatile, optimistic, and adaptable. Has loyal, imaginative, and conversational manner. Very expressive nature. Writer, dietician, and artisan in any line are possible career opportunities.

PERSONALITY INGREDIENTS: Inwardly conservative, practical, and economical. Wants constructive life-style. Appears authoritative, businesslike, and successful. Combines patience, positive attitude, and progressive outlook for happiness.

PERSONALITY EXTREME: Too changeable, or too tenacious.

DUSTIN (Old German)—M.

MAJOR TALENT: Ability to incorporate communication skills, practical organization, and responsible nature into career. Is instructive, inquisitive, and patient. Has ambition and optimism, and attracts promotional friendships. Gets financial help from women. Teacher, useful products retailer, and counselor are possible career opportunities.

PERSONALITY INGREDIENTS: Is imaginative, artistic, and versatile. Loves life and people, and wants to entertain and be entertained. Recognition, companionship, and enthusiasm are important to happiness. May clam up or go on conversational overkill. Must avoid extravagances.

PERSONALITY EXTREME: Too investigative, or too gullible.

DWIGHT (Teutonic/English)—M.

MAJOR TALENT: Ability to incorporate executive organizational skills, communications, and adventurous nature into career. Is attractive, restless, and explorative. Has sex appeal, artistic creativity, and ambition. Combines love of travel, strenuous activity, and discipline with courage and foresight for success. Government official, judge, and business analyst are possible career opportunities.

PERSONALITY INGREDIENTS: Inwardly broad-scoped, philosophical, and compassionate. Is generous, empathetic, and romantic. Appears tailor-made. Strives for businesslike judgment, efficiency, and prosperity. Attracts respect, and is sociable and persuasive. Must avoid self-doubt, sensual curiosity, and inflexibility.

PERSONALITY EXTREME: Too callous, or too burden-bearing.

DYLAN (Welsh)—M.

MAJOR TALENT: Ability to incorporate emotional sensitivity, seeing the

pros and cons, and supportive attitude into career. Is a master of detail—
exacting and striving for accuracy. Has to observe, balance input, and
come to reasonable conclusions. The bearer of this name develops and
shares. Chorus leader, legislator and union mediator are possible career
opportunities.

PERSONALITY INGREDIENTS: First impression is charming, articulate,
and expressive. Is versatile and artistic, and goes to extremes. Desires
success. Needs big challenges, confidence, and efficient management.
Wants control, respect, and the freedom that money can buy.

PERSONALITY EXTREME: Too unpredictable, or too obvious.

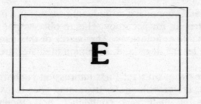

E

All names that begin with the letter *E* have the *Strong Point* of curiosity—resourcefulness—experimentation—animal magnetism—enthusiasm.

EARL (Anglo-Saxon/English)—M.

MAJOR TALENT: Ability to incorporate human understanding, disciplined artistry, and selfless service into career. Is philosophical, individualistic, and executive. Has vivid imagination, intense emotions, and magnetism. Attracts health, money, and love when positive. Doctor/lawyer, correspondent, and all artistic expression are possible career opportunities.

PERSONALITY INGREDIENTS: Desires respectability, order, and system. Believes in traditions and hard work. First impression is striking. Appears unconventional but needs structure. Strives for progressive changes, sensual pleasures, and subtle control. Sometimes negative, cold, immoral, or egocentric.

PERSONALITY EXTREME: Too talkative, or too inexpressive.

EBBA (Anglo-Saxon/English—F. & M.

MAJOR TALENT: Ability to incorporate pioneering spirit into career. Is creative, independent, and aggressive. Has courage, instigates progressive changes, and is a pacesetter. Any sales position, inventing, and promotion are possible career opportunities.

PERSONALITY INGREDIENTS: Inwardly concerned with productivity, planning, and practicalities. Wants material security, respectability, and orderly system. First impression is attractive, helpful, and responsible. Strives for family, artistic, and community attainments. Must curb impatience.

PERSONALITY EXTREME: Too procrastinating, or too stimulated.

EBENEZER (Hebrew/English)—M.

MAJOR TALENT: Ability to incorporate steady work, discipline, and practical judgment into career. Is cautious, precise, and expedient. Has materialistic goals, conventional habits, and needs spiritual/intuitional development. Service to others offers possibilities for lasting recognition. Military officer, banker, and physical therapist are possible career opportunities.

PERSONALITY INGREDIENTS: Construction and reconstruction for the material benefit of others. Inwardly perceives things sensitively. Wants peace, partnership, and a modest life-style. Appears responsible, protective, and parental. Strives for home/community security, artistic expression, and attainments. May be humanitarian powerhouse, a workaholic miser, or a born farmer.

PERSONALITY EXTREME: Too compassionate, or too unfeeling.

EDAN (Celtic/English)—F. & M.

MAJOR TALENT: Ability to incorporate creativity, cleverness, and responsibility into career. Is persevering, resolute, and ambitious. Plans artfully, handles finances, and attracts attention. Has need to serve and tends to take things too seriously. Must learn when to give in and when to ease up. Teacher, interior decorator, and all musical or art forms are possible career opportunities.

PERSONALITY INGREDIENTS: Desires family harmony, respect, and abundant life-style. Needs roots. First impression is empathetic, graceful, and romantic. Strives for humanitarian service or artistic recognition.

PERSONALITY EXTREME: Too curious, or too afraid of the unknown.

EDDA (Old Norse)—F.

MAJOR TALENT: Ability to incorporate structured administration, ambition, and cleverness into career. Is imaginative, energetic, and applies theory to reality. Learns by experience. Has sensual appetites, love of excitement, and ability to grow to be wise and understanding. Politician, entertainer, and any sales position are possible career opportunities.

PERSONALITY INGREDIENTS: Walks a tightrope between conventional behavior and experimentation. Inwardly needs to attain harmonious and gracious family/community life. First impression is efficient, authoritative, and prosperous. Must stabilize and avoid impulsivity.

PERSONALITY EXTREME: Too bold, or too timid.

EDEN (Hebrew)—F. & M.

MAJOR TALENT: Ability to incorporate intentive, independent, and broad-scoped activities into career. Is extremely energetic and capable of leading a double life. Has courage, ambition, and must learn to maintain individualism and integrity simultaneously. Designer, manufacturer, and editor are possible career opportunities.

PERSONALITY INGREDIENTS: Wants to run the show. Uncomfortable at a standstill and leaves slowpokes behind. Appears youthful, compassionate, and impressive. Can be magnetic, charming, and gentle. Philosophical and enduring nature overcomes obstacles easily.

PERSONALITY EXTREME: Too sexy, or too platonic.

EDGAR (Anglo-Saxon/German/English)—M.

MAJOR TALENT: Ability to incorporate detail analysis, sense of justice, and material judgment into career. Is orderly, articulate, and adaptable. Has sensitivity, organizational structure, and intelligence. Buyer, critic, and all communications professions are possible career opportunities.

PERSONALITY INGREDIENTS: Inwardly adventurous, unconventional, and clever. Is a freedom lover and easily bored. First impression is sociable, attention-getting, and expressive. Strives for sunshine, beauty, and humor. Enjoys outdoor activity. Needs patience, endurance, and sensual balance.

PERSONALITY EXTREME: Too indiscreet, or too disciplined.

EDITH (Anglo-Saxon/English)—F.

MAJOR TALENT: Ability to incorporate innovations, trustworthiness, and individuality into career. Is detail conscious, efficient, and adaptable. Has discrimination, courage, and direct approach. Deals in tangibles. Illustrator, idea person, and all independent creative jobs are possible career opportunities.

PERSONALITY INGREDIENTS: Appears to be, and is, progressive, understanding, experimental, freedom loving, and open-minded. Unlocks doors for others and is a catalyst for change. Needs patience, concentration, and sensual balance.

PERSONALITY EXTREME: Too status-seeking, or too disorganized.

EDMOND (Anglo-Saxon/French/Danish/English)—M.

MAJOR TALENT: Ability to incorporate material aggressiveness, sensitivity, and inventive methods into career. Is tactful, efficient, and honest. Has initiative, style, and a desire to be a trendsetter. Theater, psychiatry, and any managerial position are possible career opportunities.

PERSONALITY INGREDIENTS: Feels inspirational, idealistic, and meant to be special. Has nervous energy, strong intuition, and fast-moving ideas. First impression is businesslike, trustworthy, and affluent. Full of contradictions: impatient/careful, materialistic/generous, cooperative/independent. Needs self-control.

PERSONALITY EXTREME: Too rigid, or too reckless.

EDMUND (Anglo-Saxon/German/English)—M.

MAJOR TALENT: Ability to incorporate mental analysis, perfectionist techniques, and observation of details into career. Is adventuresome, alert, and diplomatic. Has love of nature, mobility, and quality. Photographer, researcher, and detective are possible career opportunities.

PERSONALITY INGREDIENTS: First impression is deep, honorable, and executive. Strives for position. Inwardly strong, willing, and able. Can be shrewd, resourceful, and a down-to-earth realist. Must learn from experience.

PERSONALITY EXTREME: Too square, or too rule-bending.

EDNA (Hebrew/English)—F.

MAJOR TALENT: Ability to incorporate determination, useful service, and emotional insight into career. Is acquiring, inquisitive, and quick to judge. Has to learn to discern, ease-up, and chuckle at life's inconsistencies. Good student/teacher/counselor. Ambitions may lose friends. Communications, medicine, and vocal coaching are possible career opportunities.

PERSONALITY INGREDIENTS: Wants family/community harmony, comforts, and high standards. Needs stability, responsibility, and personal involvement. Appears empathetic, philosophical, and cooperative. Strives for broad-scope, artistic expression, and emotional control. Sometimes persuasive, curious, and parental conversationalist.

PERSONALITY EXTREME: Too alone, or too dependent.

EDWARD (Anglo-Saxon/English)—M.

MAJOR TALENT: Ability to incorporate executive leadership, innovation, and direct action into career. Is explorative, ambitious, and a trendsetter. Has gentle/sensitive nature, courage and passion. Must overcome conflicting ambitions. Writer, business owner, and analyst are possible career opportunities.

PERSONALITY INGREDIENTS: First impression emits strength, self-possession, and good taste. Tunes in to others' needs. Inwardly wants love, gracious life-style, and responsibility. Is concerned, honest, and determined. Has nervous energy. Strives to organize for constructive humanitarian or artistic contributions.
PERSONALITY EXTREME: Too controlled, or too unconventional.

EDWIN (Anglo-Saxon/German/English)—M.

MAJOR TALENT: Ability to incorporate individuality, inner strength, and instigation of ideas into career. Is directive, disciplined, and orderly. Combines detail analysis, responsibility, and resourcefulness. May be a loner. Professional flyer, engineer, and any group leadership position are possible career opportunities.
PERSONALITY INGREDIENTS: Looks for new experiences, methods, and people. Tries everything and takes challenges. Needs excitement, sensual stimulation, and to avoid responsibility. Tends to handle people through clever appraisal. Bores easily and usually creates motion. May be a monster or a master.
PERSONALITY EXTREME: Too changeable, or too stubborn.

EDWINA (Anglo-Saxon/English)—F.

MAJOR TALENT: Ability to incorporate intuitional inspirations, idealistic nature, and desire to share into career. Is visionary, sensitive, and loving. Benefits from practical partner, soft approach, and commanding presence. Learns to commercialize on ideas. Psychoanalyst, inspirational writer, and social reformer are possible career opportunities.
PERSONALITY INGREDIENTS: Feels determined, conventional, and attaining. Wants roots, a loving family, and to be needed. Appears easygoing, friendly, and up to date. Strives to be noticed.
PERSONALITY EXTREME: Too ambitious, or too wishful.

EDYTHE (English: Edith)—F.

MAJOR TALENT: Ability to incorporate positive attitude, practical organization, and competitive spirit into career. Is methodical, positive, and articulate. Has pride, nervous energy, and generous/loving/dramatic nature. Secretary, builder, and waitress are possible career opportunities.
PERSONALITY INGREDIENTS: First impression is friendly, attractive, and sunny. Wants beauty, self-expression, and congeniality. Inwardly needs independence. Feels ambitious, instigative, and inventive. Is a survivor.
PERSONALITY EXTREME: Too self-indulgent, or too amiable.

EFFIE (Scottish: diminutive; Greek, Euphemia)—F.

MAJOR TALENT: Ability to incorporate gift of gab, individuality, and common sense judgments into career. Is sensible, optimistic, and bold. Has charm, administrative skills, and down-to-earth philosophy. Benefits from diplomatic touch, concentration, and letting the other guy win one. Performing artist, medical secretary, and real estate salesperson are possible career opportunities.
PERSONALITY INGREDIENTS: Inwardly wants artistic self-expression, tenderness, and harmonious family/community life. Needs to counsel,

instruct, and take responsibility. First impression is individualistic, assertive, and creative. Remembers everything.

PERSONALITY EXTREME: Too eccentric, or too bland.

EGAN (Celtic: Edan/English)—M.

MAJOR TALENT: Ability to incorporate inventiveness, efficiency, and artistic or humanitarian service into career. Is compassionate, impressionable, and tolerant. Material values and charitable nature cause diffusion of physical energy. Benefits from physical fitness regimen. Medicine, government, and welfare work are possible career opportunities.

PERSONALITY INGREDIENTS: First impression is expressive, imaginative, and kind. Strives to be optimistic and inwardly wants security. Needs to give love and sympathy, and to be useful. Must avoid scattering and losing sleep over superficial or impractical ambitions.

PERSONALITY EXTREME: Too cultivated, or too experimental.

EGBERT (Anglo-Saxon/German/English)—M.

MAJOR TALENT: Ability to incorporate self-expressive activities, conventional methods, and perfection of craft into career. Handles major commitments, is versatile, and sharp. Has sex appeal, charm and affability. Science, arts, and philosophical research are possible career opportunities.

PERSONALITY INGREDIENTS: Appears modest, but has subtle control over others. Strives to see alternatives and be decisive. Inwardly very independent, ambitious, and clear thinking. Attracts good luck, romance, and fertility.

PERSONALITY EXTREME: Too self-centered, or too giving.

EGON (Celtic: Edan/English)—M.

MAJOR TALENT: Ability to incorporate crafty intellect, practical imagination, and adaptability into career. Is observant, physically tuned, and articulate. Has a way with people that attracts boosters. Maintains an air of confidence. Sports reporter, art director, and promoter are possible career opportunities.

PERSONALITY INGREDIENTS: Is charming, sunny, and colorful. Inwardly feels special. Needs inspirational companions, serenity, and constructive outlets for innovative ideas. May exaggerate, be fanciful, and seem to see things through rose-colored glasses. Rarely down for long. A smile, honesty, and helpfulness attract success.

PERSONALITY EXTREME: Too heavy, or too light.

EILEEN (Gaelic-Irish: Greek, Helen)—F.

MAJOR TALENT: Ability to incorporate communications skills, sensitivity to details, and mobility into career. Is multifaceted, expressive, and adaptable. Has active energy, engaging charm, and strong sense of self. Respects conventions, but has unconventional ideas. Politics, theater, and legislative research are possible career opportunities.

PERSONALITY INGREDIENTS: Inwardly responsible, practical, and strong-willed. Needs security, family, and abundant life-style. Appears businesslike, capable, and reassuring. Strives for the freedom that money can buy and loved ones that can share the attainment.

PERSONALITY EXTREME: Too sensual, or too mental.

ELAINE (Greek: Helen/French/English)—F.

MAJOR TALENT: Ability to incorporate unclouded observations, independent action, and efficient organizational skills into career. Is courageous, inspirational, and gentle. Has sensual attraction, progressive ideas, and trusting nature. Balances pride with generosity and gains from patiently experiencing the unexpected. Scientist, musician, and any business partnership are possible career opportunities.

PERSONALITY INGREDIENTS: Contradictory nature. Inwardly easygoing, supportive, and sensitive. First impression is organized, strong, and ambitious. Strives for affluence, status, and diplomacy. Springs between wanting to control and needing to be cooperative.

PERSONALITY EXTREME: Too busy, or too bored.

ELEANOR (Greek: Helen/English)—F.

MAJOR TALENT: Ability to incorporate cultural interests, analytic mind, and conventional methods into career. Seeks perfection. Is articulate, optimistic, and organized. Has sharp intellect, frequent travels, and an honest, patient, philosophical approach. Research, technical skills, and all communications professions are possible career opportunities.

PERSONALITY INGREDIENTS: Fortunate in private pursuits, sometimes disappointed in love. Appears to be, and is, efficient, capable, and tailor-made. Feels in control of things. Is a persuasive, imaginative, enthusiastic, hard worker. Makes the impossible, possible.

PERSONALITY EXTREME: Too emotionally governed, or too physically active.

ELEANORA (Greek: Helen/English)—F.

MAJOR TALENT: Ability to incorporate physical and mental vitality, imagination, and self-confident approach into career. Is charming, considerate, and progressive. Attracts inheritance, executive position, and expansive goals. Must rein ambitions to maintain success. All banking, building, and political professions are possible career opportunities.

PERSONALITY INGREDIENTS: First impression is sharp, businesslike, and custom-made. Strives for status, influence, and material possessions. Inwardly needs broad horizons, artistic expression, and romance. Feels determined, compassionate, and philosophical. Must avoid self-indulgence.

PERSONALITY EXTREME: Too aggressive, or too receptive.

ELEANORE (Greek: Helen/English)—F.

MAJOR TALENT: Ability to incorporate magnetic, optimistic, and artistically discerning personality into career. Is a romantic, poetic, idealistic dreamer and doer. Has love of justice, humanity, and serving or entertaining. Gives and receives attention. All theater arts, spiritual professions, and publishing are possible career opportunities.

PERSONALITY INGREDIENTS: Inwardly a visionary and a builder. Feels philanthropic, determined, and unlimited. Solves problems, is practical, and works. First impression is dignified, strong, and distinctive. Should aim for the stars.

PERSONALITY EXTREME: Too physical, or too mental.

ELEAZAR (Hebrew: Lazarus/Greek/Latin/French/Danish/English)—M.

MAJOR TALENT: Ability to incorporate vital, imaginative, diplomatic way with people into career. Is charming, self-assured, and persuasive. Has unconventional, progressive, or speculative ideas and goes after them from within the structure of society. Business organizer, talent agent, and detective are possible career opportunities.

PERSONALITY INGREDIENTS: Supported by a dependable sense of humor. Needs variety, beauty, and recognition. First impression is sensitive, modest, and cooperative. May be accident prone, scattered, and introverted/extroverted.

PERSONALITY EXTREME: Too empathetic, or too unfeeling.

ELENA (Greek: Helen/Italian/Spanish/English)—F.

MAJOR TALENT: Ability to incorporate creative, instigative, and communication ideas into career. Is helpful, compassionate, and individualistic. Has organizational, material, and artistic interests. Intensely emotional. Theater arts, psychiatry, and all repair work are possible career opportunities.

PERSONALITY INGREDIENTS: Inwardly sensitive, idealistic, and highstrung. Wants to restructure reality, and is sometimes in another world. First impression is materialistic, controlled, and executive. Strives for affluence and influence. May be secretive due to inability to reveal independent beliefs/needs/loves.

PERSONALITY EXTREME: Too courageous, or too weak.

ELFRIEDA (Teutonic: Alfreda/English)—F.

MAJOR TALENT: Ability to incorporate practical judgment, correct behavior, and generous, sociable artistic nature into career. Is responsible, adaptable, and hospitable. Has cooperative, creative and loving attitude. Teaching, restaurant/hotel management, and musical professions are possible career opportunities.

PERSONALITY INGREDIENTS: Inwardly easy-going, peaceful, sensitive. Is kind, devoted, and can be studious. Appears solid, conventional, and masterful. Strives for improvement.

PERSONALITY EXTREME: Too active, or too placid.

ELI (Hebrew/English/independent-diminutive)—M.

MAJOR TALENT: Ability to incorporate mental analysis, creative ideas, and executive organization into career. Is culturally stimulating, cleverly humorous, and intellectually curious. Has dignity, pride, and courage. Statistical, literary, and scientific professions are possible career opportunities.

PERSONALITY INGREDIENTS: Inwardly needs adventure, sensual excitement, and constant activity. Appears charming, articulate, and entertaining. Strives for beauty, refinement, and optimism. Stubborn beliefs cause delays, pessimism, and stunt the growth of this multifaceted name.

PERSONALITY EXTREME: Too broad-minded, or too narrow.

ELIA (Hebrew: Elijah/Italian/German/Danish/English)—M.

MAJOR TALENT: Ability to incorporate individuality, efficient organization, and broad-scoped creative imagery into career. Has depth of universal understanding and material analysis to commercialize. Is courageous, ambitious, and empathetic. Multifaceted, highly energetic, and works through dreams which influence potential. Medicine/law, writing, and social work are possible career opportunities.

PERSONALITY INGREDIENTS: First impression is fashionable, expressive, charming, witty, imaginative, and entertaining. Inwardly strong willed, and tuned to home/family responsibility, comforts, and attainments. Precocious child and philosophical adult.

PERSONALITY EXTREME: Too daring, or too disguised.

ELIAS (Hebrew: Elijah/Latin/English)—M.

MAJOR TALENT: Ability to incorporate bold concepts, executive leadership, and carefuly structured actions into career. Is articulate, expressive, and resourceful. Has vitality, magnetism, and faith. Success comes through courage to learn from mistakes. Performer, scientist, and farmer are possible career opportunities.

PERSONALITY INGREDIENTS: Feels protective, determined, and family oriented. Wants security, harmony, and growth. Appears dependable, reasonable, and conventional. Must avoid harsh judgment, jealousy, and impracticality.

PERSONALITY EXTREME: Too emotional, or too detached.

ELIHU (Hebrew: Elijah/English)—M.

MAJOR TALENT: Ability to incorporate independence, uniqueness, and mental activity into career. Is able to lead/follow, hang in/move quickly, detail slowly/organize efficiently. Talents inspire others. Kindness, generosity, and adaptability broaden horizons. Selects direct course and patiently profits. Composer, illustrator, and designer are possible career opportunities.

PERSONALITY INGREDIENTS: Inwardly ambitious, driving, and businesslike. Feels best wheeling and dealing. Appears different. Strives for idealistic principles and may forget reality. First impression is imaginative, high-strung, and sensitive. May be torn between self-expression or earning a living.

PERSONALITY EXTREME: Too tenacious, or too flighty.

ELIJAH (Hebrew/English)—M.

MAJOR TALENT: Ability to incorporate intellectual/spiritual/logical insights, a personal presence, and diplomatic approach into career. Is artistic, adaptable, and inspirational. Has broad philosophy, cooperative nature, and humanitarian instincts. Welfare work, all arts, and science/ministry are possible career opportunities.

PERSONALITY INGREDIENTS: Totally self-expressive. Feels resourceful, optimistic, and flexible. Appears parental, responsible, and conventional. Strives for wisdom to counsel, teach, and encourage. Has practical intuitional gifts and magnetism to bring about recognition.

PERSONALITY EXTREME: Too businesslike, or too disorganized.

ELINOR (Greek: Helen/English)—F.

MAJOR TALENT: Ability to incorporate optimism, refined analysis, and inventive ideas into career. Is a loner or a joiner by mood. Has leadership, orginality, and courage. Combines communications, cleverness, and decision-making gifts. Can be a pacesetter. Telephone operator, manager, and designer are possible career opportunities.

PERSONALITY INGREDIENTS: Desires cooperative partnership/loving
mate. Feels supportive, sensitive, and perceptive of little things. First
impression is capable, sociable, and tailored. Is direct, to the point, and
organizing. Can combine business and personal relationships to advantage.
PERSONALITY EXTREME: Too romantic, or too cold.

ELISA ((Hebrew: Elizabeth/Italian/French/English)—F.

MAJOR TALENT: Ability to incorporate innovative ideas, daring, and
universal service into career. Is compassionate, independent, and managerial. Has vitality, faith, and intellectual curiosity. True independence
attracts honors, money, and happiness. Ecologist, charity administrator,
and all art forms are possible career opportunities.
PERSONALITY INGREDIENTS: Inwardly a self-starter. Is inconsistent,
mentally curious, and self-expressive. Appears to be helpful, broad-minded, and stimulating. Needs emotional control, freedom, and patience.
PERSONALITY EXTREME: Too aggressive, or too irresolute.

ELISABETH (Elizabeth/German/French/English)—F.

MAJOR TALENT: Ability to incorporate beauty, wisdom, and humanitarian service into career. Is empathetic, noble, and determined. Has
broad viewpoint, natural leadership, and amazing intuition. Assumes
burdens. Welfare worker, teacher, and doctor are possible career opportunities.
PERSONALITY INGREDIENTS: First impression is thoughtful, refined,
and quiet. Is socially insecure. Appears to be a loner. Inwardly wants
partnership, softness, and peace. Needs sensitive understanding, cultural stimulation, and self-confidence.
PERSONALITY EXTREME: Too materialistic, or too unproductive.

ELISE (Hebrew: Elizabeth/German/French/English)—F.

MAJOR TALENT: Ability to incorporate sharp observations, analysis,
and wit into career. Is entertaining, adaptable, and active. Has passion
for change, progress, and honesty. Enthusiastically exaggerates to promote, enlighten, or ease suffering. Advertising, politics, and communications are possible career opportunities.
PERSONALITY INGREDIENTS: Inwardly independent, ambitious, and
creatively broad-scoped. Needs liberty, innovations, and physical activity. Appears conventional, capable, and practical. Strives for respectability, security, and constructive life-style. Attracts love, family, and
material success.
PERSONALITY EXTREME: Too confident, or too unsure.

ELISHA (Hebrew/English)—M.

MAJOR TALENT: Ability to incorporate fertile mind, sensitivity to details, and broad-scoped self-expression into career. Is charitable, compassionate, and adaptable. Has intellectual, spiritual, and artistic gifts.
Original concepts need tangible outlets. Attracts supporters. Publishing,
chemistry, and judicial reform are possible career opportunities.
PERSONALITY INGREDIENTS: Is a communicator. Needs beauty, love,
and domestic harmony. Is companionable, attaining, and sensible. Ap-

pears attractive, entertaining, and optimistic. Strives for attention. Too hard on self.

PERSONALITY EXTREME: Too ambitious, or too lazy.

ELISSA (Hebrew: Elizabeth/English)—F.

MAJOR TALENT: Ability to incorporate sensitive temperament, detail analysis, and diplomatic touch into career. Is supportive, adaptable, and sees the pros and cons. Has a need to balance opposites and maintain cooperative atmosphere. Administrative assistant, group dancer/musician, and legislator are possible career opportunities.

PERSONALITY INGREDIENTS: First impression is outgoing, sexy, and adventurous. Inwardly needs family/community attainments, warmth, and roots. Is protective, comforting, and responsible. Appears unconventional, but is conservative.

PERSONALITY EXTREME: Too bossy, or too compromising.

ELIZA (Hebrew: Elizabeth/Danish/English)—F.

MAJOR TALENT: Ability to incorporate administrative organization, protective instincts, and adaptability into career. Is efficient, responsible, and strong-willed. Has ambition, outer-confidence, and desire for self-improvement. Promoter, school administrator, and public official are possible career opportunities.

PERSONALITY INGREDIENTS: Sparkles at first meeting. Is enticing, individualistic and perceptive. Inwardly needs family harmony, responsibility, and respectability. Is self-expressive, determined, and generous. Enjoys ambitions, touch sports, communications, and partnerships.

PERSONALITY EXTREME: Too impatient, or too slow-moving.

ELIZABETH (Hebrew/Scottish/Danish/English)—F.

MAJOR TALENT: Ability to incorporate communications, materialism, and intellectual analysis into career. Is culturally attaining, introspective, and practical. Has common sense, organizational awareness, and sense of justice. Teacher, technical expert, and investment counselor are possible career opportunities.

PERSONALITY INGREDIENTS: Has a way with people, clever observations, and unforgettable first impression. Inwardly wants sensitive mate, opportunity to share, and an easy-going life-style. Loyal, tolerant, and sympathetic nature. Knows when to keep silent, think, and persevere. Over-indulgences affect emotions, health, and mental capabilities. Needs moderation.

PERSONALITY EXTREME: Too ambitious, or too careless.

ELLA (Anglo-Saxon/English diminutive of *el/al* names)—F. & M.

MAJOR TALENT: Ability to incorporate innovations, resourcefulness, and self-expression into career. Is optimistic, independent, and sensitive. Has uncommon presence, philosophy, and wisdom. Martyrs while striving for approval. Clergy, lecturing, and all communications professions are possible career opportunities.

PERSONALITY INGREDIENTS: Is a giver. Displays good taste, comfortable style, and mature approach. Is understanding, comforting, and family oriented. Maintains high personal standards. May talk too much, dramatize, or avoid confrontations. Needs **sense of humor.**

PERSONALITY EXTREME: Too individualistic, **or too** conventional.

ELLAMAY (Hebrew-English)—F.

MAJOR TALENT: Ability to incorporate common sense, cooperation, and practical service into career. Is adaptable, generous, and organized. Has artistic appreciation, protective instincts, and imagination. Teaching, selling and servicing home products, and nursing are possible career opportunities.

PERSONALITY INGREDIENTS: Inwardly analytic, refined, and culturally attaining. Needs privacy, perfection, and intellectual stimulation. First impression is capable, careful, and businesslike. Strives for affluence, efficiency, and authority. Attracts family harmony, help from admirers, and success.

PERSONALITY EXTREME: Too questioning, or too gullible.

ELLEN (Greek: Helen/French: Elaine/English: Helen)—F.

MAJOR TALENT: Ability to incorporate self-expression with words, writing, or acting into career. Is creative, inspirational, and artistic. Likes to entertain, laugh, and raise spirits. Is extravagant and lucky. Model, receptionist, and hairdresser are possible career opportunities.

PERSONALITY INGREDIENTS: Always leaves an impression. Strives for personal ideals, is high-strung, and visionary. Needs attractive people, surroundings, and plans. Inwardly independent, ambitious, and intelligent. Attracts leadership, liberty, and change. Multifaceted, but must control impulsivity/impatience, and concentrate for success.

PERSONALITY EXTREME: Too free, or too tied down.

ELLERY (Teutonic/English)—M.

MAJOR TALENT: Ability to incorporate detailed perceptions, writing, and unconventional scheduling into career. Is investigative, progressive, and adaptable. Has sensitive understanding, artistic expression, and mental analysis. Loves adventure. Physical therapist, diplomatic courier, and gambler are possible career opportunities.

PERSONALITY INGREDIENTS: Desires authority, power, and affluence. Is fine judge of character. First impression is concerned, helpful, and respectable. Seems conservative, responsible, and steadfast. Persuasive, humorous, clever nature attracts success.

PERSONALITY EXTREME: Too shrewd, or too innocent.

ELLIE (Greek: Helen/English)—F.

MAJOR TALENT: Ability to incorporate reasoning mind, perfectionist nature, and scientific, technical, spiritual investigation into career. Is meant for professionalism, not manual or commercial focus. Has quality-conscious, logical, questioning nature. Photographer, educator, and all areas of expertise are possible career opportunities.

PERSONALITY INGREDIENTS: Inwardly dislikes taking orders. Desires freedom of speech, thought, and action. Strives for artistic surroundings, harmonious, warm, attaining life-style, and respect. Grows to be a wise counselor after overcoming personal obstacles.

PERSONALITY EXTREME: Too irresponsible, or too controlled.

ELLIN (Greek: Helen/Welsh/English)—F.

MAJOR TALENT: Ability to incorporate serious thinking, inventive techniques, and inspirational ideas into career. Is sensitive, analytic, and adventurous. Has fear of loneliness and poverty, but seeks introspective privacy. Spends thoughtlessly for quality. May be considered strange. Researcher, lawyer, and analyst are possible career opportunities.

PERSONALITY INGREDIENTS: Appears energetic, impulsive, and friendly. Has a way with people. Inwardly a dreamer. Is impractical, seeks peace and tolerance. Wants partnership, but needs solitude; tends to be an escapist.

PERSONALITY EXTREME: Too intense, or too lackadaisical.

ELLIOT (Hebrew: Elijah/French/English)—M.

MAJOR TALENT: Ability to incorporate fresh ideas, diplomacy, and desire for tangible results into career. Is ambitious, executive, and constructive. Has visionary creativity, inventive methods, and sound judgment. Attracts women, and improves with partnerships. Writer/agent/performer, repairman, and co-pilot are possible career opportunities.

PERSONALITY INGREDIENTS: First impression is businesslike, direct, and persuasive. Is inwardly receptive, balances opposites, and is emotionally sensitive. Feels things personally but appears controlled. Strives for the independence that power gives. Often contradicts, gets suspicious, and places trust in the wrong people.

PERSONALITY EXTREME: Too self-sacrificing, or too envious.

ELLIS (Hebrew: Elijah/English)—M.

MAJOR TALENT: Ability to incorporate communications, charm, and detail work into career. Is administrative, creative, and adaptable. Has artistic expression, individuality, and inspiration. Succeeds through change and renewal. Gossip columnist, animal trainer, and any art form are possible career opportunities.

PERSONALITY INGREDIENTS: Inwardly charitable, compassionate, and broad-minded. Is romantic, impressionable, and dramatic. Appears sunny, friendly, and imaginative. Admires beauty, humor, and extravagances. Must balance personal ambitions and responsibilities.

PERSONALITY EXTREME: Too demanding, or too disinterested.

ELMER (Anglo-Saxon/English)—M.

MAJOR TALENT: Ability to incorporate good judgment, material power, and organizational approach into career. Is persuasive, expansive, and strong. Has communications skills, studies, and pays attention to details. Likes outdoor sports, efficiency, and appears self-confident. Government, manufacturing, and college administration are possible career opportunities.

PERSONALITY INGREDIENTS: First impression is false. Must be known to be loved/understood. Feels ambitious, courageous, and strives for perfection. Needs independence, innovations, and to be boss. May seem aloof, but opens up when personal area of expertise/interest comes up. Must gain confidence. Self-improvement courses, money, and authority in one area builds inner-security.

PERSONALITY EXTREME: Too understanding, or too intolerant.

ELMIRA (Anglo-Saxon/French/English)—F.

MAJOR TALENT: Ability to incorporate stability, hard work, and common sense into career. Is dramatic, independent, and determined. Has system, administrative ideas, and positive attitude. Civil service, accounting, and building trades are possible career opportunities.

PERSONALITY INGREDIENTS: Inwardly very determined, protective, and responsible to family/community. Has good memory, discipline, and ambition. First impression is subdued. Strives for culture, refinement, and perfection. May lack polish/academic credentials/social self-confidence. Extremely competitive. Loner appearance should be tempered with cooperative, diplomatic, and more relaxed approach.

PERSONALITY EXTREME: Too arrogant, or too humble.

ELMO (Italian-Greek: Erasmus)—M.

MAJOR TALENT: Ability to incorporate efficient organization, individuality, and empathetic service into career. Is active, imaginative, and emotional. Has humanitarian instincts. Inner vitality causes physical strain. Must maintain health regimen. Often develops concepts while dreaming. Never inactive. Medicine, law, and art/theater are possible career opportunities.

PERSONALITY INGREDIENTS: Inwardly idealistic, high strung, and sensitive. Appears unruffled. Strives for dignity, culture, and perfection in all things. Prefers not to get hands dirty.

PERSONALITY EXTREME: Too protective, or too irresponsible.

ELOISE (Latin: Louise/English)—F.

MAJOR TALENT: Ability to incorporate inspiration, idealism, and intuition over intellect into career. Is visionary, special, and a dreamer. Has futuristic, often zany, ideas that when put in the hands of a practical partner come to reality. High strung, emotional, and belongs in the limelight. Advertising, theatrical promoting, and any film-oriented industry are possible career opportunities.

PERSONALITY INGREDIENTS: Could be an accountant, or a universally respected economic reformer. May become famous and should aim high. Asks questions and wants to know the why of everything; investigates, and analyzes. Needs culture, dignity, and refinement. Appears conventional, practical, and materially inclined. Don't judge this name by its neat first impression.

PERSONALITY EXTREME: Too quick, or too slow.

ELROY (Latin/Old French)—M.

MAJOR TALENT: Ability to incorporate broad-scoped, cultivated, communication skills into career. Is a perfecting artist in any line. Has orderly mind, attracts attention, and aims for conventional living. Has sex appeal, charm, and entertaining style. Opera, literature, and science are possible career opportunities.

PERSONALITY INGREDIENTS: Strives to be first. Pioneers, takes the initiative, and appears unique. Inwardly leads in spiritual/inspirational ways. Feels special. Needs loving partner and the limelight. May abuse sexual attraction, scatter energy, and bog down in petty emotions if pessimistic. Must aim for crowds, sunshine, and applause.

PERSONALITY EXTREME: Too serious, or too shallow.

ELSA (Teutonic: Elsie/diminutive: Alice/Elizabeth)—F.

MAJOR TALENT: Ability to incorporate into career unclouded perceptions, productive leadership, and intuitional grasp of mass needs, feelings, futuristic desires. Is an original. Has courage, ambition, and resourcefulness. Theatrical producer, sales manager, and automotive designer are possible career opportunities.

PERSONALITY INGREDIENTS: Inwardly family/community focused. Needs love, roots, and material attainments. Appears solid, respectable, and conventional. Strives for security, feels protective, and gives wise counsel. Needs to be decisive, firm and self-controlled.

PERSONALITY EXTREME: Too impatient, or too accommodating.

ELSBETH (Hebrew: Elizabeth/Swiss/English)—F.

MAJOR TALENT: Ability to incorporate strength, self-sufficiency, and business/money focus into career. Is ambitious, responsible, and a keen judge of character. Has impartiality, sociability, and physical coordination. Communications, arbitration, and all executive positions are possible career opportunities.

PERSONALITY INGREDIENTS: May appear stuck-up/aloof/mysterious at first meeting. Must be known to be understood. Inwardly determined, original, and individualistic. Is a planner. Needs concentration, self-control, and a strong mate.

PERSONALITY EXTREME: Too confident, or too uncertain.

ELSIE (Teutonic/diminutive: Alice-Elizabeth-Elsa/English)—F.

MAJOR TALENT: Ability to incorporate sensitivity, charm, and versatility into career. Is promotional, sensual, and has a way with people. Specializes in ideas for tangible results. Progresses through changes, adventure, and gift of human understanding. Advertising, politics, and investigative professions are possible career opportunities.

PERSONALITY INGREDIENTS: Inwardly needs courage to be the pace setter. Feels capable of overcoming any obstacles. Appears clean cut, solid, and conservative. Strives for conventional, respected, materially attaining life-style. Hides any unconventional activities until true independent nature grows to maturity. Must stop making comparisons and experience own destiny.

PERSONALITY EXTREME: Too impulsive, or too controlled.

ELTON (Old English)—M.

MAJOR TALENT: Ability to incorporate creative energy, adaptability, and communications skills into career. Is sensitive to little things. Has independence, ambition, and individuality. Finds silver linings everywhere. Writing, entertaining, and fashion are possible career opportunities.

PERSONALITY INGREDIENTS: Inwardly expansive, emotional, and romantic. Ignores limitations. Has good memory, enjoys variety, and attracts admiration. Appears sunny, entertaining, and expressive. May have a cross to bear but has a special decision making wisdom, gives and gets protection, and enjoys unique artistic gift.

PERSONALITY EXTREME: Too impulsive, or too unchanging.

ELVINA (Old English)—F.

MAJOR TALENT: Ability to incorporate impersonal service, romantic ideals, and artistic creativity into career. Is generous, compassionate, and culturally attaining. Has humanitarian instincts, magnetism, and extreme desire for self-perfection. Expects the best. Legislator, artist, and welfare worker are possible career opportunities.

PERSONALITY INGREDIENTS: First impression is friendly, sociable, and stylish. Strives for optimism, beauty, and humor. Inwardly loves comfort. Is parental, centered on family, and helpful. May give more than is received.

PERSONALITY EXTREME: Too innovative, or too traditional.

ELVIRA (Latin: Albinia/Italian/English)—F.

MAJOR TALENT: Ability to incorporate independence, positive approach, and practicality into career. Is ambitious. Works, plans, and economizes for tangible results. Highly competitive. Tenacious worker. Skilled crafts person, office administrator, and dentist are possible career opportunities.

PERSONALITY INGREDIENTS: May not shine socially. Strives for quality life-style. Appears cool, feels warm. Needs harmonious, gracious, respected home. Should cultivate softer approach, concentrate on a specialty, and enjoy the pleasures of the moment. Is hyper-active from ages nine to twelve, broadens scope, and makes major change at thirty-one. Learns that life begins at forty.

PERSONALITY EXTREME: Too bossy, or too submissive.

ELWIN (Anglo-Saxon/variant: Alvin/English)—M.

MAJOR TALENT: Ability to incorporate cooperation, intellectual analysis, and wide-scoped vision into career. Is unassuming, problem solving, and influential. Has originality, refinement, and quality. Public service, all artistic professions, and medicine are possible career opportunities.

PERSONALITY INGREDIENTS: Inwardly lively, but appears conservative. Feels adventurous, experimental and sensual. First impression is solid, dignified, and practical. Sparks progress. Attracts rewards.

PERSONALITY EXTREME: Too expectant, or too pessimistic.

ELY (English variant Hebrew: Eli)—M.

MAJOR TALENT: Ability to incorporate aptitude for learning, strong judgments, and service to others into career. Has ambition, determination, and high standards. Attracts feasts or famines. Teaching, vocal training, and interior design are possible career opportunities.

PERSONALITY INGREDIENTS: May overwork, connive, or seduce for appearances. Learns quickly, prospers from another's mistakes and must decide at some point in life, whether it is better to strive for tangibles or enjoy experiencing freedom of choice. Must look beneath the surface of commitments, and use care before signing away precious time for money. Takes things too seriously. Must loosen up.

PERSONALITY EXTREME: Too cunning, or too gullible.

ELYCE (Hebrew: Elizabeth/English)—F.

MAJOR TALENT: Ability to incorporate enthusiasm, mental curiosity, and friendliness into career. Is changeable, up-to-date, and adventurous. Has sex appeal, winning manner, and impulsive nature. Combines sensitivity to detail, communications gifts, and free spirit. Advertising, theater, and politics are possible career opportunities.

PERSONALITY INGREDIENTS: First impression is out of this world.

Seems dreamy, mystical, and inventive. Strives for idealistic reform, spiritual uplift, and lasting innovative conceptual improvements. Inwardly optimistic, clever, and artistically/scientifically self-expressive. Likes to talk, and is congenial. Desires beauty, popularity, and to enjoy living. Makes a game of life, but has the ambition to inspire through farsighted, sometimes impractical, invention. At best channeled in nonmanual, creative, attention-getting work. When negative, is temperamental, selfish, and patronizing. Attracts rewards for ideas, inheritances, and passionate/dedicated marriage/partnerships.

PERSONALITY EXTREME: Too experimental, or too cautious.

ELYSE (Hebrew: Elizabeth/English)—F.

MAJOR TALENT: Ability to incorporate originality, adaptability, and self-expression into career. Is optimistic, talkative, and determined. Not always practical. Has agile mind, extraordinary imagination, and social consciousness. Social secretary, beautician, and entertainer are possible career opportunities.

PERSONALITY INGREDIENTS: Inwardly wants influence, affluence, and respectability. Appears conventional, sturdy, and trustworthy. Combines creativity and common sense.

PERSONALITY EXTREME: Too impromptu, or too preresolved.

ELYSIA (Greek/English)—F.

MAJOR TALENT: Ability to incorporate ambition, communication gifts, and physical fitness focus into career. Is efficient, articulate, and perceptive of details. Geared for self-improvement, financial judgment, and maintaining self-confident facade. Orchestra leader/arranger, C.P.A., and consultant are possible career opportunities.

PERSONALITY INGREDIENTS: Wants to work for peace and prosperity. Applies common sense, organization, and administration to everything. Gets things done. Appears solid, tasteful, and capable. Must control impulses and persevere.

PERSONALITY EXTREME: Too courageous, or too fearful.

EMERY (Old German/Anglo-Saxon: Amalric/French/English)—M.

MAJOR TALENT: Ability to incorporate quality communication skills into career. Is organized and practical in an imaginative, expressive, skillful interest. Tackles big projects, attracts applause, and releases energy through mental and physical travel. Lecturer, transportation promoter, and editor are possible career opportunities.

PERSONALITY INGREDIENTS: Desires commercial/business success. Feels organized, efficient, and authoritative. Appears solid, practical, and dependable. Should avoid speculation and take conventional course.

PERSONALITY EXTREME: Too perfecting, or too careless.

EMIL (Gothic/Teutonic/English)—M.

MAJOR TALENT: Ability to incorporate sensitivity to details, self-expression, and creative independence into career. Is structured, adaptable, and charming. Has sense of timing, ambition, and love of beauty. Sharp observations couple with super-imagination. Writer, diplomat, and entertainer are possible career opportunities.

PERSONALITY INGREDIENTS: Inwardly sensual, experimental, and progressive. Understands people. Appears dignified, poised, and unflap-

pable. Strives for quality, quietude, and perfection. May have fear of
loneliness and poverty. Has escapist tendencies.

PERSONALITY EXTREME: Too attention-getting, or too unsociable.

EMILE (Teutonic/French)—M.

MAJOR TALENT: Ability to incorporate physical and mental agility,
communications, and learning from observation into career. Is expressive, strong-willed, and protective. Assumes responsibility with a
confident air. May be a tiger or a lamb. Music publisher, football coach,
and manufacturer are possible career opportunities.

PERSONALITY INGREDIENTS: Inwardly ambitious, individualistic, and
strong. Leaves the details to others. Appears authoritative, aloof, and
intellectual. Strives for refinement, perfection, and inspirational relationships. Attracted to mystery, innovations, and affluence.

PERSONALITY EXTREME: Too sensual, or too mental.

EMILIA (Teutonic: Emil, M./Italian/English)—F.

MAJOR TALENT: Ability to incorporate charm, originality, and down-
to-earth judgments into career. Is ambitious, energetic, and determined.
Has independent, questioning, and assertive approach. Wants to win.
Real estate sales person, manager, and nurse are possible career opportunities.

PERSONALITY INGREDIENTS: Needs family ties, abundance, and position. Is responsible, protective, and generous. Appears controlled.
Strives for perfection, intellectual stimulation, and cultural growth. Impatient with phonies. Should focus upon diplomatic touch, organization
of goals, and practical research to speed success and happiness.

PERSONALITY EXTREME: Too aggressive, or too exhausted.

EMILY (Gothic/Teutonic: Emil, M./English)—F.

MAJOR TALENT: Ability to incorporate good judgment, adaptability,
and originality into career. Is resourceful, persuasive, and courageous.
Has an inventive mind. Organizes, inspires, and attracts men. Excels as
group leader. Designer, psychiatrist, and idea person are possible career
opportunities.

PERSONALITY INGREDIENTS: Inwardly hopeful, passionate, and fun-
loving. Feels emotional, generous, and extravagant. Appears refined,
cool, and graceful. Strives for poise, position, and quality life-style.
Keen mind, dramatic nature, and proud spirit.

PERSONALITY EXTREME: Too authoritative, or too intellectually insecure.

EMLYN (Teutonic: Emil, M./Gothic: Emily, F./English variant)—
F. & M.

MAJOR TALENT: Ability to incorporate detailed perceptions, practical
organization, and instructive communication skills into career. Influences others, loves pleasure, and has parental attitudes. Gives and
needs harmonious, gracious, and loving family/community life-style.
Musician, teacher, and marriage counselor are possible career opportunities.

PERSONALITY INGREDIENTS: Is extravagant, optimistic, and artistic.
Inspires and needs beauty, wit, and up-to-date fads and fashions. Is

charm personified. May scatter interests, gossip, or be temperamental. Attracts financial and social success.

PERSONALITY EXTREME: Too eccentric, or too conventional.

EMMA (Teutonic/independent-variant: Emily/French/Italian/German/ English)—F.

MAJOR TALENT: Ability to incorporate clever observations, practical analysis, and independent learning by experience into career. May overload easily. Is capable, resourceful, and has an understanding way with people. Is progressive, inventive, and incautious. Grows wise, and stays youthful. Travel agent, politician, and pilot are possible career opportunities.

PERSONALITY INGREDIENTS: Finds conventional routines boring. Is exposed to down-to-earth experiences. Needs to adapt desires to reality. Strives for the freedom that money and power can buy. Looks efficient, authoritative, and as affluent as possible. Inwardly family rooted. Assumes responsibility, protects, and inspires gracious home life. Intensifies physical activity until lessons are learned.

PERSONALITY EXTREME: Too active, or too lazy.

EMMANUEL (Hebrew/French/English)—M.

MAJOR TALENT: Ability to incorporate creative and artistic self-expression into career. Is imaginative, good humored, and entertaining. Tends to live conventionally, but strives for uniqueness in work, dramatic impression, and to make the best of everything. Gains through social relationships. Fashion, writing, and performing arts are possible career opportunities.

PERSONALITY INGREDIENTS: Inwardly progressive, sensual, and investigative. Has sex appeal. Understands people. First impression is reserved, refined, and a bit mysterious. Strives for perfection. Impulsive gestures scatter efforts, money, and loves.

PERSONALITY EXTREME: Too optimistic, or too pessimistic.

EMMET (Middle English/English)—M.

MAJOR TALENT: Ability to incorporate sensitivity to detail, group adaptability, and a modest approach into career. Doesn't need to be up front; has no need for display. Prefers an easy-going routine. Has refinement, tender emotions, and exerts subtle control. Quality artisian, dietitian, and any service job are possible career opportunities.

PERSONALITY INGREDIENTS: Influences, masters, and brings people together through tactful arbitration, and respected individualism. Has faith, creativity, and the courage to support untried ventures. Appears to be and is, an original.

PERSONALITY EXTREME: Too burden-bearing, or too uncooperative.

ENGELBERT (Greek/German)—M.

MAJOR TALENT: Ability to incorporate dependability, determination, and skilled work into career. Is practical, artistically imaginative, and secretively analytic. Has refinement, communication gifts, and a need for authority and perfection. Understands the power of silence, privacy, and quality. Lecturer, architect, and appraiser are possible career opportunities.

PERSONALITY INGREDIENTS: Inwardly authoritative, sensual, and a cosmic parent. Wants domesticity, stability, and respectability. First impression is easy-going, affluent, and individualistic. Strives for originality, is an instigator, and pace setter. Is a gentle, sympathetic, loyal friend. Never does things halfway. May overindulge in fun, foods, and females.
PERSONALITY EXTREME: Too petty, or too superior.

ENID (Celtic/English)—F.
MAJOR TALENT: Ability to incorporate adaptability, self-expression, and mental curiosity into career. Is understanding, clever, and progressive. May inherit money or power. Has intellectual/physical skills and a passionate nature. Politics, investigative professions, and advertising are possible career opportunities.
PERSONALITY INGREDIENTS: First impression is classic, noble, and empathetic. Strives for romance, artistic expression, and humanitarian service. Inwardly is adventurous. Wants constructive changes, and gains from varied experiences. Learns easily and is an idea person.
PERSONALITY EXTREME: Too structured, or too unconventional.

ENRICO (Old German: Henry/Italian)—M.
MAJOR TALENT: Ability to incorporate intellectual/spiritual concentration, self-expression, and individuality into career. Is reserved, controlled, and internally extravagantly emotional. Has strong ties to home/family, desires cultural and financial success, and finds travel/foreign lands advantageous and interesting. Inventor, designer, and individual musical/artistic/acting jobs are possible career opportunities.
PERSONALITY INGREDIENTS: Inwardly loving, sensitive, and orderly. Likes control, and may judge by appearances. First impression is authoritative, successful, and self-reliant. Strives for refinement, quality, and respect. Can be cunning, jealous, and bullying if negative. Attracts prominence when friendly, cooperative, and expansive.
PERSONALITY EXTREME: Too protective, or too detached.

EPHRAIM (Hebrew/Greek/Late Latin/English)—M.
MAJOR TALENT: Ability to incorporate practical hard-work, expressiveness, and introspective analysis into career. Has technical, scientific, spiritual gifts. Enjoys quietude, accuracy, and variety. Thinker, doer, and communicator. University administrator, auditor, and historian are possible career opportunities.
PERSONALITY INGREDIENTS: First impression is energetic, creative, and individualistic. Strives to be authoritative, pioneering, and in control. Assumes burdens for family/community. Feels protective, attaining, and determined to raise standards. Is articulate, constructive, and knows the importance of silence.
PERSONALITY EXTREME: Too rigid, or too self-indulgent.

ERASMUS (Greek/German/Danish/Dutch/English)—M.
MAJOR TALENT: Ability to incorporate studiousness, endurance, and counseling into career. Is practical, harmonious, and just. Has charm, friendliness, and pride. Attracts respect, luck with women, and fruitful family relationships. School administration, union shop steward, and economist are possible career opportunities.

PERSONALITY INGREDIENTS: First impression is comfortable, comforting, and sympathetic. May be overweight, but dresses neatly. Feels like big brother to the world. Is empathetic, artistic, and philanthropic. Enjoys romance, drama, and material comforts. Must avoid being too protective and smothering loved ones.

PERSONALITY EXTREME: Too impatient, or too placid.

ERIC (Scandinavian/French/English)—M.

MAJOR TALENT: Ability to incorporate method, speaking, and uplifting advice into career. Is instructive, artistic, and responsible. Has keen mind, efficient attitudes, and imagination for business success. Combines adaptability, inner strength, and an aura of self-confidence. Executive, athlete, and commentator are possible career opportunities.

PERSONALITY INGREDIENTS: Has interesting voice, attraction for powerful people, and focus upon justice. Feels sensual, experimental, and loyal. Appears attractive, congenial, and expressive. Must be patient, persevering, and emotionally controlled. Profits from continued education.

PERSONALITY EXTREME: Too "on stage", or too uncommunicative.

ERICA (Old Norse: Eric, M./English)—F.

MAJOR TALENT: Ability to incorporate artistic ability, empathy, and charm into career. Is emotional, culturally attaining, and broad-scoped. Assumes leadership through perceptive philosophy, analytic approach, and sensitivity to details. Has magnetism and attracts influential boosters. Recognition possible when disciplined to specific purpose. Lawmaker, communications expert, and artist are possible career opportunities.

PERSONALITY INGREDIENTS: Wants to make a game out of life. Is conversational, up-to-date, and creatively expressive. First impression is sensible, interested, and carefully attired. Strives to be helpful. Expects the best from self and others. Should be tolerant.

PERSONALITY EXTREME: Too innovative, or too structured.

ERIK (Scandinavian: Eric/Danish/Swedish/English)—M.

MAJOR TALENT: Ability to incorporate progressive ideas, recall for details, and technical/scientific/spiritual research into career. Is introspective, factual, and refined. Seeks perfection, peaceful working atmosphere, and expertise. Photographer, writer, and psychoanalyst are possible career opportunities.

PERSONALITY INGREDIENTS: Childhood experiences affect mature judgments. Learns to depend upon self. First impression is unique. Strives for recognition, idealistic beliefs, and exotic interests. Inwardly sexy, free, and inquiring. Needs stimulating people, travels, and challenges. Not conventional, dull, or mundane. Thrives upon mental/physical/emotional activity.

PERSONALITY EXTREME: Too zealous, or too aimless.

ERIKA (Old Norse: Erik, M./Swedish)—F.

MAJOR TALENT: Ability to incorporate confident air, physical agility, and efficient organizational skills into career. Is receptive, sensitive, and helpful. Has firmness, sympathy, and encourages harmony. Strives for self-improvement. Columnist, purchasing agent, and business consultant are possible career opportunities.

PERSONALITY INGREDIENTS: Needs people, interaction, and idealistic self-expression. Feels protective, home-loving, and expansive. Is attaining, and appears refined, tasteful and uncommon. Has a far-away/high energy/visionary quality at first meeting. Extremely perceptive, imaginative, and loving.

PERSONALITY EXTREME: Too rebellious, or too weak.

ERIN (Irish/English)—F.

MAJOR TALENT: Ability to incorporate progressive leadership, clear judgment, and bold resourcefulness into career. Is adaptable, cooperative, and efficient. Has honest approach. Patience brings material success. Quality manufacturer, illustrator, and diplomat are possible career opportunities.

PERSONALITY INGREDIENTS: First impression is energetic, fashionable, and sexy. Has humor, versatility, and adventurous nature. Wants travel, human interest experiences, and to relate to all people. Has human understanding of a special quality. Must rein impulsivity.

PERSONALITY EXTREME: Too restless, or too restricted.

ERLE (Anglo-Saxon: Earl/Old Norse: Erling/English variant)—M.

MAJOR TALENT: Ability to incorporate highly developed intuition, organizational skill, constructive analysis and conclusive results into career. Is a master builder with vision to coordinate practical goals. Has understanding of human nature and may serve humanity. Workaholic nervous energy can be directed for positive or negative ends. This name offers power. Building trades, government, and professional work are possible career opportunities.

PERSONALITY INGREDIENTS: Strives for clear communication, tolerance for divergent beliefs, and optimistic reconstruction. Appears attractive, imaginative, and sociable. Likes to be in control, handling major issues, and to be proud of family/community relationships. Is individualistic, creative, and innovative. Must aim high.

PERSONALITY EXTREME: Too quick, or too procrastinating.

ERMA (Old German: Armina/English)—F.

MAJOR TALENT: Ability to incorporate personal magnetism, artistic/humanitarian self-expression, and generous philosophy into career. Is individualistic, innovative, and bold. Has understanding, ambition, and desire for broad marketplaces. Succeeds through courage to maintain inventive independence. Idea person, buyer, and business owner are possible career opportunities.

PERSONALITY INGREDIENTS: Inwardly parental, trustworthy, and interested. Likes to give advice. Needs harmonious, secure, gracious home. Appears solid, capable, and conventional. Strives for respectability, orderliness, and discipline. Enjoys the simple pleasures.

PERSONALITY EXTREME: Too bossy, or too submissive.

ERNA (Old German: Ernestine/English: nickname & alone)—F.

MAJOR TALENT: Ability to incorporate subtle manipulating, arbitration techniques, and adaptability into career. Is sensitive, friendly, and conscious of details. Best with partners. Is a collector/gatherer/assimilator.

Must ingest/digest before acting. Librarian, secretary, and data processing programmer are possible career opportunities.

PERSONALITY INGREDIENTS: Appears exciting, adventurous, and clever. Strives for multi-interests, travel, and experimentation. Inwardly needs security. Wants harmonious, beautiful, abundant home and lifestyle. Needs to be needed.

PERSONALITY EXTREME: Too hasty, or too hesitant.

ERNEST (Teutonic/German/French/English)—M.

MAJOR TALENT: Ability to incorporate concern for the comfort, welfare, and pleasure of others into career. Is perceptive of details, technical, and logical. Has empathy, compassion, and broad philosophy. Tuned to emotional, practical, and spiritual/intellectual awareness. Creative ideas motivate others to give financial and moral support. Bartender, doctor, and artist/musician/performer are possible career opportunities.

PERSONALITY INGREDIENTS: Wants to be in control. Feels independent, instigative, and courageous. First impression is businesslike. Attracts power people and has the mental endurance to meet difficulties. Must reach out to the world. Personalized small ideals/goals create a hard life.

PERSONALITY EXTREME: Too burden-bearing, or too insensitive.

ERNESTINE (Old German: Ernest, M./German/English)—F.

MAJOR TALENT: Ability to incorporate uplifting personal standards, performance, and authoritative leadership into career. Is charming, persevering, and protective. Gives emotional, practical, and spiritual support with the purest motives. May be naive, trusting, and unaware of the envy of others. Attracts financial, emotional, and intellectual security. Inventor, explorer, and any independent creative interest are possible career opportunities.

PERSONALITY INGREDIENTS: First impression is organized, directed, and conservative. Inwardly desires material comforts, enlightening people/experiences, and a loving mate and family. Is intense at work or play. Gains from inheritance, past experiences, and unique personality. Wants center stage and usually gets applause.

PERSONALITY EXTREME: Too involved, or too alone.

ERROL (Latin/Anglo-Saxon: Earl/variable/English variant of Earl)—M.

MAJOR TALENT: Ability to incorporate the gift of evoking emotional response from others into career. Is an adaptable, adventurous, progressive communicator. Has a sense of duty, human understanding, and mobility. Always in action, confident, and charming. May gamble, but generally tries to keep a conventional pattern. Politician, foreign correspondent, and marine radio operator are possible career opportunities.

PERSONALITY INGREDIENTS: Strives to be special. Feels dynamic energy. Needs a cause. First impression is optimistic, entertaining, and attractive. Likes fashion, beauty, and what some may consider trivia. Should enjoy life's pleasures and not try to become mundane. Is a born opportunist.

PERSONALITY EXTREME: Too cowardly, or too brave.

ERVIN (Anglo-Saxon/variant: Erwin)—M.

MAJOR TALENT: Ability to incorporate perception of details, artistic self-expression, and clever ideas into career. Is adaptable, entertaining, and attractive. Has understanding, love of travel/adventure/sensual pleasure, and investigative instincts. Song writer, airline steward, and legislator are possible career opportunities.

PERSONALITY INGREDIENTS: Desires to be free to touch, taste, smell, feel, and hear all that life has to offer. Charming manner attracts supporters for promotions. First impression is cosmopolitan, noble, and empathetic. Appears polished, cultural, and conforming to fashion in a conventional way. May be too modest or too confident. Always in motion.

PERSONALITY EXTREME: Too established, or too changeable.

ERWIN (Anglo-Saxon/English)—M.

MAJOR TALENT: Ability to incorporate helpfulness, compassion, and strong will into career. Bases everything on personal/universal love. Is inspired to assume parental role, burdens, or beautification for the good of others. When fired to perform universal service, geared for recognition. When family oriented, creates a protected life-style. Instructor, counselor, and nursing home administrator are possible career opportunities.

PERSONALITY INGREDIENTS: Desires travel, excitement, and sensual pleasure. Feels impatient, progressive, and energetic. First impression is determined, individualistic, and independent. Seems broad-scoped, empathetic, and self-advancing. Must avoid sacrificing emotional stability for devotion to responsibilities.

PERSONALITY EXTREME: Too immediate, or too futuristic.

ERWINA (Anglo-Saxon: Erwin-Irwin, M./English)—F.

MAJOR TALENT: Ability to incorporate communications, common sense practicality, and intellectual analysis into career. Is charming, honest, and culturally attaining. Has direct approach, investigative instincts, and artistic self-expression. Writer, antique dealer, and lawyer are possible career opportunities.

PERSONALITY INGREDIENTS: Desires love, comfort, and security. Needs to feel needed, rooted, and involved in a gracious life-style. First impression is independent, original, and positive. Enjoys wit, authority, and respect. Must avoid extravagances, unconventional behavior, and selfish cunning. Should be physically, mentally, and spiritually tuned.

PERSONALITY EXTREME: Too blunt, or too inoffensive.

ESAU (Hebrew)—M.

MAJOR TALENT: Ability to incorporate instigation, originality, and positive leadership into career. Is courageous, inventive, and has faith. Wants things now. Brings forceful attitude to unique projects. Upgrades for future use. Designer, architect, and position that is self-directed are possible career opportunities.

PERSONALITY INGREDIENTS: Desires wide horizons, compassion for all, and the quality of beauty, expression, and technique. Is romantic, intuitive, and emotionally dramatic. Appears different; is an original. Is stimulated, fast moving, and self-starting. Dislikes being told how to do things. May feel emotional, but succeeds when decisions are based upon fact.

PERSONALITY EXTREME: Too inferior, or too superior.

ESMERELDA (Hebrew/Spanish/English)—F.

MAJOR TALENT: Ability to incorporate good taste, desire for perfection, and individuality into career. Is attractive, questioning, and imaginative. Has high aspirations, initiative, and a desire to be different. Calm exterior, love relationships, and foreign travel aid success. Inspector, sales person, and writer are possible career opportunities.

PERSONALITY INGREDIENTS: Keeps a secret self. Fears loneliness, poverty, and showing ignorance. Must concentrate upon a specialty to form authority which inspires self-confidence. First impression is friendly, expressive, and sunny. Has strong family allegiances.

PERSONALITY EXTREME: Too ambitious, or too lazy.

ESTELLE (Persian: Esther/French/English)—F.

MAJOR TALENT: Ability to incorporate detail, order, system, work, responsibility, and protection . . . and an artistic, ambitious, strong-willed temperament into career. Basically, a "cosmic parent" whose common sense, diplomatic touch, and love of life attract financial, family, and creative attainment. May have personal, and universal love through sympathetic, helpful, intuitive nature. Marriage counselor, actors' agent, and home beautification specialist are possible career opportunities.

PERSONALITY INGREDIENTS: Appears compassionate, noble, and gracious. Seems understanding, independent, and broad-scoped. Desires secure, respectable, attaining life-style. Needs harmonious, creative, and comfortable home. Relationships govern the happiness and success of this name.

PERSONALITY EXTREME: Too impulsive, or too calculating.

ESTES (Latin/Italian family name: Este)—M.

MAJOR TALENT: Ability to incorporate originality, common sense practicality, and progressive thinking into career. Is exacting, dependable, and stands alone when necessary. Keen judge of human nature, adaptable, and understanding. Enjoys travel, freedom and the company of the opposite sex. Lawyer, geographer, and politician are possible career opportunities.

PERSONALITY INGREDIENTS: First impression is conservative, trustworthy, and neat. Slow, sure, and definite approach. Desires to be aggressive, forceful, and in control. Vitality may be spent in over-work and sexual variety which causes problems at home and in career. Caution, patience, and mental analysis further ambitions.

PERSONALITY EXTREME: Too energetic, or too worn-thin.

ESTHER (Persian/Hebrew/Latin: Stella/German/English)—F.

MAJOR TALENT: Ability to incorporate self-expression with words, congeniality, and imagination into career. Has emotional associations, may flirt, and enjoys humor. Works well with children, animals, and men/women. Generally optimistic, seeking quality, and capable of large assignments. Dressmaker/designer, lawyer, and artist/musician/performer are possible career opportunities.

PERSONALITY INGREDIENTS: First impression is refined, unimposing, and gracious. Seems cooperative, adaptable, and serving. Desires independence, family pride, and to be boss. Dislikes detail work, inactivity,

and to be embarrassed. Feels determined, and wants to get things started
and keep them moving.

PERSONALITY EXTREME: Too generous, or too self-centered.

ETHAN (Hebrew/Latin/English)—M.

MAJOR TALENT: Ability to incorporate beauty, utility, and innovation
into career. Is imaginative, attentive to details, and courageous. Strives
to be first, authoritative, and to tell the world. Is extravagant, articulate,
and witty. Combines artistic self-expression, visionary professionalism,
and inspirations that serve a mass need. Writing, acting, and crafts are
possible career opportunities.

PERSONALITY INGREDIENTS: Desires to benefit home, family, and community. Protects, advises, and sympathizes while building for respectability, security, and gracious life-style. Understands people, and
attracts financial and moral support.

PERSONALITY EXTREME: Too experimental, or too provincial.

ETHEL (Anglo-Saxon/Old German: Athele, Adela, Elsie/English)—F.

MAJOR TALENT: Ability to incorporate clever, quick, retentive mental
analysis, imagination, and sensitivity to details into career. Is cooperative, agile, and on-the-go. Has progressive ideas, communications gifts,
and attraction for admirers who help to further ambitions. Confident,
understanding, congenial style adds to this expressive name. Advertising, science, and theater are possible career opportunities.

PERSONALITY INGREDIENTS: First impression is conventional, neat
and routined. Desires creative action, individual recognition, and intellectual stimulation. Is physically tuned, artistically skilled, and usually
lucky. Must maintain self-confidence and concentration.

PERSONALITY EXTREME: Too socially insecure, or too attention-
getting.

ETTA (Teutonic: variant-diminutive/English: alone)—F.

MAJOR TALENT: Ability to incorporate leadership, determination, and
instigation of creative ideas into career. Is courageous, fast to act, and
prefers not to be told how/when/why to do things. Self-disciplined. May
select to be introvert or extrovert. Sales, service, or entertainment fields
in managerial positions are possible career opportunities.

PERSONALITY INGREDIENTS: Conventional outlook. Desires abundant,
beautiful, growing homelife. Wants to provide and enjoy family/
community security. First impression is capable, practical, and down-to-
earth. No-nonsense person, has realistic style. Must learn to relax with
progressive changes.

PERSONALITY EXTREME: Too controlling, or too submissive.

EUGENE (Greek/French/English)—M.

MAJOR TALENT: Ability to incorporate polished, imaginative, systematized skills/techniques into career. Strives for classic perfection. Is
philosophical, intelligent, and clever with words, music, and impersonat-
ing. Takes the actor to the thespian. Surgeon, professor, and bishop are
possible career opportunities.

PERSONALITY INGREDIENTS: Desires to reach a universal audience or
need. Feels empathetic, gracious, and charitable. Has deep and fluctuating emotions. Appears carefully attired, accessorized, and agreeable.

Imaginative, charming, and optimistic door-opener attracts people who
want multi-faceted companionship. Has sex appeal, high ideals, and romantic nature. Security depends upon following a conventional course.
PERSONALITY EXTREME: Too self-indulgent, or too disciplined.

EUGENIA (Greek: Eugene, M./German/Italian/Spanish/English)—F.

MAJOR TALENT: Ability to incorporate businesslike nature, imagination, and nonroutined scheduling into career. Prefers to get right to the
problem, sees variable solutions, decides on one, and follows efficient
course of action to bring tangible results. Has inherited authority,
money, or status. Is a persuasive, vital, and sociable leader. May need to
learn to control personal desire for freedom. Newspaper executive, business analyst, and real estate investor are possible career opportunities.
PERSONALITY INGREDIENTS: Desires to be free to experience the five
senses. Needs people, intellectual stimulation, and physical pleasure.
First impression is friendly, entertaining, and good humored. Resourceful attitude changes disappointments to successes. Likes to flirt, but once
committed, is loyal friend and lover. Rarely at a loss for words, new
ideas, or grand schemes for material gain.
PERSONALITY EXTREME: Too tied-down, or too unconventional.

EULALEE (Greek/English)—F.

MAJOR TALENT: Ability to incorporate learning from experience, attention to details, and refined mental analysis into career. Is cooperative,
cultural, and progressive. Has human understanding, exceptional intuition, and diplomacy to keep secrets. Perseveres for inner peace, concentration, and expertise. Photographer, florist, and researcher are possible
career opportunities.
PERSONALITY INGREDIENTS: First impression is dependable, harmonious, and helpful. Is family/home/community focused. Desires individuality, stimulation, and to take the initiative. Needs courage, faith, and self-
respect for innovative ideas. Must be independent, firm, gracious, and
control wanderlust.
PERSONALITY EXTREME: Too changeable, or too settled.

EUNICE (Greek/Biblical)—F.

MAJOR TALENT: Ability to incorporate skill, routine, security into a
communication based career. Is articulate, reasoned, and perfecting.
Has well ordered, philosophical, and versatile gifts that should be applied to a conventional profession. Law, medicine, and creative arts are
possible career opportunities.
PERSONALITY INGREDIENTS: Tackles broad-scoped, complicated, unimaginative jobs and efficiently organizes for exciting, appealing, material results. Desires authority, honesty, and dependability. Is all of those
things and more. Appears well-tailored, respectable, and ready to work.
Can communicate when necessary, but not prone to wasting words,
energy, or money. Basically a common sense, parental, dedicated idealist.
PERSONALITY EXTREME: Too imprudent, or too careful.

EUSTACE (Greek/Old French/English)—M.

MAJOR TALENT: Ability to incorporate adaptability, diplomacy, and
attention to details into career. Is peace-loving, seems modest, but clev-

erly strives for subtle control. Gathers facts, reactions, and must reconcile for cooperative efforts. Has influence in group activity, maintains sensitivity to balance the pros and cons. Arbitrator, diplomat, and accountant are possible career opportunities.

PERSONALITY INGREDIENTS: Wants to climb the highest unexplored mountain and be first to view the horizon. Desires adventure, freedom, and sensual pleasures. Impatient with petty projects, people, and structures. Appears conventional, sturdy, and protective. Could be like a helpful, sensitive, unobtrusive bull in a china shop. A power for cooperation when emotionally controlled.

PERSONALITY EXTREME: Too purposeful, or too inconsistent.

EVA (Hebrew/Danish/Italian/German/Portuguese/Spanish/English)—F.

MAJOR TALENT: Ability to incorporate independent ideas, action, and philosophy into career. Is sharp and has a way of mingling people. Strives to be recognized as an individual. Makes a major life-style change every nine years. Choreographer, editor, and idea person are possible career opportunities.

PERSONALITY INGREDIENTS: First impression is conventional. Appears conservative, capable, and practical. Desires comfortable, gracious, and abundant life-style. Feels protective, strong-willed, and sympathetic. Family rooted, helpful, and parental nature. Very tenderhearted, must guard against giving too much.

PERSONALITY EXTREME: Too insistent, or too dependent.

EVAN (Welsh/English)—M.

MAJOR TALENT: Ability to incorporate social service, independent leadership, and clever ideas into career. Is responsible, literate, and attracts people. Has strong will, sincerity, and a desire for self-improvement. May take things too seriously. Teacher, marriage counselor, and choral leader are possible career opportunities.

PERSONALITY INGREDIENTS: First impression is romantic, empathetic, and noble. Seems comfortable. Desires respectability, roots, and attaining life-style. Needs love, harmony, and to achieve emotional balance. Must avoid being opinionated.

PERSONALITY EXTREME: Too quick, or too cautious.

EVANGELINE (Greek/English)—F.

MAJOR TALENT: Ability to incorporate material work and humanitarian goals into career. Has strong, just, and emotional character. Is imaginative, artistic, and practical. Strives for the best of everything and with perseverance, honesty, and control of physical appetites can make dreams come true. Building trades, quality manufacturing, and landscape design suggest opportunities.

PERSONALITY INGREDIENTS: Desires cultural, serene, classy environment. Keeps secrets, needs privacy, and strives for perfection. First impression is gracious, helpful, and displays good taste. Is family/community/universally focused. Has mature approach, wisdom, and organizes everything. Tends to make people and situations fit personal fantasies. Tackles projects realistically, but emotionally makes a silk purse out of a sow's ear. Is self-deluding.

PERSONALITY EXTREME: Too experimental, or too cautious.

EVE (Hebrew/English)—F.

MAJOR TALENT: Ability to incorporate learning by trial and error into career. Academic experiences are a plus, but not a necessity. Focus is upon physical sensations, pleasures, and experimentations. Has progressive ideas, unconventional approach, and a clever understanding of people. Attracts unconventional job offers. Politics, theater, and personnel work are possible career opportunities.

PERSONALITY INGREDIENTS: Desires authority, innovations, and advancements. Feels very individualistic, proud, and instigative. First impression is not unusual. Seems honest, trustworthy, and structured. Needs to curb impulsivity to maintain desired respectability, material security, and cooperation from boosters.

PERSONALITY EXTREME: Too sensual, or too mental.

EVELINE (Hebrew: Eva/English)—F.

MAJOR TALENT: Ability to incorporate instructive and wide-scoped self-expression into career. Is a persevering pupil, and a concerned counselor. Provides a universal service, hangs in until the job is completed, and rises to leadership although there may be a cross to bear throughout the intensely passionate climb.

PERSONALITY INGREDIENTS: First impression is attractive, charming, and entertaining. Strives for fashionable interests, beauty, and optimism. Inwardly wants love, harmonious relationships, and the welfare of family. Is responsible, protective, and strong-willed. May have hot temper.

PERSONALITY EXTREME: Too understanding, or too thoughtless.

EVELYN (Hebrew: Eva/Old French/Celtic/English, variant: Eva)— F. & M.

MAJOR TALENT: Ability to incorporate adaptability, humanitarian instincts, and idealistic creativity into career. Is sensitive to details, empathetic, and romantic. Has desire for quality, high nervous energy, and a feeling of being different. Desires to uplift, educate, and inspire. Is intuitional, seeks accomplishment, and attracts recognition. Teaching, preaching, and public affairs are possible career opportunities.

PERSONALITY INGREDIENTS: First impression is expressive, optimistic, and attractive. Seems congenial, clever, and imaginative. Really wants to get down-to-business. Self-reliant, diplomatic, and efficient. Desires discrimination, dependability, and to be in control. Gets involved in partnerships, needs multi-faceted cultural interests, and is constantly called upon to make decisions. Has courage of convictions, and is very convincing . . . can sell capitalism to communists.

PERSONALITY EXTREME: Too sensual, or too mental.

EVERETT (German: Everard/English)—M.

MAJOR TALENT: Ability to incorporate unconventional ideas, receptive nature, and self-expression into career. Is adaptable, sensitive, and understanding. Multi-facted, clever, and dutiful. Always in motion, aiming for progress, optimism, and respect. Legislator, detective, all non-routine professions are possible career opportunities.

PERSONALITY INGREDIENTS: Can't wait for success. Desires security, love, and action. First impression is businesslike. Is authoritative, strong-willed, and ethical. Attracts supporters, knowledge, and tangibles. Must learn to let others help. Too much confidence alienates friends.

PERSONALITY EXTREME: Too picky, or too disinterested.

EVITA (Hebrew: Eva/Spanish)—F.

MAJOR TALENT: Ability to incorporate charm, individuality, and diplomacy into career. Is optimistic, innovative, and sensitive to details. Has communications gifts, artistic imagination, and attracts attention. Writing, medicine, and beautician are possible career opportunities.

PERSONALITY INGREDIENTS: Blossoms at twenty-one. Appears to be, and is, parental, generous, and attaining. Desires roots, and gives generous support, guidance, and emotional uplift. Must avoid using keen perceptions for material gains only. Must strive toward a humanitarian role to avoid disappointment.

PERSONALITY EXTREME: Too proud, or too humble.

EWALD (Teutonic/Old English/English)—M.

MAJOR TALENT: Ability to incorporate inventive ideas, leadership, and wide-scoped/humanitarian service into career. Is interested in quality, efficiency, and eliminating problems. Is honest, just, and romantically faithful. Combines mental and physical energies and must keep a well-balanced health routine. Hospital administrator, scout master, and publisher are possible career opportunities.

PERSONALITY INGREDIENTS: First impression is efficient, authoritative, and custom-made. Not a time, money, or emotions waster. Inwardly is strong-willed, parental, and generous to family/community. Can do quality work/artistry or limitless damage. Powers of persuasion should be used for honest, uplifting, and charitable goals.

PERSONALITY EXTREME: Too ingratiating, or too direct.

EZEKIAL (Hebrew/English)—M.

MAJOR TALENT: Ability to incorporate uplifting, responsible, and protective social service into career. Is helpful, generous, and wise. Enjoys counseling, teaching, and all forms of communications. When providing for humanitarian/universal needs, may leave a lasting mark on humanity. If family focused, is intensely attaining, supportive, and discriminating. Union organizer, missionary, and any job that helps people are possible career opportunities.

PERSONALITY INGREDIENTS: Desires to serve, unify and follow an outstanding leader, cause, or crusade. Sensitive to everything. Is gentle, resists change, and inspires/influences/cajoles to get results. Is subtle. First impression is practical, capable, and structured. Combines adaptability, material aims, and becoming a support-system for others.

PERSONALITY EXTREME: Too talkative, or too reticent.

EZRA (Hebrew/Latin/English)—M.

MAJOR TALENT: Ability to incorporate free thinking, versatility, and sensitivity into career. Is companionable, careful, and understands people. Has ability to experiment, learn from the experience, and dare to introduce and promote unknowns. Is a font of ideas, passions, and self-confidence. Gambler, advertising executive, and lawyer are possible career opportunities.

PERSONALITY INGREDIENTS: Tends to exaggerate, be possessive, and give advice. Desires comfortable, happy, gracious life-style. Feels responsible, strong-willed, and protective. First impression is businesslike, well-groomed, and directive. Enjoys family, material power, and adventure. Gains from friendliness, unconventional investments, and inheritances.

PERSONALITY EXTREME: Too bossy, or too compliant.

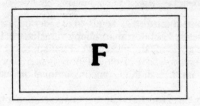

F

All names that begin with the letter *F* have the *Strong Point* of parental nature—personalized service—responsibility—musical aptitude.

FABIAN (Latin/English)—M.

MAJOR TALENT: Ability to incorporate adaptability, conscientiousness, and communications skills into career. Is idealistic, understanding, sympathetic. Has a need to counsel, uplift, and convince others. Attracts rewarding partnerships, women, and love. Blends cooperation, practical judgment, and companionability. Restaurant management, song writing, and home improvement sales are possible career opportunities.

PERSONALITY INGREDIENTS: Wants dreams to come true, no matter how impractical. Feels special, inventive, and intuitive. Appears clean-cut, studious, and neat. Has magnetic attraction when following personal fancies. Basically, home-based, conventional, and ambitious.

PERSONALITY EXTREME: Too impulsive, or too studied.

FAITH (Latin/Middle English)—F.

MAJOR TALENT: Ability to incorporate perception of details, structured thinking, and organizational efficiency into career. Strives for confident authority. Is zealous, self-reliant, and dependable. Has executive diplomacy, group compatibility, and courage. Combines physical and mental balance. Statistician, judge, and financial advisor are possible career opportunities.

PERSONALITY INGREDIENTS: Desires optimism, beauty, and entertaining people and experiences. Is humorous, charming, and sociable. First impression is sensual, open-minded, and adventurous. Seems physically tuned, clever, and attention-getting. Is curious, mentally in motion, and has a way with people. Bites the bullet in times of trouble and maintains enthusiasm for the future.

PERSONALITY EXTREME: Too materialistic, or too impractical.

FANNY (German: diminutive Frances and alone)—F.

MAJOR TALENT: Ability to incorporate disciplined work, orderly perception for details, and emotional response into career. Is concerned, sympathetic, and influences/guides others. Has conventional methods, bright outlook, and sincerity. Combines strong-will, sound business judgment, and social generosity. Nurse, teacher, and economist are possible career opportunities.

PERSONALITY INGREDIENTS: First impression may seem aloof/introspective, or unfriendly. A quirk of fate has not given the cultural opportunities necessary for this name to appear socially confident. When an area of expertise is established, the inner person shines out. Just knows how to wheel and deal with money. Has practical financial judgment, administrative horse sense, and integrity. Enjoys the freedom that money can buy. Manages everything diplomatically and finds supporters in the business community.

PERSONALITY EXTREME: Too silent, or too expounding.

FARLEY (Teutonic: Fairley/English)—M.

MAJOR TALENT: Ability to incorporate conventional, structured, administrative work, independent action, and communication gifts into career. Is determined, ambitious, and willing to fight for creative ideals. Has charm, common sense, and imagination. Instructor, bricklayer, and dentist are possible career opportunities.

PERSONALITY INGREDIENTS: First impression is dignified, cultured, and introspective. Strives for perfection, intellectual stimulation, and privacy. Desires family/group harmony, and assumes burdens for others. Feels protective, sympathetic, and domestically attaining. Inwardly emotional, appears aloof.

PERSONALITY EXTREME: Too melancholy, or too jocular.

FARRAH (Old English: Faer, family name/Old French: Ferrand)—
F. & M.

MAJOR TALENT: Ability to incorporate realistic judgments, communication gifts, and technical/scientific/spiritual refinements into career. Is analytic, investigative, and discriminating. Combines charm, discretion, and material ambition. Enjoys physical activity, travel, and quick wit. Analyst, stock broker, and lawyer are possible career opportunities.

PERSONALITY INGREDIENTS: Desires emotional peace, harmony, and support. Is thoughtful, loving, and devoted. Wants cooperative mate, easy-going life-style, and to collect facts, people, and things. Appears to be a fighter. Seems straight-forward, clean-cut, and well thought out. Prefers conventional living and open-ended thinking. Can be cunning.

PERSONALITY EXTREME: Too organized, or too careless.

FAWN (Latin/English)—F.

MAJOR TALENT: Ability to incorporate ambitious leadership, keen perceptions, and the drive to find perfect solutions into career. Is inquisitive, probing, and assertive. Has individuality, refinement, and depth. Combines material, intellectual, and spiritual awareness. Knows the power of introspective questioning. Aerospace research, financial counseling, and corporate law are possible career opportunities.

PERSONALITY INGREDIENTS: Desires personal control. Feels individualistic, proud, and assertive. Appears difficult to approach. May be too aloof, authoritative, or melancholy. Disappointments, social discomfort, or simple shyness create false impression of disinterest. A bit of kindness brings out the energetic, bright, innovator locked inside.

PERSONALITY EXTREME: Too cautious, or too inquisitive.

FAY (Old French/English, F./Celtic: diminutive Fayette, M.)—F. & M.

MAJOR TALENT: Ability to incorporate non-routine planning, timing, and end results into career. Is progressive, speedy, and mentally curious. Understands how to deal with people, likes travel, change, and off-beat experiences. Enthusiastic nature sparks activity for others. Best when concentrated. Advertising, politics, and writing are possible career opportunities.

PERSONALITY INGREDIENTS: Desires innovative, instigating, independent action. Feels energetic, positive, and forceful. May be a loner, but is a clever, directive, and self-disciplined pace setter. First impression is conventional, capable, and trustworthy. Is reconstructive, and bounces back when things go wrong.

PERSONALITY EXTREME: Too confident, or too anxious.

FAYE (Old French: Fay/English)—F.

MAJOR TALENT: Ability to incorporate inventive concepts, quality results, and leadership skills into career. Is a unique character. Expressive, organizational, and assertive. Must be prepared to stand alone for personal ideals. Inventor, psychiatrist, and fashion designer are possible career opportunities.

PERSONALITY INGREDIENTS: Desires family/community pride. Needs comfort, congeniality, and gracious living. Concerned about others, wise, and helpful. First impression is sure-building, conservative, and dignified. Likes to appear clean-scrubbed, neat, and tasteful. Runs the distance and can win any race if emotions are checked at the starting line. Can have personal and professional happiness by courageously accepting the uniqueness of this name.

PERSONALITY EXTREME: Too impulsive, or too cautious.

FELICE (Latin: Felicia/Italian)—F.

MAJOR TALENT: Ability to incorporate material judgment, structured work, and reconstructive attitude into career. Likes imaginative, bright, beautiful people. Has need for independent action, and is best when left to work alone. Is down-to-earth, but must organize, be cooperative, and concentrate for desired security. Bookkeeper, builder, and drama coach are possible career opportunities.

PERSONALITY INGREDIENTS: Is ambitious. Feels competitive, and persevering, but may be stubborn, haughty, and demanding. Always at survival level. First impression is sociable, tuned to the times, but a bit dreamy. Strives for a beautiful life but needs to develop sensitivity, and calm down.

PERSONALITY EXTREME: Too understanding, or too belligerent.

FELICIA (Latin: Felix, M./English)—F.

MAJOR TALENT: Ability to incorporate broad-scoped, quality conscious, imaginative artistic/scientific/humanitarian interests into career. Reaches out to people; to serve, entertain, or uplift. Has empathy, romance, and determination. Inspirational, dependable, down-to-earth leader. May assume or have personal problems that are overcome with optimism and emotional balance. Doctor, entertainer, and minister are possible career opportunities.

PERSONALITY INGREDIENTS: First impression is sunny, charming, and imaginative. Likes fashion, humor, and variety. Desires secure, attaining, gracious life-style. Feels sympathetic, and tries to maintain harmony in family/community. May sacrifice personal ambitions. Can be totally unselfish, or very possessive.

PERSONALITY EXTREME: Too strong, or too weak.

FELICITY (Latin: Felicia/English)—F.

MAJOR TALENT: Ability to incorporate long-term material results, practical perceptions, and efficient/organized/dependable work habits into career. Is disciplined, adaptable, and deals with useful products and services. This name has strength and promise of recognition when workaholic nature is tempered with understanding of the spiritual/inspirational side of life. Physical therapist, military leader, and farmer are possible career opportunities.

PERSONALITY INGREDIENTS: Desires beautiful, imaginative, and cheerful conventional life-style. Strives for quality performance, security, and broad-scoped projects. Appears adventurous, enthusiastic, and youthfully progressive. Has energy to burn, sex appeal, and a wonderful understanding of people. Must learn that meditation time is productive work; although it may not produce tangibles, it does increase productivity.

PERSONALITY EXTREME: Too deep, or too obvious.

FELIX (Latin/Danish/French/German/Spanish/ English)—M.

MAJOR TALENT: Ability to incorporate unselfish service, sensitivity to details, and personal ideals into career. Has artistic/humanitarian concepts, cooperative spirit, and high nervous energy. Strives for commercial success, and to retain individualism. Clever, innovative, progressive mind vies with programming for conventional security. These ingredients produce obvious anxieties. Firm decisions alleviate vacillations and give this name possibilities of lasting recognition. Evangelist, reformer, and inspirational writer are possible career opportunities.

PERSONALITY INGREDIENTS: Is curious, impulsive, and impatient. Desires adventure, companionship, and physical pleasures. Appears interested, articulate, and dignified. Attracts favors, is strong-willed, and maintains subtle or bomb-dropping control.

PERSONALITY EXTREME: Too protective, or too judgmental.

FERDINAND (German/French/Danish/English)—M.

MAJOR TALENT: Ability to incorporate communications, executive authority, and practical technology into career. Is attractive, artistically gifted, and ambitious. Has material vision. Strives for possessions, honor, and integrity. Gives and gets attention. Any art form, any business, and any welfare project are possible career opportunities.

PERSONALITY INGREDIENTS: First impression is cultured, introspective, and classy. Is quality conscious, graceful, and a perfectionist. Desires abundant, loving, gracious life-style. Feels protective, sympathetic, and conventional. Feels pride in family/community, a desire for self-improvement, and a sympathy for all beings less fortunate. Is a materialistic, creative humanitarian with a dramatic, extravagant, driving character.

PERSONALITY EXTREME: Too disciplined, or too unconventional.

FERGUS (Irish-Gaelic/English)—M.

MAJOR TALENT: Ability to incorporate hard working nature, artistic communications skills, and independent ambition into career. Is exacting, demanding, and conscientious. Has imagination, self-assertion, and practical perceptions. Vies for prominence and may lose emotional softness in the winning. Administrator, builder, and technician are possible career opportunities.

PERSONALITY INGREDIENTS: First impression is curious, friendly, and freedom-loving. Likes off-beat experiences, people, and ideas. Is self-promoting, articulate, and tends to gamble. Desires affluence, influence, and community respect. Wants to get going and does things in a big way.

PERSONALITY EXTREME: Too self-contained, or too dependent.

FERN (Anglo-Saxon)—F.

MAJOR TALENT: Ability to incorporate keen perception of details, facts, and people into career. Is tuned to serenity, silent analysis, and cultural stimulation. Has strong concerns about loneliness and poverty and strives for expertise, dignity, and open-ended experiences. Integrates non-routine happenings/people into ambitions and overcomes mundane obstacles. Sharp observations speed success. Journalistic photographer, traveling technician, and high class bartender are possible career opportunities.

PERSONALITY INGREDIENTS: Desires adventure, physical sensations, and unconventional opportunities. Needs change, mobility, and liberty. First impression is modest, refined, and tactful. Wants to apear genteel. Has vivid childhood memories that govern adult decisions.

PERSONALITY EXTREME: Too curious, or too cautious.

FERNANDO (German: Ferdinand/Spanish)—M.

MAJOR TALENT: Ability to incorporate fertile, progressive, unconventional thinking, enthusiasm, and practical application to work into career. Senses a fresh opportunity and takes gambles. Has courage to instigate vigorous changes, structure their progress, and hang-in/or reorganize to complete commitments. Promoter, politician, and explorer are possible career opportunities.

PERSONALITY INGREDIENTS: Desires beauty, love, and fashionable life-style. Wants dramatic, witty, uncommon variety. First impression is electric. Appears refined, perceptive, and high-strung. May be inspired with passionate authority to change, uplift, or entertain. Is different.

PERSONALITY EXTREME: Too helpful, or too unconcerned.

FIDEL (Latin)—M.

MAJOR TALENT: Ability to incorporate humanitarian philosophy, perception of details, and perfecting intellect into career. Is empathetic, helpful, and intends to demonstrate love in broad terms. Has magnetic attraction. Combines romantic outlook, love of freedom, and disciplined practicality. With unselfishness, emotional control and purpose, this name reaches out to uplift humanity. Welfare worker, doctor, and lecturer are possible career opportunities.

PERSONALITY INGREDIENTS: Appears conservative. Inwardly desires freedom, adventure, and physical pleasures. Seems trustworthy, neat, and premeditated. Is careful of appearance, but is not ostentatious. Wants to work and expects the same of associates. Aspires to cultural refinements, tangible results, and broad-scoped ideals.

PERSONALITY EXTREME: Too talkative, or too uncommunicative.

FIELDING (English)—M.

MAJOR TALENT: Ability to incorporate communication skills, practical administration, and sharp mind into career. Is articulate, romantic, and sincere. Has high ideals, visionary goals, and silent determination to give and get a fair deal. Strives to relieve suffering, express talents, and use power wisely. Decorator, chemist, and artist/writer/musician are possible career opportunities.

PERSONALITY INGREDIENTS: First impression is unruffled, refined, and observant. Is introspective, cool, and impatient with superficiality. Desires exploration, physical pleasures, and experimentation. Needs unrestricted thinking, time, and people. May choose to serve or squander. Attracts success.

PERSONALITY EXTREME: Too skeptical, or too gullible.

FIONA (Irish: Finn/English)—F.

MAJOR TALENT: Ability to incorporate humanitarian service, intellectual questioning, and sensitivity to details into career. Is inventive, expressive, and empathetic. Has spiritual depth, cooperative nature, and cultural interests. Welfare worker, philosopher, and doctor are possible career opportunities.

PERSONALITY INGREDIENTS: May appear far-away/dreamy/different. First impression is high strung, creative, and often mystical. Desires perfection from self and others. May sound like sour-grapes if exposed to one-up-manship. Needs education/area of authority to shine. Is very bright, impressive, and wants to save the world. Must be known to be understood.

PERSONALITY EXTREME: Too independent, or too submissive.

FLETCHER (Old French/Middle English)—M.

MAJOR TALENT: Ability to incorporate experimental ideas, structured planning, and independent action into career. Is flexible, promotional, and courageous. Has pioneering energy, enjoys people and has a knack for making others comfortable. Fertile mind and body. Advertising, travel business, and detective agency are possible career opportunities.

PERSONALITY INGREDIENTS: Is clear thinking, individualistic, and confident. Wants to be the boss. First impression is conservative, tasteful, and neat. Is a competitor. Must balance personal ambitions and emotional relationships. Has dramatic overreactions, and may be too aggressive in youth. Grows to inspire, comfort, and protect home/community.

PERSONALITY EXTREME: Too serious, or too philosophical.

FLORA (Latin: Florence/English)—F.

MAJOR TALENT: Ability to incorporate analytic, detailed, and progressive thinking into career. Is cooperative, refined, and juggles non-routine scheduling. Has cleverness, perseverance, and quality consciousness. Gets to the root of things. Journalist, librarian, and lawyer are possible career opportunities.

PERSONALITY INGREDIENTS: Desires dignified life-style. Sees all sides of a question, knows when to keep silent, and hides emotions. First impression is commanding. Seems understanding, expressive, and sometimes dramatic. Needs privacy, but fears loneliness and poverty.

PERSONALITY EXTREME: Too independent, or too accommodating.

FLORENCE (Latin/French/English)—F. & M.

MAJOR TALENT: Ability to incorporate uplifting counseling, cooperative nature, and artistic expression into career. Is strong-willed, imaginative, and generous. Has interest in children/animals/family, integrity, and a passion for harmonious surroundings. Adds a dollop of love to everything. Teacher, hotel/restaurant owner, and receptionist are possible career opportunities.

PERSONALITY INGREDIENTS: Desires polished life-style. Feels self-depreciating and tries too hard. Appears physically tuned, sociable, and as affluent as possible. Has unusual speaking or musical voice. Needs specialized skill, companionship, and recognition to feel totally secure.

PERSONALITY EXTREME: Too confident, or too stammering.

FLOYD (Celtic: Lloyd/English)—M.

MAJOR TALENT: Ability to incorporate material ambition, physical energy, and group associations into career. Is focused upon strength, adaptability, and instructional communication. Has love of outdoors, self-improvement, and expansive ideas. Athletic coach, orchestra leader, and military officer are possible career opportunities.

PERSONALITY INGREDIENTS: First impression is supportive, unassuming, and refined. Seems to be modest. Desires position of trust, protection, and respect. Needs family/group/community serenity, gracious living, and pride in instructional abilities/accomplishments. Has strong-will and tests courage repeatedly by forcing issues. Appears confident, but has high standards which are difficult to maintain.

PERSONALITY EXTREME: Too disciplined, or too rule-bending.

FORD (Teutonic/Old English)—M.

MAJOR TALENT: Ability to incorporate cultural growth, perfectionist nature, and a searching intellect into career. Is sensitive, cooperative, detail conscious. Has wanderlust, progressive ideas, and desire for challenge/change/quality. Scientific/technical experimenter, philosophy teacher, and science fiction writer are possible career opportunities.

PERSONALITY INGREDIENTS: Desires family/community harmony, artistic stimulation, and romance. Needs roots, warmth, and pride in life-style. Appears different, individualistic, and energetic. Tends to be outgoing, untraditional, and strong-willed. Thirsts for knowledge, learns, and shares the wealth.

PERSONALITY EXTREME: Too neat, or too sloppy.

FORREST (Teutonic/Old French)—M.

MAJOR TALENT: Ability to incorporate desire for creative/spiritual/intellectual beauty into career. Is idealistic, expressive, and imaginative. Has vision, attraction for material success, and inspiration for others. Film/radio producer, telephone operator, and biographer are possible career opportunities.

PERSONALITY INGREDIENTS: Wants to save the world. Needs a practical, loving, supportive partner. First impression is magnetic, comfortable, and understanding. Seems philosophical, articulate, and charming. May daydream, be mystical, or bounce from one idea to another. Needs patience to make dreams come true.

PERSONALITY EXTREME: Too tender, or too tough.

FOSTER (Teutonic/English)—M.

MAJOR TALENT: Ability to incorporate creative imagery, wide-scoped vision, and supportive nature into career. Is intuitive, inventive, and idealistic. Can be fanatical when trying to improve, create, or market ideas. Has need for stimulating companionship and expands from peer partnerships. Combines beauty, cooperation, and revealing outlook. Political reformer, character analyst, and musician are possible career opportunities.

PERSONALITY INGREDIENTS: Wants to be seen and heard. Desires emotional security, and recognition of ideas. Appears appealing, attractive, and comfortably sociable. Seems to have nobility of purpose, quality tastes, and dramatic nature. May personalize and over-react to petty inconveniences/people. Needs to maintain altruistic goals to achieve potential.

PERSONALITY EXTREME: Too relaxed, or too self-conscious.

FRANCES (German/English)—F.

MAJOR TALENT: Ability to incorporate communication gifts, conventional routines, and high quality standards into career. Is a people person. Has charm, imagination, and shines out in a group. Voice, appearance, or social manner attract attention. Combines optimism, humor, and creative artistry. Writing, entertaining, and legal professions are possible career opportunities.

PERSONALITY INGREDIENTS: Makes a home out of a hotel room. Adds a touch of sex appeal, comfort, and abundance to everything. Is a "cosmic mother" . . . gives wisdom, love, and protection. Strives for harmony, respectability, and beauty. Relaxes by traveling, philosophizing, and sharing abundances. Must avoid being overly protective, too determined, and over eating.

PERSONALITY EXTREME: Too courageous, or too fearful.

FRANCINE (German: Frances/English)—F.

MAJOR TALENT: Ability to incorporate mental analysis, practical procedures, and communications skills into career. Is questioning, imaginative, and structured. Has perfectionist ideals, schemes, and working style. Combines charm, dependability, and tactful silence. Concentration produces exceptional expertise. Physical therapist, statistician, and editor are possible career opportunities.

PERSONALITY INGREDIENTS: First impression is individualistic, straight-spined, and capable. Seems definite, inventive, and creative. Desires friends/family/material attainments in abundance. Feels devoted, protective, and conventional. Strives for comforts, and to be comforting. Enjoys teaching, learning, and observing. Needs moderation.

PERSONALITY EXTREME: Too sensual, or too mental.

FRANCIS (German/Latin/English)—M.

MAJOR TALENT: Ability to incorporate investigative ideas, cultural growth, and concentrated mental energy into career. Is very bright, determined, and knows the power of silence. Has dignity, introspective moments, and spiritual/intellectual gifts. Unconventional thinker with conventional standards. Very intuitive, direct, and expressive. Executive administrator, lawyer, and researcher are possible career opportunities.

PERSONALITY INGREDIENTS: Strives for family/group/community harmony, leadership, and respect. Is strong-willed, concerned with justice, and tries to raise standards, and counsel/inspire others. Desires individuality of thought, action, and speech. Must realize true courage in lifetime and fight for progressive goals. May have to walk alone but usually finds admiring supporters.

PERSONALITY EXTREME: Too impulsive, or too premeditated.

FRANCISCA (German/Danish/Portuguese/Spanish/English)—F.

MAJOR TALENT: Ability to incorporate self-expression, practical judgments, and idealistic concepts into career. Is high-strung, imaginative, and attracts supporters. Has charm, exemplary attitudes, and turns dreams to realities. Combines metaphysics, artistic creativity, and universal integrity. Inspirational writing, beauty specialties, and charity organizing are possible career opportunities.

PERSONALITY INGREDIENTS: Desires to change, uplift, save, and educate humanity to personal persuasions. Is a born evangelist. Needs tenderness, sensitive mate, and serene environment. Has great inner strength. Needs faith. First impression is charming, empathetic, and quietly classy. Is artistic, romantic, and youthful. Attracts gracious family life-style, admirers, and a chance to educate humanity.

PERSONALITY EXTREME: Too lofty, or too retiring.

FRANK (English diminutive: Frances/Francis/Franklin)—F. & M.

MAJOR TALENT: Ability to incorporate unconventional, progressive, and adventurous ideas into career. Is versatile, mentally curious, and a sharp analyst of people. Has need to experience all the five senses. Combines sensitivity to details, communications skills, and daring. Travel agent, investigator, and psychologist are possible career opportunities.

PERSONALITY INGREDIENTS: Strives to work for lasting construction. Can be a workaholic and expects everyone to keep up. Appears practical, straight-forward, and dynamic. Inwardly feels special. Has desire to conquer new horizons. Needs freedom, leadership, innovations . . . and patience.

PERSONALITY EXTREME: Too high-pitched, or too low-key.

FRANKLIN (Middle Latin/German/English)—M.

MAJOR TALENT: Ability to incorporate hard work, exactitude, and orderliness into career. Is honest, dependable, and methodical. Has material, economical, conscientious approach. Usually invests wisely and leaves a heritage. Mathematician, statistician, and builder suggest opportunities.

PERSONALITY INGREDIENTS: Strives for quality of self-expression, sociability, and beauty. Seems imaginative, clever, and is especially appealing to women. Needs complete freedom to try innovative ideas and experiments. Feels different and cannot be told what to do or how to do it. Finds a universal need and creates/glamorizes common sense solutions for everyday problems. Theater, science, and law interest this multi-faceted name.

PERSONALITY EXTREME: Too sensual, or too mental.

FRED (diminutive: Old German; Frederic/English)—M.

MAJOR TALENT: Ability to incorporate gift of gab, group leadership, and practical ambitious temperament into career. Has generous, determined, strong-willed instincts. Is sensitive to details, firm, and advisory. Best when able to balance family and business relationships. Life-support products/services, instruction, and showmanship professions are possible career opportunities.

PERSONALITY INGREDIENTS: Has memorable voice, energy level, and enthusiasms. First impression is assertive, different, and courageous. Strives to be inventive. Desires sensual pleasures, progressive experimentation, and freedom to satisfy curiosity. Likes to be mobile, adventurous, and should be an opportunist. Can promote, convince, and deliver.

PERSONALITY EXTREME: Too conventional, or too unrestrained.

FREDA (German/English)—F.

MAJOR TALENT: Ability to incorporate introspective planning, sensitivity to details, and experimental ideas into career. Is reflective, and draws heavily on past experience. Has cultural aspirations, adaptability, and sense of visualization. Combines cooperation, cleverness, and quest for knowledge. Psychoanalyst, engineer, and librarian suggest opportunities.

PERSONALITY INGREDIENTS: May want to explore unknowns, but gets involved with family/community burdens. Wants roots and independence. Appears energetic, assertive, and managerial. Needs harmonious home and business environment to enjoy peace of mind. Is strong-willed, bold, and must balance loves and career.

PERSONALITY EXTREME: Too bossy, or too noncommittal.

FREDERIC (Old German/English)—M.

MAJOR TALENT: Ability to incorporate exceptional understanding of human nature into career. Is promotional, convincing, and eloquent. Combines appreciation of beauty, pleasure, and perceptive analysis. Has self-confidence and will either be too responsible or irresponsible. Best when self-disciplined to practical, economical, and conventional goals. Entrepreneur, politician, or press agent are possible career opportunities.

PERSONALITY INGREDIENTS: First impression is solid, dependable, and clean-cut. Strives for stable, respectable, financially secure life-style. Desires creative leadership, individuality, and innovations. Has strong need for freedom and wants to curb impulsivity. Needs to recognize intuitional danger signals, avoid escapism, and become accountable for own mistakes. May effect progressive universal change when logical and not governed by base instincts.

PERSONALITY EXTREME: Too talkative, or too quiet.

FREDERICA (German: Frederic/Portuguese/English)—F.

MAJOR TALENT: Ability to incorporate militant love of justice, artistic self-expression, and knack of exacting respect, group harmony, and social uplift into career. Is strong-willed, firm, and cleverly perceptive. Has gracious manner, individuality, and practical discrimination. Government, medicine, and counseling are possible career opportunities.

PERSONALITY INGREDIENTS: Desires easy-going, genteel, and companionable life-style. Needs love, serenity, and cooperation. First impression is capable, honest, and well-groomed. Wants to get down to brass tacks, reconstruct, and get results. Often judges by appearances, and puts up charming front. May be an Archie Bunker, or a biblical King Solomon.

PERSONALITY EXTREME: Too changeable, or too cautious.

FREDERICK (Old German/English)—M.

MAJOR TALENT: Ability to incorporate uncommon and perfecting intellect into career. Is cultural, discerning, and poised. Has quick, clever, innovative perceptions. Combines research, contemplation, cooperation. Best in academic, spiritual, or humanitarian service work. Psychiatrist, clergyman, and historian are possible career opportunities.

PERSONALITY INGREDIENTS: First impression is gracious, helpful, and comfortable. May care little for current fashions, and may appear genuinely concerned, protective, and uplifting. Desires creative action, independence, and feels above the crowd. Has dignity, nobility, and confidence to silently stand alone.

PERSONALITY EXTREME: Too imposing, or too humble.

FREDRIC (Old German/English)—M.

MAJOR TALENT: Ability to incorporate broad-scoped, humanitarian, artistically expressive service into career. Is understanding, helpful, and generous. Has high energy, determination, and social consciousness. Combines innovations, common sense, and charitable philosophy. Missionary, thespian, or political reformer are possible career opportunities.

PERSONALITY INGREDIENTS: Marries early in life, or not at all. Strives for major constructive planning, contributions, and results. Is extremely active. Desires freedom to enjoy travel, people, and the five senses. Is a catalyst for change in others' lives. Can be a workaholic, or a beach bum. Will leave a mark from either direction.

PERSONALITY EXTREME: Too extravagant, or too restrained.

FRIEDA (German)—F.

MAJOR TALENT: Ability to incorporate mental analysis, facts/figures, refinement into career. Is sure, or knows the diplomacy/power of silence. Has cultural/spiritual intuitive instincts. Combines material practicality, self-expression, and sense of authority. Architect, investment counselor, school administrator are possible career opportunities.

PERSONALITY INGREDIENTS: First impression is different. Seems individualistic, capable, and sociable. Desires strong family ties. Feels protective, persevering, and attaining. Attracts happiness, conventional structure, and respect. Needs to ease up and allow for human frailty. Expects perfection from self and others.

PERSONALITY EXTREME: Too instigative, or too unchanging.

FRITZ (German/diminutive: Frederic and alone)—M.

MAJOR TALENT: Ability to incorporate unconventional analytic mind, practical structure, and self-expression into career. Is culturally attaining, perfecting, and investigative. Combines formality, refinement, and keen intellectual perception. Has determination, optimism, and discretion. Writer, technical administrator, and referee/umpire are possible career opportunities.

PERSONALITY INGREDIENTS: Desires philosophical, noble, quality-conscious life-style. Is empathetic, generous, and humanitarian. First impression is introspective, dignified, and aloof. Speaks when knowledgeable and authoritatively. Strives for expertise, concentration and enjoyment of nature. May be silent but is never mentally idle.

PERSONALITY EXTREME: Too controlling, or too incompetent.

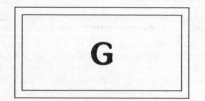

G

All names that begin with the letter *G* have the *Strong Point* of asking questions—giving answers—quality consciousness—need for privacy.

GABE (Hebrew: Gabriel/English variant)—M.
MAJOR TALENT: Ability to incorporate instructive, responsible, inspirational nature into career. Is a communicator. Combines progressive ideas, individuality, and social service. Aims for group harmony through generous, sympathetic, perceptive understanding of people. Teacher, marriage counselor, and musician are possible career opportunities.
PERSONALITY INGREDIENTS: First impression is magnetic. Strives to be noble, empathetic, and comfortable with everyone. Desires respectable, gracious, and materially attaining life-style. Wants to feel proud, protective, and loved by family. Best when careful in business agreements, and looking for more than surface values.
PERSONALITY EXTREME: Too busy, or too bored.

GABRIEL (Hebrew/French/German/Portuguese/Spanish/English)—M.
MAJOR TALENT: Ability to incorporate artistic self-expression, instructional guidance, and broad-scoped social welfare into career. Is trustworthy, inspirational, and intent upon polishing skills. Has empathy, kindness, and humanitarian philosophy. Combines dramatic, imaginative, and entertaining inclinations. Has the common sense to work out difficulties and may have or assume a heavy load. Welfare worker, artist, and lecturer are possible career opportunities.
PERSONALITY INGREDIENTS: Feels protective, parental, and trustworthy. Needs harmonious home, creative stimulation, and variety of interests. Has imagination, and strives for the limelight. First impression is attractive, sunny, and friendly. Has humor, sympathy, and strong-will. Will give last penny for a thing of beauty, a less fortunate friend, or to make people happy.
PERSONALITY EXTREME: Too talkative, or too reticent.

GABRIELLE (Hebrew: Gabriel/French/English)—F.
MAJOR TALENT: Ability to incorporate practical routines, administrative structure, and concrete results into career. Is disciplined, determined, and efficient. Has executive diplomacy, integrity, and intellectual judgment. Tuned to businesslike approach, but when spiritually aroused can reach out to labor for humanitarian purposes. Missionary, physical therapist, and banker are possible career opportunities.
PERSONALITY INGREDIENTS: Desires peace, love, and sensitivity. Is

modest, refined, and concerned with the little things. First impression is parental, responsible, and conservative. Strives for family/group harmony, gracious/attaining life-style, and respect. Is a willing counselor, fair competitor, and resourceful planner/worker. Appears confident in times of stress.

PERSONALITY EXTREME: Too innovative, or too reflective.

GAIL (Anglo-Saxon: alone/Hebrew diminutive: Abigail/English)—F. & M.

MAJOR TALENT: Ability to incorporate attention to details, adaptability, and cooperative spirit into career. Is a creature of proven habit and faces a variety of decisions to further growth. Has modesty, refinement, and is emotionally fine tuned. Health food expert, watchmaker and accountant are possible career opportunities.

PERSONALITY INGREDIENTS: Strives for independence, inventions, and freedom to take the lead. Creates new ways to do conventional jobs. Appears individualistic, energetic, and original. Is fast paced, and often a trendsetter. May do exacting work, but needs patience in other ways.

PERSONALITY EXTREME: Too optimistic, or too anxious.

GALE (Anglo-Saxon: Gail/English)—F. & M.

MAJOR TALENT: Ability to incorporate mental analysis, refined tastes, and need for perfection into career. Is investigative, careful, and factual. Has dignity, calm, and reserve. Knows how to keep a secret. Has self-doubt and may put too big or too small a price on services. Best not taking financial or romantic gambles, or accepting contracts/leases/handshake agreements without getting a sixth sense okay. May experience disappointments until authority/expertise is established. Engineer, college administrator, and publisher are possible career opportunities.

PERSONALITY INGREDIENTS: Appears to be a loner, and very independent. Strives for originality, freedom, and unrestricted leadership. Desires harmonious, artistically expressive, and respectable family attainments. May appear cool but wants warmth. Must not let emotions override logic.

PERSONALITY EXTREME: Too adventurous, or too cautious.

GARDINIA (Latin/German)—F.

MAJOR TALENT: Ability to incorporate adaptability, mental curiosity, and keen judgment of people into career. Is conservative, independent, and companionable. Has love of travel, change, and freedom. Combines pioneering efforts, productivity, and relationship to the five senses. Advertiser, airline employee, and theatrical manager are possible career opportunities.

PERSONALITY INGREDIENTS: Needs self-confidence. Strives for intellectual/spiritual/cultural attainments but lacks concentration. Becomes comfortable when established as an authority/expert through working/perfecting/researching a subject or job. Appears classy, aloof, and calm. May be an escapist and indulge in physical pleasures. Would prefer a world in which nobody burped, but has a destiny heaped with real people.

PERSONALITY EXTREME: Too trendsetting, or too uninfluential.

GARNET (Latin/English)—F. & M.

MAJOR TALENT: Ability to incorporate tact, sensitivity to details, and idealistic enthusiasms into career. Has high creative energy, magnetism, and self-expression that attracts admirers. May be a dreamer, intuitive and inspirational. Ambitions get help when ideals are maintained. Charity worker, beauty specialist, and metaphysician are possible career opportunities.

PERSONALITY INGREDIENTS: First impression is exciting, adventurous, and sexy. Seems friendly, open-minded, and clever. Desires family harmony, conventional, respectable life-style. Feels protective, strong-willed, and parental. Strives for material returns but gets the best things without trying.

PERSONALITY EXTREME: Too considerate, or too thoughtless.

GARTH (Teutonic/English)—M.

MAJOR TALENT: Ability to incorporate artistic expression, humanitarian service, and broad-scoped philosophy into career. Is detail conscious, mentally analytic, and understanding. Combines inventive ideas, sense of justice, and emotional output. Welfare worker, doctor, and artist are possible career opportunities.

PERSONALITY INGREDIENTS: First impressions is businesslike, affable, and as affluent as possible. Seems capable, trust-worthy, and efficient. Desires individuality. Needs freedom, innovations, and activity. Is a problem-solver.

PERSONALITY EXTREME: Too materialistic, or too unsubstantial.

GARY (Old German: diminutive; Gerald/Garvey/Garvin)—M.

MAJOR TALENT: Ability to incorporate group harmony, concerned counseling, and musical/communication aptitude into career. Is conventional, sympathetic, and self-improving. Has a strong sense of right/wrong, sensitivity to people/details, and determination to change/uplift/educate. Gets help from women. Intense emotions and ambition may be channeled for others' welfare or harm. Hotel/restaurant manager, school/youth group advisor, and performing artist are possible career opportunities.

PERSONALITY INGREDIENTS: Visual impression is introspective. Must be heard to be appreciated. Strives for perfection, dignity, and poise. Desires organized, affluent, and influential life-style. Wants to get down to business. Cannot be power hungry or finds disappointment in financial or love relationships. Attracts influential supporters when cheerful, optimistic, and friendly.

PERSONALITY EXTREME: Too unaffected, or too polished.

GASTON (Teutonic/French/English)—M.

MAJOR TALENT: Ability to incorporate foresight, broad philosophy, and practical, economical, administrative workaholic procedures into career. Has high energy to create, execute, and promote projects. Wants lasting tangibles, peaceful partnerships, and each detail perfected. Building trades, government, and mining export/import are possible career opportunities.

PERSONALITY INGREDIENTS: Appears solid, dependable, and polite. Strives for material attainment, respectability, and family/community pride. Desires perfection. Needs meditative time, spiritual/intellectual stimulation, and cultural environments. Wants to be welcomed as an authority and may relax conversationally only when expert. Has innate fear of loneliness and poverty. May be too materialistic, penny-pinching, or ingratiating.

PERSONALITY EXTREME: Too sensual, or too mental.

GAY (Old High German, M./English, F)—F. & M.
MAJOR TALENT: Ability to incorporate responsibility, useful service, and showmanship into career. Is artistically creative, individualistic, and experimental. Has gracious manner, sympathy, and enjoys counseling. Takes charge, and sees commitments through. Hotel management, professional housekeeper, and interior decorator are possible career opportunities.

PERSONALITY INGREDIENTS: Desires innovations, leadership, and individuality. Has courage, pioneering spirit, and pride in capabilities. First impression is enthusiastic, energetic, and at ease. Has a natural compatibility with everyone. Wants travel, foreign vistas, and to enjoy the five senses. Gets into everything . . . needs to learn discernment.

PERSONALITY EXTREME: Too skeptical, or too gullible.

GAYLE (Teutonic: alone/Anglo-Saxon variant; Gail)—F. & M.
MAJOR TALENT: Ability to incorporate unconventional material ideas, clever adaptations, and physical energy to bring concepts to form into career. Is intense, bold, and adventurous. Has confidence, honesty, and an uncommon way with people. Learns by experience. Politician, navigator, and communications expert suggest opportunities.

PERSONALITY INGREDIENTS: First impression is businesslike. Strives for efficiency, authority, and affluence. Desires secure, loving, peaceful homelife. Needs roots, beauty, and conventional successes. May expect inheritance or achieve recognition and become self-important which alienates supporters. When in tune with associates all good things happen.

PERSONALITY EXTREME: Too physical, or too mental.

GEMMA (Latin/Italian)—F.
MAJOR TALENT: Ability to incorporate self-expression, perception for details, and inspirational ideas/actions into career. Is optimistic, patient, and independent. Has charm, wit, and personal sensitivity. Combines adaptability, versatility, and resourcefulness. Entertainer, crafts designer, and writer are possible career opportunities.

PERSONALITY INGREDIENTS: Has showmanship. First impression is tasteful, sympathetic, and sociable. Has a knack for putting compatible people together. Is musical, dignified, and attaining. Needs roots, gracious home, and pride in family/community. Gives advice, protects, and loves. Scatters interests and energy. Needs concentration.

PERSONALITY EXTREME: Too ambitious, or too placid.

GENE (Greek: diminutive; Eugene/Eugenia)—F. & M.
MAJOR TALENT: Ability to incorporate long term planning/results, constructive energy, and dedication to humanitarian or life-support needs into career. Is a practical, honest, organized worker. Has economical,

administrative, and persuasive approach. Should aim high and take care not to burn the candle at both ends. Insurance planner, laboratory technician, and real estate investor suggest opportunities.

PERSONALITY INGREDIENTS: Is a problem-solving individualist. Wants to instigate new ideas, gain status, and be free to do it again. Needs to be boss, be innovative, and take challenges. Appears friendly, attractive, and imaginative. Strives to make a game out of life and take the good with the bad. Must learn to take a vacation from productivity. Works at playing.

PERSONALITY EXTREME: Too unconventional, or too proper.

GENEVA (Latin/Celtic: diminutive; Guinevere/French)—F.

MAJOR TALENT: Ability to incorporate skillful artistry, empathetic service, and broad outlook into career. Is magnetic, gracious, and romantic. Has strong intuition, perfectionist nature and sensitivity to details. Chemist, correspondent, and artist are possible career opportunities.

PERSONALITY INGREDIENTS: First impression is withdrawn. Lacks social confidence and must communicate to be appreciated. Strives for dignity, culture, and refinement. Feels special. Needs idealistic self-expression, recognition, and loving mate. Has nervous energy, visionary insights, and is futuristic. Has unique ideas, but expects too much of self and others and may alienate supporters.

PERSONALITY EXTREME: Too individualistic, or too submissive.

GENEVIEVE (Celtic: Gwen/French/English)—F.

MAJOR TALENT: Ability to incorporate practical planning, organized work effort, and material approach into career. Has common sense values, communication gifts, and determination. Is straight-forward, charitable, and compassionate. Wants to give constructive humanitarian service. Economist, nurse, and plumber suggest opportunities.

PERSONALITY INGREDIENTS: Desires inventive, fast moving, easy-going life-style. Feels special. Has high nervous energy, idealistic goals, and a need for recognition. Can be modest, sensitive, and attentive to details when calm. Seeks the perfect mate/partner, and often creates qualities that don't exist. Is a dreamer. May be disappointed in romance and career until able to not judge a book by its cover, be selective, and accept reality.

PERSONALITY EXTREME: Too adventurous, or too cautious.

GEOFFREY (Old German: Jeffrey/English)—M.

MAJOR TALENT: Ability to incorporate assuming broad-scoped responsibilities, group accord, and protective nature into career. Is a teacher, showman, and expressive musically/artistically. Has unconventional ideas, independent ambitions, and courage to explore new vistas. Is intelligent, perceptive and discriminating. Appears confident/relaxed in stressful times and fights for justice. Costume designer, union official, and all that serve or entertain the public are possible career opportunities.

PERSONALITY INGREDIENTS: First impression is dynamic, businesslike, and trustworthy. Strives for influence, affluence, and authority. Inwardly lacks confidence. Wants cultural refinements, thinking time, and perfection in all things. Dislikes the mundane, earthy, practicalities. Tries to escape or rise above the strata of unmatched dishes, milk containers on the table, and unmanicured fingers holding the wrong fork. Finds inner security through expertise and recognition.

PERSONALITY EXTREME: Too unemotional, or too melancholy.

GEORGE (Greek/French/English)—M.

MAJOR TALENT: Ability to incorporate public contact, empathetic service and positive approach into career. Wants to make this a better world through laughter, beauty, ar ¹ ˜acious living. Is easy-going, affectionate, and dotes upon love. Has sharp intellect, compassionate nature, and humanitarian instincts. Salesman, clergyman, and detective story writer are possible career opportunities.

PERSONALITY INGREDIENTS: First impression is sensual, open, and enthusiastic. Understands people. Wants adventure, innovations, and mental stimulation. Needs understanding. Is a seeker of perfection, and has logical instincts. Needs serenity, leather-bound books, and all timeless treasures. Feels a lack of polish, or is too self-confident. Tries to escape conventional standards/mundane practices. Must avoid gambles. Concentration on constructive day to day labor brings success.

PERSONALITY EXTREME: Too unconventional, or too proper.

GEORGIA (Greek: George/French/English)—F.

MAJOR TALENT: Ability to incorporate dedicated, structured, organized, practical humanitarian service into career. Is a reconstructive builder. Has conventional approach, stable judgment, and wants material results and rewards. Combines efficiency, executive capabilities, and high energy. Physical therapist, Peace Corps skilled craftsperson, and co-op farmer are possible career opportunities.

PERSONALITY INGREDIENTS: Desires beauty, optimism, and variety. Enjoys people, artistic expression, and humor. First impression is exciting, clever, and tuned to the five senses. Is curious, impulsive, and accident prone. Never has enough time. Seems confident, but must learn to roll with the punches.

PERSONALITY EXTREME: Too independent, or too accommodating.

GEORGINA (Greek: George/German/English)—F.

MAJOR TALENT: Ability to incorporate organization, system, and a broad philosophy into career. Is controlled, businesslike, and geared to helping others. Succeeds in business/arts/government through steady work effort. Tends to relax and may overindulge with food. Bank officer, military instructor, and nurse are possible career opportunities.

PERSONALITY INGREDIENTS: Has large capacity for happiness. Wants optimistic, beautiful, and imaginative life-style. Finds a ray of sunshine, dramatic reactions, and entertainment in everything. First impression is individualistic. Strives for self-assertion, responsibility, and to assume a position of control. Is inventive, courageous, and ambitious. May be impatient, but always feels loving.

PERSONALITY EXTREME: Too blunt, or too ingratiating.

GERALD (Old German/English)—M.

MAJOR TALENT: Ability to incorporate evangelistic approach, idealistic refinements, and a need for service to others into career. Is out to change or save the world. Has off-hand manner, but is high-strung and nervous.

Sees every detail, attracts admirers, and can be a dreamer. When decisive, can change the course of thinking for others. When seeing life through rose-colored glasses, loses creative, spiritual, broad-scoped recognition. Must have a practical partner to keep feet on the ground. Character analyst, welfare worker, and lawyer suggest opportunities.

PERSONALITY INGREDIENTS: Desires harmonious, gracious, respected life-style. Is family/community focused, protective, and attaining. First impression is unconventional, but is motivated toward conventionality. Strives for adventure, travel, and experimentation. Is physical, curious, and clever. Does some serious thinking in mid-forties and makes personality changes.

PERSONALITY INGREDIENTS: Too direct, or too plodding.

GERALDINE (Old German/French/English)—F.

MAJOR TALENT: Ability to incorporate communications gifts, down-to-earth approach, and understanding of public acceptance into career. Is authoritative, self-reliant, and intelligent. Has diplomacy, social awareness, and persuasive material power. Kennel operator, private school owner, and artisan are possible career opportunities.

PERSONALITY INGREDIENTS: Inwardly a bit gullible, peace-loving, and modest. First impression is assertive, direct, and individualistic. Strives for independence, innovations, and leadership. Has sympathetic, generous, and poetic/spiritual/artistic nature, and reaches for the depth of life. Is fortunate and should curb materialistic anxieties.

PERSONALITY EXTREME: Too unconventional, or too conservative.

GERARD (Old German/Danish/French/English)—M.

MAJOR TALENT: Ability to incorporate executive efficiency, persuasive communications, and tremendous energy into career. Likes work and play equally. Is imaginative, understanding, and consistent. Has expansive nature, material ambitions, and inherited strength. Theatrical producer, manufacturer, and public official are possible career opportunities.

PERSONALITY INGREDIENTS: Shines a different light at any gathering. Seems near, yet far away. Strives for individualism, sensitivity, and to bring about uplifting changes. Inwardly is home/family focused. Feels strong-willed, protective, and responsible. Likes comfort, artistic beauty, and loving/happy life-style. Wants the exotic, but needs conventions.

PERSONALITY EXTREME: Too neat, or too sloppy.

GERTRUDE (Old German/Italian/English)—F.

MAJOR TALENT: Ability to incorporate organizational efficiency, keen judgment, and common sense into career. Is careful, determined, and dedicated. May work for humanitarian and life-support expertise, or financial power. Has self-reliance, integrity, and energy. Practicality, economy, and exactness may be carried to extremes. May need to learn to relax. Speech therapist, charity organizer, and business administrator are possible career opportunities.

PERSONALITY INGREDIENTS: Desires secure, enduring, respected lifestyle. Appears well-groomed, natural, and dependable. Strives for material comforts, orderliness, and traditions. Strengths gain recognition when working to improve standards for others. Is a doer.

PERSONALITY EXTREME: Too confident, or too unsure.

GIDEON (Hebrew)—M.

MAJOR TALENT: Ability to incorporate communication skills into career. Is imaginative, responsible, and determined. Has drama, humor and common sense. The struggle of life may weigh heavy but this name can carry any burden. Teacher, writer, and performing artist are possible career opportunities.

PERSONALITY INGREDIENTS: May seem to be a fish out of water. Has difficulty getting attention. Appears dignified, but feels comforting, adaptable, and sensitive to the little things. Strives for intellectual/spiritual/cultural perfection. Needs to be known to be loved.

PERSONALITY EXTREME: Too self-promoting, or too retiring.

GILBERT (Old German/French/German/English)—M.

MAJOR TALENT: Ability to incorporate creative, independent, progressive action into career. Has will-power, drive, and individual style. Combines imagination, philosophical approach, cultural interests, and a defensive instinct. Lawyer, theatrical director, and psychologist suggest opportunities.

PERSONALITY INGREDIENTS: Needs experimentation, travel, and physical pleasures. Is clever, adventurous, and curious. Appears understanding, stimulating, and quietly sensual. Needs family love, and is very protective.

PERSONALITY EXTREME: Too sensitive, or too impersonal.

GILDA (Anglo-Saxon)—F.

MAJOR TALENT: Ability to incorporate cooperation, discipline, and concerned service into career. Is compatible, sensitive to details, and orderly. Attracts admirers, material profits, and honors. Has to touch upon communication, art, and love of beauty. Art gallery manager, voice teacher, and marriage counselor are possible career opportunities.

PERSONALITY INGREDIENTS: First impression is enthusiastic, venturesome, and understanding. Has a knack with people. Desires to be independent, unique, and innovative. Feels progressive, curious, and experimental. Sees good/pleasure in everything, or is a complainer.

PERSONALITY EXTREME: Too active, or too lazy.

GILLIAN (Latin/Celtic/English)—F. & M.

MAJOR TALENT: Ability to incorporate imaginative, analyzed, inventive actions into career. Is managerial, sociable, and refined. Has ambitions but isn't overtly aggressive. Combines friendships, introspection, and pioneering spirit. Travel agent, legal secretary, and business owner are possible career opportunities.

PERSONALITY INGREDIENTS: First impression is noble, youthful, and empathetic. Strives for wide-scoped planning, service, and artistry. Feels different. Desires independence, activity, and control. Wants leadership in humanitarian or creative ventures.

PERSONALITY EXTREME: Too enthusiastic, or too unresponsive.

GINA (Latin: Regina/German diminutive)—F.

MAJOR TALENT: Ability to incorporate inspired ideas, long-term planning, and fantastic results into career. Is sensible, organized, and economical. Has sensitivity to detail, emotions, and humanitarian ideals.

Strives for major coordination of constructive programs. Must aim high. Government agent, stage manager, and translator are possible career opportunities.

PERSONALITY INGREDIENTS: First impression is fetching, imaginative, and friendly. Combines old world charm and today's fashion. Desires individuality. Feels different, determined, and ambitious. Has courage, inventive nature, and innovative ideas. Is a doer, but must learn not to worship surface values. This name reconstructs goals in middle life.

PERSONALITY EXTREME: Too assertive, or too submissive.

GINGER (Latin: Gingiber/variant; Latin: Virginia/English)—F.

MAJOR TALENT: Ability to incorporate sense of responsibility, justice, and group harmony into career. Knows how to make people comfortable. Has common sense, parental nature, and communication gifts. Teaches, protects, and uplifts. Is an aggressive and receptive person. Marriage counselor, receptionist, and home economist are possible career opportunities.

PERSONALITY INGREDIENTS: Desires experimentation, travel, and physical pleasures. Feels curious, impulsive, and full of ideas. First impression is energetic, progressive, and individualistic. Likes to take the lead. Is cooperative, perceptive of details, and impatient for success.

PERSONALITY EXTREME: Too purposeful, or too aimless.

GIRL (often in place of first name on birth certificate)—F.

MAJOR TALENT: Ability to incorporate inventive mind, adaptable nature, and material results into career. Likes to be praised, feel pride, and move forward. Is sensitive to others, thoughtful, and attracts/collects things and people. Actress, psychiatrist, and buyer are possible career opportunities.

PERSONALITY INGREDIENTS: Feels universally sympathetic, loving, and protective. Enjoys sharing knowledge, talents, and philosophies. Appears individualistic, independent, and energetic. Combines innovations, planning, and unlimited potential.

PERSONALITY EXTREME: Too talkative, or too quiet.

GISELLE (Teutonic/English)—F.

MAJOR TALENT: Ability to incorporate authoritative counseling, conventional refinement, and concern for education/artistry/social uplift into career. Is imaginative, dramatic, and a communicator. Either very funny, or too serious. Feels the harmony in music/people/humanity. Should reach out to a broad audience/market. Government, theater arts, and useful product sales are possible career opportunities.

PERSONALITY INGREDIENTS: Likes the limelight but has a retiring quality. Is individualistic, explorative, and progressive. Strives to be, and seems to be, fetching, friendly, and noticeable. Has verve, wonder, and lightness. Inwardly exerts force, is driving, and needs controls.

PERSONALITY EXTREME: Too impulsive, or too cautious.

GLADYS (Latin/English)—F.

MAJOR TALENT: Ability to incorporate clever perceptions, intensity of interest, and adaptability to changes/experiments into career. Has a good memory, imagination, and direct approach. Is physical, cooperative, and sensitive. Combines progressive inventions, enthusiastic attitude, and forceful energy. Politics, advertising, and theater are possible career opportunities.

PERSONALITY INGREDIENTS: Wants efficiency, fair judgments, and material success. Feels managerial, discriminating, and dependable. First impression is helpful, understanding, and sympathetic. Strives for family/community harmony, respect, and attainments. Wants to advise, uplift, and improve living conditions. May get too parental, or avoid emotional relationships. Happiest when affluent, loving, and experiencing new vistas.

PERSONALITY EXTREME: Too individualistic, or too dependent.

GLEN (Celtic/English)—M.

MAJOR TALENT: Ability to incorporate diplomacy, compatibility, and sensitivity to details into career. Is too decisive, or trying to please everyone. Is helpful, reserved, and adapts to partnership/groups. Musical/dance ensembles, astronomy, and any job providing service are possible career opportunities.

PERSONALITY INGREDIENTS: Needs excitement. Feels curious, clever, and enthusiastic. Likes physical pleasure, fads and fancies. Appears interested, responsible, and wise. Strives for home/family growth, respectability, and material attainments. Needs a deep/abiding love . . . over and over again.

PERSONALITY EXTREME: Too free, or too committed.

GLENN (Old Irish/English)—M.

MAJOR TALENT: Ability to incorporate mental analysis, deep perceptions, and perfectionist approach into career. Is intellectual/spiritual, logical, and poised. Has refined tastes, investigative instincts, and looks at all angles. Either an authority, appointed leader, or refrains from light conversation. Can be quiet or can speak with enviable expertise. Needs solitude, and can keep a secret. Photographer, skilled technician, and engineer are possible career opportunities.

PERSONALITY INGREDIENTS: Appears to be calm, unassuming, and refined. Strives for easy-going, peaceful, cooperative home/family life. Wants to be free to taste all that the physical senses offer. Is full of ideas, changes, and moods. Has a long memory for childhood experiences, and refers to them for guidance. Likes to travel, has sensitivity to details, and a wanderlust.

PERSONALITY EXTREME: Too sensual, or too mental.

GLENNA (Celtic/English)—F.

MAJOR TALENT: Ability to incorporate obvious self-confidence, executive organizational aptitude, and showmanship into career. Is adaptable, protective, and sensitive to details. Has discrimination, companionability, and physical interests. Combines control, dependability, and material attainments. Should aim high to gain strength. Ski instructor, military officer, and statistician are possible career opportunities.

PERSONALITY INGREDIENTS: First impression is refined, adaptable, and retiring. Strives for easy-going life-style, cooperation, and emotional control. Inwardly parental, strong-willed, and family/community focused. Needs to give and get love, guidance, and comforts. May be scared, impulsive, and indecisive, but appears confident in shaky situations.

PERSONALITY EXTREME: Too independent or too accommodating.

GLORIA (Latin/Italian/English)—F.

MAJOR TALENT: Ability to incorporate efficiency, organization, and material values into career. Is sociable, imaginative, and progressive. Has adaptability, executive diplomacy, and resourcefulness. Combines curiosity, communication skills, and forceful mind. Office manager, insurance agent, and editor are possible career opportunities.

PERSONALITY INGREDIENTS: First impression is individualistic, understanding, and confident. Feels a need for culture, refinement, and perfection. Has lack of self-confidence, but may cover it with authoritative conversation. Needs education/expertise/social position to feel secure. Is intelligent, analytic, and can be cunning.

PERSONALITY EXTREME: Too submissive, or too assertive.

GODFREY (Old German: Jeffrey/English)—M.

MAJOR TALENT: Ability to incorporate practical work, economical thinking, and broad-scoped material power into career. Strives for humanitarian service, influential status, and everyday authority. Reaches to accumulate, execute, and feel worthwhile. Physical therapist, charity organizer, and political reformer are possible career opportunities.

PERSONALITY INGREDIENTS: Feels idealistic, zealous, and evangelistic. Wants to build a better mousetrap, or may daydream unrealistically, and attempt to redesign the wheel. First impression is quietly authoritative, concerned, and can be a showman. Strives to better life-support conditions, family/community comforts, and to be a wise counselor. Assumes responsibility, is protective, and needs a worthy cause to promote.

PERSONALITY EXTREME: Too gullible, or too skeptical.

GOLDA (Middle English: Goldie)—F.

MAJOR TALENT: Ability to incorporate articulate, charming, and imaginative personality into career. Is optimistic, dramatic, and has a sense of humor. Combines sensitivity to details, people, and individuality in a variety of interests. Has a superior memory, patience, and administrative approach. Writer, interior decorator, and scientist are possible career opportunities.

PERSONALITY INGREDIENTS: Desires time to think, plan, and build an area of expertise. Feels logical, analytic, and culturally ambitious. First impression is open-minded, progressive, and enthusiastic. Likes adventure, cleverness, and physical pleasures. Combines the introverted loner, and the ability to be at home with everyone. Scatters energy.

PERSONALITY EXTREME: Too aggressive, or too receptive.

GOLDIE (Middle English/English)—F.

MAJOR TALENT: Ability to incorporate keen intelligence, introspective analysis, and desire for perfection into career. Is imaginative, philosophical, and structured. Has humor, honest approach, and optimism. Combines appearance, common sense, and designed planning. Is wise, direct, and culturally attaining. Writer, communications technician, and librarian are possible career opportunities.

PERSONALITY INGREDIENTS: First impression is progressive, striking, and off-beat. Strives for mobility, change, and sensual stimulation. Is curious, quick, and has a spontaneous rapport with people. Inwardly feels easy-going, loving, and adaptable. Wants partnerships/mate, emotional serenity, and is sensitive. Needs quiet retreat when decisions are to be made. Wants recognition, but will not forsake personal freedom to get it.

PERSONALITY EXTREME: Too busy, or too bored.

GOLDY (Middle English: Goldie)—F.

MAJOR TALENT: Ability to incorporate artistic, humanitarian, and inventive services into career. Is perceptive of details, intellectually analytic, and philosophical. Has empathy, broad-scope, and emotional reactions. Attracts admirers, is inspirational, and expects perfection from self and others. Medicine, legislature, and performing arts are possible career opportunities.

PERSONALITY INGREDIENTS: Feels conservative, and appears unconventional. Needs security, respected life-style, and practical approach. Strives for freedom, travel, and physical pleasure. First impression is attention-getting. Should have non-routine schedule, cultural stimulation, and traditional standards.

PERSONALITY EXTREME: Too authoritative, or too detached.

GORDON (Old English/English)—M.

MAJOR TALENT: Ability to incorporate innovations, inventions, and individuality into career. Is an original. Combines communication talents, mental analysis, and courage to be the first. Has leadership, active energy, and strong convictions. Designer, salesman, and pilot are possible career opportunities.

PERSONALITY INGREDIENTS: First impression is calm, cool, and collected. Strives for intellectual stimulation, refined environments, and perfection in everything. Enjoys beauty, fun, and imaginative people. Bounces through adversity, likes children/pets, and flirts but is rarely unfaithful. Desires to be extroverted, and appears to be introverted. Wants recognition, invests wisely, and is focused upon home/family/community service.

PERSONALITY EXTREME: Too adventurous, or too responsible.

GOTTFRIED (Old German: Jeffrey/German)—M.

MAJOR TALENT: Ability to incorporate freedom of self-expression, mental curiosity, and a need for variety into career. Is clever, quick, and promotional. Has a knack for handling people, identifying progressive changes, and tackling innovative jobs. Combines non-routine ideas/schedules/social activities, mobility, and enthusiastic approach. Politics, advertising, and theater are possible career opportunities.

PERSONALITY INGREDIENTS: First impression is friendly, imaginative, and tastefully fashionable. Strives for artistry, conversational compatibility, and love. Feels cooperative, adaptable, and retiring. Wants easygoing days, beauty, and emotional calm. Is sensitive to details, orderly, and habitual. Looks for conformation before making major changes.

PERSONALITY EXTREME: Too self-disciplined, or too unstructured.

GRACE (Latin/English)—F.

MAJOR TALENT: Ability to incorporate intellectual/spiritual analysis, cultural attainments, and perfectionist nature into career. Is dignified, cooperative, and experimental. Takes things in stride, needs thinking time, and an area of expertise. Investigates, ponders, and intuitively concludes. Gets things down to a science. Librarian, florist, and antique dealer are possible career opportunities.

PERSONALITY INGREDIENTS: Desires abundant, harmonious, attaining family/community life-style. Needs roots, responsibility, and to give protection and counsel. Has a knack of making people comfortable. Is a born theatrical producer and showman. First impression is individualistic. Strives for independence, innovations, and strength. Seems different, assertive, and definite. Likes to have control.

PERSONALITY EXTREME: Too kaleidoscopic, or too stereotyped.

GRANT (Old French/Middle English)—M.

MAJOR TALENT: Ability to incorporate helpful, just, and comforting service into career. Is protective, responsible, and concerned with home/community attainments. Has sympathetic, sensitive, practical nature. Combines talent for communications, attention to details, and showmanship. Teacher, home decorating salesman, and talent agent are possible career opportunities.

PERSONALITY INGREDIENTS: First impression is clever, friendly, and open to everything. Strives for experimentation, freedom, and sensual pleasures. Feels ambitious, individualistic, and innovative. Has courage, strength, and high spirits. May be domineering, too protective, or intolerant when saddled with too much responsibility. Must recognize need for mobility.

PERSONALITY EXTREME: Too burden-bearing, or too unfaithful.

GREG (Greek: diminutive; Gregory/Celtic: alone/English)—M.

MAJOR TALENT: Ability to incorporate individualistic, assertive actions into career. Is businesslike, adaptable, and inventive. Has courage, keen judgment, and sensitivity to details. Combines cooperation, executive organization, and ambitious innovations. Producer, scientist, and idea instigator are possible career opportunities.

PERSONALITY INGREDIENTS: Needs freedom, sensual pleasures, and changing experiences. Bores easily. First impression is attention-getting, enthusiastic, and self-promoting. Creates an air of excitement and with progressive interests becomes a catalyst for change in the lives of others.

PERSONALITY EXTREME: Too questioning, or too gullible.

GREGORY (Greek/English)—M.

MAJOR TALENT: Ability to incorporate far-sighted and far-reaching progressive ideas into career. Is curious, eloquent, and promotional. Attracts leadership, admirers, and unconventional experiences. Has mathematical, scientific, and investigative approach. Is compassionate, clever, and a great diagnostician. May not dig deeply enough to work out a problem, but intuitionally knows when one exists. Photographer, electrical specialist, and critic are possible career opportunities.

PERSONALITY INGREDIENTS: First impression is attractive, sociable, and imaginative. Strives for beauty, variety, and love. Inwardly is futuristic, idealistic, and creative. Aspires to make this a better world. May be impractical. Wants spiritual values and material comforts.

PERSONALITY EXTREME: Too confident, or too concealing.

GRETA (Latin: Margaret/Lithuanian diminutive/Lettish)—F.

MAJOR TALENT: Ability to incorporate sympathy, nurturing guidance, and comforting service into career. Is conscientious, firm, and magnetic. Has family/community focus, parental instincts, and is protective. Combines sensitivity to details, practical economy, and wise counseling. Inspired to beautify, express artistically, and enjoy nature. Teacher, nurse, and musical/acting coach are possible career opportunities.

PERSONALITY INGREDIENTS: First impression is noble, romantic, and graceful. Strives to be youthful, well-groomed, and dramatic. Feels strong-willed. Sets exemplary personal standards and expects everyone to live up to them. Needs gracious, abundant, respected life-style. Can be possessive, stubborn, and too helpful. Must have peace, truth, and justice in environment or suffers emotionally.

PERSONALITY EXTREME: Too individualistic, or too ordinary.

GRETCHEN (Latin: Margaret/German)—F.

MAJOR TALENT: Ability to incorporate efficiency, sharp judgment, and self-reliance into career. Is a broad-scoped, organized, administrative hard-worker. Has humanitarian instincts, orderly approach, and plans for tangible results. Has material power for commercial success, but is gifted with the drive to benefit others in universal service. Physical therapist, diabetic nutritionist, and hospital fund raiser are possible career opportunities.

PERSONALITY INGREDIENTS: First impression is dignified, calm, and authoritative. Strives for cultural attainments, academic/technical/scientific expertise, and perfection. Needs independence. Feels determined, inventive, and ambitious. May play the piano, dance, or be drawn to athletics. Should select a cause and use extraordinary material power wisely.

PERSONALITY EXTREME: Too impulsive, or too cautious.

GRETEL (Latin: Margaret/German)—F.

MAJOR TALENT: Ability to incorporate practical, structured, and ambitious ideas into career. Is individualistic, dramatic, and generous. Has determination, energy, and competitive spirit. Combines communication talents, inventive approach, and hard work. Real estate sales, dentist, and waitress are possible career opportunities.

PERSONALITY INGREDIENTS: First impression is sociable, attractive, and accessorized. Usually vivacious, imaginative, and optimistic. Feels independent, aggressive, and courageous. Needs to be in control. Should avoid scattering interests, being too forceful, and being too routined.

PERSONALITY EXTREME: Too unimaginative, or too illusionary.

GROVER (Anglo-Saxon/English)—M.

MAJOR TALENT: Ability to incorporate orderliness, system, and disciplined thinking into career. Is a planner. Combines exactitude, economical analysis, and construction. Has endurance, integrity, and conservative instincts. If motivated wisely, may contribute to wide-scoped lasting results. Architect, military officer, and economist are possible career opportunities.

PERSONALITY INGREDIENTS: Has high nervous energy. Is idealistic, and may put workaholic drives into impractical dreams. Feels modest, retiring, and peace-loving. Is not a personality kid, but can attract sup-

porters. Is an impressive salesman for a personal crusade or worthy cause. Attracts creative peer relationships, and needs a sensitive mate.
PERSONALITY EXTREME: Too empathetic, or too unfeeling.

GUINEVERE (Celtic/English)—F.

MAJOR TALENT: Ability to incorporate nobility of purpose, intellectual analysis, and perfection of ideals into career. Is culturally attaining, introspective, and confident. Has progressive ideas, uncommon wisdom, and love of natural beauty. May be patient/kind/adaptable or petty/picky/skeptical . . . has choice. Needs quiet/solitude but may not be friendless. Is a bit above the crowd, but does not have to be a loner. University historian, religious authority, and watch designer are possible career opportunities.

PERSONALITY INGREDIENTS: First impression is refined, calm and distinctive. Strives for discretion, discernment, and fastidiousness. Inwardly is generous, romantic, and non-materialistic. Has a magnetism that comes with animation. Visually seems aloof. Feels for others and will share everything. Happiest in rustic environment away from urban noises.

PERSONALITY EXTREME: Too changing, or too tied-down.

GUNTHER (Teutonic/English)—M.

MAJOR TALENT: Ability to incorporate determination to serve, entertain, or beautify into career. Is the knight in shining armor. Has romantic, loving, imaginative nature. Combines relaxed approach, empathy for others, and optimism. Has leadership, warmth, and sociability. Reporter, lawyer, and postal service reformer are possible career opportunities.

PERSONALITY INGREDIENTS: Inwardly is efficient, organized, and businesslike. Feels managerial, intellectually keen, and impatient with indecisive people. First impression is sturdy, neat, and classic. Strives for respectability, security, and traditional attainments. May be very competitive. Needs unselfish focus.

PERSONALITY EXTREME: Too broad-scoped, or too narrow.

GUSTAVE (Swedish/French/English)—M.

MAJOR TALENT: Ability to incorporate all forms of freedom into career. Is mentally curious, progressive, and a communicator. Has sex appeal, companionability, and cleverness. Learns by experience. Has unique understanding of human nature, is at home with everyone, and has the courage to be different. Advertising, politics, and writing are possible career opportunities.

PERSONALITY INGREDIENTS: Desires beauty, nobility and culture. Feels empathetic, generous, and romantic. Sees a great lover when he looks in the mirror. First impression is striking, energetic, youthful. Is vigorous, changeable, and headstrong. Attracts recognition and inheritances.

PERSONALITY EXTREME: Too eccentric, or too average.

GUY (Old French/English)—M.

MAJOR TALENT: Ability to incorporate executive organizational instincts, efficiency, and sharp material judgment into career. Is careful, analytic, and perceptive of details. Has tact, discrimination, and authority. Combines resourcefulness, individuality, and a perfectionist approach. Finance, government, and science are possible career opportunities.

PERSONALITY INGREDIENTS: Likes to entertain and be amused. Feels imaginative, dramatic, and loving. Needs self-expression and may be a talker. First impression is exciting, enthusiastic, and sensual. Strives for freedom, adventure, and progressive activities. Appears confident, and relates to most people. Has obvious depth, and seems mysterious at times. Should retain optimistic attitude and avoid moodiness and melancholy.

PERSONALITY EXTREME: Too authoritative, or too probing.

GWEN (Celtic/Welsh/English/variant; Celtic: Guinevere-Gwyn)—F.

MAJOR TALENT: Ability to incorporate strong practical work habits into career. Is dependable, honest, and economy conscious. Has problem-solving instincts, strong beliefs, and humanitarian tendencies. Can work for universal constructive growth, or immoral ends with equal strength. May serve universal needs and leave a lasting mark. TV production, real estate, and any profession are possible career opportunities.

PERSONALITY INGREDIENTS: First impression is efficient, managerial, and as affluent as possible. Wants to get down to business, and have a constant change of pace. Enjoys adventure, liberty, and many enthusiasms. Needs patience, to release control, and to divide responsibilities. Cannot burn the candle at both ends without physical drain causing emotional reactions. May be a workaholic.

PERSONALITY EXTREME: Too physical, or too mental.

GWENDOLEN (Celtic: Gwyn/Welsh/English)—F.

MAJOR TALENT: Ability to incorporate service, responsibility, and discipline into career. Is empathetic, emotional, and intuitive. Has charm, administrative instincts, and an unconventional approach. Combines limitless inner resources, mobility, and conservative attitude. Welfare worker, missionary, and doctor are possible career opportunities.

PERSONALITY INGREDIENTS: Strives for realization of ideals. Has a special quality at first meeting. Is adaptable, loving, and cooperative. Inwardly may be disappointed in personal ambitions, realities of everyday living, and the imperfections of people. Feels culturally attaining, dignified, and analytic. Dwells upon the past and may miss the now. Could marry early and produce a large family, or may go it alone and administer to the needy.

PERSONALITY EXTREME: Too progressive, or too retrospective.

GWYN (Celtic/Welsh/English)—F. & M.

MAJOR TALENT: Ability to incorporate life-support responsibilities, instructional instincts, and focus upon family/community improvements into career. Is helpful, kind, and generous. Has need for group harmony, attention to details, and practical approach. Combines ambition, cooperation, and conventional attitude. Marriage counselor, theatrical performer, and hotel manager are possible career opportunities.

PERSONALITY INGREDIENTS: Needs refined, intellectually stimulating, unhurried environment. Enjoys being respected as an authority, and a perfectionist. Appears businesslike. Strives for efficiency, integrity, and power in the establishment. Is persuasive, artistic, strong-willed, and can be a financial and social success.

PERSONALITY EXTREME: Too adventurous, or too placid.

GYPSY (Egyptian/English/American)—F.

MAJOR TALENT: Ability to incorporate artistic inspiration, instinct for bettering mankind, and initiation into commercial ventures into career. Is a visionary, a dreamer, and an original. Has vitality, understanding, and generosity. Combines sensitivity to details, mass market ideas, and a unique characteristic that attracts admiring supporters. Inspirational writer, beauty specialist, and political reformer suggest opportunities.

PERSONALITY INGREDIENTS: Feels adventurous, freedom-loving, and changeable. Has ideas that are unconventional, but appears gracious, comforting, and parental. Can be a promoter, a showman, and a loving responsible parent. Enjoys family/community attainments, self-expression, and an abundant/comfortable life-style. Has many opportunities to grow culturally and may evolve to intellectual/spiritual power.

PERSONALITY EXTREME: Too unruffled, or too temperamental.

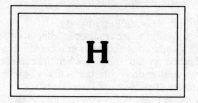

H

All names that begin with the letter *H* have the *Strong Point* of self-reliance—management—material judgment—efficiency—control.

HALEY (Anglo-Saxon/English: Hollis-Holly)—F. & M.

MAJOR TALENT: Ability to incorporate responsibility, group/family focus, and artistic or social welfare work into career. Is sympathetic, protective, and practical. Has emotional sensitivity, gracious manner, and a drive for uplift. Combines learning, teaching, and counseling. Nurse, restaurant manager, and musician are possible career opportunities.

PERSONALITY INGREDIENTS: First impression is refined, noble, and magnetic. Appears to be graceful, dramatic, and romantic. Is charming, broad-scoped, and youthful. Desires to give and receive love, companionship, and accommodations. Is a loyal friend, strong-willed achiever, and generally enjoys a conventional life-style.

PERSONALITY EXTREME: Too self-confident, or too insecure.

HANNAH (Hebrew/Greek: Anna)—F.

MAJOR TALENT: Ability to incorporate individualism, instigation, and leadership into career. Is active, cooperative, and organized. Has courage, faith, and artistic appreciation. Combines ideas, mental organization, and tangible results. Designer, buyer, and editor are possible career opportunities.

PERSONALITY INGREDIENTS: First impression is businesslike. Strives for influence, affluence, and position. Inwardly is peaceful, loving and easy-going. Feels sensitive, reserved, and retiring. Happiest when mated, helping, and learning.

PERSONALITY EXTREME: Too ambitious, or too impractical.

HANS (Hebrew: John/Danish/German)—M.

MAJOR TALENT: Ability to incorporate instruction, orderliness, and pride in helping others into career. Is clever, independent, and protective. Has strong judgments, wisdom, and a lack of discernment. Grows to learn not to judge a book by its cover. Airline steward, interior decorator, and stage performer are possible career opportunities.

PERSONALITY INGREDIENTS: First impression is speedy, open, and physical. Appears friendly, enthusiastic, and progressive. Inwardly wants control. Feels ambitious, innovative, and forceful. Enjoys leadership, freedom, and material comforts. Has a tendency to use people, and must avoid conniving. Should take things less seriously and chuckle at life's ironic twists.

PERSONALITY EXTREME: Too assertive, or too accommodating.

HARDING (Teutonic: Harden/English)—M.

MAJOR TALENT: Ability to incorporate intellectual questioning, logical perceptions, and quality consciousness into career. Is introspective, determined, and a gifted speaker. Knows when to keep silent. Has imagination, practicality, and a drive for perfection. Teacher, scientist, and skilled technician are possible career opportunities.

PERSONALITY INGREDIENTS: Inwardly an independent, aggressive idea man. Needs to lead, be up front, and instigate changes. Appears parental, helpful, and conservative. Strives to upgrade major family/community comforts. Assumes responsibility, guides, and perseveres. May instigate the formation of a credit union on the job, or start a neighborhood youth center . . . feels a kinship and serves a need.

PERSONALITY EXTREME: Too close-mouthed, or too authoritative.

HARLAN (Teutonic/English)—M.

MAJOR TALENT: Ability to incorporate artistic, humanitarian, or spiritual service into career. Is understanding, philosophical, and compassionate. Has romantic nature, magnetic charm, and a broad outlook. Combines attention to details, mental analysis, and contributions to society. College professor, doctor, and humorist are possible career opportunities.

PERSONALITY INGREDIENTS: First impression is dignified, calm, and classy. Strives for culture, natural beauty, and quality. Feels a need for perfection. Inwardly sensitive, peace-loving, and easy-going. Needs companionship, moral support, and to share. Has a font of original ideas, attracts admiration, but may be picky, fence-sitting, or mixed-up. Best when not doing physical labor.

PERSONALITY EXTREME: Too unconventional, or too limited.

HARLEY (Old English/English)—M.

MAJOR TALENT: Ability to incorporate inspiration, constructive power, and a desire to raise standards into career. Is understanding, helpful, and instructive. Has charm, artistic self-expression, and gift with words. Combines domestic/community focus, wise discernments, and selfless sacrifice. Union leader, educational reformer, and medical therapist suggest opportunities.

PERSONALITY INGREDIENTS: First impression is engaging, classic, and youthful. Strives for quality of performance, broad philosophy, and to see/share romance and beauty. Inwardly is protective, strong-willed, and sympathetic. Needs respected, abundant, comfortable life-style. Requires harmonious/peaceful environment or suffers emotionally. When over-burdened, becomes jealous, possessive, and goes for the throat.

PERSONALITY EXTREME: Too refined, or too down to earth.

HARMONY (Greek/English)—F.

MAJOR TALENT: Ability to incorporate structured work, discipline, mental and physical accuracy into career. Is conscientious, practical, and exacting. Has devotion, dignity, and great literary possibilities. A natural talent for the piano. Combines peace, study, and conservative approach. Accountant, proofreader, and landscaper are possible career opportunities.

PERSONALITY INGREDIENTS: First impression is well-groomed, controlled, and businesslike. Inwardly is adventurous, sexy, and en-

thusiastic. Has high material energy. Likes travel, experimentation, and
influential/affluent associates. Has mathematical instincts and balances
relationships, goals, and pleasure as a good bookkeeper should. Is a
person of substance.

PERSONALITY EXTREME: Too confident, or too questioning.

HARRIS (Teutonic/Old English)—M.

MAJOR TALENT: Ability to incorporate innovative leadership, progressive ideas, and instant action into career. Is sociable, perceptive, and
controlled. Has urge to travel, love of beauty, and need to be first.
Combines originality, self-expression, and keen mental analysis. Designer, lawyer, and salesperson are possible career opportunities.

PERSONALITY INGREDIENTS: First impression is strong, positive, and
impressive. Attracts boosters, broad-scoped contacts, and prosperity.
Inwardly feels independent, ambitious, and capable. Needs to be boss.
Has extraordinary ideas.

PERSONALITY EXTREME: Too aggressive, or too indecisive.

HARRISON (Teutonic/Old English)—M.

MAJOR TALENT: Ability to incorporate creative self-expression, disciplined writing, and congeniality into career. Is imaginative, inspirational,
and can be a talker. Has determination, dedication, and material ambitions. Combines talent, work, and executive judgment. Fiction writer,
promoter, and advertising salesperson are possible career opportunities.

PERSONALITY INGREDIENTS: First impression is persistent, enthusiastic, and experimental. Strives for physical pleasures, clever innovations, and unconventional challenges. Appears confident, but is
unsure unless there is an authority or designated leader present. Inwardly needs quality, natural beauty, and cultural refinements. Is never
rich enough or loved enough. Needs solid intellectual/spiritual education.

PERSONALITY EXTREME: Too adventurous, or too cautious.

HARRY (English diminutive of Henry/Harold/Harris/Harrison/alone)—
M.

MAJOR TALENT: Ability to incorporate mental analysis, perfectionist
nature, and conventional procedures into career. Is culturally attaining,
logical, and unflappable. Has charm, gift of gab, and imagination. Combines common sense, communication, and quality research. Lawyer,
electrical engineer, and librarian are possible career opportunities.

PERSONALITY INGREDIENTS: Wants affluence, influence, and respected
position. Feels fair, honest, and willing to work. First impression is well-
tailored, controlled, and solid. Strives for money, family pride, and community respect. Wins when ambitions are not purely materialistic. Loses
reputation/emotional happiness/possessions after tasting success if ambitions remain power oriented. Position is maintained when, after basic
goals are attained, focus shifts to enjoying work for its contribution to
society.

PERSONALITY EXTREME: Too gullible, or too cunning.

HAROLD (Anglo-Saxon/Danish/French/English)—M.

MAJOR TALENT: Ability to incorporate disciplined work, exacting routines, and competitive instincts into career. Is organized, expressive, and independent. Has artistry, imagination, and conscientiousness. Combines determination, communication, and individuality. Architect, builder, and fashion manufacturer are possible career opportunities.

PERSONALITY INGREDIENTS: Desires perfection. Needs cultural attainments, quality, and thinking time. Feels mentally analytic, dignified, and investigative. Appears businesslike, well-tailored, and conservative. Strives for material accumulation, position, and integrity. At best when organized, concentrated, and cooperative.

PERSONALITY EXTREME: Too unscheduled, or too routined.

HARRIET (Old German: Henrietta/Middle English/English)—F.

MAJOR TALENT: Ability to incorporate discriminating tastes, perceptive mind, and desire for perfection into career. Is artistic, expressive, and materially practical. Has determination, poise, and constructive approach. Combines discipline, inspiration, and mental analysis. Researcher, accountant, and scientific/technical expert are possible career opportunities.

PERSONALITY INGREDIENTS: Desires gracious, abundant, conventional life-style. Wants to be responsible, sympathetic, and understanding. Needs warmth, love, and protection, but first impression is a bit cool. Seems refined, poised, and confident. Knows how to keep a secret, aspires to cultural refinements, and enjoys being authoritative.

PERSONALITY EXTREME: Too sensitive, or too indifferent.

HARVEY (Old French/Celtic/English)—M.

MAJOR TALENT: Ability to incorporate mental analysis, keen powers of observation, and intuitional judgments into career. Is articulate, practical, and structured. Has dignity, perseverance, and a desire for perfection. Combines quality consciousness, love of beauty, and authoritative manner into career. Lecturer, psychoanalyst, and appraiser are possible career opportunities.

PERSONALITY INGREDIENTS: First impression is individualistic. Appears energetic, instigative, and positive. Inwardly needs home/family/social attainments, responsibilities, and sympathetic understanding. Feels parental, firm, and conscientious. Happiest in cultural, busy, and domestic life-style. Needs moral support, intellectual stimulation, and originality to achieve ambitions.

PERSONALITY EXTREME: Too skeptical, or too gullible.

HATTIE (Old German: Henrietta/English: diminutive)—F.

MAJOR TALENT: Ability to incorporate empathetic, responsible, independent nature into career. Is romantic, generous, and capable. Has talent for love. Combines humanitarian instincts, emotional sensitivity, and detailed mental analysis. Doctor, teacher, and all forms of artistic expression are possible career opportunities.

PERSONALITY INGREDIENTS: First impression is authoritative, efficient, and managerial. Strives to be businesslike, influential, and wealthy. Inwardly is an original. Needs change, innovations, and to take charge. Happiest when busy, up front, and progressing.

PERSONALITY EXTREME: Too unconventional, or too conservative.

HAYDEN (Anglo-Saxon/English)—M.

MAJOR TALENT: Ability to incorporate artistic, scientific, and technical skills into career. Is versatile, expressive, and imaginative. Has charm, sex appeal, and resourcefulness. Combines constructive planning, practical administration, and universal values. Surgeon, judge, and any communications profession are possible career opportunities.

PERSONALITY INGREDIENTS: Appears to be, and is, comforting and comfortable. Needs love, warmth, and harmony. Strives to improve conventional family/community standards, takes responsibility, and wants respect. May be strong-willed, opinionated, and prone to first impressions. Needs to protect, and may be too self-protective. By putting blinders on, the things that do not live up to personal standards can be ignored. Happiest after learning to live and let live.

PERSONALITY EXTREME: Too self-satisfied, or too changeable.

HAZEL (Anglo-Saxon/English)—F.

MAJOR TALENT: Ability to incorporate analytic mind, logic, and desire for expertise into career. Is intuitional, sensitive, and culturally attaining. Has questioning nature. Combines wanderlust, adaptability, and concentration. Keen powers of observation, perseverance, and hard work attract material security. Accountant, technical expert, and appraiser are possible career opportunities.

PERSONALITY INGREDIENTS: Strives for independence, progressive change, and innovations. Feels ambitious, individualistic, and managerial. Likes to be in control. Inwardly needs love, harmonious family life-style, and artistic self-expression. Feels protective, serving, and responsible. Unforgettable childhood experiences remain as guideposts throughout life.

PERSONALITY EXTREME: Too chatty, or too withdrawn.

HEATH (Anglo-Saxon/Middle English/English)—F. & M.

MAJOR TALENT: Ability to incorporate responsible, sympathetic, and sharing nature into career. Is an idealistic romantic. Has concern for home/family/community, artistic self-expression, and conservative values. Is interested in raising standards, adjusting problems, and seeking beauty. Teacher, divorce lawyer, and interior decorator are possible career opportunities.

PERSONALITY INGREDIENTS: First impression is classic, congenial, and empathetic. Strives for broad contacts, universal markets, and worthwhile projects. Inwardly needs companionship, love, and encouragement. Can be a showman and has an unusual voice. Interests surround health, music, theater, and comforting improvements.

PERSONALITY EXTREME: Too status seeking, or too backward.

HEATHER (Anglo-Saxon/English)—F. & M.

MAJOR TALENT: Ability to incorporate inventive, idealistic, and intuitive ideas into career. Has high energy, practicality, and imagination. Combines vision, love of beauty, and methodology. Can be inspirational as a financial and spiritual success. Political reformer, social worker, and publicist are possible career opportunities.

PERSONALITY INGREDIENTS: First impression is neat, harmonious, and romantic. Appears to have engaging manner, nobility, and understand-

ing. Inwardly is fluctuating on ideas, sensitivity, and attention to the little
things. Can sense a feather floating in the wind. Needs love, peace, and
easy-going life-style. Strives for a broad philosophy and humanitarian
contributions to society.

PERSONALITY EXTREME: Too emotional, or too withdrawn.

HECTOR (Greek/English)—M.

MAJOR TALENT: Ability to incorporate concern for reforms in home/
community education, health, and material life support into career. Is
imaginative, nature loving, and steadfast. Has strong protective instincts, problem solving ideas, and compassion. Combines determination, commitment, and strong convictions. Social work, marriage counseling, and home improvement sales are possible career opportunities.

PERSONALITY INGREDIENTS: Serves family, community, universal
needs. Feels idealistic, creative, and energetic. May be impractical. First
impression is dependable, honest, and hard-working. Strives for self-
assurance, organization, and material results. Has exceptional intuition,
and progressive ideas. May martyr to relieve the suffering of others.

PERSONALITY EXTREME: Too generous, or too selfish.

HEDDA (German: Hedwig/Scandinavian/English)—F.

MAJOR TALENT: Ability to incorporate extreme energy for broad-
scoped, far-sighted constructive work into career. Is attentive to details,
organized, and determined. Combines communication gifts, intellectual
probing, and drive for tangible results. Has originality, a personal code of
ethics, and persuasive powers. Is wise, outspoken, and has outstanding
mass market potential. Real estate, politics, and any profession are possible career opportunities.

PERSONALITY INGREDIENTS: Visual impression is dignified, poised,
and classy. Strives for prestige, authority, and cultural growth. Inwardly
feels sympathetic, domestically attaining, and devoted to raising standards, sharing wisdom, and protecting loved ones. Can get too personal.
Potentially an innovator, builder, and wants material success.

PERSONALITY EXTREME: Too hurried, or too unruffled.

HEDY (Greek/English/Slavic variant; Old German: Hedwig)—F.

MAJOR TALENT: Ability to incorporate artistic, entertaining, or social
service into career. Is diplomatic, gentle, and sympathetic. Has strong-
will, firmness, and poise. Combines willing counsel, practicality, and a
winning approach. Teacher, nurse, and cosmetician are possible career
opportunities.

PERSONALITY INGREDIENTS: Wants to play at life and is resilient and
sociable. Needs beauty, variety, and unstructured routine. Has imagination, humor, and congeniality. Needs to give and receive love, pleasure,
and optimism. At best when conservative, concentrated, and economical.

PERSONALITY EXTREME: Too analytic, or too thoughtless.

HELAINE (English/Greek: Helen)—F.

MAJOR TALENT: Ability to incorporate affection, empathy, and material expressions of love for humanity into career. Is generous, artistic,
and gracious. Has wit, charm, and firm judgment. Combines self-
expression, responsibility, and human understanding. Romance novel

writer, social reformer, and physician are possible career opportunities.

PERSONALITY INGREDIENTS: Visual impression is introspective, cool, and refined. At first word, warmth, magnetism, and cooperative nature shine out. Needs companionship, sensitivity, and orderliness. Feels modest, adaptable, and easy-going. Best when skilled/educated to a specialty. Aspires to culture and often unreasonably fears loneliness and poverty.

PERSONALITY EXTREME: Too experimental, or too cautious.

HELEN (Greek/Scottish/English)—F.   *LIGHT*

MAJOR TALENT: Ability to incorporate organizational efficiency, sharp material judgment, and executive diplomacy into career. Is discriminating, attentive to details, and conscientious. Has adaptability, understanding, and potential power for material success. Needs to develop inner confidence, but appears to be in control. Buyer, critic, and communications specialist are possible career opportunities.

PERSONALITY INGREDIENTS: Desires individuality, change, and innovations. Feels independent, influential, and special. Brings people together, has a presence, and clear mental perspective. First impression is refined, unruffled, and introspective. Strives for quality, classic beauty, and perfection. Observes, knows when to remain silent, and comments after analysis. May appear to be a snob, but doesn't realize at the moment that a lack of confidence is showing. Comfortable when respected for expertise, authority, or material power.

PERSONALITY EXTREME: Too sensual, or too mental.

HELENA (Greek: Helen/Latin/German/Irish/Spanish)—F.

MAJOR TALENT: Ability to incorporate original, empathetic, and detailed universal solutions into career. Quality of problem solving ideas attracts followers. Combines mental analysis, positive thinking, and perfectionist energy. Fashion design, hospital administration, and government are possible career opportunities.

PERSONALITY INGREDIENTS: Tries to change long standing attitudes to create a better world. Is an idealist whose enthusiasm can usually sell anything. Appears quiet, noble, and refined at first glance. Is magnetic when evangelizing. Needs peace, orderliness, and sensitive loving companionship. May have romantic notions, not allow for the natural course of events, and feel disappointment. Should aim for realism, tolerance, and practicality. Attracts security, stature, and true happiness through emotional rewards.

PERSONALITY EXTREME: Too sure, or too indecisive.

HELENE (Greek/French/German/English)—F.

MAJOR TALENT: Ability to incorporate regular, enduring, organized work into career. Is exacting, economical, and energetic. Has competitive drive, independence, and communication gifts. Combines self-expression, ambition, and practicality. Nurse, office administrator, and skilled laborer are possible career opportunities.

PERSONALITY INGREDIENTS: Strives for quality life-style. First impression is confident, refined, and unruffled. Inwardly feels sympathetic, understanding, and parental. Is home loving, strong-willed, and determined to raise standards. Needs constant routines, education/expertise, and to balance ambitions with reality. Needs individuality, but loses through over-confidence, speculation, and overly aggressive attitudes. At best when concentrated.

PERSONALITY EXTREME: Too self-indulgent, or too thoughtful.

HELGA (Old Norse/Old German)—F.

MAJOR TALENT: Ability to incorporate protective attitude, sympathetic nature, and firm judgment into career. Is attentive to details, administrative, and conscientious. Has diplomacy, organized mind, and conservative tastes. Combines loyalty, dependability, and artistic/life support service to others. Teacher, home economist, and counselor are possible career opportunities.

PERSONALITY INGREDIENTS: Desires comfortable, loving, well ordered life-style. Feels protective, trustworthy, and giving. Appears cool, poised, and refined. Strives for cultural, intellectual, and traditional goals. Is analytic, questioning, and aims for perfection.

PERSONALITY EXTREME: Too independent, or too accommodating.

HENRIETTA (Old German/English)—F.

MAJOR TALENT: Ability to incorporate leadership, originality, and idealistic inventions into career. Is courageous, charming, and strong-willed. Has showmanship, practical structure, and dominating influence. Combines artistic/scientific interests, innovative ideas, and instigation. Doctor, illustrator, and musician suggest opportunities.

PERSONALITY INGREDIENTS: Inwardly needs peace, companionship, and easy-going routine. Wants reasonable comforts, friends, and to feel supportive. First impression is managerial, sharp, and self-reliant. Strives to be practical about money, successful, and influential. Is intense, persuasive, and may tend to relate too much to childhood values. Generally lucky and should live in the now.

PERSONALITY EXTREME: Too aggressive, or too compliant.

HENRIETTE (Old German: Henrietta/French/German)—F.

MAJOR TALENT: Ability to incorporate personal contact with people, variety, and unconventional ideas/routines/relationships into career. Is emotional, active, and creative. Has instinctive understanding, sex appeal, and cleverness. Combines progressive attitudes, adventurous spirit, and companionability. Airline steward, scuba diving instructor, and performing artist are possible career opportunities.

PERSONALITY INGREDIENTS: First impression is efficient, controlled, and as affluent as possible. Wants to get down to business. Strives for financial success, executive leadership, and practical accomplishments. Inwardly wants home, family, and gracious life-style. Feels parental, responsible, and willing to give love/service/devotion. Needs to think before acting and to be discerning in relationships/commitments.

PERSONALITY EXTREME: Too busy, or too bored.

HENRY (Old German/English)—M.

MAJOR TALENT: Ability to incorporate logical, analytic, and unemotional perceptions into career. Is trustworthy, direct, and prone to conventional procedures. Has instinct for authority, secretive nature, and investigative approach. Combines communication gifts, determination, and discretion. Bridge expert, lawyer, and writer are possible career opportunities.

PERSONALITY INGREDIENTS: Inwardly needs beauty, variety, and to
play at life. Feels optimistic, imaginative, and sociable. First impression
is durable, neat, and traditional. Strives for universal/humanitarian
marketplace, material progress, and respectable life-style. May be torn
between amusements and work. Is wise, and, even when diversified,
keeps to a long term goal. Conceals depth of emotions.
PERSONALITY EXTREME: Too silent, or too questioning.

HERBERT (Anglo-Saxon/Danish/French/German/English)—M.

MAJOR TALENT: Ability to incorporate method, administrative economy, and practical concern for material values into career. Is honest,
trustworthy, and disciplined. Has emotional control, substantial goals,
and planning techniques. Combines conventions, conscientiousness, and
hard work. Accountant/lawyer, builder, and craftsman are possible
career opportunities.
PERSONALITY INGREDIENTS: First impression is attractive, congenial,
and kind. Likes humor, entertainment, and beauty. Inwardly is independent, forceful, and ambitious. Wants to come first in business/family.
Has inner faith, inventive ideas, and mixed feelings of isolation and
compatibility. When personalized, loses optimism, common sense, and
may become a conniving schemer. Best when optimistic, compassionate,
and on the up and up.
PERSONALITY EXTREME: Too petty, or too unconcerned.

HERMAN (Old German/English)—M.

MAJOR TALENT: Ability to incorporate untried ideas, cleverness, and
understanding of people into career. Is freedom-loving, active, and
physical. Has sensuality, adaptability, and curiosity. Combines attention
to details, communication gifts and unconventional instincts. Advertiser,
politician, and detective are possible career opportunities.
PERSONALITY INGREDIENTS: Strives for efficiency, executive authority, and material power. Appears businesslike, dignified, and as well-
tailored as possible. Inwardly wants harmonious, gracious, respectable
family/community life-style. Feels devoted, protective, and happy to
help/guide/assume responsibilities. When overconfident, may be over-
bearing, self-indulgent, and tasteless. Needs love, patience, and conventional sense of duty.
PERSONALITY EXTREME: Too eccentric, or too sober-minded.

HERMIONE (Greek/English)—F.

MAJOR TALENT: Ability to incorporate wise/firm authority, protective
instincts, and musical/literary communication gifts into career. Is idealistic, progressive, and vigorous. Has sympathetic, understanding, comforting approach. Combines love of innovations, individuality, and
responsible service to home/family/community. Innkeeper, entertainer,
and interior decorator are possible career opportunities.
PERSONALITY INGREDIENTS: Desires quality, refinement, and culturally stimulating life-style. Feels mentally analytic, logical, and intellectually confident. Appears to be direct, efficient, and businesslike. Strives
for status. Will appear cool, confident, and in control in times of stress.
Usually perceptive, strong-willed, and alert for advancement.
PERSONALITY EXTREME: Too sensual, or too mental.

HESTER (Persian: Esther/Hebrew/English)—F.

MAJOR TALENT: Ability to incorporate traditional standards for artistic/
skillful self-expression into career. Is imaginative, conversational, and
ready to laugh. Has sex appeal, charm, and congeniality. Combines
broad philosophy, optimism, and structure geared to security. Theater,
law, and medicine are possible career opportunities.

PERSONALITY INGREDIENTS: Visual impression is retiring, modest, and
refined. Appears supportive, peace loving, and as if trying to be un-
noticed. Inwardly feels independent, assertive, and ambitious. Needs
change, innovations, and individuality. Strives to balance introvert/
aggressive instincts. Has far-reaching potential when on a conventional
course.

PERSONALITY EXTREME: Too philosophical, or too narrow-minded.

HETTIE (Hebrew: variant; Esther/Hester/Old German: variant;
Henrietta)—F.

MAJOR TALENT: Ability to incorporate organized, enduring, practical
common sense and hard work into career. Is loyal, conscientious, and
logical. Has individuality, independence, and artistic self-expression.
Combines discipline, courage, and good memory. Nurse, farmer, and
skilled laborer are possible career opportunities.

PERSONALITY INGREDIENTS: First impression is congenial, optimistic,
and friendly. Strives to entertain, and be entertained. Looks for the
sunshine. Inwardly feels managerial, impatient, and proud. Is inventive,
progressive, and ambitious. When nervous, may be too competitive,
intense, and argumentative. Best when sure of goals and working
cooperatively.

PERSONALITY EXTREME: Too changeable, or too persistent.

HEZEKIAH (Hebrew/English)—M.

MAJOR TALENT: Ability to incorporate independence, instigation, and
originality into career. Is a forceful, positive, and courageous leader. Has
practicality, responsibility, and idealism. Combines work, energy, and
service. Editor, credit worker, and business owner are possible career
opportunities.

PERSONALITY INGREDIENTS: Desires sensitive partner/mate, tactful
support, and cooperative relationships. Feels modest, shy, and concerned with details. Has a way of using subtle control. First impression is
confident even under stress. Strives for material power, executive organization, and efficient handling of large projects. Sometimes unhappy
experiences turn the potential for too much ambition into strong
humanitarianism. This name may be mercenary.

PERSONALITY EXTREME: Too dominant, or too passive.

HILARY (Greek/English)—F. & M.

MAJOR TALENT: Ability to incorporate aspiration for creative, expansive, refined leadership into career. Is independent, sociable, and mentally analytic. Has courage, determination, and companionability.
Combines unruffled management, variety of interests, and drive to be
first. Stock broker, idea person, and analyst are possible career opportunities.

PERSONALITY INGREDIENTS: First impression is supportive. Inwardly

feels efficient, trustworthy, and businesslike. Retiring appearance belies
self-reliant approach. Has adaptability, business judgment, and diplomacy. Can be straightforward, but is tactful. Is charming, poised, and
aims for perfection.

PERSONALITY EXTREME: Too skeptical, or too gullible.

HILDA (Old Anglo-Saxon/German/Norse/English)—F.

MAJOR TALENT: Ability to incorporate mental analysis, attention to
detail, and keen powers of observation into career. Is investigative, introspective, and factual. Has strong intuition, authoritative attitude, and
the judgment to keep confidences. Combines sensitivity, curiosity, and
perfectionist outlook. Photographer, bartender, and psychoanalyst are
possible career opportunities.

PERSONALITY INGREDIENTS: Seems protective, advisory, and helpful.
First impression is conventional, tasteful, and dependable. Wants home/
family ties, attainments, and abundant living. Enjoys sharing hospitality,
raising standards, and instructing others. Inwardly is independent, determined, and inventive. Needs to lead, manage, and do things quickly.
Likes adventure, travel, and nature. At best when practical, economical,
and hard-working.

PERSONALITY EXTREME: Too active, or too lazy.

HILDEGARDE (Teutonic/English)—F.

MAJOR TALENT: Ability to incorporate individuality, pioneering ideas,
and ambition to contribute to society into career. Is clear-seeing, ethical,
and channeled to communicate. Has wit, curiosity, and self-expression.
Combines independent intellect, research, and action. Any business/
profession that inspires/entertains others is a possible career opportunity.

PERSONALITY INGREDIENTS: First impression is attention getting, and
businesslike. Emits a vibration of understanding and love. Has confidence, high energy, and exceptional perceptions. Inwardly emotional
and sensitive. Wants adoration, moral support, and thoughtfulness.
Needs to curb hasty judgments, sensuality, and tendency to drop people/
projects before they are understood/completed. Very prolific. May generate large family, celebrated offspring, or universally cherished
memories.

PERSONALITY EXTREME: Too careful, or too impulsive.

HILLARY (Greek/English)—M.

MAJOR TALENT: Ability to incorporate common sense, economical administrative techniques, and practical work into career. Has expansive
ideas, physical endurance, and mental concentration. Is honest, loyal,
and dependable. Combines skillful labor, structure, and routine. Comptroller, confidential secretary, and piano player are possible career opportunities.

PERSONALITY INGREDIENTS: First impression is sensual, energetic,
and venturesome. Wants travel, freedom, and physical pleasures. Inwardly feels businesslike, materially attaining, and efficient. Needs executive authority, substance, and influence. Likes the freedom that
money can buy.

PERSONALITY EXTREME: Too aloof, or too inquisitive.

HILLIARD (Teutonic/English)—M.

MAJOR TALENT: Ability to incorporate practical, responsible, inventive, and independent leadership into career. Is forceful, intense, and persuasive. Has showmanship, strong idealism, and methodical approach. Combines discipline, concern for others, and a need to lead the way. Inventor, musician, and doctor suggest opportunities.

PERSONALITY INGREDIENTS: Appears magnetic, noble, and genteel. Wants broad-scope, quality of performance, and to express humanitarian instincts. Inwardly needs to feel artistically or scientifically useful. Has courage, but needs to be prepared to stand alone for unique beliefs or life-style. Is a reasonable person.

PERSONALITY EXTREME: Too conventional, or too immoral.

HIRAM (Phoenician/Hebrew/English)—M.

MAJOR TALENT: Ability to incorporate work, discipline, and practicality into career. Is exacting, structured, and conservative. Has energy, determination, and common sense. Combines unemotional decisions, individuality, and communication gifts. Mechanic, farmer, and accountant are possible career opportunities.

PERSONALITY INGREDIENTS: Desires independence. Feels in control, capable, and proud. First impression is sociable, charming, and imaginative. Needs concentration, organization, and mature approach. Highly competitive nature should be curbed to encourage stability.

PERSONALITY EXTREME: Too dignified, or too earthy.

HOBART (Old German: Hubert/English variant)—M.

MAJOR TALENT: Ability to incorporate self-assertion, instigation, and independent action into career. Is inventive, progressive, and stimulating. Has will power, drive, and cleverness. Combines executive leadership, sensitive perceptions, and individuality. Designer, business owner, and inspector suggest opportunities.

PERSONALITY INGREDIENTS: Wants quality, cultural attainments, and natural beauty. Is an investigative, silent perfectionist. Appears sociable, attractive, and engaging. Strives for artistic self-expression, fashionable interests, and light variety. Is an introvert/extrovert with the courage to be different.

PERSONALITY EXTREME: Too unassuming, or too demanding.

HOLLIS (Old English/English)—F. & M.

MAJOR TALENT: Ability to incorporate artistic/entertaining, and humanitarian self-expression into career. Is articulate, charming, and may be talkative. Has optimism, good taste, and kindliness. Combines sociability, imagination, and variety of interests. Can reach a broad marketplace and leave a lasting impression. Writer, beautician, and cartoonist are possible career opportunities.

PERSONALITY INGREDIENTS: Is a cosmic parent. Tries to protect, assumes responsibility, and raises standards for everyone. Appears comfortable, comforting, and hospitable. Needs and provides family/community pride, harmony, and generosity. Is helpful, dramatic, and emotional. Has sex appeal and attracts love, respectability, and security.

PERSONALITY EXTREME: Too innovative, or too traditional.

HOLLY (Anglo-Saxon: Hollis)—F. & M.

MAJOR TALENT: Ability to incorporate empathetic, creative, humanitarian service into career. Is compassionate, charming, and individualistic. Has sensitivity to details, analytic perceptions, and quality consciousness. Combines cooperation, investigation, and philosophical outlook. Welfare worker, editor, and art dealer are possible career opportunities.

PERSONALITY INGREDIENTS: Appears adventurous, but feels conventional. First impression is understanding, friendly, and progressive. Inwardly is a practical, determined, and disciplined worker. Inspires originality and is strong, positive, and impressive. Must not be too self-critical. Expects the best from everyone.

PERSONALITY EXTREME: Too confident, or too fearful.

HOMER (Greek/English)—M.

MAJOR TALENT: Ability to incorporate freedom, progressive ideas, and action into career. Is adventurous, curious, and understanding. Has clever perceptions, sociability, and physical appetites. Combines imagination, attention to details, and unconventional approach. Newscaster, interpreter, and politician are possible career opportunities.

PERSONALITY INGREDIENTS: Inwardly an idealistic crusader. Wants to improve/change moral attitudes, products, or services. Needs tenderness, understanding, and low-pressure family life. Is filled with nervous energy. Appears friendly, expressive, and sunny. Enjoys beauty, mentally stimulating companionship, and variety. Is a charmer and attracts supporters.

PERSONALITY EXTREME: Too compassionate, or too selfish.

HONEY (Anglo-Saxon/English: diminutive; Honoria)—F.

MAJOR TALENT: Ability to incorporate charm, individuality, and regulated work into career. Is exacting, economical, and dependable, or the opposite. Has logical, concentrated, unemotional approach, or the opposite. Tends to have a good memory, expressive artistic talent, and pride. Combines strong competitive spirit with material ambitions and has a choice. When undisciplined, scatters interests. When decisive and able to work with others, is capable of financial success. Nursing, office management, and building trades are possible career opportunities.

PERSONALITY INGREDIENTS: First impression is extremely sensitive, supportive, and gentle. Inwardly feels special. Has dreams that may not be practical. With a down to earth partner, all things are possible. May have material ambitions that are too unrealistic. Is a magical, loving, generous person.

PERSONALITY EXTREME: Too gullible, or too scheming.

HONORIA (Latin/English)—F.

MAJOR TALENT: Ability to incorporate logic, hard-work, and conscientiousness into career. May serve major health, social, or environmental improvements. Is loyal, practical, and trustworthy. Has mental and physical drive, dignity, and concentrated focus. Aims for executive authority, efficiency, and concrete results. Dietitian, child psychologist, and physical therapist are possible career opportunities.

PERSONALITY INGREDIENTS: Wants to, and should, construct and be prepared to reconstruct for the good of others. Appears conservative,

tailored, and powerful. Inwardly needs material security, natural beauty, and down to earth life-style. May seem plain at times, but radiates high energy in humanitarian pursuits. Organizes, controls, and adds skill to routine matters. Has choice of materialistic or charitable life-style.
PERSONALITY EXTREME: Too different, or too ordinary.

HOPE (Anglo-Saxon/English)—F.

MAJOR TALENT: Ability to incorporate executive diplomacy, efficiency, and discriminating judgment into career. Is self-reliant, practical, and sensitive to details. Has workaholic drives, impatience, and insightful, persuasive powers. Combines orderliness, firmness, and material success. Communications, government, and commerce are possible career opportunities.
PERSONALITY INGREDIENTS: First impression is warm, interested, and harmonious. Strives for respectable, artistic, domestic attainments. Inwardly feels a highly creative/idealistic energy. Needs easy-going environments, stimulating companionship, and inspirational interests. Has capacity to envision, work, and receive material rewards.
PERSONALITY EXTREME: Too enthusiastic, or too unexcitable.

HORACE (Latin/English)—M.

MAJOR TALENT: Ability to incorporate progressive attitudes, actions, and ideas into career. Is in a hurry to try everything. Has confidence, understanding, and a sense of duty, justice, and responsibility. Aims to shed knowledge or improve existing conditions. Is a sensitive, imaginative, catalystic authority for universal growth. Advertising, navigation, and psychology are possible career opportunities.
PERSONALITY INGREDIENTS: First impression is retiring, refined, and quiet. Inwardly feels youthful, optimistic, and interested. Wants to enjoy beauty, artistic stimulation, and people. Notices details, emotional reactions, and praise. Needs to help, collect, and keep the peace. May make rash judgments before maturity. Speculations, dreams, and philosophy bring changes and expansion.
PERSONALITY EXTREME: Too unconventional, or too responsible.

HORATIO (Latin/English)—M.

MAJOR TALENT: Ability to incorporate enthusiasm, inspirational ideas, and untried ventures into career. Is unafraid, speculative, and pioneering. Has faith in times of stress. Combines confidence, promotional approach, and practical hard work. Brings concepts to reality. Promoter, politican, and investigator are possible career opportunities.
PERSONALITY INGREDIENTS: Visualizes, perfects, and masters relationships, challenges, and depth of understanding. Feels orderly, methodized, and determined. Appears individualistic. Strives to be different, forceful, and emotionally controlled. Tackles big jobs and cleverly works out problems. Wants to reach the top and succeeds by following intuition.
PERSONALITY EXTREME: Too interfering, or too personalized.

HORTENSE (Latin/French/English)—F.

MAJOR TALENT: Ability to incorporate versatility, enthusiasms, and perceptions of people into career. Is clever, quick, and progressive. Has mental curiosity, physical appetites, and individualistic approach. Com-

bines common sense, experimentation, and courage. Journalism, personnel work, and theatrical production are possible career opportunities.

PERSONALITY INGREDIENTS: First impression is introspective, aloof,
and refined. Strives to be and appear classic, cultural, and perfect. Has a
secret self and privately fears loneliness and poverty. Is moody, analytic,
and questioning. Best when concentrated on academic/technical/sci-
entific expertise to avoid self-doubt/disappointment. Tendency to investigate everything should be noted in youth and applied intellectually.
High untapped mental energy may cause impractical approach to life.

PERSONALITY EXTREME: Too physical, or too mental.

HOWARD (Teutonic/English)—M.

MAJOR TALENT: Ability to incorporate idealistic concern for people
into career. Is an inspired, instructive, protective service worker. Has
sympathy, generosity, and showmanship. Combines mass market communication gifts and a variety of activities. Uses dedicated energies to
benefit family, immediate community, or the world. This name assumes
burdens. Public health, environmental conservation, and all transporta-
tion/electronic/communication networks are possible career opportunities.

PERSONALITY INGREDIENTS: First impression is businesslike, authoritative, and controlled. Strives for power. Inwardly is analytic, investigative, and a loner. Wants calm environments, natural beauty, and
perfection. Enjoys quality and timelessness. Values privacy, silence, and
research. May be a martyr or obsessed with personal idealism . . . or
both.

PERSONALITY EXTREME: Too immoral, or too honest.

HUBERT (Old German/French/German/English)—M.

MAJOR TALENT: Ability to incorporate sensitivity to details, humanitarian approach, and creative energy into career. Is diplomatic, adaptable, and peace-loving. Has generous nature, vitality, and individualistic
attitude. Combines partnership, determination, and sometimes impractical dreams. Crusader, publicist, and lecturer are possible career opportunities.

PERSONALITY INGREDIENTS: First impression is friendly, imaginative,
and optimistic. Enjoys humor, beauty, and love. Inwardly is businesslike, efficient, and impatient with pettiness. Needs practical work,
authority, and respect. Tuned to courage, arbitration, and resourcefulness. Must persevere.

PERSONALITY EXTREME: Too studious, or too disorderly.

HUGH (Old German/Scottish/English)—M.

MAJOR TALENT: Ability to incorporate diplomatic executive judgment,
management, and control into career. Is practical, efficient, and discriminating. Has intelligence, dependability, and ambitions. Combines
cooperation, discipline, and business interests. Communications specialist, athlete, and school administrator are possible career opportunities.

PERSONALITY INGREDIENTS: Inwardly optimistic, imaginative, and
usually finds the best in people and experiences. First impression is
enthusiastic, venturesome, and energetic. Strives for physical pleasures,

progressive changes, and constant activity. Bores easily, needs variety, and devours beauty. Is a charmer.

PERSONALITY EXTREME: Too mercenary, or too extravagant.

HUGO (Old German/Latin/German)—M.

MAJOR TALENT: Ability to incorporate counseling, artistic/social service, and instinct for improvement into career. Is responsible, concerned, and parental. Has understanding, sympathy, and sensitivity to details. Combines work, orderliness, and musical/vocal interests. Entertainer, hotel/restaurant executive, and personnel director are possible career opportunities.

PERSONALITY INGREDIENTS: Inwardly is wide-scoped, philosophical, and concerned with the skill/quality of performance/service. Feels dramatic/emotional, imaginative, and helpful. Appears proper, dignified, and solid. Strives for artistic expression, family/community attainments, and gracious/respectable life-style. May be a showman/promoter. Generally practical, generous, and optimistic.

PERSONALITY EXTREME: Too stubborn, or too disinterested.

HUMBERT (Teutonic/French/English)—M.

MAJOR TALENT: Ability to incorporate life support service, responsibility, and family/community uplift into career. Is protective, sympathetic, and devoted. May raise standards through an idea, instruction, or performance. Combines imagination, faith, and tolerance. Has potential for a depth of universal or domestic love, and commitment. Uses extraordinary energy when a just cause is identified. Credit union reformer, nutritionist, and counselor are possible career opportunities.

PERSONALITY INGREDIENTS: Inwardly efficient, discriminating, and self-reliant. Feels businesslike. First impression is refined, quiet, and unruffled. Strives for quality, intellectual stimulation, and perfection. Has artistic/scientific/technical approach. Analyzes, plans, executes, and works for personal ideas.

PERSONALITY EXTREME: Too unassuming, or too demanding.

HUME (Teutonic)—M.

MAJOR TALENT: Ability to incorporate adaptability, cooperation, and diplomacy into career. Is loving, sensitive, and gentle. Has patience, friendliness, and instinct for detail and orderliness. Combines unassuming pose, rhythm/musical aptitude, and thoughtfulness. Teacher, poet, and collector are possible career opportunities.

PERSONALITY INGREDIENTS: Inwardly businesslike, realistic, and self-sufficient. Needs to be decisive. First impression is imaginative, entertaining, and optimistic. Enjoys beauty, skillful artistry, and quality craftsmanship. Has subtle control, material judgment, and sharp perceptions. Compliments partnership/group work and takes the lead.

PERSONALITY EXTREME: Too changeable, or too habitual.

HUMPHREY (Anglo-Saxon/English)—M.

MAJOR TALENT: Ability to incorporate professional/artistic/musical public service, firmness, and concern into career. Is protective, strong-willed, and idealistic. Has showmanship, active mind, and individuality. Combines family/community devotion, cleverness, and desire to raise standards. Instructor, union official, and physican are possible career opportunities.

PERSONALITY INGREDIENTS: First impression is introspective, observant, and refined. Strives for quality, authority, and technical/scientific perfection. Inwardly direct, controlled, and businesslike. Needs executive power, but has a way of directing without obvious manipulation. Wants justice, truth, and to win. Fights for beliefs, and may be involved with legal actions. Attracts happiness with the right mate, and becomes too self-indulgent when home life is inharmonious.

PERSONALITY EXTREME: Too confident, or too questioning.

HYACINTH (Latin/French/English)—F.

MAJOR TALENT: Ability to incorporate facts, logic, and mental analysis into career. Is a self-expressive, conscientious, exacting worker. Has a need for culture, refinement, and perfection. Business analyst, librarian, and accountant are possible career opportunities.

PERSONALITY INGREDIENTS: Is efficient, independent, and artistic. Needs gracious, protected, creative life-style. Gives service, sensitivity, and is adaptable. Has strong sense of right and wrong and aims to raise standards, teach, and guide others. At best working on major issues, leaving the details to others.

PERSONALITY EXTREME: Too ambitious, or too undisciplined.

HYMAN (Hebrew/English)—M.

MAJOR TALENT: Ability to incorporate sharp observations, appreciation of details, and mental analysis into career. Is investigative, questioning, and introspective. Has need for privacy, quiet, and cultural stimulation. Combines cooperative spirit, changing interests, and strong intuitional insights. Photographer, appraiser, and engineer suggest opportunities.

PERSONALITY INGREDIENTS: Can be all business, or charm, diplomacy, and understanding personified. Appears to be, and is, a product of past experience. Has wisdom and is a fine judge of character. Needs travel, mobility, and opportunity to individualize. At best when concentrated, working, and balancing physical appetites.

PERSONALITY EXTREME: Too speculative, or too practical.

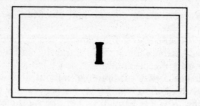

I

All names that begin with the letter *I* have the *Strong Point* of philosophical humor—humanitarian instincts—artistic/social service—compassion.

IAN (Hebrew: John/Scottish)—M.

MAJOR TALENT: Ability to incorporate concern for other people into career. Is protective, instructive, and responsible. Has individuality, courage, and cleverness. Combines student/teacher/parent approach, mobility, and trustworthiness. Sailing instructor, chef, and public service employee are possible career opportunities.

PERSONALITY INGREDIENTS: Inwardly wants to explore, challenge, and win. Feels pioneering, forceful, and energetic. First impression is understanding, physical, and unconventional. Should not be hampered by traditions, personal ties, or responsibilities, but will assume them. Travel, freedom, and adventure will bring welcome changes when immature dependencies are released and experiences become the teacher. Needs to develop a sense of humor.

PERSONALITY EXTREME: Too venturesome, or too careful.

IDA (Old German/French/German/Greek/English)—F. & M.

MAJOR TALENT: Ability to incorporate human understanding, adventurous nature, and love of life into career. Is a fine judge of people, mentally curious, and physically experimental. Has clever, progressive, and adaptable approach. Combines individuality, practical down to earth logic, and versatility. Politician, detective, and critic are possible career opportunities.

PERSONALITY INGREDIENTS: First impression is conventional, sturdy, and neat. Strives for material security, quiet dignity, and just rewards. Inwardly original, courageous, and inventive. Feels independent, proud, and definite. Likes to be boss, be depended upon, and have everything immediately. Must have activity, changes, and be part of whatever is happening.

PERSONALITY EXTREME: Too assertive, or too submissive.

IGNATIUS (Latin/English)—M.

MAJOR TALENT: Ability to incorporate trend-setting ideas, independence, and mental stimulation into career. Is quick, clever, and imaginative. Has spiritual/intellectual/artistic self-expression. Combines inspiration, perfectionist instincts, and individualism. Writer, geographer, and architect are possible career opportunities.

PERSONALITY INGREDIENTS: Inwardly a visionary with practical, humanitarian, workable ideas. Feels drawn to help people and recognizes life support improvements. First impression is protective, responsible, and comforting to family and community. Strives to instruct, guide, and face life as a mature, serious, sensible companion. Can be articulate, quality conscious, and a crusader for the underdog. Needs discernment, balanced work habits, and dramatic challenges.

PERSONALITY EXTREME: Too indefinite, or too decisive.

IKE (nickname)—M.

MAJOR TALENT: Ability to incorporate mental analysis, cultural aspirations, and perfectionist instincts into career. Is successful when on logical, researched, factual ground. Is bound to disappointment when speculative, gullible, and overly confident. Has individuality, parental nature, and determination. Should be the analyst for planning innovative group activities. Engineer, university administrator, and judge are possible career opportunities.

PERSONALITY INGREDIENTS: First impression is special. Has an air of infectious enthusiasm. Inwardly mentally alert, clever, and changeable. Wants adventure, sensual pleasures, and variety. Aims to bring innovative reforms to people and becomes the ear-catching evangelist when a personal belief is to be sold. Easy-going, supportive, and retiring when uninspired.

PERSONALITY EXTREME: Too moody, or too placid.

ILENE (Greek: Helen/English)—F.

MAJOR TALENT: Ability to incorporate unselfishness, zealous assistance, and romantic nature into career. Is trusting, empathetic, and quality conscious. Has intuitional insights, artistic/spiritual interests, and soothing counseling techniques. Combines sensitivity to details, mental analysis, and magnetic influence over others. Entertainer, welfare worker, and lawyer are possible career opportunities.

PERSONALITY INGREDIENTS: First impression is geared for wheeling and dealing. Appears efficient, controlled, and businesslike. Strives for position, security, and life's advantages. Inwardly inventive, aggressive, and independent. Wants to be number one. Needs to instigate innovations, and attracts financial and moral supporters. Should not be indecisive, gullible, or expect that everyone has pure motives. Courts disappointment if intolerant of human frailty.

PERSONALITY EXTREME: Too traditional, or too unconventional.

ILKA (Scottish)—F.

MAJOR TALENT: Ability to incorporate protective counseling and responsible parental nature into career. Is concerned, helpful, and expressive. Has determination, individuality, and unconventional ideas. Combines literary/musical/social studies, conscientiousness, and companionship. Marriage counselor, social director, and publisher are possible career opportunities.

PERSONALITY INGREDIENTS: First impression is striking, spirited, and enthusiastic. Wants to travel, diversify activities, and enjoy physical pleasures. Inwardly feels instigative. Likes to be a pace setter and stimulate change. Is clever and understands human nature. Must avoid aggressively using people to gain ambitions. Has a knack of mingling groups and creating hospitable/gracious life-style.

PERSONALITY EXTREME: Too alone, or too sociable.

ILONA (Hungarian/Greek/English)—F.

MAJOR TALENT: Ability to incorporate artistic, instructional, and uplifting service into career. Is understanding, firm, and just. Has strong domestic ties, material approach, and practical instincts. Combines sympathy, partnership, and love of people. Cosmetician, merchant, and economist are possible career opportunities.

PERSONALITY INGREDIENTS: Inwardly investigative, concentrated, and culturally attaining. Needs quality, dignity, and serenity. Not geared to noise/confusion/commercialism. First impression is influential, self-reliant, and controlled. Strives for material comforts, harmonious relationships, and perfection in all things. May seem stuck-up/aloof/cool. Must be known to be understood. Education/speciality provides needed sense of authority to ease strong fears of loneliness/poverty/unworthiness.

PERSONALITY EXTREME: Too domineering, or too humble.

ILSA (Teutonic/German)—F.

MAJOR TALENT: Ability to incorporate unconventional thought, words, and actions into career. Is curious, versatile, and companionable. Has physical consciousness, understanding, and cleverness. Combines independence, practical work, and learning from life experiences. Travel agent, psychologist, and communications specialist are possible career opportunities.

PERSONALITY INGREDIENTS: Inwardly inventive, courageous, and forceful. Appears conservative, natural, and honest. Strives for respectability through determined work. May be too impulsive, sensual, and adventurous. Needs to balance work/pleasure interests.

PERSONALITY EXTREME: Too assertive, or too submissive.

IMOGENE (Latin/English)—F.

MAJOR TALENT: Ability to incorporate infectious enthusiasm, mental curiosity, and sharp evaluations of people into career. Is versatile, sociable, and adaptable. Has individuality, common sense, and structural approach. Combines discipline, initiative, and unconventional ideas. Politician, detective, and writer are possible career opportunities.

PERSONALITY INGREDIENTS: First impression belies mentally analytic and adventurous personality. Visually seems aloof/unsociable. May be too socially confident or retiring. Inwardly tuned to quality, culture, and perfection. Needs privacy, quiet, and natural beauty. Is pleasure-seeking and wonders why. Best when accepting good fortune as it comes and avoiding ambitious speculations. Wins authority when concentrated. Faces disappointment if greedy, irresponsible, or conniving.

PERSONALITY EXTREME: Too busy, or too bored.

INA (Latin/English)—F.

MAJOR TALENT: Ability to incorporate responsible, protective, understanding, and artistic/social service into career. Is helpful, firm, and loving. Has stability, individuality, and mental curiosity. Combines learning from experience with studious approach and tries to raise standards for family/friends/community. Teacher, musician, and nurse are possible career opportunities.

PERSONALITY INGREDIENTS: Appears to enjoy people, new experiences, and spontaneity. Strives for travel, adventure, and to be different. Needs freedom to pioneer new ideas and respect for being an innovator. Has pride, courage, and ambitions. Has strong opinions and may become emotionally involved in helping others. Magnetically attracts supporters and favors when not martyring. Is able to accept things as they are.

PERSONALITY EXTREME: Too assertive, or too accommodating.

INEZ (Portuguese/Spanish/English/Greek)—F.

MAJOR TALENT: Ability to incorporate understanding, intuition, and impartial love into career. Is charitable, empathetic, and emotional. Has sensitivity, mental analysis, and cultural appetites. Combines romantic, creative, and materialistic aspirations. Entertainer, doctor, and designer are possible career opportunities.

PERSONALITY INGREDIENTS: First impression is conservative, but feels adventurous. Needs physical pleasures, travel, and innovations. Inwardly unconventional. Strives for respectability, financial security, and planned life-style. May have difficulty curbing sensual curiosity or feel torn between eccentricities and propriety.

PERSONALITY EXTREME: Too scheming, or too unambitious.

INFANT (often in place of first name on birth certificate)—F. & M.

MAJOR TALENT: Ability to incorporate leadership, quick actions, and pioneering ideas into career. Is progressive, ambitious, and responsible. Has clear insights, strong independence, and resourcefulness. Combines positive instigation, executive diplomacy and material success. Idea person, salesperson, and inventor are possible career opportunities.

PERSONALITY INGREDIENTS: First impression is noble, neat, and youthful. Strives for empathetic, impressive, and emotionally tuned humanitarian service. Inwardly impatient, forceful, and aggressive. Needs to be boss. May be selfless one day, and selfish the next. Is full of contradiction. May be an inspirational genius with the ability to produce tangible results.

PERSONALITY EXTREME: Too easy-going, or too sensitive.

INGA (Norse: Ingrid-Ingeborg)—F.

MAJOR TALENT: Ability to incorporate high energy, practical vision, and organizational activities into career. Is a skilled coordinator, detail analyst, and charmer. Has tact, adaptability, and conscientiousness. Combines cooperation, construction, and humanitarian instincts. May plan and achieve major results. Stage manager, architectural engineer, and real estate broker are possible career opportunities.

PERSONALITY INGREDIENTS: First impression is attractive, expressive, and sociable. Strives for imaginative interests, constant optimism, and popularity. Inwardly independent, aggressive, and ambitious. Needs a fast pace, innovations, and to be different. Tactful approach covers strong desire to lead. May be too structured.

PERSONALITY EXTREME: Too self-centered, or too dependent.

INGE (Anglo-Saxon, M./German variant, F.)—F. & M.

MAJOR TALENT: Ability to incorporate power, authority, and recognition into career. Is efficient, capable, and purposeful. Has concern for details, parental approach, and physical balance. Combines confident attitude, attraction to money, and integrity. Born supervisor. Private secretary, banker, and athletic coach are possible career opportunities.

PERSONALITY INGREDIENTS: Inwardly adventurous, sensual, and resourceful. Needs change, foreign travel, and constant new interests. Feels restless. First impression is sunny, fashionable, and attention getting. Strives for self-expression, good conversation, and optimistic approach. Conscious of words. May be very sensitive to what is said. Has strong feelings of self-importance which may bring success or enemies. Flexibility adds to happiness.

PERSONALITY EXTREME: Too easy-going, or too critical.

INGRID (Old Norse/English)—F.

MAJOR TALENT: Ability to incorporate inner development, questioning, and logic into career. Is refined, reserved, and proud. Has strong personal values. Combines practical work, communication gifts, and perfectionist approach. Researcher, technical/scientific professional, and analyst are possible career opportunities.

PERSONALITY INGREDIENTS: First impression is dignified, aloof, and quality conscious. Strives to enjoy natural beauty, cultural attainments, and knowledge. Inwardly empathetic, emotional, and broad-scoped. Needs to serve universal, artistic, or charitable interests. Gentle nature hides strong determination. Knows the importance of silence.

PERSONALITY EXTREME: Too moralistic, or too unconventional.

IRA (Hebrew/English)—M.

MAJOR TALENT: Ability to incorporate original ideas, independent leadership, and exploration into career. Is instigative, assertive, and aggressive. Has large scale approach, human understanding, and high energy. Combines positive force, personal style, and fast/clever decision making. Promoter, salesperson, and psychiatrist are possible career opportunities.

PERSONALITY INGREDIENTS: Strives to be everyone's big brother. Appears friendly, impressive, and expressive. Wants drama, strong emotions, and nonroutine experiences. Inwardly a pace setter. Needs freedom, definite purpose, and progress. May lead a double life if true desires are unexpressed. Succeeds when courageous enough to let go of past proven methods to materialize creative concepts.

PERSONALITY EXTREME: Too changeable, or too steadfast.

IRENE (Greek/English)—F.

MAJOR TALENT: Ability to incorporate strong principles, wholesome thought, and harmonious nature into career. Is affectionate, protective, and responsible. Has love of people and beauty. Combines useful service, imagination, and gracious approach. Reformer, teacher, and artist are possible opportunities.

PERSONALITY INGREDIENTS: First impression is striking, enthusiastic, and adventurous. Strives for physical pleasures, travel, and mental exploration. Inwardly individualistic, creative, and progressive. Needs activity, unique interests, and controlling influence. Attracts off-beat experiences, love, and money.

PERSONALITY EXTREME: Too restless, or too plodding.

IRIS (Greek)—F.

MAJOR TALENT: Ability to incorporate individuality, controlling influence, and creative concepts into career. Is ambitious, determined, and different. Has executive diplomacy, sensitivity to details, and organizational approach. Combines cooperation, material goals, and inspirational ideas. Any business, science, and statistics are possible career opportunities.

PERSONALITY INGREDIENTS: Inwardly emotional, understanding, and helpful. Needs wide-scope of friends, interests, and experiences. Feels passionate drives and emotions. First impression is proud, assertive, and busy. Strives to be first. Should avoid impatience with less energetic, efficient, and aggressive associates.

PERSONALITY EXTREME: Too indecisive, or too sure.

IRMA (Old German: Armina/English variant)—F.

MAJOR TALENT: Ability to incorporate adaptability, mental curiosity, and physical attraction into career. Is sensitive, imaginative, and versatile. Has understanding of human frailty, gentleness, and self-expression. Combines cooperation, a knack with words, and learning from life experience. Amusement industries, commercial art, and sportscasting are possible career opportunities.

PERSONALITY INGREDIENTS: First impression is neat, conventional, and natural. Strives for material security, respectability, and constructive interests. Inwardly independent, determined, and supervisory. Needs progressive activity, innovations, and to feel important. May be temperamental. Attracts ambitions with friendly, unselfish, warm attitudes.

PERSONALITY EXTREME: Too different, or too ordinary.

IRVIN (Anglo-Saxon/English)—M.

MAJOR TALENT: Ability to incorporate artistic and humanitarian self-expression into career. Is imaginative, empathetic, and broad-scoped. Has dramatic emotions, romantic notions, and spans the oceans. Born philosopher, artist, and poet. Combines imagination, showmanship, and important enterprises. Attracts well-known personalities. Song writer, public defender, and commentator are possible career opportunities.

PERSONALITY INGREDIENTS: Appears to be, and is, helpful, concerned, and youthful. Feels intense about everything. Strives for uncommercial approach, but is businesslike when necessary. Attracts burdens, but has vast inner resources. Inspires followers when optimistic, honest, and just.

PERSONALITY EXTREME: Too earthy, or too aesthetic.

IRVING (Anglo-Saxon/English)—M.

MAJOR TALENT: Ability to incorporate clear perceptions, mental analysis, and perseverance into career. Is pensive, meticulous, and quality conscious. Has material judgment, communication techniques, and desire for perfection. Combines self-expression, down to earth constructive planning, and cultural aspirations. Investment counselor, dentist, and historical writer are possible career opportunities.

PERSONALITY INGREDIENTS: First impression is quiet, dignified, and unruffled. Strives for nature's pleasures, peace, and the time to enjoy meditative silence. Inwardly a sympathetic, emotional romantic. Wants personal love but gets involved helping everyone. Really feels for others, and wants to share beliefs, talents, and worldly wisdom. Generally non-materialistic. Attracted to guide, inform, uplift family/community/universe. Should avoid physical over-indulgences. May be too easy-going and have to fight fat.

PERSONALITY EXTREME: Too analytic, or too superficial.

IRWIN (Anglo-Saxon: Irvin/English)—M.

MAJOR TALENT: Ability to incorporate individualistic opinions, initiative, and self-assertion into career. Is innovative, firm, and geared to one love at a time. Has sense of immediacy, inner faith, and a desire to be different. Combines use of words, sharp mental analysis, and progressive ideas. Sales manager, travel agent, and designer suggest opportunities.

PERSONALITY INGREDIENTS: Inwardly generous, understanding, and kind. Feels romantic and wants to be a great lover. First impression is energetic, direct, and fast-paced. Strives for speed, stimulation, and independence. May talk too much or too little. Attracts support and stability from harmonious marriage. Should avoid impulsive emotional outbursts.

PERSONALITY EXTREME: Too curious, or too satisfied.

ISAAC (Hebrew/Latin/Greek/English)—M.

MAJOR TALENT: Ability to incorporate group participation, responsibility, and parental approach into career. Is protective, instructive, and counseling. Has strong home/family ties, determination, and conventional material goals. Combines adventurous nature, independence, and service to others. House painter, hospital technician, and hotel manager are possible career opportunities.

PERSONALITY INGREDIENTS: Inwardly idealistic, inventive, and inspired to introduce reforms. Needs love, sensitive relationships, and gentle understanding. Is high-strung and visionary. First impression is hard-working, trustworthy, and natural. Strives for practical, constructive, financially secure life-style. May be too helpful and impose personal standards upon others.

PERSONALITY EXTREME: Too talkative, or too unsociable.

ISABEL (Hebrew/Spanish/English)—F.

MAJOR TALENT: Ability to incorporate oral self-expression, charm, and imagination into career. Is versatile, sociable, and kind. Has congenial approach, an eye for beauty, and youthful interests. Combines instigation of creative ideas, attention to detail, and communication. Jeweler, entertainer, and dressmaker are possible career opportunities.

PERSONALITY INGREDIENTS: Wants to be, and is, protective, trustworthy, and ambitious for home/family. Strives for respectability, material comforts, and abundant life-style. Needs love, harmonious environments, and conventional advantages. Remembers everything.

PERSONALITY EXTREME: Too revealing, or too inexpressive.

ISABELLA (Hebrew: Isabel/Danish/Italian/English)—F.

MAJOR TALENT: Ability to incorporate intellectual approach, quality consciousness, and strong intuition into career. Is poised, sensitive, and attentive to details. Has confidential nature. Combines adaptability, mobility, and desire for perfection. Very resourceful. Journalistic photographer, appraiser, and accountant are possible career opportunities.

PERSONALITY INGREDIENTS: First impression is magnetic, sympathetic, and graceful. Strives for humanitarian principles, romantic pleasures, and artistic beauty. Inwardly is self-questioning. Confident one moment and unsure the next. Needs education or long-standing expertise to maintain inner security. Fears loneliness and poverty. Keeps secrets.

PERSONALITY EXTREME: Too courageous, or too cowardly.

ISADORA (Greek/English)—F.

MAJOR TALENT: Ability to incorporate structured routines, competitive nature, and determination to overcome all obstacles into career. Is a hard-working, imaginative individualist. Has drive, but must focus upon organization and diplomacy to maintain material security. Combines self-expression, originality, and constructive planning. Mnemonics instructor, television performer, and gymnast are possible career opportunities.

PERSONALITY INGREDIENTS: Needs to feel influential. Wants money, authority, and prestige. First impression is striking, adventurous, and understanding. Strives for travel, sensual pleasures and to be different. High mental and physical energies need outlets. Should adopt cooperative attitude to uncomplicate life-style.

PERSONALITY EXTREME: Too aggressive, or too intimidated.

ISAIAH (Hebrew/English)—M.

MAJOR TALENT: Ability to incorporate decision-making, will power, and individuality into career. Is forward thinking, original, and ambitious. Has courage, executive diplomacy, and modesty. Combines cooperation, materialistic instincts, and activity. Writer, engineer, or diagnostician are possible career opportunities.

PERSONALITY INGREDIENTS: First impression is noble, charming, and understanding. Strives for quality of self-expression, service to humanity, and camaraderie. Inwardly driving for tangible results for independent ideas. Wants to be first to climb the highest mountain. Needs to be different and may be too daring. Best when investigative, patient, and cautious.

PERSONALITY EXTREME: Too self-sufficient, or too dependent.

ISIDORE (Greek/Danish/French/English)—M.

MAJOR TALENT: Ability to incorporate cultural aspirations, mental probing, and perfectionist attitudes into career. Is analytic, investigative, and refined. Has quality taste, high intuition, and confidential instincts. Combines a knack with words, practical work approach, and perseverance to become technically/scientifically expert. Secret agent, astronomer, and auditor are possible career opportunities.

PERSONALITY INGREDIENTS: Inwardly inventive, idealistic, and often impractical. Wants to save/change/reform and raise spiritual standards. First impression is engaging. Strives for physical pleasures, travel, and new experiences. Has a way with strangers that puts them at ease. Emotionally cannot let go of childhood experiences and maintains a constant comparison between then and now.

PERSONALITY EXTREME: Too eccentric, or too conservative.

ISRAEL (Hebrew/Greek/English)—M.

MAJOR TALENT: Ability to incorporate independence, self-assertion, and progressive ambitions into career. Is positive, direct, and applied to tangible results. Has decisive approach, unclouded perceptions, and sensitivity to details. Combines cooperative efforts, material power, and individuality. Should avoid recklessness and practice self-control to maintain stability. Inventor, politician, and business owner are possible career opportunities.

PERSONALITY INGREDIENTS: First impression is down to earth, dignified, and conventional. Strives for practical construction, respectability, and conventional standards. Inwardly is protective and materially attaining for home/family/community. Wants to raise standards, live graciously, and maintain harmonious relationships. Needs love, comfort, and mature companionship. Wants peace but not at the price of independence. Is full of contradictions, pride, and strong opinions. Will misplace trust, suffer, and refuse to do anything resembling that experience again. May be inflexible.

PERSONALITY EXTREME: Too talkative, or too uncommunicative.

IVAN (Hebrew: John/Russian)—M.

MAJOR TALENT: Ability to incorporate courage, independence, and broad-scoped attitudes into career. Is inventive, pioneering, and forceful. Has emotional instincts, swift perceptions, and active energy. Combines individuality, humanitarian principles, and human understanding. Attracts love, money, and family contentment, but may lead a double life. Credit advisor, editor, and architect are possible career opportunities.

PERSONALITY INGREDIENTS: First impression is expansive, noble, and youthfully vigorous. Strives for brotherly love, drama, and romance. Inwardly aggressive, assertive, and materially ambitious. Needs freedom, control, and to be boss. Has little patience for details and concentrates on major issues. Is proud and cannot tolerate embarrassment.

PERSONALITY EXTREME: Too physical, or too mental.

IVY (Greek/English)—F. & M.

MAJOR TALENT: Ability to incorporate tact, cooperative efforts, and orderliness into career. Is analytic, attentive to details, and studious. Has supportive instincts, charm, and emotional sensitivity. Excels in partnership. When making decisions, tends to judge by appearances. Maintains stability when tuned to the work, not to the appearance of a person. Private secretary, accountant, and skilled craftsman are possible career opportunities.

PERSONALITY INGREDIENTS: Inwardly aspires to cultural attainments, quality products, and perfection in everything. Needs expertise/authority/education to assure self-confidence. Wants prestige, thinking time, and natural beauty in people/surroundings. First impression is classic, well-tailored, and dynamic. Strives for broad-scoped constructive planning, actions and results. Is a visionary builder with commercial and humanitarian potential. Hard-working, ethical, practical nature is at home instigating policy.

PERSONALITY EXTREME: Too cunning, or too gullible.

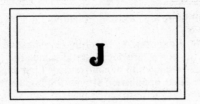

J

All names that begin with the letter *J* have the *Strong Point* of creative leadership—self-development—balanced judgment—mental analysis.

JACK (diminutive; James/John/independent)—M.

MAJOR TALENT: Ability to incorporate mental isolation, analysis, and creativity into career. Is an unconventional thinker. Has intuitive hunches. Combines cultural aspirations, quality consciousness, and perfectionist instincts. Governed by the mind, this name will dislike manual labor, contemplate many philosophies, and put love on a pedestal. Computer industries, lawyer, and authority on any subject are possible career opportunities.

PERSONALITY INGREDIENTS: First impression is comfortable, helpful, and quiet. Strives for conventional home/family security, harmony, and respectability. Inwardly individualistic, impatient, and proud. Needs to invent, assert, and control. Happiest investigating and meditating in natural/refined/serene environment. Should not over-exert physically, speculate commercially, or dwell upon retrospective self-criticism. Is inclined to moodiness/melancholy which sap physical energy. Usually a secretive loner. Torn between needing companionship and fearing closeness.

PERSONALITY EXTREME: Too impractical, or too exact.

JACKIE (Hebrew: diminutive of Jacqueline/Jane/Jacinta, etc./independent)—F. & M.

MAJOR TALENT: Ability to incorporate imagination, self-expression, and words into career. Is optimistic, pleasure seeking, and flirtatious, but not unfaithful. Attracts popularity, friendships, and applause. Combines cooperation, individuality, and variety of interests. Entertainer, author, and receptionist are possible career opportunities.

PERSONALITY INGREDIENTS: First impression is responsible, companionable, and interested. Strives for the ideal mate, job, and life-style. Needs and offers emotional support. Inwardly conservative, family/community focused, and inspired to raise standards. Wants to advise, assist, and teach. Supplies and gets protection, but has extreme fear of poverty. Attracts love and general good fortune.

PERSONALITY EXTREME: Too sensual, or too mental.

JACKSON (Old English)—M.

MAJOR TALENT: Ability to incorporate originality, progressive concepts, and courageous leadership into career. Is ego oriented. Has pride, determination, and ambition. Is capable, strong, and drawn to major issues. Combines broad vision, compassionate nature, and aggressive individuality. Editor, organization executive, and inventor suggest opportunities.

PERSONALITY INGREDIENTS: Inwardly investigative, withdrawn, and mentally analytic. Needs privacy, cultural stimulation, and refined environments. Must be known to be understood. First impression is charming, expressive, and optimistic. Strives for popularity, pleasure, and attention. Combines the introverted planner and the extroverted entertainer. Life may be a kindergarten game of show and tell if this name does not have the courage of its pioneering convictions.

PERSONALITY EXTREME: Too honest, or too promotional.

JACOB (Hebrew/Danish/Dutch/French/Portuguese/English)—M.

MAJOR TALENT: Ability to incorporate constructive, practical, tangible work into career. Is earthbound. Has dignity, exactitude, and organization. Combines independence, self-expression, and disciplined physical/mental hard-working nature. Has reconstructive lifetime changes. Learns to transform the useless into the useful. Carpenter, bricklayer, and landscaper are possible career opportunities.

PERSONALITY INGREDIENTS: Appears sympathetic, conscientious, and conventional. Strives for warm family relationships, material attainments, and roots. Inwardly a loner. Enjoys peace, privacy, and mental stimulation. Wants thinking time, refined environments, and cultural growth. Aims for perfection, expertise, and confidence. High intelligence may not be recognized in youth. Devours all sorts of information and is at best when academically polished.

PERSONALITY EXTREME: Too vain, or too unfashionable.

JACQUELINE (Hebrew/French/English)—F.

MAJOR TALENT: Ability to incorporate intellectual questioning, refined instincts, and drive for perfection into career. Is poised, imaginative, and materially practical. Has artistic/scientific/technical interests, friendliness, and gentle, but determined nature. Combines self-expression, devotion, and silent wisdom. Researcher, photographer, and psychoanalyst are possible career opportunities.

PERSONALITY INGREDIENTS: First impression is modest, retiring, and supportive. Strives for peace, cooperation, and loving partnership. Inwardly strong, sensual, and curious. Needs physical pleasures, travel, and progressive change. May be secretive, overindulgent, and attracted to off beat people. Usually earns and gets rewards.

PERSONALITY EXTREME: Too unconventional, or too controlled.

JAIME (Spanish)—M.

MAJOR TALENT: Ability to incorporate adaptability, personal service, and attention to details into career. Is considerate, charming, and gentle. Has tact, balances pros/cons, and tends to subtle control as the power behind the throne. Combines craftsmanship, maintaining peace, and concern for open communication. Cabinet maker, comptroller, and private secretary are possible career opportunities.

PERSONALITY INGREDIENTS: Inwardly conservative, but appears to be venturesome. Wants steadfast love, gracious home, and roots. Seems cosmopolitan, adventurous, and sensual. Strives for travel, physical

pleasures, and freedom. Happiness is based upon family harmony in a
progressive life-style.

PERSONALITY EXTREME: Too irresponsible, or too tenacious.

JAMES (Hebrew/French/Scottish/English)—M.

MAJOR TALENT: Ability to incorporate self-expression, cooperation,
and custom tailored viewpoint into career. Is attractive, imaginative, and
geared to communication techniques. Observes, reflects, then maintains
a unique philosophy. Combines independent thinking, quest for a soul
mate, and artistic/scientific/literary interests. Interior decorator, writer,
and actor are possible career opportunities.

PERSONALITY INGREDIENTS: Desires beauty, love, and harmonious
home life. Content when responsible, protective, and materially attaining. Appears dignified, comfortable, and interested. Strives for respectability, good taste, and conventional growth. Enjoys music, gracious
living, and showmanship. Cannot be pressured. Is helpful/conscientious/
motherly when kindled emotionally. Can be too personalized, self-
deluding, and accusing. Prone to reversals while developing character.
Success stabilizes when realistic, ethical, and accepting.

PERSONALITY EXTREME: Too egocentric, or too subordinate.

JAMIE (Hebrew: James/Scottish nickname)—F. & M.

MAJOR TALENT: Ability to incorporate sensitivity to details, patience,
and adaptability into career. Is modest, shy, and supportive. Has subtle
controlling influence over others. Combines cooperative spirit, skilled
craftsmanship, and ingrained habits. Private secretary, musician, and
statistician are possible career opportunities.

PERSONALITY INGREDIENTS: Inwardly protective, responsible, and
loving. May want independence, adventure, and progressive community
activity. Basically parental, strong-willed, and uplifting. Appears open-
minded, adventurous, and friendly. Strives for freedom, change, and
travel. First sensual impression is a bit deceiving. Needs conventional
life-style and unconventional interests.

PERSONALITY EXTREME: Too changeable, or too loyal.

JAN (Hebrew: Jane-John)—F. & M.

MAJOR TALENT: Ability to incorporate concentrated study into career.
May be a dreamer/visionary/philosopher. Has investigative approach,
poise and perseverance. Combines trust, faith, and a desire for quality/
refinement/perfection. Aims for expertise/authority. Technology, religion, and science are possible career opportunities.

PERSONALITY INGREDIENTS: Inwardly inventive, direct, and instigative. Wants independence, leadership, and to be outstanding. Appears
helpful, sensible, and classic. Strives for justice, uplift, and service to
others. Enjoys domesticity but needs privacy. At best when not materialistic.

PERSONALITY EXTREME: Too busy, or too bored.

JANE (Hebrew: John/English)—F.

MAJOR TALENT: Ability to incorporate talk, writing, or visual self-
expression into career. Is fashion conscious, entertaining, and optimistic. Has charm, imagination, and congeniality. Combines sensitivity,

individuality, and extravagant/dramatic emotions. At best in easy-going,
innovative, multi-interested partnership. Sales, theater, and artist in any
line are possible career opportunities.

PERSONALITY INGREDIENTS: First impression is retiring, refined, and
cooperative. Inwardly family/community oriented, protective, and instructional. Feels special/different. Needs to believe in something and
strive to surface a personal ideal. Has high nervous energy which, when
unused/introverted, breeds lazy, impractical, pie in the sky attitudes.
Radiates enthusiasm when heralding a mate, just cause, or universal
reform. Has potential to inspire new concepts and, through compassionate self-expression, gain recognition.

PERSONALITY EXTREME: Too unconventional, or too conventional.

JANET (Hebrew: Jane/Scottish/English)—F.

MAJOR TALENT: Ability to incorporate clever understanding of people,
uncluttered thinking, and adaptability to unconventional exposures into
career. Is energetic, physical, and adventurous. Has knack of appearing
confident while learning by experience. Combines independence, inventive ideas, and a blend of intellect/feelings. Lawyer, detective, and travel
agent are possible career opportunities.

PERSONALITY INGREDIENTS: First impression is businesslike, efficient,
and well-groomed. Strives for executive authority, affluence, and prominence. Inwardly family/community oriented, responsible, and protective. Wants mature relationships, respectability, and abundant/gracious
life-style. Is either very virginal or intensely sensual. Must learn to balance physical appetites. Is obsessed when in love. Becomes mental when
disillusioned. Has a talent for sex, and usually doesn't know it.

PERSONALITY EXTREME: Too personalized, or too unfeeling.

JANICE (Hebrew: Jane/English)—F.

MAJOR TALENT: Ability to incorporate sympathetic understanding, artistic self-expression, and instructional guidance into career. Is geared to
love/home/helping others. Has firm opinions, emotional approach, and
personalized ideals. Combines work ethic, sensitivity to details, and a
need to keep the feel of a balanced rhythm to life-style. Marriage counselor, teacher, and songwriter are possible career opportunities.

PERSONALITY INGREDIENTS: Strives to inspire quality, skill, and
elevated practices. Is attention getting, noble, and youthful. Aspires to
live an ideal life. Needs conventional roots. Tends to manage, advise,
and assume burdens. Is tender-hearted. Attracts romance, admirers, and
the helpless. At best when ambitions and temperament are balanced.
May take on more than can be handled.

PERSONALITY EXTREMES: Too experimental, or too cautious.

JANINE (Hebrew: Jane/English)—F.

MAJOR TALENT: Ability to incorporate material efficiency, judgment,
and power into career. Is self-reliant, intelligent, and discriminating. Has
executive diplomacy, protective instincts, and sensitivity. Combines
cooperation, responsibility, and control. Buyer, orchestra leader, and
consultant are possible career opportunities.

PERSONALITY INGREDIENTS: First impression emits high nervous energy. Strives for creative, uplifting, idealistic self-expression. May seem

impractical, but projects a special infectious quality that attracts supporters. Inwardly sympathetic, helpful, and geared to family roots. Wants
love, beauty, and harmonious relationships. Strives for a better life-style
for self and others. Has musical voice/gifts. Needs artistic, imaginative,
dramatic interests. Takes things too personally and must have relaxing/
attention getting/physical activity to provide emotional release.

PERSONALITY EXTREMES: Too impulsive, or too enduring.

JARED (Hebrew/English)—M.

MAJOR TALENT: Ability to incorporate emotional sensitivity, detail/
order, and analytic study into career. Is gentle, charming, receptive. Has
modesty, adaptability, and easy-going approach. Combines supportive
actions, subtle control, and collecting. Accountant, musician, and novelist are possible career opportunities.

PERSONALITY INGREDIENTS: Has a way with people that puts them at
ease. Seems understanding, open-minded, and enthusiastic. Strives for
experimentation, change, and freedom to enjoy physical pleasures. Inwardly protective, responsible, and family/community attaining. Desires
mature love, gracious living, and respectability. Assumes burdens and
wants to have non-routine experiences. May be torn by adventurous
reliable extremes of nature.

PERSONALITY EXTREMES: Too proper, or too immoral.

JARVIS (Teutonic/English)—M.

MAJOR TALENT: Ability to incorporate research, facts, and sharp
analysis into career. Is analytic, clever, and meditative. Has sensitivity,
confidential approach, and perfectionist instincts. Combines attention to
details, unconventional ideas, and confident authority. Photographer,
private detective, and travel consultant are possible career opportunities.

PERSONALITY INGREDIENTS: First impression is helpful, interested,
and parental. Strives for conventional marital attainments, respectability, and to raise standards. Has strong opinions, firm judgments, and
needs to counsel/teach/protect. Inwardly wants to control, lead, and
have the final say. Feels aggressive, inventive, and forceful. May be
jealous, cunning, and vindictive. Needs harmonious, serene, supportive
home life to still insecurities. Relives youthful experiences, and may
seem moody when reflective.

PERSONALITY EXTREME: Too assertive, or too submissive.

JASMINE (Persian/English)—F.

MAJOR TALENT: Ability to incorporate material focus, efficiency, and
executive organization into career. Is tactful, adaptable, and discriminating. Has self-reliance, control, and good judgment. Combines responsibility, concerned service, and vision. Insurance agent, critic, and
financial advisor are possible career opportunities.

PERSONALITY INGREDIENTS: Appears self-confident even when unsure. Inwardly protective, strong-willed, and family/community attaining. Wants artistic self-expression, loving mate, and respectability.
Appears different. Strives for realization of personal ideals. Aims for
inventive approach, subtle insistence, and farsighted/broad-scoped reforms. May seem impractical, dreamy, or out of this world when using

high nervous energy crusading for a cause. Refined, modest, and gentle at first meeting. Has determination, enthusiasm, and courage.

PERSONALITY EXTREME: Too impulsive, or too cautious.

JASON (Greek)—M.

MAJOR TALENT: Ability to incorporate inquisitive, nature, keen judgments of people, and clever innovations into career. Is freedom loving, pleasure-seeking, and adventurous. Has adaptability, understanding, and sex appeal. Combines hard work, individuality, and learning from life experience. Politician, promoter, and advertising executive are possible career opportunities.

PERSONALITY INGREDIENTS: Is very intelligent. Desires natural beauty, quality products, and cultural stimulation. Strives for refinement, authority, and expertise. May be cunning, scheming, and secretive. On the other hand, may be totally open and trusting. Needs a concentrated goal to achieve potential. Early specialized education and/or marriage may stabilize this multi-faceted perfectionist. Has tendencies to escape from mundane reality. Best when self-disciplined.

PERSONALITY EXTREME: Too sensual, or too mental.

JASPER (Persian: Gaspar/English)—M.

MAJOR TALENT: Ability to incorporate sympathy, counseling, and responsibility to others into career. Is firm, just, and strong-willed. Has sensitivity to detail, method, and discipline. Combines constructive work, patience, and artistic/social service. Teacher, songwriter, and decorator are possible career opportunities.

PERSONALITY INGREDIENTS: First impression is attractive, empathetic, and noble. Strives for quality/skill, universal understanding, and a broad philosophy. May be magnetic and attract followers. Inwardly loving, concerned, and protective. Wants mature companionship, gracious life-style, and roots. Attracts success.

PERSONALITY EXTREME: Too sentimental, or too disillusioned.

JAY (Latin/Old English/Old French/English)—M.

MAJOR TALENT: Ability to incorporate sympathy, compassion, and high quality skill/service into career. Is empathetic, creative, and broad-scoped. Has human understanding, charity, and magnetic personality. Combines artistic discipline, romantic nature, and selflessness. Welfare work, any profession, and philosophy are possible career opportunities.

PERSONALITY INGREDIENTS: Desires independence. Wants to lead, direct, and control. Has ambition. Appears businesslike, influential, and as affluent as possible. Strives for prominence, organizational efficiency, and material power. Very dramatic, emotional, and wise. At best when maintaining high standards and avoiding self-indulgences.

PERSONALITY EXTREME: Too confident, or too insecure.

JAYNE (Hindustani/Hebrew: Jane/English)—F.

MAJOR TALENT: Ability to incorporate originality, positive attitude, and individuality into career. Is a dominant influence. Has broad philosophy, humanitarian instincts, and little patience for unimportant issues. Combines magnetism, forcefulness, and trend setting leadership. Inventor, salesperson, and newspaper editor are possible career opportunities.

PERSONALITY INGREDIENTS: First impression is neat, groomed, and down to earth. Strives for material accomplishments, appreciation, and respectability. Works for rewards. Inwardly emotional, sympathetic, and home/family oriented. Wants love, protection, and artistic self-expression. Enjoys companionship, ease, and attention. At best when courageous and true to personal ideals.

PERSONALITY EXTREME: Too adventurous, or too conservative.

JEAN (Hebrew: Jane/Scottish/English, F./French: John, M.)—F. & M.

MAJOR TALENT: Ability to incorporate all forms of self-expression into career. May be literary, artistic, scientific, dramatic . . . the key is imagination. Has charm, congeniality, and a variety of friends/interests. Combines individuality, sensitivity to detail, and the joy of living. Entertainer, receptionist, and model are possible career opportunities.

PERSONALITY INGREDIENTS: Loves love, beauty, and attention. Strives for family growth, community respect, and abundant life-style. Wants to help, raise standards, and counsel. Has a personal psychology/poise/code of ethics. Is governed by emotions, must learn to accept reality, and thrives with a soul mate. Needs harmonious home life, and to live and let live.

PERSONALITY EXTREME: Too self-indulgent, or too outgoing.

JEANNE (Hebrew: Jane/French)—F.

MAJOR TALENT: Ability to incorporate hard work, original problem solving concepts, and constructive solutions into career. Is intellectually, spiritually, and materially tuned. Has strong opinions, persuasive methods, and broad-scoped philosophy. Combines human understanding, gentleness, and potential for universal productivity. Political reformer, diplomat, and business consultant suggest opportunities.

PERSONALITY INGREDIENTS: Desires to express ideals and bring them to the attention of the public. Appears to be, and is, different. May appear modest, shy, and impractical/mystical. When inspired, the intensity of belief turns this retiring personality to a zealous/passionate salesperson. Attracts supporters, expresses inventively, and needs partner/follower to bring ideas to reality. Highly nervous, artistic, and personalized. Requires moderate life-style, and stable health program. May be a power for social change.

PERSONALITY EXTREME: Too adaptable, or too impatient.

JEANNETTE (Hebrew: Jane/French)—F.

MAJOR TALENT: Ability to incorporate a strong determination to be independent into career. Is assertive, aggressive, and articulate. Has a good memory, dramatic reactions, and ambition. Combines material practicality, high energy, and a fighting spirit. Real estate broker, shopkeeper, and musician are possible career opportunities.

PERSONALITY INGREDIENTS: First impression is interested, comfortable, and conventional. Strives for family attainments, gracious living, and artistic self-expression. Inwardly questioning, analytic, and culturally ambitious. Desires natural beauty, refined associates, and privacy. Needs to learn concentration. Lacks self-confidence and either talks too much or too little. Best when organized and calm.

PERSONALITY EXTREME: Too impulsive, or too cautious.

JEB (Hebrew: Jedediah/English; diminutive)—M.

MAJOR TALENT: Ability to incorporate executive ability, efficiency, and organizational approach into career. Is discriminating, polite, and self-reliant. Has managerial authority, practicality, and sharp perceptions. Combines dependability, effort, and businesslike instincts. Banker, military officer, and tax lawyer are possible career opportunities.

PERSONALITY INGREDIENTS: Inwardly adventurous, sensual, and impulsive. Desires freedom, travel, and non-routine life-style. Appears attractive, fashionable, and optimistic. Wants the limelight, popularity, and a worry free existence. Is a charmer with material ambitions.

PERSONALITY EXTREME: Too easy-going, or too trouble making.

JEFF (diminutive: Old German; Jeffrey/English)—M.

MAJOR TALENT: Ability to incorporate brotherly love, empathy, and quality/skill of performance into career. Is understanding, compassionate, and attractive. Has self-expressive instincts, philosophical approach, and inspirational manner. Combines individuality, executive efficiency, and uncommercial attitude. Welfare worker, thespian, and advisor are possible career opportunities.

PERSONALITY INGREDIENTS: Inwardly adventurous, pleasure seeking, and changeable. Wants freedom, life experience, and travel. Appears dependable, practical, and sure. Strives for material security, respectability, and quiet dignity. May be a workaholic or lazy. May be a promoter or extremely honest. May give everything to someone needier or charge all that the traffic will bear. Home loving/traveler, loyal/swinger, non-routined/conventional . . . not easy to tie down or understand. At best in communications industry.

PERSONALITY EXTREME: Too responsible, or too careless.

JEFFERSON (Teutonic/English)—M.

MAJOR TALENT: Ability to incorporate common sense, work methods, and discipline into career. Is persevering, conforming, and down to earth. Has resourcefulness, orderliness, and material plans. Combines physical, mental, and emotional growth through material productivity. Government, military, and medicine suggest opportunities.

PERSONALITY INGREDIENTS: Inwardly analytic, refined, and culturally ambitious. Desires timeless beauty, perfection, and privacy. Is emotional, but won't let loose. Appears forceful, independent, and different. Strives to individualize, invent, and be first. Never feels good enough to maintain confident self-image. Has a secret self that escapes from ordinary routine. Best when academically oriented.

PERSONALITY EXTREME: Too sensual, or too mental.

JEFFREY (Old German/English)—M.

MAJOR TALENT: Ability to incorporate all forms of artistic/scientific/literary/technical self-expression into career. Is a charmer. Attracts attention, is friendly/animated/expressive, and imaginative. Has wit, love of music/beauty, and broad philosophy. Combines human understanding, quality consciousness, and turning fantasy to fact. Writer, news commentator, and interpreter are possible career opportunities.

PERSONALITY INGREDIENTS: Inwardly independent, innovative, and forceful. Desires individuality, control, and pride in work/home/family. Appears to have special qualities. May be easy-going, but comes to life when sparked by personal enthusiasms. Strives for products or creations with lasting and uplifting message. Drawn to film work, helpful partnerships, and good will projects. Should avoid scattering energy, impracticality, and frivolous self-indulgence.

PERSONALITY EXTREME: Too questioning, or too guileless.

JENNIFER (Celtic: Gwen/Guinevere/English)—F.

MAJOR TALENT: Ability to incorporate emotional understanding, practical common sense work, and unconventional ideas into career. Is sympathetic, heroic, and inspirational. Has curiosity, quality consciousness, and love of innovations. Combines materialistic, romantic, non-routine characteristics. Works tirelessly to achieve ideals, has boundless resources, and resilient attitude. Missionary, foreign correspondent, and electrical engineer are possible career opportunities.

PERSONALITY INGREDIENTS: First impression is physically tuned, controlled, and as affluent as possible. Strives for prominence, efficiency, and businesslike life-style. Inwardly creative, determined, and aggressive. Desires liberty, individuality, and to be first. Enjoys activity, challenges, and home/family/community pride. Observes or participates in most of life's experiences, and will learn the true meaning of brotherly love.

PERSONALITY EXTREME: Too empathetic, or too unfeeling.

JENNY (English/Scottish/diminutive; Celtic, Jennifer)—F.

MAJOR TALENT: Ability to incorporate a variety of unconventional thoughts, words, and actions into career. Is able to handle unknowns. Has adaptability, cleverness, and curiosity. Is a sharp people watcher and understands human frailty. Thrives on change, adventure, and sociability. Combines cooperative nature, a communication instinct, and learning from experimentation. Politician, journalist, and entertainer are possible career opportunities.

PERSONALITY INGREDIENTS: Inwardly optimistic, fashion conscious, and imaginative. Desires beauty, drama, and extravagances. First impression is refined, retiring and ethereal. Strives for expression of artistic, spiritual, or socially reforming ideals. Wants invention, quick decisions, and mental stimulation. Usually enjoys poetry, visionary planning, and non-manual work. Needs love, crowds, and sunshine.

PERSONALITY EXTREME: Too expert, or too silent.

JEREMIAH (Hebrew/English)—M.

MAJOR TALENT: Ability to incorporate fair minded spirit of give and take into career. Is strong-willed, responsible, and protective. Has musical gifts, appreciation for artistic balance, and hospitable nature. Combines helpful service, disciplined work, and tact/sensitivity/charm. Interior decorator, restaurant manager and marriage counselor are possible career opportunities.

PERSONALITY INGREDIENTS: First impression is tailor made, energetic, and dignified. Strives for broad-scoped work, respectability, and lasting results. Inwardly is easy-going, supportive, and gentle. Desires peace, orderliness, and attention to details. Wants love, is emotional, and personally sensitive. Best in creative business, enjoying conservative life-style.

PERSONALITY EXTREME: Too unambitious, or too power hungry.

JEREMY (Hebrew/English)—M.

MAJOR TALENT: Ability to incorporate intense determination, consci-entiousness, and energetic fighting spirit into career. Is methodical, imaginative, and individualistic. Has physical/mental drives, common sense, and logic. Combines hard work, communication gifts, and inventive approach. Best when goal oriented, tactful, and organized for practical construction. Building trades, landscaper, and pianist are possible career opportunities.

PERSONALITY INGREDIENTS: First impression is enthusiastic, adventurous, and noticeable. Has a way with people, adaptability, and understanding manner. Strives for physical experience, travel, and authority. Is curious, changeable, and clever. Seems unconventional. Inwardly businesslike. Desires affluence, influence, and executive authority. Tries to be efficient, exacting, and fair. If disorganized, life can seem to be a battleground, where at every twist of the road someone opens fire. May focus upon a personal philosophy of survival of the fittest.

PERSONALITY EXTREME: Too analytic, or too thoughtless.

JEROME (Greek/French/English)—M.

MAJOR TALENT: Ability to incorporate system, skill, and broad-scoped projects into a communication career. Is imaginative, versatile, and charming. Has sex appeal, quality consciousness, and desire for travel. Most successful when optimistically expressing talents in a conventional life-style. Songwriter, choreographer, and writer are possible career opportunities.

PERSONALITY INGREDIENTS: Inwardly questions own abilities. Needs specialty/education to establish authority and inner serenity. Needs privacy, cultural stimulation, and natural beauty. Appears energetic, sensually attractive, and adventurous. Strives for freedom to experience all the five senses. Bores easily when too diversified. At best when concentrated, but not compulsive. Has a distaste for vulgarity/ugliness and will try to escape from mundane exposures. Must maintain methodical/practical approach. Potentially a powerhouse.

PERSONALITY EXTREME: Too adaptable, or too inflexible.

JERRY (nickname/variant of names beginning with *Jer/Ger*)—F. & M.

MAJOR TALENT: Ability to incorporate patient, practical, exacting work into career. Is mentally/physically active, conscientious, and loyal. Has economical focus, organizational instincts, and devotion. Combines independence, self-expression, and discipline. Quality manufacturing, real estate, and law are possible career opportunities.

PERSONALITY INGREDIENTS: Appears energetic, styled, and different. Strives for inventive ideas, fast action, and cleverness. Inwardly imaginative, up to date, and emotional. Desires beauty, congeniality, and happiness. Would play at life, but ambition, pride, and the need to be first spark assertiveness. Is high strung, nervous, and always on the go. Needs calm planning to eliminate rash, uncooperative, scattered involvements. Should specialize.

PERSONALITY EXTREME: Too skeptical, or too gullible.

JESSE (Hebrew/English)—M.

MAJOR TALENT: Ability to incorporate regular, methodized, practical work into career. Is dependable, enduring, and loyal. Has energy, logic, and accuracy. Combines individuality, communication instincts, and hard work. Farmer, builder, and pianist are possible career opportunities.

PERSONALITY INGREDIENTS: Makes a major change every five years and rebuilds life-style. Desires leadership, independence, and to win. Inwardly aggressive, determined, and proud. Appears friendly, imaginative, and charming. Strives for fun, variety, and popularity/limelight. Succeeds when conservative, conventional, and ethical. Should cultivate self-discipline.

PERSONALITY EXTREME: Too impulsive, or too cautious.

JESSICA (Hebrew/English)—F.

MAJOR TALENT: Ability to incorporate expression of talents, charm, and congeniality into career. Is imaginative, clever, and optimistic. Has rhythm, color/fashion consciousness, and strong emotional reactions. Combines independence, sensitivity to detail, and communication. Designer, entertainer, and journalist are possible career opportunities.

PERSONALITY INGREDIENTS: Expects/needs group/family harmony, attainment, and comfort. Desires beauty, gracious living, and material growth. Appears concerned, helpful, and instructional. Enjoys mature, sensible, responsible companionship and gives the same. Aims to learn, educate others, and offer warmth, protection, and wisdom. Enjoys being hospitable, and creates a home-like atmosphere anywhere. May be too idealistic and judge others by personal high standards.

PERSONALITY EXTREME: Too impatient, or too self-controlled.

JESSIE (Hebrew: Jessica; diminutive/independent/Scottish: Janet-Jane; diminutive)—F.

MAJOR TALENT: Ability to incorporate broad-scoped, farsighted, practical planning into career. Is a mental/physical workaholic. Has high energy, poise, and determination. Combines attention to details, understanding of what people need/want, and trustworthy control/leadership. Building trades, mining, and government are possible career opportunities.

PERSONALITY INGREDIENTS: Must be free, truly courageous, and maintain pride to achieve high potential. Inwardly inventive, individualistic, and ambitious. Must never feel sorry for self, or give up independence for money. Appears engaging, sociable, and attention getting. Entertains others and makes the best of situations. May leave a mark for future generations.

PERSONALITY EXTREME: Too impulsive, or too deliberate.

JESUS (Hebrew/Latin)—M.

MAJOR TALENT: Ability to incorporate evangelistic salesmanship into career. Is idealistic, reforming, and enthusiastic. Has love of peace, justice, and cooperation. Combines work, action, and reaction (the law of cause and effect). Has great personal energy which may be used wisely or thoughtlessly. When positive, may change human concepts for future generations. When used immorally, may cause accidents, legal involvements, and suffering. Preacher, writer, and educator are possible career opportunities.

PERSONALITY INGREDIENTS: Inwardly strong, motivated, and ready to work. Desires material leadership, down to earth accomplishments, and self-reliance. First impression is gracious, optimistic, and attention getting. Strives for beauty, self-expression, and travel. Is imaginative, determined, and attracts admirers. May overreact, or live for the moment when self-indulgent. Needs a worthy cause.

PERSONALITY EXTREME: Too independent, or too passive.

JEWEL (Late Latin/Anglo-Saxon/English)—F.

MAJOR TALENT: Ability to incorporate initiative, independent leadership, and originality into career. Is assertive, definite, and a problem solver. Has ambition to stand out in a crowd, but must have the courage to be different. Idea person, designer, and architect are possible career opportunities.

PERSONALITY INGREDIENTS: First impression is magnetic, understanding, and classic. Strives for broad-scoped approach, helpful service, and quality of skill or artistry. Inwardly independent, aggressive, and determined. Desires control, respect, and fast paced activity. Needs self-awareness and practicality.

PERSONALITY EXTREME: Too superficial, or too unpolished.

JEZEBEL (Hebrew)—F.

MAJOR TALENT: Ability to incorporate foresight, individualism, and idealism into career. Is attention getting, energetic, and sparked with ideas. Has charm, romantic nature, and broad philosophy. Combines diplomacy, broad-scoped planning, and inventive approach. Beauty specialist, musician, and poet are possible career opportunities.

PERSONALITY INGREDIENTS: First impression is striking, enthusiastic, and sensual. Strives for cosmopolitan experiences, experimentation, and physical pleasures. Inwardly responsible, protective, and focused upon home/family/community attainments. Desires gracious living. Must learn to be decisive, less impulsive and stubborn. Attracts partnerships, recognition, and rewards.

PERSONALITY EXTREME: Too vain, or too modest.

JILL (Latin: Julia/English)—F.

MAJOR TALENT: Ability to incorporate research, logic, and specialization into career. Is questioning, sensitive, and able to keep secrets. Has poise, perseverance, and quality consciousness. Combines individuality, strong-will, and desire for perfection. Lawyer, hospital administrator, and appraiser are possible career opportunities.

PERSONALITY INGREDIENTS: Desires romance, beauty, and to help others. Feels empathetic, emotional, and impulsive. First impression is unruffled, refined, and dignified. Strives for timeless beauty, authority, and privacy. Wants love, but rarely shows feelings. Needs encouragement, education, and to learn to value quality above material possessions.

PERSONALITY EXTREME: Too friendly, or too intolerant.

JIM (nickname of: James)—M.

MAJOR TALENT: Ability to incorporate learning from experience into career. Is adventurous, adaptable, and curious. Has understanding of human nature, cleverness, and subtle controlling influence upon others. Combines routined methods, independent leadership, and unconventional ideas. Airline pilot, photographer, and detective are possible career opportunities.

PERSONALITY INGREDIENTS: Desires travel, artistic self-expression, and universal interests. Is romantic, generous, and empathetic. Enjoys natural beauty, quality, and wide-scoped philosophy. First impression is attractive to women. Needs security, but wants nonroutine life-style. Must avoid self-indulgence, sensual impulsivity, and escapist gambles. Attracts surprises, accidents, and sensationalism. May have "haste makes waste but he who hesitates is lost" decisions to make throughout lifetime.

PERSONALITY EXTREME: Too conventional, or too eccentric.

JOAN (Hebrew: Jane/Scottish/English)—F.

MAJOR TALENT: Ability to incorporate planning, structure, and practical hard work into career. Is determined, ethical, and trustworthy. Has loyalty, common sense, and material values. Combines individuality, communication techniques, and discipline. Building trades, medicine, and finance are possible opportunities.

PERSONALITY INGREDIENTS: Inwardly questioning, investigative, and a perfectionist. Desires cultural attainments, refinement, and logical approach. Knows how to keep secrets, values quality, and speaks with quiet authority when sure. First impression is tasteful, concerned, and dignified. Fears poverty/loneliness and aims for financial security, gracious life-style, and to provide artistic/social service. May be too helpful, judgmental, or personalized. Is strong-willed and has firm opinions. Often reconstructs goals and has the perseverance to build through down to earth instincts. Loses all when immoral, unconventional, and vulgar. Changes every five or six years to prevent lifetime stabilization. Best with sober-minded mate.

PERSONALITY EXTREME: Too eccentric, or too colorless.

JOANN (Hebrew: Jane/English)—F.

MAJOR TALENT: Ability to incorporate artistic, scientific, or humanitarian service into career. Is energized for imaginative, emotional, broad-scoped activities. Has generous, empathetic, and efficient nature. Combines individuality, material results, and skilled/high level performance. Doctor, lecturer, and dream analyst are possible career opportunities.

PERSONALITY INGREDIENTS: Inwardly questioning, analytic, and logical. Desires facts, quality, and cultural stimulation. Appreciates quiet thinking time, natural beauty, and privacy. May dislike loneliness, but needs uninterrupted meditation. First impression is refined, cooperative, and retiring until a personal interest comes up. Can be an effective speaker for the right subject. Aims to be or to do something special. Best when striving for technique and unconcerned about commercialization.

PERSONALITY EXTREME: Too tied down, or too fast moving.

JOANNA (Hebrew: Jane/Scottish/English, from Jane)—F.

MAJOR TALENT: Ability to incorporate creative leadership, direct approach, and trendsetting ideas into career. Is progressive, original, and courageous. Has no time for pettiness, idle minds, and stupidity. Combines broad-scoped thinking, inspirational instincts, and individuality. Service products salesperson, diagnostician, and musician are possible career opportunities.

PERSONALITY INGREDIENTS: Personally unconventional, but publicly proper. Desires a businesslike life-style. Needs organizational expansion, display of affluence, and family pride. Seems dreamy or mystical until conversation indicates a let's go to work attitude. Strives for memorable achievements, reforms, and inventions. Has fluctuating energies/ideas/emotions. Has intense loves/hates. Motivation varies from intuition to intellect.

PERSONALITY EXTREME: Too assertive, or too accommodating.

JOANNE (Hebrew: Jane/English)—F.

MAJOR TALENT: Ability to incorporate quick/clever mind, catalystic ideas, and unconventional approach into career. Is strong, energetic, and a gifted communicator. Has honesty, understanding, and adaptable instincts. Combines free spirit, self-expression, and sensitivity to details. Maintains loyal/passionate/uplifting relationships. Advertising copywriter, actor's agent/manager, and journalistic photographer are possible career opportunities.

PERSONALITY INGREDIENTS: Strives to be an innovator, reformer, and champion for a just cause. Appears special, mystical, often radiant, and attracts admirers. At times, too evangelistic, high strung, and energized. Desires optimism, artistic beauty, and fashionable interests. Feels emotional, loving, and resourceful. Spreads happiness, and is usually on the telephone. Aims to leave a lasting mark and may do it on film. Not meant for manual labor, boredom, or structured conventions.

PERSONALITY EXTREME: Too restrained, or too impulsive.

JOCELYN (Latin: Justus/English)—F. & M.

MAJOR TALENT: Ability to incorporate broad-scoped, skilled, methodized communication techniques into career. Is versatile, practical, and charming. Has a gift with words. Combines sex appeal, sparkle, and artistic/scientific/technical self-expression. Writing, entertaining, and nursing are possible career opportunities.

PERSONALITY INGREDIENTS: First impression is perky, pleasant, and animated. Strives for optimism, extravagance, and good taste. Inwardly empathetic, generous, and tuned to the quality of work and play. Desires to serve worthwhile, humanitarian, charitable causes. Has the soul of the thespian. May be careless about conventional material attainments. Values the quality of performance in any personal interest.

PERSONALITY EXTREME: Too physical, or too mental.

JODY (Latin/English/Hebrew: Judith/Latin/Welsh: Jocosa; variable)—F. & M.

MAJOR TALENT: Ability to incorporate personal magnetism, quality of performance, and brotherly love into career. Is kind, sympathetic and tries to live by the golden rule. Has individuality, emotional approach, and need for self-expression. Combines executive diplomacy, originality, and human understanding. Welfare worker, doctor, and artist are possible career opportunities.

PERSONALITY INGREDIENTS: Inwardly conventional, practical, and determined to work. Wants to be dependable, respected, and traditional. At first sight, emits adventurous, sensual, free spirited impression. Strives for physical pleasure, unrestricted experimentation, and new horizons. Walks a fine line between impulsivity and caution.

PERSONALITY EXTREME: Too aloof, or too lonely.

JOE (Hebrew: Joseph; diminutive)—M.

MAJOR TALENT: Ability to incorporate unique self-image, imaginative ideas, and communication techniques into career. Is friendly, loving, and diversified. Has charm, rhythm, and congenial approach. Combines personal sensitivity, independence, and appreciation for beauty. Newscaster, telephone repairman, and crafts designer are possible career opportunities.

PERSONALITY INGREDIENTS: Inwardly idealistic, inventive, and attentive to details. Desires recognition for innovative/reforming ideas. Appears energetic, strong, and individualistic. Strives for leadership, fast paced activity, and progressive changes. Needs to be decisive, concentrated, and just.

PERSONALITY EXTREME: Too changeable, or too tied down.

JOEL (Hebrew/English)—M.

MAJOR TALENT: Ability to incorporate protective, responsible, life support service into career. Likes showmanship. Is home/family oriented, instructional, and conscientious. Has strong-will, desire to raise standards, and maintain harmonious relationships. Combines independent leadership, adventurous nature, and volunteering instincts. Restaurant owner, youth/marriage counselor, and songwriter are possible career opportunities.

PERSONALITY INGREDIENTS: First impression is solid, down to earth, and conservative. Strives for material security, respectability, and to work for tangible results. Inwardly impractical where inventive ideas are concerned. Desires to uplift motivation, artistic quality, or intellectual perceptions for others. Wants to convince, sell, inspire when promoting a just cause. Must avoid pie in the sky schemes.

PERSONALITY EXTREME: Too talkative, or too reticent.

JOHAN (Hebrew: John/Bavarian/Danish/Esthonian)—M.

MAJOR TALENT: Ability to incorporate imagination, sensitivity to detail, and originality of self-expression into career. Is versatile, persuasive, and fashionable. Has optimism, charm, and knack for attracting attention. Combines cooperation, invention, and congeniality. Fiction writing, entertaining, and animal handling are possible career opportunities.

PERSONALITY INGREDIENTS: Seeks perfection and attracts unconventional experiences. Dislikes mundane necessity and tries to escape facing practical issues. Desires cultural stimulation, natural beauty, and polished companionship. Needs privacy, serenity, and silence. Keeps secrets, fears loneliness/poverty, and rarely shares true feelings. Seems enthusiastic, open-minded, and understanding. Strives for progressive change, sensual pleasures, and to be different. At best when concentrated and not involved with manual labor.

PERSONALITY EXTREME: Too eccentric, or too proper.

JOHN (Hebrew/English)—M.

MAJOR TALENT: Ability to incorporate attention to detail, easy-going approach, and sensitive perceptions into career. Faces decisions constantly. Is adaptable, reserved, and retiring. Has modest attitude, supportive instincts, and conservative tastes. Combines cooperative spirit, gentleness, and patience. Statistician, club organizer, and any job providing service are possible career opportunities.

PERSONALITY INGREDIENTS: Has a knack for making friends, learning from experience, and raising standards for home/family/community. Appears approachable. Understands human nature, is venturesome, clever, and enthusiastic. Aims to travel, experiment, and enjoy sensual pleasures. Wants to be responsible, respectable, and prosperous. Feels protective, instructive, and helpful. Can be fabled sugar daddy who enjoys pleasing someone who pleases him. Must avoid judging by appearances, temperamental outbursts, and staying in a rut. At best when able to let go of familiar patterns and habits.

PERSONALITY EXTREME: Too irresponsible, or too self-controlled.

JOHNNY (English: John; diminutive)—M.

MAJOR TALENT: Ability to incorporate speculative ideas, unconventional approach, and clever perceptions into career. Is experimental, sexy, and curious. Has confidence, imagination, and adaptability. Combines sharp sense of what people need and want, promotional instincts, and progressive ambitions. Gambler, detective, and lawyer are possible career opportunities.

PERSONALITY INGREDIENTS: Desires respectability, conventional attainments, and material security. Is better suited to being an opportunist and taking things as they come. Will reconstruct life-style more than once while aiming for normalcy. First impression is different, original, and gently assertive. Enjoys innovations, leadership, and control. May seem to have superior attitude, but inwardly feels lacking educationally, culturally, or financially. Has a bravado that should be used constructively. Wins through patience, determination, and intuitional decisions.

PERSONALITY EXTREME: Too skeptical, or too gullible.

JON (Hebrew: John; variable)—M.

MAJOR TALENT: Ability to incorporate original and detailed communication techniques into career. Is self-expressive, imaginative, and optimistic. Has liking for the limelight, humor, and unique personal philosophy. Combines individuality, sensitivity, and presence of mind. Actor, salesman, and journalist are possible career opportunities.

PERSONALITY INGREDIENTS: Wants roots, respected/gracious, and upgrading life-style. Needs to be trusted. Inwardly loving, generous, and helpful. Volunteers talents, guidance, and moral support. Appears sturdy, tasteful, and conventional. Strives for showmanship, harmonious relationships, and comfort. Motivated by love, joy of living, and need for variety. Benefits from telephone and mail contacts.

PERSONALITY EXTREME: Too busy, or too bored.

JONAH (Hebrew)—M.

MAJOR TALENT: Ability to incorporate patience, good memory, and words into career. Is a communicator. Has optimism, administrative approach, and originality. Combines charm, need for freedom, and self-expression. Writer, decorator, and animal groomer are possible career opportunities.

PERSONALITY INGREDIENTS: First impression is striking, sexy, and adventurous. Attracts accidents, off beat incidents, and good luck. Inwardly questioning, reserved, and culturally attaining. Desires natural beauty, serenity, and thinking time. Is a perfectionist who learns from life experience.

PERSONALITY EXTREME: Too self-reliant, or too dependent.

JONAS (Hebrew: Jonah/English)—M.

MAJOR TALENT: Ability to incorporate mental curiosity, unconventional approach, and learning from experience into career. Is understanding, adaptable, and clever. Has a knack of handling people, getting under the skin, and changing habitual thinking to innovational concepts. Has imagination, practical structure, and work/play-aholic tendencies. Entrepreneur, scientist, and politician are possible career opportunities.

PERSONALITY INGREDIENTS: Appears to be, and is, unruffled, reserved, and introspective. Strives for perfection, cultural stimulation, and private thinking time. Enjoys natural/timeless beauty, country/waterside environments, and respect for expertise or authority. Is an adventurous questioner. May be an escapist, hermit, punster, or Casanova. At best channeled in a temperate life-style.

PERSONALITY EXTREME: Too active, or too lazy.

JONATHAN (Hebrew/Irish/English)—M.

MAJOR TALENT: Ability to incorporate vision/ideas, sharp analysis, and quick decisions into career. Is a dreamer with commercial ambitions. Has individuality, wide philosophy, and strong intuition. Attracts influential supporters with enthusiasm for personal ideas for inventions. Combines retiring but magnetic personality, new approaches to business, and sensitivity to detail and people. Political reformer, inspirational lecturer, and social worker are possible career opportunities.

PERSONALITY INGREDIENTS: Inwardly efficient, organized, and self-reliant. Desires control of major projects, community respect, and businesslike approach. First impression is fashionable, cheerful, and attention getting. Strives for popularity, variety, and gracious living. Loves a party, power, and nobility of purpose. Is filled with nervous energy and should look to film work for recognition.

PERSONALITY EXTREME: Too changeable, or too indecisive.

JORDAN (Hebrew/English)—M.

MAJOR TALENT: Ability to incorporate businesslike approach, efficiency, and executive diplomacy into career. Is organized, practical, and self-reliant. Has sociability, discrimination, and intelligence. Combines protective service, attention to detail, and material ambition. Business manager, corporation lawyer, and insurance agent are possible career opportunities.

PERSONALITY INGREDIENTS: Wants to be dignified, refined, and logical. Needs cultural stimulation, natural beauty, and perfection. Dislikes crude, ugly, tasteless display. First impression is definite, controlled, and active. Strives to pioneer, compete, and not have to answer to anyone. Is clever, impatient with trifles, and inquiring. Is athletic and maintains an air of confidence even under stress. Must learn to control impulsive loves and instinct to judge and discard others according to personal overly responsible standards.

PERSONALITY EXTREME: Too physical, or too mental.

JOSE (Hebrew: Joseph/Portuguese/Spanish)—M.

MAJOR TALENT: Ability to incorporate hard work, discipline, and endurance into career. Is energetic, conscientious, and mentally/physically active. Has awareness for detail, punctuality, and accuracy. Combines individuality, artistic/scientific self-expression and practical instincts. Skilled technician, farmer, and contractor are possible career opportunities.

PERSONALITY INGREDIENTS: Inwardly inventive, idealistic, and filled with high nervous energy for progressive change. Desires decisive action for social reform or spiritual uplift. May see problems through rose-colored glasses at times, but has the inspiration, enthusiasm, and noble quality that attracts boosters. Appears modest, dignified, and easygoing. Strives for loving partnership/mate, service to others, and peace. Aims to unobtrusively make friends out of enemies and be the power behind the throne. Is very sensitive. Needs praise, tactful encouragement, and companionship.

PERSONALITY EXTREME: Too impulsive, or too passive.

JOSEPH (Hebrew/German/English)—M.

MAJOR TALENT: Ability to incorporate progressive ideas, responsible leadership, and material ambitions into career. Is pioneering, trendsetting, and forceful. Has courage, resourcefulness, and sharp perceptions. Combines attention to detail, executive efficiency, and inspirational instincts. Inventor, psychiatrist, and manufacturer are possible career opportunities.

PERSONALITY INGREDIENTS: First impression is businesslike. Strives for prominence, authority, and commercial success. Inwardly desires easy-going life-style but has high energy, idealistic instincts, and a feeling of being destined to do something special. Aims to uplift and change people's concepts and standards. Wants to be decisive, fast-paced, and is impatient. When inspired with the truth, shows enthusiasm, nobility, and attracts followers. At best when cautious, tolerant, and unselfish. Attracts emotional and financial happiness.

PERSONALITY EXTREME: Too ruthless, or to undetermined.

JOSEPHINE (Hebrew: Joseph/French/English)—F.

MAJOR TALENT: Ability to incorporate imagination, high powered magnetism, and adaptability into career. Is ESP inspired and a dreamer, but with emotional control, practical approach, and strong-will can make miracles. Has romantic/charming nature, financial practicality, and illusions about love. Combines flexibility, determination, and grand schemes for worldly attainments. Beautician, musician, and political reformer are possible career opportunities.

PERSONALITY INGREDIENTS: First impression is dynamic, radiant, and self-assured. Strives for respectability, prominence, and organizational leadership. Inwardly culturally attaining, refined, and quality conscious. Desires a world of leather-bound books/antiques/cashmere sweaters . . . things of timeless beauty and perfection. Aims for large scale projects, analyzes, and can accomplish almost anything when able to balance emotional and practical desires. Succeeds when sure of material goals and unclouded by devotion to another.

PERSONALITY EXTREME: Too irresponsible, or too down to earth.

JOSHUA (Hebrew/English)—M.

MAJOR TALENT: Ability to incorporate cooperative ventures, attention to details, and musical/artistic/statistical service into career. Is a creature of habit and benefits from flexibility. Has tact, charm, and knack for orderliness. Combines emotional sensitivity, gentleness, and retiring nature. Sculptor, accountant, and theatrical producer are possible career opportunities.

PERSONALITY INGREDIENTS: Appears to be, and wants, individualistic, independent, and forceful actions. Desires freedom, change, and inventions. Will compete and strive to be first. Wants to be boss and adds innovations to common practices. Needs to be decisive without taking control. Is a master craftsman. Attracts supportive, creative, and determined partner/mate.

PERSONALITY EXTREME: Too impatient, or too controlled.

JOY (Latin: Jove/English)—F.

MAJOR TALENT: Ability to incorporate cleverness, adapability, and gaining from life experience into career. Is curious, flexible, and sociable. Has sex appeal, progressive ideas, and unconventional approach. Combines practical disciplines, independence, and adventurous free spirit. Travel agent, private investigator, and personnel director are possible career opportunities.

PERSONALITY INGREDIENTS: Inwardly home/family/community oriented. Desires artistic self-expression, gracious life-style, and to help raise standards for everyone. Is the cosmic mother. Assumes burdens, counsels, and protects. Appears businesslike, influential, and as affluent as possible. Strives for material security, admiration, and efficiency. May be obsessed with sensual pleasure and self-indulgent, or may be physically unconscious. Must avoid over-work, and over-play.

PERSONALITY EXTREME: Too authoritative, or too silent.

JOYCE (Latin: Jove—Joy/English)—F. & M.

MAJOR TALENT: Ability to incorporate workaholic energy, organized wide-scoped planning, and universal artistic/scientific/technical approach into career. Is a bundle of nervous energy, self-assurance, and good taste. Has ideas, sensitivity to detail, and adaptability. Combines logical analysis, intuition, and common sense. In service business or charitable work, may leave a lasting mark. Government, the arts, and any profession are possible career opportunities.

PERSONALITY INGREDIENTS: Inwardly is, and appears to be, refined, modest, and retiring. Desires an ideal world and strives to invent, conceive, or evangelize to contribute reforms. Appears to be in another

world/dreaming/intense but has the enthusiasm, imagination, and honest
dedication to patiently study, teach, and promote for personal ideals.
May be stubborn, too quick, and seem impractical as a child. Grows to
inspire others when given the companionship of peers. Learns when
interested and may not excel in early years. Best suited to structured
procedures in creative interests.

PERSONALITY EXTREME: Too adventurous, or too conventional.

JUANITA (Hebrew: Jane/Spanish)—F.

MAJOR TALENT: Ability to incorporate practical and selfless constructive service into career. Is inspired to bring ideas for the welfare of others
to material results. Has understanding of human nature, organization for
work, and down to earth approach. Combines diplomacy, sensitivity to
detail, and keen mental analysis. Efficiency expert, job counselor, and
translator are possible career opportunities.

PERSONALITY INGREDIENTS: Inwardly clever, adventurous, and sensual. Desires travel, varied activities, and unconventional life-style. First
impression is sociable, managerial, and as affluent as possible. Strives
for prosperity, admiration, and commercial interests. To achieve lasting
good, this name cannot focus upon material power alone. In addition,
worldly success should have a humanitarian aspect.

PERSONALITY EXTREME: Too assertive, or too submissive.

JUD (Hebrew: Hudah/English)—M.

MAJOR TALENT: Ability to incorporate disciplined action, determination, and willingness to maintain efficiency/punctuality/methodology into
career. Is a zealous worker. Has management approach, inspires others,
and perseveres mentally/physically. Combines total dedication, creativity, and material power. Athlete, legislator, and banker are possible
career opportunities.

PERSONALITY INGREDIENTS: Inwardly imaginative, optimistic, and
congenial. Wants to enjoy, amuse, and express talents. Appears physical, adventurous, and attention getting. Strives to satisfy curiosity, promote new ideas, and never be bored. Has basics for being a promoter/
entrepreneur/stock specialist. Must exercise self control.

PERSONALITY EXTREME: Too practical, or too careless.

JUDAH (Hebrew/English)—M.

MAJOR TALENT: Ability to incorporate executive judgment, diplomacy
and discrimination into career. Is efficient, organized, and self-reliant.
Has original ideas, concern for quality, and material ambitions. Combines initiative, perfectionist approach, and keen observations. Stock
market analyst, military officer, and communication technician are possible career opportunities.

PERSONALITY INGREDIENTS: Inwardly likes routine, dependable people, and conventional structure. Appears conservative, sturdy, and natural. Dislikes pretension, gaudiness, and unconventional activity. Strives
to be definite, honest, and punctual. Demands the best from self and
others. Has manual dexterity, concentration, and strong need for tangible results.

PERSONALITY EXTREME: Too jealous, or too unemotional.

JUDITH (Hebrew/English)—F.

MAJOR TALENT: Ability to incorporate artistic, empathetic, and broad-scoped interest in the education or welfare of others into career. Is romantic, efficient, and responsible. Has empathy, discipline, and independence. Combines sensitivity to detail, perfectionist instincts, and human understanding. Attracts supporters for inventive commercial ideas. All communication techniques, decorating, and legislative reform are possible career opportunities.

PERSONALITY INGREDIENTS: Inwardly methodical, practical, and traditional. Desires punctuality, economy, and thoroughness. Has pride in family, common sense, and a distaste for pretension. Appears comfortable, comforting, and conventional. Strives for abundant, gracious, materially attaining life-style. Has intellectual, artistic, and emotional strengths, needs only to be decisive, and to refrain from aimless dreaming and selfish intolerance.

PERSONALITY EXTREME: Too ambitious, or too uncompetitive.

JUDY (Hebrew: Judith/Irish/English)—F.

MAJOR TALENT: Ability to incorporate responsibility, protection, and helpfulness to others into career. Is conscientious, strong-willed, and musical. Volunteers, assumes burdens, and makes a production out of everything. Has sympathy, firmness, and idealism. Combines independence, cleverness, and an instinct to learn/teach/counsel. Nursing, food products sales/management, and any artistic profession are possible career opportunities.

PERSONALITY INGREDIENTS: Inwardly direct, aggressive, and ambitious. Desires change, innovations, and to be boss. First impression is free spirited, enthusiastic, and friendly. Strives for travel, experimentation, and sensual pleasures. Learns from experience and has a knack of handling people. At best when able to laugh at problems and go on to investigate the next move more carefully. Needs to be less judgmental and more discerning.

PERSONALITY EXTREME: Too conniving, or too uncalculating.

JULIA (Latin: Julius/Spanish/English)—F.

MAJOR TALENT: Ability to incorporate keen business judgment, persuasive communication, and organizational efficiency into career. Is diplomatic, discriminating, and self-reliant. Combines individuality, perfectionist instincts and executive authority. Promoter, consultant, and public official are possible career opportunities.

PERSONALITY INGREDIENTS: Carries the ball for others and is a reconstructer. Wants material security, respectability, and dignity. Is a hard worker and strives to have everyone do the same. Desires a tailor made life-style and, if not careful, may get into a creatively limiting rut. Must balance work/play/rest and keep an open mind. Is a conventional planner. Prone to routine, structure, and being proper.

PERSONALITY EXTREME: Too assertive, or too accommodating.

JULIAN (Latin/German/Spanish/English)—M.

MAJOR TALENT: Ability to incorporate large scale planning, work, and results into career. Is a practical visionary with highly developed intuition. Has sociability, mobility, and down to earth analytic judgment.

Combines sensitivity to details, humanitarian instincts, and skilled leadership. Government administrator, economist, and job counselor are possible career opportunities.

PERSONALITY INGREDIENTS: Attracts notables, and appears noble, understanding, and worldly. Seems empathetic, graceful, and brotherly. Inwardly a material hard worker with conservative desires. Wants solid, respectable, orderly life-style. Strives for a broad philosophy, tolerance, and service to others. Is a sympathetic, generous, dependable person. Should aim high.

PERSONALITY EXTREME: Too busy, or too bored.

JULIE (Latin: Julius/French, F. & M./German, F./English, F.)—F. & M.

MAJOR TALENT: Ability to incorporate communication techniques, charm, and optimistic approach into career. Is concerned with structure, self-expression, and joy of living. Has good memory, imagination, and artistic interests. Combines patience, individuality, and youthful spunk. Actor, writer, and animal handler are possible career opportunities.

PERSONALITY INGREDIENTS: First impression is traditional, sensible, and dignified. Strives for respectability, material security, and to do the right thing. Inwardly wants executive authority, prominence, and high powered control. Desires efficient, organized, businesslike activity. Feels determined to have the freedom that money can buy. Keen judge of character and expects to work for rewards.

PERSONALITY EXTREME: Too sensual, or too mental.

JULIET (Hebrew: Judith/English)—F.

MAJOR TALENT: Ability to incorporate mental curiosity, unconventional ideas, and instinct for progressive change into career. Is adaptable, clever, and daring. Has sensual vulnerability, honesty, and passionate emotional reactions. Combines sensitivity to detail, communication talents, and uncompromising aim for freedom of thought, word, and action. Researcher, entertainer, and politician are possible career opportunities.

PERSONALITY INGREDIENTS: Desires the liberty, power, and stature that money can buy. Wants to get down to business, work, and see tangible results. Is mentally and physically energetic. Appears tasteful, comfortable, and interested. Strives for gracious, abundant, and loving homelife. Enjoys helping, counseling, and raising standards for others. Is a showman and loves a parade.

PERSONALITY EXTREME: Too shy, or too critical.

JULIUS (Latin/Danish/German/Spanish/English)—M.

MAJOR TALENT: Ability to incorporate attention to detail, diplomacy, and orderliness into career. Is gentle, patient, and aims to arbitrate differences. Has need for peace, quiet study, and careful pacing. Combines subtle control, emotional judgment, and master craftsmanship. Publisher, musician, and bookkeeper are possible career opportunities.

PERSONALITY INGREDIENTS: Basically domestic but appears adventurous. Inwardly protective, responsible, and materially attaining for loved ones. Feels sympathetic, mature, and wise. Enjoys giving advice. First impression is enthusiastic, friendly, and understanding. Has a knack for promoting ideas, speculating, and attracting physical pleasures. Wants to travel, experiment, and be a swashbuckler. Must expect the unexpected and understand that every change brings progress.

PERSONALITY EXTREME: Too inventive, or too imitative.

JUNE (Latin: Junius/English)—F. & M.

MAJOR TALENT: Ability to incorporate imaginative ideas, vitality, and learning from experience into career. Grasps tempo/lingo of people and situations. Is clever, adaptable, and curious. Has open mind, gambler's instinct, and knack for seizing the opportunity of the moment. Combines practical organization, individualized discipline, and adventurous nature. Entertainer, detective, and salesman are possible career opportunities.

PERSONALITY INGREDIENTS: Inwardly businesslike, efficient, and self-reliant. Desires influence, affluence, and prestige. First impression is parental, dignified, and hospitable. Strives to teach, serve, and raise standards for others. Enjoys comfortable, harmonious, artistic/musical life-style. Has strong will, firm opinions, and idealistic principles. At best on conventional/conservative course. Has impulsive sensual experiences and must temper impetuous physical desires. May over-work or over-play.

PERSONALITY EXTREME: Too self-indulgent, or too unfulfilled.

JUSTIN (Latin/French/German/English)—M.

MAJOR TALENT: Ability to incorporate engaging personality, communication techniques, and good memory into career. Is optimistic, clever, and sensitive to detail. Has individuality, patient determination, and artistic/scientific approach to self-expression. Combines cooperative instincts, inventiveness, and animated personality. Writing, entertaining, and designing are possible career opportunities.

PERSONALITY INGREDIENTS: First impression is magnetic, empathetic, and brotherly. Strives for humanitarian principles, broad-scoped philosophy, and to improve the minds and lives of others. Inwardly wants to make a game out of life. Enjoys humor, beauty, and imaginative interests. May be torn between family responsibilities and personal desires. Needs travel, non-routine life-style, and love.

PERSONALITY EXTREME: Too stubborn, or too flexible.

JUSTINE (Latin/French/German/English)—F.

MAJOR TALENT: Ability to incorporate practicality, management, and executive diplomacy into career. Is articulate, generous, and sensitive to details. Has self-reliance, control, and discrimination. Combines sense of balance, responsible service, and material ambitions. Athletic coach, musician, and insurance agent are possible career opportunities.

PERSONALITY INGREDIENTS: Appears graceful, empathetic, and classic. Strives to share and learn the true meaning of brotherly love. Enjoys art, drama, and being kind to others. Inwardly efficient, practical, and businesslike. Desires respect, leadership, and commercial success. Has material ambitions and attracts supporters with air of self-confidence, even in times of stress. Positive thinking brings success.

PERSONALITY EXTREME: Too impulsive, or too cautious.

JYNX (Latin/Greek/English/American/diminutive; Latin: Virginia)—F.

MAJOR TALENT: Ability to incorporate independence, originality, and courageous leadership into career. Is an organizer, communicator, and humorist. Has artistic interests, humanitarian principles, and high vitality. Combines pioneering spirit, attention for happy marriage, and pride in accomplishments. Idea person, editor, and psychiatrist are possible career opportunities.

PERSONALITY INGREDIENTS: Inwardly quality conscious, culturally attaining, and a perfectionist. Desires intellectual stimulation, privacy, and logical answers. Appears friendly, optimistic, and cheerful. Strives for popularity, enjoyment, and love. Is introvert/extrovert. Rarely shares all thoughts and knows how to keep a secret. Has fears of loneliness and poverty, often unrealistically. Needs to take independent needs seriously or health may suffer. Keeps one face to the world, and another inward.

PERSONALITY EXTREME: Too smug, or too anxious.

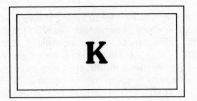

K

All names that begin with the letter *K* have the *Strong Point* of intuitional inspirations—feeling special—subtle control—quick decisions—dignity.

KAREN (Greek: Catherine/Danish/Norwegian)—F.

MAJOR TALENT: Ability to incorporate broad-scoped, humanitarian, practical work and service into career. Has great energy, plans and potential. Is a problem solver, has integrity and initiative. Combines patience, attention to detail, and firm opinions. Job counselor, efficiency expert, and builder are possible career opportunities.

PERSONALITY INGREDIENTS: Inwardly generous, loving, and protective. Desires gracious, comfortable, attaining life-style. Needs roots, family/community pride, and artistic self-expression. Outwardly unruffled, refined, and reserved. Strives for quality, natural beauty, and cultural interests. Needs to be respected and loved. At best when concentrated, educated, and taking time for silent introspection. Needs perfection and is rarely satisfied with self.

PERSONALITY EXTREME: Too analytic, or too impulsive.

KARIN (Greek: Catherine/Danish/Norwegian)—F.

MAJOR TALENT: Ability to incorporate efficiency, practical methods, and good business judgment into career. Is tactful, self-reliant, and polite. Has confident approach, handles problematic situations, and communicates well. Combines perception of details, responsibility, and material ambitions. Band leader, banker, and estate advisor/lawyer are possible career opportunities.

PERSONALITY INGREDIENTS: Inwardly independent, innovative, and daring. Desires praise, honesty, and to be boss. Strives for quality, cultural attainments, and intellectual stimulation. Visually introspective, aloof, and refined. Has feelings of self-doubt, which bring hesitation to social situations. First impression indicates insecurity. Knows the value of silence and speaks when sure. Academic degrees or technical expertise help to eliminate inner questioning. At best when exercising self-control, patience, and persistence.

PERSONALITY EXTREME: Too impulsive, or too cautious.

KARL (Old German: Charles/Danish/Swedish)—M.

MAJOR TALENT: Ability to incorporate parental attitude, instructional guidance, and sense of justice into career. Is sympathetic, generous, and firm. Has showmanship, poise, and devotion to responsibilities. Combines curiosity, independent ideas, and performance of duty. Teacher, doctor, and public or artistic servant are possible career opportunities.

All names that begin with the letter *K* have the *Strong Point* of

226   intuitional inspirations—feeling special—subtle control—quick decisions—dignity.

PERSONALITY INGREDIENTS: Inwardly aggressive, assertive, and individualistic. Desires freedom, stimulation, and to pioneer new concepts. Appears different, adventurous, and enthusiastic. Attracts and understands women. Strives for sensual pleasure, travel, and experimentation. Is a conventional planner who intuitively takes gambles. Is helpful and tends to assume another's burdens and overload emotionally.

PERSONALITY EXTREME: Too optimistic, or too worried.

KARLA (Greek: Caroline/German)—F.

MAJOR TALENT: Ability to incorporate logical, thoughtful, perfecting attitude into career. Is questioning, refined, and culturally curious. Has respect for confidences, perseverance, and quality consciousness. Combines individuality, sense of responsibility, and potential for expertise. Technical/scientific teacher, librarian, and antique appraiser are possible career opportunities.

PERSONALITY INGREDIENTS: Inwardly shy, modest, and easy-going. Desires comfort, peace, and loving partner. First impression is enthusiastic, friendly, and adventurous. Seems confident but is emotionally sensitive, gentle, and concerned about little things. Must avoid being a jack-of-all-trades.

PERSONALITY EXTREME: Too changeable, or too compulsive.

KATE (Greek: Catherine/Scottish/English)—F.

MAJOR TALENT: Ability to incorporate independent action, originality, and progressive attitudes into career. Is inventive, aggressive, and assertive. Has mental/physical strength, leadership instincts, and a dislike for waiting. Combines direct approach, provocative searching, and pride in accomplishments. Retail manager, travel guide, and architect are possible career opportunities.

PERSONALITY INGREDIENTS: First impression is classic, sturdy, and traditional. Strives for secure, conventional, respectable life-style. Inwardly helpful, protective, and counseling. Desires mature, responsible, loyal associations. Is determined, protective, and generous. Basically parental and domestic but not easy to live with. May be impatient, stubborn, and strong-willed. Has a horror of embarrassment and vulgarity, but may choose to live by individual code of ethics.

PERSONALITY EXTREME: Too changeable, or too routined.

KATERINA (Greek: Catherine/Latin/English)—F.

MAJOR TALENT: Ability to incorporate questioning nature into career. Is analytic, open-minded, and intellectually probing. Has poise, quiet authority, and good fortune through air travel. Combines communication techniques, conventional material approach, and quality consciousness. Psychotherapist, statistician, and fashion consultant are possible career opportunities.

PERSONALITY INGREDIENTS: Needs education/specialty. Appears sisterly, youthful, and understanding. Enjoys the arts, helping others, and broadening scope. Inwardly a private person. Desires calm, timeless beauty, and refinement. Strives for perfection and is self-critical. Has objective humor, and subjective seriousness.

PERSONALITY EXTREMES: Too bold, or too invisible.

KATHARINE (Greek: Catherine/English)—F.

MAJOR TALENT: Ability to incorporate emotionally responsive, hospitable, helpful approach into career. Is understanding, stable, firm. Has artistic flair, poise, and mature attitude. Combines attention to detail, down to earth values, and loving nature. Theater, teaching, and home services are possible career opportunities.

PERSONALITY INGREDIENTS: First impression is organized, efficient, and businesslike. Strives for material authority, executive diplomacy, and self-reliance. Inwardly analytic, quality conscious, and private. Enjoys natural beauty, intellectual stimulation, and research. Best when mentally concentrated, away from noise and superficiality. Must be known to be understood.

PERSONALITY EXTREME: Too passionate, or too passive.

KATHERINE (Greek: Catherine/German/English)—F.

MAJOR TALENT: Ability to incorporate independent action, inventiveness, and bulldog courage into career. Is assertive, innovative, and mentally sharp. Has energy, different style, and a sense of urgency. Combines practicality, conventional standards, and attention getting leadership. Analyst, musical entertainer, and telephone operator are possible career opportunities.

PERSONALITY INGREDIENTS: Desires peace, partnership, and easygoing life-style. Feels helpful, modest, and retiring. Is shy and sensitive, but has a knack for subtle control. May judge others too quickly, make mountains out of molehills, and become submissive in love relationships. Presents a businesslike impression. Appears organized, controlled, and managerial. Is ambitious.

PERSONALITY EXTREME: Too progressive, or too old fashioned.

KATHIE (Greek: Catherine/Katherine, diminutive)—F.

MAJOR TALENT: Ability to incorporate understanding, generous humanitarian/artistic uplift into career. Is concerned, selfless, and broadscoped. Has quality of professionalism, attraction for people, and cultivated taste. Combines sensitivity to details, intellectual analysis, and empathy. Missionary, nurse, and journalist are possible career opportunities.

PERSONALITY INGREDIENTS: First impression is up to date, sunny, and imaginative. Strives for popularity, humor, and optimism. Loves to party, entertain others, and tries to make the best of everything. Inwardly desires domesticity, warmth, and loving partnership. Enjoys family/community attainments, hospitable environment, and musical/creative self-expression. Expects the best from self and associates. Attracts materially/culturally successful admirers and widens philosophy throughout lifetime.

PERSONALITY EXTREME: Too head-strong, or too indecisive.

KATHLEEN (Greek: Catherine/Irish)—F.

MAJOR TALENT: Ability to incorporate practicality, common sense, and discipline into career. Is honest, economical, and punctual. Has independence, sociability, and candor. Combines free will, survivalist approach, and unconquerable nature. Real estate salesperson, social secretary, and waitress are possible career opportunities.

PERSONALITY INGREDIENTS: First impression is retiring, modest, and refined. Strives for subtle control, easy-going approach, and tranquility. Inwardly materially ambitious, efficient, and managerial. Is money conscious, organized, and a sharp judge of people. At best when cooperative, impersonal, and allowing others to win a few. Wants security and will fight to maintain respectable life-style.

PERSONALITY EXTREME: Too provocative, or too prim.

KATHRYN (Greek: Catherine/English)—F.

MAJOR TALENT: Ability to incorporate questioning research, quality consciousness, and perfectionist attitude into career. Is refined, culturally attaining, and structured. Has intellectual honesty, need for authority, and a knack with words. Combines self-expression, practicality, and active mind. Medicine, mathematics, and music are possible career opportunities.

PERSONALITY INGREDIENTS: Desires and appears to be businesslike. Wants affluence, influence, and the freedom that power can buy. Likes custom-made clothes and life-style. Combines real world control and well calculated planning. Is persevering and attracts success when unselfish, honest, and avoiding speculative ventures.

PERSONALITY EXTREME: Too impatient, or too procrastinating.

KAY (Roman/English, M./Greek: Catherine; diminutive, F.)—F. & M.

MAJOR TALENT: Ability to incorporate trend setting ideas, initiative, and individualistic style into career. Is inventive, progressive, and determined. Has spunk, vitality, and independence. Combines indomitable spirit, innovations, and sharp mental analysis. Advertising, performing arts, and new products sales are possible career opportunities.

PERSONALITY INGREDIENTS: Inwardly wants to be boss. Appears helpful, noble, and selfless. Strives for broad-scope, large marketplace, and universal understanding. Is magnetic, creative, and classic. Reaches for quality, natural beauty, and the best for everyone. May be too serving or too selfish.

PERSONALITY EXTREME: Too authoritative, or too silent.

KEANE (Middle English/Irish)—M.

MAJOR TALENT: Ability to incorporate an instinct to sympathize, heal, and raise standards into career. Is artistic, quality conscious, and noble. Has humanitarian approach, individuality, and magnetic attraction as a public speaker. Combines broad-scoped philosophy, innovative ideas, and efficient organization. Publisher, parole officer, and charity administrator are possible career opportunities.

PERSONALITY INGREDIENTS: First impression is quiet, refined, and classy. Wants quality, timeless beauty, and cultural stimulation. Inwardly a dreamer. Feels inventive, mentally active, and tuned to bettering mankind. Is futuristic, deeply intuitive, and ignited by nervous energy. Has a firm sense of right and wrong and may be a force for creative, artistic, scientific, or religious reforms. May have sleepless nights if materialism interferes with need to serve.

PERSONALITY EXTREME: Too gutsy, or too afraid.

KEENAN (Middle English: Keane/English)—M.

MAJOR TALENT: Ability to incorporate unconventional ideas, clever

methods, and physical energy into career. Is an understanding, sharp
judge of human nature. Has sensitivity to details, love of pomp, and
sense of responsibility to family/community/craft. Combines adventurous nature, need for self-expression, and innovative personality. Foreign
correspondent, lecturer, and theatrical director are possible career opportunities.

PERSONALITY INGREDIENTS: First impression is optimistic, encouraging, and conversational. Wants to appear fashionable, interesting, and
entertaining. Inwardly wants to inspire or uplift, gain recognition, and
live modestly/graciously/without concern for practical realities. May be a
pie in the sky dreamer or an inventive genius. Learns from experiences
and after recognizing need for self-control, will succeed.

PERSONALITY EXTREME: Too busy, or too bored.

KEIR (Celtic: Kerr/English)—M.

MAJOR TALENT: Ability to incorporate intellectual analysis, attention
to details, and sensitivity to people into career. Is questioning, adaptable, and mobile. Has progressive ideas, curiosity, and learns from experience. Combines poise, perseverance, and perfectionist nature. Photographer, detective, and bartender are possible career opportunities.

PERSONALITY INGREDIENTS: Inwardly sensual, experimental, and
quick. Desires change, life experience, and companionship. Appears retiring, dignified, and supportive. Wants to be easy-going, artistically expressive, and on good terms with everyone. Needs to be practical and
down to earth. Learns to investigate after being too trusting. Has strong
childhood recall throughout lifetime.

PERSONALITY EXTREME: Too sentimental, or too hardened.

KEITH (Gaelic/Scottish/English)—F. & M.

MAJOR TALENT: Ability to incorporate executive, efficient, intellectually perceptive approach into career. Is organized, discriminating, and
self-reliant. Has communication gifts, showmanship, and personal sensitivity. Combines instinct to counsel others, attention to details, and
willingness to work. Business advisor, theatrical producer, and athlete
are possible career opportunities.

PERSONALITY INGREDIENTS: First impression is attention getting,
friendly, and encouraging. Wants to be self-expressive, optimistic, and
up to date. Inwardly desires mobility, liberty, and physical enjoyments.
Needs travel, progressive changes, and experimentation. Aims for
prominence and financial success through unconventional ideas. May
charm the skin off a snake and cleverly ad lib while doing it.

PERSONALITY EXTREME: Too self-controlled, or too impatient.

KELLY (Celtic/Modern English)—F. & M.

MAJOR TALENT: Ability to incorporate emotional sensitivity, desire for
peace, and adaptability into career. Slides into comfortable habits and
tends to avoid taking actions. Has charm, dignity, and knack for subtle
control over others. Combines easy-going approach, modesty, and an
instinct for nesting and collecting. Is observant but avoids personal involvement whenever possible. Skilled crafts, statistics, and music are
possible career opportunities.

PERSONALITY INGREDIENTS: Inwardly wants to take things as they come, enjoy, and make everyone happy. Desires humor, gracious living, and up to date interests. Appears controlled, tailor made, and businesslike. Strives to be influential, efficient, and self-reliant. Attracts commercial interests and is financially successful when cooperative, practical, and able to adapt to reconstructive changes. May need a push.

PERSONALITY EXTREME: Too silent, or too authoritative.

KELVIN (Celtic/English)—M.

MAJOR TALENT: Ability to incorporate inventive nature into career. Is independent, direct, and ambitious. Has initiative, detailed perceptions, and efficiency. Combines individuality, competitive spirit, and need to be first. Designer, buyer, and salesperson are possible career opportunities.

PERSONALITY INGREDIENTS: Wants to be, and is, curious, adventurous, and pleasure seeking. Enjoys travel, experimentation, and change. Seems confident, progressive, and has a knack with people. May be flirtatious, glib, and full of surprises. Strives to be different, and usually is.

PERSONALITY EXTREME: Too sensual, or too mental.

KENDALL (Celtic/English)—F. & M.

MAJOR TALENT: Ability to incorporate open-mindedness, adaptability, and speculative ideas into career. Is versatile, sociable, and intuitive. Has sharp perceptions about people, sensitivity to details, and a gift of gab. Combines sense of humor, love of pleasure, and unconventional interests. Advertising executive, detective, and traveling salesman are possible career opportunities.

PERSONALITY INGREDIENTS: First impression is businesslike, influential, and self-reliant. Strives for prominence, material ambitions, and executive control. Inwardly responsible, protective, and family/community focused. Desires to have gracious home, surrounded by secure, happy, artistically accomplished loved ones. Needs non-routine career, and conservative life-style. Has vivid imagination and should avoid exaggerations and flights of fancy.

PERSONALITY EXTREME: Too up to date, or too unfashionable.

KENNEDY (Celtic)—M.

MAJOR TALENT: Ability to incorporate visionary social/artistic/scientific service into career. Is family/community attaining, protective, and guiding. Combines responsibility, domesticity, and usefulness. Has humor, charm, and attraction for others. Is either dedicated to home or the life support needs of less fortunate community members. Credit union organizer, remedial reading teacher, and nutritionist lecturer are possible career opportunities.

PERSONALITY INGREDIENTS: Inwardly efficient, materially ambitious, and businesslike. Desires accuracy, practicality, and executive control. Visual impression is introspective, aloof, and refined. Must speak with authority to relax. Not comfortable with small talk, but is a gracious listener when not expert on topic. Enjoys cultural attainments, natural/timeless beauty, and perfection in all things. Is a private person with intellectual goals and communication gifts. Has a touch of bravado, showmanship, and martyrdom. Never dull.

PERSONALITY EXTREME: Too skeptical, or too gullible.

KENNETH (Celtic/English)—M.

MAJOR TALENT: Ability to incorporate innovative ideas, communication techniques, and sensitivity to detail into career. Is clever, quick, and observant. Has versatility, energy, and understanding of human nature. Combines learning by experience, attractiveness, and confident/proud nature. Promoter, psychologist, and pilot are possible career opportunities.

PERSONALITY INGREDIENTS: First impression is dynamically constructive. Strives for large projects, and works with structure, common sense, and broad-scoped planning. Inwardly ambitious, inventive, and explorative. Wants to be different, daring, and courageous. Has high energy, style, and self-assurance. May be hyperactive, sensually unconventional, and too speculative. Must avoid temperamental or personalized manner. Attracts travel, surprises, and good luck.

PERSONALITY EXTREME: Too businesslike, or too impractical.

KENT (Celtic/English)—M.

MAJOR TALENT: Ability to incorporate mental curiosity, experimentation, and progressive ideas into career. Is freedom loving, clever, and understanding. Has vitality, a wanderlust, and desire to touch, taste, feel, smell, and hear all that life can offer. Combines independent thinking, practical working structure, and adventurous nature. May be too unconventional, self-indulgent, or sensual. At best when balancing work and play. Politician, travel agent, and lawyer are possible career opportunities.

PERSONALITY INGREDIENTS: Appears noble, brotherly, and empathetic. Strives for a broad-scope, humanitarian service, and gracious life-style. Is magnetic, impressive, and wants quality of performance. Desires non-routine days, changing interests, and uncommon people to probe. Takes gambles, is enthusiastic, and bores easily. Not the best prospect for conventional marriage.

PERSONALITY EXTREME: Too critical, or too unconcerned.

KERMIT (Celtic/English)—M.

MAJOR TALENT: Ability to incorporate sincere, down to earth, solid citizen motivation into career. Is industrious, loyal, and enduring. Has practicality, orderliness, and plans economically. Combines sociability, communication gifts, and independent nature. Newspaper editor, real estate broker, fireman, and builder are possible career opportunities.

PERSONALITY INGREDIENTS: First impression is self-reliant, efficient, and authoritative. Competes for material power, executive capacity, and to make interests pay off. Inwardly wants adventure, change, and innovations. Feels sensual, curious, and experimental. Will speculate, but uses common sense methods to turn a profit. Is a persuasive talker, confident, and clever.

PERSONALITY EXTREME: Too persistent, or too considerate.

KERRY (Celtic: Kerr/Irish/English)—F. & M.

MAJOR TALENT: Ability to incorporate gracious, clever, understanding nature into career. Is venturesome, enthusiastic, and optimistic. Has restless mind that learns from experience and is open to try anything new. Combines adaptability, sensitivity to little things, and unconventional approach. Theatrical agent, advertising copywriter, and store detective are possible career opportunities.

PERSONALITY INGREDIENTS: First impression is modest, gentle, and retiring. Doesn't look for the limelight, but attracts attention through charming personality. Inwardly wants beauty, variety, and artistic self-expression. Is an intuitive gambler and a positive catalyst for change in the lives of others. May be a late bloomer, but will expand scope considerably throughout lifetime.

PERSONALITY EXTREME: Too quiet, or too authoritative.

KERWIN (Celtic/English)—M.

MAJOR TALENT: Ability to incorporate executive capabilities, healthy ego, and mental organization into career. Is a delegator. Has enthusiasm, strength, and control. Combines unconventional approach, communication gifts, and material drive. Businessman, horse trainer, and financial consultant are possible career opportunities.

PERSONALITY INGREDIENTS: Has spunk, optimism, and usually inherits power or money. Inwardly speculative, understanding, and sensually tuned. Wants freedom, change, and challenges. Appears friendly, up to date, and youthful. Strives to be happy, entertaining, and resourceful. Best when confident, but not unrealistic about get rich quick schemes or pleasure seeking.

PERSONALITY EXTREME: Too busy, or too bored.

KEVEN (Celtic/English)—F. & M.

MAJOR TALENT: Ability to incorporate artistic, scientific, and verbal self-expression into career. Is versatile, entertaining, and ready to be entertained. Has optimism, humor, and sensitivity to details. Combines independent spirit, cooperation, and imaginative approach. Writer, model, and artist in any form are possible career opportunities.

PERSONALITY INGREDIENTS: Inwardly ambitious, creative, and individualistic. Wants to be different, self-motivating, and decisive. Has courage, leadership, and strong ego. Appears enthused when excited about a personal idea or dreamy when contemplative. Strives to inventively raise standards or uplift goals for others. Is a crusader for unique ideas and can sell them. Has high energy, artistic gifts, and futuristic vision.

PERSONALITY EXTREME: Too impulsive, or too stubborn.

KEVIN (Irish/English)—F. & M.

MAJOR TALENT: Ability to incorporate mental analysis, attention to details, and mobility into career. Is curious, quality conscious, and refined. Has adaptability, pensive nature, and air of mystery. Combines helpfulness, open-minded approach, and perfectionist instincts. Photographer, researcher, and mathematician are possible career opportunities.

PERSONALITY INGREDIENTS: Inwardly sensual, spunky, and speculative. Desires travel, experimentation, and freedom of speech and action. Appears dramatic, vibrant, and high-strung. Strives for realization of personal ideals, and the company of equally inventive people. Must be practical, persevering, and down to earth to achieve high potential.

PERSONALITY EXTREME: Too impatient, or too procrastinating.

KIM (Latin: Caesar-King; variable, M./Scottish: Ken/Welsh/English)—F. & M.

MAJOR TALENT: Ability to incorporate mature approach, protection, guidance, and innovative group leadership into career. Is sympathetic, responsible, and focused upon financial, and cultural growth for family/ community. Has firm moral/ethical standards, musical/artistic interests, and perseverance when solving problems. Interior decorator, doctor, and all types of reformists and educators are possible career opportunities.

PERSONALITY INGREDIENTS: Inwardly wants to better conditions for anyone who seems inferior. Ignores petty issues and follows commitments to a conclusion. Feels a sense of brotherly love. Takes a personal interest in everything/everyone. May prefer comfort to style, offer strong opinions, and appear conventional. Strives to have loving partner/mate, emotional security, and gracious life-style. Can be quite a showman, hospitable, entertaining, and lavish.

PERSONALITY EXTREME: Too rigid, or too yielding.

KIMBALL (Anglo-Saxon/Modern English)—F. & M.

MAJOR TALENT: Ability to incorporate problem solving nature, responsibility, and instinct for harmony into career. Is musical, servicing, and moralistic. Has sensitivity, parental approach, and firmness. Combines common sense, cooperation, and knack for adjusting group differences. Marriage counselor, teacher, and restaurant manager are possible career opportunities.

PERSONALITY INGREDIENTS: First impression is restless, sexy, and adventurous. Strives for travel, innovations, and activity. Inwardly independent, aggressive, and ambitious. Wants control, direction action, and praise. Dislikes waiting, comforming, and being second best. Gets help from admirers and may be self-insistent, meddlesome, or temperamental. Attracts success.

PERSONALITY EXTREME: Too fashionable, or too sloppy.

KIMBERLY (Old English/Modern English)—F. & M.

MAJOR TALENT: Ability to incorporate understanding of human nature, learning from experience, and a font of progressive ideas into career. Is clever, intuitive, and adaptable. Combines initiative, practicality, and adventurous pioneering spirit. Reporter, lawyer, and any job with an atmosphere of action and variety suggest opportunities.

PERSONALITY INGREDIENTS: Inwardly imaginative, resourceful, and kind. Desires beauty, pleasure, and to be happy. Appears modest, refined, and helpful. Strives for peace, love, and easy-going life-style. Seems subdued, but can tackle anything.

PERSONALITY EXTREME: Too logical, or too unrealistic.

KING (Latin/English)—M.

MAJOR TALENT: Ability to incorporate innovative ideas, mental curiosity, and unconventional nature into career. Is sharp judge of character, intuitive, and adaptable. Has knack of learning by trial and error. Combines sensitivity to detail, communication techniques, and need for adventure. Aviation, journalism, and politics are possible career opportunities.

PERSONALITY INGREDIENTS: Inwardly wants to understand everything. Desires to give guidance, help, and broaden vistas for others. Impressive speaker, compassionate, and inspired to set and live by universal high standards. Appears attention getting, restless, and gutsy. Strives to tackle everything and avoid boredom. Needs freedom, entertainment, and to avoid self-satisfied manner. Attracts changes, surprises, and sensuality.

PERSONALITY EXTREME: Too regal, or too earthy.

KINGSLEY (Old English)—M.

MAJOR TALENT: Ability to incorporate attraction to admirers, instinct to entertain or serve, and promotion through social contacts into career. Is romantic, resourceful, and loving. Has knack for forgetting unpleasantness, creating beauty, and friendliness. Combines imagination, justice, and various forms of self-expression. Writer, entertainer, and charity organizer are possible career opportunities.

PERSONALITY INGREDIENTS: Appears calm, cool, and collected. Inwardly adventurous, adaptable, and apt. Strives for refinement/culture/mental stimulation and feels experimental/progressive/physical. Is quality conscious, up to date, and philosophical. Must avoid laziness, gullibility, and physical self-indulgences.

PERSONALITY EXTREME: Too authoritative, or too vague.

KIP (German/English)—M.

MAJOR TALENT: Ability to incorporate inspirational leadership, compassion, and energetic service to others into career. Is philanthropic, empathetic, and romantic. Has deep emotions, artistic imagination, and broad range of interests. Combines efficiency, individuality, and instinct for seeing the big picture. Engraver, publisher, and all health, travel, and education professions are possible career opportunities.

PERSONALITY INGREDIENTS: Appears noble, magnetic, and sympathetic. Desires to improve conditions for less fortunates and sees most people as candidates for tenderhearted nurturing. Best when free of personal restrictions, tolerant, and able to give, expecting little or nothing in return. Is a humanitarian.

PERSONALITY EXTREME: Too reflective, or too unreasoning.

KIRBY (Teutonic/English)—F. & M.

MAJOR TALENT: Ability to incorporate non-materialistic inspirations, visionary artistic expression, and avant-garde ideas into career. Is a dreamer with potential to inspire, reform, or create so that others may improve their quality of life. Is sensitive, broad-scoped, and diplomatic. Always sees both sides of a question. Lucky with film oriented industries. Designer, promoter, and critic are possible career opportunities.

PERSONALITY INGREDIENTS: Feels confident one moment and unsure the next. Wants authority, respect, and perfection. Must hang in with one specialty, conventionally build a reputation, and let exceptional researching intellect attract supporters. Visual impression is classic, capable, and down to earth. Is a true individualist but needs to be realistic. Must maintain nobility of purpose, and systematize, plan, and direct area of concentration to bring ideas to form.

PERSONALITY EXTREME: Too questioning, or too gullible.

KIRK (Old Norse/Scottish)—M.

MAJOR TALENT: Ability to incorporate practical idealism into career. Is a constructive dreamer, who works to reform/reshape for the use/appreciation/uplift of others. Attracts money, recognition, and power. Combines cooperation, attention to details, and high-strung workaholic drive to turn ideas into reality. Has potential for international fame. Government, communications, and art are possible career opportunities.

PERSONALITY INGREDIENTS: Inwardly understanding, generous, and intuitive. Desires broad horizons, quality of product/performance, and justice for all. Appears sturdy, classic, and conventional. Strives for honesty, economy, and realism. May change roles in life from materialist to philanthropist. Grows to a broad education.

PERSONALITY EXTREME: Too sensitive, or too self-protective.

KIRSTIN (Greek: Christina/Scandinavian)—F.

MAJOR TALENT: Ability to incorporate independent leadership, inventive ideas, and direct/decisive actions into career. Is ambitious, forceful, and pace setting. Has courage, determination, and personal reserve. Combines charm, perfectionist approach, and individuality. Editor, architect, and lawyer are possible career opportunities.

PERSONALITY INGREDIENTS: Wants to serve humanitarian purposes and strive for new ideas that will promote quality of product/performance. Desires romance, artistic interests, and to reach a broad range of life experiences. May appear to be a noble loner or decidedly extroverted. Changes between introvert and audience seeker. May be sociable, imaginative, and humorous. Cultivates a multi-faceted personality through travel, questioning mental analysis, and tolerant philosophy.

PERSONALITY EXTREME: Too understanding, or too unsympathetic.

KIT (Greek: Catherine—Christian—Christopher; diminutive)—F. & M.

MAJOR TALENT: Ability to incorporate work, discipline, and practicality into career. Is a builder and may reconstruct a life plan repeatedly. Has structure, organization, and system. Combines independence, self-expression with words/art/music, and common sense. Piano player, technical writer, policeman, and contractor are possible career opportunities.

PERSONALITY INGREDIENTS: Desires broad horizons, quality of performance, and to feel that others benefit from talents/generosity. Appears conservative, classic, and capable. Strives for conventional, secure, respectable life-style. Does what must be done, but has magnetic charm and creative gifts that need an audience.

PERSONALITY EXTREME: Too self-pitying, or too emotionally detached.

KRISS (Greek: Christopher/German/English)—F. & M.

MAJOR TALENT: Ability to incorporate dynamic ideas, foresight, and energy into career. Is a worker, builder, and humanitarian. Has persuasive approach, executive diplomacy, and adaptability. Combines attention to detail, knack for arbitration, and material mastery. Has potential for fame. Building trades, government, and social reform are possible career opportunities.

PERSONALITY INGREDIENTS: Wants peace, prosperity, justice for all, and practices ideals. Appears natural, conservative, and retiring. Strives for honesty, endurance, and to be a solid citizen. Feels empathetic, generous, and philosophical. Is a broad-scoped universalist with drive to introduce constructive changes.

PERSONALITY EXTREME: Too stubborn, or too undecided.

KRISTINE (Greek: Christina; variable)—F.

MAJOR TALENT: Ability to incorporate responsible nature, problem solving parental instincts, and artistic/social service into career. Is conscientious, moralistic, and firm. Has musical interests, balance, and strong will. Combines sensitivity to details, self-discipline, and aptitude for learning and counseling. Singing teacher, interior decorator, and nurse are possible career opportunities.

PERSONALITY INGREDIENTS: Wants freedom, change, and physical activity. Feels understanding, open-minded, and adventurous. First impression is different. Seems individualistic, direct, and daring. Has high energy, accepts challenges, and strives to be first. Attracts harmonious marriage and is happiest when unselfish and careful not to judge solely by appearances. Puts love/family on a pedestal.

PERSONALITY EXTREME: Too experimental, or too frustrated.

KURT (Old High German: Conrad/German)—M.

MAJOR TALENT: Ability to incorporate questioning nature, quality consciousness, and perfectionist approach into career. Is logical, analytic, introspective to a fault and never satisfied with personal accomplishments. Combines individuality, protectiveness, and can turn on showmanlike charm. At best when polishing expertise and not focusing upon commercial ambitions. Should use magnetic attraction and authoritative delivery cautiously. Actor, appraiser, and scholar suggest opportunities.

PERSONALITY INGREDIENTS: Desires fun, humor, and pleasure. Wants youthful optimism, variety, and beauty. Appears sturdy, classic, and conventional. Strives for material security, practical reality, and respectability. Materialistic ambitions increase possibilities of romantic, business, and life-style disappointments until inner confidence grows to rely upon timeless/spiritual/intellectual, not tangible, possessions. Has potential for fame and fortune.

PERSONALITY EXTREME: Too sensitive, or too superficial.

KYLE (Irish)—M.

MAJOR TALENT: Ability to incorporate organization, executive drive, and practical judgment into career. Is investigative, strong, and trustworthy. Has commercial ambitions and efficient approach. Combines mental analysis, pioneering spirit, and instinct to delegate responsibility and maintain control. Athlete, detective, and commercial problem solver are possible career opportunities.

PERSONALITY INGREDIENTS: Inwardly physically tuned, explorative, and open-minded. Feels sensual, curious, and freedom loving. Appears friendly, attractive, and entertaining. Strives to be individualistic, unlimited, and courageous. Has potential for fame when wise to the powers of positive thinking; is progressive, and loyal to personal ideals.

PERSONALITY EXTREME: Too physical, or too mental.

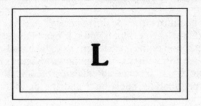

L

All names that begin with the letter *L* have the *Strong Point* of communications—artistic techniques—engaging personality—up-to-date interests.

LAIRD (Celtic: Lord/English)—M.

MAJOR TALENT: Ability to incorporate material, power drive, executive control, and businesslike approach into career. Is organized, efficient, and trustworthy. Has strength, self-reliance, and authoritative and persuasive manner. Combines responsibility to duty, sensitivity to details, and desire for personal power. Consultant, corporation lawyer, and franchise owner are possible career opportunities.

PERSONALITY INGREDIENTS: Desires individuality, freedom from mental restrictions, and never to rate "second best" in romance or business. Is a nonconformist. Appears refined, unruffled, and classy. Strives for cultural stimulation, quality products, and respect for intellect. May seem to live "in an ivory tower." Keeps secrets, fears loneliness, but needs private thinking time. Benefits from formal education.

PERSONALITY EXTREME: Too proper, or too unconventional.

LAMAR (Latin)—M.

MAJOR TALENT: Ability to incorporate tolerance, justice, and compassion into career. Is empathetic, imaginative, and romantic. Has magnetism, emotional commitment to universal needs, and broad philosophy. Combines individual style, material ambitions, and instincts for forgiveness, inspiration, brotherly love. Lecturer, religious reformer, and parole officer are possible career opportunities.

PERSONALITY INGREDIENTS: Inwardly modest, gentle, and easygoing. Desires consideration, friendliness, and loving partner/mate. First impression may be aloof, serious, and stuck-up until adaptable, patient, sensitive nature seeps through conversationally. Appears confident, then shifts to become ill at ease. Wants to be perfect, and cannot relax and accept the fact that nobody is. Needs expertise, specialty, education to attain authoritative image, which stabilizes secret insecurities.

PERSONALITY EXTREME: Too generous, or too possessive.

LAMONT (Scandinavian)—M.

MAJOR TALENT: Ability to incorporate words, retentive memory, and variety of self-expressive pursuits into career. Is imaginative, optimistic, and attention getting. Has resourcefulness, humor, and love of beauty. Combines individuality, consideration, and good luck through social contact. Model, literary critic, and business/social organizer are possible career opportunities.

PERSONALITY INGREDIENTS: Desires privacy, thinking time, and quality in everything. Is selective, aloof, and self-examining. First impression is sensual, restless, and enthusiastic. Strives to be broad-minded, unconventional, and free to challenge the unknown. Seems confident, but is most comfortable when specialized/educated/technically expert. Combines the introvert analytic questioner and the extrovert experimental "doer."

PERSONALITY EXTREME: Too sensitive, or too calloused.

LANA (Greek—Finnish: Helen/Irish: Alanna/English)—F.

MAJOR TALENT: Ability to incorporate pacesetting ideas/activities, daring, and pioneering spirit into career. Is inventive, courageous, and direct. Has positive approach, initiative, and willpower. Combines self-motivation, innovation, and unconventional personal ideals. Attracts success/happiness when patient and sure of goals. Promoter, designer, and lawyer are possible career opportunities.

PERSONALITY INGREDIENTS: Inwardly wants love, peace, and uncompetitive easygoing life-style. Feels supportive, gentle, and sensitive. Is attentive to details, persistent. Appears tailor-made, controlled, and as affluent as possible. Strives to be materially powerful, businesslike, and strong. Financial success and self-reliance invite dependent relationships.

PERSONALITY EXTREME: Too independent, or too accommodating.

LANCE (Latin: Lancelot/English)—M.

MAJOR TALENT: Ability to incorporate practical, executive, trustworthy judgment into career. Is organized, mentally analytic, and ambitious. Has initiative, loyalty, and drive. Combines independence, probing intellect, and businesslike attitude. Manufacturer, financier, and corporation lawyer are possible career opportunities.

PERSONALITY INGREDIENTS: Inwardly family/community focused, protective, and responsible. Feels strong willed, just, and ethical. Appears different, and mystical. Strives to realize personal ideals and create a vibrant and quality-conscious life-style. Has nervous energy, creative ideas, and always does two things at one time. May be moody, but succeeds when positive, concentrated, and down-to-earth.

PERSONALITY EXTREME: Too changeable, or too stubborn.

LANE (Old English)—M.

MAJOR TALENT: Ability to incorporate innovative ideas, a knack of making people comfortable, and learning by doing into career. Is gutsy, different, and adventurous. Has curiosity, cleverness, and energy. Combines independent nature, conventional instincts, and changeableness. Advertiser, politician, and contact person are possible career opportunities.

PERSONALITY INGREDIENTS: Desires domestic tranquillity, stability, and conventional standards. Wants love, gracious living, and family/community respect. Appears controlled, businesslike, and as affluent as possible. Strives to be influential, wealthy, and powerful. May reconstruct life-style due to sensual self-indulgence or some escapist technique. This name must follow a conservative course to maintain stability.

PERSONALITY EXTREME: Too bored, or too sociable.

LANG (Teutonic/English)—M.

MAJOR TALENT: Ability to incorporate introspective, analytic, intuitive
nature into career. Is quiet, refined, and culturally attaining. Has individuality, poise, and keeps secrets. Combines showmanship, inventiveness, and desire for perfection. Best when not materialistic and
developing a specialty. Researcher, analyst, and metaphysician are possible career opportunities.

PERSONALITY INGREDIENTS: Appears dignified, concerned, and conservative. Strives to be responsible, protective, and have gracious, domestically secure life-style. Inwardly desires control, free will, and to be
first. Has ambitions, trend-setting ideas, and daring. Potential is limitless
when expert/trained/schooled and known for expertise. Has feelings of
insecurity that need bolstering. Must get down to earth and concentrate
for rewards.

PERSONALITY EXTREME: Too confident, or too afraid.

LARAINE (Latin/English)—F.

MAJOR TALENT: Ability to incorporate showmanship, conscientiousness, and willing service into career. Is protective, responsible, and
ethical. Has firm ideals, artistic gifts, and appreciation for rhythm/music/
group harmony. Combines communications techniques, sympathetic
understanding, and domestic/parental focus. Is an interested parent/wife,
or a dedicated supporter for community improvement. Must share with
others. Vocal coach, union delegate, and educational reformer are possible career opportunities.

PERSONALITY INGREDIENTS: Appears businesslike and influential.
Strives to delegate work, give orders, and make money. Inwardly desires
quiet, culture, and privacy. May be torn between commercialism, and
quality consciousness. Needs to be known to be understood.

PERSONALITY EXTREME: Too sensual, or too mental.

LARISSA (Latin)—F.

MAJOR TALENT: Ability to incorporate self-control, logic, and aristocratic instincts into career. Is introspective, analytic, and questioning.
Has dignity, refinement, and sensitivity to details. Combines learning by
experience, mobility, and self-examining nature. Librarian, photographer, and skilled technician are possible career opportunities.

PERSONALITY INGREDIENTS: Inwardly secretive, pensive, and culturally attaining. Appears efficient, custom-made, and managerial. Strives
to be businesslike, organized, and influential. Best when focused upon
quality of performance and not commercially ambitious. Concentration
on an interest and a degree of expertise attracts authority, inner
confidence, and money. Must learn to be alone but not lonely, and eliminate need for ego-bolstering possessions. Grows through travel, hard
work, and independence.

PERSONALITY EXTREME: Too inventive, or too imitative.

LARRY (Latin: Laurence/English; diminutive)—M.

MAJOR TALENT: Ability to incorporate nonmaterial, inspired, visionary
ideas into career. Is able to see both sides of things. Has creative impulses, diplomacy, and strong personal ideals. Combines broad planning/
philosophy, sensitivity/attention to details, and restless energy. Writer,
evangelist, and geriatric specialist are possible career opportunities.

PERSONALITY INGREDIENTS: First impression is attractive, friendly, and beauty-conscious. Strives for imaginative, entertaining, pleasurable life-style. Desires material possessions, authority, and wealth. Feels efficient, organized, and businesslike. Partnerships may be good when quality of work, not money, is the common cause. Needs to be decisive, determined, and unselfish to attract desired prominence.

PERSONALITY EXTREME: Too quiet, or too commanding.

LARS (Etruscan/Swedish: Laurence; diminutive)—M.

MAJOR TALENT: Ability to incorporate adventurous nature, confident style, and progressively changing concepts into career. Is physical, versatile, and adaptable. Has cleverness, enthusiasm, and structure. Combines individuality, discerning observations, and understanding of people. Public servant, reporter, and travel agent are possible career opportunities.

PERSONALITY INGREDIENTS: Inwardly won't be "second best." Wants independence, innovations, and challenges. Needs to be secure, solid, and respectable. Strives to plan, work, and build. Has self-discipline, but invites impulsiveness. Must curb escapist sensual excursions that unsettle stability. Needs unregimented life-style to face daily realities. Best when free of responsibility, but drawn to live up to expected conventions.

PERSONALITY EXTREME: Too stubborn, or too indecisive.

LAURA (Latin/German/English)—F.

MAJOR TALENT: Ability to incorporate organizational instincts, self-reliance, and material awareness into career. Is trustworthy, practical, and fair. Has executive approach, initiative, and individuality. Combines quality consciousness, drive, and ambition. Administrator, financial consultant, and retail manager are possible career opportunities.

PERSONALITY INGREDIENTS: First impression is up-to-date, animated, and entertaining. Strives to be attractive, fashionable, and popular. Inwardly wants physical pleasures, freedom to experiment, and progressive interests. Comfortable when active, unrestrained, and enjoying unconventional people/experiences. Attracts recognition when investigative, intuitive, and not stretching the truth.

PERSONALITY EXTREME: Too assertive, or too submissive.

LAUREL (Latin: Laura/English)—F.

MAJOR TALENT: Ability to incorporate graciousness, conscientious attitude, and artistic/domestic/rhythmical aptitudes into career. Is stable, proper, and determined to help others. Has sincerity, kindness, and charm. Combines sensitivity to details, practicality, and problem solving. Marriage counselor, teacher, and insurance agent are possible career opportunities.

PERSONALITY INGREDIENTS: Inwardly empathetic, generous, and aware of universal/humanitarian needs. Desires broad-scoped interests, philosophy, and relationships. Dislikes petty bickering, narrow-mindedness, and intolerance. Appears dignified, solid, comfortable. Strives to be protective, respected, and musically/artistically self-expressive. Could seem like a "cosmic mother." Needs to give and receive love.

PERSONALITY EXTREME: Too talkative, or too tight-lipped.

LAUREN (Latin: Laurence/English)—F. & M.

MAJOR TALENT: Ability to incorporate confident, controlled, assured attitude into career. Is efficient, organized, and ambitious. Has sensitivity to details, social awareness, and group adaptability. Combines executive diplomacy, initiative, and practical/dependable/responsible instincts. Theatrical agent, magazine editor, and consultant are possible career opportunities.

PERSONALITY INGREDIENTS: Desires wide range of activities. Wants to reach a broad marketplace to express artistry, quality of performance, and empathetic feelings. Appears physically balanced, attractive, dominant, and self-assured. Strives to maintain a position of influence, affluence, and "big business" power. Should be patient, loyal, and respect conventions. Enjoys outdoor sports, possessions, and to make things "pay."

PERSONALITY EXTREME: Too impulsive, or too contrived.

LAURENCE (Latin/Irish/English)—M.

MAJOR TALENT: Ability to incorporate drive for perfection, research, and intellectual questioning into career. Is introspective, quality conscious, and cool in a crisis. Has refinement, dignity, and self-control. Combines attractiveness, practical organization, and public modesty. Editor, data processing, and detective are possible career opportunities.

PERSONALITY INGREDIENTS: Inwardly adventurous, sensual, and broad minded. Desires physical pleasure, experimentation, and challenges. Appears to be quiet, retiring, and easygoing. Strives to be gentle, cooperative, and friendly. Maintains conventional image, is discreet, and determined. Has love of nature, outdoor activity, and humor. Is wise, honest, and direct. May need patience and to refrain from gambles, but should attract authoritative position.

PERSONALITY EXTREME: Too impulsive, or too restrained.

LAURETTA (Latin: Laura/English)—F.

MAJOR TALENT: Ability to incorporate efficient, practical, self-reliant nature into career. Is enthusiastic, energetic, and dependable. Has honesty, initiative, and strength. Combines protective instincts, attention to detail, and organizational power. Enjoys the freedom that money can buy. Band leader, corporate planner, and communications consultant are possible career opportunities.

PERSONALITY INGREDIENTS: Desires perfection. Needs quality, natural beauty, and privacy. Feels mentally analytic, wise, and aristocratic. Appears to be a confident nonconformist, even under pressure. Strives for independence, originality, and to be first. Is an intellect in search of authority, respectability, and progress. Must avoid melancholy, impatience, and possessiveness. At best when busy, self-improving, and enjoying sports or solitude out of doors.

PERSONALITY EXTREME: Too assertive, or too submissive.

LAURIE (Latin: Laurence-Laura)—F. & M.

MAJOR TALENT: Ability to incorporate imagination, resourcefulness, and knack for creating beauty/joy/entertainment into career. Is kind, pleasure seeking, and up-to-date. Has humor, animation, and artistic interests. Combines broad-scoped ideas, restless energy, and extravagant gestures. Entertainer, salesperson, and fashion designer are possible career opportunities.

PERSONALITY INGREDIENTS: Assumes domestic and business responsibilities and aims to improve standards for everyone. Has strong will, morals, and ethics. Aims to be mature, hospitable, and gracious. Strives for material attainments, respect, and to maintain harmonious relationships. May be too giving, stubborn, or meddlesome. Is a font of self-expression with words/music/social uplift. Has great sex appeal.

PERSONALITY EXTREME: Too impulsive, or too tied down.

LAVERNE (Latin/Old French)—F.

MAJOR TALENT: Ability to incorporate experimentation, constant need to change, and cleverness into career. Is adventurous, gutsy, and versatile. Has sensual appetites, initiative, and sociability. Combines optimism, sensitivity to details, and learning from experience. Gambler, promoter, and travel consultant are possible career opportunities.

PERSONALITY INGREDIENTS: May seem impractical, but has inventive, idealistic, visionary feelings. Wants to save humanity or redesign the wheel . . . and has the energy to do either. Appears up-to-date, animated, and attention getting. Strives to be popular, entertaining, and fashionable. May be too picky, stubborn, or extravagant. Needs to serve a worthwhile cause, laugh at failures, and persevere until the right combination of circumstances attracts success. Best when governed by established conventions.

PERSONALITY EXTREME: Too confident, or too unsure.

LAVINIA (Latin/English)—F.

MAJOR TALENT: Ability to incorporate gracious manner, cleverness, and understanding of people into career. Is versatile, broad minded, and adventurous. Has nerve, confidence, and adaptability. Combines attention to details, self-expression, and unconventional/changeable approach. Lawyer, public servant, and airline hostess are possible career opportunities.

PERSONALITY INGREDIENTS: Desires peace, consideration, and tactful relationships. Wants comfort, friendliness, and easygoing life-style. Is a collector of everything. Appears animated, charming, and attractive. Strives to be entertaining and an appreciative audience. May feel that dreams are messages and they may be very helpful to this name. Should aim high, keep active, and step out to travel, experiment, and explore.

PERSONALITY EXTREME: Too independent, or too accommodating.

LAWRENCE (Latin: Laurence/Scottish/English)—M.

MAJOR TALENT: Ability to incorporate fine quality artistic/scientific/charitable performance/service into career. Is able to assume heavy responsibility, persist, and attain authority/position. Has human understanding, selflessness, and inspired imagination. Combines protective/idealistic/conscientious problem solving, optimistic/humorous approach, and magnetic universal attractiveness. Fantastic potential may be lost through escapist overindulgences, stubborn/misplaced sympathy, or ostentatious/superficial scattering of interests. Humanitarian reformer, thespian/artiste, and government agent are possible career opportunities.

PERSONALITY INGREDIENTS: First impression is aloof, refined, and poised. Strives to be cultured, self-analytic, and private. Needs quality

rather than quantity, fast pace, and to remain above "the crowd." May
have emotional extremes, impractical dreams, and take things too personally. Is founded upon kindness, and will face some self-sacrificing
tribulations that bring down-to-earth problems into life-style.

PERSONALITY EXTREME: Too speculative, or too cautious.

LAZARUS (Hebrew: Eleazar/German/English)—M.

MAJOR TALENT: Ability to incorporate commercial ideas, executive
approach, and showmanship into career. Is efficient, zealous, and
strong. Has confident manner, self-reliance, and control. Combines diplomacy, protective responsibility, and building toward material attainments. Quality manufacturer, banker, and theatrical producer are
possible career opportunities.

PERSONALITY INGREDIENTS: Appears fashion conscious, attention getting, and sunny. Strives to be popular, charming, and to live to enjoy the
moment. Inwardly is challenged by life. Desires freedom, sensual pleasures, and instant gratification. Wants travel, adventure, and progressive
change. Is energetic, helpful, and physically coordinated. Must avoid
impulsiveness, temperamental outbursts, and becoming power hungry.

PERSONALITY EXTREME: Too aggressive, or too apathetic.

LEA (Hebrew: Leah/French/Anglo-Saxon: Lee/English)—F. & M.

MAJOR TALENT: Ability to incorporate empathetic, wide-range, quality
service into career. Is magnetic, inspirational, and compassionate. Has
unlimited faith in own resources, and will give to those less fortunate.
Combines selflessness, generosity, and humanitarian instincts. Welfare
worker, actor, and doctor are possible career opportunities.

PERSONALITY INGREDIENTS: Desires domestic harmony, artistic self-
expression, and gracious life-style. Needs mature, loving, appreciative
family/friends. Is willing counselor, parental protector, and determined
idealist. Appears animated, entertaining, and fashionably comfortable.
Strives to be the life of the party. Must avoid selfishness, scattering
energy, and extravagant emotionalism.

PERSONALITY EXTREME: Too changeable, or too unprogressive.

LEAH (Hebrew/English)—F.

MAJOR TALENT: Ability to incorporate organizational efficiency, executive leadership, and practical judgment into career. Is controlled,
energetic, and dependable. Has drive, independence, and quality consciousness. Combines mental analysis, refinement, and material awareness. Investment counselor, consultant, and franchise owner are
possible career opportunities.

PERSONALITY INGREDIENTS: Appears different, emotionally expressive, and on the go. Strives to be dignified, original, and tuned to the finer
things of life. Switches from supportive booster for loved ones to enthusiastic evangelist for personal ideals and causes. Is a powerhouse
with futuristic vision.

PERSONALITY EXTREME: Too materialistic, or too ambitionless.

LEE (Anglo-Saxon/English)—F. & M.

MAJOR TALENT: Ability to incorporate structure, practical organization, and hard work into career. Is industrious, loyal, and self-

disciplined. Has trust, honesty, and calm. Combines innovative ideas, self-expression in many forms, and building, and rebuilding, to be a solid citizen. Technical expert, piano player, and policeman are possible career opportunities.

PERSONALITY INGREDIENTS: Desires universal marketplace for unique/ pioneering ideas. Appears attractive and strives to bring beauty, entertainment, or humor to others. Needs admiration, love, and security. Should maintain conventional course. Sensual overindulgences/radical changes may cause financial setbacks/loss of dignity. Must accept new circumstances and have faith in the belief that each reconstruction of lifestyle brings a deepened sense of security and a broader range for innovative concepts.

PERSONALITY EXTREME: Too temperamental, or too controlled.

LEIF (Teutonic/Norse/English)—M.

MAJOR TALENT: Ability to incorporate curiosity, daring, and adventurous nature into career. Is physically energetic, sensual, and enthusiastic. Has understanding of people, cleverness, and love of freedom. Combines cooperation, self-expression, and progressive change. Politician, traveling salesman, and foreign correspondent are possible career opportunities.

PERSONALITY INGREDIENTS: Appears noble, classic, and impressive. Strives to be broad scoped, cultural, and to selflessly serve humanitarian needs. Would give the shirt off his back, feeling that others are needier. Is strong, resourceful, and determined to offer quality performance and "see things through." Desires mental and physical freedom. Wants unconventional experiences, variety, and experimentation. Dislikes to wait, narrow-mindedness, and boredom. Learns by trial and error, is quick, and authoritatively adapts new knowledge. Is headstrong, confident, and thrives upon challenge.

PERSONALITY EXTREME: Too idealistic, or too unprincipled.

LEIGH (Anglo-Saxon: Lee/Lea/English)—F. & M.

MAJOR TALENT: Ability to incorporate clever, instructional, and adaptable perceptions of others into career. Is quick, gutsy, and intuitive. Has gracious manner, curiosity, and unconventional approach. Combines sensitivity to details, self-expression, and attraction to progressive change. Theater, government, and transportation are possible career opportunities.

PERSONALITY INGREDIENTS: Appears classic, noble, and magnetic. Strives to be generous, helpful, and forgiving. Wants quality work, broad range, and romance. Inwardly intense, impulsive, and impatient. Is restless, energetic, and mentally sharp. Needs challenges and to try new experiences each day. Relates to everyone, hopes to improve/uplift the world, and may find realism hard to handle.

PERSONALITY EXTREME: Too ambitious, or too unaspiring.

LEILA (Arabic/English)—F.

MAJOR TALENT: Ability to incorporate imagination, resourcefulness, and varieties of self-expression into career. Is ready to laugh, attention-getting, and affectionate. Has charm, convenient memory, and appreciation for all forms of beauty. Combines detail consciousness, independent nature, and popular style. Model, writer, and critic are possible career opportunities.

PERSONALITY INGREDIENTS: Desires family warmth, gracious living, and material attainments. Feels protective, responsible, and helpful. Self-image is mature, wise, and unselfish. May get too personal with others, but sincerely tries to sympathize and right all wrongs. Appears tasteful, dignified, and comfortable. Strives to be considerate and expects others to live up to personal ideals. Must avoid gossip, over anxious emotionalizing, and possessiveness.

PERSONALITY EXTREME: Too proud, or too inferior.

LEILANI (Hawaiian)—F.

MAJOR TALENT: Ability to incorporate leadership, sharp mental analysis, and executive organizational ambitions into career. Is efficient, self-reliant, and energetic. Has physical/emotional strength, persuasive/charming personality, and attraction for inherited money/influence/prestige. Combines free spirit, friendliness, and confidence to aim high. Is multifaceted. Any business, art form, and government office offer possible career opportunities.

PERSONALITY INGREDIENTS: Desires home/family/community, material and spiritual attainments. Feels ethical, protective, and responsible. Appears different, retiring, and idealistic. Can be dramatic, vibrant, dreamy. At times, may seem to be "out of this world." Is an inspirational visionary with subtle control and an enthusiasm that attracts supporters for inventions or uplifting ideas.

PERSONALITY EXTREME: Too giving, or too possessive.

LELAND (Old English/English)—M.

MAJOR TALENT: Ability to incorporate charm, imagination, and optimistic resourcefulness into career. Is restless, affectionate, and kind. Has a need for attention, enjoys beautiful people/surroundings, and has good fortune from women. Can sell anything, including self. Combines persistence, detail consciousness, and pioneering ideas/ambitions. Performing artist, promoter, and business organizer are possible career opportunities.

PERSONALITY INGREDIENTS: Needs balanced life-style. Desires home/business harmony, gracious living, and material security. Appears concerned, sturdy, and responsible. Prefers comfort to fashion, but is dignified, tasteful, and coordinated. Keeps promises, protects/serves/helps others, and has strong will/firm opinions. Assumes burdens, and should focus upon home-related activities.

PERSONALITY EXTREME: Too rigid, or too unstructured.

LENA (Greek: variable-diminutive: Helen; Madalene; Magdalena/alone)—F.

MAJOR TALENT: Ability to incorporate attraction for change, adventure, and unrestricted thinking/action into career. Is curious, clever, and sensual. Has adaptability, nerve, and knack of relating to everyone. Opts to try new ideas, learns from experience, and moves on to challenge the unknown. Is inspirational, youthful, and a catalyst for progressive change. Combines practicality, common sense, and individuality. Politician, advertising executive, and any people-oriented profession are possible career opportunities.

PERSONALITY INGREDIENTS: First impression is controlled, dominant, and as affluent as possible. Strives to be influential, authoritative, and businesslike. Desires a happy home, family attainments, and gracious living. Wants comfort, harmony, and to give/receive sympathy, kindness, and protection. Should enjoy domesticity, travel, and spicy variety.

PERSONALITY EXTREME: Too assertive, or too submissive.

LENORA (Greek: Helen/English)—F.

MAJOR TALENT: Ability to incorporate gentle nature, idealism, and productive partnerships into career. Is adaptable, peace loving, and visionary. Has nervous energy, diplomacy, and broad philosophy. Combines empathetic approach, sensitivity to details, and inventive/different ideas. Arbitrator, film maker, and advisor to the elderly are possible career opportunities.

PERSONALITY INGREDIENTS: Strives to be materially successful, desires to attract attention, and has inspirational gift of gab. Wants beauty, joy, and pleasure. Appears genial, direct, and self-assured. Is responsible, progressive, and proud. Should avoid being indecisive, stubborn, or personally sensitive to attract supporters for innovative reforming ideas.

PERSONALITY EXTREME: Too ambitious, or too lazy.

LENORE (Greek: Helen/German/English)—F.

MAJOR TALENT: Ability to incorporate sympathetic, responsible, protective social service into career. Is family/community focused, strong willed, and moralistic. Has musical interests, comforting manner, and enjoys solving problems for others. Combines friendliness, self-expression, and parental approach. Teacher, union delegate, and hospital administrator are possible career opportunities.

PERSONALITY INGREDIENTS: Desires quality, culture, and perfection. Needs position of authority to feel self-confident. Fears loneliness/poverty and maintains a secret self. Appears efficient, impressive, and managerial. Strives to be influential, wealthy, and in control. Happiest when expert/educated/respected. Should avoid materialistic/speculative ventures, stubbornness, and envy.

PERSONALITY EXTREME: Too busy, or too bored.

LEO (Latin/English)—M.

MAJOR TALENT: Ability to incorporate unconventional, progressive, and clever approach into career. Is changeable, intuitive, and sensual. Has resourcefulness, curiosity, and sociability. Combines independent nature, down-to-earth practicality, and learning from experience. Politician, advertising executive, and actor are possible career opportunities.

PERSONALITY INGREDIENTS: Appears entertaining, attractive, and attention-getting. Strives to be popular, fashionable, and optimistic. Is motivated to do more than the average person. Wants to see personal ideals realized and to reach out to influence others. Has luck with filmed products. Must avoid impulsiveness, gambling, and impracticality. Has high nervous energy, versatility, and eye for details. Should balance desire for drink/food/sex. Prone to overindulgences.

PERSONALITY EXTREME: Too smug, or too anxious.

LEON (French/Latin/Greek/Italian/Russian/English)—M.

MAJOR TALENT: Ability to incorporate independence, originality, and broad-scoped planning into career. Is inventive, aggressive, and forceful. Has leadership, decisive approach, and active energy. Combines humanitarian instincts, romantic nature, and pioneering spirit. Artist, chemist, and lawyer are possible career opportunities.

PERSONALITY INGREDIENTS: Appears genial, businesslike, and dominant. Strives to be a material success. Inwardly idealistic, gentle, and peace loving. Needs easygoing relationships, quality, and refinement. Best when not making comparisons with others. Meant to be a true individualist and should not avoid taking responsibility for unique personal desires.

PERSONALITY EXTREME: Too enthusiastic, or too nonchalant.

LEONA (Latin/English)—F.

MAJOR TALENT: Ability to incorporate tact, patience, and attention to details into career. Is orderly, friendly, and gentle. Has persistence, receptivity, and sensitivity. Combines subtle control, group planning, and refinement. Private secretary, nurse, and musician/singer/dancer are possible career opportunities.

PERSONALITY INGREDIENTS: Appears self-reliant, tailor-made, and businesslike. Aspires to be affluent, influential, and respected. Inwardly pleasure/beauty/humor seeking. Wants to forget anything unpleasant, be popular, and keep occupied with a variety of imaginative interests. Needs creative self-expression, attention, and love.

PERSONALITY EXTREME: Too bossy, or too unassertive.

LEONARD (Old German/French/English)—M.

MAJOR TALENT: Ability to incorporate instructional approach, inspiration to better conditions for others, and dedicated leadership into career. Is either very domestic or very determined to improve the quality of life for others. Is sympathetic, self-disciplined, and strong willed. Combines showmanship, creative imagination, and burden-bearing instincts. Has quiet, mature authority which commands attention and respect. Teacher, conservationist, and union leader are possible career opportunities.

PERSONALITY INGREDIENTS: Appears to be, and is, a versatile person. Strives to be optimistic, entertaining, and witty. Is motivated to set an example for others, spread happiness, and forget blunders quickly. May flirt, tease, and keep talking, but can be studious and attentive to the needs of children, animals, the elderly. Attempts to make life simple, harmonious, and worthwhile for loved ones and anyone who needs protection.

PERSONALITY EXTREME: Too proper, or too immoral.

LEONORE (Greek: Helen/German/English)—F.

MAJOR TALENT: Ability to incorporate expression of beauty, imagination, and fashionable activities into career. Is youthful, versatile, and entertaining. Has charm, humanitarian instincts, and wide-range philosophy. Combines empathetic nature, sociability, and knack for getting attention. Sales, theater, and writing offer possible career opportunities.

PERSONALITY INGREDIENTS: Is motivated to work, plan, and build for the future. Wants honest, ethical, and respectable life-style. Appears

strong, self-confident, and tailor-made. Strives to be efficient, highly organized and businesslike. Wants wealth, power, and to do things quickly. At best when structured, conventional, and able to complete commitments. Is responsible, family focused, and loving problem solver.
PERSONALITY EXTREME: Too tenacious, or too changeable.

LEONTYNE (Latin: Leontine/English)—F.
MAJOR TALENT: Ability to incorporate idealistic, quality-conscious, and refined nature into career. Is high strung, evangelistic, and different. Has gentleness, patience, and concern for details. Combines magnetic charm, humanitarian philosophy, and individuality. Group musician/dancer, union arbitrator, and religious leader are possible career opportunities.
PERSONALITY INGREDIENTS: Motivated to question, cultivate, and polish. Needs authority, privacy, and calm. Likes timeless beauty, nature, and to attract respect, rather than be aggressive. Appears dynamic, dignified, and classic. Strives to work, build, and leave a lasting mark. Has organization, gift with words, and strong personal beliefs. Affects others by example, and must avoid extravagant gestures.
PERSONALITY EXTREME: Too superstitious, or too logical.

LEOPOLD (Old German/French/German/English)—M.
MAJOR TALENT: Ability to incorporate concentrated study, cultural instincts, and striving for perfection into career. Is questioning, analytic, and structured. Has need for formal education, quality performance, and private time. Combines creative self-expression, work, and refinement of interests. Musical conductor, mathematician, and financial advisor are possible career opportunities.
PERSONALITY INGREDIENTS: Strives to be influential, controlled, and discriminating. Is organizational, commanding, and confident. Wants honesty, integrity, and efficiency. Has persuasive, dominant, logical capacities for solving major problems, gaining recognition, and heading straight to the heart of things. May be too blunt, unemotional, and ambitious. Is an intellectual workaholic.
PERSONALITY EXTREME: Too "square," or too nonconforming.

LEROY (French)—M.
MAJOR TALENT: Ability to incorporate skillful and far-reaching methods of creative self-expression into career. Is geared to orderliness when working, entertaining, or giving affection. Has engaging manner, wit, and style. Combines imagination, multiple interests, and knack for gaining recognition, money, and pleasure from social contacts. Doctor, theatrical performer/producer, and any word/language oriented profession are possible career opportunities.
PERSONALITY INGREDIENTS: Hopes to add personal ideals to uplift/change/enlighten. Desires a quality-conscious, peaceful, cooperative world. May defend impractical/unconventional causes. Has high nervous energy and usually takes on two commitments at one time. Appears to be daring, different, and in control. Strives to be pioneering and may be aggressively assertive and annoyed with little details/unaccomplished people. Is charming, attractive, and prone to scattering energy/kindness/money on fads/fashions, fantasies, and loves.
PERSONALITY EXTREME: Too technical, or too unquestioning.

LESLEY (Celtic/English)—F. & M.

MAJOR TALENT: Ability to incorporate steadfast, conscientious, group stabilizing approach into career. Is kind, problem-solving, and a student teacher. Has sympathetic, helpful, and idealistic nature. Combines structure, cooperation, and protective/responsible/parental instincts. Hotel/restaurant manager, music teacher, and marriage counselor are possible career opportunities.

PERSONALITY INGREDIENTS: Feels inventive, mentally alert, and self-motivated. Wants freedom of choice, control, and decisive action. Appears sexy, energetic, and enthusiastic. Strives to be adventurous, well traveled, and sensually stimulated. May seem dogmatic, too quick to judge, or disloyal. Has a need for unconventional interests, but assumes burdens within conventional confines. Must expect to sacrifice ego needs for weaker/needier, domestic/community relationships. Attracts admiration, showmanship, and success.

PERSONALITY EXTREME: Too introspective, or too shallow.

LESLIE (Celtic/English)—F. & M.

MAJOR TALENT: Ability to incorporate executive efficiency, control, and judgment into career. Seems confident under all circumstances, organized, and alert to details. Has sensitivity, common sense, and energetic nature. Combines cooperation, self-discipline, and material ambitions. Sports, transportation, and investing are possible career opportunities.

PERSONALITY INGREDIENTS: Motivated to invent, originate, and lead. Is mentally sharp, decisive, and individualistic. Strives to be cultured, authoritative, and intellectually polished. Appears unruffled, dignified, and classy. Aims for perfection and may find emotional/commercial realities painful. Best when academically skilled and on a clear course. Internalizes problems and must avoid moodiness/melancholy.

PERSONALITY EXTREME: Too understanding, or too unsympathetic.

LESTER (Anglo-Saxon/English)—M.

MAJOR TALENT: Ability to incorporate research, mental analysis, and specialized study into career. Is intuitive, refined, and self-controlled. Has intellectual curiosity, refined tastes, and quality consciousness. Combines attention to fine points, sensitivity, and mobility. Needs to continually polish techniques. Photographer, librarian, and detective are possible career opportunities.

PERSONALITY INGREDIENTS: Appears comfortable, dignified, and concerned. Strives to be protective, pleasing, and responsible. Aims to have loving mate, gracious home, and domestic tranquillity. Inwardly individualistic, ambitious, and creative. Wants to lead, direct, and control. Feels decisive and should not be driven. Draws heavily on childhood experiences for guidance. Best when free to travel and rooted in countrified environment.

PERSONALITY EXTREME: Too empathetic, or too self-pitying.

LETICIA (Latin: Letitia/English)—F.

MAJOR TALENT: Ability to incorporate innovative ideas, progressive leadership, and confident nature into career. Is curious, clever, and adventurous. Has understanding of people, friendly approach, and sensitivity. Combines attention to detail, creative self-expression, and free-thinking. Politician, airline stewardess, and reporter are possible career opportunities.

PERSONALITY INGREDIENTS: Wants to influence others, assume responsibility, and enjoy harmonious domestic relationships. Needs to feel loved and needed. Appears to be a born leader. Strives for position, power, and wealth. Seems businesslike, efficient, and organized to work. Has a knack with words and should persist with personal ideals to achieve high potential.

PERSONALITY EXTREME: Too original, or too imitative.

LEVY (Hebrew/English)—M.

MAJOR TALENT: Ability to incorporate original, pioneering, progressive ideas and leadership into career. Is independent, direct, and active. Has self-assertion, daring, and will power. Combines universal/humanitarian philosophy, quality of performance, and individuality. Inventor, explorer, and business owner are possible career opportunities.

PERSONALITY INGREDIENTS: First impression is quiet, unruffled, and refined. Strives to be culturally polished, mentally analytic, and perfect. Inwardly optimistic, creatively expressive, and resourceful. Wants beauty, charming companionship, and pleasure. Must be forceful to bring innovative ambitions to reality. Imitation, stagnation, and a know-it-all attitude stunt growth and cause domestic unhappiness. Combines the introverted questioner and the extroverted authority.

PERSONALITY EXTREME: Too faultfinding, or too trusting.

LEW (English: Lewis; diminutive/Russian-English: independent, M./Hebrew-Pennsylvania Dutch: Lewanna; diminutive, F.)—F. & M.

MAJOR TALENT: Ability to incorporate planning, work, and constructive attitude into career. Is practical, independent, and creatively expressive. Uses common sense, realistic methods, and instinct for solving problems. Combines imagination, pioneering spirit, and structure. Fireman, contractor, and piano player are possible career opportunities.

PERSONALITY INGREDIENTS: Desires adventure, challenge, and physical experimentation. Wants life experience. Appears self-assured, genial, and businesslike. Strives to impress, enthuse, and direct. Aims for excitement, changes, and material power. Must avoid impulsiveness, gambles, and immorality. Will experience at least one rise to/fall from prominence and reconstructs each time for a more meaningful life-style. Rarely maintains "9–5" schedule.

PERSONALITY EXTREME: Too busy, or too bored.

LEWIS (Old German/English)—M.

MAJOR TALENT: Ability to incorporate clever adaptations, adventurous nature, and learning from experience into career. Is promotional, gutsy, and quick. Has honest approach, sociability, and understanding of people. Combines attention to details, creative self-expression, and progressive ambitions. Traveling salesman, public servant, and advertising copywriter are possible career opportunities.

PERSONALITY INGREDIENTS: First impression is classic, magnetic, and noble. Strives to be broad scoped, helpful, and quality conscious. Inwardly curious, unconventional, and sensual. Wants to travel, experiment, and taste all that life has to offer. May expect inheritances, marriage, and constant change. Has fresh ideas, humanitarian philosophy, and may be a catalyst for change for others.

PERSONALITY EXTREME: Too daring, or too fearful.

LIBBIE (Hebrew: Elizabeth; diminutive/independent)—F.

MAJOR TALENT: Ability to incorporate imagination, resourcefulness, and appreciation of beauty into career. Is entertaining, optimistic, and kind. Has knack of bouncing back and seeing the lighter side in time of stress. Combines wide-range planning, conventional/practical/structured instincts, and communications gifts. Theater, sales, and fashion are possible career opportunities.

PERSONALITY INGREDIENTS: Appears refined, calm, and poised. Inwardly enthusiastic, adventurous, and spunky. Strives to be cultured, specialized, and quality conscious. Desires sensual pleasures, progressive changes, and constant activity. Gains through social contact, sex appeal, and magnetic charm.

PERSONALITY EXTREME: Too passionate, or too indifferent.

LILA (Arabic: Leila/Latin: Lillian/Sanskrit/English)—F.

MAJOR TALENT: Ability to incorporate quality consciousness, aristocratic approach, and questioning instincts into career. Is a private person when working. Best when educated to a specialty. Has mental analysis, pride, and dignity. Combines introspection, independence, and conscientiousness. Any profession, religion, and mathematics are possible career opportunities.

PERSONALITY INGREDIENTS: Desires mental and physical freedom. Wants leadership, innovations, and to be a trend setter. Appears comfortable, comforting, and concerned. Strives for domestic happiness, gracious living, and to teach, counsel, and help others. May be meddlesome, too aggressive, or disappointed in people/work until dreams of perfection come down to earth. Would like to create a world where nobody burped and everyone was protected/responsible/loved. Is secretive and dreads loneliness and poverty.

PERSONALITY EXTREME: Too sure, or too anxious.

LILLIAN (Latin: Lily/Scottish/English)—M.

MAJOR TALENT: Ability to incorporate responsible service to others into career. Is sympathetic, instructional, and protective. Has knack for problem solving, group harmony, and showmanship. Combines parental nature, strong personal beliefs, and power to inspire beauty, life-support improvements, and stability. Uses personal idealism to benefit family/community or mankind. Teacher, musician, and public defender are possible career opportunities.

PERSONALITY INGREDIENTS: Inwardly individualistic, inventive, and mentally active. Wants leadership, control, and not to be driven. Appears to be different, energetic, and enthusiastic. Strives to be adventurous, experimental, and to taste all physical life experience. Has courage, trend-setting ideas, and pioneering spirit. Must avoid escaping from reality, overindulgence in food/drink/sensuality, and procrastinating . . . self-pity, or martyrdom. May play a compassionate, law-upholding, and self-sacrificing role that accepts burdens for missionary reform.

PERSONALITY EXTREME: Too busy, or too bored.

LILY (Latin/English)—F.

MAJOR TALENT: Ability to incorporate practical, organized, common sense approach, and charitable instincts into career. Has working energy and dreamer's spirit. Is disciplined, patient, and diplomatic. Combines self-expression, understanding, and responsibility for self, family, community stability. Can turn ideas to reality and, when educated, create products of lasting improvement. Business executive, architect/builder, and uplifting/down-to-earth products inventor are possible career opportunities.

PERSONALITY INGREDIENTS: Appears warm, tasteful, and solid. Strives to be helpful, instructional, and hospitable. Inwardly quality conscious, culturally attaining, and questioning. Wants refinement, privacy, and natural beauty. Specialization improves potential for rewards and recognition.

PERSONALITY EXTREME: Too authoritative, or too quiet.

LINCOLN (Celtic-Latin/Old English)—M.

MAJOR TALENT: Ability to incorporate mental analysis, research, and quiet study into career. Is a perfectionist, attention getter, and practical worker. Has poise, eye for natural beauty, and intuitional approach. Combines pride, dignity, and cultural attainment. Lawyer, detective, and radio technician are possible career opportunities.

PERSONALITY INGREDIENTS: First impression is active, direct, and nonconforming. Strives to be first, unique, and boss. Inwardly sympathetic, helpful, and instructional. Wants gracious/loving home, respectability, and creative self-expression. Desires domesticity and assumes responsibilities, but needs reflective privacy and freedom from conventionality to "fight City Hall" for innovative beliefs. May be an escapist or a loner.

PERSONALITY EXTREME: Too brave, or too cowardly.

LINDA (Spanish/English)—F.

MAJOR TALENT: Ability to incorporate high powered energy/emotions, practical work structures, and constructive planning into career. Is an organizer and visionary. Has determination, perseverance, and common sense resources. Combines detail consciousness, gracious diplomacy, and need to work to improve standards and products. Can strive for anything and make it pay. May be humanitarian or power seeker. Contributes beauty/benefit to others to achieve high potential. Public relations expert, charity administrator, and government legislator are possible career opportunities.

PERSONALITY INGREDIENTS: Strives to be popular, fashionable, and optimistic. Appears attractive, entertaining, and self-expressive. Inwardly ambitious, inventive, and independent. Wants to be first, in control, and different. Has nervous energy that must be used constructively or can turn to self-destructive outlets. Must keep busy.

PERSONALITY EXTREME: Too self-centered, or too obliging.

LINDSEY (Teutonic/English)—F. & M.

MAJOR TALENT: Ability to incorporate proper procedures, creative self-expression, and analytic intellect into career. Is culturally attaining, refined, and intuitive. Has common sense, love of nature, and down-to-earth wisdom. Combines conventionality, optimism, and quality consciousness. Aims for perfection. Respects education/expertise/authority. Detective, lawyer, and mimic are possible career opportunities.

PERSONALITY INGREDIENTS: Visual impression is modest, shy, and gentle. Strives to be refined, easygoing, and in harmony with everyone. Inwardly curious, experimental, and unconventional. Wants sensual pleasures, nonroutine life-style, and challenges. Is a strong, clever, gutsy "survivor," and is discreet. Prefers a retiring, discriminating, adaptable facade. May be the winning "dark horse" in any race.

PERSONALITY EXTREME: Too questioning, or too authoritative.

LINNE (Anglo-Saxon/Celtic/English)—F. & M.

MAJOR TALENT: Ability to incorporate skill of performance, sympathetic service, and inspirational leadership into career. Is concerned with fine points, logic, and seeking perfection. Has creative mind, loving nature, and sees both sides of an issue. Combines cooperation, intellect, and broad-scoped philosophy. Judge, union arbitrator, and political reformer are possible career opportunities.

PERSONALITY INGREDIENTS: First impression is honest, determined, and dignified. Strives for material security, respectability, and disciplined life-style. Inwardly fiery, progressive, and sensual. Wants adventure, challenges, and change. Expects the best from everyone and must avoid playing "Pollyanna," or "Archie Bunker." Attracts support for original ideas and can bring a variety of interests to successful conclusions.

PERSONALITY EXTREME: Too accident prone, or too careful.

LINUS (Latin/English)—M.

MAJOR TALENT: Ability to incorporate optimism, words, and imagination into career. Is individualistic, adaptable, and lucky. Has charm, wit, and attracts attention. Combines gentleness, direct action, and sociability. Lecturer, journalist, and model are possible career opportunities.

PERSONALITY INGREDIENTS: First impression is kind, noble, and understanding. Strives for wide variety of interests, contacts, and skills. Likes romance, to counsel others, and to improve standards. Inwardly seeks popularity, love, and to keep busy. Feels restless, sharing, and eager to forget anything ugly/unpleasant. Desires beauty, pleasure, and fun. May be extravagant and enlarge upon truths, but rarely realizes that these fabrications bother anyone. Wants to be entertaining or promote friendships. Can be a joy and a pest.

PERSONALITY EXTREME: Too submissive, or too assertive.

LIONEL (Latin-French: Leon/English)—M.

MAJOR TALENT: Ability to incorporate industrious nature, systematized self-discipline, and tireless practical effort into career. Is geared to routine, reality, and correctness. Has endurance, individuality, and acquires technical expertise in creative interests. Combines competitive nature, innovations, and down-to-earth work. Piano player, electrician, and ecologist are possible career opportunities.

PERSONALITY INGREDIENTS: Wants easygoing, friendly, modest, family/community relationships. Feels the rhythm of life and likes comfort and refinement. Appears attention-getting, special, and enthusiastic.

Strives to bring personal ideas to reality. Has high energy and aims to inspirationally improve upon conventional standards. Can sell anything that supports dreams. Has potential to leave a mark of quality for future generations.

PERSONALITY EXTREME: Too amused, or too tragic.

LISA (Hebrew: Elizabeth/Lusatian/English)—F.

MAJOR TALENT: Ability to incorporate learning from experience into career. Is adventurous, experimental, and freedom-loving. Has nerve, adaptability, and clever perceptions about people/futuristic ideas. Combines individuality, organizational structure, and unconventional nature. Advertising, politics, and travel businesses are possible career opportunities.

PERSONALITY INGREDIENTS: First impression is classic, scrubbed, and tasteful. Strives to be proper, secure, and respectable. Inwardly independent, forceful, and decisive. Wants to materialize mental/physical pace-setting ideas. Attracts leadership. Is a nonconformist, with conventional image. Best when patient, and not overindulging in sex, food, passing fads. Is changeable, and should learn when to hang in, and when to move on.

PERSONALITY EXTREME: Too ambitious, or too nonaggressive.

LIZ (Hebrew: Elizabeth/English)—F.

MAJOR TALENT: Ability to incorporate cooperative attitude, consideration, and need to form alliances into career. Is attentive to details, rhythmical, and friendly. Has persistence, tact, and desire for peace. Combines loyal nature, appreciation of delicacy/fine points, and an unconscious drive to collect things. Musician, bookkeeper, and homemaker are possible career opportunities.

PERSONALITY INGREDIENTS: Inwardly broad scoped, compassionate, and charitable. Wants top notch quality for self/everyone, and to have a "yes" or "no" conclusion to everything. Dislikes being in limbo. Is a finisher. May seem mystical, enthusiastic, or dreamy at first glance. Has a special poise that attracts boosters. Strives to interest others in supporting personal ideas, and can sell anything when on a "crusade." Must learn not to judge by appearances, and to accept the "grays" between "black and white" solutions.

PERSONALITY EXTREME: Too power hungry, or too self-satisfied.

LLEWELLYN (Celtic/Welsh/English)—M.

MAJOR TALENT: Ability to incorporate humanitarian love, kindness, and youthful optimism into career. Is gracious, charming, and resourceful. Has imagination, emotional highs and lows and a let's-try-again approach. Combines quality/skilled creativity, empathy for others, and verbal self-expression. Missionary, entertainer, and author are possible career opportunities.

PERSONALITY INGREDIENTS: Appears to be a solid citizen. Strives to have roots, beauty, and comfort. Inwardly efficient, self-reliant, and disciplined. Wants position, power, and large tangible results. Aims to teach, uplift, and sympathetically uphold responsible ideals. May be lazy, insensitive, or sensually self-indulgent. Must finish projects to feel happy.

PERSONALITY EXTREME: Too enthusiastic, or too depressed.

LLOYD (Celtic/Welsh)—M.

MAJOR TALENT: Ability to incorporate a variety of clever, fast moving, offbeat ideas that appeal to the public into a career. Is tuned to fine points, humor, and adventure. Has wit, ambition, and knack for promoting a job, bluffing through, and learning by the experience. Relates to people, is gutsy, curious, and sensually tuned. Combines creative self-expression, adaptability, and unconventional planning, speech, and routine. Advertising, theater, and gambler are possible career opportunities.

PERSONALITY INGREDIENTS: First impression is stylish, affluent, and self-reliant. Strives for prominence, power, and control. Inwardly domestic, loving, and helpful. Wants luxurious, respectable, and harmonious life-style. Is a showman, a businessman, and a sympathetic friend. Must avoid too much temperament, self-indulgence, or arrogance.

PERSONALITY EXTREME: Too genteel, or too uncouth.

LOGAN (Scottish)—M.

MAJOR TALENT: Ability to incorporate wide range planning, workaholic dedication, and knack for solving problems into career. Is honest, ethical, and charitable. Has ambition, initiative, and sensitivity to people/fine points/details. Combines cooperative nature, strong opinions, and practical disciplines. Any business, medicine, and aeronautics offer possible career opportunities.

PERSONALITY INGREDIENTS: Wants quality, natural beauty, and cultural attainments. Inwardly seeks private thinking time, intellectual stimulation, and expertise/education/authority. Appears concerned, dignified, and comfortable. Strives to be instructional, helpful, and protective. Has showmanship and aims to serve the life-support needs of others. Should strive for gracious life-style, family/community respect, and policymaking positions. May leave tangible results for future generations.

PERSONALTY EXTREME: Too busy, or too bored.

LOIS (Greek: independent/Latin: Louise; diminutive/English)—F.

MAJOR TALENT: Ability to incorporate independent nature, ideas, and style into career. Is aggressive, assertive, and ambitious. Has courage, wide range of interests, and empathy for anyone who seems inferior. Combines humanitarian instincts, innovations, and need to instigate progressive changes. Must be willing to fight for beliefs, avoid contradictory image or compromise for security. This name introduces new concepts and attracts followers. Inventor, explorer, and promoter are possible career opportunities.

PERSONALITY INGREDIENTS: Wants love, domestic tranquillity, and gracious life-style. Needs musical/creative self-expression, and to inspire, teach, and advise. Wants to help/serve/raise standards. Appears conventional, dignified, and classic. Strives to be a solid citizen; patriotic/ethical/trustworthy. Attracts success.

PERSONALITY EXTREME: Too egotistical, or too selfless.

LOLA (Spanish: Carlota/English: independent)—F.

MAJOR TALENT: Ability to incorporate hard work, routine, and structure into career. Is down to earth, individualistic, and charming. Has integrity, self-discipline, and perseverance. Combines imagination, ambition, and manual dexterity. Technically skilled musician/writer/repairperson, accountant, and receptionist are possible career opportunities.

PERSONALITY INGREDIENTS: Appears interested, tasteful, and comfortable. Strives for a happy home, creative self-expression, and group/family harmony. Wants the best. Desires quality products, timeless beauty, and perfection from self and others. Inwardly logical, analytical, and culturally attaining. Must expect to plan, build, and rebuild for success.

PERSONALITY EXTREME: Too impatient, or too passive.

LOLITA (Spanish: Lola/English)—F.

MAJOR TALENT: Ability to incorporate sympathetic nature, helpful service, and desire to learn/instruct/advise into career. Is generous, dependable, and conscientious. Has mature/parental instincts, sociability, and creates group harmony. Combines attraction for partnerships, down-toearth material values, and emotional responsiveness. Nurse, waitress, and entertainer are possible career opportunities.

PERSONALITY INGREDIENTS: Lacks inner security. Needs education/specialized skill to feel "perfect." Wants cultural refinements, quality people/products, and privacy. Appears groomed, dominant, and genial. Strives to be influential, wealthy, and self-reliant. Cheerful/optimistic/loving outlook attracts happiness, protection, and security. Jealousy, stubbornness, and exaggerations cause stress.

PERSONALITY EXTREME: Too submissive, or too assertive.

LONA (Middle English)—F.

MAJOR TALENT: Ability to incorporate strong will, perseverance, and understanding of human foibles into career. Is sympathetic, individualistic, and ambitious. Has showmanship, capacity for teaching/learning/counseling, and a knack for strategic/subtle authority. Combines creative self-expression, unconventional nature, and domestic instincts. Marriage counselor, animal trainer, and interior decorator are possible career opportunities.

PERSONALITY INGREDIENTS: Wants refinement, intellectual stimulation, and to get to the "root" of everything. Seeks quality, wisdom, and perfection. Fears loneliness/poverty but needs privacy. Forms dependent, emotional relationships to ease unrealistic conflicts. Appears tailormade, businesslike, and as affluent as possible. Assumes burdens, raises standards, and must learn to do these things for worthwhile causes. Is inspirational, but may take responsibilities too seriously and become a martyr. Must learn not to "judge a book by its cover."

PERSONALITY EXTREME: Too ambitious, or too lazy.

LORAINE (Old High German: Louis/French/English)—F.

MAJOR TALENT: Ability to incorporate personal sensitivity, creative ideas, and high nervous energy into career. Is emotional, intuitive, and inspirational. Has detail consciousness, domestic instincts, and pride. Combines imagination, desire for beauty, and quality consciousness. Critic, teacher, and arbitrator are possible career opportunities.

PERSONALITY INGREDIENTS: Desires freedom to play, entertain, and maintain a variety of fashionable interests. Wants attention, love, and fun. Appears tailor-made, controlled, and prominent. Aspires to wealth, status, and authority. Tends to impracticality, scattering energy, and nosiness. Best when supportive, patient, and tactful. Attracts admirers and is a collector.

PERSONALITY EXTREME: Too impulsive, or too passive.

LORELEI (Teutonic: Lurline/German/English)—F.

MAJOR TALENT: Ability to incorporate organizational routines, structured thinking, and desire for tangible results into career. Is honest, sincere, and determined. Has industrious nature, discipline, and economy consciousness. Combines conventions, work, and respectability. Statistician, real estate broker, and piano player are possible career opportunities.

PERSONALITY INGREDIENTS: Appears comforting, helpful, and solid. Strives for domestic harmony, gracious living, and creative/musical self-expression. Inwardly analytical, logical, and culturally attaining. Wants quality, refinements, and perfection. Dislikes noise, confusion, and urban living. Has emotional and intellectual wisdom. Attracts successful business investments, polished relationships, and an orderly life-style.

PERSONALITY EXTREME: Too indiscreet, or too guarded.

LOREN (Latin: Laurence/English)—F. & M.

MAJOR TALENT: Ability to incorporate pace-setting ideas, initiative, and clear thinking into career. Is progressive, energetic, and resourceful. Has sex appeal, adaptability, and appreciation of fine points. Combines executive organizational efficiency, emotional generosity, and pioneering spirit. Architect, scientist, and editor are possible career opportunities.

PERSONALITY INGREDIENTS: Wants the realization of creative ideals. Inwardly quick, imaginative, and quality conscious. Feels out of the ordinary, and inspired to change/improve existing standards/concepts. Appears businesslike, controlled, and tailor-made. Strives for material advantages, dominance, and farsighted/enduring commercial success. Has enthusiasm, diplomacy, and sociability. Attracts recognition.

PERSONALITY EXTREME: Too multifaceted, or too single-minded.

LORETTA (Anglo-Saxon/Latin: Laura; diminutive/English: independent)—F.

MAJOR TALENT: Ability to incorporate independence, originality, and courage to make progressive changes into career. Is detail conscious, efficient, and direct. Has inspirational ideas, impressive manner, and learns how to adapt in partnerships. Combines humility, executive organizational efficiency, and daring. At best when patient, decisive, and emotionally balanced. New product promoter, business owner, and designer are possible career opportunities.

PERSONALITY INGREDIENTS: First impression is quiet, calm, and refined. Strives for cultural attainments, natural beauty, and perfection. Inwardly fun loving, optimistic, and filled with youthful passions. Combines the introverted analyst, and the extroverted attention getter. Opposing characteristics are alert to fight proudly for personal goals until life experience sorts out priorities. It would be easier as a youth, to pare

down variety of ambitions, seek a specialty, and try to recognize over-
sized fears of loneliness and poverty.

PERSONALITY EXTREME: Too ambitious, or too lackadaisical.

LORNA (Anglo-Saxon/Latin: Laura; variable/English)—F.

MAJOR TALENT: Ability to incorporate harmonious attitude, subtle persuasive approach, and emotional generosity into career. Is fair, kind, and
vocally/musically expressive. Has strong will, determination, and domestic instincts. Combines sensitivity to delicate issues/details, practical
hard work, and responsible protective nature. Marriage counselor, youth
group instructor, and interior decorator are possible career opportunities.

PERSONALITY INGREDIENTS: Wants refined, authoritative, quality-
perfect life-style. Inwardly analytic, intuitive, and intellectually aggressive. Strives for prominence, financial power, and organizational
efficiency. Appears tailor-made, managerial, and businesslike. Is a good
student/teacher/mature advisor. Must avoid flights of fancy, jealousy,
and getting think-stuck in childhood experiences. Must let go of past, and
make judgments based upon investigation and/or present lifestyle. Needs
to love, be loved, and experience mutual trust.

PERSONALITY EXTREME: Too independent, or too imitative.

LORNE (Irish/Scottish: Lorn/English)—M.

MAJOR TALENT: Ability to incorporate individuality, direct action, and
pioneering ideas into career. Is affectionate, capable, and strong. Has
pride, definite manner, and fast-paced approach. Combines sensitivity to
details, sound business judgment, and ambition to instigate innovative
changes. Organization executive, promoter, and theatrical performer are
possible career opportunities.

PERSONALITY INGREDIENTS: First impression is commanding,
efficient, and as affluent as possible. Strives to be respected, powerful,
and acknowledged. Inwardly imaginative, instinctual, and out to save the
world. Wants to be special and attempts to attract followers for personal
idealistic beliefs. Has personality appeal, "electricity," and refinement.
When emotionally balanced, motivated by uplifting concepts, and decisive, may leave a mark on humanity.

PERSONALITY EXTREME: Too unconventional or too standardized.

LORRAINE (Old High German: Louis/French/English)—F.

MAJOR TALENT: Ability to incorporate attention to details, inspirational leadership, and visionary ideas into career. Is quick to act, may be
brilliant, but benefits from partnership to keep feet on the ground. Has
diplomacy, gentleness, and sees both sides of an issue. Combines intellectual analysis, organizational routines, and extraordinary creative instincts. Photography, writing, and psychology are possible career
opportunities.

PERSONALITY INGREDIENTS: Visual impression is dominant, efficient,
and businesslike. Strives for affluence, influence, and recognition. Inwardly optimistic, restless, and pleasure seeking. Wants love, joy, and
kindness. Is a romantic. Prone to illusions, dreaming, and intuitional
foresight. Best when decisive, selective, and emotionally balanced.
Tends to let desire for peace dull ambitions.

PERSONALITY EXTREME: Too sensual, or too mental.

LOTTIE (French: Charlotte/English: nickname)—F.

MAJOR TALENT: Ability to incorporate appreciation for quality skills/ performance, empathetic/helpful nature, and wide range of interests into career. Is enterprising, detail conscious, and mentally analytic. Has philosophical humor, tolerance, and refined tastes. Combines resourcefulness, cultural growth, and convincing manner. Charity leader, parole officer, and any creative specialty are possible career opportunities.

PERSONALITY INGREDIENTS: Wants love, beauty, and gracious living. Inwardly strong willed, idealistic, and parental. Appears youthful, expressive, and optimistic. Strives to be attention getting, popular, and entertaining. Enjoys advising, raising standards, and all forms of originality. Best when following intuition, decisive, and accepting reality.

PERSONALITY EXTREME: Too adventurous, or too tied down.

LOU (Old German: diminutive Louis/Lewis, M./German-Anglo combination, F.)—F. & M.

MAJOR TALENT: Ability to incorporate speech, writing, and decorative ideas into career. Is creatively self-expressive and maintains a unique personal philosophy. Has charm, individuality, and kindness. Combines adaptability, attention to fine points, and uncommon eye for beauty. Finds own peace of mind. Promotion, selling, and accessorizing are possible career opportunities.

PERSONALITY INGREDIENTS: Wants to serve, educate, and improve cultural quality for a broad scope of people. Needs to promote tolerance, advise, and deal with humanitarian issues. First impression is youthful, optimistic, and attractive. Strives to be entertaining, and an appreciative audience. Adds artistry to a variety of interests, is a romantic, and in love with love. At best when aware of being set apart from mass thinking/ values and able to avoid scattering energy.

PERSONALITY EXTREME: Too styled, or too unfashionable.

LOUELLA (Latin: Louise/Hebrew-German: modern combination/ independent)—F.

MAJOR TALENT: Ability to incorporate problem solving, social consciousness, and musical/vocal showmanship into career. Is conscientious, helpful, and sympathetic. Has parental instincts, material practicality, and sensitivity to details. Combines conventionality, steadfast work, and firm opinions. Teacher, entertainer, and radio commentator are possible career opportunities.

PERSONALITY INGREDIENTS: Visually magnetic, convincing, and quality conscious. Wants to have wide scope, opportunity to benefit humanity, and romance. Inwardly domestic/loving, protective, and stable. Needs harmonious relationships, gracious/luxurious lifestyle, and to have personal ideals upheld. May be meddlesome, judgmental, and jealous. Aims to study, teach, and share knowledge. May get emotionally involved with everything. Best when tactful, considerate, and easygoing.

PERSONALITY EXTREME: Too inventive, or too uninspired.

LOUIS (Old German: Lewis/French/English)—M.

MAJOR TALENT: Ability to incorporate futuristic/humanitarian planning, work, and construction into career. Is a determined, strongly opinionated, energetic builder. Has powers of persuasion, practicality, and down-to-earth problem solving. Combines attention to details, idealism, and service to others. May be highly moral/ethical, or equally destructive/immoral. Government, science, and business are possible career opportunities.

PERSONALITY INGREDIENTS: Inwardly romantic, helpful, and empathetic. Wants to improve, serve, and may be selfless or selfish in ambitions. Strives to be, and appears, conventional, conservative, and a solid citizen. Would like to see order, system, and discipline, and may repel shows of affection by hiding feelings. A workaholic, inspirational, and materially masterful name.

PERSONALITY EXTREME: Too ruthless, or too inoffensive.

LOUISA (Latin: Louise/English)—F.

MAJOR TALENT: Ability to incorporate unconventional routine, curious nature, and appreciation of physical pleasures into career. Is quick witted, progressive, and tuned to a changing scene. Has enthusiasm, nerve, and convincing honesty. Combines creative self-expression, attention to details, and learning by experience. Short-order cook, detective, and reporter are possible career opportunities.

PERSONALITY INGREDIENTS: Inwardly independent, assertive, and self-motivated. Wants to be boss. Dislikes detail, indecision, and being ignored. Appears conventional, scrubbed, and natural. Strives to be respectable, proper, and materially secure. May be too confident, hard, and temperamental. Best when not forcing issues, and maintaining humor and open mind.

PERSONALITY EXTREME: Too bossy, or too submissive.

LOUISE (Latin: Aloysius/Old German: Louis/French/English)—F.

MAJOR TALENT: Ability to incorporate broad-scoped philosophy, tolerance, and top quality performance into career. Is a universal person. Feels empathetic, intellectually questioning, and sensitive to fine points. Has wisdom, integrity, and inspirational ideas. Combines mental control, emotional generosity, and magnetic attraction. Improves culturally throughout lifetime. Lawyer, artist/musician/actor, and teacher are possible career opportunities.

PERSONALITY INGREDIENTS: First impression is dignified, conservative, and precise. Strives to be practical, disciplined, and a solid citizen. Inwardly adventurous, clever, and understanding of human nature. Wants sensual pleasures, unconventional routine, and unusual experiences. Likes to try everything new, travel, and learn through changing experiences. Is open minded, speculative, and enthusiastic. Maintains youthful appearance, and attracts notables, affluence, and influential relationships.

PERSONALITY EXTREME: Too sensual, or too mental.

LOWELL (Old English: Lovell/English)—M.

MAJOR TALENT: Ability to incorporate intellectual analysis, adventurous nature, and questioning instincts into career. Is observant, logical, and diplomatic. Has poise, adaptability, and wants mobility. Combines need for perfection, aristocratic bearing, and self-control. Researcher, musical/radio technician, and photographer are possible career opportunities.

PERSONALITY INGREDIENTS: First impression is understanding, friendly, and open minded. Strives to learn anything new. Is curious, clever, and grows from experience. Inwardly inspired to rise above the ordinary. Wants to pioneer, polish, and promote quality expectations in public tastes and concepts. Is a visionary dreamer, tuned to expertise in all interests, and determined to survive any challenges that cross unconventional path. May have difficult childhood memories that develop uncommon human insight.

PERSONALITY EXTREME: Too talkative, or too confidential.

LUCAS (Latin/Portuguese/Spanish)—M.

MAJOR TALENT: Ability to incorporate personal idealism, enthusiasm, and attention to details into career. Is high strung, innovative, and creative. Has tact, charm, and sensitivity. Combines pioneering ideas, courage, and inspirational leadership. Minister, welfare reformer, and critic are possible career opportunities.

PERSONALITY INGREDIENTS: Appears to be refined, calm, and pensive. Strives for quality, timeless beauty, and intellectual stimulation. Aims to receive and give perfection. Inwardly conventional, structured, and routined. Feels trustworthy, realistic, and willing to work. Combines aristocratic self-image and down-to-earth motivation.

PERSONALITY EXTREME: Too stubborn, or too wishy-washy.

LUCIAN (Latin: Lucius/English)—M.

MAJOR TALENT: Ability to incorporate sympathetic, creative, and instructional service into career. Is musical, sociable, and protective. Has attraction for family/community harmony, financial security, and listeners. Combines adaptability, understanding of life-support practicality, and knack for solving problems. Restaurant/hotel manager, youth counselor, and minister are possible career opportunities.

PERSONALITY INGREDIENTS: Wants structure, organization, and to be a solid citizen. Is motivated to plan, work, and build for tangible results. Appears to be outstanding. May be flamboyant, mystical, or enthusiastically evangelistic. Strives for quality of performance, inventions, and spiritual uplift. Aims to inspire others to a better way of life. Receives help, love, and attention . . . and gives time, energy, money to maintain personal standards for others.

PERSONALITY EXTREME: Too temperamental, or too unresponsive.

LUCILLE (Latin: Lucy/French)—F.

MAJOR TALENT: Ability to incorporate inspirational, imaginative, and infectious enthusiasms into career. Is a dreamer/leader/educator. Has adaptability, sky-high ideals, and empathy for all. Combines human understanding, quality of performance and joy in accomplishment. Writer, preacher, and any profession that includes film processing are possible career opportunities.

PERSONALITY INGREDIENTS: Wants controlling responsibility, recognition, and businesslike efficiency. Feels trustworthy, organized, and willing to work. Appears fashionable, friendly, and expressive. Strives to be optimistic, resourceful, and pleasure seeking. Is a realist, with futuristic vision, and desire for peace.

PERSONALITY EXTREME: Too busy, or too bored.

LUCINDA (Latin: Lucy/English)—F.

MAJOR TALENT: Ability to incorporate initiative, drive, and new ideas into career. Is aggressive, organized, and ambitious. Has courage, receptivity, and efficient executive authority. Combines leadership, pride, and explorative approach. Business owner, designer, and program planner are possible career opportunities.

PERSONALITY INGREDIENTS: Wants security, respect, and structure. Is motivated to work, be trustworthy, and persistent. Appears tasteful, interested, and comforting. Strives for love, harmony, and creative self-expression. Should aim to have a cooperative manner, down-to-earth desires, and inner strength. Must hang in to achieve individuality.

PERSONALITY EXTREME: Too competitive, or too unoriginating.

LUCIUS (Latin/English)—M.

MAJOR TALENT: Ability to incorporate long-term planning, work, and structure into career. Is a practical idealist. Has constructive ideas, dependable habits, and high energy. Combines executive tact, sensitivity to details, and the visionary mind of the master architect/builder. Any business, law, and government reform offer possible career opportunities.

PERSONALITY INGREDIENTS: Wants logic, intellectual stimulation, and the highest quality in all interests. Seeks quiet thinking time, refinements, and natural beauty. Appears dignified, aloof, and introspective. Tuned to family, home, and comfortable/respectable/creatively expressive lifestyle. Wants love, but hides feelings and must be known to share emotions.

PERSONALITY EXTREME: Too innovative, or too unoriginal.

LUCRETIA (Latin: Lucretius/English)—F.

MAJOR TALENT: Ability to incorporate executive authority, self-reliance, and energetic organizational abilities into career. Is determined, self-motivated, and strong. Has businesslike, efficient, no-nonsense attitude. Combines youthful imagination, cleverness, and drive. Financial consultant, athlete, and politician are possible career opportunities.

PERSONALITY INGREDIENTS: Wants wide-range contacts, attention, and to serve universal interests. Feels compassionate, romantic, and conscious of quality of performance/skill. Needs a broad education/marketplace, and to give and receive "brotherly love." Appears direct, influential, and tailor-made. Strives to be in control, affluent, and recognized. Has innovative ideas, personal sensitivity, and magnetic charm. Must keep busy and avoid selfishness.

PERSONALITY EXTREME: Too independent, or too submissive.

LUCY (Latin: Lucius, M./English)—F.

MAJOR TALENT: Ability to incorporate introverted questioning nature and extroverted sociability into career. Is mentally analytic, quality conscious, and culturally attaining. Has strategic approach, facility with words/voice, and inventive ideas. Combines intuitional guidance, individuality, and authoritative manner. Succeeds through specialization, researching ideas, and "doing homework." Mimic, detective, and editor are possible career opportunities.

PERSONALITY INGREDIENTS: Desires family/community harmony, creative self-expression, and gracious living. Feels responsible, protective, and able to learn/teach/counsel. First impression is non conforming, energetic, and independent. Strives to be innovative, influential, and first in everything. Aims for leadership, control, and to implement pioneering/progressive changes. May be stubborn, too assertive, or too helpful. Success comes when non material values are established, depth of character emerges, and fears of loneliness/poverty/worthlessness are erased.

PERSONALITY EXTREME: Too confident, or too insecure.

LUKE (Latin: Lucius/English: diminutive)—M.

MAJOR TALENT: Ability to incorporate organization, dependability, and manual dexterity into career. Is honest, direct, and practical. Has loyalty, sincerity, and self-discipline. Combines independence, imagination, and down-to-earth nature. Builder, mechanic, and policeman are possible career opportunities.

PERSONALITY INGREDIENTS: Appears sexy, physically tuned, and adventurous. Strives to be understanding, broad minded, and unroutined. Wants material accomplishments, money, and prestige. Feels efficient, high powered, and far thinking. Wants the freedom that financial independence allows and doesn't mind working to secure respectable lifestyle.

PERSONALITY EXTREME: Too impulsive, or too passive.

LUTHER (Old German/German/English)—M.

MAJOR TALENT: Ability to incorporate a knack with words, youthful charm, and broad-scoped imagination into career. Is pleasure seeking, attention getting, and entertaining. Has resourcefulness, eye for beauty, and gift of laughing at life's vicissitudes and bouncing back from adversity. Combines restlessness, intense emotions, and good fortune when self-promoting. Writer, entertainer, and any people-oriented business are possible career opportunities.

PERSONALITY INGREDIENTS: First impression is dynamic, realistic, and dignified. Strives to plan, work, and build for lasting enjoyment/humanitarian benefit. Inwardly efficient, organized, and businesslike. Wants prestige, control, and executive authority. Feels self-reliant, and enjoys money, status, and power. Should leave a lasting mark on humanity when concentrated, open minded, and skirting "get-rich-quick" schemes.

PERSONALITY EXTREME: Too romantic, or too impersonal.

LYDIA (Greek: Lydios/English)—F.

MAJOR TALENT: Ability to incorporate sympathetic, conscientious, and dependable nature into career. Is kind, domestic, and problem solving. Has musical/creative gifts, hospitable approach, and strong will to improve/instruct/comfort others. Combines conventional methods, sensitivity to details, and desire to maintain harmonious relationships. Nurse, educational reformer, and civil servant are possible career opportunities.

PERSONALITY INGREDIENTS: Visually self-reliant, sociable, and as affluent as possible. Strives to be authoritative, respected, and commercially successful. Inwardly questioning, private, and quality conscious. Wants a perfect world and finds disappointments. Needs specialized education/technical expertise. Should avoid materialism and strive for knowledge. Money comes through establishing a reputation for concentrated work. Best when not judging by appearances or looking enviously into others' life-styles. Needs self-confidence.

PERSONALITY EXTREME: Too assertive, or too passive.

LYLE (French-Latin: Lisle/English)—M.

MAJOR TALENT: Ability to incorporate magnetic personality, broad human understanding, and imaginative nature into career. Is noble, charitable, and kind. Has creative ideas, organizational efficiency, and ambition. Combines brotherly feelings for everyone, tolerance, and desire for top-notch performance or craftsmanship. Is attractive to groups, has philosophical humor, and offers unselfish service. Doctor/dentist/lawyer, college administrator, and quality artist in any medium are possible career opportunities.

PERSONALITY INGREDIENTS: Wants conventional attainments, honest/ethical relationships, and to be a pillar of society. Needs work, routine, and structure. Appears quick, venturesome, and sexy. Strives to be versatile, progressive, and clever. Enjoys new experiences, travel, and unconventional people. Attempts to be gambler, but is comfortable betting the favorite.

PERSONALITY EXTREME: Too gutsy, or too cautious.

LYNETTE (Latin: Linnet/Welsh/English)—F.

MAJOR TALENT: Ability to incorporate broad-scoped idealism, unusual enthusiasms, and sensitivity to the needs of others into career. Is peace-loving, kind, and multi-faceted. Has patience, charm, and magnetic attraction for groups. Combines inventive nature, individualism, and desire to awaken others to the need for quality improvements. Film producer, psychoanalyst, and inspired teacher are possible career opportunities.

PERSONALITY INGREDIENTS: Appears expressive, attractive, and imaginative. Strives to be fashionable, happy, and pleasure seeking. Inwardly efficient, organized, and materially ambitious. Wants authority, control, and to enjoy the things that money can buy. Best when decisive, open to fresh ideas, and working compatibly with others.

PERSONALITY EXTREME: Too changeable, or too stagnating.

LYNN (Anglo-Saxon/Gaelic/English)—F. & M.

MAJOR TALENT: Ability to incorporate knack for becoming the "power behind the throne" into career. Is persistent, adaptable, and attentive to details. Has charm, diplomacy, and an instinct for arbitrating differences between opposing factions. Combines personal sensitivity, gentleness, and consideration. Private secretary, bookkeeper, and group musician/dancer are possible career opportunities.

PERSONALITY INGREDIENTS: Wants cultural attainments, polished lifestyle, and perfection. Feels private, mentally analytic, and questioning. Appears neat, dignified, and conventional. Strives for honesty, material growth, and respectability. Is a probing intellect aiming to live sensibly. Best when open minded, fine tuning artistic craftsmanship, and willing to adjust to unplanned progressive changes.

PERSONALITY EXTREME: Too understanding, or too demanding.

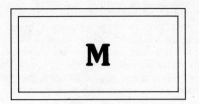

M

All names that begin with the letter *M* have the *Strong Point* of noting procedures—doing the right thing—practical administration—love of nature.

MABEL (Latin/English)—F.

MAJOR TALENT: Ability to incorporate educational, artistic, or family/home/comforting service into career. Is sympathetic, strong willed, and individualistic. Has nerve, problem-solving instincts, and protective nature. Combines originality, progressive thinking, and conscientiousness. Waitress, interior decorator, and nurse are possible career opportunities.

PERSONALITY INGREDIENTS: Appears personable, empathetic, and romantic. Strives to better conditions for anyone who seems inferior, be convincing, and attain quality of skill/performance. Aims to finish commitments and tie up loose ends. Inwardly idealistic, materially attaining, and creatively/musically expressive. Wants gracious living, respectability, and to be a refuge/counselor/"mother" to everyone. Is personally conservative, but broad minded for others. Needs to travel and have a solid home base.

PERSONALITY EXTREME: Too talkative, or too antisocial.

MAC (Irish/Scotch/Gaelic: "son"; MacDonald, MacAdam, etc.)—M.

MAJOR TALENT: Ability to incorporate mental organization, material awareness, and self-reliance into career. Is practical, energetic, and strong. Has determination, executive drive, and expanding goals. Combines down-to-earth realism, physical endurance, and pride in family and possessions. Athlete, banker, and any managerial position are possible career opportunities.

PERSONALITY INGREDIENTS: Wants to be first, in control, and inventive. Is motivated to inspire new concepts, be independent, and to make progressive changes. Appears to be cool, refined, and introspective. Strives for cultural stimulation, natural beauty, and broad scope of interests. Expects to reach a wide marketplace, work for prestige/wealth/recognition, and enjoy the finer things in life. May be a perfectionist and never personally satisfied.

PERSONALITY EXTREME: Too sunny, or too cheerless.

MADELINE (Greek/English)—F.

MAJOR TALENT: Ability to incorporate imagination, philosophical humor, and quality of skill/performance/taste into career. Is generous, empathetic, and charitable. Has charm, magnetism, and creative artistic instincts. Combines need to share, love of beauty, and humanitarian/universal understanding. Thespian, government reformer, and philosopher are possible career opportunities.

PERSONALITY INGREDIENTS: Appears refined, unruffled, and poised. Strives for privacy, natural beauty, and cultural polish. Seeks perfection, and needs education/authority/area of concentration to feel socially comfortable. Inwardly wants warmth, comforts, and easygoing relationships. Feels gentle, peace loving, and geared to being the "power behind the throne." Best when unconcerned with money, avoiding gambles, and allowing reputation to attract material gain.

PERSONALITY EXTREME: Too undisciplined, or too self-confining.

MADGE (Latin: Margaret/English)—F.

MAJOR TALENT: Ability to incorporate expressive personality, appreciation of beauty, and fortunate social relationships into career. Is creative, sensitive to details, and versatile. Has humor, charm, and resourcefulness. Combines progressive ideas, diplomatic awareness, and attention to appearances. Beautician, model, and any word-oriented profession are possible career opportunities.

PERSONALITY INGREDIENTS: Appears to be helpful, comforting, and conventional. Strives for respect, material security/family attainments, and mature love. Wants harmony, artistic self-expression, and to share. Best when involved helping others, depended upon, and maintaining personal ideals. May let emotions govern and ignore personal necessities. Should not allow dependent people to lean.

PERSONALITY EXTREME: Too understanding, or too unsympathetic.

MADISON (Hebrew: son of Matthew/English)—M.

MAJOR TALENT: Ability to incorporate organizational system to artistic/scientific/literary focus into career. Is charming, attractive, and optimistic. Has imagination, knack with words, and good luck through social contacts. Combines ambitious planning, sex appeal, and quality consciousness. Author, child psychologist, and surgeon are possible career opportunities.

PERSONALITY INGREDIENTS: Motivated to seek perfection. Wants timeless beauty, privacy, and intellectual stimulation. Feels a distaste for mundane practicalities and may be secretive or an escapist. Appears to be physically exciting, understanding, and tolerant. Strives to be youthfully progressive, adventurous, and confident. Seeks freedom, travel, and anything untried. Best on conventional course and not strategically employing sensuality. Attracts success and recognition, but immoral conduct invites loss of reputation/bankruptcy.

PERSONALITY EXTREME: Too eccentric, or too conforming.

MAE (Latin: May/English)—F.

MAJOR TALENT: Ability to incorporate independent nature, progressive ideas, and courage to change into career. Is forceful, inventive, and direct. Has willpower, initiative, and ambition. Combines individuality, activity, and leadership decisions. Designer, architect, and business owner/manager are possible career opportunities.

PERSONALITY INGREDIENTS: Appears neat, practical, and conservative. Strives for material security, orderly life-style, and to be a solid citizen. Inwardly loving, sympathetic, and family/community focused. Is motivated to raise standards, teach/guide/uplift others, and maintain personal high ethics/morals. May be dogmatic, meddlesome, and selfish.

Needs to take one step at a time, keep calm, and put energies to mental
analysis before taking action.

PERSONALITY EXTREME: Too unrealistic, or too factual.

MAGDELAINE (Greek: Madeline/French)—F.

MAJOR TALENT: Ability to incorporate steady work, discipline, and
practical service into career. Is an intuitively inspired thinker, planner,
and builder. Has high nervous energy, enthusiasm, and structure. Combines commercial focus, executive efficiency, and down-to-earth common sense. Must aim high and avoid selfish materialism. Potential
requires contribution of humanitarian/artistic/legislative improvement to
leave a lasting mark. Any business, government, and art/science are
possible career opportunities.

PERSONALITY INGREDIENTS: First impression is different, open, and
understanding. Strives to be adventurous, free, and unconventional. Inwardly wants self-expression, humor, and social contact. Needs beauty,
variety, and entertaining people/experiences. May scatter energy, be
extravagant, or impulsive. Needs unclouded compassionate goal, dedication, and then the law of supply and demand takes over to bring recognition. This name may make great demands upon the bearer, but may
change universal values.

PERSONALITY EXTREME: Too investigative, or too consistent.

MAGGIE (Latin: Margaret; diminutive-nickname)—F.

MAJOR TALENT: Ability to incorporate accommodating, protective,
and persevering service into career. Is strong willed, firm, and counseling. Has imagination, communications gifts, and appreciation of family
or group harmony/pressures. Combines versatility, idealistic principles,
and potential to leave a lasting mark for selfless service. Literary agent,
inspired teacher, and credit union organizer are possible career opportunities.

PERSONALITY INGREDIENTS: Must maintain emotional balance, temper
responsibilities, and be romantically discerning. Appears dignified, comforting, and interested. Strives to be protective, mature, and stable. Inwardly wants gracious, abundant, harmonious family/community life-
style. Is motivated to enjoy music, domestic pleasures, and correcting
others' mistakes. May be meddlesome, judgmental, and too brave. Has
far-reaching prospects when able to conserve energy and emotions.

PERSONALITY EXTREME: Too busy, or too bored.

MAHALIA (Muslim: Mahasin; expression "How beautiful" of spirit,
mind, body)—F.

MAJOR TALENT: Ability to incorporate top quality artistic, humanitarian, or religious skill/performance/research into career. Is sensitive to
details and people's physical, emotional, and spiritual needs. Has compassion, far-reaching philosophy, and forgiving nature. Combines gentleness, magnetism, and love of humanity. Health, exploration, and
educational reform are possible career opportunities.

PERSONALITY INGREDIENTS: Strives to be comforting, helpful, and
problem-solving. Appears comfortable, tasteful, and dignified. Inwardly
optimistic, creatively self-expressive, and beauty-loving. Wants to be
up-to-date, entertaining, and imaginative. Has depth of understanding,

strong intuitional guidance, and material ideas that produce tangible/
financial results. Best when decisive, adaptable, and inclined to realistic
expectations.

PERSONALITY EXTREME: Too inspirational, or too unoriginal.

MAISIE (Latin: Margaret/Scottish)—F.

MAJOR TALENT: Ability to incorporate inventive ideas into career. Is
creative, sensitive, and often impractical. Has nervous energy,
humanitarian instincts, and sharp perception of details. Combines adaptability, human understanding, and a sense of individualism. Welfare
work, film industry, and private secretary are possible career opportunities.

PERSONALITY INGREDIENTS: Inwardly conventional, but appears to be
adventurous, different, and progressive. Strives to experience travel,
sensual pleasures, and changing routines. Is motivated to be sympathetic, respectable, and protective. Aims for gracious living, domestic-
artistic self-expression, and to have everyone live up to personal
standards. Appears confident and may be anxious or too emotional. Best
when decisive and determined.

PERSONALITY EXTREME: Too gutsy, or too scared.

MALACHI (Hebrew/English)—M.

MAJOR TALENT: Ability to incorporate visionary ideas, strong individualism, and opportunities for partnership into career. Is gentle, sensitive, and enthusiastic. Has vitality, generosity, and magnetic
personality. Combines humanitarian tolerance, instinct to crusade, personal ideals, and regal bearing. Costume designer, psychologist, and film
writer are possible career opportunities.

PERSONALITY INGREDIENTS: Inwardly wants to "build a better mousetrap," inspire quality-conscious reforms, and find the "fountain of
youth." Is a dreamer and has a dual nature. May be orderly/detailed/
cooperative or may be on "cloud nine." Appears noble, understanding,
and attractive. Strives for wide range of interests, compassionate understanding, and to tie up loose ends. Aims to better conditions for anyone
who seems inferior or needy. Enjoys peer relationships, impulsive
creativity, and recognition.

PERSONALITY EXTREME: Too philosophical, or too intolerant.

MALCOLM (Celtic/English)—M.

MAJOR TALENT: Ability to incorporate domestic interests, responsibility, and protective nature into career. Is sympathetic, instructional, and
strong willed. Has problem-solving instincts, showmanship, and firm
idealistic notions. Combines sensitivity to details, practical organization,
and group accountability and harmony. Teacher, chef, and marriage
counselor are possible career opportunities.

PERSONALITY INGREDIENTS: Inwardly intuitional, analytic, and investigative. Wants privacy, polish, and perfection in all areas. Appears to be
materially aware, businesslike, and managerial. Strives to be efficient,
self-reliant, and recognized/wealthy/controlling. Needs quality and quantity. Best when discerning and able to make judgments based upon research, not emotional reaction.

PERSONALITY EXTREME: Too structured, or too immoral.

MALLORY (French/Irish/English)—M.

MAJOR TALENT: Ability to incorporate domestic/community service, music/showmanship, and concern for life-support reforms into career. Is concerned, parental, and group/family/household-oriented. Has responsible nature, communications gifts, and love of love/beauty/justice. Adds mature approach to any task that demonstrates improved conditions for others. May leave a mark on humanity. Politician, social worker, and spiritual or physical healer are possible career opportunities.

PERSONALITY INGREDIENTS: First impression is efficient, dominant, and as affluent as possible. Strives to be businesslike, mentally organized, and materially wide ranged. Inwardly wants thinking time, privacy, and discretion. Is motivated to seek intellectual stimulation, quality/natural beauty, and perfection. Best when dedicated to use intellect and practical power for uplifting purposes.

PERSONALITY EXTREME: Too confident, or too insecure.

MALVINA (Teutonic/Celtic/English)—F.

MAJOR TALENT: Ability to incorporate understanding charitable nature, and quality of artistry/skill/performance into career. Is gentle, introspective, and sympathetic. Has romantic ideas, instinct to heal/better existing conditions, and inspire others through wide range of interests and imaginative ideas. Combines patience, mental analysis, and broad/unbiased philosophy. Doctor, musician, and educator are possible career opportunities.

PERSONALITY INGREDIENTS: Not suited to commercial world. Attracts finances when helping others. Inwardly feels special. Wants to uplift, create, and maintain a supportive position. Appears aloof, refined, and quiet. Strives for poise, authority, and social confidence. Needs to specialize, concentrate, and keep feet on the ground. Seeks peer relationships, justice, and may be a bit impractical.

PERSONALITY EXTREME: Too independent, or too passive.

MAMIE (Hebrew: Mary/English: variable)—F.

MAJOR TALENT: Ability to incorporate enthusiasm for travel, change, and unconventional people into career. Is curious, experimental, and pleasure-seeking. Has sensuality, sensitivity to details/orderliness/refinements, and nerve. Combines adaptability, communications gifts, and cleverness. Travel agent, politician, and reporter are possible career opportunities.

PERSONALITY INGREDIENTS: Desires loving/secure/attaining family and mate. Wants to be respectable, informative, and to live graciously. Appears tailor-made, influential, and as affluent as possible. Strives for prestige, material power, and self-reliance. Attracts fortunate marriage, inheritance, and adventurous interests.

PERSONALITY EXTREME: Too self-indulgent, or too accommodating.

MANFRED (Teutonic/English)—M.

MAJOR TALENT: Ability to incorporate research, mental analysis, and instinct for perfection into career. Is questioning, aristocratic, and proud. Has self-control, gift with words, and sincerity. Combines communications techniques, material results, and need to get to the "root" of everything. Scientist, detective, and data processing programmer are possible career opportunities.

PERSONALITY INGREDIENTS: First impression is nonconforming, energetic, and hurried. Strives to be creative, original, and in the lead. Seeks progressive changes, decisiveness, and praise. Inwardly domestic/sharing, sympathetic, and firmly idealistic. Wants to protect, provide, and assume mature responsibilities. Maintains high standards and expects everyone to live up to them. May be domineering, fussy, and anxious, but maintains "cool" when expert/educated/in authority.

PERSONALITY EXTREME: Too precise, or too unstructured.

MANUEL (Hebrew: Emmanuel/Portuguese/Spanish)—M.

MAJOR TALENT: Ability to incorporate a knack with words into career. Is imaginative, pleasure-seeking, and optimistic. Has charm, wit, and individuality. Combines cooperative nature, creativity, and resourcefulness. Theatrical performer, writer, and fashion professional are possible career opportunities.

PERSONALITY INGREDIENTS: Inwardly tolerant, broad scoped, and compassionate. Wants top-notch performance, completed commitments, and wide range of interests. Needs to benefit others, heal, and educate. Appears up-to-date, animated, and expressive. Strives for beauty, optimism, and to forget anything unpleasant. Has a convenient memory. Best suited to working with people, and attracting financial recognition through self-expression.

PERSONALITY EXTREME: Too attention-getting, or too unobtrusive.

MARA (Hebrew: Mary; variable/English)—F.

MAJOR TALENT: Ability to incorporate fondness for luxury, sympathetic nature, and knack of being a stabilizing group influence into career. Is steadfast, kind, and musical. Has strong will, firm ideals, and interest in solving everyone's problems. Combines individuality, cleverness, and educational/creative/artistic self-expression. Restaurant/hotel manager, interior decorator, and marriage counselor are possible career opportunities.

PERSONALITY INGREDIENTS: Inwardly shy, modest, and gentle. Wants partnership, peace, and easygoing style. Appears to be practical, dignified, and traditional. Strives to be precise, organized, and hardworking. Must avoid impulsivity and maintain conventions. Wants adventure, travel, and may be too impatient to build security.

PERSONALITY EXTREME: Too active, or too lazy.

MARC (Latin: Mark/French)—M.

MAJOR TALENT: Ability to incorporate businesslike mental organization into career. Is self-reliant, practical, and delegates responsibility. Has strength, energy, and initiative. Combines inventive ideas, investigative analysis, and material ambitions. Publishing, manufacturing, and investment counseling are possible career opportunities.

PERSONALITY INGREDIENTS: Inwardly independent, aggressive, and self-assertive. Wants to be first, unique, and progressive. Appears to be aristocratic, aloof, and mysteriously introspective. Strives for expertise, culture, and authority. Aims for perfection and is self-deprecating. At best when educated, concentrated, and residing near the water. Seeks a wide range and attracts success when self-confidence is established.

PERSONALITY EXTREME: Too superficial, or too depressed.

MARCELLA (Latin: Marcia/English)—F.

MAJOR TALENT: Ability to incorporate spontaneous inventive ideas into career. Is imaginative, energetic, and an inspirational speaker. Has ambitions set a peg above the ordinary, seeks quality, creativity, and a chance to do something special. Combines sensitivity to fine points, wide-range philosophy/interests, and vibrant personality. Actor, psychoanalyst, and antique expert are possible career opportunities.

PERSONALITY INGREDIENTS: Inwardly investigative, analytic, and aloof. Wants privacy, cultural stimulation, and perfection in all things. Appears dynamic, masterful, and tasteful. Strives to be resourceful, sensible, and to put visionary plans on a realistic footing. Aims to raise standards, build for lasting good, and to create a solution for what may appear to be impractical/problematic. Should aim high.

PERSONALITY EXTREME: Too assertive, or too indecisive.

MARCIA (Latin: Mark/English)—F.

MAJOR TALENT: Ability to incorporate instinct to heal, sympathy, and forgiveness into career. Is romantic, supportive, and mentally analytic. Has tolerance, creative inspiration, and magnetic personality. Combines patient understanding, unrealistic drive for perfection, and humanitarian counsel/service. Medical profession, government reform, and parole officer are possible career opportunities.

PERSONALITY INGREDIENTS: Feels idealistic and out to save the world. Wants ideals realized, quality/not quantity, and to rise above mundane reality. May be impractical, vague, and indecisive, but may come up with ideas that have lasting influence upon others. First impression is thoughtful, refined, and aloof, until conversation begins, then becomes helpful, supportive, and enthusiastic. Strives to be an authority and to be relieved of fears of loneliness and poverty. Needs education/expertise to relax confidently.

PERSONALITY EXTREME: Too decisive, or too overanxious.

MARCUS (Latin: Mark/English: variable)—M.

MAJOR TALENT: Ability to incorporate communications, inventive ideas, and orderliness into career. Is expressive, optimistic, and when positive, progressively changeable. Has charm, imagination, and resourcefulness. Combines trend-setting concepts, patient administration, and a knack with words. Writer, actor, and organizer are possible career opportunities.

PERSONALITY INGREDIENTS: Positively patterns personality changes for others when emotions are controlled and responsibilities are accepted in perspective to creativity. This name joins inspiration/productivity and attracts all around success. Inwardly structured, practical, and mentally systematized to work. Appears businesslike, custom-made, and influential. Strives to be materially powerful and is motivated to do what must be done. A font of efficiency, common sense, and down-to-earth drives.

PERSONALITY EXTREME: Too obstinate, or too changeable.

MARCY (Latin: Marcia/Mark; English variable)—F. & M.

MAJOR TALENT: Ability to incorporate sympathetic service, domestic/parental instincts, and need for group compatibility into career. Is strong willed, protective, and fond of music/luxury/giving advice. Has sentimental/romantic/emotional approach. Combines attention to detail, practical organizational administration, and idealistic personal standards. Teacher, medical secretary, and home products sales/service are possible career opportunities.

PERSONALITY INGREDIENTS: Inwardly wants material possessions, power, and to be a solid citizen. Feels capable, worthy of recognition, and ready to work for ambitious goals. Appears reserved, refined, and authoritative. Strives to be calm, intellectual, and quality conscious. Aims to be perfect and close off the imperfect realities. Meets disappointment until fault finding ceases, inner shyness disappears, and confidence blossoms through education or technical expertise. Should learn to value privacy and not fear loneliness or poverty.

PERSONALITY EXTREME: Too argumentative, or too stoic.

MARGARET (Latin/Scottish/English)—F.

MAJOR TALENT: Ability to incorporate inspirational personality, communications talents, and an organized mind into career. Is attentive to details, strongly idealistic, and individualistic. Has presence, quality consciousness, and aims to be above the crowd. Combines material awareness, resourcefulness, and visionary ideas. May leave a lasting image. Critic, diplomat, and philosopher are possible career opportunities.

PERSONALITY INGREDIENTS: Appears traditional, tasteful, and neat. Strives to be a solid citizen. Inwardly investigative, analytical, and logical. Wants cultural stimulation, timeless beauty, and perfection/quality to everything. Should have privacy, meditative time, and spiritual/intellectual area of concentration. Attracts admiration and happiness.

PERSONALITY EXTREME: Too picky, or too unfeeling.

MARGARITA (Latin: Margaret/Portuguese/Spanish/English)—F.

MAJOR TALENT: Ability to incorporate mental investigation, analysis, and strategic planning into career. Is culturally attaining, quality conscious, and logical. Has kindness, determination, and communications gifts. Combines down-to-earth work, resourcefulness, and desire for wisdom/polish. Lecturer, undercover detective, and government agent are possible career opportunities.

PERSONALITY INGREDIENTS: Has a sense of privacy. Wants beauty, optimism, to ignore unpleasant realities, and to go forward to visualizations of more pleasant times. Likes to entertain and be entertained. Appears traditional, dignified, and classically attractive. Strives to be respectable, dependable, and a solid citizen. Is creative, expressive, and tied to a strong sense of justice. Is spicy, classy, and has deep emotions.

PERSONALITY EXTREME: Too independent, or too sustained.

MARGE (Latin: Margaret; diminutive/English)—F.

MAJOR TALENT: Ability to incorporate mental efficiency, attention to details, and group compatibility into career. Is self-reliant, practical, and willing to work. Has executive diplomacy, determination, and responsible attitude. Combines friendliness, confidence, and enthusiasm for material results. School administrator, beautician/decorator, and professional athlete are possible career opportunities.

PERSONALITY INGREDIENTS: Appears modest, subtle, and refined. Strives to be supportive, easygoing, and to avoid conflicts. Inwardly domestic, instructional, and guiding. Wants gracious, respected, expressive life-style. Likes showmanship, music/dance, and family/community cooperation. Attracted to joint ventures and does well in partnership after adjustments.

PERSONALITY EXTREME: Too impulsive, or too cautious.

MARGERY (Latin: Margaret/English)—F.

MAJOR TALENT: Ability to incorporate domestic, parental/protective, and conventionally responsible nature into career. Is sympathetic, cooperative, and practically imaginative. Has showmanship, creative expression, and graciousness. Combines easygoing manner, strong idealism, and desire to love and be loved. Ensemble musician/dancer/actor, interior decorator, and homemaker are possible career opportunities.

PERSONALITY INGREDIENTS: Appears different, vibrant, and gentle. Has a presence, drama, enthusiasm that pops up when personal interests are discussed. Strives to be above the crowd, inventive, and uncluttered by material ambitions. Inwardly wants structure, routine, and security. Feels realistic, dependable, and ready to work. Attracts the law of "give and take." Best when understanding, adaptable, and receptive.

PERSONALITY EXTREME: Too authoritative, or too quiet.

MARGO (Latin: Margaret/English)—F.

MAJOR TALENT: Ability to incorporate tolerance, artistic/scientific/philosophical top quality, and broad-scoped/empathetic/generous nature into career. Is detail conscious, sensitive, and creatively expressive. Has magnetic personality, graciousness, and diplomatic touch. Combines dramatic temperament, logical/technical analysis, and a drive to complete commitments perfectly. Thespian/artiste, physician/judge, and reformer in all areas are possible career opportunities.

PERSONALITY INGREDIENTS: Appears modest, refined, and subtle. Strives to be unhurried, tactful, and supportive. Aims for easygoing lifestyle. Inwardly private, questioning, and selective. Wants timeless/natural beauty, physical comfort, and to keep feelings/emotions under wraps. Enjoys education, nature, and one-to-one relationships. Is a classy lady.

PERSONALITY EXTREME: Too suspicious, or too protective.

MARIA (Hebrew: Mary/Latin-Spanish: F. & M./English, F.)—F. & M.

MAJOR TALENT: Ability to incorporate need for harmonious family/group relationships, protective/instructional/responsible nature, and detailed organizational approach into career. Is sensitive, emotional, and down-to-earth. Has showmanship, creative expressiveness, and strong personal ideals. Combines problem solving, raising standards, and desire to take a personal interest in everything/everyone. Teacher, psychologist, and marriage counselor are possible career opportunities.

PERSONALITY INGREDIENTS: Appears to be traditional, classic, and dignified. Strives to be respectable, materially secure, and trustworthy. Inwardly visionary, inventive, and high strung. Wants to be special, uplifting, and original. Combines impractical idealism, and common sense. Has subtle magnetism and control. Attracts influential supporters, social/financial success, and home-/community-oriented life-style.

PERSONALITY EXTREME: Too aggressive, or too passive.

MARIAN (Hebrew-Latin/English)—F.

MAJOR TALENT: Ability to incorporate imagination, visionary insights, and gifted artistry into career. Is a diplomat, dreamer, and crusader. Has nervous energy, inspirational ideas, and instinct to see both sides of an issue. Combines sensitivity to details, desire for top quality skill/performance, and spontaneous imagery that opens doors for the future. Inventor, TV/film/data processing technician, and writer are possible career opportunities.

PERSONALITY INGREDIENTS: Seems empathetic, philosophical, and romantic. Strives to be tolerant, generous, and forgiving. Feels supportive, hurried, and above the masses. Wants to contribute to better the world. Is exacting, patient, and on the go and must maintain emotional balance. Has potential to leave a lasting image.

PERSONALITY EXTREME: Too adventurous, or too tied down.

MARIANNE (Hebrew-Latin: Marian/French)—F.

MAJOR TALENT: Ability to incorporate structured, wide-ranged, voice-oriented communications gifts into career. Is charming, humorous, and optimistic. Has imagination, drive to perfect skill, and clever versatility. Combines attention-getting personality, love of children/animals/people, and fashionable tastes and up-to-date ideas. Performing artist, scientist, and lawyer are possible career opportunities.

PERSONALITY INGREDIENTS: Inwardly questioning, analytic, and unruffled. Wants natural beauty, quality, and to remain removed from earthy realities. Feels secretive, selective, and private. Appears adventurous, striking, and physically tuned. Strives for freedom, travel, and to satisfy curiosity. Aims for unconventional interests, romantic/extravagant emotions, and to balance introvert/extrovert characteristics. Can make dreams come true.

PERSONALITY EXTREME: Too sensual, or too mental.

MARIE (Hebrew: Mary/French)—F.

MAJOR TALENT: Ability to incorporate originality, independence, and ideas for pioneering progressive change into career. Is direct, active, and assertive. Has strong opinions, nonconformist tastes, and impatience. Combines efficient/organized/materially aware approach and accommodation to partnership while maintaining individuality. Designer, salesperson, and credit worker are possible career opportunities.

PERSONALITY INGREDIENTS: Inwardly domestic, creatively expressive, and luxury loving. Wants traditions, harmonious family/community life-style, and material/scholastic attainments. Is a mature counselor and concerned friend. Appears classic, tasteful, and dignified. Strives to be honest, trustworthy, and respectable. Aims for structure, conventional standards, and to prosper through hard work. May dare to be different and seem confusing at times, but regains self-control when harmony of life-style is disrupted.

PERSONALITY EXTREME: Too sensual, or too mental.

MARIETTA (Hebrew: Mary/English)—F.

MAJOR TALENT: Ability to incorporate creative, sympathetic, and culturally reforming service into career. Is determined, strong willed, and protective. Has domestic and community focus, desire to help, and showmanlike instincts. Combines attractive/up-to-date personality, wide-ranged communications gifts, and the need to promote personal ideals. When dedicated to a common cause, may leave a mark on humanity. Credit union organizer, motel/hotel manager, and teacher/counselor are possible career opportunities.

PERSONALITY INGREDIENTS: Inwardly probing, analytic, and secretive. Wants to feel confident, poised, and culturally secure. Needs quiet, solitude, natural/timeless beauty. Appears to be custom designed, influential, and self-reliant. Strives to be businesslike, efficient, and to work for big results. Is sensitive, expansive, and attracts family/community/universal problems. May be a martyr for family or a just cause.

PERSONALITY EXTREME: Too selfish, or too selfless.

MARIETTE (Hebrew: Mary; variable/English)—F.

MAJOR TALENT: Ability to incorporate nonconformist attitude, verbal self-expression, and confident/reserved/refined impression into career. Is individualistic, daring, and forceful. Has charm, analytic mind, and perfectionist instincts. Combines cultural stimulation, imagination, and courage to be "a first." Inventor, explorer, and photographer are possible career opportunities.

PERSONALITY INGREDIENTS: Inwardly shy, retiring, and modest. Wants peace, love, and easygoing comforts. Appears to be businesslike, custom-made, and managerial. Strives to be influential, affluent, and prominent. Is friendly, generous, and geared to harmonious/fruitful partnerships. Must avoid stubbornness, conniving, and competitive aggressiveness.

PERSONALITY EXTREME: Too curious, or too satisfied.

MARILYN (Hebrew: Mary-Gaelic: Linne/English)—F.

MAJOR TALENT: Ability to incorporate visionary ideas, influential relationships, and organized communications skills into career. Is sociable, up-to-date, and practical. Has animated personality, self-reliance, and imagination. Combines inspirational leadership, resourcefulness, and success as a "power behind the throne." Executive secretary, telephone/TV/camera director, and diplomat are possible career opportunities.

PERSONALITY INGREDIENTS: Wants prestige, wealth, and executive leadership. Feels organized, efficient, and determined. Appears fashionably groomed, optimist, and entertaining. Strives for popularity, beauty in people/surroundings, and to keep occupied. Has high energy and a wide range of ambitions. Can have it all. Needs only to develop unselfish life-style as an example to others to maintain family pride, romantic love, material fortune, and dreams realized.

PERSONALITY EXTREME: Too gutsy, or too intimidated.

MARINA (Latin/Italian/Spanish/English)—F.

MAJOR TALENT: Ability to incorporate visionary ideas, individualism, and idealistic principles into career. Is creative, convincing, and daring. Has enthusiasm for beliefs, gentle supportive instincts, and empathy for others. Combines diplomacy, quality of skill/performance, and keen intuition. Publicist, film maker, and psychoanalyst are possible career opportunities.

PERSONALITY INGREDIENTS: First impression is magnetic, noble, and classic. Strives to be helpful, understanding, and self-expressive. Inwardly mentally active, dreamy, and filled with ideas that may, or may not, be practical. Not at best in commercial competition, but gets help from admirers/partnerships. Should aim for down-to-earth assessments and practical goals.

PERSONALITY EXTREME: Too impatient, or too procrastinating.

MARION (Hebrew-Latin: Marian; F./Old French: Mary; M./English)— F. & M.

MAJOR TALENT: Ability to incorporate logical analysis, conventional structure, and communications techniques into career. Is quiet, private, and introspective. Has charm, practicality, and desire for perfection. Combines strategic approach, creative self-expression, and quality consciousness. Radio performer, historian, and technical expert are possible career opportunities.

PERSONALITY INGREDIENTS: Appears magnetic, gracious, and classic. Strives to be expansive, conclusive, and charitable. Aims to serve humanity's needs, cultivate and polish artistic interests, and to reach a broad marketplace. Inwardly needs to be expert/educated/authoritative to feel confident. Wants an "ivory tower" and may find everyday reality disappointing. Should seek privacy, spiritual/intellectual stimulation, and cultural attainments.

PERSONALITY EXTREME: Too impulsive, or too cautious.

MARISSA (Hebrew: Mary; variable)—F.

MAJOR TALENT: Ability to incorporate mental organization, attention to fine points, and showmanship into career. Is materially aware, self-reliant, and managerial. Has domestic/parental instincts, refinement, and executive judgment. Combines cooperative spirit, responsibility, and desire to work for ambitious goals. Music school administrator, financial advisor, and family/home product manufacturer are possible career opportunities.

PERSONALITY INGREDIENTS: Attracts attention, protection, and dependent relationships. Strives to assume burdens, educate, and bring everyone up to personal standards. Is comforting, hospitable, and attracted to luxury. Inwardly nonconforming, inventive, and impassioned to change/uplift/direct others to a better quality of life. Feels either very enthusiastic or very easygoing. Expects to be special, and when practical, positive, and independent, meets expectations.

PERSONALITY EXTREME: Too changeable, or too indecisive.

MARJORIE (Latin: Margaret/Scottish)—F.

MAJOR TALENT: Ability to incorporate dedicated planning, work, and humanitarian results into career. Is practical, honest, and structured. Has determination, endurance, and realistic values. Combines material power, mental efficiency, and manual dexterity. Physical therapist, military officer, and professional athlete are possible career opportunities.

PERSONALITY INGREDIENTS: Appears confident, striking, and enthusiastic. Strives for physical experimentation, travel, and unconventional experiences. Inwardly wants beauty, humor, and a variety of interests. Feels optimistic, expressive, and resourceful. Finds sun on a gloomy day and makes the best of everything. Is kind, inspirational, and potentially a power for good.

PERSONALITY EXTREME: Too materialistic, or too uninspired.

MARK (Latin/English)—M.

MAJOR TALENT: Ability to incorporate technical/scientific/intellectual investigation into career. Is logical, aristocratic, and proud. Has analytic mind, poise, and secretive instincts. Combines competitive nature, showmanship/luxurious desires, and expectation of quality/perfection. Best when expert/educated, not materialistic, and allowing reputation to attract recognition. Any delicate work, electronics technician, and detective are possible career opportunities.

PERSONALITY INGREDIENTS: Strives to be domestically secure, comfortable, and respectable. Aims to protect, assume responsibility, and maintain personal ideals. Appears tasteful, conventional, and dignified. Inwardly independent, competitive, and nonconforming. Wants to be in the lead and not forced to follow precedents. Needs action, originality, and to take challenges. Meets disappointment until depth of character is established.

PERSONALITY EXTREME: Too aloof, or too involved.

MARLA (Hebrew: Mary; variable/Bavarian/English)—F.

MAJOR TALENT: Ability to incorporate tolerant philosophy, broad-scoped interests, and elevated skills/performances into career. Is creative, expressive, and individualistic. Has practical organization, efficiency, and material awareness. Combines daring ideas, self-reliance, and empathetic approach. Doctor, theatrical performer, and fireman are possible career opportunities.

PERSONALITY INGREDIENTS: Best suited to noncommercial focus. Inwardly gentle, modest, and diplomatic. Feels quiet, supportive, and easygoing. Appears introspective, quality conscious, and aloof. Strives to be culturally attaining, expert, and self-confident. Needs creative/artistic education/technical concentration to establish authority. Should not fear loneliness or push for money. Success comes through inner security. Tends to moodiness.

PERSONALITY EXTREME: Too aggressive, or too passive.

MARLENE (Hebrew/English)—F.

MAJOR TALENT: Ability to incorporate curious, active, clever mind into career. Is able to adapt to situations and people. Has understanding of human feelings, sensuality, and knack of learning by experiencing. Combines imagination, friendliness, and benefiting from surprises/changes/accidents. Politician, lawyer, and reporter are possible career opportunities.

PERSONALITY INGREDIENTS: Inwardly idealistic, intuitional, and a visionary. Feels different and geared to create a special cause to uplift the quality of life for others. May get lost in dreams of a better world. Appears sociable, fashionable, and engaging. Strives to be popular, imaginative, and pleasure seeking. Makes the best of everything generally unless personal sensitivity is touched. Notices little things and should avoid making much of minutiae. May be a font of inspirational ideas.

PERSONALITY EXTREME: Too impulsive, or too careful.

MARLO (Old English: Marlow; variable/English)—F. & M.

MAJOR TALENT: Ability to incorporate unconventional, changeable, adventurous personality into career. Is adaptable, understanding, and cooperative. Has communications gifts, optimism, and gracious manner. Combines friendliness, persistence, and clever knack of learning by experience. Politician, entertainer, and advertising copywriter are possible career opportunities.

PERSONALITY INGREDIENTS: Expects perfection and may not want to accept mass market tastes. Would prefer an aristocratic world. Wants timeless/natural beauty, intellectual stimulation, and pride in everything. Appears aloof, and may be shy until reputation/expertise is established. Must be known to be loved and is romantically selective. Needs privacy, time for mental analysis, and "perfect" mate. Not suited to sharing a bathroom with just anyone. Wants family traditions, but may, quite rightfully, avoid marriage.

PERSONALITY EXTREME: Too domestic, or too unconforming.

MARLOW (Old English/English)—M.

MAJOR TALENT: Ability to incorporate inventive, daring, and progressively changing personality into career. Is decisive, individualistic, and positive. Has willpower, self-assertion, and initiative. Combines efficient organizational approach, takeover control, and ambition. Inventor, explorer, and independent business owner are possible career opportunities.

PERSONALITY INGREDIENTS: Inwardly investigative, secretive, and unruffled. Wants privacy, peace, and quiet. Appears attention-getting, fashionable, and optimistic. Strives to be sociable, imaginative, and entertaining. Wants physical comfort, beauty, and changes between quality/fads/quantity. Never dull, but may become moody/melancholy at times. Is introvert/extrovert combo and should have an exciting life.

PERSONALITY EXTREME: Too adventurous, or too cautious.

MARSHA (Latin: Marcia/English)—F.

MAJOR TALENT: Ability to incorporate protective, responsible, instructional instincts into career. Is domestic/parental/concerned, musical/artistic, and detail conscious. Has sympathetic, generous, practical/hardworking nature. Combines understanding, strong will, and desire for harmony in everything. Theater arts, home products, and restaurant/hotel management are possible career opportunities.

PERSONALITY INGREDIENTS: Appears dynamic, tasteful, and precise. Strives for long-term planning, building, and tangible results. Inwardly is independent, inventive, and courageous. Attracts dependent relationships and should be careful not to "judge a book by its cover." Feels progressive, proud, and ready to take the lead. Has firm personal ideals and must avoid expecting others to live up to them.

PERSONALITY EXTREME: Too assertive, or too passive.

MARSHALL (Old French/English)—M.

MAJOR TALENT: Ability to incorporate creative, structured, quality communications techniques/skills into career. Is imaginative, versatile, and entertaining. Has humor, optimism, and kindness. Combines beauty, charm, and self-expression. Should reach a broad/humanitarian marketplace. Surgeon, theatrical performer, and fashion professional are possible career opportunities.

PERSONALITY INGREDIENTS: Inwardly gentle, easygoing, and adaptable. Wants quiet, modesty, and peace. Appears individualistic, active, and definite. Strives to be assertive, aggressive, and inventive. Aims to take the lead in an original plan or style. Must avoid scattering, extravagances, and dramatic enlarging of the truth. Expects to have prestige, wealth, and cultural quality. Can be a powerhouse for perfection.

PERSONALITY EXTREME: Too talkative, or too unsociable.

MARTHA (Aramean/Biblical/Danish/German/Latin: Patricia; diminutive/English)—F.

MAJOR TALENT: Ability to incorporate aristocratic nature, quality consciousness, and instinct for perfection into career. Is questioning, investigative, and analytic. Has sensitivity to details, diplomacy, and progressive ideas. Combines nerve, learning from observation, and cultural ambitions. Mimic, photographer, and data processing are possible career opportunities.

PERSONALITY INGREDIENTS: Inwardly shy, retiring, and a keenly sensitive soul. Wants compatability, consideration, and is persistent. Appears striking, enthusiastic, and venturesome. Strives to be adventurous, speculative, and unconventional. Wants freedom and a quiet home base. Reflects heavily on youthful experiences and should avoid getting thinkstuck.

PERSONALITY EXTREME: Too ambitious, or too lazy.

MARTIN (Latin: Mark/French/German/Spanish/English)—M.

MAJOR TALENT: Ability to incorporate personality, words, and broad ambitions into career. Is kind, conventional/structured, and expressive. Has optimism, sociability, and love of beauty. Combines quality skills, resourcefulness, and communications techniques. Performing artist/musician/actor, surgeon, and cosmetics salesperson are possible career opportunities.

PERSONALITY INGREDIENTS: Appears retiring, refined, and modest. Strives for gentleness, attention to details, and easygoing style. Aims to keep the peace. Inwardly inventive, assertive, and ambitious. Wants to be boss and pioneer new ideas. Feels decisive, imaginative, and proud. Likes to entertain and be entertained. Has sex appeal, romantic dreams, and attracts recognition/rewards.

PERSONALITY EXTREME: Too confident, or too cautious.

MARVIN (Anglo-Saxon: Irvin/English)—M.

MAJOR TALENT: Ability to incorporate progressive changes, adventurous nature, and understanding of people into career. Is clever, quick, and adaptable. Has versatility, boldness, and unconventional ideas. Combines communications techniques, attention to detail, and learning from life experience. Lawyer, actor, and travel agent are possible career opportunities.

PERSONALITY INGREDIENTS: Is motivated to pioneer, take challenges, and follow own conscience. Wants independence, freedom, and to be a trend setter. Appears dynamic, traditional, and tailor-made. Strives to be an organized, practical, humanitarian worker. Aims to plan, buiild, and

produce lasting tangible results. Has high energy and desire to reshape/
improve/inspire better material conditions for the masses. Must take
action, but should be sure to avoid self-indulgence, haughtiness, and
sensual impulsiveness when leading others.

PERSONALITY EXTREME: Too physical, or too mental.

MARY (Hebrew/English)—F.

MAJOR TALENT: Ability to incorporate all forms of self-expression,
orderliness, and original ideas into career. Is imaginative, versatile, and
positive. Has charm, awareness of details, and initiative. Combines
pioneering spirit, inspirational leadership, and a balance between
creativity and productivity. Scientific/artistic/promotional skills, entertaining, and fashion are possible career opportunities.

PERSONALITY INGREDIENTS: Inwardly mentally efficient, industrious,
and materially ambitious. Wants influence, affluence, and the freedom
that money can buy. Appears dignified, traditional, and tasteful. Strives
to be structured, practical, and down-to-earth. Has all ingredients for
business acumen, recognition, and financial success in any people-
oriented industry.

PERSONALITY EXTREME: Too skeptical, or too gullible.

MARYANN (Hebrew-Latin: Marian/English)—F.

MAJOR TALENT: Ability to incorporate learning from experience into
career. Is clever, energetic, and gutsy. Has gift of gab, sensitivity to
details, and confidence. Combines unconventional interests, conventional routines, and succeeds when persistent, expansive, and following
intuition/spiritual directions. Detective, reporter, and promoter are possible career opportunities.

PERSONALITY INGREDIENTS: Inwardly tolerant, philosophical, and
geared to finishing commitments. Wants quality performance/skill, to
help/serve/reform inferior conditions, and a broad education. Is a romantic. Appears enthusiastic, striking, and venturesome. Strives for travel,
untried experiences, and sensual pleasures. Attracts victory over challenges when willing to hang in, be persuasive, and maintain friendships.

PERSONALITY EXTREME: Too busy, or too bored.

MARYE (Hebrew: Mary; variable/English)—M.

MAJOR TALENT: Ability to incorporate confidence, drive, and executive organizational approach into career. Is strong willed, idealistic, and
dependable. Has strength, good judgment, and desire for power. Combines voice/musical gifts, enthusiasm for work, and commercial
awareness. Athletic coach, manufacturer, and financial counselor are
possible career opportunities.

PERSONALITY INGREDIENTS: Inwardly domestic, protective, and attracted to luxury. Wants respectable, abundant, helpful life-style. Appears modest, refined, and supportive. Strives for love, partnership, and
subtle control. Forces issues to strengthen personal standards. Wants
love and may take impulsive gambles. Best controlled and developing
ambitions patiently.

PERSONALITY EXTREME: Too challenging, or too threatened.

MARYLOU (Hebrew–Old German modern combination/English)—F.

MAJOR TALENT: Ability to incorporate responsibility, sympathetic nature, and life-support service into career. Is domestic, instructional, and protective. Has knack for entertaining, promoting, and selling. Combines up-to-date methods/ideas/interests, communications techniques, and concern for social/artistic/public uplift. Nurse, credit union organizer, and inspired teacher are possible career opportunities.

PERSONALITY INGREDIENTS: Wants leadership, originality, and to be boss. Feels mentally progressive, inventive, and ambitious. Appears sensual, adventurous, and engaging. Strives to travel, experiment, and satisfy curiosity. May attract "leaners" and assume overpowering burdens, but has potential to serve mankind if dedication to uplift is tied to a cause. Works to better family or community and may be a martyr for either. Should constantly rekindle sense of humor, optimistic nature, and socialize to attract supporters.

PERSONALITY EXTREME: Too superficial, or too depressed.

MARYLYN (Hebrew: Mary-Gaelic: Linne/English)—F.

MAJOR TALENT: Ability to incorporate top quality artistic/scientific/humanitarian self-expression into career. Is imaginative, entertaining, and responsible. Has instincts to teach, comfort, and uplift. Combines magnetic personality, love of people, and empathetic nature. Welfare work, charity organizations, and police/fire/postal departments are possible career opportunities.

PERSONALITY INGREDIENTS: Is motivated to create a happy home, assume mature attitude, and maintain stability for family/everyone. Wants "roots," luxury, and idealistic life-style. Appears attention getting, fashionable, and imaginative. Strives for pleasure, variety, and popularity. Needs people to serve, love, and counsel. Must remember to be fair to self.

PERSONALITY EXTREME: Too busy, or too bored.

MASON (Latin)—M.

MAJOR TALENT: Ability to incorporate inventive ideas, efficiently organized mind, and logical executive judgment into career. Is persuasive, self-reliant, and a delegator. Has no time to waste. Sees long-term plans, established procedures, and works to produce tangibles. Combines pioneering, quality conscious, and businesslike nature. Statistical consultant, band leader, and any administrative position are possible career opportunities.

PERSONALITY INGREDIENTS: Inwardly spiritually/intellectually probing, aristocratic, and culturally attaining. Wants natural beauty, quiet, and privacy. Appears to be nonconforming, energetic, and direct. Strives for independence, progressive changes, and to do/have everything "now." Needs quality, quantity, and freedom of thought and direction. Should attract recognition for strength and depth of character.

PERSONALITY EXTREME: Too enthusiastic, or too pessimistic.

MATHILDA (Old German/English)—F.

MAJOR TALENT: Ability to incorporate unconventional ideas, sensitivity to fine points, and fashionable approach into career. Is clever, adaptable, and quick. Has flexibility, opportunistic instincts, and knack of taking advantage of unexpected happenings. Combines orderliness, communications talents, and varied enthusiasms. Politician, advertising idea person, and fashion industry promoter are possible career opportunities.

PERSONALITY INGREDIENTS: Appears attention getting, sociable, and entertaining. Strives to be popular, busy, and surrounded by beauty. Aims to forget unpleasantness and find the best in everything. Inwardly creatively idealistic and visionary. Is mentally in motion, nervous, and trying to change the world. Feels a bit above the masses and gets involved with "worthy causes" to improve the quality of life for others. Needs concentration, progressive changes, and stability.

PERSONALITY EXTREME: Too individualistic, or too unoriginal.

MATT (Hebrew: Matthew/English: diminutive)—M.

MAJOR TALENT: Ability to incorporate humanitarian service, broad mindedness, and empathetic outlook into career. Is generous, helpful, and tolerant. Has creative/artistic drives and aims for top-notch quality. Combines concern for others, magnetic attraction, and breadth of scope. Welfare worker, actor/artist/writer, and policeman are possible career opportunities.

PERSONALITY INGREDIENTS: Inwardly nonconforming, independent, and pioneering. Wants to create, courageously uphold, and "get credit for" progressive ideas and change of procedures. Appears strong, dominant, and custommade. Strives to be in control, influential, and prosperous. Needs long-term and uplifting goals. Should enjoy helping others and will gain recognition.

PERSONALITY EXTREME: Too sensitive, or too unemotional.

MATTHEW (Hebrew/English)—M.

MAJOR TALENT: Ability to incorporate questioning, sensitive, and forgiving nature into career. Is creative and materially aware. Has graciousness, generosity, and breadth of scope. Combines mental/emotional/commercial characteristics, innovative ideas, and group diplomacy. Attracts notables and support. Theatrical producer/agent/performer, psychoanalyst, and forest ranger are possible career opportunities.

PERSONALITY INGREDIENTS: Inwardly protective, sympathetic, and domestically oriented. Wants "roots," comforts, and to share loving/responsible/instructional feelings. Appears friendly, attractive, and optimistic. Strives to be entertaining, versatile, and surrounded by beauty. Best suited to noncommercial focus. Attracts money, recognition, and happiness.

PERSONALITY EXTREME: Too understanding, or too self-indulgent.

MAUDE (Old German; M./English: diminutive; Mathilda-Madaline, F.)—F. & M.

MAJOR TALENT: Ability to incorporate executive organizational control, businesslike approach, and clear material judgment into career. Is individualistic, intellectually questioning, and efficient. Has self-reliance, calculated diplomacy, and sociability. Combines desire for perfection, progressive thinking, and financial/tangible goals. Buyer, accountant, and financial advisor are possible career opportunities.

PERSONALITY INGREDIENTS: Wants to give empathetic, generous, creative service. Is broad scoped, tolerant, and has philosophical humor.

Appears dominant, controlled, and as affluent as possible. Strives to be authoritative, prosperous, and acknowledged for capabilities. Is fortunate with money/power people and attracts commercial interests.

PERSONALITY EXTREME: Too virginal, or too sensual.

MAURA (Latin: Maurice/Italian/Irish/English)—F.

MAJOR TALENT: Ability to incorporate understanding, independent, organized personality into career. Is romantic, charitable, and attracts attention. Has discipline, deep emotional reactions, and desire to perform/create a quality, not quantity, of work. Combines individuality, material awareness, and follow-through. Artist, physician, and publicist are possible career opportunities.

PERSONALITY INGREDIENTS: Inwardly adventurous, curious, and clever. Wants travel, sensual/physical activity, and freedom of expression. Appears classic, tasteful, and neat. Strives to be respectable, structured, and practical. Attracts a broad scope of people and experiences, grows culturally, and attracts respect.

PERSONALITY EXTREME: Too nonconforming, or too cowardly.

MAUREEN (Hebrew: Mary-Latin: Maura/Irish)—F.

MAJOR TALENT: Ability to incorporate physical and mental freedom, curiosity, and sex appeal into career. Is adventurous, clever, and learns by experiencing. Has keen perceptions about people, adaptability, and confident facade. Combines creative self-expression, sensitivity to fine points, and fast-paced/multifaceted/changeable nature. Theater, politics, and advertising are possible career opportunities.

PERSONALITY INGREDIENTS: First impression is attracting, noble, and broad scoped. Strives to be quality conscious, helpful, and generous. Aims for travel, wide-ranged experiences/thinking, and to finish commitments. Inwardly wants excitement, unconventional interests, and sensual/physical activity. Is charming, culturally expanding, and improves upon birthright. Wants everything that life has to offer "now."

PERSONALITY EXTREME: Too self-indulgent, or too amiable.

MAURICE (Latin/French/English)—M.

MAJOR TALENT: Ability to incorporate intellectual curiosity, communications talents, and attention to details into career. Is sensitive, refined, and knows how to keep a secret. Has engaging charm, practical work habits, and appreciation for structure. Combines aristocratic, expressive, quality-conscious nature. Comptroller, detective, and appraiser are possible career opportunities.

PERSONALITY INGREDIENTS: Visually aloof, refined, and classy. Strives for authority, expertise, and privacy to think/work/analyze. Inwardly expansive, broad scoped, and compassionate. Wants romance, top-notch performance/people/experiences, and to help others. Is a magnetic speaker, emotionally generous friend, and attracts a universal range for mental analysis/business/loves. Should avoid selfishness, scheming, and temperamental relationships. Best when educated or technically expert.

PERSONALITY EXTREME: Too adventurous, or too cautious.

MAURY (Latin: Maurice/English: variable)—M.

MAJOR TALENT: Ability to incorporate family/home/community instruction, welfare, and counsel into career. Is sympathetic, structured, and practical. Has showmanship, companionability, and enjoyment of luxury. Combines conventions, attention to details, and responsibility to everything/everyone. Marriage counselor, teacher, and musician/artist/actor are possible career opportunities.

PERSONALITY INGREDIENTS: Inwardly feels energized to serve, invent, or crusade for a better quality of life. Wants cultured tastes, ideals realized, and quick decisions. Appears to be dignified, neat, and traditional. Strives for material stability, conventional appearance, and to work for rewards. Builds security, helps others, and brings a special endowment to life.

PERSONALITY EXTREME: Too skeptical, or too gullible.

MAVIS (Celtic: Mab/French)—F.

MAJOR TALENT: Ability to incorporate inventive concepts, leadership, and wide-ranged thinking into career. Is a creator, instigator, and pacesetter. Has confident nature, courage, and empathetic viewpoint. Combines active energy, human understanding, and individuality. Should have integrity of personal beliefs to achieve potential. Designer, architect, and telephone operator are possible career opportunities.

PERSONALITY INGREDIENTS: Wants to uplift others, enlarge scope, and give/receive tolerance. Feels generous, compassionate, and inclined to seek quality of personal performance, and expect the best from everyone. Appears to be nonconforming. Strives to be independent, aggressive, and assertive. Aims to take the lead, get recognition, and maintain originality. Needs to be comfortable in unique desires, and not fake a facade or fool self.

PERSONALITY EXTREME: Too bossy, or too accommodating.

MAX (Latin/Anglo-Saxon/English: variable; diminutive; independent)—F. & M.

MAJOR TALENT: Ability to incorporate individualistic personality, diplomatic partnership/group activity, and inspirational ideas into career. Is high strung, mentally/physically able to do two things at one time, and capable of creating havoc or peace. Has dual personality traits and may be a supportive "power behind the throne" or a "fiery evangelistic crusader" for spiritual uplift. Combines detail consciousness, powers of arbitration, and cooperative efforts. Fashion designer, preacher, and private secretary are possible career opportunities.

PERSONALITY INGREDIENTS: Wants independence, originality, and progress. Feels courageous, daring, and impatient. Strives to be assertive, aggressive, and nonconforming. Is a positive forceful pacesetter, director, and solitary worker. May be a loner, but is sociable and adapts when necessary.

PERSONALITY EXTREME: Too jealous, or too unresponsive.

MAXIMILIAN (Latin/English)—M.

MAJOR TALENT: Ability to incorporate comforting service, innovations, and unconventional ideas into career. Is a strong-willed, protective leader. Has sense of justice, firm opinions, and a militance when home/family/community responsibility and loves are concerned. Combines showmanlike creative self-expression, desires for group harmony, and sincere concern/sympathy/understanding for people. Marriage counselor, teacher, and public defender/physician/servant are possible career opportunities.

PERSONALITY INGREDIENTS: Has high visionary intuition. Wants to rise above mass market tastes, philosophy, and material goods. Feels special, energized, and inventive. Needs sensitive, stimulating, friendly peer relationships. Appears dynamic, custom-made, and dignified. Strives for broad-scoped planning, work, and tangible results. Is aimed for, and has potential to be, "a master architect and builder." This name has inspirational and practical power, adds hyperactivity to the personality, and may leave a lasting mark.

PERSONALITY EXTREME: Too sensual, or too mental.

MAXINE (Latin: Maximus/English)—F.

MAJOR TALENT: Ability to incorporate words, beauty, and social contact into career. Is structured, skillful, and self-expressive. Has charm, kindness, and capacity to take on large assignments or humanitarian projects. Combines optimism, communications techniques, and inspired imagination. Writer, entertainer, and plastic surgeon are possible career opportunities.

PERSONALITY INGREDIENTS: Wants to enjoy harmonious, mature, comfortable, domestic life-style. Is motivated to help, teach, and counsel to raise standards for others. Feels responsible, protective, and sympathetic. Is a hospitable, showmanlike, luxury-loving musical/artistic/entertaining person. Attracts success through friendly relationships, conventional procedures, and sunny outlook.

PERSONALITY EXTREME: Too busy, or too bored.

MAXWELL (Anglo-Saxon/Old English)—M.

MAJOR TALENT: Ability to incorporate service that benefits the masses, attention to details, and investigative analysis into career. Is a convincing talker, magnetic, and diplomatic. Has poise, perfectionist approach, and communications gifts. Combines appreciation for beauty/art/finesse, intuitional guidance, and inspirational leadership. Artisan/thespian/author, lawyer, and social worker are possible career opportunities.

PERSONALITY INGREDIENTS: Inwardly responsible, protective, and domestic. Wants family/community harmonious relationships, gracious living, and creative self-expression. Needs honorable, respected, materially/educationally/emotionally uplifting life-style. Appears to be attention getting, up-to-date, and friendly. Strives to be optimistic, kind, and pleasure seeking. Attracts success through quality and quantity of talents.

PERSONALITY EXTREME: Too glib, or too close mouthed.

MAY (Latin/English: independent, F./Latin: Magnus; diminutive, M.)—F. & M.

MAJOR TALENT: Ability to incorporate beauty, self-expression, and a communication with words into career. Is imaginative, versatile, and original. Has individuality, detail consciousness, and diplomacy. Combines initiative, unique philosophy, and memory for "good" and "forgetting" the "bad." Entertainer, writer, and social organizer are possible career opportunities.

PERSONALITY INGREDIENTS: Wants progressive, inventive, fast-paced activity. Inwardly independent, aggressive, and strongly opinioned. Appears to be different, enthusiastic, and refined. Strives to inspire others, maintain peace, and "save the world" through personal ideals. Aims to rise above mass tastes and introduce new concepts. May be impractical, petty, or scattered. Is an energy force looking for a cause. May leave a lasting image.

PERSONALITY EXTREME: Too secretive, or too informative.

MEGAN (Greek/Irish: independent/Latin: Margaret; diminutive/English)—F.

MAJOR TALENT: Ability to incorporate wide-range futuristic planning, work, and tangible results into career. Is practical, conscientious, and dedicated. Has high energy, sensitivity to fine points, and cooperative spirit. Combines strong opinions, endurance, and constructive nature. Real estate, public service, and stage managing are possible career opportunities.

PERSONALITY INGREDIENTS: Inwardly domestically focused, instructional, and helpful. Wants harmonious relationships, companionship, and stability. Appears unruffled, cool, and refined. Strives for respect, authority, and cultural attainments. Aims for timeless/natural beauty, privacy, and quiet contemplation. Best self-image when educated/technically expert.

PERSONALITY EXTREME: Too experimental, or too cautious.

MELANIE (Greek/French/English)—F.

MAJOR TALENT: Ability to incorporate mental curiosity, originality, and creative self-expression into career. Is open minded, understanding, and kind. Has sex appeal, ambition, and initiative. Combines optimism, enthusiasm, and social progress through unconventional ideas. Advertiser, inventor, and theatrical director are possible career opportunities.

PERSONALITY INGREDIENTS: Inwardly modest, sensitive to fine points, and gentle. Wants peace, quiet, and to be a supportive mate/partner. Appears attention getting, sociable, and up-to-date. Strives to be popular, entertaining, and pleasure-seeking. Seems confident, and should be patient, cooperative, and concentrated to achieve potential.

PERSONALITY EXTREME: Too busy, or too bored.

MELBA (Old English/Celtic/English)—F.

MAJOR TALENT: Ability to incorporate studious/instructional aptitudes, pioneering spirit, and unconventional patterns into career. Is protective, responsible, and strong willed. Has musical/creatively expressive gifts, domestic/parental focus, and mature/stable nature. Combines leadership, curiosity, and showmanship. Teacher, marriage counselor, and interior decorator are possible career opportunities.

PERSONALITY INGREDIENTS: First impression is magnetic, noble, and gracious. Strives to be understanding, generous, and tolerant. Aims for universal awareness, humanitarian contributions, and to work for quality performance. Attracts emotional burdens, boosters, and prestige. At best when not judgmental or too serious.

PERSONALITY EXTREME: Too assertive, or too passive.

MELINDA (Greek/English)—F.

MAJOR TALENT: Ability to incorporate practical approach, initiative, and communications techniques into career. Is down-to-earth, hard working, and honest. Has kindness, charm, and competitive spirit. Combines doggedness, independent/pioneering/inspirational ideas, and direct attitude. Administrator, salesperson, and theatrical agent are possible career opportunities.

PERSONALITY INGREDIENTS: Appears cool, refined, and poised. Wants to be cultured, private, and intellectually tuned to rise above earthy realities and assume responsibility to uplift and serve. Inwardly emotional, protective, and domestically oriented. Desires hospitable, abundant, companionable homelife. Wants tangible, educational, luxurious attainments. Is willing to work but has perfectionist illusions. Should keep harmonious relationships/surroundings and feet on the ground.

PERSONALITY EXTREME: Too aggressive, or too passive.

MELISSA (Greek/Italian/English)—F.

MAJOR TALENT: Ability to incorporate sense of justice, responsibility, and household/domestic focus into career. Is attentive to details, practical, and hard working. Has showmanship, emotional generosity, and discipline. Combines gentleness, organization, and parental nature. Interior decorator, marriage counselor, and vocal coach are possible career opportunities.

PERSONALITY INGREDIENTS: First impression is broad scoped, classic, and empathetic. Strives to be tolerant, concerned/involved/serving universal reforms/needs, and to give full quality/skill of performance. Aims to complete commitments, keep harmonious relationships, and be a "cosmic mother."

PERSONALITY EXTREME: Too changeable, or too uninspired.

MELODIE (Greek: Melody/English)—F.

MAJOR TALENT: Ability to incorporate perseverance, imagination, and broad scoped approach into career. Is concerned about quality, dependable, and strong willed. Has deep emotional responses, magnetic personality, and musical/artistic/literary talents. Combines appreciation of beauty, optimism, and human understanding. Welfare worker, doctor, and fine artist/thespian are possible career opportunities.

PERSONALITY INGREDIENTS: Appears modest, genteel, and subtle. Strives to enthuse/inspire with unique/uplifting/inventive ideas, and to be different. Rises above mass market tastes and may find commercial acceptance elusive. Has imagery, faith, and compassion. Must balance daily reality, dreams, and sense of "fair play."

PERSONALITY EXTREME: Too impetuous, or too unexcitable.

MELVIN (Celtic: Malvin/English)—M.

MAJOR TALENT: Ability to incorporate skilled, imaginative, structured communications techniques into career. Is up-to-date, kind, and pleasure seeking. Has charm, wit, and versatility. Combines humanitarian or mass market focus, entertaining approach, and artistry through self-expression. Plastic surgeon, author/artist/actor, and travel authority are possible career opportunities.

PERSONALITY INGREDIENTS: Wants sensual pleasure, unconventional interests, and adventure. Feels curious, mentally free, and observational. Learns by "trial and error." Appears gracious, classic, and understanding. Strives to be tolerant, empathetic, and broad scoped. Aims to entertain, help, and enjoy.

PERSONALITY EXTREME: Too eccentric, or too ordinary.

MELVYN (Celtic: Malvin/English)—M.

MAJOR TALENT: Ability to incorporate instigating, original, and trendsetting ideas into career. Is a leader, pioneer, and rebel. Has drive, detail analysis, and material awareness. Combines commercial power focus, improvement through partnership, and creative energy. Store owner, designer, and editor are possible career opportunities.

PERSONALITY INGREDIENTS: Appears to be observing others. First impression is serious, introverted, and refined. When comfortable in company, is stimulating, charming, and analytic. Motivated to be entertaining, optimistic, and pleasure seeking. Strives to be authoritative, confident, and perfect. Has introverted and extroverted characteristics. Needs area of expertise/education, concentration, and easygoing attitude to fulfill potential.

PERSONALITY EXTREME: Too irresponsible, or too devoted.

MENDEL (Latin/English)—M.

MAJOR TALENT: Ability to incorporate financial focus, executive judgment, and self-reliance into career. Is confident, attentive to detail, and responsible. Has instructional approach, companionability, and athletic energy. Combines adaptability, helpful service, and organizational efficiency. Clothing business, accounting, and financial advising are possible career opportunities.

PERSONALITY INGREDIENTS: Inwardly inventive, ambitious, and in control. Wants positive, fast action, leadership, and creative opportunities. Appears quiet, refined, and pensive. Strives to be investigative, cultured, and perfect. Takes things in stride when in authority. At best when not materialistic and well educated.

PERSONALITY EXTREME: Too attention-getting, or too unattractive.

MERCER (French/English)—M.

MAJOR TALENT: Ability to incorporate executive approach, businesslike attitude, and understanding of people/self-expression/communications techniques into career. Is quick, self-reliant, and optimistic. Has humor, charm, and desire for progressive changes. Combines kindness, cleverness, and sense of public acceptance. Band leader, business analyst, and newspaper publisher are possible career opportunities.

PERSONALITY INGREDIENTS: Appears introspective, refined, and classy. Strives for cultural attainments, timeless beauty, and perfection. Inwardly nonconforming, ambitious, and inventive. Wants control, praise, and competition. Dislikes pettiness, slowness, and intolerance. May inherit money/influence/status. Is multifaceted and has many choices.

PERSONALITY EXTREME: Too empathetic, or too unfeeling.

MERCY (Latin/English)—F.

MAJOR TALENT: Ability to incorporate material ambitions, sensitivity to fine points, and individualism into career. Is gentle, cooperative, and daring. Has resilience, self-reliance, and direct approach. Combines diverse characteristics of leadership and cooperation. Attracts supporters through thoughtful ways, and loses them if self-important. Has potential for financial success when patient, emotionally responsive, and creatively inspirational. Designer, pilot, and business owner are possible career opportunities.

PERSONALITY INGREDIENTS: Inwardly imaginative, optimistic, and sociable. Wants popularity, beauty, and up-to-date interests. Appears introspective, refined, and quiet. Strives for cultural attainments, quality, and perfection. Feels restless and aims for professional authority. Best when concentrated and not scattering energy.

PERSONALITY EXTREME: Too analytic, or too thoughtless.

MEREDITH (Celtic/English)—F. & M.

MAJOR TALENT: Ability to incorporate instigational leadership, traditional routine, and creative talents into career. Is structured, strong willed, and a rebel. Has sense of justice, integrity, and showmanship. Combines idealistic opinions, method, and fortunate progressive changes. Musician/artist, inventor, and psychiatrist are possible career opportunities.

PERSONALITY INGREDIENTS: Inwardly self-oriented, but strives to be a humanitarian. Wants to avoid details, have control, and receive recognition for daring. Appears to be understanding, tasteful, and noble. Aims for romance, top quality skill/performance, and to help/educate/uplift others. Is a dominant, magnetic, and engaging personality.

PERSONALITY EXTREME: Too materialistic, or too imprudent.

MERLE (Latin/English)—F. & M.

MAJOR TALENT: Ability to incorporate executive material judgment, rhythm/music/showmanship, and organizational efficiency into career. Is overtly confident, responsible, and self-reliant. Has communications gifts, gentleness, and strength. Combines physical energy, easygoing approach, and ambition. Athletic coach, band leader, and business executive are possible career opportunities.

PERSONALITY INGREDIENTS: Visual impression is aloof, dignified, and quiet. Strives for good taste, privacy, and cultural stimulation. Benefits from self-improvement courses. Inwardly optimistic, restless, and pleasure seeking. Wants beauty, entertaining people, and to forget any unpleasantness. Desires to be an extrovert and appears to be introspective. Challenges self and needs education/expertise/respect to sustain self-confidence. When positive, can expect success.

PERSONALITY EXTREME: Too sensual, or too mental.

MERLIN (Old German/Middle English/French/Welsh/English)—M.

MAJOR TALENT: Ability to incorporate influence, affluence, or prestige as a legacy into career. Is efficient, practical, and clever. Has unconventional approach, method, and communications talents. Combines strength, imagination, and material awareness. Athlete, banker, and airline executive are possible career opportunities.

PERSONALITY INGREDIENTS: Inwardly gutsy, adventurous, and sensually fine tuned. Wants change, stimulating challenges, and to be different. Appears attention getting, up-to-date, and expressive. Strives to be entertaining, popular, and kind. Combines intuition, vision, and fortunate gambles. Aims high and gets to the top through perseverance.

PERSONALITY EXTREME: Too eccentric, or too conservative.

MERRY (Celtic: Meredith: variable/English)—F.

MAJOR TALENT: Ability to incorporate mental analysis, communications techniques, and conventional methods into career. Is quality conscious, investigative, and persevering. Has poise, charm, and practicality. Combines structure, optimism, and logic. Researcher, radio performer/technician, and lawyer are possible career opportunities.

PERSONALITY INGREDIENTS: Travels intellectually and physically culturally upward. Appears dynamic, custom-made, and dignified. Strives for idealistic planning, work, and lasting tangible results. Inwardly restless, pleasure-seeking, and humorous. Wants to share beauty, joy, and love. Has high energy, intuition, and wisdom. Is articulate, and should temper honesty with tact.

PERSONALITY EXTREME: Too skeptical, or too gullible.

MERTON (Anglo-Saxon/English)—M.

MAJOR TALENT: Ability to incorporate method, practicality, and economy into career. Is conscientious, routined, and dramatic. Has originality, communications gifts, and common sense. Combines hard work, imagination, and competitive spirit. Contractor, accountant, and dentist are possible career opportunities.

PERSONALITY INGREDIENTS: Appears modest, refined, and reserved. Strives to be supportive, cooperative, and peaceful. Inwardly creative, inventive, and idealistic. Wants quality, uplift, and to rise above the crowd. May be overtly evangelistic, then shyly controlling. Has a duality of purpose and needs firm decisions, actions, and goals.

PERSONALITY EXTREME: Too impulsive, or too cautious.

MERVIN (Anglo-Saxon: Irvin/English)—M.

MAJOR TALENT: Ability to incorporate human understanding, broad mindedness, and communications techniques into career. Is generous, kind, and helpful. Has charm, showmanship, and artistry/quality/skill. Combines self-expression, protective responsibility, and humanitarian/mass market focus. Theatrical producer, judge, and comedy writer are possible career opportunities.

PERSONALITY INGREDIENTS: Inwardly unconventional, curious, and experimental. Wants sensual pleasures, travel, and progressive changes. Appears dynamic, strong, and well turned out. Strives to inspire, plan, work, build, and leave a lasting image. Has down-to-earth common sense, but may assume, or carry, heavy responsibilities/burdens due to empathetic/compassionate nature. Best when not speculative.

PERSONALITY EXTREME: Too impulsive, or too controlled.

MERYL (Greek: Muriel/English)—F.

MAJOR TALENT: Ability to incorporate original ideas, faith, and executive diplomacy into career. Is efficient, trend setting, and stimulating. Has sensitivity to detail, sense of immediacy, and cleverness. Combines independence, initiative, and progressive action. Business owner, artist/actor, and bank administrator are possible career opportunities.

PERSONALITY INGREDIENTS: Strives for timeless natural beauty, solitude, and cultural attainments. Appears unruffled, refined, and thoughtful. Inwardly fun loving, optimistic, and artistic. Thrives on beauty, imagination, and variety. Wants social, entertaining, up-to-date interests. At best when concentrated/specialized. Sizes up situations and may seem cool at first glance. Brightens when at ease. True extrovert/introvert.

PERSONALITY EXTREME: Too animated, or too inexpressive.

MEYER (Teutonic)—M.

MAJOR TALENT: Ability to incorporate communications techniques, optimism, and imagination into career. Is skilled, methodized, and expansive. Has charm, up-to-date interests, and humor. Combines creative self-expression, people contact, and a knack with words. Plastic surgeon, writer, and theatrical performer are possible career opportunities.

PERSONALITY INGREDIENTS: Appears retiring, quiet, and gentle. Strives to be cooperative, diplomatic, and easygoing. Inwardly inventive, assertive, and ambitious. Wants to lead, be decisive, and pioneer new concepts. Is a rebel for progressive changes. Is analytic, quality conscious, and understanding of people. Needs an audience, perfection, and praise.

PERSONALITY EXTREME: Too broad minded, or too intolerant.

MICHAEL (Hebrew/Latin/German/English)—M.

MAJOR TALENT: Ability to incorporate service, devotion, and protective/responsible/sympathetic feelings into career. Is parental, domestic, and strong willed. Has sense of justice, firm ideals, and instructional instincts. Combines communications gifts, showmanship, and personal interest in everything. Teacher, marriage counselor, and public servant are possible career opportunities.

PERSONALITY INGREDIENTS: Appears noble, romantic, and youthful. Strives to be empathetic, impressive, and kind. May exaggerate. Has dramatic emotions, broad-scoped aims, and strong need to serve a worthy cultural or life-support cause. Has sex appeal, magnetism, and potential to leave a lasting contribution. Gives selfless family/community uplift when emotionally balanced. Has compulsive need for involvement, to counsel others, and to attain material security/comforts/perfection.

PERSONALITY EXTREME: Too optimistic, or too depressed.

MICHAELA (Hebrew: Michael)—F.

MAJOR TALENT: Ability to incorporate logical analysis, quality taste, and organized up-to-date activities into career. Is practical, methodized, and sociable. Has engaging manner, determination, and communications gifts. Combines creative self-expression, material approach, and probing intellect. Researcher, librarian, and fashion consultant are possible career opportunities.

PERSONALITY INGREDIENTS: First impression is gracious, tasteful, and magnetic. Strives to be a cosmopolitan, empathetic, and generous person. Inwardly self-questioning. Needs a show of confidence/expertise/authority to be socially at ease. Wants polish, timeless quality/beauty, and refinements. Needs to cultivate faith, conventional standards, and personal discrimination. Attracts dependent personalities.

PERSONALITY EXTREME: Too independent, or too accommodating.

MICHELLE (Hebrew: Michael/French)—F.

MAJOR TALENT: Ability to incorporate practicality, method, and economy into career. Is dependable, honest, and constructive. Has material awareness/analysis/needs, orderliness, and precision. Combines confidence, work, and attraction to business. Corporate administrator, mathematician/statistician, and skilled communications technician are possible career opportunities.

PERSONALITY INGREDIENTS: First impression is attracting, friendly, and current. Strives to be popular, entertaining, and optimistic. Aims for beauty, pleasure, and kindness. Inwardly individualistic, changeable, and a rebel. Wants to pioneer, lead, and set the pace. Feels impatient, ambitious, and forceful. Should focus upon social or artistic self-expression.

PERSONALITY EXTREME: Too curious, or too cautious.

MICKEY (Hebrew: Michael; diminutive/English; nickname)—F. & M.

MAJOR TALENT: Ability to incorporate broad-scoped and skillful communications artistry into career. Is creatively expressive, charming, and attention getting. Has optimism, humor, and organizational structure. Combines cleverness, entertainment, and imagination. Plastic surgeon, animal/children specialist, and organizer are possible career opportunities.

PERSONALITY INGREDIENTS: First impression is aloof, refined, and introspective. Strives to be authoritative, cultured, and quality conscious. Aims for perfection/natural beauty, and air of confidence. Inwardly physically focused, adventurous, and unconventional. Wants freedom of choice, sensual pleasures, and progressive changes. Best when specialized/educated and involved with nonroutine/people-oriented interests.

PERSONALITY EXTREME: Too analytic, or too unquestioning.

MIKE (Hebrew: Michael; diminutive/English)—M.

MAJOR TALENT: Ability to incorporate tact, tidiness, and knack of joining opposing forces into career. Is attentive to details, sensitive, and thoughtful. Has cooperative spirit, easygoing approach, and emotional tenderness. Combines studious instinct, compulsive collecting, and respect for confidences. Psychologist, repair/service businesses, and statistician are possible career opportunities.

PERSONALITY INGREDIENTS: Inwardly sensual, curious, and unconventional. Wants challenges, change, and mental stimulation. Appears to be conventional, sympathetic, and dignified. Strives for material comforts, family/community respectability, and to teach/counsel/guide others. At best when decisive, patient, and practical. Needs tolerance for loved ones and is broad minded for everyone else.

PERSONALITY EXTREME: Too adventurous, or too tied down.

MILDRED (Anglo-Saxon/English)—F.

MAJOR TALENT: Ability to incorporate inspirational personal ideals, communications techniques, and methodized/efficient approach into career. Is high strung, spontaneous, and often "in another world." Has grand schemes, enthusiasm to promote, and magnetism to attract followers. Combines creative self-expression, commercial focus, and visionary intuition. Song writer, theatrical promoter, and political reformer are possible career opportunities.

PERSONALITY INGREDIENTS: Appears dignified, comfortable, and interested. Strives to be domestic/parental, harmonious, and to set/maintain high standards. Aims for respectability, abundant life-style, and to be a mature/helpful counselor to all. Inwardly unconventional, changeable, and adventurous. Wants sensual pleasures, constant variety/travel, and never to be bored. Will try to be "rooted" but really needs freedom.

PERSONALITY EXTREME: Too tidy, or too disorganized.

MILES (Greek/English)—M.

MAJOR TALENT: Ability to incorporate visionary energized planning, work, and tangible results into career. Is structured, practical, and ambitious for money, power, and humanitarian ideals. Has creative inspirations, drive to develop skills/human understanding, and tremendous self-confidence or lack of confidence. Efficiency expert, government reformer, and building trades/utilities/transportation administrator are possible career opportunities.

PERSONALITY INGREDIENTS: First impression is businesslike, managerial, and as affluent as possible. Strives to be recognized, trustworthy, and self-reliant. Inwardly sensual, unconventional, and mentally curious. Wants changing routine, travel, and exciting companionship. Has nerve, drive, and workaholic energy. Aims to leave lasting results.

PERSONALITY EXTREME: Too impatient, or too procrastinating.

MILLARD (Teutonic)—M.

MAJOR TALENT: Ability to incorporate sympathetic community work and life-style reform into career. Is responsible, protective, and creatively self-expressive. Has showmanship, determination, and firm ideals. Combines appreciation for beauty, education, and emotional needs. Credit union investigator/leader, doctor, and writer/artist/actor are possible career opportunities.

PERSONALITY INGREDIENTS: Inwardly pioneering, managerial, and independent. Wants pride in family/community, activity, and to be boss. Appears friendly, understanding, and unconventional. Strives to be progressive, nonroutined, and experimental. Needs "roots" and freedom to satisfy impatience and curiosity. When inspired to serve, may leave a lasting social welfare improvement.

PERSONALITY EXTREME: Too proper, or too immoral.

MILLICENT (Greek: Melissa/English)—F.

MAJOR TALENT: Ability to incorporate confidential nature, social contact, and concentrated skills into career. Is analytic, persevering, and perceptive. Has optimism, kindness, and sense of duty. Combines discipline, creative self-expression, and cultural attainments. College professor, author, and scientist are possible career opportunities.

PERSONALITY INGREDIENTS: Appears refined/modest/subdued, and desires titillation/uniqueness/experimentation. Strives to be peaceful, cooperative, and genteel. Aims for partnership and needs to be free to experience/observe/progress. Has choices, is multifaceted, and should be decisive.

PERSONALITY EXTREME: Too patient, or too fidgety.

MILO (Greek: Miles/Latin)—F. & M.

MAJOR TALENT: Ability to incorporate large-scale ideas, practical application, and lasting values into career. Is inspired to create, plan, invest energy, and see solid results. Has human understanding, diplomacy, and sensitivity to details. Combines cooperative spirit, communications techniques, and material focus. Professional athlete, psychiatrist, and architectural engineer are possible career opportunities.

PERSONALITY INGREDIENTS: Inwardly protective, responsible, and family/community focused. Wants luxurious/admired/attaining lifestyle, mature/stable relationships, and to give sympathetic/supportive service. Appears quiet, refined, and unruffled. Strives for quality tastes, timeless treasures, and perfection in people/experiences/self. Seems confident/aloof, but is a softy. Intellectual, practical and emotional drives are combined and should leave tangibles for future generations.

PERSONALITY EXTREME: Too meddlesome, or too uninterested.

MILTON (Old English)—M.

MAJOR TALENT: Ability to incorporate idealistic, romantic, inspirational ideas into career. Is creative, orderly, and empathetic. Has individuality, ambition, and spontaneous enthusiasms. Combines visionary intuition, nervous energy, and diplomatic approach. Lawyer, artist, and political/religious reformer are possible career opportunities.

PERSONALITY INGREDIENTS: Inwardly domestic, instructional, and materially attaining. Wants mature relationships, abundant life-style, and respectability. Appears unconventional, striking, and alert. Strives for adventure, travel, and sensual pleasures. Aims to be commercially successful, to rise above mass tastes, and to raise everyone's standards.

PERSONALITY EXTREME: Too busy, or too bored.

MINERVA (Latin/Italian/English)—F.

MAJOR TALENT: Ability to incorporate independence, self-analysis, and pioneering communications techniques into career. Is skillful, expressive, and nonconforming. Has charm, refinement, and method. Combines imagination, technology, and desire for perfection. Goodwill ambassador, architectural engineer, and antique dealer are possible career opportunities.

PERSONALITY INGREDIENTS: Inwardly domestic, strong willed, and firmly idealistic. Wants mature/stable/harmonious relationships, material comforts, and respectability. Appears custom-made, efficiently radiant, and self-assured. Strives to be a solid citizen who plans/works/builds to amass tangibles. Has strength to leave a lasting result and may do great humanitarian work. Best when not self-indulgent, stubborn, and impatient.

PERSONALITY EXTREME: Too rebellious, or too passive.

MINNA (Old German/English)—F.

MAJOR TALENT: Ability to incorporate responsibility, protective nature, and sympathetic service into career. Is interested, sensible, and strongly opinionated. Has sensitivity to fine points, diplomacy, and determination. Combines home/family focus, justice/honesty, and devotion. Teacher, marriage counselor, and restaurant manager are possible career opportunities.

PERSONALITY INGREDIENTS: Inwardly individualistic, forceful, and trend setting. Wants freedom, progressive changes, and to take the initiative. Appears to be unconventional, understanding, and enthusiastic. Strives to be busy, experimental, and companionable. Has set ways, sex appeal, and impatience. Uses subtle control and can be domineering. Assumes burdens for less capable people.

PERSONALITY EXTREME: Too alone, or too imitative.

MINNIE (Scottish: independent/Latin: Minerva; variable-diminutive/ English)—F.

MAJOR TALENT: Ability to incorporate individualistic, entertaining, logical personality into career. Is assertive, pacesetting, and courageous. Has optimism, charm, and desire for perfection. Combines questioning analysis, creative self-expression, and a desire to be different. Theatrical performer, salesperson, and architectural designer are possible career opportunities.

PERSONALITY INGREDIENTS: Appears striking, unconventional, and enthusiastic. Strives to be adventurous, sensual, and changeable. Inwardly instigative, controlling, and rebellious. Wants a broad/unique scope, stimulating activity, and never to wait. Aims for quality of performance, skill, and to grow culturally. Must keep active, maintain humanitarian focus, and expect many surprising events.

PERSONALITY EXTREME: Too self-indulgent, or too understanding.

MIRANDA (Latin)—F.

MAJOR TALENT: Ability to incorporate domestic/community/life-support service into career. Is artistically expressive, hospitable, and concerned. Has sympathetic nature, strong will, and firm ideals. Combines social uplift, dedicated performance, and showmanship. May perform lasting work in the behalf of others. Credit union organizer, theatrical producer, and inspired teacher are possible career opportunities.

PERSONALITY INGREDIENTS: Has high nervous energy, futuristic intuition, and vivid imagination. Wants to enhance the quality of thinking/ artistry. Feels different, inspired, and "above the crowd." Appears dynamic, carefully tailored, and self-assured. Strives to plan, work, and build for material results. May be a powerhouse of mature wisdom, or a meddlesome force for troublemaking.

PERSONALITY EXTREME: Too individualistic, or too imitative.

MIRIAM (Hebrew: oldest form of Mary/English)—F.

MAJOR TALENT: Ability to incorporate empathetic, generous, creative nature into career. Is tolerant, broad scoped, and protective. Has determination, nobility, and love of humanity. Combines self-expression, domestic/parental/firm instincts, and concern for quality improvement/ welfare of others. Artiste/thespian, Peace Corps volunteer, and doctor are possible career opportunities.

PERSONALITY INGREDIENTS: Inwardly wants to take the lead. Feels daring, courageous, and inventive. Appears well tailored, influential, and direct. Strives to be businesslike, organized, and practical. Aims to progress through farsighted planning, material results, and high-powered authority. Will assume depth of responsibility/problem solving during

All names that begin with the letter *M* have the *Strong Point* of

296   noting procedures—doing the right thing—practical administration—love of nature.

lifetime and will have the gumption to achieve personal goals while serving selflessly. Is inspirational, just, and kind.

PERSONALITY EXTREME: Too uncautious, or too self-protective.

MITCHELL (Hebrew: Michael; variable/English)—M.

MAJOR TALENT: Ability to incorporate individuality, self-expression, and mental analysis into career. Is inspired to pioneer, imaginative, and a perfectionist. Has need for interaction, introspection, and nonconforming activities. Combines ambition, changeable drives, and desire to be different. Theater/music, manager, and editor are possible career opportunities.

PERSONALITY INGREDIENTS: Wants adventure, physical stimulation, and progressive interests. Feels curious, unconventional, and fascinated by people/life/unexplored vistas. Appears energetic, striking, and understanding. Strives to be on the go, traveling, and unrestricted. Is materially aware, philosophical, and multifaceted. Best when tuned to a variety of interests, in command, and unlimited by conventions.

PERSONALITY EXTREME: Too talkative, or too antisocial.

MOIRA (Hebrew: Mary/Celtic/Greek/Irish)—F.

MAJOR TALENT: Ability to incorporate inspirational original ideas, diplomacy, and broad mindedness into career. Is sensitive, attentive to fine points, and orderly. Has magnetism, human understanding, and spontaneous enthusiasms. Combines cooperation, compassion, and desire to improve the quality of man's concepts. Musician/dancer, educational reformer, and publicist are possible career opportunities.

PERSONALITY INGREDIENTS: Aims to work, structure, and build. Appears solid, dignified, and classic. Inwardly culturally attaining, analytic, and a perfectionist. Wants practicality, but has difficulty coming down to earth. Is a dreamer, a traditionalist, and needs education/specialization to achieve highest potential.

PERSONALITY EXTREME: Too rebellious, or too weak.

MOLLY (Hebrew: Mary/English: variable)—F.

MAJOR TALENT: Ability to incorporate unconventional, enthusiastic, changeable personality into career. Is nonroutined, gentle, and understanding. Has creative self-expression, knack with words, and sex appeal. Combines charm, wit, and keen judgment of people. Learns quickly and by experiencing. Travel agent, politician, and party organizer are possible career opportunities.

PERSONALITY INGREDIENTS: Inwardly practical, organized, and determined. Wants material results, discipline, and workable structure. Appears individualistic, active, and assertive. Strives for progressive changes, pioneering ideas, and to be a trend setter. Has force, adaptability, and endurance. Attracts security, friends, and adventure.

PERSONALITY EXTREME: Too aloof, or too confiding.

MONA (Teutonic/English)—F.

MAJOR TALENT: Ability to incorporate questioning nature, quality consciousness, and confidential approach into career. Is analytic, investigative, and individualistic. Has domestic/protective instincts, ambition, and need for education/expertise/authority. Combines need for perfection, logic, and creative self-expression. Must be down-to-earth to achieve potential. Writer, psychologist, and florist are possible career opportunities.

PERSONALITY INGREDIENTS: Inwardly poised, thoughtful, and aloof. Wants cultural attainments, refined/intellectually stimulating relationships, and timeless beauty. Appears to be magnetic, classic, and romantic. Strives to be graceful, gracious, and compassionate. Aims for a wide range and to help or serve humanitarian needs.

PERSONALITY EXTREME: Too aggressive, or too passive.

MONICA (Latin/English)—F.

MAJOR TALENT: Ability to incorporate initiative, inventive ideas, and executive diplomacy into career. Is bold, managerial, and capable. Has courage, sensitivity to fine points, and pride. Combines mental organization, thoughtfulness, and individuality. Architect, business owner, and lawyer are possible career opportunities.

PERSONALITY INGREDIENTS: Inwardly questioning and appears to be sure. Wants confident authority, perfection, and quality lifestyle. Needs solitude, but fears loneliness. Is impractical, but fears poverty. Needs .education/expertise. Appears to be optimistic, fashionable, and friendly. Strives for popularity, beauty, and lighthearted pleasure. Seems kind, youthful, and entertaining. Best when concentrated.

PERSONALITY EXTREME: Too daring, or too fearful.

MONROE (Celtic/English)—M.

MAJOR TALENT: Ability to incorporate mental organization, efficiency, and control into career. Is self-reliant, expressive, and adventurous. Has charm, physical endurance, and businesslike approach. Combines communications techniques, unconventional ideas, and material results. Stock broker, athlete, and business executive are possible career opportunities.

PERSONALITY INGREDIENTS: Inwardly wants prestige, money, and recognition. Feels strong, determined, and dominant. Appears noble, youthful, and understanding. Strives to reach a broad marketplace, attract attention, and serve worthwhile goals. Aims to give quality skill/performance, endure, and complete commitments. Has confidence.

PERSONALITY EXTREME: Too expansive, or too limited.

MONTE (Latin/English)—M.

MAJOR TALENT: Ability to incorporate wide-scoped/visionary structure, work, and results into career. Is a strong, opinionated, dynamic, practical workaholic humanitarian. Has sensitivity to details, musical/dance talents, and diplomacy. Combines nervous energy, dignified tastes, and self-assurance. Construction, business organizer/owner, and supper club/stage manager are possible career opportunities.

PERSONALITY INGREDIENTS: Feels, and appears to be, inspirational, spontaneously creative, and quick to think/act. Strives to be different, raise cultural standards, and to bring a quality product or performance to a market. Wants magic, refinement, exotic/dramatic presentations. Needs peer relationships, quiet, and peace to stimulate imagery, and to keep feet on the ground. Should face practical responsibilities and maintain traditional codes and duties. May be a universal influence for uplift or for immorality. This name has choice and power to leave a lasting impression.

PERSONALITY EXTREME: Too unconventional, or too conforming.

MONTGOMERY (Latin)—M.

MAJOR TALENT: Ability to incorporate pioneering, clever, sensitive perceptions, initiative, and unique high-minded inspirational leadership into career. Is physically/mentally active, quick, and dominating. Has sense of justice, discrimination, and human understanding. Combines confidence, guts, and the most dynamic form of individuality. Creates, investigates, communicates, and upholds intellectual beliefs. Judge, writer, and any profession/business are possible career opportunities.

PERSONALITY INGREDIENTS: Inwardly responsible, protective, and stable. Wants mature, harmonious, creatively expressive life-style. Feels like a showman, a teacher, a parent to all. Appears traditional, dignified, and precise. Strives to be enduring, organized, and direct. Is competitive and fights for beliefs. This name must not waste superior leadership qualities by scattering, self-indulgence, or becoming smug.

PERSONALITY EXTREME: Too aloof, or too confiding.

MORGAN (Celtic/English)—F. & M.

MAJOR TALENT: Ability to incorporate gambler's nerve, progressive change, and unconventional ideas into career. Is adventurous, confident, and sensitive to details. Has communications gifts, imagination, and a knack for handling/understanding/relating to people. Combines diplomacy, charm, and learning by experience/clever observation. Promoter, politician, and literary agent are possible career opportunities.

PERSONALITY INGREDIENTS: Inwardly strives for polish, culture, and self-confidence. Wants perfection in everyone/everything and courts disappointment, loneliness, and unrealistic fears of poverty. Appears authoritative, reserved, and unruffled. Strives to appear confident, aloof, and expert. Dislikes vulgarity, superficiality, and senseless noise. Needs privacy and must be known to be loved.

PERSONALITY EXTREME: Too sensual, or too mental.

MORRIS (Latin: Maurice/English)—M.

MAJOR TALENT: Ability to incorporate lasting image, individuality, and inspiration for inventive ideas into career. Is high strung, communicative, and quality conscious. Has material awareness, love of beauty, and imagination. Combines spiritual/creative expression, sociability, and a sense of being above the masses. Has potential for fame when enthusiasms have a practical approach. Any film industry, inspirational movements, and hair/cosmetics business are possible career opportunities.

PERSONALITY INGREDIENTS: Inwardly home/family oriented, protective, and responsible. Wants gracious living, material attainments, and to teach/serve/counsel. Is sympathetic, sharing, and strongwilled. Feels idealistic and encourages everyone to live up to personal standards. Appears different, understanding, and adventurous. Strives to be sexy, experimental, and gutsy. Aims to try everything and enjoys unconventional experiences/people. May be on "cloud nine."

PERSONALITY EXTREME: Too aggressive, or too passive.

MORTIMER (Latin/French/English)—M.

MAJOR TALENT: Ability to incorporate engaging personality, common sense, and executive self-reliance into career. Is imaginative, clever, and optimistic. Has integrity, determination, and materialistic approach. Combines creative self-expression, romantic ideals, and earning money by using words. Newspapers, theater, and law/medicine are possible career opportunities.

PERSONALITY INGREDIENTS: Inwardly gentle, retiring, and modest. Wants peace, refinement, and easygoing love relationships. Appears direct, individualistic, and energetic. Strives to be quick, progressive, and in control. Needs to be supportive and aims for active leadership. Happiest when desire for prestige/affluence is dispersed and quality of performance/talents is emphasized.

PERSONALITY EXTREME: Too empathetic, or too selfish.

MORTON (Anglo-Saxon)—M.

MAJOR TALENT: Ability to incorporate striking, progressive, and inspirational personality into career. Is sensitive to details, diplomatic, and imaginative. Has adventurous nature, confidence, and creative self-expression. Combines unconventional thinking, sharp perceptions about people, and sex appeal. Theatrical performer, politician, and promoter are possible career opportunities.

PERSONALITY INGREDIENTS: Appears modest, reserved, and subdued. Strives to be easygoing, comfortable, and at peace with everyone. Inwardly optimistic, kind, and pleasure-seeking. Wants beauty, stimulating conversation, and popularity. Is a genial, resourceful, and entertaining person. Has unique philosophy and combines subtle control, excitement, and good taste.

PERSONALITY EXTREME: Too faithful, or too irresponsible.

MOSES (Egyptian/Greek/German/English)—M.

MAJOR TALENT: Ability to incorporate executive, efficient, organized mental analysis into career. Is direct, inventive, and pioneering. Has material awareness, spiritual/intellectual perceptions, and attraction for recognition/respect/authority. Combines influence, affluence, and the wisdom to question/research/meditate before drawing conclusions. Corporate leader, commercial pilot, and military officer are possible career opportunities.

PERSONALITY INGREDIENTS: Appears strong, proud, and different. Strives to be original, progressive, and daring. Aims to be decisive, capable, and on the move. Inwardly quality conscious, confidential, and culturally attaining. Wants privacy, natural beauty, and serious study. Should avoid uncompromising ideals, impatience, and spiritual skepticism/materialism.

PERSONALITY EXTREME: Too self-centered, or too accommodating.

MURIEL (Greek/English)—F.

MAJOR TALENT: Ability to incorporate protective, instructional, and responsible social service into career. Is sympathetic, family/home/community focused, and firmly idealistic. Has showmanship, imagination, and a knack with words/fashion/appearances. Combines determination, integrity, and loving concern for everyone. Teacher, credit union organizer, and useful products salesperson are possible career opportunities.

PERSONALITY INGREDIENTS: Inwardly mentally organized, self-reliant, and managerial. Wants influence, affluence, and prestige. Feels capable, confident, and discriminating. Appears refined, gracious, and tasteful. Strives to be cultured, polished, and respected for quality, not quantity, of possessions. Aims to be unruffled, perfect, and wise. Needs expertise/education to soften fears of loneliness/poverty/insecurity. Through raising life-style standards for others, personal influence will endure.

PERSONALITY EXTREME: Too superficial, or too depressed.

MURRAY (Celtic/English)—M.

MAJOR TALENT: Ability to incorporate mature, compassionate, helpful nature into career. Is uplifting, creative, and geared to quality of skill/performance. Has engaging personality, resourcefulness, and quiet authority. Combines inspiring, teaching, and working to share emotional understanding/artistic perceptions/problem-solving talents. Assumes protective/responsible attitude to everyone and may go on overload to lose personal emotional control. Must guard against temper tantrums. Musician, physician, and social worker are possible career opportunities.

PERSONALITY INGREDIENTS: Inwardly traditional, practical, and down-to-earth. Wants respectability, dignity, and to work for tangible results. Appears youthfully enthusiastic, reserved, and tasteful. Strives to raise the quality of universal expectation. Aims to originate concepts that inspire unconventional thinking, eliminate the mundane, and bring about spiritual changes. Is a dreamer and may seem to be "out of this world" at times. Best in group/partnership, nonmaterialistic, and subduing high-strung energy. May leave a lasting image.

PERSONALITY EXTREME: Too skeptical, or too gullible.

MYRA (Latin: Mira/English)—F.

MAJOR TALENT: Ability to incorporate communications gifts, imagination, and individuality into career. Is kind, charming, and optimistic. Has sensitivity to fine points, love of people/animals/children, and creative self-expression. Combines originality/leadership, adaptability, and talent for bringing inspirations to form. Writer, model, and surgeon are possible career opportunities.

PERSONALITY INGREDIENTS: Inwardly self-reliant, efficient, and materially aware. Wants wealth, power, and prestige. Appears traditional, neat, and dignified. Strives to be respectable, secure, and down-to-earth. Should get financial rewards through artistic/creative avenues.

PERSONALITY EXTREME: Too selfish, or too unworthy.

MYRNA (Celtic: Morna/English)—F.

MAJOR TALENT: Ability to incorporate material awareness, excutive diplomacy, and attraction to service businesses into career. Is efficient, self-reliant, and sensitive to details. Has love of luxury/showmanship/music, sympathetic nature, and businesslike instincts. Combines administrative organization, devotion to commitments, and wheeling and dealing. Stage manager, bank loan officer, and cashier are possible career opportunities.

PERSONALITY INGREDIENTS: Appears understanding, youthful, and noble. Strives to be helpful, empathetic, and broad-scoped. Is magnetic, philosophical and romantic. Inwardly wants material power, admiration,

and a position of control. Wants to enjoy the things/freedoms that money
can buy. Appears confident, but at best when not inflicting the strain of
personal challenges upon self.

PERSONALITY EXTREME: Too aggressive, or too passive.

MYRON (Greek/English)—M.

MAJOR TALENT: Ability to incorporate common sense, practical work,
and determination into career. Is honest, competitive, and enduring. Has
logic, communications gifts, and imagination. Combines self-discipline,
traditional expectations, and material results. Administrator, accountant, and skilled laborer are possible career opportunities.

PERSONALITY INGREDIENTS: Appears empathetic, classic, and gracious. Strives to be broad-scoped, philosophical, and humanitarian.
Aims to reach a wide marketplace, bring quality of skill/performance to
others, and serve worthwhile causes. Inwardly a solid citizen. Wants
order, system, and thoroughness. Is unpretentious, mental, and hides
deep emotions. Must avoid becoming a workaholic.

PERSONALITY EXTREME: Too experimental, or too cautious.

MYRTLE (Latin/English)—F.

MAJOR TALENT: Ability to incorporate wide-ranged, structured, skillful
creative self-expression into career. Is artistically inspired, imaginative,
and tuned to beauty/charm/fashion. Has kind/romantic/cheerful instincts, traditional approach, and knack of handling broad commitments.
Combines versatility, resourcefulness, and attention-getting personality.
Plastic surgeon, lawyer, and theatrical producer are possible career opportunities.

PERSONALITY INGREDIENTS: Appears magnetic, youthful, and classic.
Strives to be philosophical, tolerant, and empathetic. Aims for humanitarian service, quality performance, and to attain idealistic goals. Inwardly
pleasure-seeking, humorous, and entertaining. Wants to forget unpleasant happenings and go on to brighter thoughts/experiences. Feels loving,
generous, and dramatic. Inspires, raises standards, and attracts admiration.

PERSONALITY EXTREME: Too sensual, or too mental.

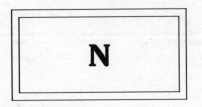

N

All names that begin with the letter *N* have the *Strong Point* of unconventional attitude—vivid imagination—stimulating communications—sensual/mental curiosity.

NADINE (Slavic: Nada/French/English)—F.

MAJOR TALENT: Ability to incorporate visionary ideas, spontaneous enthusiasms, and polished skill/performance into career. Is imaginative, attentive to details, and exotic/mysterious/avant garde. Has refinement, broad scope, and cosmopolitan ambitions. Combines empathetic service, keen observation, and a feeling of being "above the masses." Beauty/fashion design, social reform, and photography/TV/tape recording/data processing are possible career opportunities.

PERSONALITY INGREDIENTS: Inwardly "rooted," protective, and strong willed. Wants family/community attainments, gracious living, and respectability. Appears adventurous, striking, and progressive. Strives to be unencumbered, versatile, and changeable. Aims for current styles, stimulating relationships, and physical pleasure. At best when decisive, practical, and balancing self-indulgences.

PERSONALITY EXTREME: Too enthusiastic, or too long-suffering.

NANCY (Hebrew: Ann-Hannah; variable/English)—F.

MAJOR TALENT: Ability to incorporate writing in particular, but all forms of imaginative communications into career. Is inventive, sensitive to fine points, and clever. Has attractive/attention-getting/upbeat personality, and active social interests. Combines orderliness, pioneering ideas, and gift of putting thoughts to tangible results. Reporter, cosmetician, and any unconfining and self-expressive business/profession are possible career opportunities.

PERSONALITY INGREDIENTS: Inwardly mentally organized, efficient, and managerial. Wants the time/luxuries/influence that money or a powerful position can furnish. Appears to be traditional, dignified, and tasteful. Strives for security, conventional standards, and properness. Aims to be dependable, practical, and on a straight course. Attracts all needs and desires when optimistic, friendly, and self-confident. Must avoid moodiness/melancholy, and aloofness.

PERSONALITY EXTREME: Too questioning, or too gullible.

NANETTE (Hebrew: Ann-Hannah/French/English)—F.

MAJOR TALENT: Ability to incorporate mental analysis, exacting nature, and understanding of people into career. Is refined, curious, and adventurous. Has diplomacy, sharp powers of observation, and knack of learning by doing. Combines cooperative spirit, enthusiasm, and introspective questioning/study to elevate intellect. Researcher, detective, and photographer are possible career opportunities.

PERSONALITY INGREDIENTS: Inwardly "out of this world." Wants fast pace, inventive reforms, and peer relationships. Feels special and promotes idealistic purposes. Appears to be striking, engaging, and alert. Strives to be noticed, different, and changing. Wants constant activity, progress, and physical experiences. Keeps childhood memories for reference and should remember that attitudes should change with the times. Must avoid hyperactivity, impracticality, and impatience.
PERSONALITY EXTREME: Too impulsive, or too careful.

NAOMI (Hebrew/English)—F.
MAJOR TALENT: Ability to incorporate logic, emotional detachment, and instinct for perfection into career. Is analytic, questioning, and reserved. Has detailed perceptions, clever adaptability, and understanding of human foibles. Combines diplomacy, need for adventure, and studied opinions. Librarian, school administrator, and psychoanalyst are possible career opportunities.
PERSONALITY INGREDIENTS: Seems noble, romantic, and ageless. Strives to be empathetic, broad-scoped, and tolerant. Aims for poise, quality of skill/performance, and to reach a wide range of life. Inwardly aloof, secretive, and pensive. Wants natural beauty, privacy, and stimulating cultural interests. Has difficulty establishing career priorities. Practicality conflicts with wanderlust. Best when educated/technically expert.
PERSONALITY EXTREME: Too emotional, or too dispassionate.

NAT (Hebrew: Nathan; diminutive, M./Latin: Natalie; diminutive F.)—F. & M.
MAJOR TALENT: Ability to incorporate organized, efficient, decisive mental approach into career. Is self-reliant, sharp, and administrative. Has practicality, discrimination, and control. Combines strength, determination, and desire for material success. Band leader, corporation lawyer, and financial advisor are possible career opportunities.
PERSONALITY INGREDIENTS: Inwardly independent, aggressive, and pioneering. Wants to create, initiate, and lead. Appears calm, poised, and reserved. Strives to be investigative, analytic, and perfect. Attracts commercial interests. May be a bookie or a banker. Must avoid intolerance, materialism, and personalizing everything.
PERSONALITY EXTREME: Too inoffensive, or too critical.

NATACHA (Latin: Natalie/Russian: Natasha/English)—F.
MAJOR TALENT: Ability to incorporate up-to-date ideas, artistic/sensitive self-expression, and individuality into career. Is kind to animals/children, optimistic, and tuned to beauty/youthful pleasures/variety. Has desire for nonroutine scheduling, pioneering spirit, and gift of bringing imagery to form. Combines ambition, adaptability, and need for attention. Entertainer, decorator, and welfare/social organizer are possible career opportunities.
PERSONALITY INGREDIENTS: Appears magnetic, understanding, and classically neat. Strives for tolerance, humanitarian consciousness, and broad-scoped/skillful/romantic life-style. Inwardly makes the best of everything. Wants love, laughter, and entertaining relationships. Attracts success.
PERSONALITY EXTREME: Too independent, or too accommodating.

NATALIE (Latin/French/English)—F.

MAJOR TALENT: Ability to incorporate sensitivity to details, protective responsible service, and efficient/organized/practical approach into career. Is geared to executive judgment, delegating, and accountability. Has self-reliance, sociability, and showmanship. Combines domestic/business/personal comforts focus, determination, and zealousness. Interior decorator, retailer, and athletic coach are possible career opportunities.

PERSONALITY INGREDIENTS: Has self-doubt. Inwardly wants authority, cultural prominence, and natural/timeless good taste/beauty. Feels logical, analytic, and confidential. Needs quality, but does not feel deserving unless educated/expert/prepositioned by job/marriage. Appears independent, energetic, and nonconforming. Strives for progress, free expression, and to be a trend setter. Has firm opinions, and should not judge by appearances, or be overly critical in group/partnership activities.

PERSONALITY EXTREME: Too self-indulgent, or too adaptable.

NATHAN (Hebrew: Nathaniel; diminutive/English: independent)—M.

MAJOR TALENT: Ability to incorporate visionary ideas, planning, hard work, and tangible conclusions into career. Is spiritual, humanitarian, and materially powerful. Has strong beliefs, determination, and endurance. Combines sensitivity to details, executive diplomacy, and potential to leave a lasting impression. Building trades comptrolling, quality manufacturing, and theatrical production are possible career opportunities.

PERSONALITY INGREDIENTS: Inwardly shy, refined, and peace loving. Wants cooperative ventures, companionship, and easygoing approach. Appears subdued, retiring, and supportive. Strives to be agreeable, considerate, and patient. Attracts broad scope, must be decisive, and aim for large long-term results.

PERSONALITY EXTREME: Too speculative, or too cautious.

NATHANIEL (Hebrew/French/English)—M.

MAJOR TALENT: Ability to incorporate creative artistry, self-expression, and the importance of words into career. Is philosophical, broad scoped, and romantic. Has fashionable ideas, optimism, and love of beauty/humor/pleasure. Combines empathetic service, idealistic sense of justice, and fantasies of being the "knight in shining armor." Writer, organizer, and post office manager are possible career opportunities.

PERSONALITY INGREDIENTS: Inwardly quiet, pensive, and striving for perfection. Wants privacy, quality, and natural environments. Feels questioning, secretive, and logical. First impression is engaging, adventurous, and sexy. Strives to be open minded, progressive, and nonroutine. Aims to be free to taste/touch/feel/hear/see all that life has to offer. "Everyone loves a lover," and this name needs only to give love to receive the same.

PERSONALITY EXTREME: Too talkative, or too antisocial.

NEAL (Irish/English)—M.

MAJOR TALENT: Ability to incorporate instinct for spontaneous change, action, and adventure into career. Is sensual, curious, and flexible. Has initiative, common sense, and traditional values. Combines independence, determination, and desire to strike out to touch the rainbow. Advertising, theater, and navigation are possible career opportunities.

PERSONALITY INGREDIENTS: Inwardly domestic/"rooted," sympathetic, and protective. Wants mature/stable relationships, gracious living and music/beauty/material attainments. Appears to be businesslike, self-reliant, and managerial. Strives for influence, affluence, and recognition. Aims to be free and assumes responsibilities.

PERSONALITY EXTREME: Too amused, or too serious.

NED (Anglo-Saxon: Edward; diminutive/English)—M.

MAJOR TALENT: Ability to incorporate progressive ideas, adaptability, and learning from experience into career. Is experimental, adaptable, and understanding. Has gambler's instinct, sociability, and wanderlust. Combines self-assertion, discipline, and a need to be different. Reporter, detective, and politician are possible career opportunities.

PERSONALITY INGREDIENTS: Requires varied interests and experiences for inner growth. Feels probing, clever, and is drained of enthusiasm/vigor by monotony. First impression is classic, magnetic, and tolerant. Strives to achieve quality, serve worthwhile causes, and complete commitments. May be temperamental, speculative, and too impulsive. Must avoid self-indulgence, irresponsibility, and extravagant gestures.

PERSONALITY EXTREME: Too proper, or too unstructured.

NEIL (Irish: Neal/English)—M.

MAJOR TALENT: Ability to incorporate farsighted ideas, planning, and work into career. Is structured, sensitive to details, and determined. Has power to build for humanitarian or material purposes. Combines rhythm of cooperation, personal refinement, and nervous practical energy. Piano player, legislator, and stage manager are possible career opportunities.

PERSONALITY INGREDIENTS: First impression is efficient, controlled, and as affluent as possible. Strives for prestige, executive leadership, and financial freedom. Inwardly impulsive, unusually understanding, and temperamental. Wants activity, new challenges, and nonroutine days. Has workaholic approach to everything, and must not "burn the candle at both ends."

PERSONALITY EXTREME: Too optimistic, or too depressed.

NELL (Greek: Helen/Irish: diminutive-variable/English)—F.

MAJOR TALENT: Ability to incorporate need and appreciation for perfection into career. Is analytic, clever, and poised. Has polished tastes, individuality, and domestic/luxurious/artistic focus. Combines ambition, firm ideals, and intellectual observation. May not use practical judgment. Appraiser, librarian, and florist are possible career opportunities.

PERSONALITY INGREDIENTS: First impression is enthusiastic, mystical, and reserved. Strives to be above the masses, inventive, and decisive. Inwardly tempestuous, opportunistic, and adventurous. Wants challenges, excitement, and nonroutine activities. Enjoys authority, travel, and new experiences. Needs to come down to earth.

PERSONALITY EXTREME: Too noticeable, or too understated.

NELLIE (Greek: Helen/Irish: diminutive-variable/English)—F.

MAJOR TALENT: Ability to incorporate skilled and broad-scoped communications techniques into career. Is versatile, resourceful, and optimistic. Has traditional approach, appreciation for structured procedures, and abundant creative/artistic self-expressive opportunities. Combines humanitarian instincts, universal appeal, and attractive personality. Plastic surgeon, charity fund raiser/party organizer, and high fashion designer are possible career opportunities.

PERSONALITY INGREDIENTS: Wants independent, pioneering, and controlling leadership. Feels forceful, alone, and aggressive. Needs to be willing to "fight city hall" for unique desires. Appears enthusiastic, avant garde, and reserved. Strives to be "above the crowd" and to uplift the quality of expectation for others. May be too unmaterialistic, but attracts supporters and recognition.

PERSONALITY EXTREME: Too changeable, or too enduring.

NELSON (Irish: "Neal's son"/Greek: Cornelius; variable)—M.

MAJOR TALENT: Ability to incorporate research, logic, and intellectual analysis into career. Is adventurous, attentive to fine points, and diplomatic. Has reserve, polished tastes, and desire for authority/expertise/education. Combines observation, quality/perfection, and instinct for collecting everything. Librarian, editor, and antiques dealer are possible career opportunities.

PERSONALITY INGREDIENTS: Inwardly decisive, inventive, and emotionally idealistic. Wants to improve the world and uplift men's minds and souls. Inspires, and supports unusual causes. Appears engaging, sexy, and nonjudgmental. Strives to be progressive, unrepressed, and noticeable. Aims for clever, stimulating, changing experiences, and not to miss a trick. Emotionally unsettling childhood memories are unrelenting. At best when focused upon "today."

PERSONALITY EXTREME: Too physical, or too mental.

NERO (Italian)—M.

MAJOR TALENT: Ability to incorporate detailed, perceptive, unemotional analysis into career. Is aloof, calm, and introspective. Has quality taste, quantity of curiosity, and introverted feelings. Combines questioning intellect, researcher's approach, and spontaneously combustible nature. Is personalized, impetuous, and strategic. Detective, photographer, and college professor are possible career opportunities.

PERSONALITY INGREDIENTS: Wants a haven where the unvarnished, ordinary, earthy folks never enter. Strives for adventure, unrestricted activity, and timeless/natural beauty. Is observant/decisive/visionary, seizes challenges, and clashes with "no holds barred." Takes responsibility/protective instincts too seriously and may crash emotionally. May be torn between serving humanitarian uplift, and self-indulgences.

PERSONALITY EXTREME: Too suspicious, or too trusting.

NETTA (Latin: Natalie/English; variable)—F.

MAJOR TALENT: Ability to incorporate parental approach, sympathetic service, and individuality into career. Is protective, responsible, and instructional. Has companionable, creatively expressive, luxury-loving nature. Combines pioneering spirit, art/music/decorating, and knack of solving problems for others. Marriage counselor, teacher, and lawyer are possible career opportunities.

PERSONALITY INGREDIENTS: Seems compassionate, romantic, and

broad scoped. Strives to be philosophical, cosmopolitan, and conscious of quality/skill/completeness. Inwardly feels personal concern for everyone, gets involved, and may not be appreciated, or may be praised as a saint. Needs to determine what is "helpfulness," and what is "meddling." May be torn between self-interests and service to others. Needs a sense of humor.

PERSONALITY EXTREME: Too assertive, or too passive.

NEVIL (Latin/English)—M.

MAJOR TALENT: Ability to incorporate businesslike attitude, sensitivity to details, and showmanship into career. Is responsible, protective, and sympathetic. Has knack of guiding group activities to learning, sharing, and problem solving. Combines artistic/musical/self-expressive nature, material growth, and conscientiousness. Teacher, actor, and marriage counselor are possible career opportunities.

PERSONALITY INGREDIENTS: Appears friendly, attention-getting, and up-to-date. Strives to be kind, popular, and entertaining. Enjoys wit, beauty, and light hearted pleasures. Inwardly speculative, nonconforming, and changeable. Wants freedom, travel, and life experience. Learns by doing and absorbs knowledge. Seems self-assured, even in times of insecurity. Can be magnetic, athletically superior, and a workaholic. Succeeds when temperament is controlled.

PERSONALITY EXTREME: Too "on stage," or too depressed.

NICODEMUS (Greek/English)—M.

MAJOR TALENT: Ability to incorporate practical methods, attitudes, and investments into career. Is dignified, orderly, and economically/statistically analytic. Has understanding, consideration, and integrity. Combines steadfast work, intuitional research, and determination. Architectural engineer, military officer, and economist are possible career opportunities.

PERSONALITY INGREDIENTS: Inwardly curious, experimental, and mentally progressive. Wants changing pace, sensual stimulation, and speculation. Appears efficient, controlled, and businesslike. Strives to be materially successful, influential, and recognized. May take on too many projects and diversify interests. Best when optimistic, structured, and disciplined.

PERSONALITY EXTREME: Too individualistic, or too imitative.

NICHOLAS (Greek/English)—M.

MAJOR TALENT: Ability to incorporate top quality, imaginative, parental approach into career. Is protective, charming, and optimistic. Has persistence, firm ideals, and romantic notions. Combines broad philosophy, creative artistry, and wide-ranged responsibility. Welfare worker, thespian, and public defender are possible career opportunities.

PERSONALITY INGREDIENTS: Inwardly too aloof, perfecting, and unrealistic. Expects integrity, good taste, and timelessness. Courts disappointment until imagination comes down to earth. Appears to be retiring, supportive, and subdued. Strives to be diplomatic, easygoing, and decisive. Introspective analysis and desire to be equitable often put actions in limbo. At best when able to accept failure or imperfect solutions and adapt new goals to circumstances. Must be known to be understood.

PERSONALITY EXTREME: Too stubborn, or too unresisting.

NICOLA (Greek/Italian/English)—F.

MAJOR TALENT: Ability to incorporate broad-scoped philosophy, compassion, and quality of skill/artistry into career. Is detail conscious, mentally analytic, and introspective. Has nobility, grace, and generosity. Combines adaptability, appreciation of timeless/natural beauty, and selfless service. Doctor, publisher, landscape gardener are possible career opportunities.

PERSONALITY INGREDIENTS: Strives to inspire, enthuse, and convince others to rise above mass market expectations. Appears refined, modest, shy until personal ideals come into play. Inwardly expects perfection and attracts disappointment. Wants a world without vulgarity and earthiness. At best when educated/expert and bolstered by sense of authority. Should avoid criticisms and indecisive time wasting. Must learn to accept mistakes as a learning experience, not as a judgment of imperfection.

PERSONALITY EXTREME: Too aggressive, or too defensive.

NIGEL (Latin/Scottish/English)—M.

MAJOR TALENT: Ability to incorporate supportive approach, highminded ideals, and quality consciousness into career. Is attentive to fine points, refined, and considerate. Has charm, vision, and individualistic personality. Combines diplomacy, expansive philosophy, and ambition to commercialize upon inventive inspirations. Film maker, beauty specialist, and publicist are possible career opportunities.

PERSONALITY INGREDIENTS: Appears dignified, comforting, and comfortable. Strives to serve, educate, and uplift others. Aims for domestic harmony, gracious living, and creative self-expression. Inwardly adventurous, sensual, and unconventional. Wants travel, change, and challenges. Is above the crowd, impulsive, and strong willed. At best when sure of goals.

PERSONALITY EXTREME: Too talkative, or too unsociable.

NILES (Greek: Nocholas/Finnish/Irish: Neal; variable)—M.

MAJOR TALENT: Ability to incorporate inspirational ideas, adaptability, and a knack with words into career. Is versatile, artistically expressive, and up-to-date. Has engaging manner, optimism, and patience. Combines nonconforming approach, progressive feelings, and unstructured/free thinking. Advertising, politics, and theater are possible career opportunities.

PERSONALITY INGREDIENTS: Attracts attention, supporters, and causes/people in need of help. Feels experimental, speculative, and individualistic. Wants to try everything, pioneer, and gain wholesale attention. Appears noble, classic, and understanding. Strives to provide skill/quality, learn by doing, and never miss a trick.

PERSONALITY EXTREME: Too independent, or too accommodating.

NINA (Spanish/Hebrew: Anne; diminutive/English)—F.

MAJOR TALENT: Ability to incorporate tact, orderliness, and subtle control into career. Is friendly, unassuming, and gentle. Has detail analysis, receptive nature, and strength as "the power behind the throne." Combines gifts for rhythm/music/dance, pleasure in partnership, and need for peaceful relationships/environments. Private secretary, accountant, and collector are possible career opportunities.

PERSONALITY INGREDIENTS: Wants to be independent, free, and progressive. Aims for creative, solitary, futuristic self-expression of leadership. Dislikes being told how to do anything and needs praise for original ideas. Feels daring, different, and nonconforming. Best working autonomously as a "vice president" with authority to make decisions.

PERSONALITY EXTREME: Too courageous, or too fearful.

NITA (Hebrew: Ann-Hannah; variable/Spanish/English)—F.

MAJOR TALENT: Ability to incorporate businesslike approach, individuality, and intellectual/spiritual nature into career. Is self-reliant, managerial, and materially aware. Has discrimination, executive diplomacy, and organizational efficiency. Combines daring, quality consciousness, and commercial ambition. Financial analyst, engineer, and merchant are possible career opportunities.

PERSONALITY INGREDIENTS: Appears sympathetic, tasteful, and dignified. Strives to be instructional, artistically/musically self-expressive, and domestically harmonious. Aims for gracious living. Inwardly impractical. Feels inspired to improve upon general tastes/expectations, and may seem to be "out of this world." Needs peer stimulation, realization of personal ideals, and supporters for inventive/spontaneous enthusiasms. Best with feet on the ground.

PERSONALITY EXTREME: Too impatient, or too unassertive.

NOAH (Hebrew/English)—M.

MAJOR TALENT: Ability to incorporate arbitration, advantageous partnerships, and diplomatic approach into career. Is adaptable, gentle, and easygoing. Has refinement, orderliness, and love of peace. Combines instinct for being the "power behind the throne," subtle controlling ambition, and cooperative spirit. Assistant director, member of orchestra, and bookkeeper are possible career opportunities.

PERSONALITY INGREDIENTS: Inwardly questioning, calm, and serious. Wants timeless/natural beauty, privacy, and quality/perfection in everything. Appears to be sensible, conventional, and neat. Strives for practical solutions, respectable life-style, and to work for rewards. Aims to "do the right thing." Must be positive, confident, and decisive to achieve potential.

PERSONALITY EXTREME: Too materialistic, or too altruistic.

NOAMI (Arabic/English: Naomi; variation)—F.

MAJOR TALENT: Ability to incorporate mental questioning and emotionally detached approach into career. Is sensitive to fine points, adaptable, and collecting. Has diplomacy, refinement, and understanding. Combines tolerance, gentleness, and need for education/technical expertise. Photographer, researcher, and auditor are possible career opportunities.

PERSONALITY INGREDIENTS: First impression is individualistic. Strives to be inventive, forceful, and a winner. Inwardly sympathetic, instructional, and domestic. Wants family/community harmony, gracious lifestyle, and respectability. Enjoys travel, but needs "roots."

PERSONALITY EXTREME: Too empathetic, or too uninvolved.

NOBLE (Latin/English)—M.

MAJOR TALENT: Ability to incorporate fortunate results when bringing an inspiration to form, creative self-expression, and resourcefulness into career. Is optimistic, independent, and original. Has charm, love of people/animals/children, and flair for entertainment. Combines attention-getting manner, up-to-date approach, and a gift with words. Writer, lawyer, and organizer are possible career opportunities.

PERSONALITY INGREDIENTS: Has spontaneous enthusiasms to change/raise concepts. Is conscious of what tomorrow will bring. Appears different, independent, and energetic. Strives to originate, promote, and lead. May be commercially impractical, but attracts boosters, progressive changes, and rewards. Needs patience, emotional detachment, and to learn from mistakes.

PERSONALITY EXTREME: Too impulsive, or too habitual.

NOEL (Latin/English)—F. & M.

MAJOR TALENT: Ability to incorporate initiative, originality, and broad-scoped ideas into career. Is instigative, driving, and on the move. Has willpower, humanitarian focus, and a need to be different. Combines fast action, inner faith, and creativity. Editor, salesperson, and pilot are possible career opportunities.

PERSONALITY INGREDIENTS: Appears businesslike, efficient, and managerial. Strives for establishment power, material possessions, and influential position. Inwardly high strung, ambitious, and feeling above the masses. Wants to lead inspirational movements and bring personal ideals to others' attention. Can sell any true belief. Happiest in commerce and respected for unique approach.

PERSONALITY EXTREME: Too sociable, or too reclusive.

NOELLE (Latin/French/English)—F.

MAJOR TALENT: Ability to incorporate empathetic service, magnetism, and drive for top quality skill/performance into career. Is generous, sensitive, and adaptable. Has investigative, logical, meditative instincts. Combines cooperative spirit, tolerance, and broad-scoped philosophy. Welfare worker, physician, and decorator are possible career opportunities.

PERSONALITY INGREDIENTS: Should concentrate on practicality. Has a lot to give and needs education/expertise/area of authority to feel confident. Inwardly a perfectionist and, without concentration of interest, may attract disappointment or self-depreciation. Appears retiring, subdued, and refined. Aims to lead personal ideals to glory and may forget that everything costs money.

PERSONALITY EXTREME: Too changeable, or too loyal.

NOLA (Celtic/Latin: Olivia; diminutive)—F.

MAJOR TALENT: Ability to incorporate responsibility, sympathy, and protection into career. Is instructional, assuming, and concerned. Has artistic/musical gifts, showmanship, and parental instincts. Combines individuality, mental activity, and strong will. Teacher, nurse, and receptionist are possible career opportunities.

PERSONALITY INGREDIENTS: Inwardly calm, logical, and clever. Wants natural beauty, privacy, and timeless values. Appears direct, efficient, and as affluent as possible. Strives to be businesslike, delegating, and prosperous. May be torn between family and commercial interests. Needs group support and time for introspection.

PERSONALITY EXTREME: Too impatient, or too unaggressive.

NOLAN (Celtic/Latin: Noble/English)—M.

MAJOR TALENT: Ability to incorporate visionary ideas, high energy, and attention to details into career. Is a collector, critic, and leader. Has refinement, cooperative spirit, and friendliness. Combines individuality, ambition, and potential to leave a lasting image. TV/film worker, private secretary, and actor/musician/dancer are possible career opportunities.

PERSONALITY INGREDIENTS: Inwardly logical, analytic, and investigative. Wants quiet, privacy, and natural/timeless beauty. Appears conventional, dignified, and sturdy. Strives to be materially secure, structured, and a solid citizen. Needs intellectual stimulation and aims for practical results. Best when on a concentrated course.

PERSONALITY EXTREME: Too experimental, or too skittish.

NORA (Greek: Helen-Eleanor-Honoria; variable-diminutive/independent)—F.

MAJOR TALENT: Ability to incorporate creativity, self-expression, and a knack with words into career. Is kind, restless, and attention-getting. Has charm, humor, and optimism. Combines independence, sensitivity to fine points, and resourcefulness. Writer, entertainer, and salesperson are possible career opportunities.

PERSONALITY INGREDIENTS: Appears enthusiastic, engaging, and energetic. Strives to be open minded, progressive, and sensually knowledgeable. Aims for travel, adventure, and must learn by experience. Inwardly reserved, introspective, and analytic. Wants quality, privacy, and timeless treasures. Inwardly aloof and seems to be ready for anything.

PERSONALITY EXTREME: Too rebellious, or too obedient.

NORAH (Greek: Helen-Eleanor-Honoria; variable-diminutive/independent)—F.

MAJOR TALENT: Ability to incorporate sensitivity, cooperation, and fast-paced original ideas into career. Is charming, philosophical, and compassionate. Has nervous energy, spontaneous enthusiasms, and desire for recognition. Combines visionary concepts, spark from peer stimulation, and potential to change another's way of thinking. Social worker, lawyer, and political reformer are possible career opportunities.

PERSONALITY INGREDIENTS: Appears custom designed and works for the best of everything. Inwardly needs timeless beauty, privacy, and intellectual stimulation. Strives to be strong, disciplined, and structured. Seeks polished life-style and is down-to-earth. Has potential to leave lasting influence. At best when intuitive.

PERSONALITY EXTREME: Too businesslike, or too uncommercial.

NORBERT (Teutonic/English)—M.

MAJOR TALENT: Ability to incorporate inventive concepts, eye for beauty, and businesslike instincts into career. Is sensitive to details, cooperative, and tactful. Has adaptability, communications gifts, and modesty. Combines partnership, originality, and enthusiasm for sharing personal ideals. Interior decorator, diplomat, and literary critic are possible career opportunities.

PERSONALITY INGREDIENTS: Inwardly conventional, practical, and hard working. Wants to be a solid citizen. First impression is calm, refined, and pensive. Strives to be cultured, investigative, and perfect. Aims for aristocratic attainments and is comfortable with down-to-earth values. Is extremely perceptive.

PERSONALITY EXTREME: Too discontent, or too agreeable.

NORINE (English: Norah; variable)—F.

MAJOR TALENT: Ability to incorporate sociable personality, empathetic service, and creative self-expression into career. Is romantic, versatile, and idealistic. Has sense of universal love and a desire to help, entertain, and uplift others. Combines striving for quality work, communications techniques, and philosophical nature. Doctor, minister, and thespian are possible career opportunities.

PERSONALITY INGREDIENTS: Inwardly modest, retiring, and easygoing. Wants peace, partnership/mate, and gentleness. Appears nonconforming, direct, and original. Strives to be independent, assertive, and a pacesetter. Should enjoy travel, humor, and relaxation.

PERSONALITY EXTREME: Too sensual, or too unresponsive.

NORMA (Latin/Italian/English)—F.

MAJOR TALENT: Ability to incorporate dignity, self-control, and fine mind into career. Is analytic, probing, and culturally ambitious. Has secretive nature, poise, and desire for quality in everything. Combines sensitivity to fine points, confidence, and recognition/contentment through education. Opera singer, photographer, and librarian are possible career opportunities.

PERSONALITY INGREDIENTS: First impression is inviting, understanding, and classic. Strives to be tolerant, broad scoped, and entertaining/serving. Aims for a broad range of interests, travel, and to inspire others. Inwardly wants privacy, quiet, and thinking/study time. Fears loneliness and poverty but requires solitude. Maturity brings concentrated work that provides companionship and displaces fears.

PERSONALITY EXTREME: Too individualistic, or too conforming.

NORMAN (Scandinavian/English)—M.

MAJOR TALENT: Ability to incorporate structure and a broad philosophy into communications career. Is creatively expressive, gifted, and resourceful. Has love of animals/children/beauty/pleasure/humor/art/music/entertainment/. . . people. Combines restlessness, optimism, and convenient memory. Remembers happiness and forgets unpleasantness. Writer, interior decorator, and organizer are possible career opportunities.

PERSONALITY INGREDIENTS: Inwardly investigative, quality conscious, and analytic. Wants cultural/educational attainments, timeless values, and natural environments. Aims to have privacy, quiet, and mental freedom. Appears different, energetic, and understanding. Strives to be enthusiastic, adventurous, and sensually stimulated. Enjoys travel, activity, and challenges. Has guts, secretiveness, and good luck through social contacts.

PERSONALITY EXTREME: Too self-indulgent, or too thoughtful.

NORRIS (Teutonic/Scandinavian/English)—F. & M.

MAJOR TALENT: Ability to incorporate artistic, generous, resourceful personality into career. Is clever, versatile, and broad scoped. Has entertaining, noble, optimistic outlook. Combines unflinching service, humanitarian instincts, and attention to and from people. Art patron, fashion/cosmetics designer, and journalist are possible career opportunities.

PERSONALITY INGREDIENTS: Inwardly domestically ambitious. Aims for possessions, education, and to instigate/maintain traditions. Wants luxury, dignity, and harmony. First impression is tasteful, concerned, and comfortable. Strives to be a stabilizing influence, responsible, and protective. Attracts love, emotional burdens, and is a font of creative talents.

PERSONALITY EXTREME: Too unconforming, or too appeasing.

NORTON (Anglo-Saxon/English)—M.

MAJOR TALENT: Ability to incorporate creative self-expression, community responsibility, and problem-solving instincts into career. Is sympathetic, conscientious, and firmly opinionated. Has dependable, protective, steadfast nature. Combines showmanship, resourcefulness, and active energy to raise or introduce life-support improvements for family/community. Is parental and will try to improve life-style for everyone. Credit union organizer, politician, and home improvement salesperson are possible career opportunities.

PERSONALITY INGREDIENTS: Has unique philosophy, and is a nonaggressive rebel. Wants love, kindness, and pleasure. Attracts boosters and disciples. Appears friendly, up-to-date, and cheery. Strives to originate, inspire, and formulate. Assumes or is given idealistic purposes, helps those less fortunate, and attracts financial security/prestige/happiness through social contact.

PERSONALITY EXTREME: Too speculative, or too investigative.

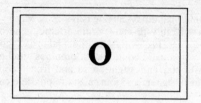

O

All names that begin with the letter *O* have the *Strong Point* of family focus—problem solving—showmanship—emotional response—firm opinions.

OCTAVIA (Latin/German/Spanish/English)—F.
MAJOR TALENT: Ability to incorporate mental efficiency, detail consciousness, and strong personal ideals into career. Is practical, organized, and managerial. Has strength, balance, and confidence. Combines physical focus, material ambition, and communications gifts. Band leader, insurance broker, and athlete are possible career opportunities.
PERSONALITY INGREDIENTS: First impression is understanding, noble, and audience catching. Strives to be tolerant, wide ranged, and to reach out to serve/entertain. Aims for philosophical humor, quality of skill/performance, and humanitarian interests. Inwardly self-improving, independent, and courageous. Wants power, challenges, and executive control. Must avoid impatience, impulsiveness, and gambling.
PERSONALITY EXTREME: Too independent, or too conforming.

OCTAVIUS (Latin/English)—M.
MAJOR TALENT: Ability to incorporate inspirational ideas, uplift, and leadership into career. Is sensitive, perceptive, and individualistic. Has vitality, firm opinions, and futuristic vision. Combines material ambition, originality, and contagious enthusiasms. Film industries, politics, and designing are possible career opportunities.
PERSONALITY INGREDIENTS: Is a leader and will have to "walk alone." Strives to be first and is a rebel. Attracts competition, conservative opposition, and praise/criticism. Feels imaginative, energetic, and decisive. Should take the initiative and keep faith in concepts that introduce progressive changes.
PERSONALITY EXTREME: Too assertive, or too passive.

ODELIA (German/English)—F.
MAJOR TALENT: Ability to incorporate initiative, originality, and nonconforming approach into career. Is peace loving, adaptable, and businesslike. Has mental organization, cooperative spirit, and daring. Combines creative leadership, imagination, and aggressive/assertive/pacesetting instincts. Lawyer, business owner, and administrative manager are possible career opportunities.
PERSONALITY INGREDIENTS: Desires pleasure, fun, and variety. Wants beauty, kindness, and love. Appears aloof, reserved, and refined. Strives to be cultured, expert, and perfect. Aims to enjoy timeless treasures, aristocratic living, and educational advantages. Combines self-

expression and introspection. Must avoid scattering energy and concentrate to make dreams come true.

PERSONALITY EXTREME: Too impatient, or too tolerant.

OGDEN (Old English/English)—M.

MAJOR TALENT: Ability to incorporate artistic, spiritual, philosophical inspirations into career. Is culturally attaining, analytic, and attentive to fine points. Has generous, empathetic, charitable nature. Combines creative activities, good business judgment, and strength of character. Preacher, doctor, and parole officer are possible career opportunities.

PERSONALITY INGREDIENTS: Appears quiet, reserved, and introspective. Strives to be cultured, poised, and investigative. Aims for quality, privacy, and intellectual growth. Inwardly inventive, idealistic, and high powered. Wants to inspire loftier concepts in another's mind and lead the way to the realization of personal beliefs. Is an evangelist and may leave a lasting image.

PERSONALITY EXTREME: Too sensual, or celibate.

OLAF (Scandinavian/Latin: Oliver; variable)—M.

MAJOR TALENT: Ability to incorporate mental curiosity, research, and analysis into career. Is intuitional, individualistic, and pioneering. Has strong will, perseverance, and quality consciousness. Combines courage, showmanship, and authoritative nature. Best when educated. Mathematician, musical technician, and data processor are possible career opportunities.

PERSONALITY INGREDIENTS: Appears broad scoped, noble, and classic. Strives to serve worthy causes, show tolerance, and expand consciousness. Attracts people and feels empathy for all. Inwardly strategic, clever, and aloof. Wants solitude, natural beauty, and cultural stimulation. Courts disappointment through speculation and materialism. Best when enjoying work and attracting rewards and recognition.

PERSONALITY EXTREME: Too protective, or too irresponsible.

OLGA (Old Norse/Latin: Olivia; variable/German/Russian/English)—F.

MAJOR TALENT: Ability to incorporate mental organization, executive control, and creative ideas into career. Is strong, self-reliant, and efficient. Has practicality, investigative approach, and material ambitions. Combines persuasive communications techniques, competitive drives, and commercial interest. Banker, franchise owner, and corporate consultant are possible career opportunities.

PERSONALITY INGREDIENTS: Appears nonconforming, determined, and decisive. Strives to be an inventive, assertive, trend setter. Inwardly refined, discreet, and geared to natural/timeless beauty. Wants privacy, quiet, and the best of everything. Expects perfection, and aims to earn top dollar through original concepts, control of activity, and unique position. Must keep faith and avoid unprogressive stubbornness.

PERSONALITY EXTREME: Too alone, or too dependent.

OLIVE (Old Norse: Olga/Latin: "the olive"/English)—F.

MAJOR TALENT: Ability to incorporate empathetic service, tolerance, and sharp analytic perceptions into career. Is questioning, adaptable, and broad scoped. Has magnetism, creative artistry, and desire for top quality skill/production. Combines attraction to partnership, discretion/reserve, and humanitarian approach. Welfare worker, physician, and publisher are possible career opportunities.

PERSONALITY INGREDIENTS: Inwardly retiring, modest, and shy. Is motivated to keep the peace. Wants love, beauty, and easygoing pace. Appears aloof, pensive, and observant. Strives to be cultured, poised, and authoritative. Wants companionship, but may seem unapproachable. Has spurts of ambition, and must maintain down-to-earth attitude, and avoid trying to please everyone to achieve potential.

PERSONALITY EXTREME: Too spontaneous, or too preconceiving.

OLIVER (Latin/Old Norse: Olaf; variable/English)—M.

MAJOR TALENT: Ability to incorporate broad-scoped creative self-expression into career. Is romantic, articulate, and imaginative. Has optimism, charm, and magnetism for assuming responsibilities. Combines compassion, sense of justice, and empathetic service/entertainment aptitudes. General practictioner, public defender, and thespian/fine artist/inspired educator are possible career opportunities.

PERSONALITY INGREDIENTS: Best in noncommercial interests. Inwardly easygoing, sensitive, and accommodating. Wants love, peace, and companionship. Appears reserved, classy, and pensive. Strives for timeless beauty, intellectual/material perfection, and privacy to study/question/analyze. Should specialize and build authority to attain inner confidence. May be inspirational leader when decisive, logical, and up-to-date.

PERSONALITY EXTREME: Too philosophical, or too narrow-minded.

OLIVIA (Old Norse: Olga/Latin: "the olive"/German/Italian/English)—F.

MAJOR TALENT: Ability to incorporate unconventional, changeable, and stimulating concepts into career. Is gutsy, adventurous, and sociable. Has optimism, sensitivity to details, and adaptability. Combines free thinking, peace loving, and creatively expressive traits. Learns by doing and is very clever. Politician, entertainer, and advertising idea person are possible career opportunities.

PERSONALITY INGREDIENTS: First impression is influential, controlled, and as affluent as possible. Strives for material success, practicality, and recognition. Inwardly domestic/"rooted," instructional, and idealistic. Enjoys luxury, artistic/musical self-expression, and hospitable lifestyle. Is confident, gracious and attracts leadership.

PERSONALITY EXTREME: Too self-centered, or too accommodating.

OMAR (Arabic)—M.

MAJOR TALENT: Ability to incorporate fine detailed craftsmanship, modesty, and patience into career. Is considerate, gentle, and cooperative. Has difficulty seeing others suffer and settles disputes. Combines diplomacy, arbitration, and knack of letting silence bring rewards. Bookkeeper, group singer/dancer/musician, and psychologist are possible career opportunities.

PERSONALITY INGREDIENTS: Inwardly pensive, questioning, and analytic. Wants privacy, serenity, and "book learning." Appears conven-

tional, dignified, and sturdy. Strives to be a solid citizen. Feels quality
conscious and a bit above mass market tastes. Aims for material security
and practical goals, but requires intellectual stimulation. Must be known
to be understood.
PERSONALITY EXTREME: Too romantic, or too unemotional.

ONA (Latin: Una/English)—F.

MAJOR TALENT: Ability to incorporate gifts of communications, individuality, and creative self-expression into career. Is versatile, up-to-
date, and charming. Has optimism, stylist flair, and kindness. Combines
sensitivity to fine points, original ideas, and love of life. Writer, entertainer, and model are possible career opportunities.
PERSONALITY INGREDIENTS: Inwardly mental, analytic, and culturally
attaining. Wants privacy, calm environment, and timeless beauty. Feels
aristocratic, confidential, and quality conscious. Appears attention-
getting, friendly, and imaginative. Strives to be popular, affectionate,
and pleasure seeking. Inwardly serious and seems lighthearted. Must
avoid scattering interests.
PERSONALITY EXTREME: Too alone, or too dependent.

OPAL (Sanskrit/English)—F. & M.

MAJOR TALENT: Ability to incorporate efficiency, mental organization,
and executive judgment into career. Is self-reliant, delegating, and persuasive. Has drive, dependability, and material ambitions. Combines
initiative, investigation, and strength. Investment advisor, newspaper
administrator, and manufacturer are possible career opportunities.
PERSONALITY INGREDIENTS: Appears different, active, and decisive.
Strives to be competitive, controlling, and a pioneer. Inwardly mentally
questioning, quality conscious, and confidential. Wants privacy, quiet,
and refinement. Finds cultured, reserved, aristocratic people and environments comfortable. At best when educated or technically expert.
PERSONALITY EXTREME: Too talkative, or too unsociable.

OPHELIA (Greek/English)—F.

MAJOR TALENT: Ability to incorporate romantic, creatively expressive, restless nature into career. Is devoted to serving others. Offers
kindness, sympathy, and expansive justice-seeking approach to major
philosophical, artistic, or charitable projects. Aims to bring quality/skill,
inspiration, and the true meaning of "brotherly love" to a broad scope.
Combines optimism, appreciation of beauty, and a gift for attracting
supporters for humanitarian causes. Charity organizer, musician/artist/
actor, and journalist are possible career opportunities.
PERSONALITY INGREDIENTS: Inwardly modest, gentle, and sensitive.
Wants companionship, peace, and easygoing life-style. Appears nonconforming, active, and self-motivated. Strives to be original, progressive,
and decisive. Attracts happiness through generous loving soul, and must
avoid impracticality, sensuality, and stagnation.
PERSONALITY EXTREME: Too ambitious, or too weak.

OREN (Greek: Orien/English)—M.

MAJOR TALENT: Ability to incorporate introspective, analytic, and detail conscious nature into career. Is self-controlled, proud, and quality
conscious. Has dignity, refinement, and high intuition. Combines adapta-

bility, wanderlust, and mental concentration. Journalistic photographer, lawyer, and detective are possible career opportunities.

PERSONALITY INGREDIENTS: Appears unconventional, enthusiastic, and understanding. Strives to be free, progressive, and challenged. Inwardly idealistic, inventive, and mentally busy. Wants to creatively inspire, improve quality, and see both sides of an issue. May have "head in the clouds," but maintains intellect. Must focus upon structure, practicality, and avoid living in the past.

PERSONALITY EXTREME: Too sensual, or too mental.

ORIEL (Latin/English)—F.

MAJOR TALENT: Ability to incorporate inquisitive, understanding, adventurous nature into career. Is flexible, unconventional, and adaptable. Has nerve, sociability, and knack of learning by doing. Combines imagination, sensitivity to details, and confidence. Travel agent, lawyer, and politician are possible career opportunities.

PERSONALITY INGREDIENTS: Inwardly parental, instructional, and determined. Wants material comforts, family/community harmony, and respect. First impression is businesslike, dominant, and as expensively dressed as possible. Strives to be in control, wealthy, and powerful. Best on a nonroutine schedule and patiently persistent.

PERSONALITY EXTREME: Too fashionable, or too sloppy.

ORSON (Latin/English)—M.

MAJOR TALENT: Ability to incorporate broad-scoped imagination, inventiveness, and intellectual probing into career. Is detail conscious, personally sensitive, and inwardly questioning. Has creative self-expression, cleverness, and drive for quality/skill/completeness. Combines need to see both sides of an issue, logic, and empathy for people and universal problems. Doctor, educational reformer, and all art/entertainment mediums are possible career opportunities.

PERSONALITY INGREDIENTS: Strives to sympathize, teach, and improve standards. Appears comfortable, dignified, and tasteful. Aims for domestic/community harmony and to solve problems for others. Inwardly creates and needs beauty, optimism, and kindness. Enjoys pets, children, and life's pleasures. Is resourceful, sociable, and articulate. Inspires admiration and commercial activity.

PERSONALITY EXTREME: Too experimental, or too fearful.

ORVILLE (Old French: Orval/English)—M.

MAJOR TALENT: Ability to incorporate communications gifts, humanitarian responsibilities, and universal kindness into career. Is creative, expressive, and intuitionally inspired to contribute to the uplift of all. Has charm, optimism, and need for quality/skill/completeness. Combines idealism, tolerance/justice/philosophy, and public attention. Has a knack with words and rarely gives up on anything. Promoter, designer, and organizer are possible career opportunities.

PERSONALITY INGREDIENTS: Inwardly subtle, retiring, and attentive to fine points. Feels sensitive, patient, and comfortable working with partner/group. Is supportive, gentle, and easygoing. First impression is nonconforming. Strives to be an aggressive, assertive, and forceful pioneer. Is inventive and may have to "walk alone" to achieve goals.

PERSONALITY EXTREME: Too adventurous, or too scared.

OSCAR (Anglo-Saxon/Norwegian/Swedish/English)—M.

MAJOR TALENT: Ability to incorporate unique personal philosophy,
detail consciousness, and collecting facts/people/things into career. Is
fortunate in business/domestic partnerships. Has friendliness, cooperative spirit, and loyalty. Forms unbending habits and may become indecisive and careless. Combines retiring nature, easygoing attitude, and
appreciation of comfort. Generally a "power behind the throne." Researcher, diplomat, and poet are possible career opportunities.

PERSONALITY INGREDIENTS: Inwardly investigative, logical, and analytic. Is motivated to seek privacy, quiet, and discretion, but has fears of
loneliness and poverty. Looks at quality, not quantity. Appears conventional, sturdy, and down-to-earth. Strives to be practical, proper, and
materially secure. Needs structure and mental victories. May be eccentric and must be known to be loved.

PERSONALITY EXTREME: Too sympathetic, or too selfish.

OSWALD (Anglo-Saxon: Oscar/English)—M.

MAJOR TALENT: Ability to incorporate tact, willingness to serve, and
attention to details into career. Is receptive, persistent, and patient. Has
personal sensitivity, devotion, and need to collect things. Combines subtle control, retiring attitude, and adaptability. Assistant manager, politician, and bookkeeper are possible career opportunities.

PERSONALITY INGREDIENTS: Needs cultural/mental stimulation and
strives for traditional respectability. Feels "above the crowd," questioning, and aloof. Appears to be a practical worker and solid citizen. Aims
to be disciplined, correct, and honorable. At best when educated and
able to put high intellect to specifics. May be difficult to understand.

PERSONALITY EXTREME: Too rule-bound, or too unconventional.

OTIS (Greek/Old German)—M.

MAJOR TALENT: Ability to incorporate independent leadership, authoritative approach, and broad-scoped communications skills into
career. Is inventive, investigative, and analytic. Has magnetism,
philosophical humor, and executive organizational approach. Combines
initiative, material power, and universal awareness. Radio engineer, religious reformer, and teacher/doctor/lawyer are possible career opportunities.

PERSONALITY INGREDIENTS: Strives to be friendly, optimistic, and up-
to-date. Appears imaginative, kind, and restless. Wants popularity, pleasure, and beauty. Inwardly strong willed, domestically attaining, and
conventional. Feels idealistic, dependable, and protective. Likes to
counsel and provide solutions. Emotions are tightly tuned to physical
well being, and must rest, balance work schedule, and guard against
nervousness.

PERSONALITY EXTREME: Too alone, or too dependent.

OTTO (German/Italian/English)—M.

MAJOR TALENT: Ability to incorporate aristocratic approach, logical
analysis, and technical/scientific expertise into career. Is mathematical,
refined, and aloof. Has discretion, originality, and determination. Combines leadership, social service, and intuitional/intellectual instincts.
Most successful when avoiding speculation, materialism, and haughtiness. Researcher, TV technician, and data-processing programmer are
possible career opportunities.

PERSONALITY INGREDIENTS: First impression is traditional, dignified, and proper. Strives to be orderly, practical, and disciplined. Wants creative self-expression, imaginative interest, and pleasure. May attract disappointment.

PERSONALITY EXTREME: Too smug, or too anxious.

OWEN (Welsh: Evan/English)—M.

MAJOR TALENT: Ability to incorporate imagination, resourcefulness, and love of people/sharing/pleasure into career. Is attention-getting, expressive, and optimistic. Has originality, leadership, and sensitivity to fine points. Combines adaptability, inventions, and the gifts of the performing artist. Literary critic, social director, and any communications position are possible career opportunities.

PERSONALITY INGREDIENTS: Appears alert, aggressive, and nonconforming. Strives to be different, first, and in control. Inwardly high pitched to instigate idealistic concepts. Wants quality, as personally perceived, for everyone. Feels futuristic, emotionally up/down, and above mass tastes. Must expect frequent changes, progressive surprises, and "never a dull moment."

PERSONALITY EXTREME: Too busy, or too bored.

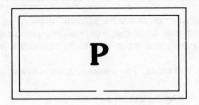

P

All names that begin with the letter *P* have the *Strong Point* of cultural attainment—nonconformity—desire for authority and/or specialization.

PABLO (Latin: Paul/Spanish)—M.

MAJOR TALENT: Ability to incorporate pioneering ideas, forceful leadership, and broad scope of interests into career. Is assertive, energetic, and original. Has creative self-expression, empathy for others, and need for progressive changes. Combines exploration, endurance, and instigation of service/products/artistry for the public benefit. Works well alone. Designer, editor, and salesman are possible career opportunities.

PERSONALITY INGREDIENTS: Appears nonconforming, ambitious, and busy. Strives to be in control, firm, and direct. Inwardly questioning, analytic, and investigative. Wants cultural attainments, natural/timeless beauty, and privacy to think/work. Feels impatient, daring, and decisive. Must have personal integrity, and maintain faith in unique ideas to achieve potential.

PERSONALITY EXTREME: Too parental, or too irresponsible.

PAIGE (Greek/French/English)—F. & M.

MAJOR TALENT: Ability to incorporate uplifting, inventive, visionary concepts into career. Is a quality-conscious dreamer, and a sensitive creator. Has high nervous energy, detailed perceptions, and broad-scoped goals. Combines generosity, adaptability, and individuality. Attracts attention. TV performer/director, literary critic, and fashion designer are possible career opportunities.

PERSONALITY INGREDIENTS: Seems clever, understanding, and adventurous. Strives for change, sensual stimulation, and challenges. Inwardly sympathetic, domestic, and protective. Needs mature, harmonious, abundant home life. Aims for freedom, and needs "roots." Must persevere, and maintain relationships/commitments to achieve potential for fame.

PERSONALITY EXTREME: Too confident, or too unsure.

PALMER (Latin/English)—M.

MAJOR TALENT: Ability to incorporate unique personal ideals, spontaneous enthusiasms, and futuristic ideas into career. Is wide ranged, ambitious, and high strung. Has elevated standards, individualism, and magnetic charm. Combines rare personal philosophy, adaptability, and variety of artistic talents. Communications, art, and diplomacy are possible career opportunities.

PERSONALITY INGREDIENTS: Appearance attracts honor/fame. Strives to be clever, adaptable, and progressive. Aims to travel, experiment, and

enjoy physical pleasures. Inwardly parental, protective, and responsible.
Wants beautiful home, artistic self-expression, and harmonious relationships. Needs to give, and receive love. At best when practical, patient, and flexible.

PERSONALITY EXTREME: Too selfless, or too uncharitable.

PAMELA (Greek/Anglo-Saxon/English)—F.

MAJOR TALENT: Ability to incorporate expressive, optimistic, and attention-getting personality into career. Is independent, adaptable, and sensitive. Has communications gifts, creativity, and resourcefulness. Combines kindness, versatility, and a knack with words. Entertainer, organizer, and model are possible career opportunities.

PERSONALITY INGREDIENTS: Inwardly reserved, analytic, and aristocratic. Wants privacy, timeless beauty, and perfection from self and others. Appears to be understanding, exciting, and open minded. Strives to be adventurous, sexy, and unencumbered. Aims to see the world, and wants the best of everything. Must be realistic, consistent, and work to attract desired recognition.

PERSONALITY EXTREME: Too assertive, or too accommodating.

PAMELLA (Greek-Anglo-Saxon: variable; Pamela/English)—F.

MAJOR TALENT: Ability to incorporate instructional, protective, responsible service into career. Is sympathetic, strong willed, and idealistic. Has showmanship, sympathy, and strong desire for harmonious relationships. Combines sensitivity to fine points, practical approach, and convincing personality. Teacher, musician, and waitress are possible career opportunities.

PERSONALITY INGREDIENTS: Appears self-reliant, managerial, and as affluent as possible. Strives to be important, controlled, and efficient. Desires quality, natural beauty, and privacy. Feels aloof, mentally analytic, and tuned to strategic planning. Best as executive in prime-product public service business.

PERSONALITY EXTREME: Too changeable, or too stubborn.

PANSY (Old French)—F.

MAJOR TALENT: Ability to incorporate creative self-expression, versatility, and resourcefulness into career. Is hopeful, up-to-date, and restless. Has attractiveness, detail consciousness, and individuality. Combines ambition, adaptability, and attention to beauty. Fashion, art/theater, and writing are possible career opportunities.

PERSONALITY INGREDIENTS: Appears dignified, practical, and classic. Strives to be structured, respectable, and solid. Inwardly efficient, organized, and materially attaining. Wants money, power, and unlimited opportunities. Attracts success and recognition when progressive in one area of concentration.

PERSONALITY EXTREME: Too questioning, or too gullible.

PARKER (Old English)—M.

MAJOR TALENT: Ability to incorporate protective, sympathetic, uplifting social service into career. Is strong willed, idealistic, and attractive. Has humor, charm, and showmanship. Combines parental nature, mature approach, and strong need to help others. Credit union organizer, inspired teacher, and parole officer are possible career opportunities.

PERSONALITY INGREDIENTS: Strives to serve humanitarian causes, be forgiving and skillful. Appears noble, attention-getting, and ageless. Inwardly loving. Wants luxury/comfort, harmony, and family/community consciousness. May be too domineering, and overdo helpfulness. May leave a lasting mark.

PERSONALITY EXTREME: Too giving, or too selfish.

PARNEL (Greek: Petra, F.-Peter, M./Celtic/Old French)—F. & M.

MAJOR TALENT: Ability to incorporate elevated artistic self-expression and conventional applications into career. Is practical, structured, and perfecting. Has sex appeal, charm, and versatility. Combines sense of justice, kindness, and romantic ideas/ideals. Plastic surgeon, legislator, and performing artist are possible career opportunities.

PERSONALITY INGREDIENTS: Feels domestic, instructional, and protective. Wants family/community respect, attainments, and comforts. Appears interested, dignified, and tasteful. Strives to be firm, expressive, and honorable. Aims to help others, and live conservatively. Grows culturally, and feels deeply for the suffering of humanity. Attracts luxury, emotional burdens, and mature relationships.

PERSONALITY EXTREME: Too talkative, or too reticent.

PARRISH (Old English)—M.

MAJOR TALENT: Ability to incorporate efficiency, executive management, and organizational skills into career. Is practical, wide ranged, and mentally sharp. Has self-reliance, determination, and spunk. Combines humanitarian instincts, conventional standards, and drive to work for tangible results. At best when intuitional as well as logical. Physical therapist, charity administrator, and financier are possible career opportunities.

PERSONALITY INGREDIENTS: First impression is reserved, calm, and observational. Strives to be classy, discreet, and private. Aims for perfection. Inwardly individualistic, aggressive, and pioneering. Wants freedom, change, and to be boss. Needs independence, timeless beauty, and ongoing growth.

PERSONALITY EXTREME: Too materialistic, or too impractical.

PASCAL (Hebrew/French/English)—M.

MAJOR TALENT: Ability to incorporate questioning, aristocratic, culturally attaining personality into career. Is discreet, reserved, and analytic. Has poise, calm, and authoritative nature. Combines individualism, uplifting service, and potential success through expertise/education. Researcher, detective, and watchmaker are possible career opportunities.

PERSONALITY INGREDIENTS: Inwardly modest, shy, and accommodating. Wants peace, love, and easygoing style. Appears enthusiastic, sexy, and adventurous. Strives to be experimental, bold, and unconventional. Seems self-assured, but is a perfectionist and is rarely self-satisfied. Should avoid gambles and materialistic career goals. Attracts money through depth of knowledge.

PERSONALITY EXTREME: Too superficial, or too depressed.

PAT (Latin/Irish: Patrick; M.-Patricia, Martha; F. diminutives/
English)—F. & M.

MAJOR TALENT: Ability to incorporate independence, daring, and competitive spirit into career. Is energetic, inventive, and forceful. Has willpower, positiveness, and nonconforming ideas. Combines fast action,
cleverness, and individuality. Shopkeeper, designer, and psychiatrist are
possible career opportunities.

PERSONALITY INGREDIENTS: Strives to be broad scoped, philosophical, and empathetic. Wants love, but usually gives more than is received. Aims to be youthful, charming, and "brotherly." Inwardly
assertive, aggressive, and proud. Needs to take the initiative.

PERSONALITY EXTREME: Too supportive, or too critical.

PATIENCE (Latin/English)—F.

MAJOR TALENT: Ability to incorporate pioneering leadership, sociability, and introspective probing into career. Is ambitious, kind, and generous. Has communications gifts, aristocratic approach, and nonconforming instincts. Combines calm reserve, imagination, and physical/mental
restlessness. Preacher, editor, and writer are possible career opportunities.

PERSONALITY INGREDIENTS: First impression is organized, managerial, and as affluent as possible. Strives to be efficient, self-reliant,
and prosperous. Inwardly retiring, adaptable, and supportive. Wants
love, cooperation, and emotional harmony. Feels sensitive, detail conscious, and inclined to partnership. Assumes protective domestic attitude, and benefits through marriage.

PERSONALITY EXTREME: Too adventurous, or too fearful.

PATRICIA (Latin/English)—F.

MAJOR TALENT: Ability to incorporate mental agility, human understanding, and unconventional ideas into career. Is individualistic, clever,
and adventurous. Has enthusiasm, versatility, and down-to-earth instincts. Combines progressive concepts, changeability, and adaptability.
Politician, investigator, and theatrical manager are possible career opportunities.

PERSONALITY INGREDIENTS: Inwardly refined, modest, and accommodating. Wants peace, emotional serenity, and easygoing life-style.
Appears attention-getting, optimistic, and charming. Strives to be up-to-
date, entertaining, and surrounded by beauty. Enjoys humor, friends,
and artistic self-expression. Has great courage in times of stress.

PERSONALITY EXTREME: Too aggressive, or too receptive.

PATRICK (Latin/Irish/English)—M.

MAJOR TALENT: Ability to incorporate far-reaching social service into
career. Is sympathetic, instructional, and responsible. Has domestic/
parental instincts, showmanship, and strong opinions/will. Combines
helpfulness, communications gifts, and uplifting imaginative activities.
Credit union organizer, teacher, and musician/artist/actor are possible
career opportunities.

PERSONALITY INGREDIENTS: First impression is unconventional, enthusiastic, and sensually exciting. Strives to be progressive, clever, and
open minded. Inwardly independent, forceful, and courageous. Needs
freedom, change, and to take the lead. At best when serving life-support

cause, and improving standards for family/community. Assumes burdens for others, and may sacrifice personal desires for the good of the majority. May leave a lasting mark.

PERSONALITY EXTREME: Too crusading, or too aimless.

PAUL (Latin/French/English)—M.

MAJOR TALENT: Ability to incorporate unconventional approach, cleverness, and knack of adapting to unfamiliar situations/people into career. Is quick, sensual, and imaginative. Has uncluttered mental powers, practical organizational structure, and pioneering courage. Combines learning by experience, sharp perceptions, and freedom of thought/action. Writer, lawyer/detective, and psychologist are possible career opportunities.

PERSONALITY INGREDIENTS: Inwardly structured, determined, and disciplined to work. Wants respectability, orderliness, and traditions. Has common sense, concentration, and distaste for pretensions. Appears different, energetic, and managerial. Strives to be a tower of strength, and to pursue unique ideas. Enjoys taking charge, and aims to keep moving forward. Should curb impatience, physical appetites, and impulsivity. May be a "swashbuckler," and overconfidently tackle confining tasks. Needs unrestricted choices, and should avoid narrowing commitments.

PERSONALITY EXTREME: Too expressive, or too uncommunicative.

PAULA (Latin: Paul/English)—F.

MAJOR TALENT: Ability to incorporate parental nature, showmanship, and responsible service into career. Is creatively expressive, sympathetic, and instructional. Has strong will, high ideals, and concern for everyone/everything. Combines courage to be different, assertiveness, and devotion to responsibilities. Teacher, marriage counselor, and nurse are possible career opportunities.

PERSONALITY INGREDIENTS: Inwardly sensual, enthusiastic, and curious. Wants adventure, travel, and excitement. First impression is active, alert, and strong. Strives to be definite, quick, and progressive. Is imaginative, and aims to be a pacesetter. At best when philosophical, and able to laugh at human foibles.

PERSONALITY EXTREME: Too aggressive, or too accommodating.

PAULINE (Latin: Paul/French/German/English: Paul, M. variable)—F.

MAJOR TALENT: Ability to incorporate uplifting family/community creative self-expression into career. Is helpful, concerned, and sympathetic. Has hospitable nature, strong opinions, and tenacity. Combines kindness to animals/children/people, self-expression, love of luxury/beauty, and desire for harmony. When properly concentrated, employs mature judgment to raise standards and provide enduring guidance for others. Home product design/sales, teacher, and personnel director are possible career opportunities.

PERSONALITY INGREDIENTS: Is motivated to give selfless service, and has magnetic charm. Feels empathetic, romantic, and broad scoped. Wants to inspire others through quality of skill/performance. Appears comforting, dignified, and tasteful. Strives to share interests, be reliable, and solve all disturbing problems. Has vivid imagination, individuality, and resourcefulness. Should avoid misplaced sympathy and meddling. Works for the good of all.

PERSONALITY EXTREME: Too sensual, or too mental.

PAYNE (Latin/English)—M.

MAJOR TALENT: Ability to incorporate questioning, perceptive, sensitive nature into career. Is intellectually/spiritually perfecting, reserved, and curious. Has keen sense of understanding, guts, and knack of inspiring change in others. Combines aristocratic ambitions, wanderlust, and progressive/energetic mind. Draws heavily upon childhood experiences. Researcher, surgeon, and editor are possible career opportunities.

PERSONALITY INGREDIENTS: Desires love, harmony, and comforts. Inwardly domestic, conventional, and strong willed. Appears different, ambitious, and self-assertive. Strives to be inventive, independent, and a pacesetter. Must avoid being too aloof.

PERSONALITY EXTREME: Too self-indulgent, or too inexperienced.

PEACE (Latin/English)—F.

MAJOR TALENT: Ability to incorporate imagination, resourcefulness, and communications techniques into career. Is entertaining, optimistic, and up-to-date. Has charm, versatility, and restless spirit. Combines independence, sensitivity to fine points, and a knack with words. Writer, salesperson, and entertainer are possible career opportunities.

PERSONALITY INGREDIENTS: Inwardly idealistic, dreamy, aiming to create a personalized Shangri-la. Wants to be unique and is intuitive and visionary. First impression is strong, individualistic, and instigating. Strives to be inventive, assertive, and aggressive. At times supportive/cooperative, but may be forceful in spontaneous enthusiasms. Attracts success.

PERSONALITY EXTREME: Too changeable, or too tenacious.

PEARL (Latin/English)—F.

MAJOR TALENT: Ability to incorporate clever and detailed mental analysis into career. Is investigative, questioning, and aristocratic. Has discretion, inner reserve, and unconventional ideas. Combines sensitivity to fine points, enthusiasm, and desire for perfection. Photographer, technical/expertise writer, and travel agent are possible career opportunities.

PERSONALITY INGREDIENTS: Inwardly protective, instructional, and parental. Wants "roots," gracious living, and family/community attainments. Feels sympathetic, stable, and enduring. Appears to be proud, progressive, and different. Strives for independence, trend-setting activities, and to win. Aims to bring truth, inventions, and peace to others. Wins through down-to-earth work.

PERSONALITY EXTREME: Too talkative, or too silent.

PEGGY (Greek/English: Margaret; dimunitive)—F.

MAJOR TALENT: Ability to incorporate creative/musical/entertaining self-expression and reforming social service into career. Is protective, responsible, and instructional. Has artistic interests, showmanship, and determination. Combines imagination, optimism, and strong personal idealism. Art patron, inspired teacher, and parole officer are possible career opportunities.

PERSONALITY INGREDIENTS: Wants beauty, joy, and pleasure. Feels sociable, resourceful, and restless. Strives to be fashionable, attention-getting, and cheerful. Is kind, discriminating, and interested. Looks for the rainbow. At best when serving an artistically uplifting or down-to-earth life support cause. Is a tireless/courageous worker to inspire family/community improvements. Carries the standard for less fortunates and may leave a lasting mark.

PERSONALITY EXTREME: Too skeptical, or too gullible.

PENELOPE (Greek/English)—F.

MAJOR TALENT: Ability to incorporate aristocratic nature, sharp mental analysis, and perfectionist approach into career. Is discreet, private, and loyal. Has tolerance, dependability, and sense of tradition. Combines creative imagination, orderly procedures, and strong introspective nature. Author, lawyer, and appraiser are possible career opportunities.

PERSONALITY INGREDIENTS: First impression is tailor-made, dynamic, and classic. Strives to plan, work, and produce lasting results. Aims to be dignified, tasteful, and self-assured. Inwardly pleasure-seeking, artistically expressive, and optimistic. Wants beauty, joy, and love. Feels affectionate, kind, and expansive. Attracts success, and should avoid self-indulgence, exaggerating, and manipulating for material power.

PERSONALITY EXTREME: Too experimental, or too cautious.

PENNY (English: Penelope, diminutive)—F.

MAJOR TALENT: Ability to incorporate visionary creativity, persuasive charm, and avant garde approach into career. Is imaginative, cooperative, and energetic. Has evangelistic zeal for personal beliefs, and attracts supporters. Combines wide-range philosophy, individualism, and sensitivity to detail. TV/data processing/photography, designer, and political reformer are possible career opportunities.

PERSONALITY INGREDIENTS: Strives to be efficient, self-reliant, and controlling. Appears influential, strong, and as affluent as possible. Inwardly kind, optimistic, and restless. Wants beauty, fun, and fashionable activity/people. Feels friendly, generous, and loving. At best when practical, investigative, and tempering desire for prestige. Wins when true to quality of purpose.

PERSONALITY EXTREME: Too questioning, or too accepting.

PERCIVAL (French-Greek/English)—M.

MAJOR TALENT: Ability to incorporate unconventional ideas, speculative instincts, and adventurous nature into career. Is clever, confident, and daring. Has physical focus, human understanding, and organizational structure. Combines pioneering spirit, self-discipline, and knack of learning through experience. Advertising, travel, and sales are possible career opportunities.

PERSONALITY INGREDIENTS: Inwardly domestic, protective, and burden-bearing. Needs family support/harmony, gracious living, and material attainments. Wants to feel needed. Strives to be respected, wealthy, and influential. Aims to work for control and has unlimited ambition/courage/potential. Is analytic, strong, and self-reliant. Attracts success, but must be discriminating when forming alliances.

PERSONALITY EXTREME: Too talkative, or too withdrawn.

PERCY (French: Percival; diminutive/English)—M.

MAJOR TALENT: Ability to incorporate practical work, structure, and organization into career. Is disciplined, determined, and dependable. Has common sense, accuracy, and loyalty. Combines independence, imagination, and system. Contractor, manufacturer, and military officer are possible career opportunities.

PERSONALITY INGREDIENTS: Inwardly optimistic, pleasure seeking, and restless. Wants beauty, creative self-expression, and variety. Feels affectionate, and romantic. Appears to be individualistic, energetic, and direct. Strives to be out front. Aims to instigate pioneering ideas, move swiftly, and progress through the courage of personal convictions. Is ambitious, and should avoid stepping over others, dividing interests, and impulsive reactions.

PERSONALITY EXTREME: Too investigative, or too unquestioning.

PERRY (Greek: Peter; variable/Old English: Peregrine/independent)—M.

MAJOR TALENT: Ability to incorporate originality, leadership, and stable approach into career. Is progressive, ambitious, and investigative. Has communications gifts, discretion, and sociability. Combines mental analysis, imagination, and individuality. Import/export business, philosophical writing, and technical/scientific products salesperson are possible career opportunities.

PERSONALITY INGREDIENTS: First impression is aristocratic, refined, and quietly authoritative. Strives to be emotionally detached, culturally polished, and perfect. Inwardly pleasure-seeking, optimistic, and resourceful. Wants beauty, joy, and love. May seem aloof, but desires friendships, fun, and fashionable activity. Attracts travel, domestic happiness, and intuitional guidance.

PERSONALITY EXTREME: Too questioning, or too gullible.

PETE (Greek: Peter; diminutive)—M.

MAJOR TALENT: Ability to incorporate progressive changes, strong independent drive, and managerial approach into career. Is distinctive, vital, and creative. Has endurance, mental agility, and communications gifts. Combines broad-scoped philosophy, service to others, and aggressiveness. Most successful when truly courageous and willing to be different and to break inherited molds. Salesman, artist, and politician are possible opportunities.

PERSONALITY INGREDIENTS: Inwardly proud, controlled, and capable. Wants freedom, action, and to leave the details to others. Appears magnetic, understanding, and noble. Strives to be a "great lover." Aims for quality of performance, to inspire good works, and to share knowledge. Is generous, talented, and should pursue nonmaterialistic interests.

PERSONALITY EXTREME: Too sensual, or too mental.

PETER (Greek/German/English)—M.

MAJOR TALENT: Ability to incorporate initiative, progressive ideas, and clear thinking into career. Is ambitious, sensitive to details, and responsible. Has many career choices and gains when sure of goals in corporate/partnership structure. Combines adaptability, self-reliance, and originality. Shopkeeper/buyer, lawyer, and theatrical director are possible career opportunities.

PERSONALITY INGREDIENTS: Appears "brotherly," empathetic, and distinctive. Strives to be philosophical, charitable, and helpful. Aims for romance, drama, and to polish skill/artistry. Inwardly bold, individualistic, and proud. Wants to take charge, and keep things moving quickly. Attracts love, and is at best when patient, practical, and decisive.

PERSONALITY EXTREME: Too sympathetic, or too self-serving.

PETUNIA (Tupi: South American Indian)—F.

MAJOR TALENT: Ability to incorporate enthusiasm, changeability, and unconventional ideas into career. Is curious, clever, and sensual. Has adaptability, individuality, and up-to-date style. Combines communications gifts, leadership, and adventurous nature. Travel agent, entertainer, and advertising executive are possible career opportunities.

PERSONALITY INGREDIENTS: Inwardly compassionate, charitable, and romantic. Wants broad-scoped interests, skill/artistry, and to help others. Appears to be striking, vital, and open minded. Strives to be unroutined, just, and confident. At best when patient, cautious, and enduring. Attracts pleasures, travel, and surprises.

PERSONALITY EXTREME: Too assertive, or too dependent.

PHIL (English: Philip-Philo; M., Phillis; F., diminutive)—F. & M.

MAJOR TALENT: Ability to incorporate polished techniques, philosophical humor, and humanitarian service into career. Is generous, empathetic, and sensitive. Has adaptability, technical/scientific approach, and analytic instincts. Combines detail consciousness, drive for perfection, and creative ideas. Designer, physician, and theatrical performer are possible career opportunities.

PERSONALITY INGREDIENTS: Wants romance, universal kindness, and "brotherly love." Feels empathetic, emotionally strong, and intuitional. Appears distinctive, understanding, and appealing. Strives to serve, heal, and broaden horizons. Is charitable, and often selfless. Attracts financial success, and may be an inspiration to others.

PERSONALITY EXTREME: Too expressive, or too taciturn.

PHILIP (Greek/English)—M.

MAJOR TALENT: Ability to incorporate introspection, quality consciousness, and perfectionist approach into career. Is dependable, intuitive, and investigative. Has up-to-date imaginative ideas, reserve, and discretion. Combines communications gifts, practical organizational common sense, and aristocratic characteristics. Has great depth, strength, and loyalty. Excels when educated/expert/"the authority." Theatrical director, political/military/medical analyst, and radio/musical technician are possible career opportunities.

PERSONALITY INGREDIENTS: Wants a broad philosophy/marketplace, and to provide/support quality skills/performances. Feels compassionate, intense, and romantic. Appears refined, aloof, and observant. Strives to get to the "root" of things, perceive fine points, and remain open to new and progressive concepts. Aims for privacy, timeless beauty, and not to show emotions. Fears loneliness/poverty, but needs solitude/expensive treasures. May be shy publicly until area of expertise comes to light. Keeps a secret self, and must be known to be understood.

PERSONALITY EXTREME: Too skeptical, or too gullible.

PHILIPPA (Greek: Philip/English)—F.

MAJOR TALENT: Ability to incorporate sense of fair play, responsibility, and firm judgment into career. Is decisive, independent, and managerial. Has showmanship, practical balance, and cleverness. Combines adventurous ideas, mature approach, and problem-solving instincts. Marriage counselor, teacher, and interior designer are possible career opportunities.

PERSONALITY INGREDIENTS: Desires leadership, originality, and mental freedom. Feels daring, energetic, and impatient. Appears striking, alert, and perceptive. Strives to be open minded, enthusiastic, and progressive. Has balanced nature, and sees two sides of an issue. At best when ambitions are tempered with kindness.

PERSONALITY EXTREME: Too confident, or too fearful.

PHILO (Greek/English)—M.

MAJOR TALENT: Ability to incorporate sympathetic service, uplifting imaginative ideas, and concern for family/group/community life-support needs into career. Is protective, responsible, and hospitable. Has charm, attractive approach, and firm beliefs. Combines sociability, resourcefulness, and mature understanding. Marriage counselor, credit union organizer, and politician are possible career opportunities.

PERSONALITY INGREDIENTS: Seems youthful, empathetic, and helpful. Strives to be brotherly, charitable, and broad-scoped. Inwardly idealistic, conventional, and materially attaining. Wants gracious living, artistic beauty, and pride in family/home. Aims to serve major issues, and attempts to provide selfless service. Is practical, but not hungry for power. May be jealous, indiscreet, and meddlesome when scattered. At best surrounded by harmonious, loving, balanced relationships.

PERSONALITY EXTREME: Too suspicious, or too trusting.

PHILOMENA (Greek/English)—F.

MAJOR TALENT: Ability to incorporate creative self-expression, words, and practical organizational approach into career. Is affectionate, imaginative, and fair. Has kind, romantic, dependable manner. Combines common sense, self-reliance, and communications gifts. Literary agent, interior decorator, and cosmetics salesperson are possible career opportunities.

PERSONALITY INGREDIENTS: Desires beauty, originality, and companionship. Inwardly optimistic, pleasure seeking, and restless. Appears noble, generous, and understanding. Seems ageless, philosophical, and magnetic. Strives to be worldly, charitable, and inspirational. Understands domestic responsibility, and needs to entertain/be entertained. Should avoid negativism, and enjoy the humorous side of changing experiences. Attracts security, love, and quality.

PERSONALITY EXTREME: Too assertive, or too squelched.

PHINEAS (Latin/Greek/Hebrew/English)—M.

MAJOR TALENT: Ability to incorporate top quality skill/performance, broad-ranged philosophy, and empathetic service into career. Is helpful, creative, and unselfish. Has charm, magnetism, and nobility. Combines imagination, firm opinions, and emotional response. Doctor, musician/artist/entertainer, and policeman are possible career opportunities.

PERSONALITY INGREDIENTS: Wants domestic harmony, gracious living, and respectability. Feels protective, responsible, and strong willed. Appears attractive, up-to-date, and optimistic. Strives to be entertaining, surrounded by beauty, and resourceful. Aims for popularity, kindness, and to bounce through adversity. Best when self-expressive, and determined.

PERSONALITY EXTREME: Too bold, or too fearful.

PHOEBE (Greek/English)—F.

MAJOR TALENT: Ability to incorporate parental approach, protective service instincts, and responsible nature into career. Is sympathetic, helpful, and imaginative. Has charm, versatility, and strong personal ideals. Combines family/community uplift, instructional focus, and selfless devotion. Musician/actor/artist, corporate personnel director, and marriage counselor are possible career opportunities.

PERSONALITY INGREDIENTS: Appears self-reliant, authoritative, and as affluent as possible. Strives to be materially powerful, efficient, and mentally organized. Inwardly questioning, confidential, and reserved. Wants privacy, quality, and perfection. Attracts personal disappointment. Expects aristocratic reactions and finds down-to-earth survival instincts of others to be surprising/distasteful. Best when realistic, and aiming for area of concentration which will invite financial rewards. Must be known to be understood.

PERSONALITY EXTREME: Too impulsive, or too cautious.

PHYLLIS (Greek/English)—F.

MAJOR TALENT: Ability to incorporate magnetic enthusiasm for original inspirations, and desire to uplift the quality of expectation for others into career. Is unique, strongly idealistic, and aims to show others a better way of living/thinking. Combines communications gifts, diplomacy, and originality. Is a forerunner. Executive secretary, education/political reformer, and TV/film performer are possible career opportunities.

PERSONALITY INGREDIENTS: Inwardly self-questioning. Wants authority, privacy, and timeless treasures. Must erase unrealistic fears of being alone through a concentrated work effort. Wants perfection, and is uncomfortable with mediocrity. Is traditional, and strives to plan, work, and build for enduring results. Can be dynamic, and attracts lasting recognition.

PERSONALITY EXTREME: Too independent, or too accommodating.

PIERCE (Greek: Peter; variable/Anglo-French/English)—M.

MAJOR TALENT: Ability to incorporate inventive, intuitive, lofty ideas into career. Is idealistic, sociable, and organizational. Has sensitivity to fine points, self-reliance, and spontaneous enthusiasms. Combines orderliness, resourcefulness, and individualism. Is a dreamer for uplifting creative service. Diplomat, designer, and evangelistic teacher are possible career opportunities.

PERSONALITY INGREDIENTS: Is very independent. Inwardly progressive, ambitious, and forceful. Wants mental freedom, pioneering interests, and to be first. Appears different, energetic, and proud. Strives to take charge, keep things moving, and maintain personal convictions. May be stubborn, bossy, and impatient. At best when able to accept leadership, withstand compromising temptations, and break with tradition.

PERSONALITY EXTREME: Too sensual, or too mental.

PIPER (Anglo-Saxon/Modern English)—F. & M.

MAJOR TALENT: Ability to incorporate creative leadership, communications techniques, and independent intellectual analysis into career. Is aristocratic, forceful, and versatile. Has expansive nature, imagination, and ambition. Combines discretion/reserve, sociability, and individualistic active energy. Comedy writer, psychiatrist, and business owner are possible career opportunities.

PERSONALITY INGREDIENTS: Inwardly very sensual or tuned to mental focus. Wants travel, unconventional structure, and changing interests. First impression is attention-getting, understanding, and enthusiastic. Strives to be progressive, confident, and different. Combines the introvert/extrovert, and attracts off beat people, artistically self-expressive outlets, and loving relationships.

PERSONALITY EXTREME: Too forgiving, or too pitiless.

PIUS (Latin/English)—M.

MAJOR TALENT: Ability to incorporate diplomacy, detailed perceptions, and subtle control into career. Is adaptable, patient, and peace-loving. Has musical/rhythmical gifts, cooperative ideas, and spiritual illumination through observation. Combines fine craftsmanship, supportive positioning, and knack of arbitrating differences of opinion. Union shop steward, private secretary, and group dancer/musician are possible career opportunities.

PERSONALITY INGREDIENTS: Appears commanding, self-reliant, and as affluent as possible. Strives to be materially efficient, recognized, and far reaching. Aims to delegate responsibility, and complete major tasks. Inwardly resourceful, optimistic, and pleasure-loving. Wants to be surrounded by people, joy, and beauty. Benefits from accepting change, avoiding pettiness and balancing emotions and logic when making decisions.

PERSONALITY EXTREME: Too indecisive, or too smug.

POLLY (Hebrew: Mary; variable/English)—F.

MAJOR TALENT: Ability to incorporate mental organization, efficiency, and self-reliance into career. Is attentive to details, idealistic, and persistent. Has material ambitions, confident facade, and showmanship. Combines knack of coordinating various interests, delegative instincts, and protective/responsible executive authority. Corporation advisor, newspaper/publishing editor, and theatrical agent are possible career opportunities.

PERSONALITY INGREDIENTS: Strives to work, and expects concrete results. Changes careers, and reconstructs life plan often. First impression is classic, dignified, and practical. Aims to be a solid citizen, and structures for enduring results. Inwardly traditional, down-to-earth, and disciplined. Dislikes pretension, insincerity, and wants love but may appear unemotional. Best when educated, or expert, and concentrated to maintain financial/emotional security. Wants quality, and fears loneliness/poverty when idle.

PERSONALITY EXTREME: Too skeptical, or too gullible.

POMEROY (Latin)—M.

MAJOR TALENT: Ability to incorporate dedicated hard work, discipline, and self-reliance into career. Is problem-solving, sensible, and determined. Has material power, executive judgment, and high ideals. Combines desire to serve humanitarian/useful purposes, logic, and wide-ranged common sense. Concert pianist, physical therapist, and construction executive are possible career opportunities.

PERSONALITY INGREDIENTS: Strives to give empathetic service, reach a broad marketplace, and inspire quality/skill of performance. Feels efficient, courageous, and determined to make efforts pay off. Wants the freedom that wealth and influence buy, and may be a strongly opinionated workaholic. Is dominant, magnetic, and dignified. Best when intuitive, and sensitive to the needs of others.

PERSONALITY EXTREME: Too authoritative, or too questioning.

POPPY (Latin/English)—F.

MAJOR TALENT: Ability to incorporate aristocratic approach, questioning nature, and technical/spiritual/intellectual analysis into career. Is resourceful, logical, and investigative. Has discretion, practical organizational instincts, and good memory. Combines up-to-date ideas, determination, and mental agility. Writer, political advisor, and lawyer are possible career opportunities.

PERSONALITY INGREDIENTS: Inwardly traditional, down-to-earth, and disciplined. Wants respectability, security, and material results. Appears attractive, charming, and kind. Strives to be popular, optimistic, and entertaining. Aims to find beauty, love, and humor in everything. Understands responsibility, conventional structure, and timeless wisdom. Is selective, fair, and very clever.

PERSONALITY EXTREME: Too secretive, or too enlightening.

PORTER (Late Latin/French/English)—M.

MAJOR TALENT: Ability to incorporate inspirational ideas, communications gifts, and mental organization into career. Is a magnetic original, and attracts followers. Has sensitivity to details, artistically/socially uplifting instincts, and futuristic vision. Combines imagination, material ambitions, and desire to enlighten others. Educational reformer, author, and individualistic artist/performer are possible career opportunities.

PERSONALITY INGREDIENTS: Inwardly a dreamer. Wants to rise above mediocrity. Desires peace, beauty, and easy-going pace. Has high nervous energy. First impression is ageless, noble, and empathetic. Strives to be philosophical, compassionate, and charitable. Seeks to exemplify top quality skill/performance. Attracts recognition, enhancing partnerships, and lasting image.

PERSONALITY EXTREME: Too indiscreet, or too polished.

PORTIA (Latin/English)—F.

MAJOR TALENT: Ability to incorporate sharp mental analysis, strategic ideas, and perfectionist instincts into career. Is practical, versatile, and resourceful. Has poise, perseverance, and traditional constructive systems. Combines expressiveness, disciplined work, and desire for authority. Researcher, radio performer, and lawyer are possible career opportunities.

PERSONALITY INGREDIENTS: Appears youthful, noble, and concerned. Strives to exemplify "brotherly love," understand human frailty, and give selfless service. Aims for a broad philosophy. Inwardly questioning, aloof, and private. Wants quiet, timeless beauty, and cultural attainments. Feels best when educated/expert and able to speak with wisdom. Needs academic/technical/scientific concentration to realize self-worth. Should be patient, cautious, and nonmaterialistic to attract success.

PERSONALITY EXTREME: Too precedent-setting, or too imitative.

PRENTICE (Latin/English)—M.

MAJOR TALENT: Ability to incorporate broad-scoped sympathetic/ instructional/artistic service into career. Is confident, determined, and forgiving. Has empathetic inner resources, constructive down-to-earth work energy, and lofty goals. Combines self-discipline, adaptability, and humanitarian nature. Religious teacher/reformer/worker, doctor, and publisher are possible career opportunities.

PERSONALITY INGREDIENTS: First impression is capable, influential, and tailor-made. Strives for material power, executive leadership, and mental organization. Aims for business acumen, lasting results, and to be generous to loved ones. Inwardly independent, pioneering, and creative. Dislikes waiting, details, and being second best to anyone. Feels controlling, ambitious, and decisive. Should set a progressive example for others.

PERSONALITY EXTREME: Too experimental, or too cautious.

PRESTON (Anglo-Saxon/English)—M.

MAJOR TALENT: Ability to incorporate far-reaching mental organization into career. Is attention-getting, vital, and experimental. Has initiative, strength, and charm. Combines inner forcefulness, efficient practicality, and zealous work effort. Gains through confident approach. Athlete, travel business leader, and newspaper executive are possible career opportunities.

PERSONALITY INGREDIENTS: First impression is dignified, comforting, and hospitable. Strives to be responsible, protective, and domestically rooted. Aims for mature judgments, showmanship/luxurious life-style, and creative self-expression. Inwardly idealistic, inventive, and individualistic. Feels special, pacesetting, and inspires followers. Accomplishes multiple goals simultaneously, and should avoid self-indulgence and overwork.

PERSONALITY EXTREME: Too sensual, or too mental.

PRISCILLA (Latin/English)—F.

MAJOR TALENT: Ability to incorporate communications techniques, nobility of purpose, and empathetic service work into career. Is philosophical, tolerant, and forgiving. Has inspirational experiences which when shared, enlighten, uplift, and support humanitarian ideals. Combines structured procedures, resourceful problem solving, and motivation to "see a glass of water half full," as opposed to half empty. Educational/medical/artistic/musical specialist, welfare worker, and parole officer are possible career opportunities.

PERSONALITY INGREDIENTS: Feels proud, independent, and courageous. Has fortitude, ambition, and spunk. Strives for influential posi-

tion, solid-citizen affluence, and executive control. May marry young,
grow to material power, and maintain prosperity through understanding
human frailty. Best when able to let go of past experiences, and change
with circumstance.

PERSONALITY EXTREME: Too assertive, or too accommodating.

PRUDENCE (Latin/English)—F.

MAJOR TALENT: Ability to incorporate understanding of people, enthusiasm, and the courage to tackle anything new into career. Is curious,
resourceful, and pioneering. Has practicality, creativity, and productive
work habits. Combines individuality, tradition, and progressive change.
Has strength of character. Civic leader, lawyer, and advertising executive are possible career opportunities.

PERSONALITY INGREDIENTS: Motivated to be a solid citizen. Wants fair
dealings, material results, and useful purposes. First impression is
energetic, different, and inventive. Strives to be assertive, independent,
and number one. Aims to be a trend setter, and has faith, courage,
endurance when things go wrong. Attracts love, protection, and fast
results.

PERSONALITY EXTREME: Too hedonistic, or too puritanical.

Q

All names that begin with the letter *Q* have the *Strong Point* of off-beat ambitions—attracting prestige—material results—investigative nature.

QUEENA (Gothic/English)—F.
MAJOR TALENT: Ability to incorporate human understanding, polished communications skills, and broad-scoped philosophy into career. Is thoughtful, compassionate, and generous. Has sensitivity to little things, analytic mind, and aristocratic nature. Combines cooperation, wisdom, and service to others. Welfare worker, educator, and artist/performer are possible career opportunities.

PERSONALITY INGREDIENTS: Inwardly sensual, curious, and enthusiastic. Wants change, progress, and challenging interests. Appears to be traditional, classic, and practical. Strives to be a conventional solid citizen. Aims for material work, planning, and structure. Feels adventurous, attracts abundant life-style, and is never dull.

PERSONALITY EXTREME: Too impatient, or too lazy.

QUENBY (Scandinavian)—F.
MAJOR TALENT: Ability to incorporate communications gifts, orderly methods, and up-to-date resourcefulness into career. Is skillful, perfecting, and imaginative. Has versatility, love of beauty/enjoyment, and high ideals. Combines optimism, organized structure, and creative/artistic self-expression. Gifted with words and sex appeal. Plastic surgeon, social organizer, and high fashion model/designer are possible career opportunities.

PERSONALITY INGREDIENTS: Is motivated to protect, serve, and teach. Wants family/home/community responsibility, harmonious relationships/environments, and to inspire justice. Appears dignified, comforting, and sympathetic. Strives to be a provider, entertainer, and to have a gracious/abundant/luxurious life. Attracts love, money, and spiritual rewards.

PERSONALITY EXTREME: Too confident, or too questioning.

QUENTIN (Latin/English)—M.
MAJOR TALENT: Ability to incorporate independent ideas, intellectual stimulation, and communications gifts into career. Is aggressive, assertive, and original. Has charm, clever wit, and aristocratic instincts. Combines words, leadership, and creative force. Writer, secret service agent, and mathematician/scientist are possible career opportunities.

PERSONALITY INGREDIENTS: First impression is refined, modest, and patient. Strives to be supportive, accommodating, and a good partner.

Inwardly self-reliant, controlled, and mentally organized. Wants material power, far reaching goals, and practical work. Is romantic, domestically protective, and sensitive to fine points. Must avoid using cleverness for deceptive material purposes.

PERSONALITY EXTREME: Too speculative, or too ascertaining.

QUINCY (French-Latin)—M.

MAJOR TALENT: Ability to incorporate organizational structure, communications gifts, and mental curiosity into career. Is efficient, self-reliant, and far-reaching. Has vitality, understanding of mass market acceptance, and enduring physical/emotional strength. Combines creative self-expression, adventurous instincts, and executive self-confidence. Finance, politics, and theater are possible career opportunities.

PERSONALITY INGREDIENTS: First impression is observing, cultured, and introspective. Strives to be analytic, private, and to speak when sure. Self-image needs bolstering, and is at best when educated to technical/scientific expertise. Wants to be independent, decisive, and assertive. Needs to control, tend to major issues, and explore new vistas. May be stubborn, impatient, and too forceful. Generallly inherits power, money, or prestige.

PERSONALITY EXTREME: Too questioning, or too assenting.

QUINN (Celtic/Irish/English)—M.

MAJOR TALENT: Ability to incorporate charming, creative, and versatile personality into career. Is a skillful communicator, and structures procedures for material results. Has respect for conventional standards, sex appeal, and desire for justice, pleasure, accomplishment. Combines optimistic approach, practical capability, and good fortune through social contact. Plastic surgeon, writer, and theatrical producer are possible career opportunities.

PERSONALITY INGREDIENTS: First impression is youthful, philosophical, and empathetic. Strives to reach a broad scope, provide quality products, and serve humanitarian needs. Inwardly wants happy home, beauty, and loving relationships. Feels resourceful, and finds pleasure in sharing. Attracts travel, quality, and success.

PERSONALITY EXTREME: Too busy, or too bored.

QUINT (Latin: Quentin/English: diminutive)—M.

MAJOR TALENT: Ability to incorporate humanitarian service, polished skill/performance, and creative/artistic self-expression into career. Is wide ranged, philosophical, and investigative. Has sensitivity to fine points, clear sightedness, and desire for fair play. Combines conceptualizing, material ambition, and unselfishness. Physician, artist, author are possible career opportunities.

PERSONALITY INGREDIENTS: Is motivated to share love, talents, and pleasure. Wants beauty, humor, and optimistic planning. Appears comfortable, dignified, and concerned. Strives to be parental, materially attaining, and to live graciously. Aims for showmanship, respectability, and to keep harmonious relationships. Is idealistic, curious, and inspirational. Should avoid rash personal judgments.

PERSONALITY EXTREME: Too faultfinding, or too passive.

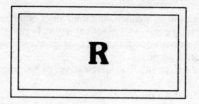

R

All names that begin with the letter *R* have the *Strong Point* of selfless service—structured communications gifts—"brotherly love"—comprehensiveness.

RACHEL (Hebrew/English)—F. & M.

MAJOR TALENT: Ability to incorporate uplifting personal ideals, inventiveness, and attention to details into career. Is high-strung, active, and sensitive. Has adaptability, tact, and empathy. Combines spontaneous enthusiasms, reforming instincts, and potential to leave a lasting image. A true individualist. Educator, designer, and film performer/technician are possible career opportunities.

PERSONALITY INGREDIENTS: Wants domestic harmony, attainments, abundance. Feels determined, instructional, and helpful. Appears to be free-wheeling, clever, and open-minded. Strives to travel, experiment, and be free. Is torn between responsible/protective/conventional soul, and adventurous self-image. Best when decisive, practical, and enduring.

PERSONALITY EXTREME: Too talkative, or too close-mouthed.

RACHELLE (Hebrew/French/English)—F.

MAJOR TALENT: Ability to incorporate creative, assertive, independent leadership into career. Is pioneering, courageous, and optimistic. Has intellectual curiosity, analytic instincts, and personal ambition. Combines words, wisdom, and originality. Business owner, spiritual counselor, and promoter are possible career opportunities.

PERSONALITY INGREDIENTS: Appears to be businesslike, tailor-made, and capable. Strives for influence, affluence, and prestige. Aims to be a very solid citizen, but inwardly a save-the-world dreamer. Wants to improve quality for everyone, and often devises impractical methods. Feels enthusiasm for personal ideals, emotional sensitivity, and overall has a nurturing/sharing/philosophical nature. Needs a down-to-earth partner/mate, material security, and self-expressive outlets to maintain ideal life-style.

PERSONALITY EXTREME: Too spontaneous, or too strategic.

RAE (Teutonic-Scandinavian/Hebrew-English: Rachel-Rachelle; diminutive)—F. & M.

MAJOR TALENT: Ability to incorporate helpful service, responsibility, and protective instincts into career. Is parental, instructional, and strong willed. Has individuality, unconventional ideas, and conservative leanings. Combines harmony, dependability, and firm opinions. Teacher, musician, and interior decorator are possible career opportunities.

PERSONALITY INGREDIENTS: Wants domestic/family structure, roots, and comfortable life-style. Feels sympathetic, emotionally generous, and inspired to give mature counsel. Appears to be ageless, noble, and understanding. Charitable, artistically/culturally polished, impressive, able to see the big picture, and eager for a wide range of interests/relationships. Is a passionate humanitarian, lover and doer.

PERSONALITY EXTREME: Too virtuous, or too wicked.

RALPH (Anglo-Saxon: Randolph/English: variable-diminutive)—M.

MAJOR TALENT: Ability to incorporate individuality, trend-setting ideas, and leadership into career. Is cooperative, businesslike, and mentally organized. Has ambition, active energy, and executive diplomacy. Combines knack of arbitrating differences, material focus, and need to be first/best/original. Uses sex appeal. Actor, government agent, and lawyer are possible career opportunities.

PERSONALITY INGREDIENTS: Wants freedom, change, and nonconformity. Feels assertive, aggressive, and different. Appears to be noble, ageless, and philosophical. Strives for quality/skill of performance, wide-ranged artistic/humanitarian uplift, and to teach or inspire others. Is romantic, resourceful, and at best when decisive. Enjoys natural beauty, optimistic/clever people, and cultural stimulation.

PERSONALITY EXTREME: Too materialistic, or too impractical.

RAMONA (Old German/Gothic/English)—F.

MAJOR TALENT: Ability to incorporate executive mental organization, practical efficiency, and diplomatic authority into career. Is self-reliant, determined, and self-improving. Has strength under fire, responsibility, and communications gifts. Combines group/partnership interaction, responsive instincts, and desire for material success. Athlete, buyer, and paymaster are possible career opportunities.

PERSONALITY INGREDIENTS: Strives to be philosophical, worldly, and polished. Seems understanding, helpful, and ageless. Inwardly protective, discriminating, and ambitious. Desires affluence, influence, and solid-citizen prestige. At best when passions are controlled, and endurance is established.

PERSONALITY EXTREME: Too impatient, or too resigned.

RANDALL (Anglo-Saxon: Randolph/English: variable-diminutive)—M.

MAJOR TALENT: Ability to incorporate authoritative manner, businesslike approach, and commercial instincts into career. Is far-reaching, discriminating, and a communicator. Has heroic strength, showmanship, and parental attitude. Combines sensitivity to fine points, firmness, and material ambitions. Publishing, banking, and musical/theatrical production are possible career opportunities.

PERSONALITY INGREDIENTS: Inwardly modest, peace-loving, and receptive. Wants domestic tranquility, gentleness, and orderliness. Appears dignified, comfortable, and solid. Strives to be responsible, protective, and instructional. Aims for respectability, luxurious family attainments, and to serve/improve/harmonize. Should avoid imposing ideals upon others, self-depreciating loves, and careless words.

PERSONALITY EXTREME: Too brave, or too cowardly.

RANDOLF (Anglo-Saxon: Randolph; variable/English)—M.

MAJOR TALENT: Ability to incorporate logic, structure, and introspection into career. Is questioning, intuitive, and quality-conscious. Has reserve, discretion, and perseverance. Combines imagination, organization, and scientific/technical approach. Researcher, aviator, and psychoanalyst are possible career opportunities.

PERSONALITY INGREDIENTS: Desires privacy, quiet, and timeless beauty. Wants refinement, cultural attainments, and intellectual stimulation. First impression is noble, empathetic, and philosophical. Strives to be broad-scoped, skillful, and helpful. Aims for universal interests, artistic/humanitarian improvements, and romantic goals. Best when unselfish, patient, and down-to-earth.

PERSONALITY EXTREME: Too blunt, or too kind.

RANDOLPH (Anglo-Saxon/English)—M.

MAJOR TALENT: Ability to incorporate intellect, imagination, and constructive planning into career. Is loyal, determined, and investigative. Has aristocratic instincts, reserve, and unclouded wisdom. Combines creative self-expression, practical organization, and introspective analysis. Excels through education. Data processing, religion, and communications are possible career opportunities.

PERSONALITY INGREDIENTS: Strives to be compassionate and unbiased, and to serve the public. First impression is magnetic, empathetic, and noble. Inwardly logical, secretive, and culturally attaining. Knows when to talk and when to remain silent, and has great strength when problems arise. May live in an ivory tower and be calculating, aloof, and sensually uncontrolled. Attracts material success when not overcompensating for fears of loneliness and poverty.

PERSONALITY EXTREME: Too materialistic, or too impractical.

RAPHAEL (Hebrew/English)—M.

MAJOR TALENT: Ability to incorporate aristocratic nature, analytic introspection, and unemotional decision-making into career. Is structured, artistically creative, and expressive. Has integrity, unbiased attitude, and a knack of speaking only when prudent/authoritative/just. Combines common sense, charm, and wisdom. Government agent, appraiser, and editor are possible career opportunities.

PERSONALITY INGREDIENTS: Wants natural/timeless beauty, serene surroundings, and refinement. Feels private, intuitive, and discriminating. Appears to be ageless, interested, and brotherly. Strives to be culturally/artistically polished, cosmopolitan, and philosophically humorous. Aims for broad-scoped planning, service, and understanding. May be selfish, temperamental, and conniving. Major change at twenty-six opens doors to adventure. Needs concentrated effort, tact, and to control possessiveness.

PERSONALITY EXTREME: Too talkative, or too unsociable.

RAQUEL (Hebrew: Rachel/Spanish)—F.

MAJOR TALENT: Ability to incorporate high inventive energy, magnetic personality, and cooperative spirit into career. Is original, quality-conscious, and geared to unique tastes. Has diplomacy, friendliness, and potential to inspire others. Combines broad-scoped professionalism/skill, attention to details, and creative artistry. Film industries, religious reform, and true artiste in any medium are possible career opportunities.

PERSONALITY INGREDIENTS: Strives to be gentle, refined, and adaptable. Appears sensitive, obliging, and modest. Inwardly passionate, empathetic, and selfless. Wants to serve humanitarian purposes, reach a wide marketplace, and share all talents/money/emotions with anyone who seems needy. Attracts business partnership/assistance and may leave a lasting image when embarked upon one career direction.

PERSONALITY EXTREME: Too attention-getting, or too reclusive.

RAY (Latin/English: Rachel/Raymond; variable-diminutive)—F. & M.

MAJOR TALENT: Ability to incorporate efficiency, self-reliance, and practical executive judgment into career. Is strong, domestically generous, and a solid citizen. Has initiative, originality, and technical/scientific instincts. Combines independence, investigative analysis, and far-reaching material focus. Bandleader, stock broker, and theatrical director are possible career opportunities.

PERSONALITY INGREDIENTS: Desires progressive changes, immediate action, and new ideas. Wants to be a pace-setter. Appears to be introspective, aristocratic, and observant. Strives for cultural attainments, private thinking time, and natural beauty. Best when specialized, and in a communications field.

PERSONALITY EXTREME: Too confident, or too questioning.

RAYMOND (Old German/French/English)—M.

MAJOR TALENT: Ability to incorporate polished skills/artistry/performance, broad scoped service, and humanitarian instincts into career. Is magnetic, philosophical, and creatively expressive. Has selflessness, strong sense of justice, and inventive mind. Combines emotional responsiveness, inspirational personality, and social uplift. Physician, parole officer, and any dedicated profession may be career opportunities.

PERSONALITY INGREDIENTS: First impression is retiring, refined, and modest. Strives to see both sides of an issue, maintain order/sensitivity/details, and use subtle control upon others. Aims to be a master craftsman. Inwardly aloof, cultural, and introspective. Wants timeless beauty/quality, refinements, and solitude to enjoy uncluttered/logical/investigative thinking. At best when decisive, specialized, and not overprotecting others.

PERSONALITY EXTREME: Too conventional, or too improper.

REAGAN (Latin/Irish Gaelic: Regan/English)—F. & M.

MAJOR TALENT: Ability to incorporate progressive ambitions, originality, and independent leadership into career. Is managerial, imaginative, and tuned to supporting/needing supporters. Has daring, sex appeal, and aristocratic feelings. Combines attention to details, executive organizational approach, and pioneering spirit. May be full of contradictions, but aims to do the expedient thing. Attracts power, prestige, and money. Business owner, salesman, and architect are possible career opportunities.

PERSONALITY INGREDIENTS: Should practice self-control. Appears to be optimistic, up-to-date, and attention-getting. Strives for humor, pleasure, and love. Inwardly discriminating, analytic, and self-contained. Wants mental challenges, discretion, and the finer things in life. Aims for authority, and spiritually resides in an ivory tower. Should avoid recklessness.

PERSONALITY EXTREME: Too experimental, or too cautious.

REBECCA (Hebrew/English)—F.

MAJOR TALENT: Ability to incorporate independence, initiative, and pioneering spirit into career. Is mentally organized/efficient, attentive to details, and progressive. Has vision, pride, and determination. Combines competitiveness, passion, and ambition. Writer, psychiatrist, and designer may be career opportunities.

PERSONALITY INGREDIENTS: Inwardly idealistic, quality-conscious, and filled with inspirational ideas geared to improving existing conditions and mundane expectations. Feels different, nervous, and personalized. Appears influential, managerial, and as affluent as possible. Strives to be self-reliant, affluent, and powerful. Aims for material goals, but often has impractical enthusiasms. Attracts worldly status.

PERSONALITY EXTREME: Too bossy, or too submissive.

REECE (Welsh/English)—M.

MAJOR TALENT: Ability to incorporate intellectual/intuitive/inspirational ideas, polished artistry, and expansive nature into career. Is questioning, adaptable, and conceptual. Has magnetic charm, understanding, and humanitarian drives. Combines introspection, cooperation, and cultural improvement. Composer, doctor/lawyer, and electrical engineer may be career opportunities.

PERSONALITY INGREDIENTS: Inwardly parental, responsible, and protective. Wants roots, family/community attainments, and to serve life-support needs. Feels instructional, sympathetic, and helpful. Appears to be up-to-date, optimistic, and kind. Strives for beauty, pleasure, and love. Should be practical, unscattered, and tolerant to achieve tangible results.

PERSONALITY EXTREME: Too unconventional, or too self-limiting.

REED (Old English: Read/English)—M.

MAJOR TALENT: Ability to incorporate confident strength, experimental nature, and cleverness into career. Is imaginative, creatively expressive, and sensitive to details. Has ambition, cooperative spirit, and futuristic ideas. Combines drive, learning by experience, and progressive enthusiasms. Scientist, lawyer, and politician may be career opportunities.

PERSONALITY INGREDIENTS: Inwardly non-conforming, aggressive, and inventive. Wants mental/physical freedom to pioneer ideas, and receive acceptance. First impression is dignified, conventional, and solid. Strives to be practical, constructive, and respected. Aims to establish traditions, and thrives upon unconventional methods. Is very investigative, physically agile, and changeable. Attracts honor.

PERSONALITY EXTREME: Too disciplined, or too unroutined.

REGINALD (Old German/English)—M.

MAJOR TALENT: Ability to incorporate intellect, common sense, and personal charm into career. Is analytic, questioning, and quality-conscious. Has discretion, reserve, and aristocratic tastes. Combines disciplined structure, electric personality, and desire for authority. Radio performer, writer, an scientific/technical expert may be career opportunities.

PERSONALITY INGREDIENTS: Inwardly domestic, parental, and loving. Wants mature companionship, luxury, and family/community respect. Appears individualistic, energetic, and nonconforming. Strives to be independent, assertive, and aggressive. Aims to pioneer, direct, and never wait for anything. Should avoid self-indulgence, pessimism, and aimlessness.

PERSONALITY EXTREME: Too proper, or too unconventional.

REGAN (Latin/English/diminutive: Regina)— F. & M.

MAJOR TALENT: Ability to incorporate love of mankind, spiritual strength, and broad inspirational ideas into career. Is philosophical, counseling, and helpful. Has artistic consciousness, romantic approach, and knack of understanding people and the big picture. Combines introspective questioning, adaptability, and energy to move mountains to raise standards. Physician, judge, and publisher are possible career opportunities.

PERSONALITY INGREDIENTS: Seems optimistic, entertaining, and fashionable. Strives to be popular, happy, and surrounded by beauty. Inwardly sympathetic, strong-willed, and idealistic. Wants domestic/family harmony, artistic self-expression, and respectability. Feels protective, responsible, and instructional. At best when down-to-earth, decisive, and just.

PERSONALITY EXTREME: Too adventurous, or too fearful.

REGINA (Latin/Italian/English)—F.

MAJOR TALENT: Ability to incorporate imagination, sense of fair play, and burden-bearing instincts into career. Is culturally attaining, empathetic, and conscious of quality/skill of performance. Has need to complete commitments, communications gifts, and emotional responsiveness. Combines optimism, determination, and humanitarian motives. Judge, social worker, and physician are possible career opportunities.

PERSONALITY INGREDIENTS: Strives to be fashionable, entertaining, and kind. Wants beauty, pleasure, and artistic/musical/showmanlike self-expression. Appears to be comforting, parental, and solid. Strives to be instructional, respectable, and domestic/rooted. Aims to serve life-support causes, inspire family/community uplift, and be down-to-earth. Attracts martydom, obstacles to ego drives, and recognition for universally accepted creativity, or humanitarianism.

PERSONALITY EXTREME: Too selfish, or too accommodating.

REGIS (Latin: Regan/English)—F. & M.

MAJOR TALENT: Ability to incorporate practical work, system, and problem-solving into career. Is strong, determined, and energetic. Has imagination, individuality, and ambition. Combines daring, communications gifts, and industrious attitude. Real estate salesperson, piano player, and administrator may be career opportunities.

PERSONALITY INGREDIENTS: Inwardly impulsive, sensual, and adventurous. Wants travel, progressive changes, and unconventional experiences. First impression is tailor-made, managerial, and self-assured.

Strives to be businesslike, influential, and organized. Seems confident, and will fight for goals. At best when concentrated, routined, and cooperative. Adds drama and competitive spirit to everything.

PERSONALITY EXTREME: Too assertive, or too submissive.

REID (Old English: Read/English)—M.

MAJOR TALENT: Ability to incorporate polished communications techniques, broad philosophy, and empathetic nature into career. Is compassionate, imaginative, and inspirational. Has healing gifts, generosity, and universal vision. Combines sensitivity to fine points, intellectual/scientific/technical expertise, and humanitarian drives. Doctor, artist/performer/musician, and educational reformer are possible career opportunities.

PERSONALITY INGREDIENTS: Inwardly adventurous, sensual, and unconventional. Wants travel, speculation, and stimulating enthusiasms. Appears to be conventional, practical, and dignified. Strives to be precise, down-to-earth, and enduring. Aims to plan, work, and see tangible results. Expects the best from everyone, and should maintain tolerance.

PERSONALITY EXTREME: Too rigid, or too unstructured.

RENATA (Latin/English)—F.

MAJOR TALENT: Ability to incorporate flexibility, unconventional ideas, and adventurous nature into career. Is expressive, accommodating, and progressive. Has keen physical appetites, human understanding, and cleverness. Combines daring, imagination, and communications techniques. Travel agent, politician, and theatrical performer may be career opportunities.

PERSONALITY INGREDIENTS: Desires technical/scientific expertise, authority, and perfection. Feels introspective, questioning, and aristocratic. Appears mysterious, cool, and observing. Strives to be confident, educated, and cultured. Aims to be discreet, tasteful, and poised, but needs concentrated study to boost inner strength. Fears loneliness/poverty, and must learn to enjoy solitude and the marvels of nature.

PERSONALITY EXTREME: Too ambitious, or too aimless.

RENE (Greek: Irene; variable, F./Latin: Renault/French: René; M.)—F. & M.

MAJOR TALENT: Ability to incorporate sympathetic concern, sense of harmony, and advisory attitude into career. Is companionable, idealistic, and attentive to details. Has financial practicality, emotional understanding, and love of family/justice/creative expression. Combines attraction for supporters, discipline, and protective responsibility. Costume/cosmetics/home products designer, therapist, and hotel/restaurant manager may be career opportunities.

PERSONALITY INGREDIENTS: Inwardly inventive, independent, and nonconforming. Desires leadership, originality, and progressive action. Appears striking, enthusiastic, and off-beat. Strives to be gutsy, clever, and free. Has sex appeal, strength, and social success.

PERSONALITY EXTREME: Too temperamental, or too controlled.

RENEE (Latin: Renata/French: Renée/English)—F.

MAJOR TALENT: Ability to incorporate inventive enthusiasms, sensitivity to fine points, and desire to inspire artistic quality into career. Is high-strung, individualistic, and accommodating. Has supportive drives, attraction for unusual causes, and persuasive communications techniques. Combines friendliness, orderliness, and potential to bring original ideas to lasting fame. Designer, reformer, and writer are possible career opportunities.

PERSONALITY INGREDIENTS: Desires domestic happiness, luxury, and respectability. Feels protective, responsible, and instructional. Aims for material security, community uplift, and companionship. Appears to be energetic, exciting, and sensual. Strives for adventure, travel, and unconventional pleasures. Wants freedom, and takes on burdens for others. Attracts recognition.

PERSONALITY EXTREME: Too changeable, or too tied-down.

REUBEN (Hebrew/English)—M.

MAJOR TALENT: Ability to incorporate inventive ideas, high energy, and sense of uniqueness into career. Is a zealous crusader for personal beliefs, futuristic plans, and intuitive feelings. Has appreciation of art, beauty, and peer relationships. Combines individuality of purpose, empathetic helpfulness, and rebellion against mediocrity. Welfare worker, promoter, and psychologist are possible career opportunities.

PERSONALITY INGREDIENTS: Desires tangible results, honesty, and down-to-earth practicality. Needs planning, work, and to be a solid citizen. Appears to be pensive, aloof, and subdued. Strives for quality, timeless values, and perfection in self and others. Finds disappointment in self-image. Needs to be nonmaterialistic and to concentrate upon an intellectual or spiritual interest. Best when attracting recognition through expertise, not manual labor. Hides true emotions under aristocratic hat.

PERSONALITY EXTREME: Too irresponsible, or too dedicated.

REX (Latin/English/diminutive: Regan-Reginald-Eric)—M.

MAJOR TALENT: Capacity for incorporating personal accommodation, devotion to peace, and diplomatic charm into career. Able to arbitrate differences, accumulate knowledge/things/friendships, and work with others. Has modesty, subdued tastes, and knack of attracting good fortune through patience/persistence. Combines sensitivity, kindness, and inspirational leadership. Politician, psychologist, and poet are possible career opportunities.

PERSONALITY INGREDIENTS: Desires adventure, sensual pleasures, and constant change. Feels open-minded, speculative, and clever. Appears interested, comfortable, and respectable. Strives for domestic harmony, gracious living, and to improve living standards for others. Seems opinionated, but works to teach, counsel, and adjust problems. Is domineering when insecure.

PERSONALITY EXTREME: Too critical, or too sympathetic.

REYNARD (Old German/Danish/English)—M.

MAJOR TALENT: Ability to incorporate dependability, hard work, and practical wisdom into career. Is honest, structured, and methodical. Combines problem-solving confidence, material accomplishments, and research/study/dedication. Mathematician, pianist, and administrator may be career opportunities.

PERSONALITY INGREDIENTS: Appears aloof, but wants love. Desires family/community harmony, comforts, and improvements. Needs companionship, and is responsible/protective. Strives to be analytic, strategic, and aristocratic. Aims for quality, culture, and perfection. Should avoid disorganization, secretiveness, and unrealistic goals. Is often misunderstood.

PERSONALITY EXTREME: Too industrious, or too lazy.

RHEA (Greek/English)—F.
MAJOR TALENT: Ability to incorporate unconventional, experimental, enthusiastic personality into career. Is sensitive to fine points, communicative, and imaginative. Has adaptability, understanding, and flexibility. Combines patience, optimism, and cleverness. Advertising, politics, and communications are possible career opportunities.

PERSONALITY INGREDIENTS: Appears to be businesslike, tasteful, and managerial. Strives to be influential, affluent, and trustworthy. Desires family/community attainments, material comforts, and to help others. Feels responsible, protective, and sympathetic. Enjoys adventure, romance, and progressive changes. Should avoid emotional outbursts of temper.

PERSONALITY EXTREME: Too independent, or too submissive.

RHODA (Oriental/Latin/Greek: Rose/English)—F.
MAJOR TALENT: Ability to incorporate individuality, initiative, and leadership into career. Has sensitivity to fine points, mental organization, and executive efficiency. Is different, pioneering, and ambitious. Combines competitive spirit, material power, and inventiveness. Business executive, lawyer, and salesperson are possible career opportunities.

PERSONALITY INGREDIENTS: Inwardly self-questioning, analytic, and culturally attaining. Wants privacy, quality, and tasteful perfection. Appears to be entertaining, up-to-date, and optimistic. Strives to be popular, kind, and surrounded by beauty. Desires discretion, and bubbles with conversation. Has conflicting characteristics. At best when educated and sociable. Has fears of loneliness/poverty, and needs recognition.

PERSONALITY EXTREME: Too dominating, or too dependent.

RICHARD (Old German/French/English)—M.
MAJOR TALENT: Ability to incorporate intellectual productivity, words, and uncluttered perceptions into career. Is kind, sympathetic, and determined. Has inventive nature, parental self-image, and instinct for perfection. Combines discipline, discretion, and professionalism. Attracts overindulgence, intuitive guidance, and admiration. Technical/scientific expert, appraiser, and editor may be career opportunities.

PERSONALITY INGREDIENTS: Desires independence and leadership. Feels ambitious, impatient, and nonconforming. Appears to be dignified, sympathetic, and comfortable. Strives to teach, pioneer, counsel, and uplift the emotional needs of others. Aims for showmanship, luxury, and family/community respect. Has strong sense of justice, loyalty, and social service. May leave a lasting image through mature concern for the welfare of the community. Enjoys gracious living, timeless beauty, and has surprising stamina for problem solving.

PERSONALITY EXTREME: Too hard-working, or too self-destructive.

RICK (Old German: Richard/English: dimunitive)—M.

MAJOR TALENT: Ability to incorporate cleverness, flexibility, and progressive changes into career. Is curious, adventurous, and attentive to details. Has unconventional appetites, sociability, and enthusiasm. Combines agility, communications techniques, and knack of learning by experience. Promoter, travel agent, and athlete are possible career opportunities.

PERSONALITY INGREDIENTS: Inwardly empathetic, generous, and broad-scoped. Wants romance, quality of skill/performance, and humanitarian interests. Appears vital, sexy, and different. Strives to be open-minded, free-wheeling, and confident. Attracts protection, inheritances, and passionate loves.

PERSONALITY EXTREME: Too impractical, or too careful.

RICKY (Old German: Richard, M./Italianate: Ricarda-Greek: Rhoda, F./English)—F. & M.

MAJOR TALENT: Ability to incorporate polished, structured, and wide-ranging communications techniques into career. Is artistic, imaginative, and kind. Has personal attractiveness, charm, and versatility. Combines skill, practicality, and production of beauty/entertainment/quality. Plastic surgeon, thespian, and philosophical writer are possible career opportunities.

PERSONALITY INGREDIENTS: Inwardly seeks perfection. Feels questioning, private, and aristocratic. Needs education/expertise to achieve potential/self-esteem. Appears to be sexy, understanding, and alert. Strives to be experimental, open minded, and progressive. Always seems youthful, energetic, and enthusiastic. Best when on conventional course.

PERSONALITY EXTREME: Too unrealistic, or too logical.

RILEY (Old English/English)—M.

MAJOR TALENT: Ability to incorporate social service, parental outlook, and strong personal ideals into career. Is sympathetic, instructional, and counseling. Has mature insight, dedication to family/community uplift, and a knack with words. Combines domestic instincts, inspirational leadership, and potential to work for lasting benefit. Musician, hotel/restaurant executive, and credit union organizer may be career opportunities.

PERSONALITY INGREDIENTS: Inwardly optimistic, pleasure seeking, and kind. Wants love, entertainment, and beauty. Appears sociable, attractive, and up-to-date. Strives to be inspirational, happy, and apart from the turmoil of materialism/suffering/angers. Aims for ease, tolerance, and acceptance. Must avoid assuming unnecessary burdens.

PERSONALITY EXTREME: Too skeptical, or too gullible.

RITA (Sanskrit/Latin-Spanish: Margaret; diminutive/English)—F.

MAJOR TALENT: Ability to incorporate words/writing/entertaining, cooperative spirit, and individuality into career. Is attention-getting, versatile, and optimistic. Has charm, wit, and cleverness. Combines ambition, desire to rise above mediocrity, and creative self-expression. Theater, fashion, and science may be career opportunities.

PERSONALITY INGREDIENTS: Inwardly independent, inventive, and competitive. Wants mental freedom, nonconforming style, and to be first/original. Appears different, enthusiastic, and exciting. Has high nervous energy, futuristic concepts, and idealistic approach. Strives to raise expectations, lead unusual causes, and universally improve expectations of quality. Must avoid impracticality, selfishness, and scattering interests. Has potential to leave a lasting image.

PERSONALITY EXTREME: Too assertive, or too submissive.

ROBERT (Old German/French/Scottish/English)—M.

MAJOR TALENT: Ability to incorporate ideas for social improvement, dedicated work, and domestic/community problem-solving into career. Is parental, instructional, and counseling. Has determination, firm personal ideals, and high nervous energy. Combines optimism, burden-bearing, and potential to raise living standards/sense of security for others. Responsible/protective/assuming nature may lead to martyrdom. Any home product/service, credit union organizer, marriage counselor, and inspired teacher are possible career opportunities.

PERSONALITY INGREDIENTS: Expects to plan, work, and achieve long-lasting results. Strives to be practical, disciplined, and resourceful. Inwardly cannot accept mediocrity. Wants quality, fine points acknowledged, and to inspire universal spiritual uplift. Is a dreamer, but has workaholic drive to bring concepts to reality. Must avoid pessimistic discontent, hardness, and taking on impossible tasks. May be a poet, or a power for humanitarian reform.

PERSONALITY EXTREME: Too personalized, or too unfeeling.

ROBERTA (Old German: Robert/English)—F.

MAJOR TALENT: Ability to incorporate self-expression, common sense, and introspective analysis into career. Is versatile, practical, and culturally ambitious. Has investigative, secretive, beauty-seeking nature. Combines nonroutine scheduling, problem solving, and strategic planning. Appraiser, university administrator, and lawyer may be career opportunities.

PERSONALITY INGREDIENTS: Self-image demands far-reaching tangible goals. Strives to be self-assured, helpful, and highly successful by traditional standards. Inwardly imaginative, sociable, and youthfully optimistic. Wants humor, pleasure, and sunny days. Appears to be direct and down-to-earth, but needs material and emotional security to burn off high nervous energy.

PERSONALITY EXTREME: Too independent, or too submissive.

ROBIN (Old German: Robert/English)—F. & M.

MAJOR TALENT: Ability to incorporate practical work, determination, and structured discipline into career. Competitive, strong, and articulate in authority. Has imagination, charm, and conscientiousness. Combines individuality, kindness, and concentrated labor. Landscaper, bookkeeper, and piano player are possible career opportunities.

PERSONALITY INGREDIENTS: Inwardly protective, responsible, and instructional. Wants family/home/community respectability, emotional harmony, and luxury/beauty in personal environments. Appears aloof, perceptive, and aristocratic. Strives to be discreet, cultured, and perfect. Aims to feel confident, and is best when educated/expert/specialized. Must be known to be understood.

PERSONALITY EXTREME: Too adventurous, or too cautious.

ROBINSON (Old German: Robert/English: variable)—M.

MAJOR TALENT: Ability to incorporate logic, research, and creative intellect into career. Is skillful, aristocratic, and introspective. Has poise, common sense, and optimism. Combines disciplined work, creative self-expression, and perfecting nature. Writer, fine artist, and data processor may be career opportunities.

PERSONALITY INGREDIENTS: Wants variety, humor, and pleasure. Feels kind, attentive to details, and individualistic. Appears to be dynamic, tailor-made, and solid. Strives to plan, build, and labor for lasting tangible results. Aims to reshape, improve, and bring progress to others. Resourceful, determined, and clever, attracts fame, friendship, and just causes.

PERSONALITY EXTREME: Too adventurous, or too fearful.

ROBYN (Old German: Robert/English)—F. & M.

MAJOR TALENT: Ability to incorporate personal idealism, sensitivity to details, and individuality into career. Is supportive, administrative, and orderly. Has nervous energy, desire for partnership and artistic/spiritual expectations. Combines refinement, modesty, and desire to inspire improvement. May leave a lasting image. Film industries, data processing, and administrative executive are possible career opportunities.

PERSONALITY INGREDIENTS: Inwardly practical, organized, and determined. Feels trustworthy, industrious, and structured. Wants to be a solid citizen. First impression is aloof, introspective, and aristocratic. Strives to be authoritative, culturally polished, and perfect. Courts personal disappointment through materialistic attitudes. At best when educated or technically skilled. Attracts success through quality of performance.

PERSONALITY EXTREME: Too unconventional, or too proper.

ROD (English: variable-diminutive)—M.

MAJOR TALENT: Ability to incorporate originality, drive, and independent leadership into career. Is aggressive, assertive, and philosophical. Has empathetic instincts, courage, and pioneering spirit. Combines humanitarian approach, daring, and inventive ideas. Writer, salesperson, and architect may be career opportunities.

PERSONALITY INGREDIENTS: Wants love, domestic harmony, and gracious living. Feels parental, sympathetic, and instructional. First impression is traditional, dignified, and neat. Strives to be a solid citizen. Aims for practicality, organization, and constructive work. Must understand uniqueness. Is meant to inspire/lead/originate and open doors to progress. Attracts followers. May tend to be a loner.

PERSONALITY EXTREME: Too conventional, or too improper.

RODERICK (Old German: Richard-Robert; combination/English)—M.

MAJOR TALENT: Ability to incorporate intellectual, practical, emotionally vibrating nature into career. Is a conflicting personality with inventive, futuristic, self-expressive gifts. Has material structure, inspirations that strive for perfection, and magnetic charm. Combines spontaneous enthusiasms, traditional ambitions, and financial success when decisive. Photographer, psychoanalyst, and geriatrics specialist may be career opportunities.

PERSONALITY INGREDIENTS: Wants peace, partnership, and love. Desires relaxation, gentleness, and refinement. Appears youthful, noble, and brotherly. Strives to bring skill, quality, and helpful service to others. Aims for a broad marketplace, tolerance, and professionalism. At best when discriminating, discreet, and logical.

PERSONALITY EXTREME: Too adaptable, or too critical.

RODGER (Old German: Roger/English)—M.

MAJOR TALENT: Ability to incorporate planning, work, and discipline into career. Is orderly, prompt, and statistical. Has integrity, modesty, and gentleness. Combines receptive nature, traditional focus, and problem-solving determination. Bookkeeper, pianist, and builder are possible career opportunities.

PERSONALITY INGREDIENTS: Wants easygoing style, inventive interests, and peaceful peer relationships. Has nervous energy, uplifting ideas, and a desire to encourage others to expect more out of life. Feels refined, empathetic, and aims for quality of skill/performance. Appears understanding, charitable, and magnetic. Attracts recognition, romantic notions, and success through system and conscientiousness.

PERSONALITY EXTREME: Too compassionate, or too unfeeling.

RODNEY (Teutonic/Anglo-Saxon/English)—M.

MAJOR TALENT: Ability to incorporate philosophical approach, imagination, and polished performance into career. Is kind, responsible, and parental. Has impressive, dramatic, and attracting personality. Combines words, creative self-expression, and wide understanding/interests/emotions. Gifted artist/entertainer, welfare worker, and clergyman are possible career opportunities.

PERSONALITY INGREDIENTS: Seems quiet, deep, and analytic. Strives to be poised, questioning, and quality-conscious. Aims for timeless beauty, privacy, and perfection. Inwardly feels unique. Wants peace, love, and stimulating relationships. Desires inventive, futuristic, high-toned activities. Radiates nervous energy that produces spontaneous enthusiasms, inspirational ideas, and attracts followers. Best when geared to original methods/concepts, and concentrated artistically. Has potential to amass money/universal recognition.

PERSONALITY EXTREME: Too insecure, or too confident.

ROGER (Old German/French/English)—M.

MAJOR TALENT: Ability to incorporate imagination, responsible/protective nature, and broad planning into career. Is determined, magnetic, and instructional. Has showmanship, artistic/musical gifts, and sense of fair play. Combines inspirational ideas/personal example, burden-bearing/problem-solving instincts, and youthful/romantic approach. Theater, religion, and education may be career opportunities.

PERSONALITY INGREDIENTS: First impression is classy, introspective, and reserved. Strives to be cultured, polished, and perfect. Aims to specialize, be discreet, and rise above mediocrity. Inwardly sensitive, detail-conscious, and intensely romantic. Wants to improve expectations and standards for others. Has emotional high/lows, drama, and need for beauty/peer relationships. Best when concentrated, calm, and confident.

PERSONALITY EXTREME: Too charitable, or too selfish.

ROLAND (German/French/English)—M.

MAJOR TALENT: Ability to incorporate originality, sensitivity to fine points, and executive leadership into career. Is inventive, self-reliant, and ambitious. Has diplomacy, organizational efficiency, and initiative. Combines orderliness, businesslike instincts, and pioneering spirit. Retailer, architect, and idea person are possible career opportunities.

PERSONALITY INGREDIENTS: Appears extroverted, while feeling reserved. Desires solitude, intellectual stimulation, and perfection. Wants to get to the root of everything. First impression is attention-getting, up-to-date, and friendly. Strives to be popular, imaginative, and self-expressive. Needs beauty, love, and cultural interests. Should specialize.

PERSONALITY EXTREME: Too traditional, or too nonconforming.

ROLANDA (German: Roland, M./English)—F.

MAJOR TALENT: Ability to incorporate inspirational enthusiasms, diplomacy, and wide creative ambitions into career. Is sensitive, romantic, and inventive. Has nervous energy, distaste for mediocrity, and standard-raising concepts. Combines patience, individuality, and reforming nature. Corporation secretary, diplomat, and film performer/technician are possible career opportunities.

PERSONALITY INGREDIENTS: Desires material rewards, prestige, and executive leadership. Feels businesslike, efficient, and determined. Appears to be sociable, entertaining, and fashionable. Strives to get attention, love, and pleasure. Aims to be happy. Attracts commercial partnerships, and success. Best when decisive, adaptable, and persistent.

PERSONALITY EXTREME: Too independent, or too accommodating.

ROLF (Anglo-Saxon-German: Ralph; Randolph, Rudolph, variable)—M.

MAJOR TALENT: Ability to incorporate responsible, protective, instructional approach into career. Is sympathetic, practical, and attentive to details. Has common sense, showmanship, and need for group/partnership harmony. Combines parental nature, service, and firm personal ideals. Teacher, theatrical producer, and home products sales/services are possible career opportunities.

PERSONALITY INGREDIENTS: Desires family/community attainments, luxury, and creative self-expression. Wants traditions, music/beauty, and to take an interest in everything. Appears helpful, understanding, and polished. Strives to be charitable, broad-scoped, and skillful. Attracts admirers, but must avoid jealousy, stubbornness, and pessimism.

PERSONALITY EXTREME: Too meddlesome, or too disinterested.

ROLLO (Teutonic: independent/Roland; variable/English)—M.

MAJOR TALENT: Ability to incorporate compassion, quality performance/skill, and attention to fine points into career. Sensitive and patient, with investigative approach, discretion, and magnetic charm. Combines creative self-expression, diplomacy, and wide-ranging philosophy. Doctor, psychologist, and publisher are possible career opportunities.

PERSONALITY INGREDIENTS: Best when serving humanitarian interests. Desires beauty, love, and kindness. Strives to protect, instruct, and counsel. Appears comforting, conventional and sturdy. Aims to improve living standards, inspire group harmony, and share talents. Attracts money through spiritual/intellectual strengths.

PERSONALITY EXTREME: Too possessive, or too relinquishing.

ROMEO (Latin/Italian/English)—M.

MAJOR TALENT: Ability to incorporate polished artistic/humanitarian self-expression into career. Is imaginative, clever, and versatile. Has sex appeal, charm, and respect for traditions/justice/domestic tranquility. Combines romantic nature, conventionality, and a knack with words. Writer, artist, and organizer may be career opportunities.

PERSONALITY INGREDIENTS: Feels above the crowd. Desires quality, beauty, and peace. Wants to be unique, inspire professionalism and implement personal ideals. Seeks perfection, and may be impractical. First impression is alert, inventive, and ambitious. Strives to be aggressive, assertive, and first. Attracts recognition, romance, and a lasting image. Best when realistic.

PERSONALITY EXTREME: Too devoted, or too uncaring.

RONALD (Old German: Reginald; variable/Old Norse/Scottish/ English)—M.

MAJOR TALENT: Ability to incorporate individuality, diplomacy, and creative businesslike approach into career. Is aristocratic, pioneering, and courageous. Has adaptability, initiative, and ambition. Combines cooperation, self-reliance, and nonconformity. Architect, musician/ actor, and inventor are possible career opportunities.

PERSONALITY INGREDIENTS: Desires timeless beauty, solitude, and cultural refinements. Feels aloof, questioning, and logical. Wants privacy, intellectual stimulation, and dignity. Appears attractive, sociable, and imaginative. Strives to be popular, entertaining and artistic. Aims for humor, optimism, attention, and love. Must be known to be understood.

PERSONALITY EXTREME: Too traditional, or too inconstant.

RONALDA (Teutonic-Old German/Old Norse/English)—F.

MAJOR TALENT: Ability to incorporate inspirational ideas, tact, and crusading enthusiasms into career. Is inventive, high-strung, and attention-getting. Has refinement, broad philosophy, and sensitivity to fine points. Combines patience, humanitarian instincts, and individuality. Poet, novelist, and religious/educational reformer may be career opportunities.

PERSONALITY INGREDIENTS: Strives to be fashionable, kind, and entertaining. Appears optimistic, affectionate, and sociable. Inwardly managerial, self-reliant, and materially attaining. Wants efficient organization, tangible results, and influence/affluence/respect. Should aim for a creative industry, be practical, and avoid indecision.

PERSONALITY EXTREME: Too aggressive, or too receptive.

ROOSEVELT (German/Dutch/English)—M.

MAJOR TALENT: Ability to incorporate unconventional ideas, practical structure, and independent, courageous leadership into career. Is organized, ambitious, and clever. Has sensuality, confidence, and faith. Combines instinct for progressive change, discipline, and mental agility. Politician, lawyer, and theatrical agent may be career opportunities.

PERSONALITY INGREDIENTS: Desires far-reaching and lasting planning, work, results. Is a masterful problem solver, organizer, and diplomatic executive. Feels firm, strong, and imaginative. First impression is nonconforming, definite, and proud. Strives to pioneer, lead, and retain individuality. Attracts all round success, but must control physical appetites.

PERSONALITY EXTREME: Too critical, or too easygoing.

RORY (Old German/Celtic/English)—M.

MAJOR TALENT: Ability to incorporate discipline, independence, and originality into career. Is attention-getting, proud, and optimistic. Has determination, practicality, and structure. Combines creative self-expression, daring ideas, and down-to-earth competitive work. Builder/contractor, printer, and farmer are possible career opportunities.

PERSONALITY INGREDIENTS: Inwardly conventional, determined, and honest. Desires material security, dignity, and tangible results. First impression is understanding, appealing, and noble. Strives to be empathetic, helpful, and broad-scoped. Aims for quality/skill of performance, humanitarian principles, and artistry. Magnetic, cooperative/diplomatic, modest, and at best when efficiently aimed toward one goal.

PERSONALITY EXTREME: Too confident, or too self-questioning.

ROSA (Latin: Rose/Italian/Portuguese/Spanish/English)—F.

MAJOR TALENT: Ability to incorporate practical executive efficiency, independent ideas, and desire for cultural growth into career. Is managerial, determined, and organized. Has integrity, initiative, investigative approach. Combines independence, introspection, and material ambition. Business administrator, banker, and engineer may be career opportunities.

PERSONALITY INGREDIENTS: Inwardly strategic, analytic, and questioning. Desires solitude, refinement, and perfection. Self-image is sensual and adventurous. Appears nonconforming, alert, and direct. Strives to be progressive, courageous, and in the lead. Should avoid stubbornness, pessimism, and self-doubt. Attracts recognition and results.

PERSONALITY EXTREME: Too assertive, or too submissive.

ROSALIE (Latin: Rose/German/English)—F.

MAJOR TALENT: Ability to incorporate introspective questioning, practical work, and sociability into career. Is analytic, intuitive, and secretive. Has refined tastes, desire for perfection and creative self-expression. Combines conventional approach, artistic/fashion conscious focus, and strong philosophical/spiritual/cultural leanings. Librarian, metaphysician/clergyman, and musical technician are possible career opportunities.

PERSONALITY INGREDIENTS: Inwardly wants beauty, love, and pleasure. Desires variety, humor, and to entertain/be entertained. First impression is conventional, down-to-earth, and honest. Strives to be materially secure, orderly and ethical. Best when traditional, educated, and optimistic. Suffers melancholy when solid-citizen self-image is disturbed. Must maintain integrity.

PERSONALITY EXTREME: Too adventurous, or too cautious.

ROSALIND (Latin-Spanish: Rosalinda/English)—F.

MAJOR TALENT: Ability to incorporate inventive, quality-conscious, inspirational ideas into career. Is diplomatic, modest, and hard-working. Has nervous energy, optimistic approach, and efficiency. Combines creative self-expression, material ambitions, and drive to uplift artistic tastes, spiritual awareness, and life-style expectations for others. Educational reformer, preacher, and poet are possible career opportunities.

PERSONALITY INGREDIENTS: Desires expertise, authority, and cultural attainments. Needs education and intellectual polish. Wants privacy, discretion, and refinements. Appears to be traditional, dignified, and realistic. Strives to be a far-reaching architect/builder for humanitarian goals. Aims to leave a lasting constructive mark. Attracts family/community burdens/responsibilities, idealistically impractical partnerships, and fame.

PERSONALITY EXTREME: Too disciplined, or too unconventional.

ROSCOE (Teutonic/English)—M.

MAJOR TALENT: Ability to incorporate creative self-expression, disciplined routine, and ambitious planning into career. Kind, optimistic, and sociable, with charm, wit, and practicality. Combines respect for conventions, attention-getting personality, and attention to beauty/quality/love. Plastic surgeon, theatrical producer, and philosophical writer are possible career opportunities.

PERSONALITY INGREDIENTS: Desires executive leadership, wealth, and prestige. Wants to control, delegate, and tackle large assignments. Appears dignified, traditional, and sturdy. Strives to be honest, fair, and conscientious. Attracts success and happiness.

PERSONALITY EXTREME: Too sensual, or too mental.

ROSE (Oriental/Latin/Greek/English)—F.

MAJOR TALENT: Ability to incorporate artistic/creative/inspirational concepts, practical sensitivity to details, and attention-getting talents into career. Is kind, sociable, and conversational. Has a knack with words, optimism, and entertaining. Combines individuality and desire to collect information/things, with attractive appearance and/or animated/charming personality. Social organizer, beautician, and writer are possible career opportunities.

PERSONALITY INGREDIENTS: Inwardly spiritually/inventively reforming. Desires to uplift quality and expectations. Feels above mediocrity, and wants peer partnership/relationships. First impression is energetic, different, and progressive. Strives to be a nonconforming, and courageous winner. Self-image is pioneering, and aims to create new vistas or break outworn traditional molds. Attracts recognition, and leaves a lasting mark through patience, unlimited ambitions, and concentration.

PERSONALITY EXTREME: Too experimental, or too tenacious.

ROSEANNA (Latin-Hebrew/English)—F.

MAJOR TALENT: Ability to incorporate life-support service, creative self-expression, and parental nature into career. Is sympathetic, helpful, and protective. Has showmanship, charm, and high energy. Combines words, warmth, and dedication. Nurse, credit union organizer, and marriage counselor may be career opportunities.

PERSONALITY INGREDIENTS: Inwardly practical, hard-working, and persevering. Desires dignity, material security, and traditional successes. Appears retiring, modest, and refined. Strives to be supportive, peaceful, and easygoing. Aims to maintain harmony, but should avoid face-value judgments.

PERSONALITY EXTREME: Too ambitious, or too uninspired.

ROSEMARIE (Latin-Hebrew: Rosemary/English)—F.

MAJOR TALENT: Ability to incorporate practical emotional balance, integrity, and strength of character into career. Is broad-scoped, generous, and capable. Has desire to give and receive material security. Combines intuitive sense of timing, conscientious perseverance, and desire for material comforts. Business administrator, lawyer, and quality manufacturer are possible career opportunities.

PERSONALITY INGREDIENTS: Strives to experience everything. First impression is vital, enthusiastic, untraditional. Aims for travel, change, and people contact. Inwardly wants material success, businesslike efficiency, and prestige. Feels trustworthy, managerial, and self-reliant. Is inspirational, clever, and philosophical. Attracts success.

PERSONALITY EXTREME: Too self-indulgent, or too easily satisfied.

ROSEMARY (Latin-Hebrew/English)—F.

MAJOR TALENT: Ability to incorporate creative imagination, musical/artistic gifts, and protective/responsible/parental nature into career. Is sympathetic, practical, and cooperative. Has sensitivity to fine points, showmanship, and discipline. Combines professionalism, sympathetic domestic/community service/uplift, and responsive emotional nature. Teacher, interior decorator, and hospital administrator are possible career opportunities.

PERSONALITY INGREDIENTS: Inwardly desires independent leadership, pioneering activities, and mental freedom. Is ambitious, and wants to instigate progressive changes. First impression is striking, enthusiastic, and sensual. Strives to be adventurous, open-minded, and on the move. Self-image encourages unconventional experiences, but must avoid physical self-indulgences, impulsiveness, and impatience.

PERSONALITY EXTREME: Too skeptical, or too gullible.

ROSS (Teutonic: Roscoe; variable/English)—M.

MAJOR TALENT: Ability to incorporate efficient businesslike instinct, independence, and sharp analytic mind into career. Is self-reliant, managerial, and materially ambitious. Has strength, control, and reserve. Combines investigative desire for perfection, creative leadership, and executive judgment. Business consultant, publisher, and manufacturer are possible career opportunities.

PERSONALITY INGREDIENTS: Desires harmonious, respectable, luxurious home/family/community lifestyle. Feels protective, responsible, and instructional. Is sympathetic, helpful, and parental. Strives to be an inspiration of quality or spiritual uplift to others. Appears different, and is enthusiastically contagious when fired to reform the expectations/thinking of others. Should maintain optimistic ideals, and be open to progressive changes. Has a unique attractive quality that offers lasting recognition.

PERSONALITY EXTREME: Too individualistic, or too imitative.

ROWENA (Celtic/Old English)—F.

MAJOR TALENT: Ability to incorporate practical work, attractive personality, and competitive spirit into career. Is conscientious, honest, and orderly. Has determination, independence, and self-assertion. Combines kindness, courage, and discipline. Bookkeeper, real estate salesperson, and landscaper are possible career opportunities.

PERSONALITY INGREDIENTS: Inwardly wants artistic expression, optimism, and love. Desires pleasure. A fighter, first impression is nonconforming, direct, and energetic. Strives to be progressive, daring and first. Aims for leadership, and never to be kept waiting. At best when concentrated, patient, and tactful.

PERSONALITY EXTREME: Too bossy, or too accommodating.

ROXANNE (Persian: Roxana/English)—F.

MAJOR TALENT: Ability to incorporate originality, aristocratic tastes, and love of beauty into career. Is reserved, charming, and independent. Has discretion, artistic interests, and analytic approach. Combines imagination, research, and progressive ideas. Designer, secret service agent, and lawyer are possible career opportunities.

PERSONALITY INGREDIENTS: Strives to be cultured, poised, and perfect. Appears observant, refined, and aloof. Desires beauty, joy, and romance. Feels restless, pleasure-seeking, and resourceful. Aims for authority/expertise, and is most comfortable dividing interests. Attracts diversification and needs to concentrate.

PERSONALITY EXTREME: Too experimental, or too unchanging.

ROY (Latin/English)—M.

MAJOR TALENT: Ability to incorporate far-reaching and humanitarian planning, work, and practical results into career. Is direct, principled, and determined. Has sensitivity to details, diplomacy, and cooperative nature. Combines inspirational ideas, self-assurance, and knack of coordinating workaholic activities. Stage manager, practical reformer, and efficiency expert may be career opportunities.

PERSONALITY INGREDIENTS: Desires family/community harmony, respect, and comforts. Wants abundant, loving, materially attaining lifestyle. Is parental, showmanlike, and musical/artistic. Appears to be refined, poised, and introspective. Strives for cultural attainments, natural/timeless beauty, and discretion. Needs specialty or education. Best when unmaterialistic, and counseling/perfecting/inspiring wisdom and/or spirituality. Loses reputation/finances when power-hungry. Must maintain inner faith.

PERSONALITY EXTREME: Too skeptical, or too gullible.

RUBEN (Hebrew: Reuben/English)—M.

MAJOR TALENT: Ability to incorporate parental nature, conscientiousness, and emotional understanding into career. Is sympathetic, protective, and responsible. Has patience, tact, and practical common sense. Combines cooperation, discipline, and stability. Teacher, nurse, and musician may be career opportunities.

PERSONALITY INGREDIENTS: Inwardly efficient, self-reliant, and materially attaining. Wants big business, admiration, and respect. Appears aloof, reserved, and aristocratic. Strives to be confident, culturally polished, and perfect. Best when expert/educated. May seem stuck up, but really feels unacceptable to others. Needs to be known to be understood.

PERSONALITY EXTREME: Too busy, or too bored.

RUBIN (Latin: Ruby/English)—M.

MAJOR TALENT: Ability to incorporate independent leadership, detailed perceptions, and executive capability into career. Is daring, determined, and self-reliant. Has tact, friendliness, and progressive ambitions. Combines dependability, adaptability, and initiative. Retail store owner, architect, and salesperson are possible career opportunities.

PERSONALITY INGREDIENTS: Seems introverted and desires popularity. Inwardly resourceful, optimistic, and pleasure-seeking. Wants beauty, variety, and imaginative love relationships. Flirts, but is not unfaithful. First impression is reserved, pensive, and aristocratic. Strives to be authoritative, polished, and perfect. Courts disappointment until a realistic self-image is developed. At best when educated or specialized. Lacks inner confidence. Must be known to be understood.

PERSONALITY EXTREME: Too sensual, or too cerebral.

RUBY (Latin/English)—F. & M.

MAJOR TALENT: Ability to incorporate attention-getting creative self-expression into career. Is kind, imaginative, and individualistic. Has sensitivity to fine points, patience, and a gift with words/entertainment/artistry. Combines independent ideas, need for peace, and talent for bringing concepts to form. Writer, model, and entertainer may be career opportunities.

PERSONALITY INGREDIENTS: First impression is unusual, vibrant, and mystical. Strives to originate and inspire. Inwardly aggressive, assertive, and ambitious. Wants mental freedom, progressive changes, and constant activity. Has high nervous energy, stimulating personality, and organized approach. Should avoid indecision, selfishness, and disregarding past mistakes.

PERSONALITY EXTREME: Too aristocratic, or too earthy.

RUDOLPH (Old German/English)—M.

MAJOR TALENT: Ability to incorporate order, practicality, and precision into career. Is dependable, honest, and traditional. Has discipline, loyalty, and hard-working nature. Combines humanitarian and charitable instincts, devotion, and structured thinking. Physical therapist, accountant, and builder may be career opportunities.

PERSONALITY INGREDIENTS: Strives to be materially secure, traditional, and structured. Appears classic, sturdy, and neat. Inwardly philosophical, generous, and willing to give selfless service. Desires quality/skill of performance, broad-ranged activity, and romance. Attracts health, money, and love through ability to understand human foibles.

PERSONALITY EXTREME: Too materialistic, or too financially imprudent.

RUDY (Old German: Rudolph; variable/English)—M.

MAJOR TALENT: Ability to incorporate unconventional approach, sensitivity to fine points, and learning by experience into career. Is diplomatic, creatively self-expressive, and curious. Has confidence, cleverness, and sensuality. Combines unassuming friendliness, inspired imagination, and understanding of human nature. Politician, advertising executive, and detective are possible career opportunities.

PERSONALITY INGREDIENTS: Appears to be conventional, dignified, and disciplined. Strives for constructive work, respect, and material security. Inwardly independent, aggressive, and impatient. Wants inventive, changing, trend-setting life-style. Has inner faith, and attracts help from superiors.

PERSONALITY EXTREME: Too analytic, or too thoughtless.

RUFUS (Latin/English)—M.

MAJOR TALENT: Ability to incorporate inspirational ideas and down-to-earth work into career. Is understanding, practical, and cooperative. Has strong opinions, determination, and skillful managerial approach. Combines sensitivity to fine points, concern for humanity, and idealistic reforms that are geared to constructive results. Builder, politician, and psychiatrist are possible career opportunities.

PERSONALITY INGREDIENTS: Desires creative self-expression, luxury, and domestic/community attainments. Feels sympathetic, instructional, and stable. Wants mature, harmonious, comforting relationships/loves. Appears introspective, reserved, and observational. Strives to be authoritative, polished, and perfect. Aims for financial power, but must first establish expertise to attract success. At best when surrounded by natural beauty, and feeling serene.

PERSONALITY EXTREME: Too ambitious, or too lazy.

RUPERT (Old German: Robert; variable/French/English)—M.

MAJOR TALENT: Ability to incorporate efficient organizational approach, self-reliance, and extraordinary leadership qualities into career. Is consistent, dedicated, and attention-getting. Has charm, unconventional ideas, and guts. Combines understanding of public acceptance, creative imagination, and material power. Inherits money or prestige. Banker, industrialist, and any position of leadership are possible career opportunities.

PERSONALITY INGREDIENTS: Inwardly strong, ambitious, and confident. Wants to be a solid citizen, and a force of power. Appears to be empathetic, philosophical, and noble. Strives to serve humanitarian/artistic uplift, improve mass market skill/performance, and take responsibility for broad-scoped improvements. Attracts physical and mental admiration.

PERSONALITY EXTREME: Too critical, or too submissive.

RUSSELL (Latin/English)—M.

MAJOR TALENT: Ability to incorporate detailed perceptions, analytic questioning, and technical/scientific/logical approach into career. Is curious, adventurous, and unconventional. Has adaptability, ambition, and desire for peace/friendliness/collection. Combines mental/physical resourcefulness, specialization, and intellectual investigation. Photographer, architectual designer, and surgeon may be career opportunities.

PERSONALITY INGREDIENTS: Strives for material success with the freedom that money/power can buy. Desires leadership, business acumen, and practicality. Enjoys natural/timeless beauty, and display. Wants influence, affluence, and businesslike relationships. A domestic pussycat and a commercial tiger, who wins through perseverance, integrity, and hard work.

PERSONALITY EXTREME: Too sociable, or too reclusive.

RUTH (Hebrew/English)—F.

MAJOR TALENT: Ability to incorporate dynamic organizational energy, practical planning, and knack of coordinating business and charitable interests into career. Is trustworthy, conscientious, and down-to-earth. Has determination, discipline, and sensitivity to fine points. Combines far-reaching ambitions, strong opinions, and resourceful problem solving. Contractor, government administrator, and farmer are possible career opportunities.

PERSONALITY INGREDIENTS: Inwardly optimistic, humorous, and imaginative. Desires beauty, kindness, and variety. First impression is nonconforming, direct, and proud. Strives to be original, independent, and in the lead. Aims to pioneer new concepts, and uplift quality of skill/performance. Is philosophical, and must avoid assuming self-depreciating burdens. May leave constructive contributions for future generations.

PERSONALITY EXTREME: Too efficient, or too careless.

RYAN (Latin/Irish-Gaelic/English)—M.

MAJOR TALENT: Ability to incorporate practical vision, kind/patient leadership, and broad-scoped accomplishments into career. Strong, firm, and positive, with determination, common sense, and dynamic constructive energy. Combines attention to details, self-assurance, and workaholic drive. Efficiency expert, political organizer, and stage manager may be career opportunities.

PERSONALITY INGREDIENTS: Inwardly materially ambitious, businesslike, and mentally organized. Wants wealth, prominence, and power. Appears to be sensual, free-spirited, and unconventional. Strives to travel, experiment, and taste all the physical pleasures. Aims to be noticed, and has a knack of making others feel at home. Must avoid impulsiveness, self-indulgence, and forgetting that money is just a means of barter. Is a powerhouse.

PERSONALITY EXTREME: Too changeable, or too loyal.

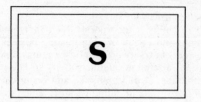

S

All names that begin with the letter *S* have the *Strong Point* of public-service ambitions—emotional reactions—competitiveness—nonconformity.

SABINA (Latin/Italian/English)—F.

MAJOR TALENT: Ability to incorporate independent spirit, originality, and initiative into career. Is fast-acting, expressive, and problem-solving. Has magnetism, faith, and empathetic understanding. Combines endurance, leadership, and progressive purpose. Lawyer, salesperson, and designer are possible career opportunities.

PERSONALITY INGREDIENTS: First impression is efficient, managerial, and as affluent as possible. Strives to be self-reliant, financially secure, and respected. Inwardly filled with inspirational nervous energy. Desires inventive, futuristic, quality interests. Wants to uplift/save the world, and may be impractical at times. At best in a personalized trend-setting style, and able to stand alone. Must have courage.

PERSONALITY EXTREME: Too daring, or too imitative.

SABRINA (Hebrew: Sabra/Italian/English)—F.

MAJOR TALENT: Ability to incorporate inventive ideas, adaptability, and efficient mental organization into career. Is daring, forceful, and energetic. Has direct approach, big plans, and sound judgment. Combines executive diplomacy, attention to details, and progressive ambitions. Balances data, and may be contradictory until logic rules emotions. Editor, business owner, and bank loan officer may be career opportunities.

PERSONALITY INGREDIENTS: First impression is businesslike, managerial, and as affluent as possible. Strives to be prosperous, influential, and in control. Inwardly wants personal ideals realized. Is motivated to improve quality and creativity for everyone. Has high nervous energy, and occasional impractical spontaneous enthusiasms. When inspired, may appear to be materially unconscious, but can be a zealous fighter for universal uplift. An original.

PERSONALITY EXTREME: Too self-motivated, or too dependent.

SADELLE (Hebrew: Sarah; variable/English)—F.

MAJOR TALENT: Ability to incorporate visionary planning, practical workaholic energy, and extraordinary coordination of projects into career. Is driven to see tangible results that bring progress and/or constructive products to a broad marketplace. Has varied talents, strong opinions, and potential to reshape/reorganize to master any situation. Combines attention to details, executive diplomacy, and material power.

Government, any profession, and business are possible career opportunities.

PERSONALITY INGREDIENTS: Has high nervous energy, inspired creative vision, and drive to rise above mediocrity. Aims to improve standards and expectations for others. Appears refined, retiring, and spontaneously enthusiastic when personal ideals are aroused. Strives to be supportive, helpful, and to keep an easygoing style, but always does at least two things at once. Should avoid wild schemes, aimlessness, and being too far removed from average tastes to understand another's suffering. Attracts recognition and financial security.

PERSONALITY EXTREME: Too adventurous, or too cautious.

SADIE (Hebrew: Sarah; variable/English: independent)—F.

MAJOR TALENT: Ability to incorporate cooperation, adaptability, and sensitivity to little things into career. Is patient, accommodating, and devoted to maintaining peace/partnerships/family unity. Has musical/rhythmical talents, sense of timing, and need to accumulate/collect things/people. Combines swift emotional judgments, concerned friendships, and gentle controlling influence. Private secretary, statistician, homemaker are possible career opportunities.

PERSONALITY INGREDIENTS: Desires family/community respect, material attainments, and comforts. Is motivated to protect, assume responsibility, and instruct/guide/counsel. Appears to be venturesome, enthusiastic, and open-minded. Strives to travel, experiment, and be free to enjoy all the physical pleasures of life. Needs roots/traditions/conventional acceptance, but self-image aims to learn from experience/increase unique understanding of people/do the unconventional.

PERSONALITY EXTREME: Too gutsy, or too fearful.

SALLY (Hebrew: Susan; variable/English: independent)—F.

MAJOR TALENT: Ability to incorporate responsible, protective, instructional service into career. Is sympathetic, independent, and clever. Has musical/artistic interests, firm ideals, and understanding of human foibles. Combines individuality, unconventional leanings, and need to take an adult attitude. Teacher, nurse, and restaurant/hotel manager are possible career opportunities.

PERSONALITY INGREDIENTS: First impression is aristocratic, reserved, and quiet. Strives to be cultured, analytic, and perfect. Desires material success, prestige, and unlimited opportunities. Feels efficient, orderly, and dignified. Is self-improving, and should keep a sense of humor to balance burden-bearing nature.

PERSONALITY EXTREME: Too questioning, or too trusting.

SALOME (Hebrew/English)—F.

MAJOR TALENT: Ability to incorporate attention to details, emotionally sensitive service, and knack for subtle control of others into career. Is gentle, charming, and companionable. Has need for order, balance, and peace. Combines cooperation, fine-point analysis, and diplomacy. Private secretary, accountant, and group singer/dancer may be career opportunities.

PERSONALITY INGREDIENTS: Wants beauty, entertainment, and imaginative relationships. Feels optimistic, kind, and up-to-date. First impression is practical, self-reliant, and intelligent. Strives to be efficient, businesslike, and materially powerful. Aims to have the fun/freedom/influence that money can buy.

PERSONALITY EXTREME: Too impulsive, or too cautious.

SALVADOR (Late Latin)—M.

MAJOR TALENT: Ability to incorporate inventive, detail-conscious, inspiring personality into career. Is high-strung, gentle, and idealistic. Has wide-ranging philosophy, regard for top quality/skill, and instant enthusiasms. Combines human understanding, perfecting discipline, and futuristic original concepts. Is zealous spiritual/artistic reformer. Composer, preacher, and publicist may be career opportunities.

PERSONALITY INGREDIENTS: Desires prestige, money, and far-reaching influence. Feels efficient, organized, and productive. Strives to be popular, attention-getting, and entertaining. Appears optimistic, up-to-date, and imaginative. An extraordinary individual, who should avoid materialism, impracticality, and scattering his interests.

PERSONALITY EXTREME: Too generous, or too selfish.

SAM (Hebrew-English: Samuel; Samson; Sampson, M-Samantha, F./diminutive & independent)—F. & M.

MAJOR TALENT: Ability to incorporate protective, responsible, instructional service into career. Is sympathetic, parental/domestic, and a born advisor. Has showmanship, sense of justice, and determination. Combines companionability, adult approach, and firm ideals. Teacher, interior decorator, and hotel/restaurant manager are possible career opportunities.

PERSONALITY INGREDIENTS: Is motivated to be independent, inventive, and brave. Wants progressive change, constant stimulation, and adventure. First impression is sensual, curious, and striking. Strives to be different, speculative, and unencumbered. Needs freedom, but assumes burdens.

PERSONALITY EXTREME: Too ethical, or too immoral.

SAMANTHA (Aramaic/English)—F.

MAJOR TALENT: Ability to incorporate freedom-loving instincts, curiosity, and unconventional experiments into career. Is changeable, clever, and sensual. Has diagnostic intuition, understanding of people, and sensitivity to fine points. Combines adaptability, optimism, and knack of being a catalyst for change in the lives of others. Tries everything first, and moves on to experience again. Politician, speculator, and travel agent may be career opportunities.

PERSONALITY INGREDIENTS: Desires pleasure, fashionable interests, and creative self-expression. Is motivated to enjoy, laugh, and attract attention. First impression is subdued, refined, and modest. Strives to be accommodating, helpful, and friendly. Gracious/stimulating nature radiates sex appeal. Best when patient, cautious, and concentrated.

PERSONALITY EXTREME: Too independent, or too clinging.

SAMPSON (Hebrew/Greek/English)—M.

MAJOR TALENT: Ability to incorporate intellectual analysis, detailed perceptions, and unconventional ideas into career. Is thoughtful, reserved, and self-controlled. Has poise, discretion, and appreciation for quality. Combines patience, curiosity, and technical/scientific/spiritual investigation. Photography, radio/data processing, and detective are possible career opportunities.

PERSONALITY INGREDIENTS: First impression is noble, understanding, and magnetic. Strives to be empathetic, broad-scoped, and charitable. Inwardly aloof, reflective, and self-questioning. Desires quiet, natural beauty, and perfection from self and others. Best when educated/specialized.

PERSONALITY EXTREME: Too inconsistent, or too loyal.

SAMSON (Hebrew/French/English)—M.

MAJOR TALENT: Ability to incorporate humanitarian instincts, individuality, and constructive material power into career. Is romantic, creative, and compassionate. Has originality, mental efficiency, and self-reliance. Combines independence, large breadth of outlook, and empathetic service. Doctor, fireman, and educational reformer are possible career opportunities.

PERSONALITY INGREDIENTS: Desires quiet, natural beauty, and to know the why of everything. Feels aristocratic, authoritative, and analytic. First impression is intense, different, and retiring. Strives to be a leader for spiritual/artistic/futuristic uplift, and to raise men's minds to higher expectations. An evangelist for personal ideals, who aims to change/save the world. May appear to be impractical, but has inspirational vision that may leave a lasting message/image.

PERSONALITY EXTREME: Too sensual, or too cerebral.

SAMUEL (Hebrew/Danish/French/German/English)—M.

MAJOR TALENT: Ability to incorporate material ambitions, efficiency, and self-reliance into career. Is individualistic, introspective, and practical. Has executive drive, competitive spirit, and desire for expertise/authority. Combines pioneering leadership, mental analysis, and businesslike instincts. Administrative executive, tax lawyer, and critic are possible career opportunities.

PERSONALITY INGREDIENTS: Has quality/skill of performance, wide-ranging interests, and desire to give helpful service. Wants romance, drama, and justice. Appears controlled, influential, and as affluent as possible. Strives to be strong, discriminating, and respected. Happiest when petty details are left to others.

PERSONALITY EXTREME: Too self-expressive, or too uncommunicative.

SANDRA (Greek: Alexandra; variable/English)—F.

MAJOR TALENT: Ability to incorporate imaginative concepts, sensitivity to details, and independent leadership into career. Is expressive, up-to-date, and adaptable. Has talent for writing, attracting people, and orderliness. Combines patience, determination, and creative work. Journalist, entertainer, and animal handler may be career opportunities.

PERSONALITY INGREDIENTS: Inwardly wants to be supportive, adaptable, and easygoing. Feels sensitive to fine points, inclined to keep the peace, and shy. Appears to be independent, assertive, and nonconforming. Self-image is progressive, forceful, and courageously individualistic. Must understand the true meaning of standing alone, in order to achieve the pioneering inspiration which attracts rewards and happiness.

PERSONALITY EXTREME: Too changeable, or too tenacious.

SANDY (diminutive Old English names beginning with "san")—F. & M.

MAJOR TALENT: Ability to incorporate independent, polished, and efficiently organized creative and/or humanitarian service into career. Is empathetic, generous, and romantic. Has discipline, drive, and self-reliance. Combines originality, material ambition, and contributions to the mental, physical, and spiritual welfare of others. Physician, artist, and counselor are possible career opportunities.

PERSONALITY INGREDIENTS: Desires prosperity, respect, and authority. Feels trustworthy, progressive, and businesslike. First impression is alert, strong, and definite. Strives to be aggressive, assertive, and nonconforming. Aims to be tolerant, assume responsibility, and take the lead.

PERSONALITY EXTREME: Too skeptical, or too gullible.

SANFORD (Old English)—M.

MAJOR TALENT: Ability to incorporate unconventional ideas, communications talents, and knack of understanding people into career. Is clever, quick, and adaptable. Has detail-consciousness, diplomacy, and imagination. Combines group/partnership support, creative self-expression, and freedom of mind, spirit, and activity. Politician, travel agent, and theatrical coach/performer/producer are possible career opportunities.

PERSONALITY INGREDIENTS: Desires perfection. Strives to be culturally, intellectually, artistically investigative and quality-conscious. Feels introspective, analytic, and logical. Hides depth of emotions, and appears appraising, authoritative, and reserved. Enjoys timeless beauty, solitude, and discretion. Best when educated/expert, and free to experience/experiment. Is a catalyst for change in the lives of others.

PERSONALITY EXTREME: Too hard-working, or too destructive.

SARA (Hebrew: Sarah; variable/French/German/English)—F.

MAJOR TALENT: Ability to incorporate engaging personality, imagination, and creative self-expression into career. Is fashionable, kind, and affectionate. Has varied talents, a gift with words, and inspirational ideas. Combines individualistic philosophy, respect for details, and social cleverness. Writer, dressmaker, and model suggest opportunities.

PERSONALITY INGREDIENTS: Desires friendliness, cooperation, and easygoing style. Feels modest, refined, and shy. First impression is nonconforming, active, and ambitious. Strives to be aggressive, assertive, and competitive. Self-image is pioneering, but is comfortable taking direction. At best when receptive and accommodating. Attracts conflicting personalities.

PERSONALITY EXTREME: Too independent, or too submissive.

SARAH (Hebrew/English)—F.

MAJOR TALENT: Ability to incorporate adaptability, patience, and tact into career. Is friendly, emotionally sensitive, and attracted to fine points. Has diplomatic control over others, drive to collect things/people, and talent for partnership. Combines supportive instincts, musical/rhythmical talents, and devotion. Nurse, psychologist, and executive assistant may be career opportunities.

PERSONALITY INGREDIENTS: Strives for independence, originality, and leadership. Can be a Mrs. Fullcharge, and take the initiative for everyone. Is ambitious, daring, and progressive. Needs to be a pace-setter, and enjoys praise. Must stick to beliefs, and clear inventive paths that provide access to change for less creative people. Should investigate before making decisions, and act on logic, not emotions.

PERSONALITY EXTREME: Too materialistic, or too impractical.

SARGENT (Latin/Hebrew/Old French/English)—M.

MAJOR TALENT: Ability to incorporate practical, creative, attention-getting, articulate/vocally attractive personality into career. Is multitalented, kind, and optimistic. Has wit, charm, and sense of tradition/orderliness/security. Feels a strong sense of right and wrong. Combines skill, social awareness, and sex appeal. Plastic surgeon, fiction writer, and lawyer/government official are possible career opportunities.

PERSONALITY INGREDIENTS: Desires roots, domestic/community respect, and gracious living. Feels responsible, protective, and instructional. Strives to be parental, sympathetic, and helpful. Enjoys showmanship, beauty, and music. Attracts pleasures, secure homelife, and material comforts. Should maintain high-mindedness.

PERSONALITY EXTREME: Too personalized, or too accommodating.

SARI (Hebrew: Sarah; variable/Hungarian/English: independent)—F.

MAJOR TALENT: Ability to incorporate tact, receptivity, and persistence into career. Is considerate, charming, and attentive to details. Has supportive approach, modesty, and refinement. Combines emotional sensitivity, patience, and need to alleviate suffering/problems for others. Psychologist, bookkeeper, and nurse may be career opportunities.

PERSONALITY INGREDIENTS: Appears compassionate, ageless, and noble. Strives to be broad-scoped, charitable, and artistically/skillfully polished. Aims to serve humanitarian purposes. Inwardly wants love, peace, and easygoing lifestyle. Is motivated to work with others, accumulate things/people, and seek comfort. Feels shy, modest, and subdued. Must avoid snap decisions, martyrdom, and making mountains out of molehills. Has subtle control over relationships.

PERSONALITY EXTREME: Too empathetic, or too unfeeling.

SAUL (Hebrew/Late Latin/English)—M.

MAJOR TALENT: Ability to incorporate executive discipline, practical work, and material ambition into career. Is organizational, managerial, and athletically balanced. Has strength, perseverance, and resourcefulness. Combines several talents, businesslike approach, and mental/physical power. Banking, sports, and band leader are possible career opportunities.

PERSONALITY INGREDIENTS: Wants down-to-earth, structured, orderly results. Feels traditional, exacting, and trustworthy. Appears to be neat, conservative, and definite. Strives to be a solid citizen, and can be a workaholic. Has originality, communications gifts, and faith. Enjoys humor, beauty, and being boss. Happiest when being paid for creative self-expression.

PERSONALITY EXTREME: Too attention-seeking, or too reclusive.

SCARLETT (Middle English)—F.

MAJOR TALENT: Ability to incorporate sensitivity to fine points, creative temperament, and practical executive efficiency into career. Is responsible, adaptable, and sympathetic. Has parental/domestic instincts, air of authority, and strength. Combines desire for peace/partnership, protective service, and material ambitions. Home products buyer, athletic coach, and financial advisor may be career opportunities.

PERSONALITY INGREDIENTS: Strives to be refined, modest, and supportive. Self-image is not aggressive, but has subtle control over others. Inwardly wants home/family/community harmony, creative self-expression, and abundant lifestyle. Feels instructional, helpful, and adult. Has understanding, and enjoys sharing prosperity/joy/beauty. Attracts difficult romantic entanglements, and should avoid sensual indulgences.

PERSONALITY EXTREME: Too critical, or too accommodating.

SCHUYLER (Dutch/English)—F. & M.

MAJOR TALENT: Ability to incorporate self-expression through words, artistry, polished professional skills and depth of human understanding into career. Is usually articulate, charming, entertaining. Has imagination, wit, and selflessness. Combines multifaceted talents, empathetic service, and strength of character. Plastic surgeon, author, and charity organizer may be career opportunities.

PERSONALITY INGREDIENTS: Is motivated to be efficient, businesslike, and organized to achieve practical results. Wants wealth, far-reaching ambitions, and influential positioning. Appears to be conservative, dignified, and solid. Aims to be trustworthy, ethical, and down-to-earth. Is a hard-working creative humanitarian.

PERSONALITY EXTREME: Too compassionate, or too unfeeling.

SCOTT (Late Latin/English)—M.

MAJOR TALENT: Ability to incorporate mental and physical curiosity into career. Is clever, adaptable, and individualistic. Has confidence, common sense, and organizational practicality. Combines pioneering independence, work ethic, and unconventional approach. Personnel director, politician, and private investigator are possible career opportunities.

PERSONALITY INGREDIENTS: Wants harmonious family/community relationships, luxurious life-style, and to help/counsel/guide everyone. Feels sympathetic, involved, and parental. First impression is strong, authoritative, and as affluent as possible. Strives to be wealthy, influential, and admired. May be dominating, jealous, and too self-indulgent. Has impulsive loves.

PERSONALITY EXTREME: Too sensitive, or too uncooperative.

SEAMUS (Irish: James)—M.

MAJOR TALENT: Ability to incorporate responsible service, individuality, and knack of understanding/handling people/situations into career. Is sympathetic, instructional, and family/domestically oriented. Has musical/showmanlike talents, determination, and independence. Combines conscientiousness, devotion, and drive to protect, improve, balance. Teacher, policeman, and songwriter are possible career opportunities.

PERSONALITY INGREDIENTS: First impression is dignified, comfortable, and interested. Strives to advise wisely, attain abundant life-style, and maintain group/community stability. Inwardly emotionally broadscoped, empathetic, and motivated to polish creative skills. A romantic, who needs to be needed.
PERSONALITY EXTREME: Too impatient, or too unambitious.

SEAN (Gaelic: John)—M.

MAJOR TALENT: Ability to incorporate creative self-expression, independent leadership, and adaptability into career. Is daring, sensitive to details, and trend-setting. Has charm, optimism, and faith in personal ideals. Combines fast action, friendliness, and words. Writer, entertainer, and salesperson are possible career opportunities.
PERSONALITY INGREDIENTS: Is motivated to serve, protect, and assume responsibility for family/community uplift. Wants abundant homelife, dignity, and mature/stable relationships. Strives to be sympathetic, understanding, and instructional. Enjoys counseling, beauty, and showmanship. Experiences a variety of unconventional incidents, but retains traditional instincts.
PERSONALITY EXTREME: Too adventurous, or too cautious.

SEBASTIAN (Greek/Spanish/English)—M.

MAJOR TALENT: Ability to incorporate unselfish service, polished skill/artistry, and broad-scoped philosophy into career. Is compassionate, diplomatic, and intellectually analytic. Has understanding, adaptability, and desire for perfection. Combines supportive instincts, investigative nature, and humanitarian approach. Doctor, welfare worker, and artist may be career opportunities.
PERSONALITY INGREDIENTS: Best when educated/technically/scientifically expert. Wants culture, refinement, and quality. Feels private, reserved, and meditative. First impression is intense, refined, and spontaneously enthusiastic. Strives to inspire/invent spiritual/creative uplift. Aims to improve tastes and expectations. Has high nervous energy, personal/emotional sensitivity, and a unique self-image. May be impractical, live in an ivory tower, and seem to have aimless visions. When unmaterialistic and dedicated to sharing wisdom, may leave a lasting image.
PERSONALITY EXTREME: Too physical, or too cerebral.

SELBY (Teutonic/Old English)—M.

MAJOR TALENT: Ability to incorporate empathetic service, pioneering ideas, and businesslike approach into career. Is helpful, understanding, and generous. Has initiative, self-reliance, and managerial responsibility. Combines courage, material efficiency, and humanitarian ideals. Artist, physician, and hotel/resort owner are possible career opportunities.
PERSONALITY INGREDIENTS: Inwardly optimistic, creatively expressive, and pleasure-seeking. Wants beauty, kindness, and love. First impression is interested, traditional, and comfortable. Strives to help, protect, and assume responsibility to raise living standards. Aims for material attainments, family unity, and gracious life-style. Attracts success through fine quality of skill/performance.
PERSONALITY EXTREME: Too confident, or too confused.

SELDON (Teutonic/Anglo-Saxon/English)—M.

MAJOR TALENT: Ability to incorporate responsible, protective, sympathetic nature into career. Is determined, idealistic, and instructional. Has adult values, sensitivity to details, and discipline. Combines patience, practicality, and domestic/parental approach. Music teacher, home products/services salesperson, and therapist are possible career opportunities.

PERSONALITY INGREDIENTS: First impression is traditional, definite, and dignified. Strives to be a solid citizen. Inwardly wants quality, inventions, and creative activity. Is motivated to uplift and reform anything that doesn't come up to personal standards. Is inclined to do two things at once, and finds spontaneous enthusiasms to pass on to others. Should avoid possessiveness, aimlessness, and judging surface values alone. May inspire futuristic improvements and leave a lasting mark.

PERSONALITY EXTREME: Too free, or too tied down.

SELENA (Greek/English)—F.

MAJOR TALENT: Ability to incorporate tact, orderliness, and sensitivity to fine points into career. Is receptive, gentle, and modest. Has unassuming friendliness, cooperative approach, and knack of seeing two sides of an issue. Combines supportiveness, love of peace, and diplomacy. Administrative assistant, group singer/dancer, and librarian are possible career opportunities.

PERSONALITY INGREDIENTS: Appears broad-scoped, youthful, and noble. Strives to be skillful, empathetic, and unselfish. Aims to serve humanitarian causes, and to show tolerance, creative expertise, and brotherly love to all. Inwardly idealistic, high-strung, often impractical. Feels special, and hopes to raise expectations/quality of life for others through inspirational ideas. Needs to be decisive, and avoid aimless dreaming. May leave lasting image.

PERSONALITY EXTREME: Too alone, or too dependent.

SELMA (Celtic/English)—F.

MAJOR TALENT: Ability to incorporate mental curiosity, cleverness, and learning by experience into career. Is adaptable, understanding, and adventurous. Has individuality, practical common sense, and desire for organization of details. Combines original ideas, conventional procedures, and unconventional approach. Lawyer, booking agent, and psychologist are possible career opportunities.

PERSONALITY INGREDIENTS: Inwardly domestic/parental, sympathetic, and responsible. Wants gracious living, material upgrading, and to be loved/needed. Appears to be managerial, efficient, and as affluent as possible. Strives to be prosperous, respected, and self-reliant. Attracts dependent people, and should be sensually cautious.

PERSONALITY EXTREME: Too aggressive, or too submissive.

SENIOR (Latin/English)—M.

MAJOR TALENT: Ability to incorporate executive authority, communications skills, and adventurous ideas into career. Is efficient, self-reliant, and strong. Usually receives inheritance of weath or influential positioning. Has businesslike instincts, creative self-expression, and mental/physical curiosity. Combines optimism, instinct for public approval, and

far-reaching ambitions. Banker, band leader, and corporation lawyer
may be career opportunities.

PERSONALITY INGREDIENTS: Inwardly shy, refined, and able to see
both sides of an issue. Wants easygoing, peaceful, companionable life-
style. Appears to be dignified, sympathetic, and comfortable. Strives for
family/community attainments, musical/creative/beautiful surroundings,
and helpfulness to others. Aims for respectability and the role of mature
advisor. Should avoid assuming unnecessary burdens.

PERSONALITY EXTREME: Too charitable, or too intolerant.

SERENA (Latin/English)—F.

MAJOR TALENT: Ability to incorporate material judgment, businesslike
mental analysis, and executive organizational efficiency into career. Is
strong/athletic, managerial, and attentive to details. Has confident air,
communications/showmanlike talents, and diplomacy. Combines supportive nature, responsible approach, and desire to be influential. Danc-
er, purchasing agent, and financial advisor are possible career opportunities.

PERSONALITY INGREDIENTS: Inwardly nervous, idealistic, and intuitive. Wants peace, superior quality, and refinement. Likes drama, unusual ideas, and daydreaming. Feels unique, and has flights of fancy.
Strives for family/community attainments, harmony, and luxurious life-
style. Has stressful unconventional experiences, and adapts personality
to rapidly changing conditions after learning to assert individuality. Attracts financial freedom.

PERSONALITY EXTREME: Too daring, or too afraid.

SERGE (Latin/Russian/English)—M.

MAJOR TALENT: Ability to incorporate broad-ranged creative artistry,
empathetic understanding, and discipline geared to polishing skills into
career. Is mathematical, logical, and introspective. Has sensitivity to fine
points, rhythm/group adaptability, and knack of seeing philosophical
humor. Combines romantic approach, intellectually questioning nature,
and a need to heal all wounds. Physician, artist, and welfare worker are
possible career opportunities.

PERSONALITY INGREDIENTS: Inwardly independent, inventive, and
courageous. Feels aggressive, managerial, and impatient. Wants to instigate progressive changes, and lead the way for others. Appears to be
self-reliant, strong, and controlled. Strives to be influential, organized for
practical efficiency and recognized. Is a font of inspirational ideas.

PERSONALITY EXTREME: Too open-minded, or too intolerant.

SERGEANT (Latin: Serge/English)—M.

MAJOR TALENT: Ability to incorporate executive judgment, material
efficiency, and the power of persuasion into career. Is attention-getting,
curious, and adventurous. Has confidence, determination, and trustworthy leadership. Combines inherited strength, cleverness, and desire
for material power. Stock broker, theatrical producer, and public official
are possible career opportunities.

PERSONALITY INGREDIENTS: Inwardly inventive, idealistic, visionary.
Wants to inspire, lead, and instigate beneficial reforms. First impression
is dignified, advisory, and traditional. Strives to be responsible, protective, and parental. Self-image is mature/sensible/reliable, and is geared to

helping, teaching, counseling others. Should avoid emotional overreactions.

PERSONALITY EXTREME: Too critical, or too retiring.

SETH (Hebrew/Greek/English)—M.

MAJOR TALENT: Ability to incorporate intellectual/spiritual analysis, pioneering ideas, and family/community service into career. Is confidential, reserved, and investigative. Has parental nature, courage, and desire for authority. Combines inner wisdom, technical/scientific questioning, and quest for perfection. Religious leader, psychoanalyst, and metaphysical researcher are possible career opportunities.

PERSONALITY INGREDIENTS: Inwardly curious, clever, and unconventional. Desires freedom, progressive changes, and constant activity. Feels enthusiastic, sensual, and free of routine. Appears to be refined, retiring, and dramatic. Has a flair for mystery, intense visionary leadership, and inspiring others to follow personal beliefs. Needs concentrated education/expertise. Must avoid materialism, gambling, and impracticality. Courts disappointment when overconfident.

PERSONALITY EXTREME: Too far-reaching, or too unambitious.

SEYMOUR (Old English/French-Latin/English)—M.

MAJOR TALENT: Ability to incorporate mental organization, communications skills, and intuitive understanding of people/mass market tastes into career. Is efficient, energetic, and socially attractive. Has imagination, sensuality, and curiosity. Combines creative self-expression, adventurous nature, and material ambition. Business executive, trial lawyer, and financial advisor are possible career opportunities.

PERSONALITY INGREDIENTS: Inwardly adaptable, versatile, and enthusiastic. Wants freedom, nonroutine experiences, and travel. First impression is friendly, up-to-date, and entertaining. Strives to be humorous, attention-getting, and kind. Has vitality, concentration, and inherited spiritual/material strengths. Should maintain discipline, and avoid self-indulgence, pessimism, and stubbornness.

PERSONALITY EXTREME: Too empathetic, or too self-serving.

SHANE (Gaelic: John)—M.

MAJOR TALENT: Ability to incorporate orderliness, tact, and sharp detail analysis into career. Is gentle, receptive, and unassuming. Has patience, musical/rhythmical gifts, and quiet contemplation. Combines cooperation, unaggressive manipulating, and subtle leadership. Private secretary, bookkeeper, band singer are possible career opportunities.

PERSONALITY INGREDIENTS: Appears unconventional, sexy, and striking. Strives to be adventurous, understanding, and on the move. Inwardly wants roots, secure/respectable homelife, and to assume responsibility for loved ones/community. Feels sympathetic, strong-willed, and protective. Makes major changes every ten years. Seems confident, aims to take challenges, and is bolstered by stable/loving/domestic relationships.

PERSONALITY EXTREME: Too busy, or too bored.

SHANNON (Irish Gaelic/English)—F. & M.

MAJOR TALENT: Ability to incorporate routine, work, and practical discipline into career. Is exacting, dependable, and conscientious. Has initiative, sociability, and imagination. Combines competitive spirit, optimism, and common sense. Real estate sales, skilled laborer, and dentist are possible career opportunities.

PERSONALITY INGREDIENTS: Desires thinking time, intellectual stimulation, and timeless beauty. Feels analytic, reserved, and aristocratic. Appears to be traditional, sympathetic, and comfortable. Strives to be responsible, protective, and helpful. Enjoys teaching, and guiding others into adopting personal ideals. Wants expertise, luxury, all-round perfection, and may sacrifice practicality to achieve high minded goals. Will fight for success.

PERSONALITY EXTREME: Too impulsive, or too determined.

SHARI (Hebrew: Sharon; variable/English)—F.

MAJOR TALENT: Ability to incorporate inventive ideas, initiative, and leadership into career. Is sensitive to details, gentle, and mentally efficient. Has businesslike instincts, self-reliance, and broad ambitions. Combines originality, material power, and active energy. Theatrical performer/director, architect, and business owner are possible career opportunities.

PERSONALITY INGREDIENTS: First impression is magnetic, interested, and helpful. Strives to be philosophical, culturally skilled/polished, and of service to life support/improvement causes. Inwardly feels aggressive, impatient, and individualistic. Desires control, praise, and will power. Has inner conflicts, and may be selfless one minute, and egocentric the next.

PERSONALITY EXTREME: Too empathetic, or too unfeeling.

SHARON (Hebrew/English)—F.

MAJOR TALENT: Ability to incorporate creative imagination, communications talents, and high-minded organizational structure into career. Is articulate, up-to-date, and versatile. Has attention-getting poise, desire to polish skills, and cleverness. Combines sex appeal, optimism, and words. Writer, plastic surgeon, and interior designer may be career opportunities.

PERSONALITY INGREDIENTS: Desires introspective, refined, cultured life-style. Wants timeless beauty, authority, and discretion/perfection in all areas. Appears to be understanding, enthusiastic, and open-minded. Strives to experience life, progress, and freedom to satisfy curiosity. Feels reserved/aloof/logical, and aims to be amiable/friendly/spontaneous. Should avoid overeating, secretiveness, and unfounded fears of loneliness/poverty. At best when technically/scientifically educated.

PERSONALITY EXTREME: Too adventurous, or too cautious.

SHAWN (Gaelic: John)—M.

MAJOR TALENT: Ability to incorporate sensitive, cooperative, diplomatic approach into career. Is peace-loving, concerned, and devoted. Has easygoing way, modesty, and capacity to be the power behind the throne. Combines attention to details, confidential nature, and gentle assertion. First violin in an orchestra, office worker, and any service job are possible career opportunities.

PERSONALITY INGREDIENTS: Is a mixture of active energy and instinct to collect data. Wants independent leadership, and appears to be aggressive. Is motivated to instigate progressive changes, new ideas, and to be a pacesetter. Feels daring, proud, and definite. Is impatient, nonconforming, and inventive. May be a powerful aggressor, or a subtly controlling influence. Best when decisive, and maintaining equality in partnerships.

PERSONALITY EXTREME: Too impulsive, or too tenacious.

SHEA (Irish: Shela; variable/English)—F. & M.

MAJOR TALENT: Ability to incorporate responsibility, protection, and devotion into career. Is parental, strong-willed, and advisory. Has communications gifts, showmanship, and initiative. Combines active ego, enthusiasm for adventure, and caring for others. Medicine, education, and home products/services are possible career opportunities.

PERSONALITY INGREDIENTS: First impression is noble, classic, and understanding. Strives to be philosophical, broad-scoped, and charitable. Aims to polish skills, and inspire quality of performance. Inwardly wants domestic harmony, gracious living, and respectability. Feels helpful, dignified, and instructional. Assumes burdens for others, and should avoid imposing personal standards, meddling, and jealousy.

PERSONALITY EXTREME: Too ambitious, or too lazy.

SHEILA (Latin: Cecilia/Irish: Cecilia-Shelah)—F.

MAJOR TALENT: Ability to incorporate philosophical nature, instinct for cultural stimulation, and sensitivity to fine points into career. Is compassionate, resigned to human foibles, and self-improving. Has communications gifts, intellectually questioning approach, and a desire to please. Combines cooperation, perfection, and humanitarianism. Medicine, the arts, and government may be career opportunities.

PERSONALITY INGREDIENTS: First impression is attention-getting, charming, and friendly. Strives to be entertaining, cheerful, and fashionable. Inwardly wants to protect, teach, and counsel. Feels responsible, dignified, and concerned about everybody/everything. Is emotional, sympathetic, idealistic, and aims to improve/reform/polish skills and standards.

PERSONALITY EXTREME: Too independent, or too subordinate.

SHEILAH (Latin: Cecilia/Hebrew: Shela/Irish: Cecilia-Sheila/English)—F.

MAJOR TALENT: Ability to incorporate material ambitions, businesslike approach, and understanding of marketable tastes into career. Is efficient, clever, and practical. Has imagination, self-reliance, and adventurous ideas. Combines strength, sociability, and knack of delegating/coordinating. Banker, broker, and band leader are potential career opportunities.

PERSONALITY INGREDIENTS: Is motivated to maintain harmony, justice, and respectable domestic/community living standards. Feels parental, advisory, and adult. Wants luxury, creative self-expression, and to be involved. First impression is refined, modest, and subdued. Emits a nonaggressive air. Strives to be gentle, supportive, and easygoing. Inner personality shines through to reveal a confident/managerial spirit that belies appearance. Is a power for achievement when logical and decisive.

PERSONALITY EXTREME: Too materialistic, or too disorganized.

SHELA (Hebrew/Celtic/English)—F. & M.

MAJOR TALENT: Ability to incorporate brotherly love, creative ideas, and mental efficiency into career. Is empathetic, philosophical, and generous. Has initiative, executive self-reliance, and uplifting ideals. Combines ambition, down-to-earth work, and wide-ranging service. Doctor, publisher, and designer are possible career opportunities.

PERSONALITY INGREDIENTS: Strives to be popular, fashionable, and pleasure-seeking. Aims to attract attention, be happy, and share imaginative interests. Inwardly wants domestic/family/community respect, love, and accomplishments. Feels protective, responsible, and sensible. Desires beauty, gracious living, and harmonious relationships. Should avoid strain, and maintain balance between emotional and physical commitments.

PERSONALITY EXTREME: Too hasty, or too patient.

SHELBY (Old English)—M.

MAJOR TALENT: Ability to incorporate material efficiency, organization, and application into career. Is self-reliant, far-reaching, and trustworthy. Has detailed perceptions, diplomacy, and sense of justice/responsibility/protection. Combines sensitivity, parental concern, and discriminating executive judgment. Banker, military officer, and merchant may be career opportunities.

PERSONALITY INGREDIENTS: Desires humor, beauty, and self-expression, and society. Appears to be adventurous, sensual, and striking. Strives to be progressive, confident, and clever. Aims to travel, be unencumbered, and taste all that life has to offer.

PERSONALITY EXTREME: Too investigative, or too unquestioning.

SHELDON (Anglo-Saxon)—M.

MAJOR TALENT: Ability to incorporate unconventional ideas, communications techniques, and perceptive detail analysis into career. Is clever, adaptable, and enthusiastic. Has optimism, imagination, and diplomacy. Combines eye for beauty/humor/pleasure, friendliness, and instinct for understanding people. Theatrical manager, salesperson, and psychologist are potential career opportunities.

PERSONALITY INGREDIENTS: Inwardly idealistic, high-strung, and capable of juggling creative ideas. Is motivated to inspire artistic/spiritual/intellectual improvements and reforms. Is visionary and, with practical application, may leave a lasting image. First impression is up-to-date, unworried, and conversational. Strives to be entertaining, kind, and affectionate. Has restless energy, and aims to touch upon a variety of interests.

PERSONALITY EXTREME: Too experimental, or too cautious.

SHELLY (Anglo-Saxon/English)—F. & M.

MAJOR TALENT: Ability to incorporate polished skills, broad-scoped philosophy, and understanding of human foibles into career. Is empathetic, patient, and helpful. Has analytic mind, desire for perfection, and quality tastes. Combines refinement, knack of arbitrating differences, and humanitarian interests. Doctor, wine expert, and theatrical producer may be career opportunities.

PERSONALITY INGREDIENTS: Strives to have gracious, beautiful, comfortable home. Appears sympathetic, stable, and dignified. Aims to protect, help, and advise everyone. Self-image is parental and mature. Inwardly optimistic, artistically expressive, and pleasure-seeking. Wants humor, entertainment, and love. Is a restless problem solver, and a tower of strength.

PERSONALITY EXTREME: Too authoritative, or too quiet.

SHERMAN (Old English/English)—M.
MAJOR TALENT: Ability to incorporate firm personal ideals, responsibility, and protective service into career. Is sympathetic, creatively self-expressive, and advisory. Has showmanship, domestic/family feelings, and drive to serve/improve/secure stability for all. Combines resourcefulness, imagination, and self-sacrifice. Credit union organizer, co-op nursery school administrator, and dedicated teacher are potential career opportunities.

PERSONALITY INGREDIENTS: Wants beauty, gracious living, and to help and be appreciated. Wants comfort, respectability, and conventional attainments. First impression is understanding, concerned, and brotherly. Strives to be tolerant, broad-minded, and humorously philosophical. At best when living up to self-image, and involved in humanitarian pursuits.

PERSONALITY EXTREME: Too adventurous, or too cautious.

SHERRI (Hebrew: Sharon; variable/English)—F.
MAJOR TALENT: Ability to incorporate unconventional approach, independent leadership, and disciplined structure into career. Is curious, adaptable, and enthusiastic. Has courage, original ideas, and focus upon tangible results. Combines progressive inspirational concepts, fast action, and versatility. Politician, travel agent, and personnel director are potential career opportunities.

PERSONALITY INGREDIENTS: Desires sensual pleasures, adventure, and change. Wants to be free to explore. First impression is noble, romantic, and harmonious. Strives to be wide-ranging, polished, and charitable. Aims for quality/skill of performance, human kindness, and to grow culturally. Should share loving nature, but avoid impulsive self-indulgence.

PERSONALITY EXTREME: Too emotional, or too philosophical.

SHERRILL (Latin/French: Charlotte; variable/English)—F. & M.
MAJOR TALENT: Ability to incorporate inspirational futuristic ideas, conflicting down-to-earth values, and wild dreams into career. Is a practical dreamer with enthusiasm that inspires supporters, trust, and luxury. Has emotional sensitivity, nervous energy, and unique tastes. Combines firm ideals, flexible interests, and potential to make dreams come true. Designer, spiritual leader, and concert pianist may be career opportunities.

PERSONALITY INGREDIENTS: Inwardly sensual, curious, and gutsy. Wants freedom, progressive changes, and never to be bored. First impression is dignified, traditional, and concerned. Strives to instigate/reform living standards, express creatively, and inspire optimism/happiness/love. Self-image is burden-bearing, protective, and respectable. Needs travel/freedom/excitement, but assumes binding responsibilities.

PERSONALITY EXTREME: Too talkative, or too unsociable.

SHERRY (Latin: Caesar/French: Charlotte/English)—F.

MAJOR TALENT: Ability to incorporate social, artistic, and skillfully structured creative outlets for self-expression into career. Is attention-getting, kind, and optimistic. Has charm, communications gifts, and imagination. Combines clever use of words, engaging personality, and a taste for humor. Hairdresser, writer, and lawyer are potential career opportunities.

PERSONALITY INGREDIENTS: Strives to be noble, tolerant, and gracious. Seems magnetic, empathetic, and dramatic/emotional. Inwardly pleasure-seeking, youthful, and fashionable. Wants sunny days. A romantic, who attracts children, animals, and invitations.

PERSONALITY EXTREME: Too skeptical, or too gullible.

SHERWIN (Anglo-Saxon)—M.

MAJOR TALENT: Ability to incorporate creative imagination, attention to details, and practical discipline into career. Is responsible, protective, and sensible. Has charm, emotional sensitivity, and firm personal ideals. Combines easygoing approach, strength of character, and loving/cooperative instincts. Marriage counselor, musician, and interior decorator may be career opportunities.

PERSONALITY INGREDIENTS: Inwardly sensual, experimental, and adventurous. Wants to experience all that life has to offer. Appears to be nonconforming, independent, and capable. Strives to be different, controlling, and an idea person. Aims to be a pacesetter, and needs freedom to investigate all that is new and progressive. Is either very lonely, or lovingly idolized.

PERSONALITY EXTREME: Too unconventional, or too restrained.

SHERYL (German: Charlotte; variable/Old English: Shirley; variable/English)—F.

MAJOR TALENT: Ability to incorporate inspirationally uplifting service, showmanship/musical/artistic expression, and responsible/adult advisory personality into career. Is sympathetic, instructional, and quietly dynamic. Has strong will, firm personal ideals, and need to provide domestic/community uplift. Combines communications gifts, imagination, and skillful problem solving. Marriage counselor, credit union organizer, and teacher may be career opportunities.

PERSONALITY INGREDIENTS: Wants beauty, entertainment, and happiness to share. Feels youthful, cheery, and restless. Strives to be up-to-date, friendly, and amusing. Appears attention-getting, animated, and charming. At best when dealing with people, and working in decorative surroundings. May be too dedicated, or seemingly irresponsible. Takes things to heart, and may be an escapist.

PERSONALITY EXTREME: Too optimistic, or too depressed.

SHIRLEE (Old English/English)—F.

MAJOR TALENT: Ability to incorporate disciplined work, organized method, and determination to perform worthwhile service into career. Is persevering, expedient, and geared to tangibles. Has strong loyalties, traditional values, and endurance. Combines common sense, orderliness, and useful goals. Physical therapist, farmer, and dentist are possible career opportunities.

PERSONALITY INGREDIENTS: Inwardly nonconforming, ambitious, and controlling. Wants leadership, dignity, and progress. First impression is up-to-date, imaginative, and friendly. Strives to be popular, entertaining, and optimistic. Attracts love, but must avoid flirting, impatience, and scattering interests to maintain productivity.

PERSONALITY EXTREME: Too sensual, or too cerebral.

SHIRLEY (Old English/English)—F. & M.

MAJOR TALENT: Ability to incorporate sympathetic, creative, companionable nature into career. Is artistically/musically expressive, instructional, and domestically protective/responsible/ambitious. Has imagination, practicality, and sensitivity to details. Combines cooperation, discipline, and desire to help others. Teacher, minister, and homemaker may be career opportunities.

PERSONALITY INGREDIENTS: Inwardly curious, clever, and eager to experience all that life has to offer. Wants physical pleasure, mental stimulation, and unconventional experiences. Appears to be independent, retiring, and traditional. Strives to be progressively changing, assertive, and in the lead. Self-image is individualistic, but needs conventional attainments, gracious living, and strong bonds of love. Attracts dependent/problematic lovers.

PERSONALITY EXTREME: Too aloof, or too questioning.

SIBIL (Greek: Sibyl/English)—F.

MAJOR TALENT: Ability to incorporate protective, responsible, instructional service into career. Is patient, practical, and sympathetic. Has rhythm/musical/artistic interests, strong will, and parental instincts. Combines adaptability, discipline, and counseling. Teacher, interior decorator, and hotel/restaurant manager may be career opportunities.

PERSONALITY INGREDIENTS: Inwardly romantic, broad-scoped, and generous. Wants polished skills, humanitarian accomplishments, and brotherly love. First impression is comfortable, dignified, and interested. Strives to be needed, just, and uplifting. Aims to share personal ideals to improve living standards for others, but must avoid face-value judgments or assuming other peoples' obligations. Attracts love and gracious living.

PERSONALITY EXTREME: Too talkative, or too uncommunicative.

SIBYL—SYBIL (Greek/Irish/Scottish/English)—F.

MAJOR TALENT: Ability to incorporate broad inspirational planning, work, and tangible results into career. Is charged with practical energy. Has organization, method, and determination. Combines detailed perceptions, instinct for coordinating, and patient/diplomatic/imaginative leadership. Architect-builder, writer-promoter-director-producer, and appraiser-salesperson-owner are potential career opportunities.

PERSONALITY INGREDIENTS: Inwardly needs intellectual/spiritual confidence. Desires aristocratic, cultured, introspective life-style. Has fears of loneliness/poverty and material disappointment until feelings of authority are substantiated by respected specialization of interest. Is motivated to material accumulation and status symbols until inner faith/security is established by recognition of natural/timeless beauty/wisdom. First impression is dignified, tasteful, and comforting. Self-image is adult, sensible, and responsible. Inwardly reserved, and apparently emo-

tionally responsive. Should be encouraged to seek education, private
thinking time, and harmonious family/community relationships.
PERSONALITY EXTREME: Too expressive, or too worried.

SIDNEY (Phoenician/English)—F. & M.

MAJOR TALENT: Ability to incorporate hard work, independent leadership, and communications techniques into career. Is practical, exacting,
and conscientious. Has dignity, imagination, and courage. Combines
individuality, creative self-expression, and discipline. Is competitive.
Builder, accountant, and administrator are possible career opportunities.

PERSONALITY INGREDIENTS: Inwardly unconventional, experimental,
and sensual. Wants travel, progressive changes, and constant activity.
Appears to be businesslike, authoritative, and influential. Strives to be
efficient, affluent, and materially ambitious. Aims for recognized power/
status. Best when organized, adaptable, and concentrated in a direction.
Attracts challenges.

PERSONALITY EXTREME: Too analytic, or too unquestioning.

SIGFRIED (Teutonic/German/English)—M.

MAJOR TALENT: Ability to incorporate focus upon the physical senses,
unconventional approach, and understanding counseling into career. Is
active, curious, and experimental. Has enthusiasm, cleverness, and
adaptability. Combines adventurous ideas, nerve, and self-confidence.
Writer, analyst, and statistician may be career opportunities.

PERSONALITY INGREDIENTS: First impression is noble, empathetic,
and brotherly. Strives to be humorously philosophical, broad-scoped,
and charitable. Is magnetic, and aims for polished skills and memorable
performances. Attracts domestic comfort, social contact, and intuitional
guidance.

PERSONALITY EXTREME: Too proper, or too untraditional.

SIGMUND (Old German/English)—M.

MAJOR TALENT: Ability to incorporate parental nature, firm ideals, and
protective/responsible/advisory service into career. Is sympathetic, mu-
sical/artistic, and creatively self-expressive. Has eye for symmetry, and
uncluttered mental analysis for problem solving. Combines sense of justice, stick-to-itiveness, and concern for others. Marriage counselor,
credit union organizer, and teacher may be career opportunities.

PERSONALITY INGREDIENTS: Strives to communicate. Wants optimism, humor, and love. Feels imaginative, restless, and poised to accept
all ways of life/people. Aims to cheer, entertain, and find serenity. May
be an escapist when overburdened. Attracts success through ability to
turn concepts to tangibles. Must avoid scattering interests, reclusiveness, and exaggeration.

PERSONALITY EXTREME: Too hard-working, or too unroutined.

SILAS (Latin/English)—M.

MAJOR TALENT: Ability to incorporate responsible, protective, sympathetic service into career. Is individualistic, adventurous, and sentimental. Has creative communications gifts, parental nature, and
instructional attitude. Combines ambition, enthusiasm, and assumption
of burdens for others. Flight attendant, theatrical producer, and musical/
vocal coach are potential career opportunities.

PERSONALITY INGREDIENTS: Wants to originate, compete, and be accountable. Needs praise, constant activity, and progressive changes. First impression is striking, interested, and ready for anything. Strives to travel, be sociable, and try all the physical pleasures that life has to offer. Is firmly idealistic, temperamental, and imaginative. Would improve personal relationships with a touch of humor.

PERSONALITY EXTREME: Too aggressive, or too smug.

SILVESTER (Latin: Silas; variable/English)—M.

MAJOR TALENT: Ability to incorporate communications skills, human understanding, and humanitarian crusading into career. Is compassionate, expressive, and burden-bearing. Has broad philosophy, imagination, and drive to polish techniques/performance. Combines brotherly love, attention-getting approach, and words. Writer, entertainer, and organizer are possible career opportunities.

PERSONALITY INGREDIENTS: First impression is modest, sensitive, and receptive. Strives to join forces, cooperate, and maintain easygoing approach. Inwardly wants independence, action, and to pioneer new ideas. Feels aggressive, different, and competitive. Must find comfort in true individuality to enjoy peace of mind. Enjoys material security, progressive changes, and optimism. Best when courageous, charitable, and unroutined.

PERSONALITY EXTREME: Too generous, or too selfish.

SILVIA (Latin: Silvester/Italian/English)—F.

MAJOR TALENT: Ability to incorporate fine-point perceptions, cultural refinement, and polished communications gifts into career. Is diplomatic, analytic, and empathetic. Has quality-consciousness, gentility, and appreciation for solitude/silence/timeless beauty. Combines cooperative nature, logic,and broad-scoped philosophy. Doctor, publisher, and musician may be career opportunities.

PERSONALITY INGREDIENTS: First impression is self-reliant, managerial, and businesslike. Strives to be efficient, trustworthy, and practical. Aims for influence, affluence, and constructive goals. Inwardly strong, independent, inventive, and forceful. Wants to be in control, progressive, and active. May be impatient, insensitive, and skeptical. Best when tolerant and decisive.

PERSONALITY EXTREME: Too positive, or too confused.

SIMON (Hebrew/French/German/Greek/Spanish/English)—M.

MAJOR TALENT: Ability to incorporate analytic, investigative, technical/scientific mind into career. Is introspective, attentive to details, and curious. Has enthusiasm, gentility, and experimental approach. Combines diplomacy and free-thinking, intellectual/cultural/quality instincts. Detective, electronics expert, and appraiser are potential career opportunities.

PERSONALITY INGREDIENTS: Desires abundant, harmonious, conservative life-style. Feels protective, responsible, and sympathetic. Wants family/community attainments, domestic tranquility, and to guide/advise/teach. Appears to be aggressive, independent, and ambitious. Strives to be explorative, inventive, and first. Aims for leadership, and may be dynamic when educated/expert/recognized for authority. Must not be controlled.

PERSONALITY EXTREME: Too adventurous, or too cautious.

SIMONE (Hebrew: Simona, F.—Simon, M./French)—F.

MAJOR TALENT: Ability to incorporate communications talents, practical routine/application, artistic/creative self-expression into career. Is versatile, sociable, and entertaining. Has charm, optimism, and sex appeal. Combines attention-getting manner, multifaceted skills, and need to share joy/romance/humor. Writer, theatrical performer, and fashion expert may be career opportunities.

PERSONALITY INGREDIENTS: Appears individualistic, quick, and in control. Strives to be original, daring, and in the lead. Inwardly wants peace, loving partner, and relaxed environments. Feels accommodating, gentle, and sensitive to little things. Gets hurt easily, but tries to hide softness. Attracts success when conservative. Should avoid habitual flirting.

PERSONALITY EXTREME: Too sensual, or too mental.

SISLEY (Latin: Cecilia; variable/English)—F.

MAJOR TALENT: Ability to incorporate efficiency, practical organization, and executive leadership into career. Is trustworthy, self-reliant, and strong. Has diplomacy, showmanship, and businesslike determination. Combines social service, knack for arbitrating differences, and commercial ambitions. Theatrical agent, fast-food franchise owner, and corporate administrator are possible career opportunities.

PERSONALITY INGREDIENTS: Seems to have a unique personal approach/philosophy. Strives to be noticed, entertaining, and kind. Inwardly unconventional, changeable, and sensual. Wants travel, freedom, and curiosity satisfied. Has up-to-date ideas, and may be a catalyst in the lives of others. Best when creatively expressive, concentrated, and cooperative.

PERSONALITY EXTREME: Too skeptical, or too gullible.

SLOAN (Celtic/English)—F. & M.

MAJOR TALENT: Ability to incorporate intellectual/social/spiritual refinements into career. Is analytic, individualistic, and family/community uplifting. Has self-control, introspection, and ambition. Combines leadership, idealistic service, and aristocratic approach. Political analyst, scientific inventor, and editor are potential career opportunities.

PERSONALITY INGREDIENTS: Appears to be understanding, noble, and magnetic. Strives for broad-scoped humanitarian interests, quality/polish of skill/performance, and brotherly love. Inwardly aloof, discriminating, and scientifically/technically questioning. Wants solitude, timeless beauty, and authority. Maintains material security when nonmaterialistic. Needs education/specialization, to attract desired wealth/prestige.

PERSONALITY EXTREME: Too busy, or too bored.

SOL (Latin, F./Hebrew: Solomon; diminutive, M./English; independent)—F. & M.

MAJOR TALENT: Ability to incorporate inventive, independent, forceful nature into career. Is creative, aggressive, and assertive. Has impatience, progressive ideas, and pride. Combines leadership, dislike for detail, and need to be left to own devices. Service business owner, designer, and promoter may be career opportunities.

PERSONALITY INGREDIENTS: Desires family/community attainments, gracious living, and to assume responsibility for the betterment of others. Feels responsible, instructional, and sympathetically concerned. Appears to be conservative, conventional, and dignified. Has a big mouth, or underplays. Strives to be a solid citizen.

PERSONALITY EXTREME: Too optimistic, or too depressed.

SOLOMON (Hebrew/Late Latin/English)—M.

MAJOR TALENT: Ability to incorporate down-to-earth practical ideas and judgment into career. Is creatively expressive, competitive, and independent. Has dignity, integrity, and need for order/structure/economy. Combines communciations gifts, originality, and a hardworking fighting spirit. Builder, piano player, and policeman are possible career opportunities.

PERSONALITY INGREDIENTS: Inwardly philosophical, compassionate, and understanding of human foibles. Wants artistry, romance, and to contribute to universal welfare. Enjoys seeing things through to conclusions, equity, and brotherly love. Appears to be traditional, classic, and upright. Strives to plan build, and achieve tangible results. Has strong sense of justice, domestic/community commitment, and drive to maintain stable/harmonious conditions.

PERSONALITY EXTREME: Too sensual, or too cerebral.

SONNY (English: nickname)—M.

MAJOR TALENT: Ability to incorporate parental nature, cooperative spirit, and practical/traditional values into career. Is sympathetic, advisory, and concerned. Has friendliness, determination, and firm personal ideals. Combines sensitivity to fine points, self-discipline, and sense of guardianship. Teacher, nurse, and therapist may be career opportunities.

PERSONALITY INGREDIENTS: Inwardly wants material security, conventional attainments, and systematized life-style. Feels thorough, honest, and loyal. Dislikes pretension. First impression is dreamy, creative, and avant-garde. Strives to be different, enthusiastic, and able to raise the quality of expectation for everyone. May be an impractical/unrestrained crusader, or a structured workaholic. Self image is out of this world, while natural instincts are earthbound. Can be a conflicting personality.

PERSONALITY EXTREME: Too confident, or too unsure.

SONYA (Greek/Russian/English)—F.

MAJOR TALENT: Ability to incorporate tact, detail consciousness, and subtle control into career. Is cooperative, personally sensitive, and peace-loving. Has modesty, refinement, and need to collect things/people/data. Combines perseverance, devotion, and desire to work with others. Bookkeeper, group dancer/musician, and psychologist may be career opportunities.

PERSONALITY INGREDIENTS: Inwardly structured, conservative, and hard-working. Wants material security, dignity, and discipline for self/

others. Appears to be aristocratic, calm, and poised. Strives for cultural, natural beauty, and perfection. Self-image is refined/introspective/calculating but needs down-to-earth endurance for success.

PERSONALITY EXTREME: Too independent, or too submissive.

SOPHIA (Greek/English)—F.

MAJOR TALENT: Ability to incorporate adventurous nature, cleverness, and understanding of people into career. Is gutsy, quick, and self-promoting. Has speculative, experimental, curious approach. Combines communications talents, keen/sensitive perception for details, and knack of appearing self-confident. Politician, entertainer, and advertising executive may offer career opportunities.

PERSONALITY INGREDIENTS: Fears loneliness/poverty/lack of power. Needs education/specialization/intellectual authority to feel secure. Appears to be aloof, refined, and discriminating. Strives to be respected, but sometimes for material accumulation, which may be the downfall of this name. Loss of reputation/wealth is possible until spiritual/natural/timeless values are focused upon. Wants perfection, quality, and privacy to think. Is extremely logical/analytic but lacks inner faith. Achieves recognition easily but must be free of mercenary judgment to maintain position.

PERSONALITY EXTREME: Too aggressive, or too anxious.

SOPHIE (Greek/French/English)—F.

MAJOR TALENT: Ability to incorporate empathetic nature, broad philosophy, and desire for top quality/skills/artistry into career. Is creative, expressive, and versatile. Has parental instincts, strong will, and determination to guide/teach/raise standards for others. Combines words, responsibility, and brotherly love. Humorist, educational reformer, and lawyer/C.P.A. may be career opportunities.

PERSONALITY INGREDIENTS: Appears to be discriminating, aristocratic, and self-examining. Wants privacy, timeless beauty, and perfection. Needs specialized education to maintain self image. Inwardly supportive, easygoing, and modest. Wants loving mate/partnership, peace, and friendliness. Attracts success through persistence, common sense, and trustworthiness. Assumes heavy responsibilities/burdens, but has unique strength of character to maintain duties/obligations.

PERSONALITY EXTREME: Too gutsy, or too scared.

SPENCER (Old French: Spenser/English)—M.

MAJOR TALENT: Ability to incorporate communications talents, instinct for understanding people, and unconventional forms of mental organization into career. Is clever, efficient, and self-reliant. Has vitality, executive diplomacy, and firm judgments. Combines strength, businesslike attitude, and individuality of ambitions. Band leader, writer, and corporate executive are potential career opportunities.

PERSONALITY INGREDIENTS: Is motivated to pioneer, instigate, and walk alone. Feels proud, free, impatient. Wants changing goals, and attracts admiration for personal uniqueness. Appears to be observing, aloof, and introspective. Strives to be questioning, logical, and culturally/intellectually stimulated. Aims for natural/timeless/spiritual beauty, quality, and perfection. Pays attention to fine points, and enjoys spontaneous enthusiasms but keeps a secret self that shuts out mundane distractions.

PERSONALITY EXTREME: Too philosophical, or too narrow.

STACEY (Latin: independent/English: Anastacia; F.-Eustace; M., diminutive)—F. & M.

MAJOR TALENT: Ability to incorporate originality, initiative, and progressive ideas/goals into career. Is philosophical, empathetic, and ambitious. Has quality-consciousness, pride, and vitality. Combines human understanding, mental freedom, and persuasive leadership. Designer, salesperson, and botanist may be career opportunities.

PERSONALITY INGREDIENTS: Needs family/community harmony, respect, material attainments. Feels protective, responsible, and instructional. Likes luxury, showmanship, and music. Appears to be classic, dignified, and enduring. Strives to be constructive, practical, and down-to-earth. Must be true to individuality, and fight for personal beliefs to maintain integrity. Is resourceful, and should instigate changes that will open doors for others.

PERSONALITY EXTREME: Too authoritative, or too insecure.

STACIE (Greek; Anastacia; diminutive/English)—F.

MAJOR TALENT: Ability to incorporate the gift of bringing creative concepts to reality into career. Is up-to-date, optimistic, and attentive to details. Has initiative, leadership, and attention-getting instincts. Combines independence, knack of seeing both sides of issues, and communications gifts. Attracts success with words. Writer, entertainer, and organizer may be career opportunities.

PERSONALITY INGREDIENTS: Desires domestic harmony, gracious living, and showmanship. Feels responsible, protective, and stable. Strives to sympathize, teach, guide others into personal ideals. Has firm beliefs, and aims to share them. Wants dignity, beauty, and love. Must avoid being too helpful or living vicariously.

PERSONALITY EXTREME: Too impulsive, or too tied-down.

STACY (Latin: Stacy; variable/Greek: Anastasia; diminutive/English)— F. & M.

MAJOR TALENT: Ability to incorporate learning through observation and experience into career. Is clever, understanding, and adaptable. Has sensual curiosity, unconventional instincts, and originality. Combines independence, practical materialism, enthusiasm for untried ventures and speculation. Reporter, detective, and travel agent are potential career opportunities.

PERSONALITY INGREDIENTS: Inwardly businesslike, self-reliant, and managerial. Wants influence, affluence, and power. Appears to be comfortable, sympathetic, and advisory. Strives for family/community attainments, gracious living, and adult approach. Aims to give and receive love/protection/guidance. Has musical/writing/creative gifts, and must avoid impulsive actions to maintain stability.

PERSONALITY EXTREME: Too analytic, or too unquestioning.

STANISLAUS (Slavonic/English)—M.

MAJOR TALENT: Ability to incorporate humanitarian instincts, drive to polish skills/performance, and detailed/analytic perceptions into career.

Is investigative, artistic, and self-questioning. Has logic, gentleness, and brotherly love. Combines knack of seeing both sides of an issue, intellectual/spiritual depth, and empathetic service to others. Doctor, philosopher, and artist are possible career opportunities.

PERSONALITY INGREDIENTS: Appears traditional, but wants unconventional interests. Strives to be practical, down-to-earth, and materially constructive. Inwardly needs physical pleasures, freedom, and constant change. Dislikes boredom, but aims for stability. Best when cautiously decisive.

PERSONALITY EXTREME: Too assertive, or too dependent.

STANFORD (Old English)—M.

MAJOR TALENT: Ability to incorporate practical/structured communications skills, and questioning intellect into career. Is analytic, investigative, and private. Has optimism, discipline, and technical/scientific instincts. Combines love of beauty, material construction, and wisdom. Computer systems consultant, preacher, and university administrator are potential career opportunities.

PERSONALITY INGREDIENTS: Strives to improve quality/performance/skills of others. Appears to be noble, understanding, and empathetic. Inwardly aloof, introspective, and aristocratic. Needs solitude, timeless beauty, and perfection. Probes to get to the root of things, and aims to share. Knows how to keep a secret, and prefers culturally stimulating relationships.

PERSONALITY EXTREME: Too rigid, or too unroutined.

STANLEY (Old English/English)—M.

MAJOR TALENT: Ability to incorporate parental instincts, showmanship, and sympathetic/musical/creatively expressive service into career. Is sensitive to fine points, practical, and structured. Has patience, gentleness, and stubborn endurance. Combines firm opinions/ideals, self-discipline, and sense of justice, responsibility/conscientiousness. Gives protection and wants love. Teacher, home decorator, and restaurant chef/hotel manager may be career opportunities.

PERSONALITY INGREDIENTS: Inwardly desires domestic/community serenity, respect, material security. Likes luxury, beauty, and mature companionship. First impression is understanding, noble, and magnetic. Strives to be philosophical, charitable, and culturally polished. Aims to put the welfare of others before self, and must avoid financial/emotional drains that result from judging by appearances, and superficial values.

PERSONALITY EXTREME: Too introspective, or too unquestioning.

STARR (Latin/English)—F. & M.

MAJOR TALENT: Ability to incorporate broad planning, hard work, and practical results into career. Is attentive to fine points, adaptable, and disciplined. Has integrity, determination, and endurance. Combines knack of coordinating multifaceted interests, common sense, and desire to create something of lasting benefit. Builder, legislator, and efficiency expert may offer career opportunities.

PERSONALITY INGREDIENTS: Wants independence, change, and constant activity. Feels aggressive, assertive, and inventive. Appears to be fashionable, charming, and entertaining. Strives to be popular, attrac-

tive, and in the spotlight. Has firm opinions, ideals, structure. Attracts
success.

PERSONALITY EXTREME: Too generous, or too selfish.

STEFAN (Greek: Stephen/English)—M.

MAJOR TALENT: Ability to incorporate attention to details, knack of
arbitrating differences, and cooperative approach into career. Is supportive, receptive, and musical/rhythmical. Has charm, orderliness, and
modesty. Combines consideration, friendliness, and subtle control over
others. Must be decisive to maintain emotional balance. Administrative
assistant, bookkeeper, and union shop steward are possible career opportunities.

PERSONALITY INGREDIENTS: Inwardly family/home focused, instructional, and protective. Feels sympathetic, helpful, and hospitable. Likes
showmanship, beauty, and justice. Appears to be unconventional,
understanding, and enthusiastic. Strives for travel, adventure, and sensual pleasures. Is often fooled by appearances and is attracted to strong
women who appear to be dependent. Must accept unexpected changes,
and break outworn habits to find happiness.

PERSONALITY EXTREME: Too speculative, or too cautious.

STEFANIE (Greek: Stephana/French/English)—F.

MAJOR TALENT: Ability to incorporate research, logic, and analysis
into career. Is thoughtful, expressive, and sensible. Has charm, practicality, and discretion. Combines talk, tenacity, and technical/scientific
approach. Engineer, dentist, and librarian may offer career opportunities.

PERSONALITY INGREDIENTS: Strives to experience all that life has to
offer. Seems open-minded, sensual, and enthusiastic. Inwardly emotional, receptive, and gentle. Feels supportive, shy, and happy to serve
as the power behind the throne. Is extremely direct, and full of surprises.
Attracts legal problems.

PERSONALITY EXTREME: Too busy, or too bored.

STELLA (Latin/Persian: Esther; variable/English)—F.

MAJOR TALENT: Ability to incorporate creative, unconventional uplift-
ing/sympathetic/protective ideas into career. Is advisory, strong-willed,
and devoted to home/family. Has communications gifts, desire for luxury, and firm ideals. Combines individuality, experimentation, and responsible community service. Flight attendant, interior decorator, and
home products salesperson are potential career opportunities.

PERSONALITY INGREDIENTS: Aims to reach a broad/universal public
need, and unselfishly work to improve standards/conditions. Strives to
be understanding, disciplined, and self-expressive. Feels concern for
everyone. Attracts gifts/financial help, and should not take advantage of
supporters. Benefits from self-improvement studies. Gains material stability when storehouse of knowledge, sense of humor, and instant appraisals broaden. Should avoid becoming smug.

PERSONALITY EXTREME: Too independent, or too submissive.

STEPHANIE (Greek: Stephana/French)—F.

MAJOR TALENT: Ability to incorporate scientific/technical analysis,

practical work, and personal charm into career. Is questioning, aristocratic, and sympathetically kind. Has optimism, dependability, and
power of strategic intellect. Combines constructive ideas, creative self-
expression, and a fine mind. Veterinarian, antique dealer, and editor are
possible career opportunities.

PERSONALITY INGREDIENTS: Inwardly modest, accommodating, and
easygoing. Feels supportive, reserved, and emotionally sensitive. Appears to be adventurous, enthusiastic, and confident. Strives to travel,
experiment, and satisfy curiosity. Would like to enjoy freedom, sensual
pleasures, and to be unconventional. Must be wary of overindulgence/
uncomplementary partnership. Should specialize to work with people in
a changing routine. Needs privacy, and is secretive, but attracts a full
life.

PERSONALITY EXTREME: Too cerebral, or too sensual.

STEPHEN (Greek/English)—M.

MAJOR TALENT: Ability to incorporate life-improving, protective, compassionate service into career. Is creative, expressive, and far-reaching.
Has self-discipline, resourcefulness, and inspirational ideas. Combines
artistic/writing/musical gifts, counseling, and instinct for domestic or social uplift. May confer lasting benefits when selflessly devoted to a
specific cause. Teacher/student, credit union organizer, and conservationist may be possible career opportunities.

PERSONALITY INGREDIENTS: Inwardly independent, forceful, and progressive. Wants to originate, direct, and lead. Is a pacesetter and a rebel.
Appears striking, enthusiastic, and vital. Strives to be open-minded,
adventurous, and understanding of human nature. Self-image is unconventional, daring, and sexy. Courts disappointment/emotional problems
when self-sacrificing for selfish motives.

PERSONALITY EXTREME: Too changeable, or too compulsive.

STERLING (Teutonic/English)—M.

MAJOR TALENT: Ability to incorporate multifaceted communications
techniques, bravery, and pioneering/adventurous/inspirational nature
into career. Is sensual, clever, and determined. Has knack of learning by
observing/experiencing, reflecting confidence, and gambling successfully. Combines down-to-earth work, originality, and understanding of
people. Any unconventional, challenging creative career offers sugges-
tions.

PERSONALITY INGREDIENTS: First impression is noble, empathetic,
and brotherly. Strives to be philosophical, culturally polished and generous. Aims for quality of skill/performance. Inwardly needs freedom,
travel, and mental stimulation. Feels impulsive, impatient and changeable, but benefits through a constant flow of new interests. Exemplifies
daring, and may be a catalyst for others. Should try everything, and
share observations.

PERSONALITY EXTREME: Too introspective, or too unquestioning.

STEVE (Greek: Stephen/English: diminutive)—M.

MAJOR TALENT: Ability to incorporate management, self-reliance, and
businesslike approach into career. Is realistic, efficient, and discriminating. Has structure, individuality, and logical analytic mind. Combines
ambition, drive for perfection, and knack for commercializing. Business

consultant, athlete, and theatrical agent are potential career opportunities.

PERSONALITY INGREDIENTS: First impression is classy, calm, and introspective. Strives to be cultured, investigative, and wise. Aims to have quality, and keeps confidences. Inwardly daring, pioneering, and controlling. Feels different, and wants to be a pacesetter. Is competitive, stubborn, and moody. Intellectual challenges add to success. Attracts powerful friends.

PERSONALITY EXTREME: Too temperamental, or too cool.

STEVEN (Greek: Stephen/English)—M.

MAJOR TALENT: Ability to incorporate ambitious planning, hard work, and tangible results into career. Is opinionated, determined, and problem-solving. Has detailed perceptions, diplomacy, and patient/enduring/ethical approach. Combines management, trusted friendships, and high constructive energy. This name has positive or negative power. Lawyer/C.P.A./doctor, architectural engineer, and stage manager may be career opportunities.

PERSONALITY INGREDIENTS: Strives to be entertaining, fashionable, and optimistic. Appears sociable, attention-getting, and creatively self-expressive. Needs people. Inwardly inventive, courageous, and proud. Wants independence, leadership, and never to wait for anything. Feels different, and aims for center stage.

PERSONALITY EXTREME: Too busy, or too bored.

STEWART (Anglo-Saxon/Scottish/English)—M.

MAJOR TALENT: Ability to incorporate detailed analysis, adventurous spirit, and intellectual probing into career. Is questioning, introspective, and diplomatic. Has aristocratic desires, confidential nature, and need for perfection in everything. Combines emotional sensitivity, physical daring, and mental surveillance. Wins through down-to-earth work, and specialization. Communications technician, detective, and data processor are possible career opportunities.

PERSONALITY INGREDIENTS: Strives to be independent, trend-setting, and fast-acting. Aims for controlling leadership, stimulating activity, and progressive changes. Inwardly conservative, domestically focused, and idealistic. Wants family/community attainments, security, and respectability. Feels protective, responsible, and advisory. Likes luxury, showmanship, and beauty. Best when educated, but will succeed through perseverance.

PERSONALITY EXTREME: Too critical, or too shy.

STORM (Anglo-Saxon/English)—F. & M.

MAJOR TALENT: Ability to incorporate projected planning, hard work, and practical results into career. Is attentive to details, tactful, and sensitive. Has strong opinions/ideals, high energy, and knack of coordinating varied interests skillfully. Combines vision, organizational analysis, and accomplishment. May inspire lasting large-scale humanitarian benefits. Construction, communications, and government may be career opportunities.

PERSONALITY INGREDIENTS: Strives for authority, quality, and perfection. Appears to be confident, investigative, and controlled. Inwardly responsible, protective, and family/community focused. Wants mature/

stable/loving mate, gracious lifestyle, and harmonious relationships.
Likes music, showmanship, and solving problems for others. Is sympathetic, but hides a secret self that feels lonely/unworthy/disappointed.
Aims for a world where nobody burps, everyone eats with the right fork,
and natural beauty rates over a plastic surgeon's perfection.

PERSONALITY EXTREME: Too disciplined or too unstructured.

STUART (Anglo-Saxon: Stewart; variable/English)—M.

MAJOR TALENT: Ability to incorporate human understanding, romantic
ideals, and quality of skill/performance into career. Is charitable,
philosophical, and individualistic. Has mental organization, businesslike
approach, and self-reliance. Combines independent creative leadership,
material power, and empathetic service. Doctor, publisher, and decorator may be career opportunities.

PERSONALITY INGREDIENTS: Inwardly practical, methodized, and conservative. Wants material security, dependability, and enduring values.
Appears to be adventurous, unconventional, and sociable. Strives for
sensual pleasures, confident reflection, and authority. Aims to be free,
and feels traditional. Has creative vitality, and must conserve energy to
eliminate nervousness and fatigue. Is an imaginative and soothing personality when cautious, calm, and down-to-earth.

PERSONALITY EXTREME: Too considerate, or too personalized.

SUE (English: Susan; diminutive)—F.

MAJOR TALENT: Ability to incorporate emotional responsiveness, inspirational attraction for others, and unlimited creative artistry into
career. Is romantic, intuitive, and tolerant. Has magnetic charm, universal understanding, and generous nature. Combines broad-scoped philosophy, drive for quality skills/performance, and commitment to
uplifting others. Welfare worker, physician, and artist/writer/entertainer
are potential career opportunities.

PERSONALITY INGREDIENTS: Inwardly wants material power, executive control, and ambitious goals. Feels self-reliant, trustworthy, and
practical. Appears to be decisive, independent, and different. Strives to
be inventive, praised, and left to own devices. Is impatient, and dislikes
details. Has conflict with selfishness, and selflessness. Best when busy.

PERSONALITY EXTREME: Too confident, or too scared.

SULLIVAN (Latin/Celtic/English)—M.

MAJOR TALENT: Ability to incorporate refinement, inventive ideas, and
stimulating enthusiasms into career. Is high-strung, quick, and perceptive. Has quality tastes, desire to inspire/lead others, and dreams of a
better world. Combines individuality, initiative, and sometimes impractical, but always consciousness-raising ideas. Evangelist, TV director, and
psychologist are possible career opportunities.

PERSONALITY INGREDIENTS: Inwardly methodized, orderly, and disciplined. Wants material security, dignity, and traditional accomplishments. First impression is aristocratic, thoughtful, and reserved. Strives
to be classy, authoritative, and confident. Aims for wisdom, timeless
beauty, and perfection. Self-image is discriminating while inner motivation is practical. Best when educated/specialized, analytic, and receptive. Attracts recognition, and supporters.

PERSONALITY EXTREME: Too open-minded, or too intolerant.

SUNNY (English-American; nickname)—F.

MAJOR TALENT: Ability to incorporate creative self-expression, imagination, and words into career. Is clever, inventive, and attentive to details. Has knack of bringing concepts to reality. Is youthful, optimistic, and ambitious. Combines independent leadership, orderliness, and literary/musical/artistic talents. Entertainer, fashion designer, and writer may offer career opportunities.

PERSONALITY INGREDIENTS: Inwardly inventive, forceful, and competitive. Wants mental stimulation, activity, and progressive changes. Appears to be adaptable, unassuming, and gentle. Strives to be special. Aims to inspire reforms, maintain peaceful relationships, and lead movements that improve the quality of life for others. Should avoid scattering interests, impatience, and exaggerating. Best when concentrated. Attracts happiness and financial success.

PERSONALITY EXTREME: Too deep, or too shallow.

SUSAN (Hebrew/English)—F.

MAJOR TALENT: Ability to incorporate supportive nature, nervous creative energy, and gifted artistry into career. Is sensitive, gentle, and diplomatic communicator. Has patience, spontaneous enthusiasms, and difficulty making decisions because of seeing both sides of an issue. Combines imagination, strong personal ideals, and a feeling of being special. Has opportunity to leave a lasting image through drive for superior quality and disapproval of mediocrity. Thespian, psychoanalyst, and crusader for uplifting causes are possible career opportunities.

PERSONALITY INGREDIENTS: First impression is aristocratic, aloof, and introspective. Strives for solitude, timeless beauty, and perfection. Inwardly wants practical, methodized, material achievements. Desires down-to-earth relationships, but may switch hit to an ivory tower. Seems confident, but is very vulnerable.

PERSONALITY EXTREME: Too sensual, or too cerebral.

SUSANNA (Hebrew: Susan/Italian/Portuguese/Spanish/English)—F.

MAJOR TALENT: Ability to incorporate efficient mental organization, material ambitions, and executive leadership into career. Is self-reliant, inventive, and intellectually analytic. Has poise, initiative, and determination. Combines courage, drive for perfection, and knack of making things pay. Band leader, investment counselor, and printer are potential career opportunities.

PERSONALITY INGREDIENTS: First impression is attention-getting, optimistic, and entertaining. Strives to be fashionable, kind, and creatively expressive. Inwardly adventurous, sensual, and clever. Wants constant activity, new experiences, and freedom of speech/interests. Appears easy to know, but is constantly changing.

PERSONALITY EXTREME: Too independent, or too submissive.

SUSANNAH (Hebrew: Susan/English)—F.

MAJOR TALENT: Ability to incorporate detailed observations, logical analysis, and curious mind into career. Is reserved, refined, and sensitive. Has tact, discretion, and desire for perfection. Combines technical/scientific interests, gentleness, and common sense. Photographer, computer programmer, and mimic are potential career opportunities.

PERSONALITY INGREDIENTS: Appears supportive, easygoing, and genteel. Strives to be friendly, accommodating, and cautious. Inwardly
clever, quick, and adventurous. Desires sensual pleasure, travel, and
freedom. Happiest when impetuous, open-minded, and confident. Leans
heavily upon past experiences, and may be a late-bloomer. In youth,
tends to dramatize mistakes, and avoid decisive action. Overcomes fears
of loneliness and poverty in mid-life, which opens doors to achieving
major goals.
PERSONALITY EXTREME: Too mercenary, or too impractical.

SUSANNE (Hebrew: Susan/Bavarian/French/German/English)—F.
MAJOR TALENT: Ability to incorporate charm, creative concepts, and
communications gifts into career. Is youthful, optimistic, and capable.
Has sensitivity to details, adaptability, and individuality. Combines
cooperative spirit, independent/original ideas, and fashionable interests.
Writer, entertainer, and model are possible career opportunities.
PERSONALITY INGREDIENTS: Inwardly compassionate, philosophical,
and broad-scoped. Wants romance, culture, and top-quality skills/
performance. Has a knack with words. Appears to be up-to-date, sociable, and imaginative. Strives to attract attention, enjoy beauty, and focus
upon sunny days. Aims to bring pleasure to others, and must avoid
scattering energy, exaggerating, and hiding from practical realities. Attracts admirers, and inspires happiness.
PERSONALITY EXTREME: Too impulsive, or too cautious.

SUZANNA (Hebrew: Susan/English)—F.
MAJOR TALENT: Ability to incorporate protective, instructional, responsible nature into career. Is parental, sympathetic, and sensitive to
fine points. Has practical approach, determination, and firm personal
ideals. Combines discipline, patience, and companionability. Homemaker, teacher, and marriage counselor may be career opportunities.
PERSONALITY INGREDIENTS: Inwardly curious, clever, and sensual.
Wants variety, adventure, and unconventional pleasures. First impression is assertive, aggressive, and independent. Strives to be different,
strong, and capable of courageous leadership. Is stubborn, and should
avoid assuming confining burdens and judging by appearances.
PERSONALITY EXTREME: Too ambitious, or too lazy.

SUZY (Hebrew-English: Susan; diminutive)—F.
MAJOR TALENT: Ability to incorporate initiative, originality, and daring
leadership into career. Is proud, wide-ranged, and philosophical. Has
ambition, competitive spirit, and problem-solving vitality. Combines human understanding, uniqueness, and pioneering ideas. Salesperson, designer, and architect may be career opportunities.
PERSONALITY INGREDIENTS: Appears magnetic, gracious, and concerned. Strives to be quality-conscious, empathetic, and charitable. Inwardly wants progressive changes, control, and praise. Must learn the
true meaning of independent courage, and will face the lessons of endurance.
PERSONALITY EXTREME: Too questioning, or too authoritative.

SYBIL—SIBYL (Greek/Irish/Scottish/English)—F.
MAJOR TALENT: Ability to incorporate broad-scoped and inspirational

planning, work, and tangible results into career. Is charged with practical energy. Has organization, method, and determination. Combines detailed perceptions, instinct for coordinating, and patient/diplomatic/imaginative leadership. Architect-builder, writer-promoter-director-producer, and appraiser-salesperson-owner are potential career opportunities.

PERSONALITY INGREDIENTS: Inwardly needs intellectual/spiritual confidence. Desires aristocratic, cultured, introspective life-style. Has fears of loneliness/poverty and material disappointment until feelings of authority are substantiated by respected specialization of interest. Is motivated to material accumulation and status symbols until inner faith/security is established by recognition of natural/timeless beauty/wisdom. First impression is dignified, tasteful, and comforting. Self-image is adult, sensible, and responsible. Inwardly reserved, and apparently emotionally responsive. Should be encouraged to seek education, private thinking time, and harmonious family/community relationships.

PERSONALITY EXTREME: Too expressive, or too worried.

SYDNEY (Phoenician: Sidney; variable/Old French/English)—F. & M.

MAJOR TALENT: Ability to incorporate idealistic principles, accommodating personality, and persistent purpose into career. Is gentle, adaptable, and imaginative. Has impulsive enthusiasms, sensitivity to details, and broad-scoped philosophy. Combines supportive instincts, quick decisions, and individuality. Must avoid impracticality. Artist, educational reformer, and psychoanalyst may be career opportunities.

PERSONALITY INGREDIENTS: Inwardly youthful, optimistic, and pleasure-seeking. Wants beauty, kindness, and love. Strives to be businesslike, efficient, and influential. Appears self-reliant, managerial, and as affluent as possible. Aims for material power. Needs sunny days. Is visionary, and ahead of mass tastes. Should come down-to-earth, to stabilize.

PERSONALITY EXTREME: Too skeptical, or too gullible.

SYLVESTER (Latin: Silvester-Silas/English)—M.

MAJOR TALENT: Ability to incorporate pace-setting leadership, will power, and inventive methods into career. Is reserved, artistically/creatively expressive, and ambitious. Has stimulating vitality, kindness, and the courage to be different. Combines communications gifts, perfectionist instincts, and competitive spirit. Theatrical performer, salesperson, and lawyer are potential career opportunities.

PERSONALITY INGREDIENTS: First impression is modest, retiring, and agreeable. Strives to be peaceful, easygoing, and cooperative. Inwardly desires financial freedom, influential lifestyle, and businesslike efficiency. Feels self-reliant, determined, and strong. Likes wheeling and dealing but has a knack for executive diplomacy. Love/homelife are important, but will stand the test of uprooting travel, progressive changes, and controlled emotions blasting loose periodically.

PERSONALITY EXTREME: Too philosophical, or too intolerant.

SYLVIA (Latin: Silvia; variable/English)—F.

MAJOR TALENT: Ability to incorporate logic, research, and analysis into career. Is perceptive of details, clever, and adventurous. Has aristocratic approach, perfectionist tastes, and authoritative manner. Combines persistence, understanding of human nature, and technical/scientific/introspective questioning. Photographer, accountant, and psychoanalyst are possible career opportunities.

PERSONALITY INGREDIENTS: Strives to be of service to others. Seems noble, compassionate, and dramatic. Aims for romance, quality of skill/performance, and unselfishness. Inwardly wants to get to the root of everything, and defensively stays aloof from strong emotions. Needs the inner security that education/expertise offer. Has drive for material status, but gains self-assurance through intellectual/spiritual focus. Enjoys travel, sensual pleasures, and privacy. Finds success when hardworking, decisive, and down-to-earth.

PERSONALITY EXTREME: Too assertive, or too unworthy.

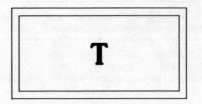

T

All names that begin with the letter *T* have the *Strong Point* of domestic/community burdens—affectionate nature—fine-point analysis—collecting.

TABITHA (Aramaic/English)—F.

MAJOR TALENT: Ability to incorporate intellectual questioning, poise, and specialization into career. Is intuitive, thoughtful, and aristocratic. Has curiosity, charm, and tact. Combines secretiveness, adventurous ideas, and need for authority. Electronics technician, data-processing programmer, and political analyst are possible career opportunities.

PERSONALITY INGREDIENTS: First impression is different, clever, and enthusiastic. Strives to be open-minded, changing, and progressive. Likes sensual pleasures, travel, and unconventional people/experiences. Inwardly idealistic, high-strung, and mentally energetic. Wants originality, quality, and to remain above the mass-market culture. May be impractical, evangelistic, and full of surprises. Never dull.

PERSONALITY EXTREME: Too aggressive, or too passive.

TAD (Hebrew: Thaddeus/Irish: independent/English: diminutive)—M.

MAJOR TALENT: Ability to incorporate investigative, analytic, pensive nature into career. Is refined, quiet, and controlled. Has logic, poise, and an air of mystery. Combines concentration, calm, and wisdom. Scientist, mathematician, and strategist may be career opportunities.

PERSONALITY INGREDIENTS: Desires independence, innovations, and leadership. Wants to take the initiative. Appears solid, comforting, and dignified. Strives to study/teach/counsel. Aims to take responsibility, enjoy family/community respect, and work for material security. Is sensitive, practical, and inventive. Needs education.

PERSONALITY EXTREME: Too structured, or too rule-bending.

TALLY (Latin/English)—F. & M.

MAJOR TALENT: Ability to incorporate questioning nature into career. Is analytic, culturally attaining, and logical. Has domestic instincts, independence, and desire for perfection. Combines strong will, inventiveness, and ambition. Best when educated/technically expert, and attracting money through expertise. Should avoid aggressive materialism. Scientist, chess expert, and librarian are potential career opportunities.

PERSONALITY INGREDIENTS: Appears to be businesslike and desires control. Strives to be affluent, influential, and self-reliant. Inwardly organized, practical, and willing to work. Aims for quality and quantity.

Should avoid gambling, bluffing, and manipulative actions. Best when receptive and letting reputation attract commerce.

PERSONALITY EXTREME: Too skeptical, or too gullible.

TAMARA (Hebrew: Tamar/English)—F.

MAJOR TALENT: Ability to incorporate imagination, tolerance, and empathetic service into career. Is generous, just, and philosophical. Has individuality, organizational efficiency, and desire to reach a universal marketplace. Combines understanding, romance, and devotion to quality/skill/top-of-the-line performance. Doctor, judge, and educational reformer may be career opportunities.

PERSONALITY INGREDIENTS: Inwardly loving, kind, and optimistic. Wants pleasure, variety, to entertain and be entertained. Finds the best in everything/everyone. Appears dignified, solid, and comforting. Strives to be artistically expressive, instructional, and wise. Aims for mature judgments, material security, and domestic tranquility. Has an open door for anyone in need and uses practicality for business only. Is all heart.

PERSONALITY EXTREME: Too decisive, or too changeable.

TAMMY (Thomas/Tamar: diminutive/English)—F. & M.

MAJOR TALENT: Ability to incorporate quality performance, wide appeal, and artistic/social/religious service into career. Is charitable, tolerant, and individualistic. Has organizational efficiency, material awareness, and philosophical humor. Combines inventiveness, enthusiasm for work, and knack of visualizing the big picture. Any creative field, doctor, and educational reformer are potential career opportunities.

PERSONALITY INGREDIENTS: Inwardly ambitious, businesslike, and self-reliant. Wants affluence, influence, and recognition. First impression is individualistic, energetic, and firm. Strives to be original, pioneering, and aggressive. Wants prominence and is willing to work and serve others to get it.

PERSONALITY EXTREME: Too self-controlled, or too argumentative.

TARA (Gaelic)—F.

MAJOR TALENT: Ability to incorporate common sense, construction, and resourcefulness to rebuild or reassess projects into career. Is practical, economical, and administrative. Has individuality, independence, and love of beauty. Combines communications gifts, competitiveness, and structure. Secretary, real estate salesperson, and technical writer may be career opportunities.

PERSONALITY INGREDIENTS: Inwardly peace-loving, gentle, and receptive. Wants comforts, partnership/mate, and easygoing life-style. Appears different, energetic, and enthusiastic. Strives to be original, idealistic, and above the crowd. May be passive or excitable as the moods change. Undergoes reversals, is persistent, and uses subtle control to restructure material security. Is a survivor.

PERSONALITY EXTREME: Too pioneering, or too imitative.

TATE (Anglo-Saxon/English)—F. & M.

MAJOR TALENT: Ability to incorporate independence, inventiveness, and daring into career. Is competitive, direct, and ambitious. Has intellectual agility, leadership, and initiative. Combines aggressiveness, assertion, and active energy. Idea person, architect, and designer are potential career opportunities.

PERSONALITY INGREDIENTS: Inwardly sympathetic, strong-willed, and family/community focused. Wants gracious living, material attainments, and high standards. Appears traditional, tasteful, and solid. Strives to be practical, structured, and proper. Dislikes vulgarity, waiting, and imitations. Best when self-employed.

PERSONALITY EXTREME: Too impulsive, or too calculating.

TAYLOR (French-Latin/American)—M.

MAJOR TALENT: Ability to incorporate initiative, assertiveness, and originality into career. Is independent, inventive, and a pioneer. Has courage, decisiveness, and willpower. Combines sensitivity to details, businesslike organization, and individuality. Writer, designer, and business owner may be career opportunities.

PERSONALITY INGREDIENTS: Inwardly calm, cool, and collected. Appears friendly, expressive, and attention-getting. Wants privacy, quiet, and perfection. Is mentally alert, clever, and investigative. Enjoys fun, parties, and pleasure. Is an escapist from mundane realities. Strives to be discriminating, precise and aristocratic. Likes puns, intellectual stimulation, and cultural attainments. Needs education.

PERSONALITY EXTREME: Too broad-minded, or too intolerant.

TED (Anglo-Saxon: Edward-Greek: Theodore; diminutive/English independent)—M.

MAJOR TALENT: Ability to incorporate visionary ideas, detailed perceptions, and desire for uplift into career. Is instructional, communicative, and inspirational. Attracts recognition. Has sense of justice and the courage to back personal beliefs. Combines need for progressive change, individuality, and originality of purpose. Lawyer, promoter, and educational reformer may be career opportunities.

PERSONALITY INGREDIENTS: Wants adventure, physical pleasures, and changing routine. Feels challenged by life. Appears tasteful, dignified, and comforting. Strives to be mature, responsible, and protective. Aims for family/community attainments, stability, and respectability but feels a drive for free expression. Should avoid feeling above the masses, impulsiveness, and temperamental overreactions.

PERSONALITY EXTREME: Too structured, or too rule-bending.

TERENCE (Latin/English)—M.

MAJOR TALENT: Ability to incorporate research, analysis, and logic into career. Is questioning, intuitive, and proud. Knows when to keep a secret, seek privacy, and time to reflect upon experiences. Combines communications gifts, practical structure, and desire to get to the root of things. Musical technician, watchmaker, and data processor are potential career opportunities.

PERSONALITY INGREDIENTS: Appears different, independent, and energetic. Strives to be first, in control, and leading others. Inwardly wants home/family respectability, gracious living, and harmonious relationships. Needs to love and be loved. Feels protective, sociable, and artistically expressive. Is an individualistic, hospitable showman.

PERSONALITY EXTREME: To thoughtless, or too understanding.

TERESA (Latin: Theresa/Italian/Spanish/English)—F.

MAJOR TALENT: Ability to incorporate daring, progressive ideas, and unconventional routines into career. Is sensitive, gentle, and optimistic. Has enthusiasm, communications gifts, and active/curious/changeable mind. Combines attention to details, friendliness, and the knack of understanding people. Politician, advertising executive, and athletic coach are possible career opportunities.

PERSONALITY INGREDIENTS: First impression is attractive, imaginative, and entertaining. Strives for social contact, variety, and self-expression. Is resourceful and learns from observation. Inwardly wants to inspire, uplift, and serve others through original personal concepts. Feels different, intuitive, and visionary. Has high energy, force, and wisdom. May be out of this world/impractical at times, but bounces back to reality when not in an ivory tower. Attracts recognition.

PERSONALITY EXTREME: Too changeable, or too persistent.

TERRY (Latin: diminutive; Terence-Theresa/English)—F. & M.

MAJOR TALENT: Ability to incorporate adventurous, curious, unconventional nature into career. Is understanding, gracious, and adaptable. Has imagination, nerve, and knack of learning from experience. Combines resourcefulness, attention to details, and progressive/changeable ideas. Politician, advertising executive, and travel agent may be career opportunities.

PERSONALITY INGREDIENTS: First impression is retiring, refined, and modest. Strives for partnership, peace, and easygoing life-style. Inwardly wants fashionable, beautiful, fun-filled experiences. Wants to be popular, entertaining, and to live for the moment. Forgets bad times and keeps moving. May be extravagant, fanciful, and superficial when daily living becomes too earthy. Best when free of serious responsibilities.

PERSONALITY EXTREME: Too confident, or too fearful.

TESS (Latin: Theresa; variable/English)—F.

MAJOR TALENT: Ability to incorporate abstract thinking, wide range of interests, and romantic/humanitarian instincts into career. Is creative, expressive, and understanding. Has charm, wit and resourcefulness. Combines drive to complete commitments, tolerance, and inspirational/magnetic/empathetic personality. Welfare worker, performer, and college professor are potential career opportunities.

PERSONALITY INGREDIENTS: Wants life experience, freedom, and unconventional interests. Inwardly sensual, curious, and adventurous. Appears conservative, dignified, and tasteful. Strives to be proper, trustworthy, and dependable. Should work to serve/entertain/heal others, and travel, study, and share experiences.

PERSONALITY EXTREME: Too accommodating, or too selfish.

THADDEUS (Hebrew/Irish/English)—M.

MAJOR TALENT: Ability to incorporate inventiveness, independence, and direct action into career. Is creative, forceful, and self-motivated. Has pride, nonconformist instincts, and pioneering spirit. Combines attention to fine points, businesslike methods, and individuality. Lawyer, salesperson, and any decision-making job may be career opportunities.

PERSONALITY INGREDIENTS: Inwardly broad-scoped, empathetic, and generous. Wants tolerance, quality of artistry/performance, and to uphold humanitarian principles. Is an old soul. Appears alert, different, and positive. Strives to be pacesetting, in control, and number one. Attracts money, sensual fulfillment, and practical life-style. Has unlimited potential when able to work compatibly with others.

PERSONALITY EXTREME: Too decisive, or too elastic.

THATCHER (Middle English/English)—M.

MAJOR TALENT: Ability to incorporate personal ideals, communications techniques, and executive organizational skills into career. Is an imaginative, efficient, sensitive communicator. Has nervous energy, detail consciousness, and self-reliance. Combines futuristic ideas, quality consciousness, and potential to change the course of thinking for others. Advertising, TV/film production, and any art field are possible career opportunities.

PERSONALITY INGREDIENTS: Wants home/family/community focus, gracious living, and mature approach. Inwardly hospitable, sympathetic, and helpful. Appears curious, gutsy, and understanding. Strives to be adventurous, sensual, and unconventional. First impression is attention getting, but needs refinements, conservative standards, and respectability.

PERSONALITY EXTREME: Too tolerant, or too narrow-minded.

THEA (Greek)—F.

MAJOR TALENT: Ability to incorporate questioning, analytic, and refined nature into career. Is a perfectionist who rarely accepts anything totally. Has quality consciousness, desire for natural beauty, and need for privacy. Combines opposing drives: independence-mating/originality-peer pressure/logical-emotional approach. Best when educated or technically expert. Librarian, radio announcer, and mathematician may be career opportunities.

PERSONALITY INGREDIENTS: Wants family warmth, comforts, and attainments. Feels domestic, artistically expressive, and idealistic. Needs to help, be involved, and raise life-support standards for others. Appears individualistic, energetic, and self-motivated. Strives for freedom to make progressive changes, lead, and be first in everything. Prefers not to be told how/when/why to do things. Aims for material success, but should concentrate on expertise to attract commercial activity.

PERSONALITY EXTREME: Too decisive, or too anxious.

THEDA (Greek: Dorothy; variable/English)—F.

MAJOR TALENT: Ability to incorporate sensitivity to details, subtle controlling nature, and knack for making friends out of enemies into career. Is diplomatic, supportive, and works well in partnership. Has gift of seeing both sides, and aims to maintain balance in surroundings. Combines consideration, patience, and musical/rhythmic gifts. Best when decisive and avoiding dependency upon another. Executive secretary, bookkeeper, and group musician/dancer may be career opportunities.

PERSONALITY INGREDIENTS: Inwardly conventional, but longs for adventure. Wants stability, material attainments, and gracious living. Appears sensual, striking, and understanding. Aims for experience, travel, and to satisfy curiosity. Is happiest when protective, responsible, and helping. Needs love, action, and to avoid personalizing.

PERSONALITY EXTREME: Too habitual, or too changeable.

THELMA (Greek/English)—F.

MAJOR TALENT: Ability to incorporate nonroutine, adaptable, adventurous nature into career. Understands people. Is sociable, imaginative, and sensual. Has versatility, nerve, and learns by experience. Combines open-mindedness, urge for change/activity/mental stimulation, and progressive ideas. Politician, theatrical manager, and detective may be career opportunities.

PERSONALITY INGREDIENTS: Desires secure home/family and to give and receive love, comfort, and sensible advice. Appears businesslike, authoritative, and as affluent as possible. Strives to be influential, organized, and efficient. Is courageous, sympathetic, and ambitious. Attracts leadership, loyalty, and inheritance. Must not live vicariously and fear experimentation. Should take a chance on self. May be inspirational to family/community/world.

PERSONALITY EXTREME: Too supportive, or too independent.

THEODORA (Greek: Dorothy; variable/English)—F.

MAJOR TALENT: Ability to incorporate enthusiasm, mental curiosity, and inspirational leadership into career. Is individualistic, concerned with tangible results, and an opportunist. Has need for change, progress, and new inventions. Combines structured work habits, creativity, and adventurous nature. Promoter, travel agent, and reporter are potential career opportunities.

PERSONALITY INGREDIENTS: Appears striking, sexy, and openminded. Strives for travel, pleasure, and a variety of things at one time. Inwardly wants romance, quality of skill/performance, and to reach a broad understanding of life/people. Needs to give love, artistry, and/or charity. Has a generous, empathetic, and philosophical outlook. Must avoid self-indulgence, impulsiveness, and jealousy.

PERSONALITY EXTREME: Too daring, or too fearful.

THEODORE (Greek/French/English)—M.

MAJOR TALENT: Ability to incorporate artistic/social service, empathetic understanding, and unbiased attitude into career. Is tolerant, generous, and philosophical. Has structure, nonroutine focus, and mental curiosity. Combines practicality, changing interests, and imagination. Artist, doctor, and publisher may be career opportunities.

PERSONALITY INGREDIENTS: Inwardly plans, works, and builds for idealistic and tangible results. Wants to master every situation, serve mass-market needs, and leave a lasting mark. Appears vital, enthusiastic, and engaging. Strives to explore all physical sensations, travel, and taste varied life experience. Is inspirational, exciting, and energetic. Happiest when giving others the benefit of personal experience.

PERSONALITY EXTREME: Too resourceful, or too defeated.

THERESA (Latin/Portuguese/English)—F.

MAJOR TALENT: Ability to incorporate common sense, work, and practical organization into career. Is administrative, structured, and methodical. Has determination, integrity, and creative ideas. Combines communications techniques, independent leadership, and dependability. Accountant, real estate salesperson, and any office work may be career opportunities.

PERSONALITY INGREDIENTS: Wants to save the world, share personal ideas, and raise standards for others. May be impractical when on a crusade. Appears gentle, modest, and refined. Strives for peaceful environments and relationships. Envisions an easygoing life-style, but high inner energy produces fast pace. Best when decisive, organized, and able to work compatibly with partner/groups. May use subtle controls, and be too bossy.

PERSONALITY EXTREME: Too changeable, or too passive.

THERESE (Latin: Theresa/French/German/English)—F.

MAJOR TALENT: Ability to incorporate executive efficiency, self-reliance, and intuitive understanding of mass-market acceptance into career. Is gutsy, forceful, and open-minded. Has optimism, charm, and adventurous spirit. Combines versatility, businesslike approach, and people contact. Stockbroker, travel agent, and business organizer may be career opportunities.

PERSONALITY INGREDIENTS: Wants roots, love, and comforts. Feels responsible, protective, and focused on family/community/group. Is motivated to study, teach, and be sympathetic. Appears retiring, accommodating, and supportive. Strives to be kind, helpful, and maintain peace at all costs. Best when persistent, but not unreasonable. Attracts prominence, expansion, and travel.

PERSONALITY EXTREME: Too confident, or too fearful.

THOMAS (Aramaic/French/Portuguese/Scottish/English)—M.

MAJOR TALENT: Ability to incorporate visionary planning, practical routine/structure, and long-term tangible results into career. Is dynamic or mundane, but is honest, determined, and hard-working. Has potential to benefit future generations. Combines high nervous energy, knack of solving problems, and strong opinions. Directs, administers, and has original ideas. Corporate executive, government/religious reformer, and any profession are possible career opportunities.

PERSONALITY INGREDIENTS: Inwardly wants privacy, quality, and perfection. Feels analytic, investigative, and authoritative. Desires expertise, natural beauty, and self-control. May be secretive and fear loneliness and poverty. Appears dignified, tasteful, and comforting. Strives for family/community harmony, gracious living, and material attainments. May aim for conventional success, but has possibility of universal recognition.

PERSONALITY EXTREME: Too bossy, or too passive.

TIFFANY (Latin/Old French/Modern English)—F. & M.

MAJOR TALENT: Ability to incorporate communications, artistry, and dedication to ideals into career. Is intensely loving, kind, and creative. Has eye for beauty, dignity, and balance. Combines self-expression, home/family/community service, and broad philosophy. Best when aimed toward humanitarian or artistic business. Welfare worker, novelist, and policeman are potential career opportunities.

PERSONALITY INGREDIENTS: Strives to be original, independent, and direct. Appears nonconforming. Inwardly efficient, self-motivated, and materialistic. Wants the things that money can buy. Has family ties, need for perfection, and quality. Must avoid impracticality, selfishness, and mundane ambitions.

PERSONALITY EXTREME: Too aloof, or too involved.

TILDEN (Old English)—M.

MAJOR TALENT: Ability to incorporate initiative, leadership, and new ideas into career. Is direct, organized, and logical. Has impatience, ambition, and resourcefulness. Combines material awareness, individuality, and pioneering spirit. Banker, salesperson, and architect may be career opportunities.

PERSONALITY INGREDIENTS: Wants action, adventure, and sensual experiences. Feels curious, gutsy, and adaptable. Appears unconventional, friendly, and open-minded. Strives to be free, challenged, and fast-moving. Must be able to decide when to hang in and when people/things are past their usefulness. Thrives upon change, travel, and understanding people.

PERSONALITY EXTREME: Too fickle, or too intense.

TIM (Greek: Timothy; diminutive/English)—M.

MAJOR TALENT: Ability to incorporate responsibility, family/community welfare, and showmanship into career. Is protective, conscientious, and instructional. Combines unconventional ideas, sense of competition, and mature approach. Theater, education, and home products/services are possible career opportunities.

PERSONALITY INGREDIENTS: Wants a broad education, scope, and range of relationships. Feels empathetic, romantic, and just. Needs to help, raise standards, and inspire. Appears solid, conventional, and comforting. Strives to be involved, stable, and to maintain personal ideals. Best when not quick to judge, too serious or impetuous. Prone to Archie Bunkerisms and should not moralize without having personal experience.

PERSONALITY EXTREME: Too rigid, or too undisciplined.

TIMOTHY (Greek/English)—M.

MAJOR TALENT: Ability to incorporate unique creative, intuitional, and visionary ideals into career. Is imaginative, intellectually zealous, and spiritually conscious of the quality of life. Has refinement, gentleness, and desire to bring dreams to reality. Combines communications techniques, businesslike approach, and potential for fame. Political campaigner, artist/performer, and religious leader may be career opportunities.

PERSONALITY INGREDIENTS: May seem stuck-up, aloof, or mysterious at first glance. Must be in authority or known to be understood. Strives for specialization, perfection, and cultural attainments. Inwardly hard-working, down-to-earth, and purposeful. Wants structure, practicality, and lasting, tangible results. Has nervous energy, efficiency, and sense of duty.

PERSONALITY EXTREME: Too skeptical, or too gullible.

TINA (English independent/designates "little" as a F. suffix; example, Justina—M. Justin)—F.

MAJOR TALENT: Ability to incorporate material awareness, efficiency, and self-reliance into career. Is strong, trustworthy, and practical. Has control, determination, and strategic approach. Combines quality consciousness, independence, and appreciation of the things that money can buy. Retailer, publisher, and administrator are potential career opportunities.

PERSONALITY INGREDIENTS: First impression is calm, refined, and introspective. Strives to be cultured, expert, and analytic. Inwardly daring, inventive, and positive. Wants to be a trend setter. Aims for recognition, praise, and to avoid petty details. Happiest when financially and intellectually prominent. Fears loneliness/poverty and stagnation.

PERSONALITY EXTREME: Too changeable, or too stubborn.

TITUS (Latin/English)—M.

MAJOR TALENT: Ability to incorporate businesslike approach, independent ideas, and cultural stimulation into career. Is efficient, organizational, and mentally analytic. Has energy, initiative, and executive control. Combines financial focus, perfectionist drive, and determination. Investment counselor, manufacturer, and politician may be career opportunities.

PERSONALITY INGREDIENTS: Strives to be speculative, progressive, and sexy. Appears adventurous, different, and understanding. Has a knack of making people comfortable. Inwardly artistically expressive, optimistic, and pleasure-seeking. Likes to entertain, be entertained, make the best of things. Is resourceful, restless, and willing to forget unpleasant memories. Wants beauty, love, and to be a swashbuckler.

PERSONALITY EXTREME: Too inventive, or too imitative.

TOBIAS (Hebrew/Late Latin/Danish/German/Greek/Spanish/English)— M.

MAJOR TALENT: Ability to incorporate words, originality, and sensitivity into career. Is imaginative, youthful, and pleasure-seeking. Has humor, charm, and optimism. Combines social contact, ambition, and self-expression. Performing artist, writer, and organizer may be career opportunities.

PERSONALITY INGREDIENTS: Inwardly investigative, analytic, and quality-conscious. Wants concentration, quiet, and privacy. Feels secretive and lacks the confidence to attract people and respect. Needs tangible assurance of self-worth. Appears friendly, understanding, and assured. Strives to be unconventional, progressive, and sensual. Aims to travel, experiment, and learn by experience. May be an escapist. Needs education/expertise.

PERSONALITY EXTREME: Too impatient, or too indecisive.

TOBY (Hebrew: Tobias; diminutive/English: independent)—F. & M.

MAJOR TALENT: Ability to incorporate mental organization, efficiency, and commercial ambitions into career. Is independent, logical, and determined. Has executive judgment, strength, and enthusiasm for business acumen. Combines drive, self-reliance, and long-term planning. Consultant, corporate administrator, and printer are potential career opportunities.

PERSONALITY INGREDIENTS: Wants conventional structure. Feels self-disciplined, proper, and practical. Appears dignified, precise, and neat. Strives to be a solid citizen. Must avoid workaholic tendencies, rigidity, and self-depreciation if not culturally/academically educated. Enjoys the things that money can buy and will gain polish through fine observational abilities.

PERSONALITY EXTREME: Too authoritative, or too shy.

TODD (Old English)—M.

MAJOR TALENT: Ability to incorporate questioning nature into career. Is mentally analytic, probing, and culturally attaining. Has confidential instincts, logic, and lacks inner confidence. Needs material results to improve self-image. Combines perfectionist, counselor, and inventor. Detective, researcher, and mimic may offer career opportunities.

PERSONALITY INGREDIENTS: Inwardly wants roots, family harmony, and comforts. Needs to love, protect, and assume responsibility. Appears nonconforming, but wants conventional attainments. Strives to be independent, original, and to instigate progressive changes. Aims to be first and dislikes being told how to do things. Best when educated and not speculative or materialistic.

PERSONALITY EXTREME: Too structured, or too impractical.

TOM (English/Thomas: independent-diminutive)—M.

MAJOR TALENT: Ability to incorporate self-expression, words, and personal charm into career. Is detail-conscious, independent, and sensitive. Has imagination, love of beauty, and restlessness. Combines unique philosophy, modesty, and promotions through social contact. Salesperson, accountant, and literary critic may be career opportunities.

PERSONALITY INGREDIENTS: Desires gracious homelife, stability, and family harmony. Needs to protect, guide, and feel responsible. Appears to be conventional, dignified, and interested in everyone. Strives to be hospitable, musical/rhythmic, and to maintain high standards. Is a showman, problem solver, reformer, and educator. Best when diplomatic, optimistic, and not assuming everyone's problems.

PERSONALITY EXTREME: Too conventional, or too improper.

TONI (Latin: Anthony; M./Antonia; F., diminutive)—F. & M.

MAJOR TALENT: Ability to incorporate visionary planning, hard work, and lasting results into career. Is industrious, organized, and determined. Has practical ideals, humanitarian instincts, and structured organizational approach. Combines tact, sensitivity to details, and potential to build commercially for the benefit of future generations. Construction trades, government reform, and the arts are potential career opportunities.

PERSONALITY INGREDIENTS: First impression is unruffled, refined, and quiet. Strives to be cultured, expert, and investigative. Inwardly emotional, but appears cool. Wants domestic tranquility, attainments, and abundant life-style. Feels protective, problem-solving, and artistically/musically self-expressive. Needs close family ties, to love/be loved, and to maintain harmony in all relationships. Must avoid domineering opinions, jealousy, and misplaced sympathy.

PERSONALITY EXTREME: Too possessive, or too generous.

TONY (Latin: Anthony; M./Antonia; F., diminutive)—F. & M.

MAJOR TALENT: Ability to incorporate personal ideals, devoted service, and appreciation of details into career. Works well in conjunction with others. Is diplomatic, subdued, and persistent. Combines subtle controlling nature, skilled/quality craftsmanship, and need for adaptability. Has powerful emotions and must not make snap judgments. Leather crafter, photographer/film/TV producer/technician/performer, and inventor may be career opportunities.

PERSONALITY INGREDIENTS: Visually aloof, refined, and poised. Strives to be authoritative/expert, analytic, and perfect. Aims for peer relationships, private emotional life, and quality comforts. Inwardly organized, orderly, and disciplined. Feels home-loving, dependable, and sincere. Wants respectability, cultural attainments, and to work for material stability. May seem confusing/impractical/on cloud nine at times. Has strong potential for achieving fame.

PERSONALITY EXTREME: Too unrealistic, or too specific.

TOR (Old Norse/English)—M.

MAJOR TALENT: Ability to incorporate self-reliance, efficiency, and mental organization into career. Is materially aware, strong, and ambitious. Has leadership, breath of vision, and self-assertion. Combines inventive ideas, investigative analysis, and desire for financial success. Banker, corporate executive, and business owner are potential career opportunities.

PERSONALITY INGREDIENTS: Wants domestic, respectable, abundant life-style. Needs to help others, express artistically/scientifically, and share personal ideas/standards with everyone. Is strong-willed, protective, and instructional. Strives to be original, uplifting, and inspirational. Seems enthusiastic, gentle, and peace-loving, but will fight to uphold justice as he sees it. May leave a unique mark on humanity.

PERSONALITY EXTREME: Too forgiving, or too unsympathetic.

TOREY (Anglo-Saxon/Latin: Terence; variable/English)—M.

MAJOR TALENT: Ability to incorporate inventive ideas, idealistic nature, and high nervous energy into career. Is sensitive, gentle, and adaptable. Has charm, broad philosophy, and human understanding. Combines tenderness for oldsters, knack of arbitrating arguments, and vibrant personality. Actor, filmmaker, and psychologist may be career opportunities.

PERSONALITY INGREDIENTS: Appears noble, magnetic, and empathetic. Strives to be charitable, unbiased, and artistically creative. Aims for quality, romance, and inspirational service to others. Inwardly wants to discover the fountain of youth, reinvent the wheel, or build a better mousetrap. Feels special and takes everything personally. Best with practical associations, following intuition, and selective when crusading for causes. Must come down to earth.

PERSONALITY EXTREME: Too secretive, or too outspoken.

TRACY (Latin: Theresa/Old French/English)—F. & M.

MAJOR TALENT: Ability to incorporate work energy, practical ideas, and drive for tangible results into career. Is a constructive dreamer. Has service, artistic, and business instincts. Is self-reliant, logical, and inspirational. May leave a lasting mark if able to rise above mundane ideas and aspire to broad-scoped humanitarian planning. Combines orderliness, sensitivity to details, and subtle control. Manual laborer, legislative reformer, and any business are potential career opportunities.

PERSONALITY INGREDIENTS: Appears curious, enthusiastic, and engaging. Strives for adventure, sensual pleasures, and progressive thinking. Inwardly businesslike, ambitious, and concerned with material success. Appears confident, striking, and may be a mental and physical powerhouse. Must avoid impulsiveness, self-indulgence, and get-rich-quick schemes.

PERSONALITY EXTREME: Too authoritative, or too introverted.

TRAVIS (Old French: Travers/English)—M.

MAJOR TALENT: Ability to incorporate audience appeal, confident approach, and business sense into career. Is detailed, responsible, and assumes challenges. Has self-reliance, determination, and tact. Combines cooperative nature, teamwork, and mental efficiency. Athlete, business analyst, and theatrical agent may be career opportunities.

PERSONALITY INGREDIENTS: Appears quiet, controlled, and refined. Strives for culture, quality, and perfection. Aims for self-improvement and achieving high standards. Should be realistic. Inwardly aggressive, decisive, and progressive. Wants to be first in an original endeavor. Best when cautious, concentrated, and patient.

PERSONALITY EXTREME: Too ambitious, or too passive.

TRISTAN (Latin/Old French/English)—M.

MAJOR TALENT: Ability to incorporate inventive, visionary, expressive personality into career. A dual personality, whose creative personal ideals may either be impractical or change the course of thinking for many. Can be persistent, detailed, and diplomatic, and attracts commercial offers of assistance. Combines individualism, broad ambitions, and peer recognition. Union arbitrator, film producer, and artistic/religious/intellectual leader are possible career opportunities.

PERSONALITY INGREDIENTS: Strives for exploration into new concepts and to lead and inspire. Appears nonconforming. Wants to be different and may have to walk alone to introduce ideas. Has high energy, is above mundane reality, and may leave a mark for future generations.

PERSONALITY EXTREME: Too adventurous, or too fearful.

TRIXIE (Latin: Beatrice; variable/English)—F.

MAJOR TALENT: Ability to incorporate method, structure, and orderliness into career. Is honest, sincere, and trustworthy. Has sound material judgment, common sense, and dependability. Combines studious approach, conservative nature, and appreciation of routine. Piano player, bookkeeper, and police officer are potential career opportunities.

PERSONALITY INGREDIENTS: Inwardly adventurous, curious, and physical. Wants challenges, off-beat people/experiences, and enthusiasms. Appears to be controlled, tailor-made, and dominant. Strives to be businesslike, affluent, and influential. Succeeds through application to down-to-earth work. Is able to learn from experience and to build for tangible results.

PERSONALITY EXTREME: Too speculative, or too conservative.

TRUDIE (Teutonic: Truda; variable/Old German: Gertrude; diminutive/English)—F.

MAJOR TALENT: Ability to incorporate learning from experience into career. Is curious, enthusiastic, and understanding. Has adventurous nature, optimism, and detailed perceptions. Combines communications gifts, adaptability, and confident nature. Politician, translator, and travel agent may be career opportunities.

PERSONALITY INGREDIENTS: Seems comforting, proper, and concerned. Strives for domestic/conventional focus, sympathetic service, and creative self-expression. Inwardly wants wealth, prominence, and businesslike efficiency. Aims to be self-reliant, controlled, and work for large/far-reaching tangible results. Is a practical opportunist, and a survivor.

PERSONALITY EXTREME: Too self-assured, or too trepidatious.

TRUMAN (Old English)—M.

MAJOR TALENT: Ability to incorporate artistic, self-expression, sense of responsibility to family/community, and focus upon truth/justice/educational priorities into career. Is sympathetic, helpful, and patient. Has sensitivity, practical organization, and strong need to love and be loved. Combines artistic temperament, problem-solving instincts, and concern for the entertainment/welfare/uplift of others. Psychologist, home products salesperson, and musician/actor/writer are possible career opportunities.

PERSONALITY INGREDIENTS: Inwardly structured, orderly, and a tireless worker. Wants self-discipline, integrity, and unpretentious relationships. May seem too proper to show strong affections. Appears modest, retiring, and supportive. Strives for loyal friendships, peace, and to be the power behind the throne. Attracts boosters through kindness, honesty, and ability to mend fences for opposing interests. Has subtle control and should serve life-support causes.

PERSONALITY EXTREME: Too unconventional, or too standardized.

TUCKER (Old French)—M.

MAJOR TALENT: Ability to incorporate showmanship, comforting approach, and down-to-earth personality into career. Is direct, generous, and parental. Has determination, patience, and sensitivity. Combines welcoming appearance, material awareness, and responsible/protective/instructional approach. Teacher, musical/theatrical performer, and guidance counselor offer potential career opportunities.

PERSONALITY INGREDIENTS: Inwardly organized, self-reliant, and motivated to work for far-reaching material results. Wants to be a solid citizen and enjoy the things that money can buy. First impression is aloof, introspective, and refined. Strives to be cultured, dignified, and perfect. May lack knack for small talk and take things too seriously.

PERSONALITY EXTREME: Too emotional, or too hardened.

TULLY (Latin/Irish Gaelic/English)—M.

MAJOR TALENT: Ability to incorporate humanitarian instincts, generous emotional temperament, and artistic/scientific/legislative uplift into career. Is empathetic, philosophical, and individualistic. Has material awareness, drive for quality of skill/performance, and imagination. Combines independence, service to others, and romantic judgments. Welfare organizer, doctor, and publisher may be career opportunities.

PERSONALITY INGREDIENTS: Seems businesslike, tailor-made, and authoritative. Strives to appear confident, self-reliant, and prominent. Inwardly pleasure-seeking, optimistic, and loving. Wants variety, beauty, and to find enjoyment in everything/everyone. May scatter interests, be practical one day and unrealistic the next. Has high vitality and needs education/expertise to achieve potential.

PERSONALITY EXTREME: Too aloof, or too questioning.

TYLER (Old English)—M.

MAJOR TALENT: Ability to incorporate executive leadership, organizational approach, and practical work into career. Is efficient, responsible, and generous. Has initiative, drive, and business acumen. Combines showmanship, confident approach, and desire for control. Athlete, banker, and insurance broker are possible career opportunities.

PERSONALITY INGREDIENTS: Inwardly optimistic, restless, and artistically expressive. Wants beauty, love, and pleasure. Appears physically tuned, open-minded, and engaging. Strives to be active, experimental, and sexy. Needs a steady self-improvement diet, new ideas and challenges. Attracts multifaceted interests and should exercise self-control.

PERSONALITY EXTREME: Too empathetic, or too unfeeling.

TYRONE (Greek/Irish/English)—M.

MAJOR TALENT: Ability to incorporate intellectual analysis, cultural improvements, and need for perfection into career. Is refined, logical, and introspective. Has charm, practical organization, and investigative approach. Combines love of timeless/natural beauty, common sense, and systematic thinking. Needs expertise or education. Technical art forms, surgeon, and data processing are among potential career opportunities.

PERSONALITY INGREDIENTS: Appears thoughtful, aloof, or uppity. Strives for authority and self-confidence to handle daily unpolished reality. May lack social confidence, but appear authoritative. Inwardly empathetic, concerned with the quality of life, and generous with emotions. Needs wide scope, humanitarian interests, and philosophical humor. Is an understanding, helpful, creative, and inspirational person. Has magnetism for groups, need for travel, and romantic notions.

PERSONALITY EXTREME: Too unconventional, or too cautious.

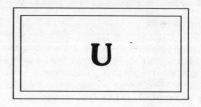

U

All names that begin with the letter *U* have the *Strong Point* of social consciousness—creative expression—emotional highs/lows—fashionable ideas.

ULA (Welsh: Cordelia; variable)—F.

MAJOR TALENT: Ability to incorporate mental analysis, precise approach, and aristocratic instincts into career. Is proud, dignified, and logical. Has poise, calm, and blanketed emotions. Combines need for physical comfort, expertise, and intellectual stimulation. Aims for perfection. Research, religion, and communications are potential career opportunities.

PERSONALITY INGREDIENTS: Appears attractive, friendly, and imaginative. Strives for beauty, love, and pleasure. Inwardly proper, structured, and down-to-earth. Wants material security, practical results, and respectability. Deals constructively with abstracts. Desires a variety of interests.

PERSONALITY EXTREME: Too impatient, or too passive.

ULRIC (Teutonic: Alaric/Bohemian/French/Swedish)—M.

MAJOR TALENT: Ability to incorporate sympathetic service, human understanding, and broad philosophy into career. Is generous, artistic, and charitable. Has empathy, imagination, and inspirational leadership. Combines sensitivity to fine points, intellectual analysis and desire to improve existing conditions. Welfare work, medical/legal profession, and educational fields may be career opportunities.

PERSONALITY INGREDIENTS: Inwardly pleasure-seeking, up-to-date, and optimistic. A romantic who wants love, beauty, and to make the best of everything. Appears comfortable, comforting, and counseling. Strives to learn/teach/advise others, live graciously, and maintain harmonious family/community relationships. Expects high standards, fair play, and quality of performance from self/others. Attracts money through expertise, should uphold personal standards and avoid social pressures to commercialize.

PERSONALITY EXTREME: Too communicative, or too silent.

ULRICK (Teutonic: Alaric/English)—M.

MAJOR TALENT: Ability to incorporate sensitivity, inventions, and inspirational activities into career. Tends to have nervous energy, multiple interests, and broad-scoped thinking. Has charm, artistic gifts, and humanitarian instincts. Combines human understanding, attention to details, and potential for fame/recognition. Must find worthy cause and lead others to seek new horizons. Government diplomat, union arbitrator, and any art form may be career opportunities.

PERSONALITY INGREDIENTS: First impression is controlled, tailor-made, and businesslike. Strives to be efficient, self-reliant, and materially powerful. Inwardly resourceful, imaginative, and in love with love. Feels restless, extravagant, and attention-seeking. Has unique philosophy and seems different.

PERSONALITY EXTREME: Too impractical, or too materialistic.

ULRICH (Teutonic: Alaric/German)—M.

MAJOR TALENT: Ability to incorporate organizational efficiency, executive leadership, and practical/structured/routined mental analysis into career. Is a zealous worker for tangible results. Has charm, nerve, and drive. Combines unconventional ideas, communications techniques, and business aptitudes. Stock market, banking, and newspaper administration are potential career opportunities.

PERSONALITY INGREDIENTS: First impression is adventurous, physically tuned, and striking. Strives for change, travel, and sexual stimulation. Enjoys new/different/offbeat people and activities. Inwardly seeks beauty, pleasure, and freedom from worry. Feels optimistic, resourceful, and energetic. Would like to be the life of the party, forget unpleasant memories, and be surrounded by youthful/versatile/expressive opportunities. Drawn to inheritances, constant activity, and self-indulgence.

PERSONALITY EXTREME: Too power-hungry, or too unambitious.

ULYSSES (Latin/English)—M.

MAJOR TALENT: Ability to incorporate writing, unusual memory, and variety of communications techniques into career. Is optimistic, resourceful, and charming. Has need for beauty, friendliness, and patience. Attracts attention, luck from friendships, and scientific/mathematical/technical education/expertise. Combines individuality, attention to details, and inspirational leadership. Entertainer, journalist, and organizer are potential career opportunities.

PERSONALITY INGREDIENTS: Desires executive position, control, and power. Wants efficiency, respect, and recognition. Appears traditional, dignified, and solid. Strives to be practical, structured, and trustworthy. Develops expertise/concentration, but may expect spontaneous/daring/accidental competitive changes throughout lifetime.

PERSONALITY EXTREME: Too brave, or too weak.

UNA (Latin/English)—F.

MAJOR TALENT: Ability to incorporate magnetic personality, tolerance, and concern for the quality/skill of performance into career. Is generous, romantic, and dramatic. Has humor, charm, and nobility. Combines selflessness, broad philosophy, and forgiving nature. Welfare worker, artist, and doctor may be career opportunities.

PERSONALITY INGREDIENTS: Desires unpretentious, practical, earthy life-style. Feels honest, determined, and ready to work. Appears open-minded, understanding, and different. Strives to be experimental, venturesome, and to satisfy curiosity. Aims for freedom, sensual pleasure, and travel/untried experiences. Needs convention but appears unconventional.

PERSONALITY EXTREME: Too assertive, or too passive.

UPTON (Anglo-Saxon/English)—M.

MAJOR TALENT: Ability to incorporate clever observations, human understanding, and learning by experience into career. Is gutsy, sensual, and adaptable. Has diagnostic gifts, graciousness, and gambler's instinct. Combines sensitivity to details, varied communications techniques, and desire for progressive change. Detective, aviator, and political lobbyist are possible career opportunities.

PERSONALITY INGREDIENTS: Wants to improve humanitarian services, promote social consciousness, and serve a broad marketplace. Feels empathetic, generous, and quality-conscious. Appears adventurous, enthusiastic, and striking. Strives to be a Sir Galahad. Best when unencumbered and free to travel, experiment, and live unconventionally. Should be catalytic in the lives of others and promote elimination of outmoded concepts.

PERSONALITY EXTREME: Too physical, or too intellectual.

URSULA (Middle Latin/English)—F.

MAJOR TALENT: Ability to incorporate gentle, diplomatic, and considerate nature into career. Is detail-conscious, sensitive, and persistent. Has charm, refinement, and friendliness. Combines knack of seeing both sides of a question, working with others, and compulsion to collect things. Succeeds when decisive. Private secretary, homemaker, and psychologist are potential career opportunities.

PERSONALITY INGREDIENTS: Desires quality, culture, and privacy. Needs to feel authoritative, expert, and intellectually stimulated. A perfectionist who is rarely satisfied. Appears classic, dignified and solid. Strives for traditional security, structure, and conventions. Uses subtle control and should avoid petty probing or becoming a creature of habit. If down-to-earth and adaptable, may overcome tendency to become introverted and intensify emotional responses.

PERSONALITY EXTREME: Too active, or too lazy.

URSULINE (Middle Latin: Ursula/English)—F.

MAJOR TALENT: Ability to incorporate idealistic enthusiasms, attention to fine points, and a feeling of being special into career. Is individualistic, nervous, and inventive. Has charm, organizational efficiency, and poetic nature. Combines romantic approach, executive diplomacy, and potential to raise standards for others. Foster parent, preacher, and TV/photographer may be career opportunities.

PERSONALITY INGREDIENTS: Inwardly shy, modest, and peace-loving. Wants partner/mate, musical expression, and easygoing life-style. Appears broad-scoped, noble, and youthful. Strives to be helpful, compassionate, and quality conscious. Aims for tolerance, service, and to give and receive attention. Can be magnetic and leave a lasting mark.

PERSONALITY EXTREME: Too changeable, or too procrastinating.

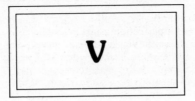

V

All names that begin with the letter *V* have the *Strong Point* of dynamic work energy—practical resourcefulness—visionary planning—lasting results.

VALENTINA (Latin/Italian/English)—F.

MAJOR TALENT: Ability to incorporate materialistic approach, unconventional ideas, and businesslike self-expression into career. Is direct, dominant, and controlled/controlling. Has enthusiasm, guts and curiosity. Combines imagination, swift perceptions, and desire for financial authority. Stockbroker, newspaper executive, and quality fashion manufacturer are possible career opportunities.

PERSONALITY INGREDIENTS: Appears different, energetic, and nonconforming. Strives to be original, forceful, and pioneering. Wants refinements, intellectual/cultural stimulation, and expertise. inwardly analytic, investigative, and out to improve self-image. Maintains an anxious secret self that fears loneliness and poverty. Needs people, but gets moody when too active and aims for physical privacy. Best when educated/technically skilled and able to attract, not seek, recognition.

PERSONALITY EXTREME: Too alone, or too dependent.

VALENTINE (Latin/French/English)—F. & M.

MAJOR TALENT: Ability to incorporate imagination, expression of beauty, and love of people into career. Is attention-getting, animated, and geared to top-quality performance/skill. Has charm, wit, and youthful optimism. Combines humanitarian/universal understanding, empathetic nature, and resourcefulness. Model, scientist, and writer are potential career opportunities.

PERSONALITY INGREDIENTS: Inwardly modest, easygoing, and adaptable. Wants peace, comfort, and to give and receive emotional support. Appears to be a nonconformist. Strives to be decisive, innovative, and independent. A romantic who serves others and tries to embody love through compassion, sharing, and creativity. Is idealistic, inspirational, and magnetically attracts an audience.

PERSONALITY EXTREME: Too physical, or too intellectual.

VALERIE (Latin: Valentina/Old French/English)—F.

MAJOR TALENT: Ability to incorporate artistic/scientific self-expression, strong will, and unforgettable voice into career. Broad-scoped and magnetic, entertains while being entertained. Has wit, charm, and high standards. Combines optimism, realistic approach, and empathetic nature. Is inspired with brotherly love, communications gifts, and tolerance for humanity. Artist, doctor, and welfare worker may be career opportunities.

PERSONALITY INGREDIENTS: Appears unruffled, dignified, and quality-conscious. Strives for perfection. Aims to analyze, research, and achieve expertise. Inwardly sensitive, gentle, and peace-loving. Dislikes emotional upheaval, tactlessness, and disorder. May be shy, self-conscious, or quick to tears if depressed. Needs romance, variety, and beauty.
PERSONALITY EXTREME: Too down-to-earth, or too adventurous.

VALERY (Latin: Valentina/English)—F.

MAJOR TALENT: Ability to incorporate attention to fine points, innovative ideas, and partnership into career. Is peace-loving, supportive, and intuitive. Has magnetic charm, spontaneous creativity, and drive to do more than the average person. Combines generosity, empathy, and a taste for quality, not quantity. Actor, TV writer, and antiques dealer may offer career opportunities.
PERSONALITY INGREDIENTS: Is motivated to plan, work, and build material security. Wants to avoid pretensions/insincerity/dishonesty. May appear stuck-up at first glance, but really fears rejection and scans a room before entering. Must be known to be appreciated. Aims for cultural attainments, natural beauty, and perfection in self/others/daily living. Faces disappointment until materialism loses its luster and depth of character emerges. May be remembered by future generations.
PERSONALITY EXTREME: Too skeptical, or too gullible.

VAN (Dutch: independent; M./Greek: Vanessa; diminutive; F.)—F. & M.

MAJOR TALENT: Ability to incorporate independence, inventions, and explorations into career. Is able to originate, stand alone, and lead others toward new horizons. Has initiative, assertion, and aggressiveness. Combines a desire to be different, fast actions, and inner faith. Salesperson, actor/actress/comic, and manager are possible career opportunities.
PERSONALITY INGREDIENTS: First impression is gracious, brotherly and refined. Strives to be compassionate, generous, and broad-scoped. Enjoys the best of everything. Inwardly wants to be boss. Feels strong, energetic, and nonconforming. Has own design for life and attracts admirers.
PERSONALITY EXTREME: Too friendly, or too arrogant.

VANCE (Dutch/English)—M.

MAJOR TALENT: Ability to incorporate quality of performance, wide-ranging philosophy, and brotherly love into career. Is emotional, romantic, and empathetic. Has charm, magnetism, and often puts the welfare of others before self. Combines individuality, courage, and executive authority. Publisher, public defender, and decorator may be career opportunities.
PERSONALITY INGREDIENTS: Appears entertaining, attractive, and friendly. Strives for popularity, creative self-expression, and optimism. Inwardly rooted, strong-willed, and idealistic. Wants luxury, respectability, and to study/teach/counsel. Aims to secure mature relationships, harmonious home/business balance, and durability in everything. May be impractical, purposeless, and superficial. Best when filling a life-support need or improving mass-market tastes.
PERSONALITY EXTREME: Too changeable, or too routined.

VANESSA (Greek/English)—F.

MAJOR TALENT: Ability to incorporate loyal, creative, compassionate nature into career. Is imaginative, faithful, and intensely emotional. Has instinct for efficiency, material power, and individuality. Combines independent thinking, realistic structure, and desire to improve standards for others. Doctor, politician, and thespian are potential career opportunities.

PERSONALITY INGREDIENTS: Strives to put personal ideals to public attention, and implement innovative progressive changes. Seems different, enthusiastic, and refined. Has an unforgettable quality and wants perfection from self/others/world. Inwardly analytic, culturally aggressive, and questioning. Wants to know the why of everything and investigates. Best when physically routined, finishing one thing before starting another, and accepting self as a unique personality. Makes many major changes during lifetime.

PERSONALITY EXTREME: Too nonconforming, or too imitative.

VAUGHN (Celtic/Irish: Paul/English)—M.

MAJOR TALENT: Ability to incorporate group participation or partnership, diplomacy, and creative ideas into career. Is independent, inventive, and determined. Has mental approach, responsible judgment/leadership, and clear-sighted progressive vision. Combines cooperation, executive organizational efficiency, and trend-setting ideas. Pioneer in anything, business promoter/owner, and all art forms are potential career opportunities.

PERSONALITY INGREDIENTS: Appears to be comfortable, comforting, and dignified. Strives for showmanship, helpfulness, and dependability. Enjoys gracious living, family/community attainments, and to give instructional service. Inwardly practical, economical, and down-to-earth. Wants orderly, calm, solid values. Is conservative, honest, and strong-willed. Bottles temperament and may be intolerant of others' emotional needs. Best when blending personal ideals and controlling impulses.

PERSONALITY EXTREME: Too impatient, or too indecisive.

VELVET (English)—F.

MAJOR TALENT: Ability to incorporate off-beat adventures, curiosity, and learning from experience into career. Is clever, quick, and sensual. Has understanding, adaptability, and enjoys people. Combines attention to details, imagination, and changing appetites. Advertising, politics, and travel professions may be career opportunities.

PERSONALITY INGREDIENTS: Wants independence, inventions, and to be first. Feels competitive, direct, and sure. Appears classic, dignified, and conservative. Strives for material security, respectability, and structured living. Best in an unconventional job on a conventional course.

PERSONALITY EXTREME: Too peace-loving, or too critical.

VERA (Latin/English)—F.

MAJOR TALENT: Ability to incorporate instigative energy, love of innovations, and human understanding into career. Is determined, self-assertive, and decisive. Has willpower, logic, and strong leadership. Combines wide range of interests, appreciation of quality, and individuality. Promoter, performer, advertising executive, and architect are potential career opportunities.

PERSONALITY INGREDIENTS: Inwardly kind, helpful, and domestic. Needs artistic self-expression, showmanship, and material attainments. Wants roots, respect, and propriety. First impression is conventional, dignified, and solid. Strives for practicality, economy, and organizational routine. Enjoys being a pillar of society, counseling others, and taking a personal interest in everything. May be a well-meaning busybody, or a burden-bearing cosmic parent.

PERSONALITY EXTREME: Too bossy, or too mild-mannered.

VERGIL (Latin: Virgil/English)—M.

MAJOR TALENT: Ability to incorporate leadership, inventive mind, and progressive change into career. Is straight-forward, firm, and individualistic. Has active energy, drive, and ambition. Combines diplomacy, communications techniques, and independence. Writer, lawyer, and editor are possible career opportunities.

PERSONALITY INGREDIENTS: Strives for adventure, physical pleasure, unconventional experiences, and freedom from all restrictions. Curious, clever, perceptive, and conscious of humanitarian needs, quality, and human frailty. Has emotional control, compassion, and high aspirations.

PERSONALITY EXTREME: Too talkative, or too unsociable.

VERNA (Latin: Verne/English)—F.

MAJOR TALENT: Ability to incorporate emotional response, subtle control, and responsible protective nature into career. Is dependable, helpful, and parental. Has graciousness, artistic expressiveness, and concern for appearances. Combines attention to details, common sense, and problem solving. Musician, nurse, and educational reformer may be career opportunities.

PERSONALITY INGREDIENTS: Appears understanding, noble, and magnetic. Strives for humanitarian principles, romance, and quality of performance. Inwardly generous, firm, and conventional. Wants gracious living, family/community attainments, and respectability. Best when helping others.

PERSONALITY EXTREME: Too instigative, or too dependent.

VERNE (Latin/variable: Verna-Vernon)—F. & M.

MAJOR TALENT: Ability to incorporate initiative, innovations, and pioneering spirit into career. Is logical, decisive, and courageous. Has executive aspirations, orderliness, and efficient approach. Combines cooperative instincts, organizational procedures, and nonconformist ideas. Designer, architect, and business owner are possible career opportunities.

PERSONALITY INGREDIENTS: Appears youthful, noble, and expressive. Holds an audience, is empathetic, and quality conscious. Inwardly self-oriented. Wants leadership, fast action, and progressive changes. Strives to reach a broad marketplace, and is creative, charming, inspirational. Attracts sensual experiences, difficult decisions, and commercial/emotional success through learning how to cooperate in partnership.

PERSONALITY EXTREME: Too confident, or too fearful.

VERNON (Latin/English)—M.

MAJOR TALENT: Ability to incorporate investigative instincts, appetite for timeless beauty, and introspective nature into career. Is a communicator, organizer, and perfectionist. Has charm, common sense, and drive for expertise. Combines creative self-expression, structure/planning/work, and development of culture/techniques/wisdom. Radio/musical performer, religious leader, and statistical analyst are potential career opportunities.

PERSONALITY INGREDIENTS: Inwardly inspired to raise standards and disseminate innovative ideas. May seem to be in another world at times. Feels special, and is sensitive. Appears to be understanding, open-minded, and adventurous. Strives for unconventional experiences, travel, and sensual pleasures. Aims to promote inventive concepts and refine life and aspirations for everyone. May be a lasting influence for improvement or destruction.

PERSONALITY EXTREME: Too progressive, or too reactionary.

VERONICA (Greek: Berenice/English)—F.

MAJOR TALENT: Ability to incorporate conscientiousness, sympathy, and instructional guidance into career. Is parental, hospitable, and caring. Has showmanship, artistic self-expression, and strong will. Combines practical structure, sensitivity to fine points, and knack for establishing group harmony. Teacher, entertainer, and restaurant manager may be career opportunities.

PERSONALITY INGREDIENTS: Attracts and enjoys attention. Is motivated to share talents, be popular, and optimistic. Strives for beauty, justice, and to entertain/be entertained. May scatter energy, be dramatic, and too imaginative. Best when conservative, routined, and unselfish. Needs love.

PERSONALITY EXTREME: Too different, or too imitative.

VICTOR (Latin/German/English)—M.

MAJOR TALENT: Ability to incorporate compassionate, creative, and uplifting service into career. Is parental, generous, and instructional. Has firm principles, determination, and self-discipline. Combines love of people, kindness, and courage to work/promote life-support reforms for others. Union leader, law maker, and personnel director are possible career opportunities.

PERSONALITY INGREDIENTS: Wants family/community welfare, gracious living, and beauty. Feels protective, responsible, and willing to serve. Appears romantic, charming, and impressive. Strives for broad-scoped planning/accomplishment, quality of performance, and creative self-expression. May be showman, healer, or martyr. Has self-sacrificing nature.

PERSONALITY EXTREME: Too empathetic, or too unemotional.

VICTORIA (Latin: Victor/English)—F.

MAJOR TALENT: Ability to incorporate mental analysis, investigative nature, and quality-consciousness into career. Is logical, thoughtful, and private. Has respect for conventions, communications gifts, and drive for perfection. Combines creative self-expression, common sense, and refinement. Specialist in a field, religious leader, and radio performer may be career opportunities.

PERSONALITY INGREDIENTS: Attracts attention, notables, and applause. Strives for broad marketplace, humanitarian uplift, and quality of performance. Inwardly questioning, sensitive, and sensual. Wants privacy, quiet and natural beauty. Has retentive memory, poise, but cannot balance introvert/extrovert qualities. Knows how to keep secrets.

PERSONALITY EXTREME: Too independent, or too accommodating.

VINCENT (Latin/French/English)—M.

MAJOR TALENT: Ability to incorporate artistic/social consciousness into career. May serve the family or universe. Is sympathetic, parental, and emotionally tuned. Has protective, responsible, conscientious nature. Combines imagination, showmanship, and life-support/comforting/uplifting wisdom. Teacher, artist, and credit union organizer are possible career opportunities.

PERSONALITY INGREDIENTS: Desires change, travel, and unconventional experiences. Feels sensual, curious, and gutsy. Appears different, nonconforming, and charged. Strives to be first. Aims to be aggressive, assertive, and ambitious. Must use dynamic energy for worthwhile/ethical/creative causes or escapist tendencies may surface.

PERSONALITY EXTREME: Too supportive, or too critical.

VIOLA (Latin: Violet/Italian/English)—F.

MAJOR TALENT: Ability to incorporate cleverness, adaptability, and instinct for progressive change into career. Is sensual, experimental, and creatively expressive. Has friendly approach, open mind, and knack of putting people at ease. Combines imagination, gentleness, and curiosity. Science, art, and music are potential career opportunities.

PERSONALITY INGREDIENTS: First impression is refined, aloof, and cultured. Strives for natural beauty, sharp mental analysis, and expertise. Inwardly wants perfection. Desires knowledge, privacy, and to be sure of everything. Needs education/technical authority. Best when concentrated.

PERSONALITY EXTREME: Too competitive, or too unaggressive.

VIOLET (Latin/English)—F.

MAJOR TALENT: Ability to incorporate creative, peace-loving, idealistic nature into career. Is adaptable, supportive, and broad-scoped. Has empathy, knack for seeing both sides of an issue, and nervous energy. Combines humanitarian service, cooperation/partnership, and desire to save/change/raise men's minds and hearts for a better quality of life. May leave a mark. Social worker, photography/TV performer/technician, and political campaigner may be career opportunities.

PERSONALITY INGREDIENTS: Inwardly shy, modest, and supportive. Wants refinement, easygoing routine, and friendliness at almost any price. Appears poised, youthful, and romantic. Strives for drama, charitable contributions, and human understanding. Best when uncommercial.

PERSONALITY EXTREME: Too picky, or too agreeable.

VIRGIL (Latin/English)—M.

MAJOR TALENT: Ability to incorporate adventure, adaptability, and physical focus into career. Is curious, clever, and understanding. Has respect for conventions, individuality, and ambition. Combines unpretentious approach, unlimited scope, and need for change/activity/

progress. Public servant, reporter, and travel agent are possible career
opportunities.

PERSONALITY INGREDIENTS: Inwardly empathetic, creative, and concerned with quality. Wants wide range of interests, romance, and to
serve/express universal reforms/needs. Appears free, open, and sensually tuned. Strives to be a swashbuckler. Aims for the new/exciting/
unconventional, and once achieved, moves on to untried experiences. Is
a catalyst and introduces others to a variety of interests. Attracts friends,
surprises, and resourcefully maintains structure.

PERSONALITY EXTREME: Too sociable, or too reclusive.

VIRGINIA (Latin: Virgil/German/Italian/English)—F.

MAJOR TALENT: Ability to incorporate efficient, organized, and self-
reliant attitude into career. Is a strong self-starter, and a good judge of
people/commercial interests. Has executive diplomacy, trustworthiness,
and attracts responsibility/recognition/respect. Combines progressive
curiosity, cleverness, and practicality. Works well with creative people.
Literary agent, business promoter, and innovative retailer are possible
career opportunities.

PERSONALITY INGREDIENTS: Appears calm, refined, and quiet. Wants
cultural attainments, thinking time, and quality in everything. Aims for
perfection. Inwardly independent, inventive, and ambitious. Wants
novelty, activity, and leadership. Has pioneering spirit, financial instincts, and knack for detailed research/investigation.

PERSONALITY EXTREME: Too assertive, or too obliging.

VITO (Latin/Italian/English)—M.

MAJOR TALENT: Ability to incorporate sociability, imagination, and
knack with words into career. Is sensitive, individualistic, and resourceful. Has humor, artistic self-expression, and love of people/pleasure.
Combines independent ideas, attention to details, and optimism. Professional organizer, any communications field and fashion/decorating may
be career opportunities.

PERSONALITY INGREDIENTS: Wants home/family/community respect,
attainments, and harmony. Is responsible, concerned, and parental.
Feels protective, firmly opinionated, and geared to be a provider. Is
sympathetic, broad-scoped, and emotionally sensitive. Must feel
needed.

PERSONALITY EXTREME: Too suspicious, or too understanding.

VIVIAN (Latin/German: M./English)—F. & M.

MAJOR TALENT: Ability to incorporate learning from experience,
clever perceptions, and nonroutined approach into career. Is sexy, unconventional, and adaptable. Has diplomacy, partnership instincts, and
physical appetites. Combines imagination, sensitivity to details, and adventurous nature. Advertising writer, detective, and lawyer are potential
career opportunities.

PERSONALITY INGREDIENTS: First impression is natural, solid, and
conventional. Strives for dignity, material security, and morally/ethically
correct life-style. Inwardly independent, ambitious, and innovative.
Wants to be first in everything, but is wise/empathetic/charitable. May
scatter interests. Best when open-minded, optimistic, and philosophical.

PERSONALITY EXTREME: Too sensual, or too cerebral.

VIVIEN (Latin/French: M./English)—F. & M.

MAJOR TALENT: Ability to incorporate creative self-expression, quality of performance/skill, and wide range into career. Is understanding, emotional, and dramatic. Has charm, love of beauty/fashion/humor, and conservative structure. Combines down-to-earth instincts, artistry, and perseverance. Charity organizer, theatrical performer, and legislative reformer are possible career opportunities.

PERSONALITY INGREDIENTS: Inwardly unconventional but appears proper. Wants freedom, change, and sensual pleasure. Strives to be practical, financially secure, and respectable. Is friendly and ready for anything that doesn't impugn reputation. Is prone to personal overindulgences when bored. Needs mental stimulation, recognition, and broad scope.

PERSONALITY EXTREME: Too impulsive, or too careful.

VIVIENNE (Latin/French/English)—F.

MAJOR TALENT: Ability to incorporate individualism, originality, and determination into career. Is structured, ambitious, and creative. Has organization, strong will, and pioneering ideas. Combines initiative, drive, and daring. Designer, retail store owner, and architect may be career opportunities.

PERSONALITY INGREDIENTS: Seems concerned, empathetic, and broad-scoped. Strives for expansiveness, romance, and quality of skill/performance. Inwardly aggressive, self-motivated, and controlling. Wants to take the lead. Appears magnetic and is passionate, charming, and entertaining, traits that cover a strong competitive spirit. Best when realistic, mature, and practical. Is an inspiration to others.

PERSONALITY EXTREME: Too busy, or too bored.

VLADIMIR (Slavic/English)—M.

MAJOR TALENT: Ability to incorporate analytic approach, investigation, and quality-consciousness into career. Is precise, logical, and refining. Has poise, drive for practical work, and communications gifts. Combines culturally attaining instincts, concentration, and conventional procedures on a self-expressive course. Musician, mathematician, and technical writer are potential career opportunities.

PERSONALITY INGREDIENTS: First impression is dignified, comfortable, and showmanlike. Strives for material goals, family/community harmony, and gracious living. Is strong-willed. persevering, and straightforward. Inwardly ambitious, competitive, and inventive. Wants to be first, different, and progressive. Can be pleasure-seeking, impulsive, and grasping when pride in self is weakened. Is lucky with physical activities, travel, and seeing the lighter side.

PERSONALITY EXTREME: Too tolerant, or too narrow-minded.

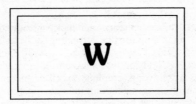

W

All names that begin with the letter *W* have the *Strong Point* of persistence—self-evaluation—love conquers all—adventure.

WADE (Teutonic/Old English)—M.

MAJOR TALENT: Ability to incorporate close scrutiny, calculated planning, and personal attraction into career. Strives for attainment and draws money/gifts/favors from others. Wants prestige and, as a gifted teacher, sets an example for others to follow. Performing arts, domestic counseling, and service businesses are possible career opportunities.

PERSONALITY INGREDIENTS: First impression is empathetic, romantic, idealistic. Family/community oriented. Inwardly protective, emotional, and discerning. Intensely ambitious; must learn to take material things less seriously. Has choice of virtue or vice.

PERSONALITY EXTREME: Too easygoing, or too driving.

WALDO (Old & Modern German/English)—M.

MAJOR TALENT: Ability to incorporate organizing projects and public image into career. Should inspire others with examples of endurance, broad philosophy, and expressive manner of speech. Succeeds through courageous changes, personal faith, and a knack for seeing the obvious answers that others ignore. Any freelance profession, editing, and inventing are potential career opportunities.

PERSONALITY INGREDIENTS: First impression is socially adept, attractive, and imaginative. Inwardly requires time for introspection, perfecting, and cultural growth. Harbors a secret self concealing self-pity or inadequate education. Wants to be the authority but never seems to stay with one thing.

PERSONALITY EXTREME: Too protective, or too irresponsible.

WALKER (Anglo-Saxon)—M.

MAJOR TALENT: Ability to incorporate nonconforming intuition, judgments based upon past life experiences, and a resourceful mind into career. Prefers mobility, progressive interests, and a calm environment for researching/investigating/intellectualizing ideas. Attention to detail attracts recognition. Scientist, detective, and clergyman may be career opportunities.

PERSONALITY INGREDIENTS: Drawn to the righting of wrongs and instigating crusades. When impulsive, adopts surface values that will produce conflict and inertia, and leave nothing accomplished. Must learn always to read the fine print. Needs secure, attractive, comfortable lifestyle. First impression is individualistic.

PERSONALITY EXTREME: Too concerned, or too uninvolved.

WALLACE (German/English)—M.

MAJOR TALENT: Ability to incorporate lucky introductions, formalized procedures, and an exceptionally attractive personality into career. When changes in plans are accepted as natural events, and greed/selfishness do not block vision, life's lessons are learned and success is assured. Attracts a following, employs excellent memory, and encourages optimism. Any communications medium, inspirational salesmanship, and social director are potential career opportunities.

PERSONALITY INGREDIENTS: Voice and delivery attract the refined/cultured/thinkers required by the inner self. Variety/offbeat people/stimulating events are enticed by the first impression. May be a cunning schemer, or a wise, loyal, and expressive friend. Balance of introvert and extrovert.

PERSONALITY EXTREME: Too sensual, or too cerebral.

WALLIS (Old German/English)—F. & M.

MAJOR TALENT: Ability to incorporate humanitarian ideas, practical construction, and stamina into career. Hard work is supported by nervous energy. Sees the overall end result and finds the economical, efficient, and effective way to get there. Ethical, honest leadership provides a power base that should not be abused, or emotional setbacks will result. Possible financial rewards allow for charitable works that leave a mark on mankind. Government, labor relations, and mass-communications executive are possible career opportunities.

PERSONALITY INGREDIENTS: May be a force for good or evil. First impression is engaging. Inwardly needs independence, originality, and a leadership role. Must know the difference between intuition and gambling. Suffers when impractical.

PERSONALITY EXTREME: Too indecisive, or too self-assured.

WALTER (Old German/Anglo-Saxon/English)—M.

MAJOR TALENT: Ability to incorporate personal perceptions, detailed analysis, and astute conclusions into career. Travel heightens resourcefulness. Successful after mastering obstacles. Followup is the key. Cultural/refined professions, photography, and communications/writing are potential career opportunities.

PERSONALITY INGREDIENTS: Must avoid impulse, indecision, and laxity. First impression is independent, executive, and aggressive. Inwardly wants a home/family/roots to rely upon. Feels protective, and assumes that everyone will live up to personal standards. Stands firm and fights for strong convictions.

PERSONALITY EXTREME: Too petty, or too philosophical.

WANDA (Old German/English)—F.

MAJOR TALENT: Ability to incorporate personal attraction, direct logic, and clever expression into career. Special gifts for writing and speaking. Authority, independent actions, and intellectual activities bring success. Risk-taking due to overconfidence brings only a modicum of the expected return. This name must learn, through disappointment in material security, which of life's experiences are transitory and which are permanent. Any spiritual work, author, and research may be career opportunities.

PERSONALITY INGREDIENTS: First impression is exciting, curious, im-

pulsive. Inwardly wants serenity, gentleness, and emotional balance.
Opposing forces in this name may cause disappointment. The key to
happiness is developing a specialty that keeps the inner person company
and makes feelings of loneliness/poverty disappear.
PERSONALITY EXTREME: Too active, or too passive.

WARD (Old English/English)—M.
MAJOR TALENT: Ability to incorporate creative leadership, communications, and problem-solving techniques into career. Tremendous vitality allows for diversification of interests. Success comes through having
the courage to follow intuition. When running scared, leads a double life.
Theater, science, agriculture may be career opportunities.
PERSONALITY INGREDIENTS: First impression is distinctive, empathetic, and emotionally idealistic. Inwardly needs to feel free to make
changes, assert individuality, and be first in everything. At best with a
supportive mate. Financial and personal rewards come through positive
thinking.
PERSONALITY EXTREME: Too structured, or too nonconformist.

WARNER (English)—M.
MAJOR TALENT: Ability to incorporate mental, physical, and artistic
skills into career. Trustworthy, honest, and patient with a logical approach to practical conventions. Drawn to philosophy and religion with
an eye to the needs of everyman. Should relate to travel and communications. Quality catering, engineering, and legal research are possible
career opportunities.
PERSONALITY INGREDIENTS: Enjoys country/waterside living. Inwardly strives for right and justice, as personally understood. Sometimes
too honest, even downright blunt. Wants roots and the good life. Appears to be aggressive, proud, and stimulating.
PERSONALITY EXTREME: Too sympathetic, or too detached.

WARREN (Teutonic)—M.
MAJOR TALENT: Ability to incorporate conventional/practical behavior, straight talk, and high regard for spiritual/intellectual beliefs into
career. Blends an open mind, intuition, and a need for immediate results.
Analytic thinking requires patience and unselfishness, for inner determination to win out. Relaxes through sports or nature study. Any specialty,
private investigation, and the savings or insurance field may be career
opportunities.
PERSONALITY INGREDIENTS: Family generosity, secure life-style, and
artistic expression are the inward responses of this apparent lone wolf.
First impression is not as emotionally tuned as the natural inclinations
dictate. Improves with age.
PERSONALITY EXTREME: Too futuristic, or too shortsighted.

WASHINGTON (Old English/English)—M.
MAJOR TALENT: Ability to incorporate mind, matter, and strength of
character into career. Senses when to act and when to wait, among many
basic attributes for financial success. However, needs to balance the
mind and the emotions. Must follow goals even after success comes,
without self-satisfaction, or overindulgence creeping in (this could lead

to a gluttonous life and aimless fantasies). All building trades, professional boxing, and laboratory technician are potential career opportunities.

PERSONALITY INGREDIENTS: First impression is extremely paternal, sensitive, and affectionate. Wants personal freedom, authority, and feels a pioneering instinct. Attracts wealth through marriage, impressive home, and material comforts. Protective attitude leads to good fortune.

PERSONALITY EXTREME: Too impulsive, or too tenacious.

WAYNE (Teutonic: Wainwright/English variable)—M.

MAJOR TALENT: Ability to incorporate physical agility, material ideas, and multiple interests into career. Clever/quick mind facilitates learning and honest approach invites supporters for ambitions. Best suited to flexible schedules. Athletics, theater, and politics may offer career opportunities.

PERSONALITY INGREDIENTS: Loyal, passionate, and responsible in immediate relationships. Wants home, abundant life-style, and artistic beauty. First impression is authoritative, trustworthy, and successful. Enthusiastically grasps chances to improve intellectually, physically, and financially. Benefits from professional advice.

PERSONALITY EXTREME: Too glib, or too silent.

WEBSTER (Old English/English)—M.

MAJOR TALENT: Ability to incorporate detailed analysis, diplomatic relationships, and futuristic vision into career. Generally supportive but takes the lead in spreading the gospel of any strong personal belief. Blends generosity, nervous energy, and must seize the opportunity of the moment. Public affairs, metaphysics, and any arbitration work may be career opportunities.

PERSONALITY INGREDIENTS: Cannot be indecisive, uncooperative, or allow emotional anxiety to rule financial decisions. Meant to learn material world structure. Appears to be, and is, very individualistic.

PERSONALITY EXTREME: Too philosophical, or too personalized.

WENDELL (Teutonic/English)—M.

MAJOR TALENT: Ability to incorporate conventional system, communications, and broad-scoped projects into career. Artistic gifts may bring enjoyment and fulfillment. Sex appeal is an asset that should be applied practically. Writing, trial lawyer, and theater are potential career opportunities.

PERSONALITY INGREDIENTS: First impression is modest, calm, and diplomatic, but inwardly wants to be the boss. Needs creative freedom, activity, and ambitious challenges. Benefits from travel, philosophical study, and a formal life-style. Expects and delivers quality.

PERSONALITY EXTREME: Too talkative, or too inarticulate.

WENDY (Teutonic/Old German: Wendla/English)—F.

MAJOR TALENT: Ability to incorporate enthusiasm, courage, and a desire for power into career. Will learn to deal with stressful situations to acquire self-confidence. Success comes through interaction with others. Should combine communications and executive business sense. Sports, theater, and savings banks are possible career opportunities.

PERSONALITY INGREDIENTS: Usually some strong focus on pregnancy/

parent-child relationship during lifetime. Impulsiveness, scattering energy, and discomfort with routine responsibility need self-control. May be naive. Appears adventurous, free-thinking, and youthful. Inwardly wants attention, imaginative people, and glitter.

PERSONALITY EXTREME: Too reserved, or too outgoing.

WESLEY (Anglo-Saxon/English)—M.

MAJOR TALENT: Ability to incorporate confident approach, physical energy, and responsible authority into career. Does well financially if very probing before investing self or money. Must learn to control impulsive love relationships and master patience and endurance. Manufacturing, financial consulting, and political official are possible career opportunities.

PERSONALITY INGREDIENTS: First impression is inconsistent: sometimes authoritative, sometimes self-deprecating. Seems to be introspective, gentlemanly, and sharp. Inwardly very sensitive to little things and personalized. Wants show of love and often repels the giver. Develops self-confidence through overcoming emotional stress.

PERSONALITY EXTREME: Too polished, or too earthbound.

WHITNEY (Anglo-Saxon)—M.

MAJOR TALENT: Ability to incorporate a myriad of concepts and a snowball of tangibles into career. Brings ideas to reality and promotes the results with faith, enthusiasm, and endless courage. Given help and protection, will find love and happiness, with a zest for living that may inspire and nurture others. The natural senses are heightened in this name and may be used for self-indulgence, to a fault. Communications, consulting, psychology may be career opportunities.

PERSONALITY INGREDIENTS: This personality can select any career that includes people, progressive ideas, and nonmonotonous structure. Appears understanding, attractive, and noble. Inwardly open-minded, youthful, and ambitious. Must maintain sensual balance to enjoy full potential.

PERSONALITY EXTREME: Too earthy, or too elegant.

WILBUR (Old German: Gilbert/English variable)—M.

MAJOR TALENT: Ability to incorporate a competitive spirit, strong will, and a dramatic nature into career. Blends vitality, pride and independence, and strives to surmount all obstacles. Blessed with a good memory and prone to a variety of interests, would be prudent to develop practicality, cooperation, and direction to achieve success. Accounting, retail automotive repair, and sculpture are possible career opportunities.

PERSONALITY INGREDIENTS: Appears to be ambitious, innovative, and in motion. Inwardly imaginative, optimistic, and sociable. Must organize for structure to relax in luxury.

PERSONALITY EXTREME: Too imperturbable, or too excitable.

WILEY (Teutonic: Wile/German/English)—M.

MAJOR TALENT: Ability to incorporate opportunities for business partnerships, independent creativity, and ambitious challenges into career. Must stay alert for trustworthy financial minds to recognize the extraordinary visionary gifts that only need commercial organization to gain recognition. Perseverance brings success. Computers, inspirational teaching, and filmmaking are potential career opportunities.

PERSONALITY INGREDIENTS: First impression is parental—interested, concerned, and protective. Inwardly dislikes responsibilities that impose restrictions, and squelch impulses. Wants youth, sexuality, and experimentation. Should be decisive and opportunistic for positive results.

PERSONALITY EXTREME: Too impersonal, or too sensitive.

WILFRED (Old & Modern German/English)—M.

MAJOR TALENT: Ability to incorporate inspiration, form, and enthusiastic promotion into career. Pioneers concepts that serve as a catalyst for change in others' lives, and courageously tackles everything. May produce many children; the key word is fertility. Very fortunate when pleasure-seeking and self-indulgence is balanced. Advertising, theater, politics may be career opportunities.

PERSONALITY INGREDIENTS: Truly gifted through the five senses and practical enough to bring this high energy into an organizational structure. First impression is magnetic, empathetic, and universal. Inwardly wants to enjoy life and experience travel, sex, family, business—you name it. Caution: beware impulsiveness, fear of change, and impatience.

PERSONALITY EXTREME: Too hidebound, or too improper.

WILHELMINA (Old German/English)—F.

MAJOR TALENT: Ability to incorporate intelligence, high-minded philosophy, and solitude into career. Not comfortable in the din of the business world. Maintains poise in times of stress and senses a reserve of humanitarian energy from which to draw quality conclusions. May have to stand alone and rise above mundane realities. Will benefit from education. Metaphysics, religion, and legal research are potential career opportunities.

PERSONALITY INGREDIENTS: First impression is individualistic, active, and assertive. Inwardly wants roots; harmonious family, abundant lifestyle, and artistic interests. Redefines faith through changing conditions and events. Must avoid symptoms of depression; jealousy, tunnel vision, and bigotry. Needs solitude and must recognize this instinct to avoid self-distructive emotionalizing.

PERSONALITY EXTREME: Too strong, or too weak.

WILLA (Old German: Wilhelmina/English variable)—F.

MAJOR TALENT: Ability to incorporate detailed administration, independent creative action, and exceptional perceptions of life and people into career. An inspiration to others through gift of self-expression. Blends talent, charm, and fortunate meetings to perpetuate changes necessary for successful growth. Patience, optimism, and originality produce commercial success. Writing, theater, and any nonroutine business are potential career opportunities.

PERSONALITY INGREDIENTS: First impression is supportive, but inwardly desires independent thinking and action. Expects more than the average from self. Nervous energy should be used constructively for presentation/selling abstract ideas. Polarity in the nature; gentle-strong. May be eccentric.

PERSONALITY EXTREME: Too unobtrusive, or too aggressive.

WILLANN (Old German: Wilhelmina/English)—F.

MAJOR TALENT: Ability to incorporate self-respect, determined will, and the ability to influence others into career. To be energized by a challenge is not enough; efficient organization, cooperation, and setting clear goals are what bring successful conclusions. Use attractive-positive personality, instant recall and ability to influence others to build financial success. Industrialist, real estate broker, and chiropractor may be career opportunities.

PERSONALITY INGREDIENTS: First impression is friendly, spontaneous, and emotionally tuned. Inwardly wants individuality, leadership, and mental analysis. Proud, hard-working, and determined to win. Must avoid scattering energy.

PERSONALITY EXTREME: Too pleasure-seeking, or too ambitious.

WILLIAM (Old German/English)—M.

MAJOR TALENT: Ability to incorporate logical thinking, social interaction, and practical planning into career. Trustworthy, honest, and introspective; either discreet or blunt, rarely in between. Enjoys sports, humor and dependable insights. Legal profession, aviation, and data-processing executive are possible career opportunities.

PERSONALITY INGREDIENTS: First impression is strong-willed, persevering, and protective. Inwardly feels lucky, wants variety, and requires attractive people and environments. Usually expressive, hopeful, and determined. Impatient, selfish, and cunning when negative.

PERSONALITY EXTREME: Too conventional, or too unorthodox.

WILLIS (Old German: son of William/English)—M.

MAJOR TALENT: Ability to incorporate versatility, cleverness, and skill into career. Brings system, order, and recognition to comprehensive projects. Blends high ideals and sex appeal to forge a practical effect. Commentator, travel consultant, any limelight profession suggests opportunities.

PERSONALITY INGREDIENTS: Extremely selective and uncompromising in terms of quality. Inwardly feels that there is a limitless supply of everything necessary to succeed. First impression is less broad-scoped but surges to attract contacts necessary to reach a universal marketplace. The key is communications, and with perseverance all doors will open.

PERSONALITY EXTREME: Too tender, or too insensitive.

WILLY (Old German: Wilhelmina-William/English variable)—F. & M.

MAJOR TALENT: Ability to incorporate creative artistic ideas, business sense, and an aura of confidence into career. Tolerance and decisive action should be cultivated to speed the promotion of a fertile mind to tangible results. Medicine, mineral research, and professorship suggest opportunities.

PERSONALITY INGREDIENTS: Magnetizing appearance and personality. Combines empathy, generosity, and mental/emotional depth. Makes others happy when successful; broad philosophy attracts supporters. This name germinates/procreates for widespread attention.

PERSONALITY EXTREME: Too cultured, or too earthy.

WILMA (Old German: Wilhelmina/English variable)—F.

MAJOR TALENT: Ability to incorporate a potential for widespread constructive vision and material achievement. Arrives at practical solutions for reconstructive purposes and then enhances the original to broader terms. Can be a great humanitarian, shape destinies, and form enduring personal relationships. This name has a chance to aim high or accept the mundane. Diplomat or government worker, architect or draftsperson, manufacturer or retailer suggest opportunities and some choices.

PERSONALITY INGREDIENTS: First impression is poised, unusual, and socially attractive. Inwardly independent, influential, and mentally energetic. Overwork causes emotional difficulties, and a desire for control over others jeopardizes unique resources.

PERSONALITY EXTREME: Too changeable, or too settled.

WILONA (Old German: Wilhelmina/English)—F.

MAJOR TALENT: Ability to combine the need to commercialize with creative expression into career. Multitalented, wise, and gifted with foresight, this name may attract renown. Others notice unique qualities, and partnerships/supporters provide stability for profitable enterprises. Indecision, anxiety, and uncooperative attitudes will cause problems, but a sure decision plus sticking to it may win a top spot. Attracts recognition and honors. Bookkeeper-C.P.A., caterer-gourmet chef, union delegate–national diplomat are possible career opportunities.

PERSONALITY INGREDIENTS: Inwardly practical, organized, down-to-earth. First impression is inconsistent: authoritative or unsure. Would like cultural refinements but instinctually focuses on necessity. High nervous energy is depleted by emotional fears.

PERSONALITY EXTREME: Too domineering, or too compliant.

WILSON (Old German: son of William/English)—M.

MAJOR TALENT: Ability to incorporate foresight, individualistic ideas, and sensitivity to the smaller issues that glue major projects together into career. This name includes wisdom and vision. Must learn to be decisive, and avoid anxieties that weaken emotions and physical well being. Friends and agreements are the key, but they must be selected with an eye to successful enterprise. Pride, stubbornness, and arrogance are the symptoms of unadmitted mistakes and should be avoided as such. This name has the potential to rise to fame. Public affairs, computer electronics, and custodial professions may be career opportunities.

PERSONALITY INGREDIENTS: First impression is conversational, sexually attractive, and progressively changeable. Inwardly parental, idealistic, and artistically expressive. Learns to commercialize through ongoing experiences.

PERSONALITY EXTREME: Too physical, or too intellectual.

WINGATE (Teutonic/English)—M.

MAJOR TALENT: Ability to incorporate practical structure, cultivated intellect, and communications into career. Blends sound judgment into straightforward advice. Most successful as an authority in technical/scientific/spiritual areas. Enjoys the outdoors, travel, and a quick wit. When negative, may be impatient, impulsive, reckless, selfish, and cunning. Archaeology, photography, and psychic investigation are potential career opportunities.

PERSONALITY INGREDIENTS: First impression is individualistic, independent, and creative. Inwardly parental, protective, and artistic. Prefers others to live up to personal standards and may be intolerant. Gifted teacher, designer, and advisor.

PERSONALITY EXTREME: Too sensual, or too cerebral.

WINIFRED (Teutonic: Winfred/Old German/Anglo-Saxon/Celtic: Wenefride/English)—F.

MAJOR TALENT: Ability to incorporate charity, nobility of ideals, and intellectual curiosity into career. Makes binding commitments, and is kind, patient, and courageous. Should learn to use solitude wisely to perfect high-minded purposes. Education is the key to eliminating destructive fears of loneliness and poverty, which weaken an uncommon comprehension of life. Metaphysics, library research, and writing are possible career opportunities.

PERSONALITY INGREDIENTS: First impression is neat, cooperative and observing. Inwardly needs freedom, progressive mental stimulation, and self-expressive interests. May not understand the innate need for private time and may react to intrusions with inappropriate jealousy, snide comments, gossip, or bigoted opinions. Philosophical/spiritual probing may fill a gap.

PERSONALITY EXTREME: Too straitlaced, or too unconventional.

WINONA (American Indian/English)—F.

MAJOR TALENT: Ability to incorporate independence, competitive instincts, and sense of pride into career. Strong determination, energy, and patience must find down-to-earth direction and develop understanding of teamwork. Dramatic, observant, and a resolute fighter. Professional numerologist, athlete, or florist may be career opportunities.

PERSONALITY INGREDIENTS: First impression is parental, accommodating, and emotional. Inwardly lacks self-understanding. Needs area of specialization to develop authority which brings out feelings of adequacy. Pomposity, disorganization, and high-strung overreaction cause legal and personal disputes. Desires privacy to develop intellect, cultural interests, and polish.

PERSONALITY EXTREME: Too sluggish, or too active.

WINSLOW (Teutonic)—M.

MAJOR TALENT: Ability to incorporate a structured technique, patience, and deep thinking to translate expertise into career. Blends inner questioning, honest evaluation, and a quick wit. Expressive, quality-conscious, and trained for practical results. Enjoys nature, philosophy, and justice. Writing, farming, and engineering are potential career opportunities.

PERSONALITY INGREDIENTS: Expansive freethinker must coexist with a saving conservative. These personality components clash and confuse others. Selects to be cautious and stable one minute, and gambling on an imaginative idea the next. Desires artistic/beautiful home, adoring family, and abundant life-style. Outwardly assertive, original, and correct.

PERSONALITY EXTREME: Too dutiful, or too irresponsible.

WINSTON (Old English/English)—M.

MAJOR TALENT: Ability to incorporate the highest levels of compassion, self-sacrifice, and charismatic teaching into career. Must accept responsibility of a special idealistic humanitarian mission to rise to this name potential. If the necessary courage, self-discipline, and inspirational personal example is not set, the name takes a purely domestic focus. Position, money, and immortality are possible in exchange for universal love. Credit union organizer, family business trustee, and transportation innovator may be career opportunities.

PERSONALITY INGREDIENTS: First impression is magnetic, empathetic, and worthy. Inwardly parental, idealistic, and artistic. Must avoid becoming an emotional doormat.

PERSONALITY EXTREME: Too physical, or too cerebral.

WINTHROP (Teutonic/Old English)—M.

MAJOR TALENT: Ability to incorporate Solomonesque perceptions, General George Patton–type authority, and a bit of Sir Lancelot into career. This name is powerful and attracts wealth, broad-scoped responsibility, and notoriety. Any injustices, dictatorial actions, or overreactions to surrounding conditions may result in extreme attempts of revenge. Judge, high political office, and the military are possible career opportunities.

PERSONALITY INGREDIENTS: Inwardly image-conscious, parental, and expressive. Desires to be discerning, prestigious, and exemplary. First impression is memorable.

PERSONALITY EXTREME: Too pretentious, or too guileless.

WOLFGANG (Teutonic)—M.

MAJOR TALENT: Ability to incorporate researched methods, financial horse sense, and mathematics into career. Is wise, confident, and considerate. Uses positive forces when receptive, meditative, and compassionately loving. Uses negative aspects when polishing the other side of the coin: creating confusion, disorder, and squandering money on illusions. Investment counselor, commercial real estate, and literature researcher are potential career opportunities.

PERSONALITY INGREDIENTS: First impression is responsible, protective, and expressive. Inwardly wants quiet time for intellectual growth and stimulation. An orderly, conservative life-style will ensure perpetuity of family fortune.

PERSONALITY EXTREME: Too obliging, or too fault-finding.

WOODROW (Anglo-Saxon)—M.

MAJOR TALENT: Ability to incorporate abstract thought with form into career. Is loving, faithful, and enthusiastically courageous. Fertile physically and mentally. Nurtures parental and philosophical tenderness. Politician, editor, and investigator may be career opportunities.

PERSONALITY INGREDIENTS: Inwardly a compassionate, humane philosopher. Is apt to give the shirt off his back to anyone who seems to need it more than he does. First impression is youthful, freedom loving, and attractive to the opposite sex. Must control sensual indulgence and impulsiveness.

PERSONALITY EXTREME: Too curious, or too bored.

All names that begin with the letter *W* have the *Strong Point* of persistence—self-evaluation—love conquers all—adventure.

427

WOODS (Anglo-Saxon: Wood/English)—M.

MAJOR TALENT: Ability to incorporate techniques for unmasking and solving problems into career. Far-reaching constructive resource: philanthropic, wise, and industrious. Strong opinions and judgments, plus practical work energy. Attracts power; should avoid workaholic tendencies or ruthless control over others. Government, university administration, and building trades are potential career opportunities.

PERSONALITY INGREDIENTS: Desires imaginative, attractive, romantic life-style. Feels optimistic, artistic, and dramatic. First impression is hard-hitting, well-positioned, and individualistic. Has a sense of poise, and an uncommon tolerance for divergent philosophies.

PERSONALITY EXTREME: Too subdued, or too conceited.

WYATT (Old French: Guy/English variable)—M.

MAJOR TALENT: Ability to incorporate investigative mind, material emphasis, and executive leadership into career. Is a traveler and attracts affluent/powerful assistance. While gifted with persuasive words, must not abuse the privilege. Organizer, financial consultant, and chemist are possible career opportunities.

PERSONALITY INGREDIENTS: Desires affluence, refinement/culture, efficient life-style. First impression is creative, learned, and empathetic. Excels when able to concentrate and hang in for most desired long-term goals.

PERSONALITY EXTREME: Too guarded, or too tactless.

WYNNE (Anglo-Saxon, M./Celtic, F./English)—F. & M.

MAJOR TALENT: Ability to incorporate originality, self-expression, and artistic judgment into career. Is concerned, impressive, and commanding. Should implement ideas that reap a benefit for everyone. When enterprising, wealth and comforts flower. Medicine, communications, and exploring suggest opportunities.

PERSONALITY INGREDIENTS: Voice, music, harmony instruments are involved in success. First impression is responsible, parental, and tastefully comfortable. Inwardly needs variety, beauty, and attractive people and environment. This name offers artistic greatness and needs supporters for commercial achievement.

PERSONALITY EXTREME: Too many eggs in one basket, or too bored.

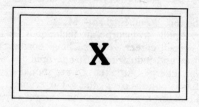

X

All names that begin with the letter *X* have the *Strong Point* of attracting affluence—excesses—poor equilibrium—teaching.

XAVIER (Arabic/English)—M.

MAJOR TALENT: Ability to incorporate keen thinking, frank and open delivery, and counseling into career. Employs a systematic approach and practical/conventional behavior to philosophical, introspective, and tangible goals. High regard for nature and spiritual values. Respected for wisdom, quick wit, and balanced judgment. Any refined/cultured atmosphere, attorney/judge, and psychic research are potential career opportunities.

PERSONALITY INGREDIENTS: First impression is individualistic, manly, and all-embracing. Inwardly wants roots. Feels that others should learn from and live up to personal standards. Desires beauty, peace, and meaningful relationships. May show impatience, impulsiveness, and selfishness when threatened.

PERSONALITY EXTREME: Too generous, or too careful.

XAVIERA (Arabic: Xavier M./Spanish Basque)—F.

MAJOR TALENT: Ability to incorporate intellectual and commercial research into career. Attracts respect, honesty, and solutions. Acquires tangibles through mental applications. Executive administration, writing, and investigative research may be career opportunities.

PERSONALITY INGREDIENTS: First impression is individualistic, vital, and worldly. Inwardly a seeker of perfection that lacks academic credits and needs an intellectual outlet. Disappointed in the mundane reality that is natural to daily living. Tries escapist tactics until self-confidence is established through expertise in one subject.

PERSONALITY EXTREME: Too self-centered, or too yielding.

XENA (Greek/English)—F.

MAJOR TALENT: Ability to incorporate positive perceptions/attitudes and research into career. Benefits from solitude for intellectual probing, and relates to tangible accomplishments. Drawn to sea and air experiences. Attracts recognition. Executive administration, exploring, and investigative services are potential career opportunities.

PERSONALITY INGREDIENTS: First impression is modest, soft, and attentive. Inwardly desires home, responsible/loving family, and material advancement. Wants to serve just causes.

PERSONALITY EXTREME: Too assertive, or too compliant.

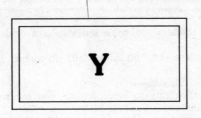

Y

All names that begin with the letter *Y* have the *Strong Point* of sudden decisions—intellectual freedom—non-commercial focus—attraction to water.

YALE (Teutonic)—M.

MAJOR TALENT: Ability to incorporate a forceful, often magnetic personality, and clever expression of ideas into career. Employs a gift for clear-sighted appraisals of situations and people, which can be used for speculation or can be researched for lasting success. Should avoid overconfidence. Good fortune is maintained when materialistic notions are balanced by comforting truths and worldly authority. Scientific, technical, or mystery writing, investigating, investment banking are possible career opportunities.

PERSONALITY INGREDIENTS: First impression is independent, courageous, and decisive. Inwardly wants a warm, abundant lifestyle that supports pride, responsibility, and attainment. Often self-righteous, but places the welfare of family/community first. Either very successful, or a complete failure.

PERSONALITY EXTREME: To experimental, or too careful.

YANCY (French/derivative: Danish; Jan-John/Early American)—M.

MAJOR TALENT: Ability to incorporate daring ideas, physical agility, and the gift of learning through observation into career. Passionate, loyal, and always in a hurry. Attracts patronage, material comforts, and community attention. Advertising executive, theater, and aviation may be career opportunities.

PERSONALITY INGREDIENTS: First impression is concerned, expressive, and sympathetic. Inwardly wants the independence that power and money allow. Impatient with less efficient people. Sensual, experimental, and energetic. Often headstrong, but sincerely helpful.

PERSONALITY EXTREME: Too spiritual, or too material.

YARDLEY (Old English)—M.

MAJOR TALENT: Ability to incorporate perseverance, dependability, and intensity of feeling into career. Assumes burdens and overcomes obstacles. Kind, just, and broad-scoped. Unafraid of challenges. Composer, judge, and domestic lawyer are potential career opportunities.

PERSONALITY INGREDIENTS: Needs social and artistic harmony and feels a strong sense of responsibility to home/family/community. First impression: attractive, witty, and charming. Appears to have star quality. Too much earthiness weakens manifestation of ideals and may bring emotional upheaval.

PERSONALITY EXTREME: Too cultured, or too coarse.

YETTA (Teutonic/English)—F.

MAJOR TALENT: Ability to incorporate astute investigation, courageous attitude, and compassionate insights into career. Organizational leadership melds with mental application for tangible results. Attracts assistance, advancements, and moral support. Can be very persuasive. Lawyer, broker, and household retailer are possible career opportunities.

PERSONALITY INGREDIENTS: Inwardly the cosmic mother. Desires family harmony, attractive surroundings, and attainment. Outwardly less directive than supportive and filled with nervous energy. Drawn to charities or causes that moralize. May be protective, touchy, or irritable when too inactive.

PERSONALITY EXTREME: Too bossy, or too dependent.

YOLANDA (Latin: Violet/English)—F.

MAJOR TALENT: Ability to incorporate artistic creativity, strong intuition, and originality into career. Impressive mind and positive attitude move others to implement ideas. Should create useful products and avoid intolerant judgments of self and associates. Any forms of self-expression, magician, and publishing may be career opportunities.

PERSONALITY INGREDIENTS: First impression is individualistic, courageous, and productive. Inwardly efficient, organized, and conscious of power and tangible results. Strong creative business personality. Must follow first thought; eliminate indecision and confusion.

PERSONALITY EXTREME: Too changeable, or too inert.

YORK (Celtic/English)—M.

MAJOR TALENT: Ability to incorporate an effective personality, ambition, and sound business judgment into career. Attracts fortunate family life-style, influential boosters, and material comforts. Sincere sense of truth and justice may cause reputation for stubbornness or bring great respect. Acting, teaching, and any service business are possible career opportunities.

PERSONALITY INGREDIENTS: Appears to be philosophical, generous, and empathetic. Dresses comfortably and attracts attention. Wants warm, abundant, artistic home and attainment for loved ones. Can be a difficult adversary.

PERSONALITY EXTREME: Too emotional, or too controlled.

YVES (Old Scandinavian/French/English)—M.

MAJOR TALENT: Ability to incorporate questioning, research, and experimentation into a career that brings tangible results. When concentrated, enduring, and a positive visualizer, may achieve lasting fame. Corporate executive, entrepreneur, and athlete are potential career opportunities.

PERSONALITY INGREDIENTS: First impression is entertaining, attractive, and sunny. Inwardly desires freedom, sensual experiences, and youthful pursuits. Intuitive diagnostician; always knows what the problem is but may lack professional expertise. Clever, impatient, and self-confident. May lose all through pessimism.

PERSONALITY EXTREME: Too daring, or too compromising.

YVETTE (Old Scandinavian: Yves/French/English)—F.

MAJOR TALENT: Ability to incorporate intuitive and practical observations, a gift for detail, and an adventurous mind into career. May lead crusades, meet difficult obstacles in childhood, and rise to leadership through resourcefulness and perseverance. Benefits from travel. Photography, archaeology, and investigative research may be career opportunities.

PERSONALITY INGREDIENTS: First impression is reliable, concerned, and secure. Inwardly needs independent action, creative freedom, and attainment. Dislikes mundane pleasures, but does not shirk any type of practical work. Enjoys life's cultural refinements.

PERSONALITY EXTREME: Too prudish, or too sexual.

YVONNE (Old Scandinavian: Yves/French/English)—F.

MAJOR TALENT: Ability to incorporate communications, intuitional judgments, and facility with language into career. May achieve highest goals through persistence, patience, and sense of duty. Progressive/expansive attitudes and seizing the opportunity of the moment may attract success easily. Guilt/haughtiness/pridefulness turn boosters into enemies. Accept acclaim gracefully. Philosophy/religion, dream interpretation, and teaching are potential career opportunities.

PERSONALITY INGREDIENTS: First impression is attractive and outgoing, but inwardly needs peaceful time for meditation. Feels special. Emotionally sensitive, high-strung, and visionary. Lucky gambler with a channel to inner light.

PERSONALITY EXTREME: Too busy, or too bored.

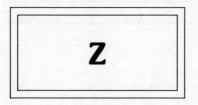

Z

All names that begin with the letter *Z* have the *Strong Point* of aspiration—perception—confidence—physical balance.

ZACH (Diminutive, Hebrew: Zachary/English)—M.

MAJOR TALENT: Ability to incorporate detailed craftsmanship, adaptability to change, and silent analysis into career. Should apply logic (not stubborn emotions) to changes that are necessary for productive growth. Successful when able to break habits and take nothing at face value. Any skilled craft, insurance adjusting, and diplomacy may be career opportunities.

PERSONALITY INGREDIENTS: First impression and inward needs are individualistic, independent, and creative. Prefers to lead the way. Life will offer many turning points, which are always beneficial when accepted and reasoned through with common sense.

PERSONALITY EXTREME: Too organized, or too lackadaisical.

ZACHARIAH (Hebrew: Zachary/English)—M.

MAJOR TALENT: Ability to incorporate a materialistic understanding to art, animal care, and science into career. Conservative sense of values, responsibility, and sympathy blend to serve a community need. Matures to release need for accumulation and aspires to higher purposes. Veterinary, trial lawyer, and art business are potential career opportunities.

PERSONALITY INGREDIENTS: First impression is understanding, magnetic, and interested. Inwardly wants a variety of imaginative interests, a cheerful atmosphere, and attention. Never satisfied. Often an impressionable worrier. Strives to relieve the suffering of others.

PERSONALITY EXTREME: Too commercialized, or too artsy-craftsy.

ZACHARY (Hebrew/English)—M.

MAJOR TALENT: Ability to incorporate defensive tactics, mature reserve, and desire for prominence into career. Offers devoted service to business, religious interests, and home/community. Possesses strength, optimism, and intuition; should aim to use these inner assets. Group leadership, military planning, and creative productions may be career opportunities.

PERSONALITY INGREDIENTS: First impression is zesty, progressive, and resourceful. Inwardly philosophical, empathetic, and noble. If negative, appears calm while planning deception. Interested in travel, love, and attainment for family/community/universe. A pioneering welfare worker.

PERSONALITY EXTREME: Too questioning, or too innocent.

ZANE (Hebrew: Jane-John/English variable)—F. & M.

MAJOR TALENT: Ability to incorporate leadership, public service, and
inventive ways and means into career. Mind and vitality blend to overcome obstacles. Should try to learn to balance opposing interests. May
lead a double life. Should cultivate courage to face daily realities. Sales
manager, production planning, and entertainment industry are possible
career opportunities.

PERSONALITY INGREDIENTS: First impression is steadfast, and the face
is etched with past experiences. The strain for financial security/power
creates lifestyle upheavals, the results of needed changes in thinking and
aspirations show in the face. Inwardly protective, nurturing, and attracted to love, beauty, and culture.

PERSONALITY EXTREME: Too sensual, or too intellectual.

ZARA (Variable Hebrew: Sarah/English)—F.

MAJOR TALENT: Ability to incorporate organizing, directing, and
managing into career. Vitality, intellect, and positive attitude to redirect-
ing goals bring success. Benefits from inspiring others and exercising
self-control. Creative ventures, recycling products, and government may
be career opportunities.

PERSONALITY INGREDIENTS: Appears efficient, concentrated, and ex-
pansive. Inwardly wants gentle, supportive, harmonious partner/mate.
Inner sensitivity takes emotional tolls when motives are misunderstood.
Attention to petty details may cause problems.

PERSONALITY EXTREME: Too energetic, or too tired.

ZEBADIAH (Hebrew/English)—M.

MAJOR TALENT: Ability to incorporate practical imagery, material investments, and influencing others into career. Relates subconscious to
conscious and sets a spiritual, parental, and useful example for others.
Invites family pride, tangible wealth, and contributions to society. Guidance counseling, writing, and space-age electronics are potential career
opportunities.

PERSONALITY INGREDIENTS: First impression is conservative, solid,
and practical. Inwardly reserved and alone in a search for perfection that
leads to personal disappointment. A balanced marriage will help.
Benefits from friendships.

PERSONALITY EXTREME: Too mercenary, or too extravagant.

ZEDEKIAH (Hebrew/English)—M.

MAJOR TALENT: Ability to incorporate a cooperative nature, creative
imagination, and trustworthy judgment into career. Mixes the mystical
and practical. Always keeps commitments. Home/love are balanced by
strong sense of give-and-take. Decorating, mediation, and children's literature are possible career opportunities.

PERSONALITY INGREDIENTS: First impression is conservative, solid,
and sensible. Inwardly very emotional, receptive, and affectionate.
Should avoid appearing too gracious and effusive. Others often misinter-
pret the natural kindness that is offered.

PERSONALITY EXTREME: Too nonmaterialistic, or too acquisitive.

ZEKE (Hebrew: Ezekiel/English diminutive)—M.

MAJOR TALENT: Ability to incorporate adaptability, silent wisdom, and a knack for detail into career. Intuitively knows truth from transitory values. Finds success and happiness through forgoing desire to control people and situations, and learning to wait and see before drawing conclusions. Grows through accepting change. Bookkeeper, architect, and the ministry may be career opportunities.

PERSONALITY INGREDIENTS: First impression and natural instincts are parallel in their focus upon independent action. Wants to be self-starter and has difficulty following set patterns. Should avoid stubborn focus on minute detail and just keep moving. Excels in skilled craft.

PERSONALITY EXTREME: Too old-fashioned, or too progressive.

ZELDA (English variable/Latin/Old German: Griselda)—F.

MAJOR TALENT: Ability to incorporate creativity, charming personality, and luck into career. Patience, positive thinking, and a good memory blend with practical organizational limitation. The arts, cosmetology, and writing are possible career opportunities.

PERSONALITY INGREDIENTS: First impression and natural instincts are parallel. Sincere, concerned, maternal, and loving nature shows at first meeting. Can be too helpful, idealistic, and aspiring, but happiest when serving the home/family/community.

PERSONALITY EXTREME: Too ambitious, or too satisfied.

ZENA (Persian)—F.

MAJOR TALENT: Ability to incorporate independent energy, empathy for others' welfare, and communications skills into career. Attracts love and money when emotions are controlled. Success comes through having the courage to follow natural desires without making comparisons. Sound reasoning and endurance aid in eliminating self-pity. Inventing, theatrical production, and any creative field are potential career opportunities.

PERSONALITY INGREDIENTS: First impression is solid, organized, and practical but loses balance when family/community are involved. Desires harmonious, abundant, and upstanding life-style. Natural teacher; expects everyone to live up to personal standards. Keeps a private/secretive life when negatively fearful of progressive changes.

PERSONALITY EXTREME: Too ambitious, or too easily satisfied.

ZENOBIA (Latin/English)—F.

MAJOR TALENT: Ability to incorporate determination and perseverance to overcome burdensome obstacles into career. Dependability leads to authoritative positions. Might be described by associates as "the salt of the earth." Musician, surgeon, and horticulturist are possible career opportunities.

PERSONALITY INGREDIENTS: Very artistic lover of beauty. First impression is sympathetic, helpful, and protective. Inwardly wants variety, cheerfulness, and sociability. Impetuous emotionalizing creates discomfort in relationships.

PERSONALITY EXTREME: Too strong-willed, or too ineffectual.

ZINNIA (Latin/English/American)—F.

MAJOR TALENT: Ability to incorporate composure and a militant sense of responsibility into career. Expansive ideas and emotional understanding should attract prominence and supporters. International experiences are attractive and emotionally rewarding. Psychologist, investment advisor, and any independent creative business are potential career opportunities.

PERSONALITY INGREDIENTS: Home is very necessary to security. May play out life experience with inward reserve and secrecy: a poker player. First impression is noble, understanding, and magnetic. Inwardly impatient, individualistic, and ego-oriented.

PERSONALITY EXTREME: Too aggressive, or too receptive.

ZITA (Hebrew/English)—F.

MAJOR TALENT: Ability to incorporate tact, patience, and shrewd powers of observation into career. Should lead group activities and make judgments based upon performance, rather than personality. Greatest strength lies in ability to adjust differences between opposing points of view. Union arbitration, legal trustee, and bill collection may be career opportunities.

PERSONALITY INGREDIENTS: May want leadership but lack courage. Appears individualistic, creative, ambitious. Wants to control but must learn not to get caught in minutiae, when making decisions. Personal sensitivity may overrule logic.

PERSONALITY EXTREME: Too impatient, or too sedentary.

ZOE (Greek/English/French)—F.

MAJOR TALENT: Ability to incorporate down-home appraisals and problem-solving leadership into career. Expressive intellect combines with a compassionate attitude. Conscious of public image. Institution head, newspaper editing/ownership, any experimental field are potential career opportunities.

PERSONALITY INGREDIENTS: Appears to enjoy money, authority, and impressing others. Inwardly intuitive, understanding, and adaptable. Crusades for causes that represent personal beliefs and usually attracts donations. Childhood values remain to enforce a responsible lifestyle.

PERSONALITY EXTREME: Too impulsive, or too enduring.

Bibliography

Campbell, Florence, M.A., *Your Days Are Numbered*, The Gateway, Ferndale, Pa., 1931.

Hitchcock, Helen, *Helping Yourself with Numerology*, Parker Publishing Co., West Nyack, N.Y., 1972.

Javane, Faith, and Bunker, Dusty, *Numerology and the Divine Triangle*, Para Research, Rockport, Mass., 1972.

Roquemore, Kathleen, *It's All in Your Numbers: The Secrets of Numerology*, Harper & Row, New York, N.Y., 1975.

Rule, Lareina, *Name Your Baby*, Bantam Books, New York, N.Y., 1963.

Sleigh, Linwood, and Johnson, Charles, *Apollo Book of Girls' Names*, Thomas J. Crowell, New York, N.Y., 1962.

United States Government, *Foreign Versions, Variations and Diminutives of English Names*, United States Department of Justice, Immigration & Naturalization Service, 1973.

Wells, Evelyn, *What to Name the Baby*, Doubleday & Co., Garden City, N.Y., 1946.